TWO IN

SURREY'S DOUBLE-WIN

by TREVOR

LIMITED NUMBERED EDITION
This is one of only 170 specially bound, hand-numbered copies

Number 19 *of 170*

Mr J.C.Lodge
28 Heathside Avenue
Bexleyheath
Kent
DA7 4PZ

TWO IN BLUE

SURREY'S DOUBLE-WINNING 2003 SEASON

Trevor Jones

TREVOR JONES

Sporting Declarations Books

www.sportingdeclarations.co.uk

PO Box 882, Sutton, Surrey, SM2 5AW

First published in 2004 by Sporting Declarations Books

ISBN 0 9535307 6 0

Cover Photographs

FRONT - TOP:
Surrey celebrate at Trent Bridge after becoming the first winners of the Twenty-20 Cup…
Photo courtesy of Surrey CCC

FRONT - BOTTOM:
…and at The Oval after being presented with the NCL Division One trophy
Photo courtesy of Surrey CCC

BACK:
James Ormond and Adam Hollioake with the Twenty-20 Cup
Photo courtesy of Surrey CCC.

Typesetting and design by Trevor Jones

Printed and bound in Great Britain by MPG Books, Victoria Square, Bodmin, Cornwall
Colour work by APG, Unit 9, Mitcham Industrial Estate, Mitcham, Surrey CR2 4AP

Contents

Introduction

It might not have been the season that people had wanted, or at one point expected, as the County Championship title slipped away, but 2003 was still a fine year for Surrey, with twenty-seven matches won and just seven lost. Two trophies were won and, for much of the summer, the treble was a distinct possibility. As ever, we were treated to some excellent cricket, with the team's displays in the limited-overs form of the game being especially impressive, particularly when the chips were down in close finishes. While the loss of the Championship was a significant blow, Surrey could justifiably claim to have become the nation's best one-day team, having claimed two cups and continued to come out on top in clashes with Gloucestershire. I hope I have convinced you that 2003 wasn't such a bad year for Surrey after all!

The fact that I have again been able to record the season's events is entirely down to the generous and greatly valued support of my Sponsor-Subscribers, who continue to 'commission' me to spend a large part of the close season holed up in my flat working long - and often incredibly stupid! - hours, turning piles of notes, newspaper clippings and taped interviews into the book that you are now holding in your hand. Many thanks to those of you who have backed me and enabled me to continue producing these hefty tomes detailing Surrey's successful campaigns.

There were so many features I wanted to include in this new volume - some of them suggested by those who support me - but time, space and finance did not allow me to go as far as I would have liked. There are two things I have deliberately tried to steer clear of including in this book, however… gossip and speculation. Towards the end of the season, and into the winter months, there seemed to be a great many stories doing the rounds as people tried to come up with reasons for the late loss of form in the Championship, and for the departures/resignations of key figures at the Club. The sole purpose of these books, however, is to record a successful season for posterity, purely by concentrating on the matches and the facts. I hope people will understand that and approve of my stance.

Finally, I should mention that, in order to accommodate increased coverage of the competitions that were won, a few of the less significant and 'dead' Championship matches are covered in slightly less detail than usual. I'm sure you will appreciate my reasons for doing this and enjoy the greater coverage of the NCL matches, as well as the inclusion of Twenty-20 Cup reporting.

The 2004 season sees Surrey entering an exciting new era. Hopefully, it will be every bit as successful as the Medlycott-Hollioake era, and I will be writing another of these introductions in March 2005!

Trevor Jones

March 2004

1 Grounds For Optimism

Having suffered the most traumatic pre-season period imaginable in 2002, the spring of 2003 dawned brightly for Surrey and a mood of optimism was understandable as the players prepared to defend their County Championship crown. A fourth title in five years was certainly a possibility and the bookmakers made Keith Medlycott's team firm favourites to prove that the loss of the 2001 title to Yorkshire had been a mere blip in a rich era of success for the Club.

There hadn't been many changes to the squad during the close season, with the only major signing being that of Azhar Mahmood, the 28-year-old Pakistani all-rounder, following the decision to allow every county to field two overseas players in 2003 and 2004, while just four men had left for pastures new - Jason Ratcliffe had retired after losing his battle with a knee injury and had taken up a post with the Professional Cricketers' Association; Michael Carberry, a talented left-handed batsman and livewire fielder, had decided to move to Kent in order to get more first-team opportunities; Rupesh Amin, the left-arm spinner whose chances of building on his early promise had been restricted by the presence of Ian Salisbury and Saqlain Mushtaq, had been signed by Leicestershire; and Ed Giddins, like Amin, released by the county at the end of the 2002 season, had joined Hampshire, the fourth first-class county of his career.

Giddins' departure had reduced the number of international cricketers on the Club's books to thirteen, though only three of these - Mark Butcher, Saqlain Mushtaq and Alec Stewart - looked certain to miss Surrey matches due to Test or One-Day International commitments during the summer. There was, however, a strong possibility of Azhar Mahmood being called up by Pakistan at some stage, while James Ormond, Mark Ramprakash, Alex Tudor and Ian Ward would all have harboured hopes of an England recall. The same applied to Graham Thorpe, whose well publicised domestic problems had resulted in him eventually opting out of England's winter commitments. Still rated by many as the best batsman in the country, he would clearly need to score plenty of runs and prove that he had regained his hunger for the game before Duncan Fletcher and Nasser Hussain would allow him to return to the fold. This was clearly going to work in Surrey's favour as there was a fair chance that they would be able to avail themselves of Thorpe's services for the entire season, further strengthening a top order that, even without Butcher and Stewart, already boasted a wealth of talent, including Ian Ward, Mark Ramprakash, Alistair Brown, Adam Hollioake and Rikki Clarke, the youngster who had shown exciting potential in 2002. On the bowling front, Saqlain and Salisbury would again form a dangerous spinning combination, while there were plenty of seam bowling options with Martin Bicknell, James Ormond, Alex Tudor, Azhar Mahmood, Tim Murtagh and Phil Sampson all battling for places in the starting eleven.

Bearing in mind that Butcher and Stewart would be available to play in some of the season's opening matches, supporters who had tried to select their eleven for the first match of the season had found the task nigh-on impossible, with fourteen or fifteen players all worthy of a place in the team. It was clear why Surrey were such hot favourites to win the Championship and equally obvious that Keith Medlycott and Adam Hollioake would face some very tough team selection decisions during the season.

So all looked good on the home front… but what of the opposition? Who were the counties most likely to threaten Surrey in their attempt to retain the Championship crown? Assessing the opposition had proved to be a very tricky task in 2002, with the two sides fancied by most 'experts', Yorkshire and Somerset, both being relegated to the second division! Twelve months later, Lancashire had emerged as the team most likely to push for the title, though Warwickshire, runners-up in the previous campaign, were also highly regarded by many.

Having lost another group of players during the winter, Leicestershire were most unlikely to mount a challenge and faced a difficult season, while Sussex, despite the signing of Mushtaq Ahmed, looked more likely to feature in the lower half of the table than the top half. Kent, an unpredictable side at the best of times, had meanwhile bolstered their bowling with the signing of the Worcestershire left-armer, Alamgir Sheriyar, and looked, at best, the dark horses of the division.

The experience of recent seasons had shown that the promoted sides usually struggled to retain first division status, so it wasn't surprising that no-one really expected any of the three new teams - Essex, Middlesex and Nottinghamshire - to be serious contenders. Middlesex, boasting a strong batting line-up, looked like they would be a tough team to beat, but were bereft of match-winning bowlers, especially once Phil Tufnell decided that he wanted to trade in his life as a cricketer in order to become a 'celebrity', while Essex didn't appear to have sufficient quality or depth in either department, despite having come up as second division champions. Their success in winning that division had been achieved largely on the back of fourth-innings run chases, and it was unlikely that they would encounter many generous captains in the rarified atmosphere of the first division. Nottinghamshire were certainly not an easy side to assess and I found myself far from alone in thinking that they could finish the season in any position between third and bottom. Clearly there was a lot of talent there but the men from Trent Bridge rarely seemed to do themselves justice and it was only a Stuart MacGill inspired surge late in 2002 that earned them their place at English domestic cricket's top table. With Shane Warne suspended from all cricket for a year after failing a drugs test at the World Cup, Nottinghamshire were clearly going to be without MacGill, Warne's natural replacement in the Australian side, for parts of the season.

The first division newcomers weren't the only side to have a problem with their overseas registrations as April arrived, however, since Lancashire revealed that they were unlikley to see their new signing, Harbhajan Singh, in action in the early weeks of the season owing to a problem with the Indian off-spinner's spinning finger. It wasn't certain how long the injury would take to heal so the Red Rose county were going to have to bide their time and hope that Singh would be able to take up his contract with the club sooner rather than later. Surrey's position as favourites for the Frizzell Championship title was strengthened as a result of this revelation from the side perceived to be their main rivals, and it seemed that complacency could be the team's biggest foe during the season ahead.

In the field of limited-overs cricket, 2003 was to see the introduction of The Twenty-20 Cup in place of the Benson And Hedges Cup. Played, as the name implied, over twenty overs a side, with a starting time, in most cases, of 5.30pm, the new competition had been designed to attract new spectators, especially children, to cricket. Two weeks had been set aside in the middle of June for a series of regional qualifying matches, with the four best sides then contesting the semi-finals and final at Trent Bridge on July 19th. It seemed to be something of a gamble by the ECB and, like many, I feared it would be something of a disaster, with spectators unable or unwilling to travel to matches during the rush hour and counties resting their top players in order to give youngersters some first-team exposure. John Emburey, the Middlesex coach, had even been quoted as saying that he felt the competition might corrupt the technique of his players and would consider fielding a team of club players, which wouldn't have been music to the ears of the marketing men at the ECB. Since the short-course duration of the games would probably prove to be something of a 'leveller', it looked tough to predict which sides might fare well in the competition and I had a sneaking suspicion that two or three really unfancied sides might emerge to reach the showpiece finals day in Nottingham.

The first division of the National Cricket League - now often abbreviated, American style, to the NCL - also looked a tough league to call. After four seasons of promotion and relegation it appeared that the top flight of the one-day league finally contained the nine counties who, day-in day-out, were the best at the 45-overs version of the game. Only Lancashire of the ten sides in division two - Scotland having been added for 2003 - had claims to being up to the standard of the nine division one teams. The league comprised of Essex, Glamorgan, Gloucestershire, Kent, Leicestershire, Surrey, Warwickshire, Worcestershire and Yorkshire, pretty much all of whom could be envisaged as potential champions come the final round of matches on September 21st. Essex and Leicestershire appeared, to me, to be in greatest danger of finishing in the relegation places and not even the 2002 champions, Glamorgan, looked safe from the drop in a highly competitive league. I felt Surrey's prospects might depend on how they started their campaign. Having bounced back and forth between the two divisions since the introduction of promotion and relegation, the one thing that had emerged as a consistent guideline to the team's chances was how they fared in their opening few matches. During their previous season in the top flight, in 2001, the team had been unable to recover from a wretched start, while their two promotion-winning campaigns of 2000 and 2002 had, to differing degrees, been characterised by a series of early confidence-boosting victories. Maybe early results would again prove influential.

The time for all the speculation to end, and for the action to start, eventually arrived when Surrey played a one-day friendly against Kent at Canterbury, with the home team emerging victorious by twenty-one runs in a 50-overs-a-side contest. Rikki Clarke, with 2-38 from his ten overs, was very much the pick of Surrey's bowlers as Kent compiled 324-7, thanks largely to Dave Fulton's eighty-nine, Michael Carberry's unbeaten eighty-four, and seventy-five from Mark Ealham. The visitors were then all out for 303 from the final ball of their allotted overs, with the top scorers being Graham Thorpe (77), Mark Butcher (69) and Ali Brown (51), while Amjad Khan took 4-52 for the hosts.

A two-day friendly was then played at The Rose Bowl against Hampshire, with each side batting for one day. On day one, Hampshire compiled 393-9 from their agreed one-hundred overs, with the major contributions coming from Alex Morris (100*), Robin Smith (80), Derek Kenway (71), and James Hamblin (53). Of the Surrey bowlers, the highly-promising 18-year-old fast bowler, Neil Saker, who had just been taken on to the staff, was the star man, taking 4-73, though Ian Salisbury showed up well in a spell of 27-12-61-2, and Alex Tudor grabbed 3-110. The visitors then romped to a six-wicket victory on the second day, scoring 394-4 from just seventy-six overs, with the main runscorers being Mark Ramprakash, who retired after making 130, Graham Thorpe, who contributed ninety-two, and Ali Brown, who ended unbeaten on seventy-five. Now it was time for the real thing.

2 A Mixed Start

The fixtures computer had certainly thrown up a mouth-watering opening encounter for Surrey, with the visit of Lancashire to The Oval. It represented a chance for the two sides rated most likely to win the Championship to flex their muscles and maybe gain a crucial early advantage. Everyone was looking forward to this curtain-raiser and, with fine weather forecast for the start of the match at least, all was set fair for an epic battle.

FRIZZELL COUNTY CHAMPIONSHIP DIVISION ONE - MATCH ONE

SURREY versus LANCASHIRE
at The Oval

First Day - Friday 18th April
Lancashire 391-2

The Teams And The Toss - *Much to Surrey's disappointment, Martin Bicknell, James Ormond and Phil Sampson are all sidelined by injuries picked up during pre-season, while Azhar Mahmood is also unavailable as he is concluding his wedding celebrations at home in Pakistan. Tim Murtagh, who has been impressive during the pre-season period, is therefore selected to take the new ball with Alex Tudor. Alec Stewart is rested by England, even though the nation's involvement in the World Cup had ended on March 2nd, while Mark Butcher is available but omitted from the County Champions' line-up. With Surrey's seam bowling resources so depleted, Rikki Clarke wins a place in the side as middle-order batsman/third seamer. Lancashire are meanwhile close to full strength, with World Cup stars Andrew Flintoff and James Anderson both included, though Peter Martin misses out because of a family bereavement and is replaced by Kyle Hogg. Close season signings, Mal Loye (ex Northamptonshire) and Iain Sutcliffe (ex Leicestershire) both play. Warren Hegg wins the toss for Lancashire and, on an absolutely beautiful late spring morning, inevitably elects to take first use of the pitch used for the historic 'Ali Brown 268' C&G match against Glamorgan.*

The glorious weather, coupled with the fact that it is the Good Friday public holiday, has helped to pull in one of the largest County Championship crowds at The Oval in recent memory - estimated at over 3,000 - and, consequently, the Surrey team takes to the field to a quite astonishing extended ovation. On a less happy note, all the home side's players are wearing black armbands as a mark of respect to former Club President, Sir John Paul Getty, who had passed away the previous day at the age of 70.

Alex Tudor and Tim Murtagh open the attack for Surrey and it is soon clear that the pitch is an excellent one that will offer little margin for error to the bowlers. The former is accurate, though not especially threatening, while the latter looks dangerous when pitching the ball up and obtaining a little swing either way. Murtagh's more attacking full length does offer run-scoring opportunities to the Lancashire openers, however, and the left-handed Iain Sutcliffe unfurls three glorious straight drives to the boundary in the young Surrey seamer's initial burst of seven overs.

With the opening bowlers withdrawn from the attack simultaneously, the home side faces an early test, since Rikki Clarke and Adam Hollioake appear to be a less than lethal combination of first-change seamers. The worst fears of the Surrey faithful appear to be confirmed immediately, too, when Clarke delivers a wayward opening over that yields two boundaries to Alec Swann and a glanced four to Sutcliffe as the total races beyond fifty.

Much to his credit, Clarke comes back well after his seventeen-run first over, though, and the two boundaries conceded in the course of his next two overs are both courtesy of thick edges to the rope at third man. With Hollioake having, meanwhile, surrendered two legside fours to Swann, things are not looking too rosy for the County Champions, so it is no great surprise when the Surrey captain removes himself from the attack after just three overs and turns to Saqlain Mushtaq at the Vauxhall end.

The off-spinner's early introduction, for the twenty-first over of the innings, merely underlines the fact that the visitors have taken the early honours, and further confirmation of this comes when Swann twice cuts, and then off-drives, Saqlain for fours in the new bowler's second over. The former Northamptonshire batsman then completes an impressive 83-ball fifty in the following over from Clarke, and celebrates by clipping the same bowler to the square-leg boundary two overs later to raise the Lancashire hundred in just the twenty-sixth over. This is certainly not the start that the reigning champions would have hoped for and it signals the end of Clarke's opening six-over spell, with Ian Salisbury chosen as his replacement at the pavilion end.

This change finally brings the breakthrough for the home side, though it is not through the efforts of the bowler as, for the third time in his last five Championship innings against Surrey, Swann finds himself run out. It's a pretty dismal mix-up that brings about the non-striking batsman's demise, too, as he calls Sutcliffe for a run to short square leg and sprints down the pitch, only to find that his partner is not interested. Having got two-thirds of the way down the track, Swann is unable to beat Jon Batty's throw back to the bowler, though there is a surprisingly long delay before umpire Vanburn Holder finally decides that the batsman hasn't made his ground and sends him on his way with an upraised finger.

As one former Northamptonshire batsman, Mal Loye, replaces another at the crease with the score standing at 108-1 in the twenty-eighth over, the home team and their supporters are breathing a sigh of relief, but, though Loye's first run for Lancashire is a very tight single to mid-on that almost brings the umpire into play again, the visitors get through to lunch without further loss. It's been a tough opening session of the season for the champions.

Lunch:- Lancashire 121-1 (Sutcliffe 47, Loye 3*) from 33 overs*

Adam Hollioake reintroduces his opening bowlers after lunch and Sutcliffe immediately cuts Murtagh for the boundary that brings up his personal half-century from 85 balls. The young Surrey bowler is then removed from the attack after just two overs, allowing Tudor to switch to the pavilion end and Saqlain to reappear at the Vauxhall end.

Unfortunately for the home captain, his new combination of bowlers doesn't initially bring any change of fortune, though Sutcliffe is rather lucky when he top-edges a hook at Tudor to the rope at fine leg to bring up the Lancashire 150. Meanwhile, at the other end, Loye looks to be settling in ominously well as he lofts Saqlain high over wide mid-on and then pulls to midwicket to notch two impressive fours and raise a fifty partnership for the second wicket. Much to Surrey's relief, some salvation arrives shortly afterwards, however, when Sutcliffe falls to Saqlain, who, by this time, is operating from round the wicket to both batsmen. The left-handed opener looks rather aggrieved to be adjudged lbw on the front foot to the off-spinner, though umpire Neil Mallender deserves credit for giving the appeal plenty of consideration before deciding that Sutcliffe is out for seventy with the score at 169.

The former Leicestershire captain's replacement at the wicket is Stuart Law, a man with a very good record against Surrey over the years. The fact that he is fresh from a wretched Australian domestic season offers the County Champions hope, though he certainly doesn't look out of form in the early stages of his innings as he drills Tudor through straight mid-on and extra cover for majestic boundaries.

With Loye continuing to play Saqlain quite comfortably and lofting him down the ground for two more fours, Surrey are in need of another breakthrough, and a chance comes their way with Law on twelve and the score 196-2. Unfortunately for the hosts, Tudor, at backward point, fails to hang on to a well-struck but loose cut from the first ball delivered by Salisbury, his replacement at the pavilion end. It's a low chance, though certainly catchable, and everyone of a Surrey persuasion begins to wonder if this could turn out to be an expensive miss.

In the immediate aftermath of this scare, Law seems content to re-establish himself by picking up singles, but the spinners are unable to keep the Lancashire pair quiet for long and Saqlain suffers at the hands of both men when his nineteenth over yields twelve runs and sees the arrival of first the fifty partnership and then Loye's half-century from 105 balls.

Although he stays on the field, Saqlain appears to be struggling with a back injury at this stage of the day, and he is therefore pulled out of the attack, with Salisbury switching to the Vauxhall end in the lead-up to tea and Hollioake returning to the fray at the pavilion end. While the Surrey leg-spinner quickly settles into a good line and length, Hollioake is instantly pulled to the rope at midwicket by Loye - these runs taking the score past 250 - and then driven through straight mid-on to the pavilion fence by Law, the prolific Australian completing an 84-ball half-century in the process. At tea, Lancashire are in complete command, with both batsmen looking in top form.

Tea:- Lancashire 265-2 (Loye 61, Law 54*) from 72 overs*

Surrey certainly need to pick up some wickets in the day's final session if they are to retain any hope of winning this opening encounter of the season, so Adam Hollioake turns to Salisbury, the pick of his bowlers to date, and Tudor.

The batsmen continue to exercise control, however, as Loye drives the paceman wide of mid-on for three to complete the century stand for the third wicket and then cuts the spinner to the cover boundary. Surrey are then further hit, after just three overs, by Saqlain's retirement from the fray to nurse his injury, and misery continues to be heaped upon misery as both Loye and Law start to find the fence with increasing regularity.

Consequently, the Lancashire three-hundred arrives in the eighty-third over, and it isn't long before the third-wicket partnership becomes worth 150 as Salisbury pays a heavy price for dropping short to Law on three separate occasions. Murtagh, after a long absence from the attack, is meanwhile given another chance as Tudor's replacement at the pavilion end and starts well with a couple of tight overs.

With Saqlain looking unlikely to reappear, the rather limited Surrey attack does look overstretched, though, and both batsmen take full advantage of the situation, especially when Salisbury is rested and the new ball is, perhaps surprisingly, taken after ninety-one overs. Since Tudor has already delivered twenty-one overs in the day, Rikki Clarke is given the responsibility of sharing the new 'cherry' with Murtagh and the young seamers make an inauspicious start with it as Law races from eighty-nine to an excellent century with three fours in rapid succession, two off Murtagh and another from Clarke's first delivery. The Queenslander celebrates his 57th first-class century, scored from 156 balls and containing 14 fours, with a yelp of delight, though the young Surrey all-rounder almost has his revenge two balls later when the triumphant batsman edges just short of second slip.

Loye has meanwhile been making rather more sedate progress towards three figures and, apart from a pulled boundary off Clarke to take his score to ninety-five, is rather becalmed in the nineties. Given that this is his debut innings for his new county this is entirely understandable.

Law keeps the scoreboard rolling round nicely in any case, at one point picking up three boundaries from a Murtagh over to take the third-wicket partnership beyond two-hundred.

Finally, in the ninety-ninth over of the day, Loye reaches his cherished landmark, clipping Clarke backward of square leg and scurrying through for a tight second run to complete a 210-ball debut century, which he celebrates with a leap in the air and an animated wave of the bat. The 30-year-old former England 'A' batsman's knock, and his partnership with Law, have put the visitors in an immensely strong position and they see off one final burst from Tudor, replacing Murtagh at the pavilion end for three overs, to leave Lancashire holding all the aces at the end of day one. They return to the dressing room to a good ovation from the big crowd, most of whom will have been very disappointed by Surrey's lacklustre efforts on the opening day of the season.

Close:- Lancashire 391-2 (Loye 104, Law 129*) from 72 overs*

Second Day - Saturday 19th April

Lancashire 599

What a difference a day makes. In stark contrast to the opening day, the weather is grim and grey at the outset and only a scattering of spectators are in the ground as the start of play is delayed for twenty minutes by poor light and a few spots of rain.

Just fourteen balls are then delivered by Tudor and Murtagh before the Lancashire overnight pair accept an offer of bad light from the umpires. Having encountered no real problems in pushing the score up to 397, it seems a strange decision, especially as the visitors will surely need all the time they can get if they are to bowl Surrey out twice on what is a typically excellent Oval pitch.

Nineteen overs are lost, to add to the five that were lopped off following the late start, before play resumes again at 12.43pm. The batsmen are soon making up for lost time, however, as Law drives Murtagh for two handsome fours during the remainder of the over that was in progress when the players had left the field, and Loye drills the same bowler to the long-on fence in his next over. The Australian then pulls Tudor over the square leg boundary for six to reach 150 from his 205th delivery and, as bat continues to dominate ball, the Lancashire pair plunder three further fours in the last fifteen minutes before lunch to take the score to 438-2 at the interval.

Lunch:- Lancashire 438-2 (Loye 118, Law 160*) from 114 overs*

Upon the resumption, Salisbury and Clarke are the Surrey skipper's chosen bowlers and it isn't long before the latter finally brings the epic Loye-Law partnership to a close. After each batsman has notched a boundary during the first three overs of the session, the opening delivery of Clarke's second over nips back into the pads of an almost static Loye and wins an lbw verdict from umpire Holder. The total is 451 and the third-wicket stand has finally been terminated at 282 as Loye makes his way back to the pavilion to a well-deserved ovation for his contribution of 126, which has included 17 fours… and before a highly eventful over is complete he is joined back in the changing room by his partner. Having seen a confident first-ball lbw appeal against the new batsman, Mark Chilton, turned down, Clarke yields a boundary apiece to each batsman before inducing Law to play on in attempting an off-side forcing stroke from the over's final delivery. The applause accorded to Loye is repeated for Law, whose outstanding 169 has been compiled from just 223 balls and included 24 fours and a six.

As if Surrey don't have enough problems with the scoreboard reading 460-4, the man now striding out to the wicket is Andy Flintoff and, after a few overs of careful reconnaissance, he is soon tucking into Clarke's bowling with relish. Three fours come from the 21-year-old all-rounder's sixteenth over, then Flintoff really goes to town two overs later by adding two mighty sixes - both flipped over the fairly short midwicket boundary - to a thunderous off-drive that fairly rattles into the pavilion fence. In spite of this savage assault, Hollioake bravely decides to keep faith with Clarke, though this merely allows Flintoff to reel off a glorious checked straight drive for four which completes a rapid fifty partnership inside ten overs.

While feeding hungrily off Clarke, the big England all-rounder has found the admirable Salisbury a much tougher proposition at the other end, however, and the Surrey leg-spinner gains long overdue reward for his efforts when the fourth ball of his thirty-second over of the innings takes the outside edge of Flintoff's defensive bat and settles in the safe gloves of Jon Batty behind the stumps.

With the dangerous Lancashire all-rounder out of the way after a typically belligerent knock of 43 from 39 balls, the home side are clearly hoping that the rest of the visitors' batting might go quietly and quickly but that doesn't prove to be the case. Chilton suddenly develops a taste for Clarke's fast-medium seam bowling, blasting him out of the attack with three legside boundaries before missing a sweep at a Salisbury leg-break and falling lbw, while Glen Chapple starts his innings in the style of Flintoff by cutting and hooking Tudor, the new bowler at the pavilion end, for three thrilling fours.

As the score hurtles up to and beyond 550, Chapple even manages something that his team-mate had been unable to do by launching a successful attack on Salisbury, taking 4-6-4 from consecutive deliveries with a square cut, a lofted straight drive and a drive wide of mid-on. It isn't long before the Surrey leg-spinner takes revenge, however, safely snaffling a return catch in the over after Tudor has had the left-handed Chris Schofield taken at the wicket after snicking a ball angled across his bows.

With eight wickets now gone for 565, Surrey's ordeal is nearly over, though Warren Hegg and Kyle Hogg do manage to add a further twenty-eight runs in eight overs before Salisbury has the latter taken at wide mid-on by the home skipper from a miscued pull to earn a well-deserved fourth wicket. The innings then ends in rather gloomy light three overs later when Murtagh returns to the attack and plucks out Hegg's off stump as the visiting skipper backs away to leg in an attempt to scythe the ball through the off side. Lancashire's final total of 599 leaves their hosts needing the small matter of 450 runs in order to avoid the follow-on when they commence their first innings after tea.

During the break the light worsens, however, and Surrey have time to reflect on their efforts in the field as they wait to start their reply. Missing the catch offered by Stuart Law when he was on just twelve has clearly proved very expensive and only one bowler can really look back on his performance with any great satisfaction. With Saqlain unable to take any part in today's play, Ian Salisbury has certainly done a great job for his side, his final figures of 42-10-116-4 representing a truly outstanding effort for a leg-spinner in early season conditions on a true pitch. Another man who can take great pride in his display is Jon Batty, since it is discovered that Lancashire's 599 is the highest total conceded by Surrey not to include a bye.

After much waiting around, the umpires conclude that the light is not going to improve and play is eventually called off for the day before the reigning champions can start their innings. Fifty-six overs have been lost in total today and Surrey might well be grateful for that if they are to escape from this game with a draw.

Tea and Close:- Lancashire 599 all out from 151.4 overs

Third Day - Sunday 20th April

Lancashire 599; Surrey 280 and 61-2

Although it is a cold day, conditions are generally much better at the start of day three as Surrey begin their pursuit of Lancashire's 599.

Ian Ward and Jon Batty cope well with some testing opening overs from Glen Chapple and James Anderson, English cricket's bright young fast-bowling hope, picking off the occasional boundary as the Lancashire pair find the task of beating the bat almost as tough as their Surrey counterparts had on the first two days.

Having made a slow but steady start, Batty looks to be stepping up a gear when taking two consecutive fours backward of point in Anderson's fourth over but the 20-year-old paceman takes revenge in his next over by spearing a fine yorker through the Surrey wicketkeeper's defences and flattening his off stump. Batty out for thirteen, Surrey 35-1.

Despite his success, Anderson is given just one more over in his opening burst before being replaced by Kyle Hogg, and, with Chapple having already given way to Flintoff at the Vauxhall end, it's all change on the bowling front as Warren Hegg seeks to pick up further early wickets. Ward and the new batsman, Mark Ramprakash, resist stoutly, though, with the left-hander doing the bulk of the scoring - including two beautiful on-driven boundaries and another drive through extra cover, all at Hogg's expense - as his new partner settles in.

Having scored just three runs in ten overs while acclimatising himself, Ramprakash finally breaks loose, however, finding the rope at extra cover off Hogg and then taking consecutive boundaries off Flintoff with further delightful strokes as the partnership extends towards fifty and the bat continues to hold sway in the match.

Consequently, the Lancashire skipper opts for a double bowling change, recalling Chapple at the pavilion end and giving his leg-spinner, Chris Schofield, an early opportunity at the Vauxhall end.

Although these changes fail to unsettle Ramprakash, who twice cuts Schofield to the rope and steers Chapple to the third-man boundary in taking the total into three figures, Ward, having suddenly found runs harder to come by, almost perishes to the Lancashire opening bowler as lunch approaches. Sparring uncertainly outside his off stump at a decent delivery angled across him, the left-handed opener edges, at a good height, to Mark Chilton at second slip but has a lucky escape as the fielder misses the opportunity to reward Chapple for some fine bowling during the morning session.

Everyone is then amazed to see Hegg instantly replacing the unlucky Chapple with Anderson at the pavilion end, but this proves to be a masterstroke as Ward fails to take advantage of his let-off on forty-eight, top-edging a rather rash square cut at the young paceman's sixth delivery, allowing Hegg to dive away to his left in front of first slip and take a fine catch. With lunch just a couple of overs away, it's a disappointing end for the Surrey opener, but Ramprakash doesn't allow this to distract him. Having driven consecutive balls from Schofield to the wide long-on boundary in the very next over, he completes a fine fifty from 74 balls from the penultimate delivery of the session when he hooks Anderson, albeit in rather uncontrolled fashion, over the rope at fine leg for six.

Lunch:- Surrey 121-2 (Ramprakash 50, Thorpe 0*) from 33 overs*

After a pretty even first session, Lancashire take control in the early stages of the afternoon as the County Champions lose three key wickets in the first six overs. Pairing Anderson with Flintoff for the first time, Warren Hegg hits upon a winning combination, though it has to be said that some indifferent batting and umpiring play a major part in Surrey's slump.

Having failed to add to his lunchtime score, Ramprakash is the first to go, wafting rather loosely outside his off stump at the third ball of Anderson's first over and being taken behind the wicket by Hegg with the score at 123.

This is clearly a serious blow for the home team, though worse is to follow when Ali Brown falls in the young speedster's next over after inexplicably padding up to what seems to be a straight delivery. From the boundary, he appears to have been saved by the fact that the ball looks to be going over the top of the stumps, but umpire Holder seemingly fails to take this into account as he raises his finger and sends Brown packing for two with the total advanced to just 129.

With all four wickets now to his name, Anderson has sent Surrey into a potentially fatal tailspin and, by adding Graham Thorpe to his bag of victims in his next over, he continues to single-handedly wreck the reigning champions' innings. It is fair to say, however, that the batsman again plays a significant part in his own downfall. Perhaps feeling over-confident after locating the cover and midwicket fences with fine strokes from the previous two balls, Thorpe takes on the almost inevitable bouncer that follows but only succeeds in top-edging his hook to Mal Loye at long leg. The fielder takes a good tumbling catch to reduce Surrey to a desperate 140-5 and Anderson's figures are suddenly reading 10.4-1-50-5. This stunning effort on a good flat pitch leaves the hosts still 310 runs short of saving the follow-on with nigh-on five sessions left for play.

Almost inevitably, however, the champions respond to adversity in positive style as Rikki Clarke and Adam Hollioake launch an instant counter-attack. With Hollioake plundering three off-side boundaries in Flintoff's fifth over of the session and Clarke pulling Anderson over midwicket for six in the following over, Hegg again decides to make a double change, reverting to the pre-lunch pairing of Chapple and Schofield.

A couple of full-tosses - one to each batsman - in the leg-spinner's opening over are both despatched efficiently to the boundary, offering a little encouragement to the beleaguered home side, and when Hollioake launches the same bowler over mid-on two overs later he completes a fifty partnership by the sixth-wicket pair at almost a run a ball. A stirring off drive for four by the Surrey skipper off Chapple then takes the total beyond two-hundred shortly afterwards, but the Lancashire paceman brings Hollioake's 43-ball innings of forty-two to a close a couple of balls later, thanks to a brilliant catch by Flintoff at first slip - gloving an attempted hook at a short delivery, Hollioake turns to see the towering all-rounder leaping high and plucking the ball out of the air one-handed in almost nonchalant fashion. At 204-6, Surrey are now even deeper in the mire, while the deserving Chapple at last has something to show for his efforts.

Showing his mettle in adversity, young Clarke responds positively to his skipper's departure by taking three fours off Schofield in the space of four deliveries, a meaty pull following drives through extra cover and wide mid-on. Despite having witnessed this assault on his former England leg-spinner at close hand, Hegg bravely opts to retain Schofield in the attack and his faith is repaid when the bowler picks up two wickets in four balls in his next over. Alex Tudor falls to the third delivery, when he fails in his attempt to thread a drive between two fielders posted in the short extra cover region and sees Chilton pull off a very good catch diving away to his left, then Clarke goes to the last ball, aiming to leg and getting a leading edge to the same fielder in the same position. The follow-on now looks inevitable with the home side in disarray at 230-8, though Ian Salisbury does at least earn his team a second batting point by taking three high-class boundaries off Kyle Hogg, a surprising replacement for Chapple at the pavilion end.

After a disappointing four-over spell, Hogg then gives way to Flintoff and the big all-rounder immediately brings Salisbury to book, though in controversial circumstances as umpire Holder upholds a rather half-hearted appeal for a catch down the legside by the sprawling Hegg. Salisbury is clearly convinced that Flintoff's short-of-a-length delivery hasn't made any contact with either bat or glove but he has to depart and, at 268-9, the end is nigh.

Saqlain Mushtaq's response to his spin twin's dismissal is to blast the first three deliveries of the next over from Schofield to the boundary but, in attempting an equally violent stroke at the next ball, he merely succeeds in skying a catch to Anderson at mid-off.

Having returned final figures of 13-2-61-5, the catcher rightly leads his side from the field, though Chapple, Flintoff and Schofield have also played their part in dismissing the County Champions for 280. Confirmation that tea will now be taken and that Surrey are to be asked to follow on for the first time since the final match of 1998, when Leicestershire clinched the title at The Oval, soon arrives via the public address system.

Tea:- Between Innings

Trailing by 319 runs on first innings, Surrey begin their second knock in indifferent light and lose an early wicket when Jon Batty cuts the first ball of the fourth over, bowled by Glen Chapple, straight to Alec Swann in the gully. With just eight runs on the board and a possible thirty-two overs still left for play today, there is a real possibility that Surrey could be staring defeat in the face by the close, though the grey clouds that are gathering around the ground offer some hope of a reprieve.

The gritty and determined Ian Ward and Mark Ramprakash stand between Lancashire and further breakthroughs in any case and, while the latter starts much more positively and confidently than in the first innings, the former takes twelve from Chapple's third over and then two fours from James Anderson's fifth before a combination of poor light and a spattering of rain drives the players from the field with the scoreboard reading 48-1 after 8.5 overs.

After a break of exactly half an hour, play is able to restart and Surrey lose Ramprakash almost immediately when Andy Flintoff, having replaced Chapple at the Vauxhall end, finds an outside edge as the batsman pushes at a delivery wide of off stump and Warren Hegg swoops low to pick up a fine catch in front of first slip.

Fortunately for the home side, the light closes in again within ten minutes and the players leave the field for the final time at 5.57pm, with Lancashire still 258 runs to the good and requiring eight wickets to force victory on the final day.

Close:- Surrey 61-2 (Ward 40, Thorpe 0*) from 12.2 overs*

Fourth Day - Monday 21st April

Lancashire 599; Surrey 280 and 379-6
Match Drawn
Surrey 7pts, Lancashire 12

On a bright but cool morning, with the pitch still in good order, the overnight batsmen make a very circumspect start against Glen Chapple and James Anderson after an early exploratory over from Chris Schofield.

Apart from a couple of nicely struck boundaries by Ian Ward in Anderson's opening over, the second of which takes him through to a fine 48-ball fifty, neither batsman attempts anything too extravagant, with just two further fours, both from deflections to third man, coming in the first forty-five minutes. Ward does eventually thump Chapple to the rope at extra cover to raise the fifty partnership but Graham Thorpe remains utterly dogged until he hooks to the fence when Andy Flintoff replaces Chapple at the pavilion end for the twenty-seventh over of the innings. In typical fashion, Warren Hegg then makes it a double bowling change by reintroducing Schofield in place of Anderson at the Vauxhall end, though this doesn't seem to bother either batsman as Thorpe becomes the principal aggressor by picking up a couple of isolated boundaries off Flintoff. Unfortunately, however, Thorpe's attempts to dominate his former England team-mate bring about his downfall as, for the second time in the match, he falls on the hook, this time hitting the ball cleanly but putting it straight down the throat of Anderson, who has been deliberately posted at deep backward square leg.

With lunch just half-an-hour away the loss of Thorpe for thirty-five, with his side still 195 runs adrift, is especially disappointing, and, as so often happens, the capture of one wicket leads to a second success for the fielding side… and, again, regrettably, the wicket is gifted to Lancashire by the batsman. Having been unable to get off the mark from the first dozen balls he faces, Ali Brown foolishly attempts an almost impossible single to mid-off and pays the ultimate price. The fielder, Mark Chilton, can scarcely believe what is happening but he stays calm, picks the ball up cleanly and returns it to the bowler, Schofield, who removes the bails at the non-striker's end with Brown still well short of the crease.

Surrey are now on the ropes at 131-4 and only a stroke of good fortune prevents them from losing a fifth wicket shortly afterwards. Having smashed a Schofield full-toss over the midwicket boundary for six in the over following Thorpe's dismissal, Ward almost comes unstuck against the leg-spinner two overs after the loss of Brown when a leg-break spins back through the left-handers 'gate' and bowls him. Lancashire celebrations are instantly muted, however, as umpire Holder has called 'no-ball'.

After Ward's lucky escape on seventy-three, the last few overs of the morning pass relatively quietly, though the Surrey total does at least reach 150 from the last ball of the session with a thick-edged single to third man by Adam Hollioake off the persevering Flintoff.

Lunch:- Surrey 150-4 (Ward 78, Hollioake 10*) from 43 overs*

Warren Hegg pulls a rabbit out of the hat for his side immediately after lunch, giving Kyle Hogg his first bowl of the innings and reaping instant dividends as Hollioake steers the youngster's innocuous third delivery straight to Chilton in the gully. The loss of their captain represents a serious blow to the home team's chances of holding out for a draw as they still trail by 169 runs, with just five wickets remaining and the small matter of sixty-six overs left to play.

Unfazed by the task that lies ahead, Rikki Clarke gets away confidently with three well-timed boundaries in his first four overs at the crease. With Hogg largely unimpressive as Ward twice whips short deliveries through midwicket for four to move his personal score into the nineties, and Anderson unable to recapture his first-innings spark at the other end, Hegg sensibly reverts to Chapple and Schofield after just eight overs.

Putting his moment of good fortune against the leg-spinner before the break to the back of his mind, Ward takes the attack to Schofield once again, driving and pulling fours in successive overs to move on to ninety-nine before whipping the 'leggie' away through square leg for a boundary that not only completes a magnificent century from 156 balls but also takes the Surrey score beyond two-hundred. Having finished the 2002 campaign with four centuries in his last five Championship innings, Ward has thus extended his run of success to five centuries in his last seven visits to the crease and, though he is happy to celebrate this latest ton, he is clearly also aware that there is still much to do if he is to steer his side to a draw. The Surrey opener is obviously seeing the ball very well now, though, and he continues to close the gap between the two sides by steering and pulling fours off Chapple and then battering a Schofield long-hop high over midwicket for the second six of his innings. Doubtless inspired by his partner's excellence, Clarke then contributes a pulled six of his own when Hogg returns at the pavilion end in place of Chapple and, as we move deep into the afternoon session, Surrey continue to improve their prospects of defying their opponents.

After another short and ineffective spell by Hogg, the Lancashire skipper turns back, rather belatedly it seems, to Flintoff, though he, too, fails to provide any instant breakthrough as Ward pulls a short ball to the rope at midwicket to simultaneously raise the hundred partnership for the sixth wicket and the Surrey 250. A third six for the left-hander off Schofield, pulled over the fence at deep midwicket, merely underlines Ward's dominance and shortly afterwards his partnership with Clarke earns a place in the record books as the highest for the sixth wicket by Surrey against Lancashire, surpassing the 116 added by Bobby Abel and Percy Fender at The Oval in 1923.

With tea imminent and his team's hopes of victory just starting to fade, Hegg attempts to pull off the rabbit-out-of-the-hat trick again by replacing Schofield with Alec Swann, the purveyor of occasional off-breaks, but this time he has no success as both batsmen reach personal milestones just before the break. Ward makes it through to 150 from 211 balls by forcing Flintoff to the extra-cover fence, while Clarke reaches an invaluable half-century from 85 deliveries when he drives Swann to the rope at long-on. The home team still trail by thirty-four runs and are certainly not out of the woods yet, but their prospects of denying Lancashire victory are looking pretty good as the not out batsmen leave the field to warm and well deserved applause from the Surrey faithful.

Tea:- Surrey 285-5 (Ward 150, Clarke 53*) from 74 overs*

Ian Ward continues to look in imperious form during the opening over after the resumption as he despatches Chapple's first and third deliveries to the cover boundary, but in attempting a similar stroke in the next over from the rested and recalled Anderson he lifts the ball into the hands of Iain Sutcliffe at cover point, thereby reviving Lancashire's hopes of victory. As Ward returns to the pavilion to a standing ovation for his superb 221-ball innings of 158, his team remain twenty-five runs in arrears with four wickets to fall and they clearly still have a battle on their hands.

The new batsman, Alex Tudor, has his own personal battle to fight, too, as this is only his second competitive innings since being struck a nasty blow in the face by a Brett Lee bouncer at Perth on England's winter tour to Australia. It is entirely predictable, therefore, that the tall Surrey paceman should receive more than his fair share of short-pitched deliveries, yet he gets right behind the ball every time, in an almost exaggerated style, while Clarke at the other end continues to narrow the gap between the two sides with pulled and on-driven boundaries off Chapple.

By the time Flintoff replaces Chapple at the pavilion end for the seventh over of the final session the seventh-wicket pair seem to have stabilised the situation again after the loss of Ward, and the home fans' belief that a draw can be achieved is confirmed by their enthusiastic applause when Clarke ties up the scores with a sublime straight-driven four in the next over from Anderson.

As he searches for another breakthrough, Hegg switches his bowlers every few overs, but Tudor remains solidly defiant and Clarke again takes a liking to the returning Schofield's leg-breaks, cutting, pulling and sweeping three boundaries in quick succession to take his personal tally into the nineties and further extend Surrey's advantage as the overs continue to tick away.

The one remaining hurdle that Surrey now have to clear is the new ball, which is taken as soon as it becomes available, with nineteen overs remaining for play. The highly impressive Clarke, on ninety-two at the time, is not to be denied a century, however, and reaches the landmark with a brace of strokes for two, through midwicket and cover, followed by a deliberate deflection to the third-man boundary in Chapple's first over with the new 'cherry'. The 21-year-old all-rounder's phenomenally mature 139-ball innings has contained 14 fours and a six, and rightly receives a hero's ovation from the crowd and his team-mates and looks increasingly likely to prove a match-saving knock.

Warren Hegg seemingly acknowledges this fact by withdrawing Chapple from the attack after just two overs, with the Surrey total having just passed 350, and, as the pressure eases on the batsmen, they ensure that the match will be drawn by firing off six assorted boundaries in the next five overs delivered by Hogg and Anderson.

Finally, at 5.30pm, Lancashire admit defeat in their attempt to force a win, with Clarke undefeated on 127 after a truly magnificent knock and Tudor still unbowed after a determined 68-ball occupation of the crease for eleven runs. Lancashire have outplayed the County Champions for the majority of the four days, of that there can be no doubt, and, but for the loss of eighty overs to bad light and rain, Surrey might well have suffered a defeat in their opening match of the season for the first time since 1990. That they have escaped is almost entirely down to the efforts of Messrs Ward and Clarke.

Lancashire 599; Surrey 280 and 379-6
Match Drawn - Surrey 7pts, Lancashire 12

TALKING POINTS - ADAM HOLLIOAKE

There seemed to be conflicting reports flying around as to whether or not James Ormond was fit to play in this match. Can you clear that one up for me, please?

AH - Jimmy could have played, but he was only just coming back from injury, and we wanted to make sure that he was right for the second game - we didn't want to bring him back too early and risk him being out for a longer period. At the same time, Timmy Murtagh was looking good in pre-season, so that was the thinking behind the decision. It was a case of being careful with Jimmy, and getting Tim in while he was going well.

TALKING POINTS - IAN SALISBURY

Conditions weren't easy for a leg-break bowler, but I suspect you must have been very pleased with how you bowled in this game. Correct?

IS - Yes, certainly not ideal conditions - the track was pretty flat, and I had to bowl a lot of the time into a howling wind on a freezing cold day… but, yes, I thought I bowled really well, which was my reward for a lot of hard work I'd put in during pre-season. Having started so well, it was especially frustrating that I then got hit on the hand by Freddie Flintoff when I batted. It didn't actually fracture the index finger on my bowling hand but it messed up all the ligaments… and I didn't realise much I used that finger in my bowling until it got damaged. But that really set me back - I missed a few games and then I had to play catch-up for a long time afterwards.

How did you feel Chris Schofield, your fellow leg-spinner, bowled? I'm not convinced that Lancashire use him very well or give him enough opportunities.

IS - He had a big opportunity to take some wickets here, with them having got such a lot of runs on the board, but I thought they were just trying to get him to bowl tightly, rather than telling him to bowl to get wickets. He still went at about three-an-over, which they seemed to be happy with, but he didn't really threaten to take a lot of wickets. He got three in the first innings but they were all very soft dismissals, really, and I think they masked how he'd bowled. I think the second innings was more of a true reflection.

SURREY v LANCASHIRE at The Oval 18th to 21st April

Lancashire won the toss and elected to bat Umpires:- Vanburn Holder and Neil Mallender

LANCASHIRE - First Innings

Fall Of Wkt	Batsman	How	Out	Score	Balls	4s	6s
1-108	**A.J. Swann**	**run**	**out**	**57**	95	11	0
2-169	**I.J. Sutcliffe**	**lbw**	**b Saqlain**	**70**	118	12	0
3-451	**M.B. Loye**	**lbw**	**b Clarke**	**126**	283	17	0
4-460	**S.G. Law**		**b Clarke**	**169**	223	24	1
6-534	**M.J. Chilton**	**lbw**	**b Salisbury**	**28**	56	5	0
5-523	**A. Flintoff**	**c Batty**	**b Salisbury**	**43**	39	6	2
8-565	**G. Chapple**	**c &**	**b Salisbury**	**32**	29	5	1
7-565	**C.P. Schofield**	**c Batty**	**b Tudor**	**1**	14	0	0
10-599	**W.K. Hegg *+**		**b Murtagh**	**14**	34	1	0
9-593	**K.W. Hogg**	**c Hollioake**	**b Salisbury**	**16**	27	3	0
	J.M. Anderson	**Not**	**Out**	**3**	9	0	0
	Extras	**(4lb, 36nb)**		**40**			
	TOTAL	**(151.4 overs)**		**599**			

Bowler	O	M	R	W	NB	Wd
Tudor	**37**	**4**	**137**	**1**	10	-
Murtagh	**21.4**	**2**	**100**	**1**	1	-
Hollioake	**8**	**0**	**27**	**0**	-	-
Clarke	**21**	**0**	**137**	**2**	5	-
Saqlain Mushtaq	**22**	**5**	**78**	**1**	1	-
Salisbury	**42**	**10**	**116**	**4**	1	-

SURREY - First Innings (Needing 450 to avoid the follow-on)

Fall Of Wkt	Batsman	How	Out	Score	Balls	4s	6s
2-106	**I.J. Ward**	**c Hegg**	**b Anderson**	**49**	101	6	0
1-35	**J.N. Batty +**		**b Anderson**	**13**	23	3	0
3-123	**M.R. Ramprakash**	**c Hegg**	**b Anderson**	**50**	80	9	1
5-140	**G.P. Thorpe**	**c Loye**	**b Anderson**	**15**	20	3	0
4-129	**A.D. Brown**	**lbw**	**b Anderson**	**2**	7	0	0
8-230	**R. Clarke**	**c Chilton**	**b Schofield**	**38**	41	6	1
6-204	**A.J. Hollioake ***	**c Flintoff**	**b Chapple**	**42**	43	9	0
7-227	**A.J. Tudor**	**c Chilton**	**b Schofield**	**9**	12	2	0
9-268	**I.D.K. Salisbury**	**c Hegg**	**b Flintoff**	**18**	36	3	0
10-280	**Saqlain Mushtaq**	**c Anderson**	**b Schofield**	**23**	48	4	0
	T.J. Murtagh	**Not**	**Out**	**0**	2	0	0
	Extras	**(4b, 5lb, 12nb)**		**21**			
	TOTAL	**(67.4 overs)**		**280**			

Bowler	O	M	R	W	NB	Wd
Anderson	**13**	**2**	**61**	**5**	1	-
Chapple	**15**	**2**	**52**	**1**	1	-
Flintoff	**13**	**2**	**42**	**1**	-	-
Hogg	**9**	**1**	**39**	**0**	4	-
Schofield	**17.4**	**4**	**77**	**3**	-	-

SURREY - Second Innings (Following on, 319 runs in arrears)

Fall Of Wkt	Batsman	How	Out	Score	Balls	4s	6s
6-294	**I.J. Ward**	**c Sutcliffe**	**b Anderson**	**158**	221	24	3
1-8	**J.N. Batty +**	**c Swann**	**b Chapple**	**4**	7	1	0
2-48	**M.R. Ramprakash**	**c Hegg**	**b Flintoff**	**13**	21	3	0
3-124	**G.P. Thorpe**	**c Anderson**	**b Flintoff**	**35**	79	6	0
4-131	**A.D. Brown**	**run**	**out**	**0**	13	0	0
5-150	**A.J. Hollioake ***	**c Chilton**	**b Hogg**	**10**	22	1	0
	R. Clarke	**Not**	**Out**	**127**	171	19	1
	A.J. Tudor	**Not**	**Out**	**11**	68	2	0
	Extras	**(11b, 6lb, 2w, 2nb)**		**21**			
	TOTAL	**(100 overs)**	**(for 6 wkts)**	**379**			

Bowler	O	M	R	W	NB	Wd
Anderson	**22**	**7**	**72**	**1**	-	-
Chapple	**20**	**1**	**100**	**1**	-	-
Flintoff	**19**	**5**	**47**	**2**	-	1
Schofield	**25**	**8**	**86**	**0**	1	-
Hogg	**12**	**3**	**46**	**1**	-	1
Swann	**2**	**0**	**11**	**0**	-	-

Other Frizzell Championship Division One Results

In the other opening matches of the campaign, Nottinghamshire made a good start to their debut season in the first division by beating Warwickshire in a fine match at Trent Bridge, while Middlesex battled back well to salvage a draw against Essex at Chelmsford. County Championship cricket received a welcome boost as excellent crowds were recorded all around the country on Good Friday.

April 18-21
***Chelmsford:-* Essex (12pts) drew with Middlesex (8)**. Middlesex 214 (Dakin 4-57) & 495 (Joyce 117, Koenig 94, Razzaq 81, Middlebrook 5-172); Essex 402 (Robinson 83, Irani 69, Jefferson 56, Dakin 52) & 41-0
***Trent Bridge:-* Nottinghamshire (19.25pts*) beat Warwickshire (3.75*) by 3 wickets.** Warwicks 222 (Wagh 73, Shreck 4-33) & 390 (Giles 94, Ostler 58, Betts 56*, Brown 52, Smith 5-98); Notts 349 (Shafayat 97, Bicknell 61, Richardson 4-85) & 264-7 (Bicknell 81, Pietersen 54, Betts 4-49). *** Nottinghamshire were deducted 0.75 pts and Warwickshire 0.25pt for their slow over-rates.**

First-Class Friendly - Centuries Galore But Loughborough Contest Fails To Inspire

As a competitive contest the first-class friendly at The Oval against Loughborough UCCE had little to commend it, with rain on the final day assisting the battling students in achieving a draw. As an opportunity for batting practice and giving a run out to players who had missed the Lancashire match through injury, absence or non-selection there was, however, something to be gained from the contest. James Ormond returned his best first-class bowling figures for Surrey in the match, and Martin Bicknell recorded a second first-class century, though, given the rather variable quality of their opponents, it is doubtful that these will rate as performances to be remembered with any great sense of pride or achievement by the players concerned.

Scores:- Loughborough UCCE 206 (White 76, Nash 54, Ormond 6-34) and 235-4 (Atri 82*, Francis 57) drew with Surrey 663-9dec (Ramprakash 205, Batty 123, Hollioake 121*, Bicknell 103*)

Frizzell Championship Division One Results

While Surrey had been playing Loughborough UCCE, a full programme of Championship matches had produced a win for Middlesex over Sussex - after they had been dismissed for just 116 in their first innings - and an enthralling tie at Edgbaston between Warwickshire and Essex, following collusion between the captains on the final day. At Old Trafford, Lancashire were again left frustrated by rain, while Kent and Leicestershire fought out a competitive draw at Canterbury.

April 23-26
***Canterbury:-* Kent (8pts) drew with Leicestershire (9)**. Kent 245 (Blewett 57, Carberry 55) & 411 (Jones 104, Ealham 82, DeFreitas 4-69); Leics 270 (Nixon 113*, Maddy 63, Saggers 4-75) & 255-6 (Nixon 53, Brandy 52).
***Old Trafford:-* Lancashire (11pts) drew with Nottinghamshire (9).** Lancashire 354 (Loye 113, Flintoff 97, Elworthy 5-71) & 41-2; Notts 275 (Cairns 57, Read 57, Martin 5-54).
***Lord's:-* Middlesex (17pts) beat Sussex (4) by 3 wickets.** Sussex 239 (Ambrose 51) & 204 (Martin-Jenkins 50, Keegan 4-36); Middlesex 116 & 330-7 (Strauss 83, Shah 61, Kirtley 4-87).
***Edgbaston:-* Warwickshire (12pts) tied with Essex (9)**. Warwickshire 446-7dec (Troughton 129*, Brown 120, Frost 59) & 2nd inns forfeited; Essex 66-0dec & 380 (Irani 87, Robinson 56, Flower 55, Giles 5-115).

NATIONAL CRICKET LEAGUE DIVISION ONE - MATCH ONE
Essex Eagles versus Surrey Lions at Chelmsford
Sunday 27th April

Setting The Scene - Surrey's opening match of the 2003 NCL season sees them taking on one of their fellow promoted sides, Essex Eagles, at Chelmsford, with the Lions' thrilling promotion-clinching two-run victory in last season's corresponding fixture still in the memory. Surrey welcome back Martin Bicknell from injury for this match, while Azhar Mahmood also plays his first game of the season after returning from Pakistan. Saqlain Mushtaq is meanwhile fit to play after recovering from the injury he sustained in the opening Championship match, though Ian Salisbury is unavailable after damaging a finger while batting in that game. While the England captain, Nasser Hussain, is permitted to play for Essex, allowing them to field what would appear to be a full-strength eleven, Surrey have been told that they cannot select their centrally-contracted players, Alec Stewart and Mark Butcher. Essex decide to field after Adam Hollioake calls incorrectly at the toss.

Surrey Lions' Innings

The visitors' NCL campaign gets away to an inauspicious start when Ian Ward, fresh from his century against Lancashire, falls lbw to Jon Dakin as he aims to leg in the third over with the total on ten.

On a pitch that is clearly offering some early assistance to the bowlers, Ali Brown and Mark Ramprakash wisely attempt to re-establish the innings, though they have to endure some uncomfortable moments against both Dakin and Scott Brant, Essex's left-arm Australian import. The second-wicket pair have been together for just six overs, adding twenty-three runs to the total, before both men are dismissed in the space of four balls - Ramprakash is bowled by a delivery from Brant that appears to keep a little low in the eighth over, then Brown flashes at a wide ball from Dakin in the next over and edges to James Foster behind the stumps to put Surrey in real trouble at 34-3.

Encouraged by these early successes, Ronnie Irani keeps both bowlers going until they are through seven overs apiece, though they fail to make another breakthrough as Graham Thorpe, supported by Rikki Clarke, makes a positive start and takes ten runs from the final over of Dakin's spell to raise the visitors' fifty.

A double bowling change, which sees the introduction of Graham Napier and Irani himself, soon puts the skids under Surrey again, however, as Clarke falls lbw to Napier in the seventeeth over after an unconvincing innings of eight. With Thorpe having just survived a very difficult chance to Foster off Irani in the previous over, and the score now 68-4, Jon Batty enters the fray at number six, ahead of his captain and Azhar Mahmood, presumably in an attempt to steady the Surrey ship.

This move doesn't pay any dividends, however, as Napier strikes twice in his fourth over - the first delivery sees Thorpe getting an inside edge that dribbles back onto his stumps via his pads, then Batty is trapped lbw when only half forward two balls later - to leave the Lions well and truly cornered at 82-6 in the twenty-first over.

Much is clearly going to depend on the two men now at the crease, Adam Hollioake and Azhar Mahmood, and the Surrey skipper makes an impressive start by driving his first ball to the extra-cover boundary and then lofting his second back over the bowler's head for another four.

These blows, plus the suspicion that one of these free-spirited batsmen might hit the self-destruct button, doubtless encourage Irani to remove Napier from the firing line, despite his three wickets, and introduce the left-arm spin of Paul Grayson. Hollioake responds to this change by driving the new bowler's sixth ball over mid-off for four to bring up the Surrey hundred in the twenty-third over, while Azhar finds the rope at midwicket and third man in the following over from Irani. The game certainly appears to be at a crucial stage as the experienced Irani and Grayson plug away in the hope that the batsmen will make a fatal mistake, but, to Essex's undoubted disappointment, Hollioake and Azhar stay cool while picking up just seven singles from the next four overs to take the score to 118-6 after 28 overs.

This period of calm soon develops into something of a storm, though, as Hollioake launches the second ball of Grayson's fourth over high over long-on, shattering a window in the press box and leaving Angus Fraser, the nearest journalist to the point of impact, peering through the resulting 'cobweb-effect' glass. Although the Surrey captain is rather fortunate when an inside edge off Irani earns him four more runs to raise the fifty partnership for the seventh wicket in the next over, the floodgates now appear to be opening up as Hollioake pulls his opposite number high over long-on for six in the final over of Irani's decent and, hitherto, restrictive spell, while Azhar joins the party by clattering the returning Napier for a four backward of square leg and a six over wide long-on.

Having succeeded in pushing the fielders back onto the boundary, plenty of singles are now on offer and the Surrey pair sensibly gather in plenty of these as Irani goes for an all-spin attack of Grayson and James Middlebrook. Neither batsman turns down an opportunity to pick off a boundary here and there, though, as Hollioake demonstrates when he lofts Middlebrook over mid-on for four to complete a 46-ball fifty and then repeats the stroke, this time for six, in the next over from Grayson. The equally destructive Azhar is only just behind his skipper in reaching fifty and, in fact, trumps him in two respects - by taking one less delivery to get there and by doing so with a six, driven over long-on off Middlebrook. This amazing burst of scoring has seen seventy-six runs added in just nine overs and, after a brief hiatus when Grayson comes up with a highly creditable over that costs him only three runs, the charge is on again.

The Surrey two-hundred - a score that had been nothing more than a pipe dream at 82-6 - comes up in the thirty-ninth over when Azhar drives Middlebrook for the first of two fours, then, when Hollioake pulls Grayson for six in the following over, the stand goes into the record books as the highest in Sunday/National League history for the seventh wicket. The previous best mark of 132 by Keith Brown and Neil Williams for Middlesex against Somerset at Lord's in 1988 is then left way behind as the carnage continues with three more fours coming from the next six balls, despite the return of Napier for the expensive Middlebrook.

With the partnership now exceeding 150 and Surrey on 233-6, Irani finally recalls his opening bowlers to complete their spells and the innings. Having compiled a stunning seventy-seven from 66 balls during a stand of 154 in just twenty-one overs, Hollioake finally perishes to Brant's fourth delivery as his unsuccessful attempt to run the ball down to third man ends with his off stump being flattened, but Azhar remains and continues to mete out some hefty punishment to the Eagles' opening bowlers - Dakin is cut to the boundary as the Lions reach 250 in the forty-third over, then he blasts a huge straight six off Brant to move his score into the nineties. Alas, he falls two runs short of a well deserved century as he has his stumps rearranged by a Dakin yorker in trying to make room to hit the penultimate ball of the innings through the off side. Like his skipper before him, the Pakistani all-rounder gets a good hand from the crowd for his scintillating knock (73 balls, 9 fours, 3 sixes) as he leaves the field and it is pretty certain that anyone who has witnessed this amazing partnership is unlikely to forget it in a hurry. A final total of 268-8, which would have been beyond their wildest dreams earlier in the afternoon, gives Surrey a good chance of starting the NCL season with a victory.

Essex Eagles' Innings

Facing a daunting asking rate of 5.98 runs per over, the Eagles need to get away to a flying start if they are to challenge Surrey's impressive final total. The 6' 10" Will Jefferson and the stocky Darren Robinson are the men entrusted with that task and they give the innings early impetus as each man finds the extra-cover boundary on a couple of occasions in the opening three overs from Martin Bicknell and Azhar Mahmood. Jefferson continues to look particularly strong off the front foot as he takes three further fours from Bicknell's third over and, with the Essex fifty clicking up from the final ball of the fifth over, and another eleven runs then coming from the next over by Azhar, Surrey are already under some pressure.

While Bicknell is withdrawn from the attack with unusually expensive figures of 3-0-28-0 and replaced by Alex Tudor, Adam Hollioake keeps faith with Azhar at the river end and is rewarded when the Pakistani deservedly removes Robinson, courtesy of a return catch via the batsman's inside edge and front pad. Bizarrely, this is the third time that Azhar has 'dismissed' Robinson in the innings, having bowled him the previous ball, as well as in the second over, with free-hit deliveries following front-foot no-ball discretions. This wicket, with the total on sixty-five, brings some welcome relief to the visitors and they are soon celebrating a second breakthrough when Jefferson, having looked much less comfortable when confronted by Tudor's greater pace and shorter length, falls lbw when barely half-forward to the big paceman.

At 71-2 after nine overs, parity seems to have been restored to the contest, though the balance shifts two overs later when Tudor strikes again to claim the vital wicket of Andy Flower. Having edged the fourth ball of the over down to the rope at third man, the former Zimbabwe international is bowled by the next delivery and, suddenly, the Eagles are struggling a little at 75-3.

With the England captain now joined at the wicket by the Essex skipper, and with some decent batting still to come, the hosts are by no means out of the game, and this point is firmly underlined as Hussain pulls and drives boundaries off Azhar, while Irani suddenly gets after Tudor, driving him for three fours and a towering six over long-on in the course of the bowler's next two overs. This positive approach sees the hundred rattling up in the fifteenth over and a quick-fire fifty partnership being completed just four overs later.

At this stage, Essex appear to be taking control, though the pairing of Saqlain Mushtaq and Martin Bicknell from the eighteenth over slowly but surely begins to even up the contest again. Hussain, in particular, is completely tied down by the off-spinner and it is no surprise when frustration finally gets the better of him with the score at 136-3 in the twenty-second over. Attempting to cut a ball that is neither short enough nor wide enough for the stroke, he is bowled for twenty-one and the game is again back in the balance.

With Saqlain and Bicknell continuing to concede nothing more than the occasional single, the pressure on Irani and his new partner, Paul Grayson, begins to mount and in the twenty-sixth over Grayson cracks, charging recklessly down the wicket to Saqlain and being comfortably stumped for just four with the total standing at 146.

At this point, Hollioake elects to break Saqlain's spell of 7-0-16-2 in order to bring himself into the attack, and the picture changes yet again as Irani launches an assault on Bicknell, twice driving him for six over wide long-on and then pulling him through midwicket for four to complete a feisty 56-ball half-century.

With Bicknell's uncharacteristically erratic spell now complete, the Surrey skipper elects to introduce Rikki Clarke at the Hayes Close end, which is a surprising and unnecessary move since there is no reason why he can't get through the rest of the innings using his front-line bowlers. There is clearly method in Hollioake's apparent madness, however, as Irani, having lofted Clarke's first ball to the wide long-on boundary, advances to the second and edges a wild drive into the safe gloves of Jon Batty. A fascinating game is nicely poised once more with the Eagles, at 178-6, needing ninety-one further runs from almost fourteen overs.

Having made a slow start after replacing Grayson at the crease, James Foster is now the key man for the home side and he doesn't disappoint the home fans as he launches into a calculated attack on Clarke's second over, picking off three boundaries during a fifteen-run over that sees the arrival of the Essex two-hundred.

Hollioake responds immediately by making a double bowling change that sees Saqlain and Tudor returning to the fray, and it isn't long before his off-spinner provides him with another important wicket. The potentially dangerous Jon Dakin is the man to go, falling lbw when missing a sweep and thereby providing Saqlain with instant revenge for an on-driven six in the Surrey spinner's previous over. It is still anyone's match, however, at 215-7 in the thirty-sixth over, though the Eagles are certainly grateful that Saqlain is now out of the equation, having completed his allotted overs with the excellent figures of 9-0-27-3.

The powerful Graham Napier is Dakin's replacement at the wicket, though it is Foster who provides Essex with their next boundary as he drives the final ball of Tudor's penultimate over for six over long-on to leave his side needing forty-four from the last eight overs to win the match.

Fortunately for Surrey, however, Tudor follows up a tight four-run over from his skipper by emulating Saqlain in dismissing the man who has just struck him for six. Foster's attempt to repeat the stroke that had brought him a 'maximum' in the Surrey paceman's previous over ends up in the hands of 'Saqi', the off-spinner having run in from the long-on fence to take a good catch that pegs the home side back to 233-8.

When James Middlebrook then falls in the next over, the fortieth, his leading-edged drive off Hollioake being well taken low down by Clarke at deepish mid-off, the Lions look virtually assured of victory, especially as the Eagles' last man, Scott Brant, is reputed to be a genuine number eleven.

In actual fact the blond Queenslander turns out to be no mug with the willow, and when he whips the returning Azhar wide of mid-on for four to raise the Essex 250 in the forty-third over it looks like there might yet be life left in the game. Surrey's Pakistani all-rounder has no intention of ending up on the losing side after his earlier heroics with the bat, however, and, with sixteen runs needed from thirteen balls, induces a skied drive from Napier which Tudor takes safely at wide mid-on to leave the Surrey Lions victorious at the end of a most entertaining match.

ADAM HOLLIOAKE'S VIEW FROM THE DRESSING ROOM

Having been put in, we slipped to 82-6. Was that mainly due to a slightly sporty surface, indifferent batting or good bowling?
AH - I think the pitch did start a little bit sporty, and the ball swung around early on, but I don't think we batted especially well. It wasn't a disastrous wicket, but it certainly wasn't a belter.

Jon Batty was promoted to number six. Was that his intended position in the order, or an attempt to steady the ship, allowing yourself and Azhar to come in for a blast late on?
AH - He's not a big striker of the ball at the end of the innings, so the idea of promoting him was to try and see off a bit of the movement - then Azhar and I would come in at the end of the innings and be destructive. As it happened it didn't work out, so when we got together we had a bit of a chat and decided that we would take the attacking option and try to put them on the back foot... and thankfully it worked.

Would you describe it as something of a do-or-die partnership then?
AH - Well, it started off that way, but then it changed from a do-or-die situation to putting them on the back foot very quickly. It didn't take us long to put them in a situation where they had to rethink their plans. We managed to spread the field, and then the game became a lot easier.

They went off like a rocket, with Jefferson blasting the ball around, then you brought on Tudes in place of Bickers and the game changed dramatically. Would you say that was key spell in the match?
AH - Yes, definitely a key spell. Tudes was basically moving the ball back into the right-hander, as opposed to Bickers moving it away, and Jefferson appeared to be liking the ball moving away from him so he could hit through the off-side, so it gave him something very different to think about. But we needed to get him out because the way he was hitting the ball the game was going to be over very quickly otherwise.

Given that early results seem especially important in the NCL, would you look back on this as being perhaps one of the most significant wins of the NCL campaign?
AH - Definitely. Traditionally, when we've done well in the NCL we've got off to a flyer and won our first three or four games, then the motivation is there each week on its own. But if you lose your first three or four games then all of a sudden the Sunday League season seems to become a very long and hard affair.

ESSEX EAGLES v SURREY LIONS at Chelmsford

Sunday 27th April — **Surrey Lions won by 15 runs**

Essex Eagles won the toss and elected to field — **Umpires:- Trevor Jesty & Allan Jones**

SURREY LIONS

Fall Of Wkt	Batsman	How	Out	Score	Balls	4s	6s
1-10	**I.J. Ward**	**lbw**	**b Dakin**	**0**	8	0	0
3-34	**A.D. Brown**	**c Foster**	**b Dakin**	**18**	21	3	0
2-33	**M.R. Ramprakash**		**b Brant**	**11**	20	1	0
5-79	**G.P. Thorpe**		**b Napier**	**26**	37	3	0
4-68	**R. Clarke**	**lbw**	**b Napier**	**8**	22	1	0
6-82	**J.N. Batty +**	**lbw**	**b Napier**	**7**	14	1	0
7-236	**A.J. Hollioake ***		**b Brant**	**77**	66	6	4
8-266	**Azhar Mahmood**		**b Dakin**	**98**	73	9	3
	Saqlain Mushtaq	**Not**	**Out**	**9**	8	1	0
	A.J. Tudor	**Not**	**Out**	**2**	1	0	0
	M.P. Bicknell	**did not bat**					
	Extras	**(5lb, 7w)**		**12**			
	TOTAL	**(45 overs)**	**(for 8 wkts)**	**268**			

Bowler	O	M	R	W	NB	Wd
Dakin	**9**	**1**	**51**	**3**	-	4
Brant	**9**	**0**	**44**	**2**	-	-
Napier	**7**	**0**	**50**	**3**	-	-
Irani	**9**	**0**	**38**	**0**	-	1
Grayson	**8**	**0**	**49**	**0**	-	1
Middlebrook	**3**	**0**	**31**	**0**	-	1

ESSEX EAGLES

Fall Of Wkt	Batsman		How	Out	Score	Balls	4s	6s
1-65	**D.D.J. Robinson**		**c &**	**b Azhar**	**12**	18	2	0
2-71	**W.I. Jefferson**		**lbw**	**b Tudor**	**47**	36	9	0
4-136	**N. Hussain**			**b Saqlain**	**21**	43	3	0
3-75	**A. Flower**			**b Tudor**	**4**	5	1	0
6-178	**R.C. Irani ***	**c Batty**		**b Clarke**	**64**	60	6	3
5-146	**A.P. Grayson**	**st Batty**		**b Saqlain**	**4**	9	0	0
8-233	**J.S. Foster +**	**c Saqlain**		**b Tudor**	**41**	37	5	1
7-215	**J.M. Dakin**		**lbw**	**b Saqlain**	**17**	21	1	1
10-253	**G.R. Napier**	**c Tudor**		**b Azhar**	**11**	16	0	0
9-235	**J.D. Middlebrook**	**c Clarke**		**b Hollioake**	**0**	4	0	0
	S.A. Brant		**Not**	**Out**	**14**	13	1	0
	Extras	**(4b, 5lb, 1w, 8nb)**			**18**			
	TOTAL	**(43 overs)**			**253**			

Bowler	O	M	R	W	NB	Wd
Bicknell	**9**	**0**	**60**	**0**	-	-
Azhar Mahmood	**8**	**1**	**54**	**2**	3	-
Tudor	**9**	**0**	**57**	**3**	-	-
Saqlain Mushtaq	**9**	**0**	**27**	**3**	1	1
Hollioake	**6**	**0**	**22**	**1**	-	-
Clarke	**2**	**0**	**24**	**1**	-	-

Other NCL Division One Results

April 27

***Bristol:-* Worcestershire Royals (4pts) beat Gloucestershire Gladiators by 35 runs (D/L method).** Gloucs 143 (43.3ov; Mason 4-35); Worcs 98-2 (24.4ov; Hick 52*).

***Canterbury:-* Kent Spitfires (4pts) beat Leicestershire Foxes by 54 runs**. Kent 254-4 (45ov; Walker 82*); Leics 200 (39.2ov; Trego 4-39).

***Edgbaston:-* Yorkshire Phoenix (4pts) beat Warwickshire Bears by 6 wickets (D/L method)**. Warwicks 158-9 (42ov; Giles 61*); Yorks 160-4 (35ov; Lumb 61).

3 Warming Up

Surrey's victory at Chelmsford had gone some way towards making up for the poor display against Lancashire, though it was disappointing to see so many of the players still looking rather 'ring rusty'. Lancashire, having played some decent, competitive cricket on a pre-season tour to South Africa, had without doubt looked much the sharper and better prepared team. Looking on the bright side, though, the team had - largely through the efforts of Ian Ward and Rikki Clarke - saved the match when the chips were down and that had made a huge difference where points were concerned. Had Lancashire won the game they would have taken twenty-two points (a win having been increased in value to fourteen points for 2003) to Surrey's three - a nineteen-point advantage - whereas the draw had resulted in a twelve points to seven outcome that scarcely reflected the visitors' superiority. It was possible that the swing of fourteen points - the difference between winning and drawing for Lancashire - could prove important come the end of the season.

For now, however, the biggest cloud on Surrey's horizon was the fallout from the first team selection of the summer, with Mark Butcher having, regrettably, publicly voiced his displeasure at having been omitted from the team. It was understandable that he should be concerned about the possible impact on his place in the England team if he wasn't selected to play for Surrey, and David Graveney hadn't helped matters by stating that "Mark needs to have played sufficient county cricket for him to be available for selection (for England)." It was rather disappointing that Butcher had felt the need to make his comments public, however, when the matter could surely have been resolved internally and behind closed doors. The England left-hander was quoted as saying, "I'm hacked off and it's fair to say that I put my point forcefully" and then, referring to his 124 at Sydney in the final Test of the Ashes series, went on to add, "The way I see it is that I'm an England player who scored a century against the best team in the world in my last game. But for some reason I'm not picked for my county."

These comments obviously hadn't gone down particularly well within the Club, with Keith Medlycott being quoted in *The Times* as saying:- "I don't think some of the things that have been said have been that helpful. Everyone needs to understand that Surrey will pick the best side for Surrey. It's not rotation, it's about balance. But we knew six months ago this would happen. This is an isolated period. Come the middle of the summer everybody will be very happy." Time alone would tell if this was to be the case or not, though it did seem likely that there would be considerably less scope for controversies once England call-ups started to take players out of the equation for the Surrey manager.

On a happier note, news came through on the eve of the next match, against Warwickshire, that Adam Hollioake had been selected as one of *Wisden's* 'five cricketers of the year' for 2002. The announcement had been delayed because of the late publication of the 2003 almanack - to allow coverage of the recent World Cup to be included - but there was no doubting that the man who had led Surrey to so many successes in his spell at the helm richly deserved the accolade that had now been bestowed upon him.

Another honour looked likely to elude him, though, with most good judges believing that, despite plenty of media support, Hollioake would not be chosen to take the reins of England's one-day side for a second spell, following Nasser Hussain's resignation of the post - not before time in the opinion of a great many people - after England's World Cup failure. With neither the outgoing skipper nor the England coach, Duncan Fletcher, believed to be Hollioake fans, the post looked much more likely to be filled by Michael Vaughan.

FRIZZELL COUNTY CHAMPIONSHIP DIVISION ONE - MATCH TWO

SURREY versus WARWICKSHIRE
at The Oval

First Day - Wednesday 30th April
Warwickshire 342-8

The Teams And The Toss *- The Surrey team shows no fewer than five changes following the disappointing display against Lancashire in the opening match. While Ian Salisbury is sidelined by his injured finger, Graham Thorpe, Rikki Clarke, Jon Batty and Tim Murtagh are all omitted from the side as James Ormond, Mark Butcher, Azhar Mahmood, Alec Stewart and Martin Bicknell are given places in the County Champions' line-up. It is clear that some very tough selectorial decisions have been required, but the omission of Rikki Clarke seems particularly harsh after his match-saving century in the opening game. The attack that had looked rather toothless against Lancashire, particularly in the seam department, is clearly boosted by the return of Messrs Bicknell, Ormond and Mahmood, however, and an interesting decision might have been required had Salisbury, Surrey's best bowler against Lancashire, been fit to play here. Warwickshire, meanwhile, have a few problems of their own, with their seam attack shorn of Shane Bond (on international duty with New Zealand in Sri Lanka), Melvyn Betts (stomach strain), Neil Carter (back) and Michael Clark, the Australian left-armer (back and groin), while skipper Michael Powell misses out with a broken toe. With both Bond and Clark unavailable to them, the visitors field a line-up that is entirely England-qualified. On a cool but reasonably pleasant morning, Ashley Giles, skippering the Bears in Powell's absence, wins the toss and elects to take first use of what looks to be another fine pitch.*

With the ball moving around quite a lot in the early stages, Martin Bicknell and James Ormond give the Warwickshire openers, Nick Knight and Tony Frost, a tough time. The ball beats the bat on numerous occasions and only one of the four boundaries that the batsmen pick up in the opening ten overs comes from the middle of the bat, while scarcely a run comes in front of the wicket. To give the batsmen credit, however, they both show good judgement of which balls to leave around their off stump and, while Knight looks rather out of sorts, Frost gradually gains in confidence as he begins to strike the ball sweetly through the covers and wide of mid-on.

It comes as something of a surprise, therefore, when it is the Bears' wicketkeeper who offers Surrey their first chance of a breakthrough, an edged drive in Ormond's sixth over being badly missed by Mark Butcher at second slip with the total on forty-four and Frost on twenty-six. This proves to be a pivotal moment as it turns out, since Frost continues to prosper and Knight suddenly finds his touch with a flowing on-drive in the last over of Ormond's fine opening burst of eight overs.

With Bicknell's replacement at the pavilion end, Azhar Mahmood, unable to locate the consistent line and length of his predecessor, runs begin to flow at an uncomfortably fast rate from the Surrey point of view. After Knight picks off two boundaries behind point during the Pakistani's third over, having just survived a confident appeal for a catch at the wicket, Frost adds to Azhar's woes with a brace of off-side fours and a hooked six in the bowler's next over. When ten runs then come from the following over, delivered from the Vauxhall end by the generally steady Alex Tudor, the home side are really losing control, and the score continues to mount rapidly as Frost reaches a fine half-century from 69 balls with a glorious cover drive, struck on the up, in Azhar's fifth over. The 27-year-old keeper then celebrates his achievement with another hooked six at the end of a poor spell by the hapless Pakistani, raising the Warwickshire hundred in the process and adding to Hollioake's headaches.

Since the visitors are now racing along at almost four runs an over, the Surrey skipper turns to the normally reliable Saqlain Mushtaq for some control. It comes as something of a shock, therefore, when the new bowler delivers a dreadful first over, costing fifteen runs, where every ball is short, played comfortably off the back foot and scored off.

Although the Surrey off-spinner locates a rather better length in three more overs up to the lunch interval, it appears that all is still not well with him as he oversteps the crease on three occasions and then, in the morning's final over, offers up a wide full-toss that Knight smashes gleefully to the boundary at extra cover to complete a battling half-century from his 107th ball.

With Warwickshire clearly in command at the break, it has been a very disappointing morning for the home side after some fine new ball bowling had threatened to bring early wickets.

Lunch:- Warwickshire 140-0 (Knight 51, Frost 70*) from 33 overs*

Adam Hollioake's decision to revert to his opening bowlers at the start of the afternoon session is entirely predictable and soon produces the breakthrough that his team needs so badly.

Things don't look too rosy initially as Frost strikes Bicknell for two off-side fours to raise the Warwickshire 150 in the fourth over after the resumption, but the 34-year-old Surrey swing bowler takes revenge in his next over when the Bears' keeper cuts straight to Hollioake at point and departs for a well-played seventy-eight with the total standing at 153.

While Ormond continues to keep the batsmen on their toes at the Vauxhall end, Bicknell then beats the new batsman, Mark Wagh, four times in one outstanding over before striking another blow for his side with a well-disguised slower ball that Knight clips, at head height, to Ian Ward at square leg. Knight out for fifty-eight, Warwickshire 158-2.

These well-deserved wickets for Bicknell have brought his side back into the contest, and his excellent post-lunch spell of 8-5-13-2 has seen him beat the bat on many occasions. Ormond, however, remains wicketless despite some moral victories of his own and he must feel there is no justice as he ends his spell with a rather weary looking over that yields three back-foot boundaries to Wagh.

Fears that Warwickshire might begin to surge forward again following a double bowling change that sees the return of Tudor and Azhar are quickly snuffed out, however, when the former's fourth delivery brings him the wicket of Ian Bell. The highly regarded young batsman's short stay at the crease ends with a miscued pull stroke that sends the ball spiralling into the legside where it is well caught by Rikki Clarke, on the field as a substitute, as he runs back towards deepish midwicket.

With the visitors now 180-3 and Bell gone for four, the picture is looking more promising for the reigning champions, though hopes of securing further breakthroughs are initially scotched by the steady Wagh and a very positive Jim Troughton, who reels off three trademark extra cover boundaries in taking the total beyond two-hundred.

Some good thinking by Tudor eventually brings about the left-hander's downfall, though it does appear that Lady Luck is smiling on Surrey as Warwickshire are pegged back to 215-5 in the course of the sixty-third over of the innings.

In an attempt to restrict Troughton's off-side strokes, the Surrey paceman switches his angle of attack to round the wicket and, forcing the batsman back with a short-of-a-length delivery, sees him dislodge a bail with his left foot as he attempts to push a single to square leg off his hip.

With the unfortunate Troughton gone for seventeen from the second ball of the over, Tudor then follows up with the wicket of Dominic Ostler from the final delivery, the veteran batsman chopping the ball down onto his stumps in attempting to cut a delivery that is not wide enough for the chosen stroke. The Surrey players and supporters are cock-a-hoop at this comeback and Tudor has good reason to feel satisfied with his efforts as he gives way to his captain at the pavilion end after a fine spell of 9-2-23-3.

While wickets have been falling at the other end, Wagh has continued to go about his business in a calm and efficient manner and, with tea fast approaching, he completes a nicely constructed fifty from 98 balls with his ninth boundary, clipped backward of square leg off the Surrey skipper.

A very good session for the home side then becomes an excellent session when they capture a sixth wicket with the first ball of the last over before the break. Having twirled away steadily from the Vauxhall end since the fifty-eighth over, Saqlain gets some reward for his efforts when Dougie Brown gloves a sweep and is well taken down the legside by the ever alert Alec Stewart. Warwickshire are now 237-6 and the game is undoubtedly back in the balance.

Tea:- Warwickshire 237-6 (Wagh 50) from 71.1 overs*

With Saqlain continuing to occupy the Vauxhall end and Bicknell now joining him in the attack, Surrey are optimistic of making further breakthroughs upon the resumption, but three early boundaries - two to Wagh and one to the new batsman, Ashley Giles - take the total past 250 and give a clear indication that Warwickshire plan to bat positively despite losing those six wickets during the afternoon session. Giles, in fine form with the willow during the opening matches of the season, survives several edgy moments against Bicknell before settling down to play some more authentic shots and, with Wagh continuing to look largely untroubled, the seventh-wicket partnership begins to prove a serious irritation for the home side.

As a result, Ormond replaces Bicknell at the pavilion end and, after immediately conceding an on-driven boundary to Wagh that makes the stand worth fifty, captures a hard-earned first Championship wicket of the season when Giles hooks his fourth delivery to Azhar at long leg. The score is 288-7 as Warwickshire's stand-in captain makes his way back to the pavilion, and the opportunity now exists for the hosts to dismiss their opponents for a total in the region of 320-330.

Things don't quite go to plan, though, as Mohammad Sheikh, a decent enough batsman to be coming in at number nine, drives and sweeps three fours off the persevering Saqlain, thereby securing the visitors' third batting point at three-hundred. He finds Ormond a much more testing proposition, however, and the sturdy Surrey fast bowler brings him to book in the ninety-first over with the score at 310, courtesy of an edged drive from the batsman and a fine catch by Stewart diving away in front of first slip.

With the light now starting to close in, Hollioake allows Wagh to take singles by spreading the field, in the hope that his bowlers can remove Neil Smith, the new man at the crease. This tactic fails to work, however, as Wagh still manages to find the boundary - moving his score into the nineties with a pull off the recalled Tudor - while Smith slashes and smears three fours of his own in the same bowler's next over.

Despite the fact that Smith seems to be seeing the ball perfectly well, Hollioake's decision to take the new ball and bring Azhar back into the attack in place of the largely ineffective Saqlain proves sufficient to persuade the umpires to offer the light to the batsmen. It comes as no surprise when Wagh, nine runs short of his century, accepts the offer.

Close:- Warwickshire 342-8 (Wagh 91, Smith 20*) from 97.2 overs*

Second Day - Thursday 1st May
Warwickshire 413; Surrey 237-4

With the outfield having been left very damp by overnight rain and a couple of short showers just before the start of play, the players are confined to the pavilion until 12.30pm. Twenty-four overs have been lost in this time, though Surrey go some way towards making up for this when

Neil Smith falls to the first ball he faces in the over that Azhar had been unable to complete last night. Twitching at a good delivery just outside off stump, Warwickshire's veteran off-spinner provides Alec Stewart with a straightforward catch and departs with the scoreboard reading 343-9.

Having secured this early breakthrough, the visitors' innings now looks likely to be terminated before lunch, but a combination of fine play by Wagh, unexpected resistance by the last man, Alan Richardson, and the employment of some baffling tactics by the Surrey captain allows the last-wicket partnership to survive and thrive until the interval.

Seemingly failing to appreciate that any batsman, no matter how good he is or how many runs he has to his name, is vulnerable at the start of a new day, Hollioake slavishly follows the tactic of setting the field back for Wagh in an attempt to get Richardson on strike - and, to compound this apparent error of judgement, he allows the front-line batsman the chance to take a single for five balls of most overs, instead of the generally accepted four. The excellent Wagh takes full advantage of this to progress serenely to a most worthy 167-ball century containing fifteen fours, while Richardson, though rarely having to face more than one ball per over, finds time to steer and slash three boundaries of his own.

Disappointingly, from Surrey's point of view, Hollioake's chosen bowling combination of Azhar and Tudor rarely looks capable of breaking the frustrating partnership as Bicknell and Ormond remain spectators in the outfield, and when Wagh pulls Tudor over midwicket for six in the penultimate over of the shortened morning session the last-wicket stand becomes worth forty-eight.

By the time the players head off for lunch a few minutes later it has passed the fifty mark and one can only reflect that, apart from the early wicket, it's been a shockingly poor 10.4 overs of cricket from Surrey.

Lunch:- Warwickshire 394-9 (Wagh 123, Richardson 15*) from 108 overs*

Despite the introduction of Ormond and Saqlain, Surrey's agony continues for another five overs after lunch. A further nineteen runs are added to the total in this time before Wagh's fine knock comes to an end when he inside-edges the second delivery of Ormond's third over onto his leg stump. The tall right-hander leaves the field to a warm ovation from the crowd, with 136 runs to his name, forty-four of which have been garnered during the last-wicket partnership of seventy.

So, for the second time in two weeks, Surrey are under pressure to perform as they commence their first innings... and it isn't long before they lose their first wicket. While Mark Butcher causes an early flutter in the home camp by edging Richardson airily between the slips and gully, Ian Ward is less fortunate as he offers an angled defensive bat to a ball from Dougie Brown and is comfortably taken behind the wicket by Tony Frost with the total on twelve in the fourth over.

The loss of this early wicket fails to inhibit Butcher's strokeplay, however, and two rasping cuts in Richardson's third over force the first bowling change, with Mo Sheikh introduced in place of the former Staffordshire paceman at the Vauxhall end. This move clearly suits Butcher, though, as he plunders two legside fours in Sheikh's third over and three off-side boundaries in the same bowler's next over to send the score racing past fifty. Meanwhile, at the other end, Mark Ramprakash, having gathered plenty of runs in the third man region at the start of his innings, begins to expand his repertoire by driving Brown first to the midwicket fence and then wide of mid-on for three to complete a half-century partnership in the sixteenth over. Although both Warwickshire seamers also manage to get a number of deliveries past the outside edge during this period, it is surprising that they are allowed to bowl in tandem for fifteen overs before we eventually see the reappearance of Richardson and the introduction of the captain himself. It is less of a surprise, however, to see the batsmen trying to impose themselves on Giles early on, each man using his feet to get down the track and drive a boundary, while Butcher is soon cutting

Richardson to the cover fence to take his score to fifty-two - made up of twelve fours and two twos - from 68 balls.

Hereafter, the bowlers manage to string together a series of tight and testing overs in the lead-up to tea, though Butcher does eventually manage to break free with two successive cover-driven fours off Richardson, while Ramprakash sweeps Giles fine for three to raise the Surrey hundred in the final over of the session.

Tea:- Surrey 104-1 (Butcher 63, Ramprakash 37*) from 31 overs*

Things start to go wrong for Surrey soon after tea as Ashley Giles pairs Richardson with Sheikh and sees the latter snap up the wicket of Ramprakash with the score advanced to 113. Two balls after taking the second-wicket stand into three figures with an incredible lofted cover drive that sails away over the boundary rope for six, the former Middlesex batsman plays solidly forward and remains blissfully unaware of what is happening as the ball bounces down from the face of his bat, trickles back gently onto the stumps and dislodges a bail. It's a desperately unlucky way for a well-played innings of forty-five to come to an end and it allows the visitors to seize the initiative in the match as Richardson strikes two further blows for his team during an impressive spell from the pavilion end.

Butcher becomes his first victim when an intelligent switch to a round-the-wicket line of attack pays instant dividends as a full-length delivery flattens the England batsman's off stump to terminate an impressive knock of sixty-four and reduce Surrey to 115-3. Then, to make matters worse for the home side, Ali Brown, having almost repeated his folly of the Lancashire match while getting off the mark with a very risky single to mid-on, pulls the Warwickshire seamer straight down the throat of Sheikh at long leg to depart for two with the total advanced to just 121.

While Richardson and his team-mates celebrate these successes joyfully, Adam Hollioake joins Alec Stewart at the crease with his side now in a spot of trouble, since they still need 143 runs to avoid having to follow on for a second successive match.

To no-one's great surprise, the two Surrey batsmen go about the task of repairing the damage inflicted by Richardson in totally different ways - Stewart, playing his first competitive innings of the summer, battens down the hatches; Hollioake, having survived a couple of edgy moments during his first two overs at the crease, tears into the bowling with bold strokes. While Richardson is taken for three boundaries - a straight drive, a pull high over mid-on and an immaculate cover drive - in the penultimate over of his spell, Sheikh is soon being thumped through extra cover for two fours to take the hosts past 150. To be fair to the bowler, the Surrey captain is also beaten twice outside the off stump in that same over, though he quickly reasserts his dominance with two further boundaries, prompting Giles to bring himself into the attack to join Richardson's replacement, Dougie Brown. Hollioake responds by immediately cutting his opposite number to the rope at backward point, though Giles is unfortunate not to take almost instant revenge when the home skipper charges down the pitch and misses a drive in the left-arm spinner's next over with his score on forty-nine. Luckily for Hollioake, wicketkeeper Frost fumbles an apparently straightforward take, allowing the astonished batsman to regain his ground and then complete a forthright 55-ball fifty two deliveries later with a cut for a single to the fielder posted on the cover boundary.

The possibility that Frost's error might prove expensive is underlined in the very next over when the home captain cracks three consecutive balls from Brown to the boundary, though he also offers a very difficult catching chance to Smith at deepish mid-off, the diving fielder getting his hands to an uppish drive from a well disguised slower ball, but being unable to cling on.

Although Hollioake has undoubtedly enjoyed a little luck, his calculated assault has eased Surrey's fears and, as Stewart gets in on the act by clipping a Giles full-toss to the rope at midwicket to take his side past the two-hundred mark, there now appears to be no chance of the home side having to follow on.

With the day drawing to a close, Richardson, possibly carrying a slight injury, returns for one expensive over, during which each batsman picks up a pulled boundary, and Smith makes a belated appearance to bowl the fifty-seventh over. The Warwickshire off-spinner fails to make any impression, though, as the fifth-wicket pair complete a century partnership - Hollioake 75, Stewart 21, Extras 4 - and the Surrey captain ends the day in style by smiting the returning Giles for a towering six which lands on the pavilion balcony.

Close:- Surrey 237-4 (Stewart 29, Hollioake 87*) from 63 overs*

Third Day - Friday 2nd May
Warwickshire 413; Surrey 349-7

The chances of an interesting contest developing appear to be greatly reduced by overnight and morning rain which prevents play from starting until 2pm.

With thirty-seven overs lost to the inclement weather, Ashley Giles opts to employ Alan Richardson and, perhaps surprisingly, Neil Smith as his first two bowlers, though neither causes the Surrey batsmen much discomfort. Adam Hollioake, in fact, simply picks up where he had left off the previous evening by spanking Richardson to the cover and midwicket ropes in the third over of the day to move his score on to ninety-seven. Thereafter, however, he becomes comparatively becalmed as Alec Stewart temporarily takes over the mantle of principal aggressor with a couple of nicely timed fours off Smith.

Finally, after requiring four overs to move from ninety-seven to ninety-nine, Hollioake pulls a Richardson delivery to midwicket for the single he needs to complete an excellent century from just 114 balls. His innings has included 15 fours and a six, and it isn't long before he adds to those tallies by twice forcing Smith to the fence at deep cover and then blasting him high over the rope at long-on for six. The fifth-wicket partnership increases in value to 150 in the midst of this strokeplay, while Stewart, in more positive mode today, completes a 99-ball half-century shortly afterwards with a single to deep backward square leg off Dougie Brown, who has replaced Richardson at the pavilion end.

The former England Test captain's innings goes no further, however, as Brown has him taken at first slip by Nick Knight in his next over, thereby ending a superb partnership of 171with the total at 292, and it isn't long before the Stirling-born all-rounder also manages to dislodge the other participant in the stand.

Gaining justified reward towards the end of a fine spell of 6-0-16-2, Brown terminates Hollioake's highly entertaining knock at 122, with the score advanced to 309, when the Surrey skipper gloves a rather half-hearted pull through to Frost behind the wicket and departs to a richly deserved ovation.

Unfortunately, rain clouds are gathering again at this stage and, after a few lusty blows from the new batting partnership of Azhar Mahmood and Alex Tudor, and a double bowling change that brings Mo Sheikh and Ashley Giles into the attack, the players are driven from the field by another short sharp shower with the scoreboard reading 331-6.

Thanks to the efforts of the ground staff, along with the positive attitude of umpires Willey and Evans, play is suspended for no more than fifteen minutes, though we get barely half-an-hour's action after the resumption before poor light on a miserable day forces an early tea.

In the seven-and-a-half overs that are possible before the interval, Warwickshire manage to capture a seventh wicket, however, when Azhar skies a drive off Sheikh high towards mid-on and sees Mark Wagh eventually cling on to a very good catch despite readjusting his position on a couple of occasions as the ball descends from the sky.

Sadly, no more play proves possible as conditions deteriorate rather than improve, and it looks like we are facing a pretty dull final day where both sides have nothing left to play for but the remaining bonus points.

Tea and Close:- Surrey 349-7 (Tudor 25, Bicknell 1*) from 92 overs*

Fourth Day - Saturday 3rd May
Warwickshire 413 and 215-7; Surrey 390
Match Drawn
Surrey 11pts, Warwickshire 12

In much better and brighter conditions than on day three, Surrey start effectively eight wickets down, as opposed to seven, with Martin Bicknell laid low by illness and unable to resume his innings. The other overnight batsman, Alex Tudor, makes light of this 'loss', however, by reeling off five magnificent boundaries - none of which would have been disowned by a top-order Test batsman - in the first four overs of the day delivered by Mo Sheikh and Dougie Brown.

He loses his new batting partner, Saqlain Mushtaq, soon afterwards, however, when Brown defeats the Pakistani's forward push and sends the off stump cartwheeling, leaving the home side down to their last pair as James Ormond walks to the crease.

Surrey's progress is subsequently slowed by the introduction of Alan Richardson in place of Sheikh, though the batsmen still manage to edge their side slowly but surely towards a final batting point and Tudor completes a fine fifty by forcing his 66th ball backward of point for two runs in the tenth over of the morning.

Alas, after another memorable cover-driven boundary by the tall paceman off Brown, the innings ends at 390, courtesy of a fine head-high catch at first slip by Nick Knight which allows the bowler to almost instantly redress the balance in his contest with Tudor.

Both participants in Surrey's last-wicket partnership are back in action, this time with the ball, ten minutes later and, in a reversal of roles from the Warwickshire first innings, Knight is the batsman who is more likely to punish the occasional lapse from the bowlers. Frost struggles quite badly, in fact, and has scored just five runs from twenty-two balls when indecision over whether to play or leave a Tudor delivery results in an inside edge and a flattened middle stump. With the visitors now 28-1 in the tenth over, the game is still going nowhere at this point, though Mark Wagh is soon providing some entertainment with a series of pleasing straight drives off Surrey's successful bowler.

Tudor is not about to let Wagh spoil his impressive morning session at this late stage, however, and instantly wreaks revenge by luring the batsman into another drive at a slightly shorter delivery and inducing an edge to second slip, where Azhar holds on to a good catch at head height.

Lunch is taken shortly after this dismissal and, with Warwickshire's lead standing at seventy-four, the draw looks inevitable.

Lunch:- Warwickshire 51-2 (Knight 18, Bell 3*) from 16 overs*

Saqlain Mushtaq joins Tudor in the attack upon the resumption and, after half-a-dozen quiet overs, this proves to be a successful combination as it brings two wickets in the space of six balls - the final delivery of Saqlain's fourth over sees Ian Bell shouldering arms and having his off stump pegged back by an off-break, while the fifth ball of the following over brings a third victim in the innings for Tudor, who again out-thinks Jim Troughton. Attacking the left-hander from round the wicket right from the outset, the Surrey fast bowler follows a third-ball bouncer with a fast straight delivery that leaves Troughton stranded on the crease and plucks out his off stump, sending it spinning away on a merry dance towards the slips.

Although the Bears are now 72-4, only fifty-eight overs remain for play so there still seems to be no realistic chance of the reigning champions forcing victory as Dominic Ostler makes his way to the middle to join a very determined-looking Knight. Saqlain appears equally ready for a scrap, however, and has already been a far more dangerous proposition for the batsmen than he had been first time around, running in and appealing with vigour and passion as the batsmen content themselves merely with survival.

The Bears' chances of repelling Surrey's late surge are then further enhanced when Tudor, having bowled fourteen successive overs either side of lunch, finally rests with figures of 3-56 and Azhar, yet to find his best bowling form in the opening games, takes over at the pavilion end.

Surrey's Pakistani pair subsequently strive hard to earn further successes for their adopted county over the course of the next hour, but Knight and Ostler resist stoutly and nudge their side towards the stalemate that has been almost inevitable since rain decimated the previous day's play.

By batting in a largely passive style, the batsmen have, however, left their side open to a degree of danger in the event of a late collapse, and when Saqlain suddenly strikes twice in three balls during the forty-first over - having both Ostler and Dougie Brown expertly taken at silly point by his captain - Surrey scent an outside chance of success.

Knight remains as unyielding as ever, though, reaching a very valuable fifty from 112 balls with a glance to the rope at fine leg off Azhar in the next over, and, with support from his stand-in captain, he ensures that no further calamities befall his side in the final five overs before tea.

Tea:- Warwickshire 127-6 (Knight 52, Giles 5*) from 46 overs*

As Warwickshire start the final session leading by 150 runs with thirty-six overs remaining for play, there is just a glimmer of a chance that a couple of quick wickets could make things interesting and set up a run chase similar to the one in the corresponding fixture in 2002.

Hollioake's chosen bowlers, Ormond and Saqlain, are unable to produce any magic on this occasion, however, and a series of boundaries by Giles off the Surrey paceman inside the first six overs of the session ensures that honours will end even.

This is acknowledged by the introduction of Ali Brown and Mark Ramprakash, who deliver sixteen overs in double-quick time to prevent their side from being deducted points for a slow over-rate. Brown also has the pleasure of picking up his second first-class wicket during this period, having Giles taken by Stewart behind the stumps from an edged defensive push.

Then, as time ticks away towards 5.30pm, the now certain time for close of play, Ian Ward and Alec Stewart take a turn with the ball and Knight makes a late charge for a century. He has only reached ninety-three, though, as the big hand on the Vauxhall end clock hits the six and, at the end of that over, the Surrey players shake hands with the other batsman, Mo Sheikh, and make to leave the field. A clearly disappointed Knight stands his ground, however, and eventually wins the sympathy vote from all concerned, earning himself another Stewart over in which to reach his goal. Demonstrating great generosity of spirit, the former Surrey and England captain immediately offers up three rank deliveries, the final one being a slow full-toss which Knight smashes high over the midwicket boundary to complete his match-saving ton from 222 balls.

As the players leave the field and Knight receives the Surrey supporters' applause, despite once again proving to be a thorn in the side of their team, one wonders what might have happened had rain not wrecked the third day with the game so evenly balanced. A good, competitive match that had seen some fine cricket might well have produced a great last day had the weather not intervened so cruelly.

Statistical footnote - In almost three-hundred overs of play, not one lbw appeal was upheld by umpires Peter Willey and Jeff Evans.

Warwickshire 413 and 215-7; Surrey 390
Match Drawn. Surrey 11pts, Warwickshire 12

TALKING POINTS - ADAM HOLLIOAKE

It must have been a very tough decision to leave Rikki Clarke out after his century against Lancashire. Looking back, with the benefit of hindsight, was it the right decision?

AH - Even with hindsight, I think it was the correct decision. It's easy to say who **shouldn't** be left out of the side but it's a lot harder to say who **should** be left out. If we had picked Clarkey then we would have had to leave out Browny out, who's been batsman of the year for something like six of the last seven years… or, if not him, then who do you leave out? I mean, we'd even left Thorpey out of that game! I believe you've got to stick with the guys who have done it for you over the years - you have to show some consistency of selection, otherwise you get into the habit of just picking the people who scored the most runs in the last game, or you end up going down the same road as England did, chopping and changing the team all the time.

TALKING POINTS - ALEX TUDOR

You must have pleased with your results against Jim Troughton, both in this Championship match and in the NCL game?

AT - Yes, I'd not bowled to Troughton before, but I remember the captain coming up to me and saying that he wanted me to try and bounce him out and make things uncomfortable for him, so I was pleased it worked out well. Then when he came out to bat in the second innings Adam got me on straight away. He was the young batsman that everyone was talking about at that time so I was pleased to be able to test myself against him and get him out in both innings here as well as in the NCL game.

After a largely poor performance against Lancashire and a difficult first couple of days here I thought we started to look like we were finally hitting our straps with our second innings bowling. Did you feel we were a bit 'undercooked' for the first week or so of the season?

AT - Yes, quite possibly - I think the batsmen could have done with more time in the middle and the bowlers could have done with some more overs under their belt. But I think the biggest problem we had with the Lancashire game was being without Bicknell, Ormond and Azhar.

SURREY v WARWICKSHIRE at The Oval 30th April to 3rd May							
Warwickshire won the toss and elected to bat			Umpires:- Jeff Evans and Peter Willey				
WARWICKSHIRE - First Innings							
Fall Of Wkt	Batsman	How	Out	Score	Balls	4s	6s
2-158	**N.V. Knight**	**c Ward**	**b Bicknell**	**58**	136	8	0
1-153	**T. Frost +**	**c Hollioake**	**b Bicknell**	**78**	117	12	2
10-413	**M.A. Wagh**		**b Ormond**	**136**	217	19	1
3-180	**I.R. Bell**	**c sub (Clarke)**	**b Tudor**	**4**	20	0	0
4-215	**J.O. Troughton**	**hit wicket**	**b Tudor**	**17**	33	3	0
5-215	**D.P. Ostler**		**b Tudor**	**0**	4	0	0
6-237	**D.R. Brown**	**c Stewart**	**b Saqlain**	**8**	21	1	0
7-288	**A.F. Giles ***	**c Azhar**	**b Ormond**	**25**	45	3	0
8-310	**M.A. Sheikh**	**c Stewart**	**b Ormond**	**14**	34	3	0
9-343	**N.M.K. Smith**	**c Stewart**	**b Azhar**	**20**	27	4	0
	A. Richardson	**Not**	**Out**	**20**	31	4	0
	Extras	**(10lb, 1w, 22nb)**		**33**			
	TOTAL	**(112.2 overs)**		**413**			

Bowler	O	M	R	W	NB	Wd
Bicknell	**20**	**9**	**62**	**2**	3	-
Ormond	**25.2**	**4**	**83**	**3**	2	-
Azhar Mahmood	**15**	**3**	**72**	**1**	3	-
Tudor	**23**	**3**	**92**	**3**	-	-
Saqlain Mushtaq	**26**	**4**	**86**	**1**	3	-
Hollioake	**3**	**1**	**8**	**0**	-	1

SURREY - First Innings (Needing 264 to avoid the follow-on)							
Fall Of Wkt	Batsman	How	Out	Score	Balls	4s	6s
3-115	**M.A. Butcher**		**b Richardson**	**64**	99	14	0
1-12	**I.J. Ward**	**c Frost**	**b Brown**	**2**	11	0	0
2-113	**M.R. Ramprakash**		**b Sheikh**	**45**	96	4	1
5-292	**A.J. Stewart +**	**c Knight**	**b Brown**	**50**	101	8	0
4-121	**A.D. Brown**	**c Sheikh**	**b Richardson**	**2**	13	0	0
6-309	**A.J. Hollioake ***	**c Frost**	**b Brown**	**122**	137	17	2
7-347	**Azhar Mahmood**	**c Wagh**	**b Sheikh**	**25**	48	4	0
9-390	**A.J. Tudor**	**c Knight**	**b Brown**	**55**	71	10	0
	M.P. Bicknell	**retired**	**hurt**	**1**	12	0	0
8-375	**Saqlain Mushtaq**		**b Brown**	**5**	18	0	0
	J. Ormond	**Not**	**Out**	**5**	18	0	0
	Extras	**(8lb, 6nb)**		**14**			
	TOTAL	**(103.3 overs)**		**390**			

Bowler	O	M	R	W	NB	Wd
Richardson	**24**	**4**	**89**	**2**	2	-
Brown	**27.3**	**4**	**96**	**5**	1	-
Sheikh	**23**	**6**	**91**	**2**	-	-
Giles	**16**	**2**	**53**	**0**	-	-
Smith	**13**	**1**	**53**	**0**	-	-

WARWICKSHIRE - Second Innings (Leading by 23 runs on first innings)							
Fall Of Wkt	Batsman	How	Out	Score	Balls	4s	6s
	N.V. Knight	**Not**	**Out**	**103**	222	13	1
1-28	**T. Frost +**		**b Tudor**	**5**	22	1	0
2-48	**M.A. Wagh**	**c Azhar**	**b Tudor**	**19**	24	4	0
3-71	**I.R. Bell**		**b Saqlain**	**13**	26	2	0
4-72	**J.O. Troughton**		**b Tudor**	**0**	4	0	0
5-117	**D.P. Ostler**	**c Hollioake**	**b Saqlain**	**25**	58	3	0
6-117	**D.R. Brown**	**c Hollioake**	**b Saqlain**	**0**	2	0	0
7-169	**A.F. Giles ***	**c Stewart**	**b Brown**	**33**	59	7	0
	M.A. Sheikh	**Not**	**Out**	**4**	47	0	0
	Extras	**(4b, 3lb, 2w, 10nb)**		**19**			
	TOTAL	**(76.3 overs)**	**(for 7 dec)**	**221**			

Bowler	O	M	R	W	NB	Wd
Ormond	**11**	**3**	**41**	**0**	3	-
Tudor	**14**	**2**	**56**	**3**	1	-
Saqlain Mushtaq	**19**	**9**	**29**	**3**	-	-
Azhar Mahmood	**9**	**1**	**34**	**0**	1	-
Ramprakash	**8**	**4**	**9**	**0**	-	-
Brown	**9**	**3**	**11**	**1**	-	-
Ward	**4**	**0**	**11**	**0**	-	-
Stewart	**2.3**	**0**	**23**	**0**	-	1

Other Frizzell Championship Division One Results

April 30 - May 2

***Hove:-* Sussex (19pts) beat Kent (3) by 133 runs**. Sussex 279 (Adams 54, Sheriyar 5-65) & 198 (Goodwin 96, Tredwell 4-48); Kent 185 & 159 (Kirtley 6-26).

April 30 - May 3

***Leicester:-* Leicestershire (8pts) drew with Essex (7).** Essex 188 (Stephenson 50) & 191-9dec (Dagnall 5-66); Leics 201 (Stevens 65, Brant 4-54, Dakin 4-64) & 104-5.

FRIZZELL CHAMPIONSHIP DIVISION ONE TABLE AT 3RD MAY

Pos	Prv		P	Points	W	D	L	T	Bat	Bwl	Ded
1	n/a	Nottinghamshire	2	28.25	1	1	0	0	5	6	0.75
2	n/a	Essex	3	28.00	0	2	0	1	5	8	0.00
3	n/a	Warwickshire	3	27.75	0	1	1	1	11	6	0.25
4	n/a	Middlesex	2	25.00	1	1	0	0	1	6	0.00
5	n/a	Sussex	2	23.00	1	0	1	0	3	6	0.00
6	n/a	Lancashire	2	23.00	0	2	0	0	9	6	0.00
7	n/a	Surrey	2	18.00	0	2	0	0	6	4	0.00
8	n/a	Leicestershire	2	17.00	0	2	0	0	3	6	0.00
9	n/a	Kent	2	11.00	0	1	1	0	1	6	0.00

NATIONAL CRICKET LEAGUE DIVISION ONE - MATCH TWO

Surrey Lions versus Warwickshire Bears at The Oval

Sunday 4th May

Setting The Scene - Surrey field the same eleven that played at Chelmsford and, with Jon Batty selected ahead of Alec Stewart, it looks possible that, barring an injury to Batty, the England wicketkeeper-batsman might have played his last limited-overs match for the county. Despite their inability to field an overseas player, the Bears are still able to put out a side that looks well suited to one-day cricket, with their eleven showing just one change from the team that contested the Championship match - Neil Smith makes way for the highly promising left-handed all-rounder, Graham Wagg. The toss sees a reversal of fortunes from the four-day encounter as Ashley Giles calls incorrectly this time, allowing Adam Hollioake's side to take first use of another fine-looking pitch.

Surrey Lions' Innings

Taking advantage of their captain's good fortune at the toss, Ian Ward and Ali Brown launch the Lions innings in fine style against Graham Wagg and Dougie Brown, with Surrey's Brown pulling the 20-year-old Wagg over the boundary at backward square leg in the third over and then collecting a second 'maximum' with a lofted off-drive at the expense of his namesake six balls later. To Wagg's credit, he recovers from his twelve-run second over by delivering a maiden to Ward, but Brown is left nursing first-spell figures of 3-0-30-0 after being battered for three fours in a costly third over which sees the Surrey total advancing from twenty-nine to forty-four.

Disappointingly for both the batsman and the decent-sized crowd at a sunny Oval, Ali Brown drills the first ball of the seventh over into the hands of Alan Richardson at mid-off and departs for twenty-eight, though Wagg, the successful bowler, finds Mark Ramprakash no easier to bowl at as the new batsman glances and drives his first two balls to the boundary to raise the home side's fifty in just 6.3 overs.

After a respectable opening over from Richardson, who has replaced Dougie Brown at the Vauxhall end, Wagg again responds well to punishment by delivering an accurate fifth over, but the Lions are soon rampant again as Ward pulls Richardson for two successive fours and then takes full advantage of a 'free hit' following a no-ball by driving the ball high over wide long-on for six to leave Surrey on 80-1 after just ten overs.

Although the tempo drops slightly in the next couple of overs as Wagg and Mo Sheikh - the latter replacing Richardson - locate a better line and length, Ward and Ramprakash still manage to complete a fifty partnership from just thirty-four balls at the end of the twelfth over.

Another expensive over from Wagg, costing twelve runs and including two further boundaries from Ramprakash, sees the Surrey hundred up after 12.4 overs, and it is only when Ashley Giles brings himself into the attack to link up with Sheikh in the fifteenth over that the visitors finally start to exercise a degree of control. Two quick wickets certainly help their cause as Ward's fine knock of forty-seven ends with a tame return catch to Giles with the total at 119 in the seventeenth over, and then Saqlain, surprisingly promoted to number four, is adjudged lbw to Sheikh for a second-ball duck with just two runs added to the score.

The loss of this third wicket brings Graham Thorpe out to the middle to join forces with Ramprakash and, showing the value of all their experience, the Lions' pair spend most of the next six overs gathering singles and ensuring that their team's blistering start is not wasted. Although Ramprakash does at one point unleash a violent slog-sweep for six off Giles on the way to completing an excellent 53-ball fifty, this more sedate approach is maintained until the 150 arrives after 24.3 overs.

Thereafter, with Sheikh having given way to Mark Wagh after a tidy spell of 7-0-27-1, the batsmen start to push on again, with drives down the ground providing a steady stream of singles while sweeps, both conventional and reverse, bring most of the boundaries. Worryingly for Warwickshire, their stand-in skipper is, by now, about to deliver his final permitted over, though he does provide his side with another breakthrough before it is completed. After conceding the most amazing reverse-swept six over backward point to the increasingly dominant Thorpe, as well as two wides, Giles redresses the balance by hanging on to a low return catch offered by Ramprakash from his penultimate delivery to complete a good, restrictive spell of 9-0-40-2. At 185-4 after thirty-one overs, the Lions still look set for a massive total, however, as their former Middlesex batsman departs to a warm ovation for his sixty-three and is replaced at the crease by Rikki Clarke.

Despite having made this breakthrough, there is no respite for the visitors as the new batsman gets away to a good start and, with runs continuing to come from almost every ball, Surrey's 200 arrives during an expensive thirty-fourth over, delivered by the part-time off-spinner, Wagh.

While Thorpe makes his way to a well-constructed fifty from 62 balls at the other end, Clarke shines briefly but brightly, taking three fours from the returning Brown and Sheikh before falling to an excellent stumping by Frost off Brown, the keeper taking a full-length delivery supremely well and whipping the bails off in a flash.

As Clarke departs for a quick-fire twenty-six, with Surrey now 229-5 after thirty-seven overs, the home fans are hoping for some fireworks from Adam Hollioake to propel their side to a total in the region of three-hundred. It isn't to be the Surrey captain's day, however, as he soon holes out to Sheikh on the extra-cover fence off the final delivery of Richardson's comeback over, though Azhar Mahmood immediately delights the crowd by smiting his second ball, bowled by Brown, high over the midwicket boundary. This mighty blow takes the total past 250 in the forty-first over and, though Thorpe goes for fifty-eight two balls later to a stumping that mirrors the earlier brilliant effort to remove Clarke, Azhar is not deflected from his task as he plunders two further boundaries in Richardson's next over.

The tall paceman has his revenge shortly afterwards, however, when he defeats the Pakistani's mighty slog and extracts middle stump, and the last three overs of the innings prove rather disappointing for Surrey as they yield just nineteen runs. This is largely due to the excellence of young Wagg, who delivers six dot balls and concedes only eleven runs - including a lucky inside-edged boundary by Alex Tudor from the last ball of the Lions' innings - after returning to bowl the forty-third and forty-fifth overs of the innings.

Surrey's brilliantly constructed total of 281-8 still looks very impressive, though, and it is clear that the Bears will have to bat out of their skins if they are to win the match.

Warwickshire Bears' Innings

Facing such a big score, the visitors need Nick Knight and Tony Frost to get them off to a good start, but the opening pair only manage to put on nineteen before Bicknell delivers an early blow to their hopes, clean bowling Frost with a ball that nips back through a rather indeterminate stroke. This loss is then compounded in the next over, the sixth of the innings, when Mark Wagh, aiming to leg, is beaten by a fine Azhar outswinger that removes the off-bail and reduces the Bears to 24-2.

Knight and the new batsman, Ian Bell, are now faced with a tricky situation and elect to try to re-establish the innings against some fine new-ball bowling from the Surrey pair. They only manage to take the total as far as thirty-six, however, before Azhar strikes again to put the Lions in complete control of the match. Bell, the man dismissed, can count himself rather unfortunate, however, as he follows a lofted cover drive for four with an equally well-timed clip off his toes from the next delivery, only to see Thorpe pull off a blinding overhead catch at short midwicket.

Warwickshire are really on the ropes now and it isn't long before Surrey are celebrating again when Tudor dismisses Jim Troughton for the third time in five days shortly after replacing Bicknell at the pavilion end. This time it's an edge to Jon Batty from a wild drive outside off stump that brings about Troughton's downfall and leaves the Bears' innings in tatters at 43-4. As Tudor celebrates his seventh-ball success, credit is also due to the Surrey captain for immediately confronting the Warwickshire left-hander with the bowler who had so tormented him during the Championship match.

The experienced combination of Knight and Dominic Ostler are now left with no alternative but to dig in for a while and, as a result, the fifty doesn't arrive until the fifteenth over and the required run-rate rises. The batsmen are, therefore, required to take some positive action when Saqlain Mushtaq enters the fray as soon as the fielding restrictions are lifted. They enjoy a degree of success in cutting and sweeping three fours during the course of the off-spinner's opening two overs but, once again, the Lions roar back with a wicket just as a partnership appears to be building. Tudor is the successful bowler again, this time luring Ostler into an uncontrolled drive which ends up in the safe hands of Brown at first slip. Credit again to Hollioake, this time for keeping a slip in place, with his reward being a scoreboard reading 74-5 after nineteen overs.

Dougie Brown's response to this crisis is to launch an immediate counter-attack - he drives his second ball, from Saqlain, to the rope at wide long-on, before taking 4-4-6 from the first three balls of the next over from Tudor, courtesy of a square drive, a lofted straight drive and a pick-up over midwicket. Knight then adds a boundary of his own off Saqlain to take the Bears' total into three figures in the twenty-second over, leaving Hollioake to decide whether to retain Tudor in the attack for the next over or make a change. He opts to keep faith in his tall paceman and nearly reaps an instant reward when Brown skies a drive almost vertically and only survives because none of the fielders in the vicinity take responsibility for getting under the ball. The Warwickshire all-rounder fails to take advantage of this escape, however, as he repeats his error two balls later and is safely held by Bicknell at mid-off.

At 108-6 in the twenty-third over, everything now depends on Knight, who is keeping remarkably cool given what has been going on at the other end, and Ashley Giles, newly arrived at the wicket. Giles immediately enjoys a stroke of luck as he edges Tudor between wicketkeeper and slip and profits by four runs, but the big fast bowler enjoys better fortune in the final over of his stint when Warwickshire's stand-in captain drives uppishly in the direction of extra cover and sees his opposite number diving away to his right to pull off a brilliant one-handed catch. Giles is left shaking his head as he departs for ten with the Bears surely down and out at 127-7, while Knight, having completed a brave fifty from 61 balls during the previous over, must be wondering if he will ever find someone to stay with him for longer than a few overs.

Hollioake's next decision is a very interesting one. With Tudor having completed a fine spell of 9-0-45-4, he makes a double bowling change, resting Saqlain after six rather disappointing overs and introducing Rikki Clarke and Ali Brown.

The Brown experiment doesn't prove successful, however, as Knight helps himself to three fours from two overs that cost seventeen runs, and, having finally found a more reliable ally in Mo Sheikh, takes the Bears to the 150 mark in the thirty-second over. Needing ten runs per over, Warwickshire still seem to have no chance of victory but, as Knight begins to get after Clarke, cutting him to the cover boundary then lifting him over wide long-on for six, one or two slight doubts arise in Surrey minds.

With the eighth-wicket partnership close to fifty and Knight now into the nineties, Bicknell and the skipper himself take over with the ball for Surrey, though this proves no problem for Knight as he instantly drives and sweeps Hollioake for two boundaries that take him through to a really impressive century - his second of the weekend, following his match-saving effort the previous day - from 91 balls. It still seems odds-against him being able to win this game for his side, however, though Warwickshire pick up the ten runs they require from the next over as Sheikh twice drives the previously ultra-economical Bicknell over mid-on for four to raise the visitors' two-hundred with thirty-seven overs completed.

A couple of good overs from the batsmen could now put the Bears in with a chance, but it turns out to be the Lions who produce the goods at the crucial time - Hollioake ends the gallant Knight's magnificent knock by having him well taken by Ramprakash on the cover boundary from a flat, skimming drive at the end of a tight thirty-eighth over, then, two balls later, Bicknell outwits Sheikh, who is bowled behind his legs as he moves across to the off side in an attempt to flick the ball to the rope at fine leg. This second wicket for Surrey's senior bowler is fitting reward at the end of an excellent spell of 9-0-30-2 and leaves Warwickshire finally out of contention at 208-9 after thirty-nine overs.

Graham Wagg clearly doesn't see it that way, however, and, with nothing to lose, he and Alan Richardson swing their bats merrily against the bowling of Hollioake and the recalled Saqlain. With Wagg driving the off-spinner for three sixes over long-on and Richardson contributing a couple of fours, they manage to bring the target down to a still unlikely twenty-six from two overs before the Lions' captain finally seals his side's victory by having Richardson safely taken by Bicknell at wide mid-on.

An entertaining afternoon's cricket on an outstanding Oval pitch, ideally suited for one-day cricket, therefore ends with Surrey triumphant by twenty-five runs and boasting a two-out-of-two record in the NCL. The Lions face a very stiff test tomorrow, however, when they visit New Road to take on the Worcestershire Royals.

ALEX TUDOR'S VIEW FROM THE DRESSING ROOM

I thought we put up a great performance with the bat in this game. What was your view?
AT - Yes, I thought we played it brilliantly with Wardy and Browny going off like a house on fire, and then we accumulated well through Ramps and Thorpey. Then we've obviously got our explosive players like Adam, Azhar and Clarkey to bang the big boundaries late on. It was a shame that Azhar got out when he did because he was going really well and I think he would have been fun to watch if he'd been around for the last two or three overs.

Considering how good the pitch was, would this rank as one of your best spells in limited-overs cricket for Surrey?
AT - Yes, I think that spell would be up there with my best in one-day cricket for Surrey. I felt really confident after the Championship game - in that week against Warwickshire I got ten wickets, and I really thought my season was going to flow from there. Then I picked up my knee injury while fielding a ball off Saqi during this match and eventually had to have keyhole surgery after the Championship game at Trent Bridge to sort out the problem with the cartilege.

Graham Wagg had a good match, bowling well at both ends of the innings and then hitting out boldly towards the end. Do you know much about him?

AT - I met him at the Academy but he was injured at the time, so he wasn't able to take any part. He's a confident lad - he mixes his pace up well when he bowls and, as he showed in this game, he's a really decent striker of the ball, too. He's definitely one to keep your eye on for the future.

They only ended up twenty-five runs short, though I felt that margin of defeat rather flattered them. Did you ever have any serious worries about us losing the game?

AT - I think we perhaps took our foot off the pedal a bit when we saw the back of Nick Knight, and the batsmen coming in after him had nothing to lose so they were bound to go for it and have some fun. But I always thought we had too many runs for them.

SURREY LIONS v WARWICKSHIRE BEARS at The Oval

Sunday 4th May — **Surrey Lions won by 25 runs**

Surrey Lions won the toss and elected to bat — **Umpires:- Jeff Evans & Peter Willey**

SURREY LIONS

Fall Of Wkt	Batsman	How	Out	Score	Balls	4s	6s
2-119	**I.J. Ward**	**c &**	**b Giles**	**47**	45	7	1
1-44	**A.D. Brown**	**c Richardson**	**b Wagg**	**28**	21	3	2
4-185	**M.R. Ramprakash**	**c &**	**b Giles**	**63**	76	9	1
3-121	**Saqlain Mushtaq**	**lbw**	**b Sheikh**	**0**	2	0	0
7-251	**G.P. Thorpe**	**st Frost**	**b Brown**	**58**	75	4	1
5-229	**R. Clarke**	**st Frost**	**b Brown**	**26**	17	4	0
6-242	**A.J. Hollioake ***	**c Sheikh**	**b Richardson**	**6**	7	0	0
8-269	**Azhar Mahmood**		**b Richardson**	**19**	12	2	1
	A.J. Tudor	**Not**	**Out**	**11**	9	2	0
	J.N. Batty +	**Not**	**Out**	**7**	7	1	0
	M.P. Bicknell	**did not bat**					
	Extras	**(4lb, 10w, 2nb)**		**16**			
	TOTAL	**(45 overs)**	**(for 8 wkts)**	**281**			

Bowler	O	M	R	W	NB	Wd
Wagg	**9**	**1**	**56**	**1**	-	5
Brown	**8**	**0**	**63**	**2**	-	-
Richardson	**5**	**0**	**47**	**2**	1	-
Sheikh	**9**	**0**	**38**	**1**	-	1
Giles	**9**	**0**	**40**	**2**	-	4
Wagh	**5**	**0**	**33**	**0**	-	-

WARWICKSHIRE BEARS

Fall Of Wkt	Batsman	How	Out	Score	Balls	4s	6s
8-207	**N.V. Knight**	**c Ramprakash**	**b Hollioake**	**105**	98	13	1
1-19	**T. Frost +**		**b Bicknell**	**8**	11	2	0
2-24	**M.A. Wagh**		**b Azhar**	**5**	7	1	0
3-36	**I.R. Bell**	**c Thorpe**	**b Azhar**	**8**	18	2	0
4-43	**J.O. Troughton**	**c Batty**	**b Tudor**	**0**	8	0	0
5-74	**D.P. Ostler**	**c Brown**	**b Tudor**	**12**	24	1	0
6-108	**D.R. Brown**	**c Bicknell**	**b Tudor**	**25**	15	3	1
7-127	**A.F. Giles ***	**c Hollioake**	**b Tudor**	**10**	15	1	0
9-207	**M.A. Sheikh**		**b Bicknell**	**25**	35	3	0
	G.G. Wagg	**Not**	**Out**	**31**	11	1	3
10-256	**A. Richardson**	**c Bicknell**	**b Hollioake**	**18**	18	2	0
	Extras	**(4lb, 3w, 2nb)**		**9**			
	TOTAL	**(43.1 overs)**		**256**			

Bowler	O	M	R	W	NB	Wd
Bicknell	**9**	**0**	**30**	**2**	-	-
Azhar Mahmood	**7**	**0**	**34**	**2**	1	-
Tudor	**9**	**0**	**45**	**4**	-	1
Saqlain Mushtaq	**8**	**0**	**67**	**0**	-	-
Clarke	**4**	**1**	**24**	**0**	-	1
Brown	**2**	**0**	**17**	**0**	-	-
Hollioake	**4.1**	**0**	**35**	**2**	-	1

Other NCL Division One Result

While the Lions had been taming the Bears at The Oval, the 2002 NCL champions had begun their attempt to retain the title with a comfortable victory over Leicestershire Foxes at Grace Road.

May 4
Leicester:- **Glamorgan Dragons (4pts) beat Leicestershire Foxes by 44 runs.** Glamorgan 249-5 (45ov; Hemp 83); Leics 205 (41.3ov; Maddy 80, Croft 3-39).

NATIONAL CRICKET LEAGUE DIVISION ONE - MATCH THREE
Worcestershire Royals versus Surrey Lions at Worcester
Monday 5th May

Setting The Scene - It really is testing time for the Lions as they face a good Worcestershire Royals side on a ground where success has proved elusive in one-day cricket over the years. Having only recorded two away wins against Worcestershire in fourteen previous attempts in the Sunday/National League, history suggests that this will be one of the most difficult assignments of Surrey's 2003 NCL campaign. Unfortunately, Alex Tudor, the four-wicket hero of the victory over the Warwickshire Bears, is forced to sit this game out after sustaining an injury to his knee, though Surrey have a perfectly good replacement in James Ormond. The rest of the team is unchanged. Worcestershire's eleven is the strongest they are able to field at this moment in time, since their second overseas player - the South African all-rounder, Andrew Hall - isn't due to arrive in England until later in the week. The pitch looks to be a good one by New Road's standards, so it is no surprise when Ben Smith elects to bat first upon winning the toss.

Worcestershire Royals' Innings

Gorgeous late-spring weather has ensured a good attendance for this Bank Holiday Monday encounter, and there is a nice atmosphere in the ground as Stephen Peters and Vikram Solanki do battle with Martin Bicknell and Azhar Mahmood at the start of the match. It turns out to be an extremely even contest, too, with the Surrey bowlers delivering highly disciplined opening spells that allow the batsmen to take very few liberties. While Solanki produces the best strokes early on, including a handsome straight six off Bicknell and a couple of wristy shots through the legside, Peters eventually cuts loose with three boundaries whipped away over square leg. It is still hard to say which side holds the advantage, however, as Bicknell and Azhar end their spells with the scoreboard reading 61-0 after twelve overs. The fact that the Royals' openers are still together is a major plus point for the home side, though the Lions will be happy to have kept the scoring rate down to five runs per over with the most demanding fielding restrictions in place.

Nothing much changes either after James Ormond and Saqlain Mushtaq enter the fray, with the equilibrium being maintained despite the seventeenth-over dismissal of Solanki, who plays back to Ormond and falls lbw after contributing an attractive forty to an opening stand of eighty-five.

With runs coming largely in singles as the new batsman, Graeme Hick, plays himself in and Peters plays an anchoring role, the run-rate never wavers far from five as the Worcestershire hundred arrives after 20.1 overs. It really is a fascinatingly even battle and no sooner have the Royals started to take the initiative - thanks to a sudden assault by Hick on Ormond, which brings the former England batsman three boundaries in the twenty-third over - than the visitors immediately hit back to restore parity with two wickets in seven balls. Peters is the first to go, for forty-eight with the total on 119, when Saqlain lures him into a sweep that is smartly picked up low down at backward square leg by Ali Brown, then Ben Smith, so often a thorn in Surrey's side, is run out in the next over. Pushing the ball into the covers, the Royals' skipper is belatedly sent back by Hick and fails to beat Bicknell's return to Jon Batty, leaving the hosts on 124-3 in the twenty-fifth over.

These wickets certainly help to peg the scoring rate back and the Lions take a slight advantage over the course of the next five overs as the new batsman, Kadeer Ali, takes the bulk of the bowling in establishing his innings.

By the time Ormond and Saqlain have completed their excellent mid-innings spells with figures of 9-0-46-1 and 9-0-32-1 respectively, Worcestershire have slipped back to 139-3 after thirty overs and it is clear that some remedial work needs to be done if they are to post a truly challenging total on what looks to be a very good wicket.

The bowlers now entrusted with maintaining control for Surrey are Rikki Clarke and the captain himself and, while Hollioake starts well, his young colleague immediately suffers at the hands of Kadeer, who shows the value of playing himself in by plundering two boundaries from a rather wayward opening over that costs twelve runs and brings up the Royals' 150.

As we move deeper into the final third of the home team's innings the Hick-Kadeer partnership continues to flourish, albeit in unspectacular fashion as Hollioake keeps things admirably tight at one end and Clarke recovers from his early mauling with two good, steady overs. The young all-rounder is unable to maintain his improvement, though, as Kadeer pulls and glances him for two further boundaries in a twelve-run thirty-seventh over that sees the fourth-wicket partnership reach fifty and the score advance to 184-3.

Predictably enough, Bicknell immediately replaces Clarke at the New Road end and starts his new spell well, even though he is unable to prevent Hick completing a half-century from 52 balls. While the former Worcestershire captain has looked in good touch, he has never really commanded his team's innings in the face of Surrey's tight bowling and fielding, though it seems highly likely that he might suddenly cut loose in the closing overs, especially as his side have so many wickets in hand.

Sure enough, with the total having finally passed the two-hundred mark in the fortieth over, Hick lashes into Hollioake, taking boundaries from the first four deliveries of the forty-second over - two through the covers and two behind square on the legside - raising the hundred partnership with Kadeer and giving the innings a belated boost.

Some fine Surrey bowling prevents the floodgates from opening during the final three overs of the innings, however, as Bicknell and the returning Azhar restrict the batsmen to singles and twos in addition to picking up a wicket apiece - Hick, having accelerated to eighty-one from 67 balls, top-edges a pull back to Bicknell with the total on 235, while Kadeer, after completing his half-century from 71 balls in the forty-third over, is comprehensively 'castled' by a fine Azhar yorker while heaving to leg with just five balls of the innings remaining.

With Surrey having produced a very tidy and efficient display in the field, Worcestershire's final score of 244-5 looks no better than par in the prevailing conditions, though it might take some getting, given the Lions' history on this ground in this competition.

Surrey Lions' Innings

The hosts' tally appears to grow in magnitude within three balls of the start of Surrey's reply as Ian Ward, having driven Kabir Ali's opening delivery to the rope at wide long-on, clips the third straight to Gareth Batty at square leg.

The next few overs are understandably tense as Ali Brown and Mark Ramprakash attempt to subdue a home team, and crowd, that have clearly been lifted by an early success. Although both batsmen enjoy a touch of luck with edges that fly to the fence at third man off Matt Mason, the opening bowler from the New Road end, they soon start to locate the middle of the bat, and the boundary rope, with increasing regularity. Brown initially steps up the run-rate by taking fourteen - including a slash over backward point and two lofted drives down the ground which all bring fours - from Kabir's fourth over, then Ramprakash emulates his partner by plundering an identical number of runs, again including three boundaries, from the opening over delivered by Nantie

Hayward, Kabir's replacement at the Diglis end. This stunning Surrey strokeplay has seen the fifty arrive in 8.4 overs and taken the total through to 68-1 after eleven overs, thereby putting the visitors well ahead of the required scoring rate.

Hayward subsequently responds with a better second over costing just five runs, but the hitherto accurate Mason then follows up with an expensive over that yields pulled, driven and glanced fours to Brown, the second of these boundary strokes completing a hugely entertaining half-century from just 43 balls. The Surrey opener's innings has thus far included ten boundaries and emphasises the bowlers' inability to stick to the sort of consistent lines and lengths that had served the Lions so well earlier in the afternoon.

Two more fours in the next over, to Ramprakash off Hayward, further underline the problem and take the Surrey total into three figures with one ball of the first fifteen overs still to be bowled, then Brown greets David Leatherdale's introduction with a pull over midwicket for six to complete a century partnership for the second wicket.

Having found the edge of Ramprakash's bat with a good delivery in his previous over, Hayward is then unlucky to see Leatherdale just failing to pull off a wondrous diving catch at extra cover with the same batsman on forty-five, and suffers further agony when Ramprakash takes twelve from the last three balls of the over - having reached a fine fifty from 47 balls by following a clip to deep midwicket for two with a drive to the same legside boundary for four, the former Middlesex batsman then picks up a free-hit delivery and deposits it effortlessly over the midwicket rope for six. A bewildered Hayward retires to the outfield with the gruesome figures of 4-0-47-0 and Surrey are cruising to victory at 126-1 after just seventeen overs.

It's now just a matter of picking off runs here and there for the visitors and, though Leatherdale and the newly introduced former Surrey man, Gareth Batty, contribute a series of more disciplined overs it seems that we are in for a very early finish as the 150 arrives just before the end of the twenty-second over. Although the 150 partnership then follows two balls later when Brown smashes a Batty full-toss high over the wide long-on boundary, the Worcestershire spinner is soon feeling happier as the Lions' opener misses a sweep at the next ball and drags his back foot forward as Steve Rhodes takes the bails off. The wicketkeeper immediately appeals for the stumping and, after a delay long enough to suggest that the batsman will be given the benefit of the doubt, John Holder, the third umpire in this televised game, declares Brown to be out. A magnificent innings of eighty-one from 68 balls is therefore terminated, along with what would seem to be a match-winning stand of 157 from 21.5 overs.

Worcestershire have no intention of giving this one up yet, though, and their hopes rise a little further when they rid themselves of their other tormentor two over later with the score advanced to 160. Like his partner before him, Ramprakash falls to a combination of Batty, Rhodes, the sweep shot, and the sixty-eighth delivery of his innings, though on this occasion there seems to be no doubt in the umpire's mind as the ball balloons up off the batsman's glove for a catch.

With Ramprakash gone for an excellent sixty-seven and two new batsmen - Graham Thorpe and Rikki Clarke - at the wicket, the Royals sense that they could be back in business, though Thorpe soon cracks three boundaries in quick succession to remind them that Surrey remain in control of their own destiny.

Encouraged by the success of Batty, Graeme Hick is now given a short spell, during which Clarke survives a referral to the third umpire following another stumping appeal, but Thorpe continues to look in good form as he takes two further fours off his former Surrey team-mate, with a reverse 'hit' and a lofted drive, the second of these strokes heralding the arrival of the visitors' two-hundred with only 30.4 overs having been bowled. With seven wickets in hand and the required run-rate just three an over, it should be plain sailing from here on in for the Lions, but suddenly an inspired piece of fielding sees everything start to unravel.

No-one gets especially excited when Hayward's brilliant direct-hit throw from deep backward square leg ends Thorpe's sensible knock of thirty-eight with the score at 209 after another lengthy third-umpire referral, but when Adam Hollioake is bowled for a second-ball duck by the South African paceman three balls later it does appear that Surrey might not yet be home and dry.

It seems impossible that any degree of panic could set in, yet that is what appears to happen when Kabir Ali - replacing Batty at the Diglis end after a good spell of 9-0-43-2 by the 25-year-old off-spinner - strikes twice in his first over back. Clarke is his first victim, falling lbw to the opening ball of the thirty-seventh over of the innings, then Azhar Mahmood drives carelessly to mid-on three balls later to reduce the visitors to 221-7 and bring the contest back to life.

Surrey's nerves are then calmed as Jon Batty and Martin Bicknell, aided by a Hayward no-ball and four byes, add sixteen runs from the next two overs, albeit with a few of the runs coming from edged strokes. With just eight now needed, they appear to have weathered the storm and secured the victory, but Hayward has other ideas and ends a much improved second spell by taking two wickets and putting the game back on a knife edge.

While the first dismissal, that of Batty, is routine enough - an edged drive is well taken low down by Rhodes behind the wicket - the second is highly controversial and, temporarily at least, makes Saqlain Mushtaq the most unpopular man in Worcester.

The incident occurs from the final ball of Hayward's spell, with just a no-ball added to the Lions' total, when Saqlain emulates Batty in edging a drive at the South African's slower delivery. To the naked eye, from the boundary, Rhodes appears to fumble the ball, though that doesn't prevent him from claiming the 'catch'... or umpire Jeremy Loyds from giving Saqlain out. The Pakistani off-spinner clearly isn't happy with what he has seen and departs slowly for the pavilion, only to be sent back by his team-mates in the dressing room who have seen the television replay confirm that the Worcestershire keeper has momentarily grassed the ball before picking it up again on the half-volley. With Saqlain consequently left standing midway between the pavilion and the pitch, uncertain of what he should do, the home crowd becomes highly agitated, while the umpires confer briefly but stubbornly refuse to entertain the idea of allowing the third umpire to give them any advice or help. It all makes for a pretty unpleasant spectacle as poor Saqlain has to return to the pavilion to a chorus of catcalls, while Surrey's last man, James Ormond, has to join Bicknell in the middle with six runs still required in order to ensure that his team doesn't end up snatching defeat from the jaws of victory.

At least there is no pressure in terms of time, since five overs are still to be bowled as Bicknell faces Kabir. With everyone in the crowd on the edge of their seats and a lot of tense cricketers out in the middle, the experienced Bicknell comes safely through the first five balls before driving the sixth wide to the left of Mason at mid-off. The big fast bowler elects to take a dive, even though the ball looks to be struck just a little too firmly for him to get down in time, and, sure enough, he is left grasping at thin air as the ball evades him and, after what seems like a lifetime for Surrey's players and fans, trundles over the boundary rope.

Two runs are now required as Ormond prepares to face his first ball, with Leatherdale the bowler, since Hayward, Mason and Batty have all finished their stints. An attempted off-drive at his first ball sees Ormond perilously close to being bowled, but, after repelling the next delivery with a solid defensive stroke, the sturdy Lions' seamer unfurls a classic extra-cover drive from the third to seal an ultimately nerve-racking victory with a stylish boundary.

With the first meeting between these two counties since the Nat West Trophy quarter-final of 1999 ending in a rare New Road triumph for Surrey, thereby maintaining the Lions' one-hundred percent start to the 2003 NCL campaign, it's no wonder that the visiting supporters are in buoyant mood as they head for home. Meanwhile, the team are set to make their way to Stone, where they will be taking on Staffordshire in the third round of the Cheltenham And Gloucester Trophy on Wednesday.

ALI BROWN'S VIEW FROM THE DRESSING ROOM

This appeared to be one of the better New Road pitches. What did you think of it?
AB - Yes, it was a fair wicket, actually. We've been used to having some wet seaming ones there in the past but this was a good wicket… and it was nice to get on the field after we'd all been woken up by a fire alarm at the hotel in the middle of the night!

You had a tremendous partnership with Ramps. I suppose he is the ideal foil for you, isn't he?
AB - I don't know about him being the ideal foil for me - I bat well with a number of players, though I do enjoy playing with Ramps because he works the ball around well, which often gets me a lot of the strike! I guess it depends how explosive you want to be - he works it around and the explodes at the end whereas I'll explode at the beginning, and, if I'm still there, I'll be exploding at the end, too! So it's not the most explosive of partnerships but it's certainly one that's worked very well for us.

With the game all but over, things started going badly wrong. What happened?
AB - We were always fairly certain that we were going to win, and sometimes when you think like that, and then lose a few quick wickets, you can be taken out of your bubble a little bit. We were cruising along one minute and then there were a few 'iffy' decisions and an 'attempted catch' by the keeper, which was a rather shoddy. I was a little bit surprised and disappointed about that - I think he got rather excited by the whole thing and the momentum of the game, realised that he'd fumbled it and then, more out of embarrassment than anything else, claimed the catch.

Even though it was early in the season this felt like a big win to me. Would you agree?
AB - Yes, I thought it was a very good win, as I felt they'd be one of the sides who could really do some damage in the competition… but they only seemed to perform well on odd occasions. I think it's very important how you begin in each competition so it was good to get some early wins under our belt.

WORCESTERSHIRE ROYALS v SURREY LIONS at Worcester
Monday 5th May — **Surrey Lions won by one wicket**
Worcestershire Royals won the toss and elected to bat — **Umpires:- Ian Gould & Jeremy Lloyds**

WORCESTERSHIRE ROYALS

Fall Of Wkt	Batsman	How	Out	Score	Balls	4s	6s
2-119	**S.D. Peters**	**c Brown**	**b Saqlain**	**48**	66	6	0
1-85	**V.S. Solanki**	**lbw**	**b Ormond**	**40**	51	5	1
4-235	**G.A. Hick**	**c &**	**b Bicknell**	**81**	67	9	0
3-124	**B.F. Smith ***	**run**	**out**	**4**	4	0	0
5-240	**Kadeer Ali**		**b Azhar**	**52**	75	5	0
	D.A. Leatherdale	**Not**	**Out**	**4**	5	0	0
	G.J. Batty	**Not**	**Out**	**2**	3	0	0
	S.J. Rhodes +	**did not bat**					
	Kabir Ali	**did not bat**					
	M. Hayward	**did not bat**					
	M.S. Mason	**did not bat**					
	Extras	**(4lb, 7w, 2nb)**		**13**			
	TOTAL	**(45 overs)**	**(for 5 wkts)**	**244**			

Bowler	O	M	R	W	NB	Wd
Bicknell	**9**	**1**	**52**	**1**	-	2
Azhar Mahmood	**8**	**0**	**37**	**1**	1	1
Ormond	**9**	**0**	**46**	**1**	-	-
Saqlain Mushtaq	**9**	**0**	**32**	**1**	-	2
Clarke	**4**	**0**	**32**	**0**	-	1
Hollioake	**6**	**0**	**41**	**0**	-	1

SURREY LIONS							
Fall Of Wkt	Batsman	How	Out	Score	Balls	4s	6s
1-4	**I.J. Ward**	**c Batty**	**b Kabir Ali**	**4**	3	1	0
2-157	**A.D. Brown**	**st Rhodes**	**b Batty**	**81**	68	12	2
3-160	**M.R. Ramprakash**	**c Rhodes**	**b Batty**	**67**	68	8	1
4-209	**G.P. Thorpe**	**run**	**out**	**38**	48	5	0
6-220	**R. Clarke**	**lbw**	**b Kabir Ali**	**16**	19	0	0
5-210	**A.J. Hollioake ***		**b Hayward**	**0**	2	0	0
7-221	**Azhar Mahmood**	**c Smith**	**b Kabir Ali**	**3**	11	0	0
8-237	**J.N. Batty +**	**c Rhodes**	**b Hayward**	**4**	8	0	0
	M.P. Bicknell	**Not**	**Out**	**11**	17	1	0
9-239	**Saqlain Mushtaq**	**c Rhodes**	**b Hayward**	**0**	5	0	0
	J. Ormond	**Not**	**Out**	**4**	3	1	0
	Extras	**(7b, 5lb, 1w, 6nb)**		**19**			
	TOTAL	**(41.3 overs)**	**(for 9 wkts)**	**247**			

Bowler	O	M	R	W	NB	Wd
Kabir Ali	**8**	**1**	**43**	**3**	-	-
Mason	**9**	**1**	**46**	**0**	-	-
Hayward	**9**	**0**	**66**	**3**	3	-
Leatherdale	**4.3**	**0**	**27**	**0**	-	-
Batty	**9**	**0**	**43**	**2**	-	-
Hick	**2**	**0**	**10**	**0**	-	1

Other NCL Division One Results

The defeats suffered by the Kent Spitfires and Yorkshire Phoenix left the Lions and the Glamorgan Dragons as the only sides still boasting an unbeaten record at this very early stage of the campaign. While Yorkshire were dismissed for their lowest-ever Sunday/National League total by Essex, both the reigning champions and the Gloucestershire Gladiators won convincingly enough to mark them out as possible contenders for the 2003 title.

May 5
Cardiff:- **Glamorgan Dragons (4pts) beat Kent Spitfires by 7 wickets.** Kent 192-9 (45ov; Key 68, Croft 3-33); Glamorgan 195-3 (36.2ov; Croft 59, Powell 58).
Bristol:- **Gloucs Gladiators (4pts) beat Leicestershire Foxes by 57 runs**. Glos 311-4 (45ov; Weston 92, Spearman 89, Hancock 82, Dagnall 3-52); Leics 254 (43.5ov; DeFreitas 90, Stevens 65, Ball 3-59).
Headingley:- **Essex Eagles (4pts) beat Yorkshire Phoenix by 157 runs**. Essex 211-6 (45ov; Jefferson 57, Habib 50, Bresnan 3-29); Yorks 54 (20.2ov; Napier 4-18, Brant 4-25).

NCL DIVISION ONE TABLE AT 5TH MAY

Pos	Prv		P	Pts	W	T	L	A
1	n/a	**Surrey Lions**	**3**	**12**	3	0	0	0
2	n/a	**Glamorgan Dragons**	**2**	**8**	2	0	0	0
3	n/a	**Essex Eagles**	**2**	**4**	1	0	1	0
=	n/a	**Gloucestershire Gladiators**	**2**	**4**	1	0	1	0
=	n/a	**Kent Spitfires**	**2**	**4**	1	0	1	0
=	n/a	**Worcestershire Royals**	**2**	**4**	1	0	1	0
=	n/a	**Yorkshire Phoenix**	**2**	**4**	1	0	1	0
8	n/a	**Warwickshire Bears**	**2**	**0**	0	0	2	0
9	n/a	**Leicestershire Foxes**	**3**	**0**	0	0	3	0

C&G Trophy 3rd Round - Surrey Subdue Plucky Staffs

Staffordshire v Surrey at Stone C.C. Played on Wednesday 7th May.
Surrey won by 9 runs

An impressive and plucky Staffordshire side - containing three players with significant first-class experience in Kim Barnett, Graeme Archer and Dave Follett - came within ten runs of defeating Surrey in front of a good crowd on a fine day at the very pleasant Stone C.C. ground… though it is fair to say that the game was never quite as tight as the margin of victory suggests.

On a slow but reliable pitch, Surrey's total of 273 was built almost entirely around Ian Ward's first-ever one-day century - reached, with the last of three successive sixes, from his eightieth delivery - and Rikki Clarke's 41-ball innings of forty-seven. After Ward had dominated the first half of the innings with his fluent knock of 108, which included no fewer than 7 sixes and 10 fours, Clarke took his place at the wicket in the twenty-fifth over and shepherded the visitors through to a decent enough score despite some fine Staffordshire fielding and an excellent spell of 10-0-39-3 by the tall left-arm spinner, Guy Bulpitt, a former international swimmer who was once on Worcestershire's books.

The promotion of James Ormond to number four in the batting order had given the impression that Surrey were not going to be operating at one-hundred percent during this match, and this was confirmed during the middle and latter stages of the Staffordshire reply as Ward (10-0-49-0), Mark Ramprakash (6-0-38-1) and Ali Brown (2-0-17-0) delivered a total of eighteen overs between them while the front-line bowlers took a back seat. The home batsmen took advantage of this to such an extent, however, that Saqlain Mushtaq (5-0-38-1) was forced to enter the fray late in the day with 108 runs needed from the last ten overs. Rather surprisingly, this move failed to halt the Staffordshire charge, as Archer, the former Nottinghamshire batsman, and Paul Shaw continued to blast the ball around the park on the way to completing valiant 44-ball half-centuries, though their target always looked just out of reach, with a requirement of 93 runs off seven overs becoming 64 off four and then twenty-five from the final over by Hollioake, who had finally introduced himself with five overs to go. Although the gallant Richard Harvey managed to heave the Surrey skipper's first and fourth balls over the legside boundary to leave himself a shot at glory, the battered Hollioake (3-0-35-0) was ultimately never likely to surrender ten runs from the last two balls when the chips were down. The minor county had done themselves proud, though, and the crowd had thoroughly enjoyed a day of attractive batting and big hitting.

Scores:- Surrey 273 (49.3ov; Ward 108, Clarke 47, Bulpitt 3-39) beat Staffordshire 264-4 (50ov; Archer 65, Shaw 55*, Womble 49) by 9 runs.

4 Off The Mark

Surrey's three NCL wins had boosted confidence and left the Club needing only three, or maybe four, further victories in order to ensure their survival in the first division of that competition. That had to be the first aim following promotion. It was certainly far too early for anyone to even think about Surrey emulating the Glamorgan Dragons, who had won the 2002 title in their first season after elevation from the second division.

The team's County Championship form had been less impressive so far, though there was no doubt that everything seemed to be coming together during the second half of the Warwickshire match, with the second-innings bowling being the best the team had produced, as a unit, during the first two matches. We'd finally seen the real Surrey in action as they had put the batsmen under serious pressure in attempting to pull off a highly unlikely last-day victory. With a win badly needed to kick-start the Championship campaign, it was to be hoped that this improved form would be carried into the next match, against Nottinghamshire, the side who were currently top of the Championship table, at Trent Bridge.

The team selection for that game would, again, be interesting. Although he hadn't gone public with his comments, it was strongly rumoured that Rikki Clarke had made the Surrey management well aware of his feelings about being discarded for the Warwickshire match after his superb century against Lancashire had helped to save the team from an opening-match defeat. I think most supporters could understand the young man's fury at being dropped in this fashion, though they disagreed with those in the media who were suggesting that Clarke was the victim of the new ruling allowing counties to field two overseas players and had lost his place in the team to Azhar Mahmood. During his time with Surrey to date, it was clear that Azhar was seen as a bowling all-rounder, whereas Clarke's performance in the Lancashire match had confirmed him as very much a batting all-rounder. While Azhar could easily be utilised as an opening bowler, Clarke didn't even look suited to the role of third seamer at this early stage of his career, though there was obvious all-round potential there. The Guildford lad was, therefore, losing out to one of the batsmen as opposed to the Pakistani all-rounder and, though he had, quite rightly, been retained in Surrey's one-day team, it was to be hoped that he would soon be reappearing in the Championship eleven as well. Given the fact that Graham Thorpe was now also in the queue for one of the batting slots it looked, sadly, as if Clarke might have to bide his time for a little while longer yet. Butcher's inclusion in the team for the Warwickshire match was an interesting one and had also provoked plenty of debate. Had England put pressure on Surrey to include him in the team? If so, then the Club's decision to accede to that request surely flew in the face of Keith Medlycott's earlier public assertion that "Surrey will pick the best side for Surrey." It was a messy business and an unwelcome distraction for all concerned.

While on the subject of selections, the issue of the captaincy of the England one-day team had been resolved in the days leading up to the Nottinghamshire game, with Michael Vaughan, as expected, given the job of succeeding Nasser Hussain. Given that the England management were said to be looking to the future, and in particular the 2007 World Cup, it seemed highly unlikely that Adam Hollioake would be selected for the forthcoming Nat West Challenge matches against Pakistan, or for the Nat West Series later in the summer, now that he had been passed over for the captaincy. It seemed likely that England's loss would be Surrey's gain.

FRIZZELL COUNTY CHAMPIONSHIP DIVISION ONE - MATCH THREE

NOTTINGHAMSHIRE versus SURREY
at Trent Bridge

First Day - Friday 9th May
Nottinghamshire 211; Surrey 159-5

The Teams And The Toss - *While Surrey name the same side that had played against Warwickshire, their opponents are some way short of full strength, with Kevin Pietersen nursing a knee injury, Russell Warren yet to make an appearance for his new county after breaking a thumb during pre-season, and first-choice overseas players, Chris Cairns and Stuart MacGill, still on international duty. Additionally, Paul Franks plays despite being handicapped by a calf injury and, since the Nottinghamshire line-up includes four other seam bowlers - Greg Smith, 'A.J.' (as he now prefers to be known) Harris, Charlie Shreck and their stand-in overseas registration, Steve Elworthy, the veteran South African - it seems possible that he is playing purely as a batsman. The pitch at Trent Bridge looks rather strange, since it has a mottled green appearance, so Adam Hollioake is probably not too disappointed when he loses the toss, leaving Jason Gallian to decide how it might play in the early stages of the match. The Nottinghamshire skipper can't be too disturbed by what he sees because he elects to bat first.*

The first-ever Bicknell-versus-Bicknell confrontation in County Championship cricket adds extra spice to the early stages of the morning's play as everyone looks closely for signs of the ball misbehaving on this rather odd-looking pitch.

Despite being beaten by movement in the air and/or off the pitch on a number occasions, Darren Bicknell and his skipper manage to survive without too many alarms against Martin Bicknell and Alex Tudor until the elder Bicknell offers a very sharp bat-pad chance to Mark Ramprakash at short leg with his score on ten, and the total sixteen, in the ninth over. While neither batsman is able to get on top of the bowling, they do a good job in seeing off the opening seven-over bursts from the Surrey pair, taking the score to 38-0 in the process.

Since there have been very few memorable strokes up until this point, Bicknell's wristy whip to the midwicket boundary from Azhar Mahmood's first delivery is warmly welcomed by the spectators, though it turns out to be the final run-scoring stroke of the tall left-hander's innings as the Pakistani claims the opening breakthrough for Surrey five balls later. It's a smart catch by Mark Butcher, taken low to his left at second slip, which ends Bicknell senior's innings on twenty-nine… and it isn't long before the same bowler and fielder are in business again.

After eight scoreless deliveries, the new batsman, Guy Welton, pushes hard at the fifth ball of Azhar's third over and edges towards first slip, though the ball doesn't reach Ali Brown, the fielder stationed in that position, as Butcher moves smartly to his left to snaffle up the chance at chest height.

With his side now pegged back to 48-2, and James Ormond proving almost as testing from the pavilion end as Azhar is from the Radcliffe Road end, Gallian knows he has a real battle on his hands but soldiers on manfully, scoring a large proportion of his runs in the area backward of point on the off side with cuts, forces and deflections. His new partner, Usman Afzaal, meanwhile unfurls what is probably the best stroke of the morning when he drives Azhar sweetly through mid-off for four in the twenty-fifth over, though Nottinghamshire's progress remains slow as the ball continues to beat the bat with some regularity.

Both batsmen are doubtless relieved, therefore, when Azhar is rested in favour of Bicknell after an outstanding eight-over burst, and Ormond, in a slightly surprising move, gives way to Butcher an over later, with lunch imminent. Adam Hollioake's decision pays off handsomely, however, as Afzaal drives loosely at the medium-pacer's second delivery, allowing an inswinging delivery to pass through a gaping 'gate' and remove the batsman's off stump. A joyous Butcher leads the Surrey celebrations as the former England left-hander departs for sixteen, leaving the home side under pressure at 83-3.

Although the new batsman, the highly regarded 18-year-old, Bilal Shafayat, starts confidently with a square-cut boundary from the final delivery of Butcher's over followed by a straight-driven four in the last over of the session from Bicknell, it is probably fair to say that it has been Surrey's morning as the players leave the field at the interval.

Lunch:- Nottinghamshire 92-3 (Gallian 38, Shafayat 8*) from 33 overs*

Mark Butcher is allowed one more over at the start of the afternoon session before the Surrey captain opts for a combination of Azhar from the Radcliffe Road end and Bicknell from the pavilion end.

Azhar is instantly successful, too, as his first ball, something of a wide loosener outside off stump, tempts Shafayat into a wild sliced drive that sends the ball flying into the hands of Ramprakash at the finer of two gullies. It's a very disappointing stroke from the young man, though it's easy to see why he has tried to adopt a positive approach on this far-from-perfect surface where 250 looks to be the approximate par score.

With both bowlers maintaining the high standards they had set during the morning session, life continues to be tough for the batsmen, as Gallian, on forty-five at the time, discovers when a magnificent outswinger from Azhar induces an edge to second slip. Fortunately for the home captain, Butcher fails to hang on to a catch to his left-hand side that looks easier than the two chances he had gobbled up before lunch.

Clearly determined to make the most of this let-off, Gallian goes on to complete a gritty half-century, from 131 balls, four overs later and, given good support by Chris Read, many people's choice as Alec Stewart's successor in the England team, eventually manages to force Hollioake into a double bowling change that sees the return of Ormond and Tudor.

This move appears to be to Gallian's liking as he pulls each new bowler to the fence to take the score past 150 and complete a most valuable fifty partnership with Read, who has contributed a couple of pleasant boundaries of his own along the way.

The former, and maybe future, England wicketkeeper saves his best till last, however, as he drives Ormond crisply down the ground from the first ball of the following over before chopping the next delivery down onto his stumps to end a battling knock of twenty-two.

With the score standing at 155-5 at the fall of this wicket, the hosts are struggling again since there doesn't appear to be a great deal of batting to come - Paul Franks, making his way out to the middle, looks as if he may be one place too high in the order, despite making an unbeaten eighty-four in Notts' C&G win at Lincoln on Wednesday, while the tail that follows him looks decidedly fragile.

With this possibly in the back of his mind, Franks digs in doggedly, attempting nothing flamboyant and leaving his captain to glance and drive boundaries in order to prevent the scoreboard from seizing up completely. Worryingly for all batsmen in the match, four byes are also added to the score when a Tudor delivery rears viciously from just short of a length and flies over the head of the leaping Stewart behind the stumps.

Tudor is then to the fore again in the next over from Ormond when Franks, still without a run to his name after twenty-five minutes at the crease, looks sure to break his duck with a blazing drive that the big paceman stops brilliantly at midwicket. This fine piece of fielding turns out to be of some significance, since Franks clearly begins to fret about getting off the mark and eventually loses patience in Ormond's next over, slashing wildly outside his off stump and getting a top edge through to Stewart. As Franks departs for a 24-ball duck with the score now 177-6, Ormond has two wickets to his name and, with a bunch of bunnies to come, must feel confident about adding to his haul.

This confidence turns out to be fully justified, too, as three more wickets tumble in the next four overs delivered by the Ormond-Tudor combination. In the sixty-second over, with the total advanced by just one run, Steve Elworthy offers a limp bat to a Tudor delivery and edges to Stewart; five balls later, Ormond brings Greg Smith to book as the Pretoria-born seamer pushes a rearing delivery tamely to Azhar in the gully; then two overs later, with the score standing at 185-8, A.J. Harris provides Stewart with another catch, and Ormond with his fourth wicket, by getting a thin outside edge to a fine ball that lifts and leaves the bat.

Poor Gallian has been left to watch helplessly from the other end as his team's innings has crumbled away, and as soon as he gets back on strike he makes his intentions clear - he will be looking to rack up some quick runs before the last man, Charlie Shreck, goes the same way as his fellow tailenders.

His first attempt to do this leads to a lucky escape when a hook off Tudor flies through the upstretched hands of Ormond at long leg, resulting in six runs rather than the end of the Nottinghamshire innings, though the extra-cover drive that follows later in the over is superbly executed and takes Gallian through to a really gutsy and hard-earned century. The extended round of applause that follows the announcement of the statistics for the home skipper's lone-hand innings - 198 balls, 16 fours and 1 six - is well deserved.

With even less to lose now that he has a century to his name, Gallian follows up by driving Ormond's slower ball over long-off for the second six of his knock, bringing up the Nottinghamshire two-hundred in the process, then finding the rope at extra cover again from the next delivery.

Ormond ends the home side's innings in his next over, however, when Shreck, having looked a more capable batsman than some of his fellow tailenders, gloves a lifter to Stewart, giving the big Surrey seamer final figures of 5-45, thanks to a final burst of 4-13 in twenty-five balls which has seen the tail swept away in double-quick time.

Gallian is the undoubted hero of the innings, though, and receives a fine ovation as he leaves the field, having carried his bat for 112 out of a total of 211 all out.

Tea:- Between Innings

After their impressive bowling and fielding display, Surrey need to bat with equal conviction and skill during the day's final session in order to build a match-winning position. Their innings gets off to the worst possible start, however, when Mark Butcher is adjudged to have got a thin edge to Steve Elworthy's opening delivery and departs looking far from happy with umpire Trevor Jesty's decision.

This is just the fillip that Nottinghamshire need after their struggles with the bat, and they receive further encouragement when Ian Ward is opened up by the second ball of Greg Smith's first over and edges low to first slip where Paul Franks takes a good catch. At 4-2, with Ward gone for three, the visitors are suddenly in danger of surrendering their advantage completely.

Seemingly unshaken by these early losses, Alec Stewart, entering at number four, gets away to a great start by glancing his first ball to the fine-leg boundary, though he almost sees his side plunged into even deeper trouble when Mark Ramprakash is badly missed at short leg by Guy Welton in Elworthy's second over. With the former Middlesex man still not off the mark at the time, Surrey have come close to being 10-3, with 211 looking a long way off.

As the ball continues to pass the outside edge of the bat almost as often as it had during the home team's innings, Ramprakash battles gamely through a sticky start, while Stewart makes the conditions look relatively easy at the other end, driving and pulling three boundaries in the same number of overs while moving his personal score to twenty-seven after just seven overs.

At this point he enjoys a slice of luck, though, when a top-edged hook off Smith seems certain to be caught by Darren Bicknell lurking out at deep backward square leg. Unfortunately for the fielder and his team-mates, however, the ball's path takes it directly into line with the sun, causing Bicknell to lose track of its flight and, consequently, end up some distance from the ball as it drops safely to earth.

Far from unsettling Stewart, this incident seems to strengthen his resolve, while simultaneously throwing Elworthy's thinking completely awry - the tall South African suddenly decides to test the England wicketkeeper-batsman's acknowledged skill on the pull shot with a series of short balls, all of which disappear to the boundary. When he then tries to pitch the ball up again, Elworthy merely produces a half-volley that Stewart despatches to the rope at long-on, thereby completing a classic fifty, from a mere 33 balls, out of a total of 63-2.

The immediate introduction of A.J. Harris in place of Elworthy, whose final over of a increasingly erratic spell has cost fourteen runs, comes as no surprise, though the replacement of the increasingly dangerous Smith with Charlie Shreck is rather unexpected.

The hitherto restrained Ramprakash is perfectly happy with the situation, however, as he instantly picks up the first two fours of his innings with a deflection to third man and a drive through extra cover at Shreck's expense. When the 6' 7" Cornishman's poor first over is then followed by an equally loose over from Harris that sees Stewart profit by eleven runs, including cut and pulled boundaries, it is clear that the hosts are being rather too generous with their hospitality towards their visitors.

After their wayward first overs, both bowlers do manage to regain a modicum of control, however, though they still leak the occasional boundary as the Surrey total storms into three figures in the twentieth over when Ramprakash cuts Shreck for four. The towering paceman's tendency to bowl too short always looks likely to cost him very dearly at some point and so it proves when the final over of his spell turns out to be the nadir of a really poor opening burst of 5-0-37-0. Having seen the first ball driven to the extra-cover fence by Stewart, he elects to bang the ball in short for the rest of the over and sees the second, third and fifth deliveries also being clattered for four, courtesy of two hooks - the first, to be fair to the bowler, top-edged over the wicketkeeper's head - and a resounding cut.

With Harris' first six overs at the other end having yielded thirty-three runs, the frustrated Gallian soon has his opening bowlers back in harness, though Elworthy's opening over offers little encouragement as Stewart drives through mid-on for four to take his score into the nineties.

Smith again looks the man most likely to break what has become a very dangerous partnership and, with the day drawing to a close, he does the trick for his skipper as Stewart attempts another pull and only succeeds in getting a bottom-edge down into his stumps with his personal tally ninety-eight and the total on 147. As he leaves the field, the former Surrey and England captain receives justified applause for a sparkling knock that has put his side in a potentially powerful position after the early loss of the openers, while the Nottinghamshire players hope that this breakthrough might lead to further successes in the final six overs of the day.

This looks unlikely, initially, as the new batsman, Ali Brown, drives each bowler down the ground for four, but a surprise change of bowling - Shreck for Elworthy at the pavilion end - proves to be an inspired piece of captaincy by Gallian and brings two late wickets for his side.

The former Cornwall seamer makes the initial breach by luring Ramprakash into an uncontrolled hook that deposits the ball in the hands of long leg with the batsman on thirty-eight and the total 157, then, six balls later, with no addition to the total, the seemingly out-of-form

Brown attempts to pull a delivery from Smith and miscues the shot high in the air over the head of Elworthy at mid-on. For a few seconds it looks as if the Surrey batsman will get away with his error of judgement, but the South African seamer shows great determination to chase back and complete a fine one-handed catch over his shoulder at full stretch. Suddenly, we have a much more even contest on our hands and a fascinating day lies ahead of us tomorrow.

Close:- Surrey 159-5 (Saqlain 0, Hollioake 1*) from 35 overs*

Second Day - Saturday 10th May
Nottinghamshire 211 and 94-6; Surrey 393

Adam Hollioake's glorious cover drive from the first ball of the day, bowled by Steve Elworthy, gives us an immediate taste of what is to come on a cool and cloudy morning as Surrey look to build a sizeable first-innings lead.

After the nightwatchman, Saqlain Mushtaq, crashes Greg Smith to the rope at extra cover in the following over, the visiting skipper makes it clear that his side will be adopting a positive approach on this pitch by launching into Elworthy's second over with gusto. While it is fair to say that the former South African international is unfortunate to see Hollioake's top-edged hook at the first ball disappear for four over Chris Read's head, there is nothing lucky about the on-drives and glances that yield further boundaries from balls two, three, five and six in an over costing twenty runs.

Charlie Shreck immediately replaces Elworthy at the pavilion end and also feels the force of Hollioake's blade as the Surrey captain drives and cuts fours to take his team's score beyond two-hundred in just the fortieth over of the innings. With Hollioake in such devastating touch so early in the day, the Cornishman is then possibly relieved to discover that he has been given this over merely to enable his captain to switch his opening bowlers around, as Elworthy reappears for the next over from the Radcliffe Road end while Smith moves to the pavilion end.

This turns out to be another good decision by Jason Gallian as the Springbok almost instantly extracts Hollioake's off stump with a fine yorker to end a quite amazing cameo innings of thirty-five runs from a mere 25 balls.

With Surrey now six down and still nine runs adrift of the Nottinghamshire total, the home side are still very much in the match, given the vagaries of a pitch that looks likely to deteriorate as the game wears on. Proof that it remains unpredictable comes shortly after Hollioake's dismissal when Saqlain is hit on the hand and requires on-field treatment.

The visitors' bold intentions look entirely sensible in these circumstances and Azhar Mahmood soon picks up where Hollioake had left off by on-driving Elworthy for a four and a six to maintain the tempo of the innings. With his overseas bowler proving so expensive and Smith lacking the spark of the previous day, Gallian is forced to turn to his first-change seamers, Harris and Shreck, with mixed results.

While both men concede boundaries to Azhar in their opening over, allowing Surrey to speed past the 250 mark in the forty-eighth over, Harris does at least provide his side with another breakthrough, removing Saqlain with a good lifting delivery that seemingly brushes the batsman's glove on its way through to Read behind the stumps. Although the visitors have already established a lead of forty by this time, the capture of a seventh wicket at least raises home hopes of restricting the opposition's first-innings advantage.

Surrey's renowned depth of batting leaves the Nottinghamshire bowlers with plenty of work to do yet, however, and while the new batsman, Alex Tudor, settles in at one end, Azhar continues to attack at the other, driving down the ground with immense power to add four boundaries to his collection in the course of two overs and complete a quite brilliant quick-fire half-century from just 42 deliveries faced.

The Pakistani all-rounder promptly celebrates by driving Harris over extra cover for the second six of his innings, while Tudor opens up and joins in the fun with successive fours off Shreck as the fifty-fifth over sees the total reaching three-hundred and the eighth-wicket partnership becoming worth fifty.

The replacement of Shreck with Smith at this point seems like a good idea but merely brings Azhar's third six, lifted high over long-on, and when Harris then follows up with another poor over that yields ten runs to Tudor the morning's stats - 162 runs added in twenty-two overs - compel Gallian to take action.

With none of his four seamers able to stem the flow of runs, Franks clearly unfit to bowl, and Usman Afzaal an unattractive spin option, the Notts captain decides that he can't do any worse if he has a go himself. And how right he is. Although fairly gentle in pace, the home captain demonstrates the value of maintaining a steady line and length by tying up one end until the lunch break and picking up the wicket of Tudor - caught by Read from a top-edged cut for twenty-seven with the total 333 - along the way.

With Smith and Elworthy almost shamed into contributing a couple of better overs apiece at the other end, even Azhar is reduced to picking off singles to deep-set fields and the scoring rate dips accordingly. This is not a problem for Surrey, since their morning onslaught has already put them in a very strong position in the match.

Lunch:- Surrey 345-8 (Azhar 82, Bicknell 6*) from 67 overs*

With a heavy shower having swept across the ground during the interval, the start of the afternoon session is delayed until 3.10pm, by which time twenty overs have been lost.

Although the state of both the pitch and the match suggests that we will not be requiring a fourth day for this contest, Surrey continue to bat as if there is no tomorrow once play resumes. Azhar pulls Elworthy's first ball over mid-on for four and his third ball over midwicket for six to secure a fourth batting point for his team, before enjoying two strokes of luck later in the over, first when he miscues another pull into a gap at midwicket, picking up two runs in the process, and then when he edges for four to third man. Within one over of the restart the Pakistani international has, therefore, moved his score on from eighty-two to ninety-eight.

Like Stewart before him, however, Azhar falls two short of his century, Elworthy gaining a small measure of revenge in his next over when a top-edged hook in the direction of square leg brings a fine catch out of Read, who sprints from his position behind the wicket and takes the ball just inches from the turf. Although the Surrey all-rounder is undoubtedly disappointed as he leaves the field to a good reception from the crowd, he has the consolation of knowing that, weather permitting, his 95-ball knock has given his team every chance of registering their first Championship win of the campaign sometime during the next two days.

Any hopes the home side have of Surrey's last pair - Martin Bicknell and James Ormond - going quietly are soon shattered as Bicknell plunders five assorted fours from the next two overs, though Ormond doesn't last too long, driving Smith's slower ball to Afzaal at mid-on with the visitors just seven runs short of a fifth and final batting point. It's fitting that Smith has secured the final wicket, since he is the only one of Nottinghamshire's four main bowlers who can look back on his performance with any pride.

An imposing Surrey lead of 182 then begins to look even more daunting for the home team when Bicknell claims Bicknell with the fifth ball of their second innings. Trapped on the crease by a ball that shapes back into his pads, Darren falls lbw to Martin following an impassioned appeal to umpire Jesty, and, while one brother celebrates his success, the other trudges disconsolately back to the pavilion with a duck to his name.

Rainfall after 3.1 overs then brings an early tea with the home side struggling on 6-1.

Tea:- Nottinghamshire 6-1 (Gallian 6, Welton 0*) from 3.1 overs*

After the loss of four further overs to the inclement weather, play restarts at 4.25pm with James Ormond continuing to share the new ball with Martin Bicknell in the absence of Alex Tudor, who is said to have aggravated a knee injury during his innings this morning.

Ormond is very much to the fore, too, as he plunges Nottinghamshire into even deeper trouble by taking two wickets in three balls during the sixth over of the innings. Having just registered his first runs of the match with a forcing stroke to the extra-cover boundary, Guy Welton holes out to Bicknell at mid-off with the total at fifteen, then Usman Afzaal gets an outside edge to a ball angled across him and sees Mark Butcher diving away in front of first slip from his position at second slip to pull off a very fine low catch. The Surrey players are understandably jubilant at having reduced their hosts to a parlous 15-3, still 167 runs in arrears, and it appears that Gallian is going to have to produce an even more impressive captain's innings second time around - and receive better support - if Notts are to have any chance at all of avoiding a heavy defeat.

With both Surrey bowlers consistently putting the ball in testing areas, the only boundaries that accrue in the next half-an-hour come via edges over the slips, and it's no great surprise when Ormond strikes again in his seventh over, courtesy of a fine delivery that Bilal Shafayat can only snick into the safe gloves of Alec Stewart. As the England Under-19 skipper departs with just ten runs to his name, and his side wobbling badly at 35-4, defeat is already looking on the cards for the current leaders of the Championship.

The fall of Shafayat reunites Gallian with Chris Read, and the pair who had produced the biggest partnership of the Nottinghamshire first innings offer a little hope to their side again as the wicketkeeper glances and drives early boundaries, while his captain stays out of trouble by demonstrating impeccable judgement of which balls to play and which balls to leave around his off stump. The fifth-wicket pair have just taken the total past fifty and seen off Ormond, whose excellent eight-over burst has earned him figures of 3 for 26, when bad light causes the suspension of play at 5.30pm with the scoreboard reading 56-4.

At this stage of the day it seems possible that we might not see any further action, but, to the batting side's undoubted disappointment, the grey clouds around the ground clear sufficiently for the umpires to order a resumption at 6pm, leaving thirteen overs to bowl in the day… if the improved light holds.

Having enjoyed a thirty-minute break, Bicknell continues from the pavilion end, while Azhar Mahmood resumes the spell that he had just started from the Radcliffe Road end when the light closed in.

Although survival until the close of play must now be the primary objective of the batsmen, Read isn't prepared to turn down opportunities to score runs, as he shows by cracking the Pakistani all-rounder for two impressive boundaries within three overs of the restart. Gallian then manages one of his own by forcing Bicknell away backward of point, only to find the fourth ball of the same over thudding into his pads and bringing forth a huge lbw appeal from the whole Surrey team. The visitors' veteran swing bowler looks distraught when umpire Jesty rejects the appeal, but he is smiling again two balls later when another fine delivery catches the home skipper on the crease and the inevitable appeal this time earns a positive verdict from the man in the white coat. With Gallian out for twenty-eight and Nottinghamshire now 71-5, with a lengthy tail to follow, all hope is gone for the home side and there is even an outside chance that Surrey could seal victory tonight if the light remains playable.

The possibility of a two-day finish then increases four overs later when Bicknell finally gets some reward for his fine bowling throughout the match as he claims the important scalp of Read for twenty-six with the score advanced only as far as seventy-six. Having edged his drive at an outswinger, the 24-year-old wicketkeeper-batsman turns to see Azhar, at third slip, snap up a very good catch at head height to his right-hand side, thereby pushing Notts ever closer to defeat.

Whether that defeat will come today or tomorrow remains unclear as Paul Franks and Steve Elworthy attempt to battle through to the close, though it is clear that, unless the weather intervenes, there will be no need for a fourth day for this one-sided contest.

As it happens, the seventh-wicket pair do actually manage to bat through the last six overs of the day and it comes as something of a surprise when, in fast-fading light at 6.50pm, Surrey claim, and are granted, the extra half-an-hour in which to try to finish the match. The umpires soon see the folly of their decision, however, offering the light to the batsmen after just one over and drawing stumps when, inevitably, Franks and Elworthy elect to retire for the day.

Close:- Nottinghamshire 94-6 (Franks 12, Elworthy 9*) from 33 overs*

Third Day - Sunday 11th May

Nottinghamshire 211 and 176; Surrey 393
Surrey won by an innings and 6 runs
Surrey 21pts, Nottinghamshire 4

With nothing to play for but pride, and no pressure of expectation, Franks and Elworthy resume, against Bicknell and Azhar, with a positive attitude on a pleasantly bright Sunday morning that suggests the game will be completed without any interruptions from the weather.

The seventh-wicket pair are clearly determined to enjoy what is left of the match, notching a boundary apiece from the day's opening two overs in advancing the total beyond a hundred, though Bicknell gives notice that batting is still going to be a hazardous affair by inducing an edge from Elworthy that flies over the slips to add another four runs to the total.

This morning's aggressive approach certainly pays dividends for the batsmen as they rattle off five more boundaries in the next four overs to complete the home side's second half-century partnership of the match. Like the Gallian-Read stand in the first innings, it doesn't go much further, though, as the left-handed Franks attempts to add to his boundary count with an expansive drive outside off stump at Azhar and only succeeds in edging to Ali Brown at first slip. With the sharp chance nicely pouched away to the fielder's left-hand side, Franks goes for twenty-five, leaving Nottinghamshire trailing by fifty-four runs with just three wickets now left standing.

Defeat is already staring the home side in the face, and it moves considerably closer over the course of the next four overs as Greg Smith perishes to his sixth ball - thick-edging a Bicknell outswinger straight down the throat of Mark Ramprakash, who had been carefully moved into a fly-gully position at the start of the over - and A.J. Harris to his fifth, when he walks into the line of a delivery from Azhar and is sent packing by umpire Holder.

With Notts still requiring forty-four runs to make Surrey bat again, the visitors' margin of victory looks sure to be an innings-plus, though the gap between the two sides narrows quite rapidly as the last-wicket pair of Elworthy and Charlie Shreck swing their bats to good effect - the Cornishman picks up three fours early in his knock, while the South African reels off a couple of pleasant drives and then a pull off Bicknell which carries over the midwicket boundary for six to complete a valiant, if inconsequential, fifty from 71 balls. Bicknell doesn't waste any time in redressing the balance and completing a five-wicket haul, however, having Elworthy caught by Azhar at a cleverly positioned fly slip from an edged drive later in the over to conclude both the batsman's innings and the match, with the hosts still six runs short of levelling the scores.

The fact that the game has ended at 12.14pm on the third day says plenty about both the poor quality of the Trent Bridge pitch - even though an ECB pitches inspector had declared himself satisfied with it on the second morning - and the lack of depth in Nottinghamshire's squad. In sharp contrast to Surrey, whose current wealth of talent had forced them to omit several high-class players from their eleven, the team that had been leading the Championship after the first two matches had clearly missed the services of Chris Cairns, Stuart MacGill and Kevin Pietersen.

Nottinghamshire 211 and 176; Surrey 393
Surrey won by an innings and 6 runs. Surrey 21pts, Nottinghamshire 4

TALKING POINTS - ALEC STEWART

This was clearly not the best of pitches at Trent Bridge. What did you think of it?
AS - It was a poor wicket. Unless two teams play badly, a four-day wicket should see the game lasting until at least the middle session of the final day. That's the sign of a good wicket. This was anything but a good wicket. It was cracked and it had grass on it, and it was summed up perfectly by the fact that neither side bowled an over of spin, even with Saqi in our side.

I thought the Nottinghamshire bowling was pretty abysmal. What was your view?
AS - I have to say that I thought their bowling was rubbish. On a pitch like that you get rewarded if you bowl line and length. They saw the excessive bounce at times and proceeded to bowl the ball halfway down the track… and then over-compensated by bowling it too full. They basically fed my hook and cut shots, and it was the dimmest bowling I'd seen in a long time, really.

TALKING POINTS - MARTIN BICKNELL

Would I be right in thinking that you changed your run-up during this game?
MBi - Yes, I had struggled a little bit with it during the first innings - I was finding that I had no real rhythm or timing - and I'd been thinking about changing it. So I tried my short run-up - which has now become my normal run-up - during the second innings, and everything clicked into place straight away and I bowled as well as I possibly can.

NOTTINGHAMSHIRE v SURREY at Trent Bridge 9th to 11th May
Nottinghamshire won the toss and elected to bat. Umpires:- John Holder and Trevor Jesty

NOTTINGHAMSHIRE - First Innings

Fall Of Wkt	Batsman	How	Out	Score	Balls	4s	6s
1-42	**D.J. Bicknell**	**c Butcher**	**b Azhar**	**29**	50	5	0
	J.E.R. Gallian *	**Not**	**Out**	**112**	204	17	2
2-48	**G.E. Welton**	**c Butcher**	**b Azhar**	**0**	8	0	0
3-83	**U. Afzaal**		**b Butcher**	**16**	36	2	0
4-96	**B.M. Shafayat**	**c Ramprakash**	**b Azhar**	**8**	8	2	0
5-155	**C.M.W. Read +**		**b Ormond**	**22**	51	3	0
6-177	**P.J. Franks**	**c Stewart**	**b Ormond**	**0**	24	0	0
7-178	**S. Elworthy**	**c Stewart**	**b Tudor**	**0**	3	0	0
8-179	**G.J. Smith**	**c Azhar**	**b Ormond**	**1**	5	0	0
9-185	**A.J. Harris**	**c Stewart**	**b Ormond**	**0**	11	0	0
10-211	**C.E. Shreck**	**c Stewart**	**b Ormond**	**5**	12	1	0
	Extras	**(4b, 9lb, 5w)**		**18**			
	TOTAL	**(68.4 overs)**		**211**			

Bowler	O	M	R	W	NB	Wd
Bicknell	**16**	**4**	**41**	**0**	-	-
Tudor	**16**	**1**	**58**	**1**	-	-
Azhar Mahmood	**16**	**4**	**46**	**3**	-	1
Ormond	**18.4**	**5**	**45**	**5**	-	-
Butcher	**2**	**0**	**8**	**1**	-	-

SURREY - First Innings							
Fall Of Wkt	Batsman	How	Out	Score	Balls	4s	6s
1-0	**M.A. Butcher**	**c Read**	**b Elworthy**	**0**	1	0	0
2-4	**I.J. Ward**	**c Franks**	**b Smith**	**3**	3	0	0
4-157	**M.R. Ramprakash**	**c Smith**	**b Shreck**	**38**	108	5	0
3-147	**A.J. Stewart +**		**b Smith**	**98**	70	17	0
5-157	**A.D. Brown**	**c Elworthy**	**b Smith**	**9**	15	2	0
7-251	**Saqlain Mushtaq**	**c Read**	**b Harris**	**24**	43	3	0
6-202	**A.J. Hollioake ***		**b Elworthy**	**35**	25	8	0
9-365	**Azhar Mahmood**	**c Read**	**b Elworthy**	**98**	95	12	4
8-333	**A.J. Tudor**	**c Read**	**b Gallian**	**27**	46	5	0
	M.P. Bicknell	**Not**	**Out**	**33**	27	7	0
10-393	**J. Ormond**	**c Afzaal**	**b Smith**	**5**	5	1	0
	Extras	**(5b, 8lb, 10nb)**		**23**			
	TOTAL	**(72.1 overs)**		**393**			

Bowler	O	M	R	W	NB	Wd
Elworthy	**21**	**2**	**136**	**3**	1	-
Smith	**22.1**	**4**	**81**	**4**	-	-
Shreck	**12**	**1**	**81**	**1**	-	-
Harris	**12**	**1**	**75**	**1**	4	-
Gallian	**5**	**0**	**7**	**1**	-	-

NOTTINGHAMSHIRE - Second Innings (Trailing by 182 runs on first innings)							
Fall Of Wkt	Batsman	How	Out	Score	Balls	4s	6s
1-0	**D.J. Bicknell**	**lbw**	**b Bicknell**	**0**	5	0	0
5-71	**J.E.R. Gallian ***	**lbw**	**b Bicknell**	**28**	66	4	0
2-15	**G.E. Welton**	**c Bicknell**	**b Ormond**	**4**	13	1	0
3-15	**U. Afzaal**	**c Butcher**	**b Ormond**	**0**	2	0	0
4-35	**B.M. Shafayat**	**c Stewart**	**b Ormond**	**10**	24	1	0
6-76	**C.M.W. Read +**	**c Azhar**	**b Bicknell**	**26**	39	4	0
7-128	**P.J. Franks**	**c Brown**	**b Azhar**	**25**	47	5	0
10-176	**S. Elworthy**	**c Azhar**	**b Bicknell**	**52**	73	8	1
8-131	**G.J. Smith**	**c Ramprakash**	**b Bicknell**	**2**	6	0	0
9-138	**A.J. Harris**	**lbw**	**b Azhar**	**3**	5	0	0
	C.E. Shreck	**Not**	**Out**	**16**	28	4	0
	Extras	**(4lb, 6nb)**		**10**			
	TOTAL	**(50.5 overs)**		**176**			

Bowler	O	M	R	W	NB	Wd
Bicknell	**25.5**	**8**	**83**	**5**	1	-
Ormond	**8**	**0**	**26**	**3**	-	-
Azhar Mahmood	**16**	**3**	**59**	**2**	2	-
Butcher	**1**	**0**	**4**	**0**	-	-

Other Frizzell Championship Division One Results

While Surrey moved up into second place in the table with their victory at Trent Bridge, Warwickshire took over at the top of the Championship following a dismal second-innings collapse by Sussex at Edgbaston that handed victory to the Bears. Lancashire were meanwhile frustrated for a third successive match when rain, coupled with a magnificent second-innings opening stand by Andrew Strauss and Sven Koenig, helped Middlesex secure a draw after they had trailed by 261 runs on first innings.

May 9-12

***Lord's:-* Middlesex (8pts) drew with Lancashire (12).** Lancashire 565-7dec (Law 198, Chilton 119, Flintoff 111); Middlesex 304 (Shah 81, Joyce 53, Keedy 6-68) & 176-0 (Strauss 100*, Koenig 71*).

***Edgbaston:-* Warwickshire (22pts) beat Sussex (7) by 234 runs.** Warwicks 422 (Trott 134, Sheikh 57*, Mushtaq 6-157) & 285-7dec (Bell 107, Troughton 105); Sussex 367 (Ambrose 85, Prior 84, Sheikh 4-60) & 106 (Cottey 55, Betts 5-43, Brown 4-17).

FRIZZELL CHAMPIONSHIP DIVISION ONE TABLE AT 12TH MAY

Pos	Prv		P	Points	W	D	L	T	Bat	Bwl	Ded
1	3	Warwickshire	4	49.75	1	1	1	1	16	9	0.25
2	7	Surrey	3	39.00	1	2	0	0	10	7	0.00
3	6	Lancashire	3	35.00	0	3	0	0	14	9	0.00
4	4	Middlesex	3	33.00	1	2	0	0	4	7	0.00
5	1	Nottinghamshire	3	32.00	1	1	1	0	6	9	1.00
6	5	Sussex	3	30.00	1	0	2	0	7	9	0.00
7	2	Essex	3	28.00	0	2	0	1	5	8	0.00
8	8	Leicestershire	2	17.00	0	2	0	0	3	6	0.00
9	9	Kent	2	11.00	0	1	1	0	1	6	0.00

5 Rain Frustrates, Lions Roar On

Having registered their first Championship victory and earned themselves some extra time off by completing their triumph at Trent Bridge with almost two days to spare, everything was now looking much rosier for Surrey. It was to be hoped, however, that we wouldn't see too many more pitches like the one in Nottingham, even though the team had become more proficient at playing on such surfaces in recent years. With a potential seam attack of Bicknell, Tudor, Ormond and Azhar to face, it seemed unlikely that too many teams would be daft enough to prepare a green pitch for Surrey's visit in any case.

While things were on the up for the reigning champions, Warwickshire, the new leaders of the Championship, had suddenly been hit by bad news concerning their overseas players. Michael Clark, the stand-in left-arm pace bowler from Australia, had been released from his contract after being diagnosed as having a stress fracture of the back, while their number one overseas 'pick', Shane Bond, had broken down in Sri Lanka and was to undergo tests, with the fear being that he had sustained the same injury as Clark. In the meantime, the Bears had secured the services of Collins Obuya, the Kenyan leg-spinner who had impressed many good judges during the World Cup in South Africa. Bowling leg-spin in Africa and bowling it in England, on lower-bouncing tracks, often in cool and damp weather, were two very different things, however, and the feeling was that the young man might struggle to adapt to conditions in a land where, history tells us, only the very best 'leggies' thrive.

While Warwickshire had gone for an inexperienced young player to fill one of their overseas vacancies, Lancashire had, by way of contrast, signed the 36-year-old former West Indies captain, Carl Hooper, as a replacement for Harbhajan Singh, whose finger injury was not showing sufficient signs of recovery. Strict ECB rules governing the replacement of injured overseas players meant that Lancashire had to seek clearance for Hooper to begin playing straight away and this was eventually granted. It seemed odd that Mike Watkinson had opted to replace a specialist off-spinner with a high-class batsman who could also bowl very respectable off-breaks, though this was probably due to the fact that there were no top-quality overseas spinners available to him at this stage of the season. Although Hooper was undoubtedly still a very fine cricketer, his signing looked more likely to boost Lancashire's chances in one-day cricket, rather than the Championship, since it was impossible to see the West Indian running through opposition batting line-ups in the way that Harbhajan might have done.

Everything was still looking rosy for the County Champions, therefore, as they prepared to take on Leicestershire at The Oval.

FRIZZELL COUNTY CHAMPIONSHIP DIVISION ONE - MATCH FOUR

SURREY versus LEICESTERSHIRE
at The Oval

First Day - Wednesday 14th May
Leicestershire 200; Surrey 182-2

The Teams And The Toss - *With Alex Tudor and James Ormond ruled out by the knee injuries that had curtailed their participation with the ball at Trent Bridge, Surrey are forced into making two changes to their side, recalling Rikki Clarke and Ian Salisbury, thereby altering the balance of their side on an Oval pitch that will clearly play very differently from the one in Nottingham. Although Ali Brown has yet to hit form in the Championship he keeps his place in the side ahead of Graham Thorpe. With Virender Sehwag making his Championship debut, Leicestershire are* *able to field what appears to be a full-strength eleven and are boosted further when Phillip DeFreitas calls correctly at the toss and elects to bat first on a typically good-looking wicket. Adam Hollioake has now lost eight out of nine tosses this season.*

With Surrey's seam attack having been depleted by the injuries to Ormond and Tudor, it is no surprise to see Martin Bicknell and Azhar Mahmood sharing the new ball. These two will need to perform well, too, since the back-up seamers - Rikki Clarke, Adam Hollioake and Mark Butcher - are unlikely to cause the opposition too many sleepless nights.

The capture of early wickets would clearly help matters, so there is much relief in Surrey circles when Azhar strikes a huge blow for his team with the opening ball of his third over, which lifts and leaves the bat of the Indian international, Virender Sehwag, inducing an involuntary nick into the hands of Ali Brown at first slip. Having bowled all of his previous twelve balls to Trevor Ward, the other Leicestershire opener, Surrey's Pakistani all-rounder is understandably jubilant at having enjoyed instant success against his Indian rival, and the reaction of the whole fielding side demonstrates how highly they value Sehwag's wicket.

The loss of the 24-year-old strokemaker with the total on fourteen certainly seems to unsettle the visitors and a catalogue of dismal strokes follows as they subside to 26-4 during a remarkable five-over passage of play.

With the score advanced to 19-1, Ward attempts to pull Azhar through midwicket but only succeeds in gloving the ball through to Alec Stewart; Darren Maddy then flails wildly at a wide delivery from Bicknell, so often his nemesis, providing the Surrey keeper with another edged catch with the total on twenty-five; and, finally, Darren Stevens snicks an ambitious off-side forcing stroke from his third ball to first slip, where Ali Brown does extremely well to complete the dismissal as Stewart, sensing the possibility of a third victim, dives across in front of him before opting out of attempting the catch. Although there has been a degree of assistance from the pitch for Surrey's opening bowlers, both of whom have maintained excellent control of line and length, it is clear that the surface is, basically, a good one and that these are not conditions in which any side should be reeling at 26-4.

The Australian, Brad Hodge, and the Foxes' wicketkeeper, Paul Nixon, attempt to restore some order by reeling off a few boundary strokes at Azhar's expense, but their fightback turns out to be a very brief one as the Pakistani all-rounder soon nips a good delivery back into the Victorian's pads and elicits a positive response from umpire Neil Mallender when the inevitable appeal goes up. With the visitors' top five all back in the hutch and only forty-seven runs on the board, Azhar, who now has four wickets to his name, appears to have put his side in a commanding position with only eighteen overs of the match completed.

The experienced and gutsy Nixon could, of course, still be a threat, as he demonstrates when he picks Bicknell up for four over square leg in the twenty-first over, but his new partner, Jeremy Snape, looks all at sea, and it is no great surprise when he offers a fairly straightforward caught-and-bowled chance to the veteran Surrey swing bowler with his score on nine and the total at sixty-eight. Bicknell fails to cling on to the catch as it comes back at waist height, however, and sustains some damage to a finger in the process, bringing a very good twelve-over spell to an end.

With Azhar also rested following an excellent opening burst that has earned him figures of 11-3-30-4, Adam Hollioake now turns to Mark Butcher at the pavilion end and Rikki Clarke at the Vauxhall end… with surprisingly rapid, and impressive, results. It would be untrue, however, to say that Butcher really deserves the wicket that he picks up with his fourth delivery, since it is a rank legside delivery that brings about Nixon's downfall. Seeing an apparently straightforward opportunity to add four, or maybe even six, runs to his score, the Leicestershire left-hander attempts to flick the ball over midwicket, but manages only to get a leading edge that sends it spiralling into the air behind the slips. Brown has the simple task of trotting back from first slip to complete the catch, sparking further Surrey celebrations, led by a highly amused Butcher, as a very unhappy Nixon departs for twenty-two, passing a scoreboard reading 68-6 on his way back to the dressing room.

As if the situation isn't already bleak enough for the Foxes, Snape, having offered a very sharp catch to a diving Mark Ramprakash at backward point in Clarke's first over, then follows Nixon back to the pavilion two overs later, ending a really dismal innings of ten in appropriate style by slapping a wide long-hop from Butcher straight to Ian Ward at backward point. 'Golden Arm' Butcher can't believe his luck - and nor can anyone else, if truth be told - as Snape departs with the visitors in dire straits at 70-7 on a blameless pitch.

The Leicestershire skipper, Phillip DeFreitas, is surely a very unhappy man at this point in time, though he does his best not to show it as he cuts and drives Clarke to the rope at cover and then picks him up over backward square-leg for six in the final over of what has been a very depressing morning for his team.

Although DeFreitas and Masters have added twenty-two to the score in the last five overs of the morning, it seems possible that we have already witnessed the decisive session of this contest.

Lunch:- Leicestershire 92-7 (DeFreitas 15, Masters 8*) from 31 overs*

As a result of their morning horror show, where they gifted five wickets to Surrey with desperately poor strokes, Leicestershire already have their backs to the wall in this match and their position almost deteriorates further in the second over of the afternoon when Ramprakash nearly manages to cling on to another difficult chance at backward point. DeFreitas' sliced drive off Bicknell, with his score still on fifteen, is struck just powerfully enough to defeat the fielder's leaping effort, however, and brings the first run of the afternoon session.

The eighth-wicket pair then show how good the pitch is and put their top-order colleagues to shame by coming through short post-lunch spells from Bicknell and Azhar unscathed, taking their partnership beyond fifty in the process.

Butcher, replacing Azhar at the pavilion end, certainly finds the going tougher after his magical morning spell of four overs, conceding a couple of well-struck off-side boundaries to DeFreitas before giving way to Saqlain Mushtaq, while Masters shows unexpected ability with the bat in keeping his captain company. The Surrey off-spinner struggles initially, twice being cut to the rope at cover by DeFreitas during his opening over, but once his compatriot rejoins him in the attack to bowl the forty-third over, Leicestershire's fightback comes to a fairly swift end.

With the total having just passed 150, Azhar makes the all-important first breakthrough at the end of a tremendous over which has seen DeFreitas complete a valuable 48-ball half-century with a thick edge to the third-man boundary. After a fighting knock of thirty-three, Masters is the man dismissed, however, as he snicks an outswinger to third slip, where Clarke takes a fine catch away to his left-hand side, thereby giving Azhar his fifth wicket of the innings.

Since he now has Charlie Dagnall for company and Devon Malcolm padding up, DeFreitas opts to move up a gear, though he only manages a couple of fours before a well flighted delivery from Saqlain tempts him into assaying a mighty slog-sweep that results in the batsman missing and the bowler hitting.

As the Foxes' captain examines the damage to his rearranged stumps and departs the scene at the end of a brave innings of sixty-five, he probably sees little prospect of his last pair being able to muster the thirty-three runs that are now required to earn a batting point - and, since both Dagnall and Malcolm have first-class career batting averages below eight, that would appear to be a reasonable assessment.

To everyone's surprise, however, Dagnall produces three fine strokes - two cover drives and a pull - in one Azhar over to advance the total by twelve runs and, assisted by a wayward legside delivery that scoots away for five wides, takes the visitors within sight of two-hundred. When Malcolm then picks up a single after a diving Clarke fails to hang on to a very difficult catch at third slip, Dagnall takes his chance, glancing and cutting boundaries to record the highest Championship score of his career and earn the vistors an unlikely, and scarcely deserved, batting point. It turns out that he has achieved these goals just in the nick of time, too, since Malcolm holes out to Butcher at backward point from a miscued drive at Saqlain in the very next over.

Having returned figures of 5-78, a weary but happy Azhar leads his team from the field to warm applause from home supporters who are well aware that their team holds all the aces after dismissing the opposition for two-hundred on what appears to be an increasingly fine pitch.

Ten minutes later, the Surrey openers are off in pursuit of the Leicestershire total and they make a flying start, blasting Dagnall out of the attack after two overs costing seventeen runs, during which Butcher helps himself to cut, straight-driven and cover-driven boundaries. To add to DeFreitas' problems, Masters, the new bowler at the pavilion end, then promptly concedes three off-side boundaries to Ward, taking the score to 36-0 after just six overs.

Luckily for Leicestershire, their former Kent seamer comes back well after his woeful opening over, while DeFreitas, steady as ever, provides his side with a much needed breakthrough when Ward plays on in the ninth over with nineteen to his name and the total advanced to thirty-nine. Thereafter, Butcher and Ramprakash accumulate runs at a steady rate up until tea, with the visiting skipper perhaps surprisingly opting to stick with Masters instead of unleashing Malcolm, who, even at the age of forty, remains the main strike bowler in his line-up.

Tea:- Surrey 66-1 (Butcher 29, Ramprakash 14*) from 18 overs*

DeFreitas pairs Dagnall with Malcolm immediately after tea, and it proves to be an interesting combination as a much improved Dagnall locates a good line and length, keeping things quiet at the pavilion end with four successive maidens, while all the action takes place at the Vauxhall end, where Malcolm proves to be as thrillingly inconsistent as ever.

After starting with a couple of relatively uneventful overs, the former England paceman concedes ten runs to Butcher, including two boundaries forced away on the off side, in his third over before bouncing back to dismiss the left-handed opener - well caught by Darren Stevens at first slip from a defensive push - with the third ball of his next over. This wicket gives the visitors something of a fillip as, with Surrey now 80-2 and Butcher gone for thirty-nine, they have just an outside chance of making amends for their feeble batting effort.

The appearance of Alec Stewart at number four to face his former England team-mate, Malcolm, adds further interest to the action, since it pits the two oldest current players on the county circuit against one another, and it's the Surrey man - by around six weeks the junior combatant - who takes the honours as he maintains his Trent Bridge form by taking three fours from the former Derbyshire fast bowler's fifth over. He then adds another boundary - a savage cut over extra over - to his side of the balance sheet two overs later with the total just past a hundred, thereby forcing Malcolm's withdrawal and the introduction of Darren Maddy.

Dagnall has meanwhile been plugging away without any luck at the other end, inducing inside and outside edges from Ramprakash, as well as a leading edge from Stewart that sees the ball dropping into space behind the bowler. The former Warwickshire man remains wicketless, though, at the end of a fine spell of 9-4-20-0, with eight of those runs having come from the aforementioned edges.

Maddy, on the other hand, proves neither very economical nor impressive, and by the thirty-eighth over, DeFreitas is ready for a double bowling change, bringing himself back into the attack and, rather surprisingly, deciding to call upon Virender Sehwag to deliver some off-breaks ahead of Jeremy Snape, regarded by most people as his principal off-spinner. Ramprakash certainly shows no respect whatsoever for Sehwag's bowling, driving him straight for four and then slog-sweeping him for six later in an opening over costing twelve runs. Then, when the part-time off-spinner is allowed a second over, Ramprakash takes full advantage again, forcing and cutting off-side boundaries to first push Surrey's total beyond 150 and then arrive at a typically well-constructed half-century from his ninety-fourth ball.

With Stewart continuing to look in fine form as he picks off a boundary in each of the three overs that DeFreitas allows himself in his second spell of the innings, and Sehwag bafflingly retained in the attack for another two overs, the home side begins to assume complete control again, and their former skipper completes a sparkling fifty from 57 balls with just six overs left for play. It is Stewart's third half-century in three Championship innings this season and he is still there at the close, with the third-wicket pair having added 102 after coming safely through three-over bursts from Masters and Darren Stevens.

Close:- Surrey 182-2 (Ramprakash 59, Stewart 58*) from 50 overs*

Second Day - Thursday 15th May
Leicestershire 200 and 14-2; Surrey 560-8dec

Phil DeFreitas and Devon Malcolm launch Leicestershire's attempt to get back into the game at the start of day two, though the Foxes' skipper soon finds Alec Stewart to be in fine fettle again as the incumbent England wicketkeeper strokes him to the boundary on three occasions during his second over. Consequently, the Surrey two-hundred arrives in the fifty-fifth over, though DeFreitas' expensive over turns out to be completely out of context with the rest of a slow opening hour that brings just thirty-four runs from fourteen overs. This can partly be explained by the loss of the free-flowing Stewart for seventy-one in the day's ninth over, DeFreitas gaining a measure of revenge for the batsman's earlier assault on him by having his former England colleague picked up in the gully by Jeremy Snape from a thick-edged drive.

Leicestershire's period of control, during which Malcolm's radar is in good order and Ali Brown proves understandably keen to establish himself after a run of low scores, doesn't last for long, however, as Ramprakash suddenly lashes into Malcolm, who has probably been given one over too many. Sweetly struck boundaries through point and mid-on, followed by a superb straight drive from a low full-toss, break the spell and force the former England fast bowler out of the attack after an impressive eight-over spell during which he has shown that he is still capable of some quick deliveries.

With his side now coming under great pressure again, DeFreitas reacts by resorting to disappointingly negative tactics, bowling virtual wides to a 7-2 off-side field, and encouraging Charlie Dagnall, Malcolm's replacement at the pavilion end, to operate in the same manner. This lack of positive ambition probably costs the visitors a wicket, however, as Brown, his score on just seven after nine overs at the crease, immediately edges the new bowler at catchable height through the untenanted second/third slip area.

The feeling that Brown might make DeFreitas pay for his overly defensive approach is then confirmed when he and Ramprakash take advantage of the skipper's need to rest after delivering eleven successive overs from the Vauxhall end. The new bowler, David Masters, proves incapable of bowling to the seven-two field during a sixteen-run opening over that sees Brown crashing the ball to the rope at cover, Ramprakash racing into the nineties with two pulls wide of mid-on, and the score suddenly surging past 250. When Brown then cuts and drives Dagnall for two fours, the first of which completes a fifty partnership, Leicestershire are really on the back foot again.

Ramprakash is on ninety-seven at this point and duly completes the sixty-second first-class century of his career in the next over from Masters when he toe-ends a cut at his 208th ball to the third-man boundary. The master craftsman's fine, measured knock, which has underpinned the Surrey innings and contained 16 fours and a six, receives warm applause from an appreciative home crowd, who are now hoping that he will go on to make this a big hundred and provide their team with an unassailable first-innings lead.

Ramprakash's hopes of doing that are immediately raised by DeFreitas' decision to keep the innocuous-looking Masters going from the Vauxhall end, while introducing Brad Hodge, another purveyor of occasional off-breaks, at the pavilion end. Brown certainly needs no second invitation to tuck into Hodge's offerings and, while his partner ticks along with a series of singles, he proceeds to power on to, and beyond, a 68-ball fifty with a sequence of 4-2-4-3 from consecutive deliveries sent down by the suffering Masters. This surge from Brown also shepherds Surrey past the three-hundred mark and the fourth-wicket pair through to a century partnership that is rapidly burying the struggling Foxes.

A couple more Brown boundaries, off Darren Stevens' medium-pace when the Leicestershire batsman appears for a short bowl in place of Hodge before lunch, merely put the icing on the cake for a dominant home side.

Lunch:- Surrey 323-3 (Ramprakash 115, Brown 67*) from 84 overs*

With the new ball just six overs away, DeFreitas recalls Hodge to the attack and, rather belatedly, gives Jeremy Snape his first bowl of the innings.

It is interesting to see these two bowl in tandem, and those who have been unable to understand the visiting skipper's decision to utilise his two occasional off-spinners ahead of Snape soon have evidence to justify their belief that DeFreitas has been getting it wrong. While the Australian is being despatched for three fours in his opening two overs, Snape concedes just two singles before ending Brown's innings at seventy-three, with the total at 345, when Darren Maddy pouches a comfortable catch at square leg, albeit from a short delivery by the former England one-day international.

Having looked capable of making a ton, the batsman departs disappointed with himself for whipping a pretty innocuous ball straight into the fielder's hands, and it isn't long before Snape is maybe having regrets about removing Brown, too, since the new batsman, Adam Hollioake, instantly takes a liking to his bowling. The Surrey skipper has only been at the wicket for a matter of balls before he takes 4-6-4 off Snape with a cover drive, a mighty blow over long-on and a late cut, and when the pair next go head-to-head two overs later Hollioake again drives the off-spinner high into the pavilion.

Having delayed the taking of the new ball by two overs, probably as a result of Snape's success in breaking the fourth-wicket partnership, DeFreitas has now seen enough and returns to the fray, accompanied by Malcolm and the new 'cherry'.

Any hopes that this might put the brakes on Hollioake are immediately dispelled, however, when the home captain produces a most amazing stroke in his Leicestershire counterpart's first over - striking cleanly through the line of a good length delivery, the batsman sends the ball soaring straight back over the head of an astonished DeFreitas for six.

A couple of miscued attempts to repeat the stroke then follow and, as the field spreads ever wider for both batsmen, singles become the norm for a few overs, apart from one pulled four by Ramprakash that brings up the four-hundred. The Surrey number three then records a personal milestone in the next over by securing his 150th run from his 285th ball, though neither he nor his captain get much further as the visitors enjoy their best spell of the match by capturing two wickets in two balls!

Dagnall, having made a surprise return to the attack after just one over from Malcolm with the new ball, makes the initial breakthrough with the last ball of his eighteenth over by having Ramprakash taken at first slip following an edged drive, then DeFreitas has Hollioake caught at the wicket from a top-edged cut with the first ball of the following over.

Understandably, both batsmen receive a warm welcome from the crowd on their return to the dressing rooms after playing hugely contrasting innings - Ramprakash's 152, a 289-ball study in concentration, has laid the foundations for a very big total, while Hollioake's brutal forty-one from just 24 balls, including 3 fours and 3 sixes, has provided a turbo-charged burst of acceleration.

It is also fair to say that both bowlers have deserved these successes that have pegged Surrey back just a little at 408-6, and there is better still to come for the Foxes captain when Rikki Clarke goes for nought four overs later, undone by a fine outswinger that takes the edge and brings a very good diving catch out of Nixon. With Azhar Mahmood having shown signs of following in his skipper's footsteps by blasting Dagnall for three fours in the over prior to Clarke's dismissal, the visitors are well aware, however, that these three wickets will count for little if they can't polish off their hosts' lower order quickly.

As it happens, they spurn a chance to capture an eighth wicket soon afterwards when Masters, diving away to his right at mid-off, fails to hang on to a tough chance offered by Salisbury off DeFreitas when on seven, and the leg-spinner then piles misery upon misery for the poor bowler by driving him for two boundaries to take the home side beyond 450 just a couple of overs later.

Deep-set fields and some accurate overs by the recalled Maddy and Snape subsequently manage to reduce the flow of runs in the lead-up to tea, as well as bringing the wicket of Azhar, who edges the off-spinner's arm ball to slip after making twenty-seven. Salisbury does, however, locate the rope a couple of times thereafter, once off each bowler, in advancing his score to thirty-eight at the interval.

Tea:- Surrey 477-8 (Salisbury 38, Saqlain 4*) from 122 overs*

With Surrey already 277 runs to the good, it seems likely that the batsmen will now press on, allowing Adam Hollioake to give his bowlers an hour or more at the opposition tonight.

While Salisbury seems to be working to this plan, striking Snape into the pavilion for two towering sixes in the space of fours overs to move through to a well-played fifty from his 90th ball, Saqlain Mushtaq finds the other bowler, Dagnall, almost impossible to score off. Consequently, progress is slower than expected, though Salisbury does manage to pick off a couple of isolated boundaries as the total passes five-hundred, before raising the tempo again with edged and cover-driven fours in what turns out to be the last over of Dagnall's restrictive post-tea spell of eight overs for sixteen runs. Perhaps inspired by his spin twin's two-boundary burst, Saqlain then picks up the first two fours of his innings, after no fewer than twenty-two overs at the crease, sweeping and driving Snape to the fence in the same over.

Although the reigning champions now have more than enough runs on the board to be able to declare, Salisbury is closing in on his second first-class century and, with two days left in the match, it doesn't seem entirely unreasonable for Hollioake to delay the closure.

Runs are still not flowing freely, however, since Snape is operating with a very defensive field and utilising the skills he has picked up in limited-overs cricket, while DeFreitas, back in place of Dagnall, is employing his wide-of-off-stump line. This does at least allow Salisbury an easy single-gathering passage into, and through, the nineties, though he chooses to reach his century in the grand manner, moving from 95 to 101 by dancing down the pitch to Snape and lofting him straight down the ground for the third six of his innings. The Surrey leg-spinner's 160-ball knock has also contained nine fours and is a career-best, just trumping the 100 not out that he recorded on the occasion of his maiden first-class century against Somerset at The Oval in 1999.

To no-one's surprise, the declaration follows immediately, allowing Salisbury to receive a fine reception from the crowd as he passes a scoreboard reading 560-8. Leicestershire are therefore facing a first-innings deficit of 360 and have to bat for seven overs tonight.

Given the long and tiring time that the visitors have spent in field, it seems fairly likely that they might not get through to the close of play unscathed, though it is probably more than Martin Bicknell can have hoped for when Trevor Ward edges his fourth ball of the innings low to second slip where Mark Butcher picks up a good catch. As poor Ward trudges disconsolately back to the pavilion, the County Champions celebrate the first of the ten wickets they need to complete a well-merited victory.

A score of 0-1 then becomes 6-2 when the fourth ball of Bicknell's next over does the trick again, nightwatchman David Masters snicking a fine, lifting delivery straight to Azhar at third slip, causing even greater jubilation in the Surrey camp.

Although Sehwag and Maddy manage to see out the last four overs, they know that their side now faces a major uphill battle if they are to take the match into a fourth day, let alone save the match. Their only hope would appear to be a forecast of unsettled weather over the next two days.

Close:- Leicestershire 14-2 (Sehwag 14, Maddy 0*) from 7 overs*

Third Day - Friday 16th May
Leicestershire 200 and 32-2; Surrey 560-8dec

Persistent rain throughout the morning and early afternoon frustrates the home team, their supporters and the ground staff as the weather forecasters' gloomy predictions prove accurate.

Eventually, however, conditions improve sufficiently for the umpires to declare that play will start at 4.45pm, with twenty-eight overs to be bowled… then it begins to drizzle again. Two further overs are therefore lost before the players finally appear at 4.53pm.

Having lost so much time, and with dark clouds still hovering around the ground, it is now important that Surrey make good use of the overs available to them, hopefully picking up at least a couple of wickets to make their victory task easier on the final day.

Azhar and Bicknell, Adam Hollioake's predictable choice of bowlers, find Sehwag in superb form, though, as fifteen runs, including on-driven, square-cut and straight-driven boundaries, come from the first two overs.

Maddy looks far less sure of himself, however, and offers a half-chance off Bicknell to Salisbury at the squarer of two gullies in the fourth over of play. The fielder manages to gets his upstretched right hand to a sliced drive but, unfortunately for everyone in the Surrey camp, the ball doesn't stick, allowing Maddy to continue his battle to get off the mark.

He still hasn't managed to do this when the rain returns after one more over and washes out play for the rest of the day. Surrey now face quite a tough task tomorrow - weather permitting - if they are to secure the win that their efforts in the match so far deserve.

Close:- Leicestershire 32-2 (Sehwag 32, Maddy 0*) from 12 overs*

Fourth Day - Saturday 17th May

Leicestershire 200 and 185-8; Surrey 560-8dec
Match Drawn
Surrey 12pts, Leicestershire 7

There is bad news for Surrey on the final morning the game, as the umpires decide that the outfield is too wet for play to start on time. The third day's rainfall has, in fact, left conditions damp enough for them to opt to take an early lunch at 12.30pm, with the intention of the game resuming, with the home side needing eight wickets for victory, at 1.10pm, provided there is no further rain.

Fortunately for everyone of a Surrey persuasion, the rain does hold off, allowing Bicknell and Azhar to continue their contest against Sehwag and Maddy with seventy-two overs remaining for play, twenty-four having been lost because of the delayed start.

Although everyone in the small crowd is fully aware that Sehwag will not be playing a blocking role as his team seeks to secure the draw, they are still amazed by his early strokeplay as he drives his first ball, bowled by Azhar, over mid-off's head for four and then picks up a second boundary, courtesy of a back-foot force through extra cover, before the over is out. Bicknell then receives the same kind of treatment as his bowling partner, with the talented Indian strokeplayer whipping two deliveries from around off stump through square leg and midwicket, for four and three respectively, before reaching his fifty, from just 52 balls, in the next over from Azhar with an upper-cut to third man. Since runs are utterly irrelevant, given the state of the game, it is a breathtaking approach that we are seeing from Sehwag, and, even though the Indian is giving the opposition a chance by playing so aggressively, you get the feeling that Bicknell and Azhar are certainly happier when bowling to Maddy. This is in spite of the fact that the Foxes' number three looks much more confident and composed today, largely as a result of finding the boundary with good shots of his own during the opening overs.

With the pitch still in fine condition and Sehwag continuing to play the seamers with some comfort - two extra-cover drives and another whip through midwicket off Bicknell particularly catch the eye - Adam Hollioake turns to spin, in the form of Saqlain Mushatq, for the thirteenth over of the afternoon.

Although this change has no immediate effect on Sehwag as he smashes the off-spinner away wide of mid-on for the fourteenth and fifteenth fours of his innings, the fact that the first of these two shots can best be described as a slog offers encouragement to a bowler who has immediately given the impression of being very much up for this afternoon's challenge.

It is not totally surprising, therefore, when Saqlain strikes with the third ball of his second over, though the manner of Sehwag's dismissal does raise a few eyebrows around the ground, umpire Mallender giving a rapid affirmative verdict to the Pakistani's lbw appeal when the batsman is beaten after advancing down the track to drive. From the boundary, Sehwag certainly appears unlucky to have fallen to what can be nothing more than an 'instinct' decision from the umpire after a super knock of eighty-one at nearly a run a ball.

Surrey's hopes that this initial breakthrough will lead to the capture of further wickets prove unfounded, however, as the new batsman, Brad Hodge, settles in confidently enough with a couple of back-foot fours off Saqlain, while Maddy reels off a succession of hooked and driven boundaries to see off Azhar.

Ian Salisbury is the predictable replacement for Azhar at the pavilion end, thereby presenting the Leicestershire batsmen with a twin spin threat for the first time in the match, and, though Maddy and Hodge initially cope pretty well with this new challenge, it still seems likely that the spinners hold the key to the game as the overs tick away faster than Surrey would like.

Hollioake and his spinners remain patient, however, and finally get their reward when Maddy gives Saqlain the charge and is beaten by a combination of flight and spin to be bowled for forty in the twenty-ninth over of the day. And this time the breakthrough does lead to further wickets.

Maddy's departure at 168-4, with a minimum of forty-three overs left for play - if the gathering grey clouds around the ground permit that many - brings Darren Stevens to the crease… but only for a short while, since he falls lbw, for a third-ball duck, to Salisbury's googly in the very next over to reduce the visitors to 171-5.

Paul Nixon then sweeps the next delivery from Salisbury for a single to retain the strike for the following over from Saqlain, only to depart to his first ball from the off-spinner when his firm push to silly point is very well parried upwards and caught by Hollioake. It's 172-6 and the Surrey spinners have captured three wickets in eight balls.

Jeremy Snape then almost plays on to Salisbury during his second over at the wicket, bringing gasps and groans from everyone around the bat, before settling down a little in support of Hodge, who is playing a fine knock for his side at the other end.

It comes as quite a shock, therefore, when it is the Victorian who becomes Saqlain's fourth victim as tea approaches with the total advanced only as far as 183. Having initially decided to get down the track and attack a nicely flighted delivery, Hodge fatally changes his mind and ends up playing a checked defensive push which results in the ball popping into the hands of Ian Ward at short leg, setting off further Surrey celebrations and taking the hosts within three wickets of what would be a well deserved victory.

When Phil DeFreitas then edges his first ball just short of slip the excitement level rises further, though by this stage the weather is looking just as likely to thwart the County Champions as the batsmen. As the eighth-wicket pair battle through the last four overs of the session surrounded by close fielders it is apparent that tea is coming at a very bad time for the home side since further rainfall is looking fairly imminent.

Tea:- Leicestershire 185-7 (Snape 5, DeFreitas 0*) from 53 overs*

As play resumes it is already clear that Surrey don't have very long in which to secure victory, since the sky is slate grey and any rain that falls now is likely to be heavy enough and prolonged enough to finish the game off for good.

Light rain is already in the air, in fact, as Salisbury completes an opening maiden to Snape, though home hopes are quickly raised again when DeFreitas pushes firmly at the second ball of the next over from Saqlain and sees Hollioake pull off a very fine reflex catch low to his right-hand side at silly point. This excellent one-handed catch not only secures the eighth Leicestershire wicket, but also completes the off-spinner's twenty-eighth five-wicket haul for his adopted county.

Unfortunately from the Surrey point of view, it also turns out to be the final ball of the match as the heavens open before DeFreitas has even reached the boundary edge, sending the umpires, players and spectators scattering for cover.

As the rain becomes increasingly heavy, puddles start to form on the outfield, giving the umpires a very easy decision to make when the downpour eventually abates, allowing an inspection just after 5pm.

Leicestershire therefore escape with a very fortunate draw, though these things do even up over a period of time as Surrey appreciate, having needed some intervention from the weather to scratch out a stalemate with Lancashire just a few weeks ago. Strangely, though, this result extends the run of recent fixtures between Surrey and Leicestershire that has seen one or other side being saved by rain, with several such instances in the last five seasons alone.

Leicestershire 200 and 185-8; Surrey 560-8dec
Match Drawn. Surrey 12pts, Leicestershire 7

TALKING POINTS - IAN SALISBURY

When you went out to bat at 423-7, I suppose all you were really aiming to do was score some quick runs ahead of the declaration, and a second first-class century must have been the last thing on your mind, really?

IS - To be honest, I'm a bit fatalistic when it comes to scoring hundreds or whatever... I just go for it, and if it happens it happens. If I remember rightly I brought up both my fifty and hundred with sixes… if I was to get the hundred then it was meant to be. So it most certainly wasn't on my mind. So, yes, I was thinking "quick runs, declaration, see what happens", simple as that.

There were some who said that we'd batted on too long, but I assume your response would be that we were desperately unlucky to only get 47 overs of play from the last two days of the match?
IS - I think it would be very harsh to say we batted on too long when we had them eight down in their second innings and lost about 170 overs in the match!

Was our inability, for one reason of another, to beat Leicestershire home or away, a significant factor in our failure to retain the Championship?
IS - I think it was more significant that we didn't compete against Lancashire - we played them twice and couldn't beat them, and we were second-best for a lot of the game against Sussex at Hove… so the two teams that played better than us finished ahead of us.

SURREY v LEICESTERSHIRE at The Oval 14th to 17th May

Leicestershire won the toss and elected to bat — Umpires:- Barry Dudleston and Neil Mallender

LEICESTERSHIRE - First Innings

Fall Of Wkt	Batsman	How	Out	Score	Balls	4s	6s
2-19	**T.R. Ward**	**c Stewart**	**b Azhar**	**14**	29	1	0
1-14	**V. Sehwag**	**c Brown**	**b Azhar**	**2**	12	0	0
3-25	**D.L. Maddy**	**c Stewart**	**b Bicknell**	**1**	16	0	0
5-47	**B.J. Hodge**	**lbw**	**b Azhar**	**14**	26	2	0
4-26	**D.I. Stevens**	**c Brown**	**b Azhar**	**0**	3	0	0
6-68	**P.A. Nixon +**	**c Brown**	**b Butcher**	**22**	37	3	0
7-70	**J.N. Snape**	**c Ward**	**b Butcher**	**10**	32	2	0
9-167	**P.A.J. DeFreitas ***		**b Saqlain**	**65**	58	11	1
8-155	**D.D. Masters**	**c Clarke**	**b Azhar**	**33**	66	6	0
	C.E. Dagnall	**Not**	**Out**	**23**	24	5	0
10-200	**D.E. Malcolm**	**c Butcher**	**b Saqlain**	**3**	8	0	0
	Extras	**(2b, 2lb, 5w, 4nb)**		**13**			
	TOTAL	**(51.3 overs)**		**200**			

Bowler	O	M	R	W	NB	Wd
Bicknell	**17**	**2**	**64**	**1**	1	-
Azhar Mahmood	**19**	**5**	**78**	**5**	1	1
Butcher	**6**	**0**	**20**	**2**	-	-
Clarke	**4**	**2**	**14**	**0**	-	-
Saqlain Mushtaq	**5.3**	**0**	**20**	**2**	-	-

SURREY - First Innings

Fall Of Wkt	Batsman	How	Out	Score	Balls	4s	6s
2-80	**M.A. Butcher**	**c Stevens**	**b Malcolm**	**39**	80	6	0
1-39	**I.J. Ward**		**b DeFreitas**	**19**	20	3	0
5-408	**M.R. Ramprakash**	**c Stevens**	**b Dagnall**	**152**	289	19	1
3-204	**A.J. Stewart +**	**c Snape**	**b DeFreitas**	**71**	88	14	0
4-345	**A.D. Brown**	**c Maddy**	**b Snape**	**73**	91	12	0
6-408	**A.J. Hollioake ***	**c Nixon**	**b DeFreitas**	**41**	24	3	3
7-423	**R. Clarke**	**c Nixon**	**b DeFreitas**	**0**	10	0	0
8-461	**Azhar Mahmood**	**c Maddy**	**b Snape**	**27**	45	4	0
	I.D.K. Salisbury	**Not**	**Out**	**101**	160	9	3
	Saqlain Mushtaq	**Not**	**Out**	**20**	68	2	0
	M.P. Bicknell	**did not bat**					
	Extras	**(6b, 5lb, 6nb)**		**17**			
	TOTAL	**(145.2 overs)**	**(for 8 dec)**	**560**			

Bowler	O	M	R	W	NB	Wd
DeFreitas	**36**	**9**	**101**	**4**	3	-
Dagnall	**28**	**8**	**95**	**1**	-	-
Masters	**20**	**4**	**93**	**0**	-	-
Malcolm	**16**	**4**	**58**	**1**	-	-
Maddy	**9**	**2**	**23**	**0**	-	-
Sehwag	**4**	**1**	**26**	**0**	-	-
Stevens	**5**	**3**	**11**	**0**	-	-
Hodge	**7**	**0**	**50**	**0**	-	-
Snape	**20.2**	**2**	**92**	**2**	-	-

LEICESTERSHIRE - Second Innings (Trailing by 360 runs on first innings)							
Fall Of Wkt	Batsman	How	Out	Score	Balls	4s	6s
1-0	T.R. Ward	c Butcher	b Bicknell	0	4	0	0
3-107	V. Sehwag	lbw	b Saqlain	81	84	15	0
2-6	D.D. Masters	c Azhar	b Bicknell	0	6	0	0
4-168	D.L. Maddy		b Saqlain	40	106	7	0
7-183	B.J. Hodge	c Ward	b Saqlain	47	69	5	0
5-171	D.I. Stevens	lbw	b Salisbury	0	3	0	0
6-172	P.A. Nixon +	c Hollioake	b Saqlain	1	2	0	0
	J.N. Snape	Not	Out	5	43	0	0
8-185	P.A.J. DeFreitas *	c Hollioake	b Saqlain	0	14	0	0
	Extras	(1lb, 10nb)		11			
	TOTAL	(54.2 overs)	(for 8 wkts)	185			

Bowler	O	M	R	W	NB	Wd
Bicknell	12	5	40	2	1	-
Azhar Mahmood	14	3	65	0	1	-
Saqlain Mushtaq	15.2	3	46	5	1	-
Salisbury	13	3	33	1	2	-

Other Frizzell Championship Division One Results

With Warwickshire not involved in this round of matches and rain also affecting the games at Old Trafford and, to a lesser extent, Canterbury, Surrey's twelve points were enough to take them to the top of the table. It meant little, however, since the gap between the top and bottom sides was a mere twenty-eight points.

May 14-17

***Canterbury:-* Kent (12pts) drew with Middlesex (8).** Kent 472 (Smith 103, Blewett 60, Carberry 53, Jones 52, Weekes 4-70, Dawes 4-90); Middlesex 221 (Hutton 74, Saggers 4-48) & 249-4 (Koenig 96, Strauss 93).

***Old Trafford:-* Lancashire (11pts) drew with Essex (8).** Essex 215 (Foster 57, Anderson 4-67) & 42-3; Lancashire 375 (Sutcliffe 109, Chilton 106, Irani 4-59).

FRIZZELL CHAMPIONSHIP DIVISION ONE TABLE AT 17TH MAY

Pos	Prv		P	Points	W	D	L	T	Bat	Bwl	Ded
1	2	Surrey	4	51.00	1	3	0	0	15	10	0.00
2	1	Warwickshire	4	49.75	1	1	1	1	16	9	0.25
3	3	Lancashire	4	46.00	0	4	0	0	18	12	0.00
4	4	Middlesex	4	41.00	1	3	0	0	5	10	0.00
5	7	Essex	4	36.00	0	3	0	1	6	11	0.00
6	5	Nottinghamshire	3	32.00	1	1	1	0	6	9	1.00
7	6	Sussex	3	30.00	1	0	2	0	7	9	0.00
8	8	Leicestershire	3	24.00	0	3	0	0	4	8	0.00
9	9	Kent	3	23.00	0	2	1	0	6	9	0.00

NATIONAL CRICKET LEAGUE DIVISION ONE - MATCH FOUR

Surrey Lions versus Kent Spitfires at The Oval

Sunday 18th May

Setting The Scene - The Kent Spitfires, NCL champions in 2001, come to The Oval with just one win from their first three games, while the Lions are defending their one-hundred percent record. The home team's line-up shows just one change from their last NCL outing almost two weeks ago, with the incapacitated James Ormond being replaced by Tim Murtagh, while Kent, who have thus far opted to register just one overseas player, field Greg Blewett as a stand-in for Andrew Symonds, who is away with Australia. Their principal absentee, though, is skipper David Fulton, who is likely to be absent for a while yet after sustaining a serious eye injury during a pre-season net when a ball from a bowling machine penetrated the gap between the visor and the grille on his helmet. With conditions looking ideal for batting, the Spitfires' captain, Mark Ealham, decides that his side will be best suited to fielding first and chasing whatever total the Lions manage to amass.

Surrey Lions' Innings

Handed first use of an excellent pitch, the Surrey openers take full advantage, with Ali Brown striking three fours in Martin Saggers' second over and then pulling Ben Trott high over the fence at midwicket to lift the score to 34-0 after the first four overs.

Ian Ward then takes ten runs from Saggers' next over, including two fine boundaries of his own, before Brown is to the fore again, bringing up Surrey's fifty from just 33 balls with another pulled four off Trott and following up by hammering another short ball for six as the former Somerset seamer shows himself to be a slow learner.

With the scoreboard reading 58-0 after just six overs and the Lions absolutely rampant, Ealham is forced into action and elects to bring himself and Peter Trego into the attack. These two fare no better than Saggers and Trott, initially, as Ward peppers the boundary boards between extra cover and midwicket with four further fours in eleven balls, but Trego's decision to come round the wicket for the final ball of his opening over instantly brings a change of fortune when the Surrey opener's attempted drive down the ground is defeated by some away movement and his off stump goes flying.

Although Ward's rapid thirty-one has given his side a great start of 78-1 from eight overs, the loss of his wicket changes the flow of the game for a while as Brown, having chopped a wide long-hop from Trego onto his stumps after making a breathtaking forty-four from a mere 24 balls, follows him back to the pavilion seven balls later and the bowlers enjoy a spell in the ascendancy. Just ten runs come from the next five overs from the Kent medium-pacers, in fact, as Mark Ramprakash and Graham Thorpe ensure their side suffers no further losses, before Thorpe breaks the spell by glancing Ealham to the rope at fine leg in the thirteenth over. A couple of classy extra-cover drives, one from each batsman, then lead to the arrival of the hundred from exactly fifteen overs, before Surrey surge on again when the Spitfires' captain surprisingly brings his opening bowlers back into the attack. Four overs yield twenty-three runs, eighteen of these coming from the last two, before Ealham sees the error of his ways and tries to take the pace off the ball by throwing James Tredwell's off-spin and Greg Blewett's gentle medium pace into the mix.

While far from threatening, these two do a good job for their skipper in restricting the batsmen to just eighteen singles and one four - a sweep by Ramprakash off Tredwell - from the next six overs, leaving the Lions on 145-2 at the twenty-five over mark. Although the last seventeen overs have brought just sixty-seven runs, Surrey certainly have a fine launching pad from which to blast off towards an imposing total.

And, sure enough, the home side's score does rocket skywards in the very next over, during which Blewett concedes eighteen runs - including Thorpe's subtle deflection and Ramprakash's cover drive and amazing pick-up/sweep hybrid over the rope at square leg, all of which bring boundaries - but this brief burst of acceleration is promptly evened up by the loss of two wickets in the next over from Tredwell. Thorpe goes first, disappointingly reverse-sweeping straight into the hands of the waiting Trott at short third man after reaching thirty-six from 61 balls, then Rikki Clarke is defeated by turn down the legside and stumped after charging down the track to his second ball.

Despite these setbacks, the Surrey skipper, Adam Hollioake, is doubtless still happy enough to enter the fray at 165-4 after twenty-seven overs, though his first two run-scoring strokes owe a fair bit to fortune, as a miscued drive and a top-edged cut both narrowly evade scrambling fielders. There is no such uncertainty about the strokeplay of the well-established Ramprakash, however, as he celebrates reaching a 53-ball half-century by pulling the returning Trego over square leg for six. Hollioake then follows up by driving the same bowler over long-on for a 'maximum' of his own two overs later, though he is run out shortly afterwards when he tries to steal a quick single and is sent back by his partner.

The home captain's demise with the total one short of two-hundred brings the equally dangerous Azhar Mahmood to the middle with thirteen overs remaining and the Lions probably looking to post a total in the region of 280-290, given that a minimum of six runs an over really ought to be possible for the rest of the innings.

The Pakistani all-rounder initially plays a watching brief, however, failing to score from his first six balls, while Ramprakash manages just one boundary in the next three overs from Trego and the impressively tidy Tredwell. This fairly barren spell puts question marks against the possibility of Surrey getting as far as 290, though the home side soon get back on track when Trott returns to the attack in place of Trego and finds Azhar just as adept at pulling a short ball for six as Brown had been earlier in the afternoon. Having got off the mark with this blow over midwicket, Azhar then drives the next ball to the long-off boundary to suggest that his blue touchpaper has now been lit, though he is a touch fortunate in the next over when an inside edge from the final delivery of Tredwell's admirable spell of 9-0-35-2 narrowly misses his leg stump.

There is nothing lucky, however, about his second pulled six off the apparently brainless Trott at the start of the thirty-eighth over, which ends up costing the hapless bowler fourteen runs, nor the two successive fours that greet Ealham on his return to the attack in place of Tredwell. With the second of these boundaries having taken the score to 253-5 at the end of the thirty-ninth over, a final total in excess of three-hundred now looks far from impossible, though two decent overs from Saggers immediately after he succeeds Trott at the pavilion end leave Surrey needing twenty-six from three overs if they are to reach this goal.

By the end of the next over from Ealham it has become a mere formality, however, as Azhar drills the first ball to the cover boundary and then, having completed a sensational 35-ball fifty with a single from the next ball, lifts the fourth and fifth deliveries clean over the rope at long-off and extra cover for successive sixes. The over ends up yielding twenty runs, leaving a battered Ealham shaking his head, and the Lions just six short of the magic three-hundred mark.

Ramprakash, now on ninety-three, must also have a personal milestone in mind at this stage and needs just three balls of the penultimate over to reach it as he powers consecutive deliveries from Saggers to the rope, moving to ninety-seven with an extra-cover drive, then 101 with a clip backward of square on the legside. His ton has come from just 96 deliveries, yet has included just 8 fours and 2 sixes, these statistics underlining how well he has worked thc ball around the field throughout his innings.

Once the applause has died down following Ramprakash's century celebrations, nine balls remain for Surrey to pile on further runs, though the sixth-wicket partners, whose stand is already worth 103, only manage one more boundary apiece, Ramprakash because he only gets to face three of the last nine deliveries, and Azhar because he drives a low full-toss to Tredwell at extra cover off Trego with four balls of the innings remaining. As he returns to the pavilion, the Pakistani master-blaster receives a rapturous reception for his incredible innings of seventy from just 41 balls, six of which he has hit for four and four of which he has hit for six.

Even though only three balls now remain in the Lions' innings there is still time for one more boundary, Jon Batty heaving a Trego full-toss way over the rope at midwicket before being caught by Rob Key on the cover fence from the last ball of the innings, by which time the score has advanced to an awesome 322-7.

The magnitude of the task that Kent now face if they are to win this match is underlined by two stats:- 1) Surrey's total is the highest ever made by either side in the history of Surrey versus Kent games in the Sunday/National League; and 2) The highest total ever made to win a

Sunday/National League match when batting second is 317-6, by Surrey against Nottinghamshire at The Oval in 1993 - the season when games were 50-overs-a-side affairs.

Kent Spitfires' Innings

Kent's hopes of pulling off a stunning victory are dealt an early blow when Mark Ealham, their stand-in skipper, top-edges a cut at the final ball of the second over and goes *caught Batty, bowled Azhar 4*, with just fourteen runs on the board.

Having made this first breakthrough, the Pakistani all-rounder then has Rob Key dropped by Ramprakash on the midwicket boundary in the sixth over with the batsman on nineteen and the total thirty-one, the brilliantly positioned fielder seemingly seeing the ball late and consequently having to try and take the catch at shin level. Worryingly for Surrey, Ramprakash leaves the field shortly afterwards, having apparently damaged his hand in missing the chance.

Although Azhar should now have two wickets to his name, he turns out to be pretty expensive during his opening spell of five overs, conceding thirty-eight runs, including three fours to both Key and Peter Trego, promoted as a pinch-hitter to number three in an attempt to get the innings away to a rapid start. The Spitfires' attempts to do this have been thwarted at the other end, however, by an outstandingly accurate spell from the experienced Bicknell, whose opening five overs have, by way of contrast, yielded just fifteen runs.

With the Kent fifty having arrived after exactly nine overs they are far from out of the match at this stage, however, though the twelfth-over introduction of Tim Murtagh for Azhar at the pavilion end brings the loss of a second wicket when Trego hits across the line of a first-ball outswinger and is comprehensively bowled for twenty-one.

Although the new batsman, Ed Smith, manages to locate the rope at long-on with a handsome stroke from the last ball of Murtagh's opening over, and Key then drives Bicknell through extra cover for another four to restore a little balance to the match at 71-2 from thirteen overs, another setback is just around the corner for Kent. After a rather frenetic and not entirely convincing innings of thirty-nine, Key departs to the second ball of Murtagh's second over, repeating Trego's error in aiming across the line of a good delivery, though, unlike his team-mate, getting his pads in the way of the ball and falling lbw.

In an attempt to put further pressure on the visiting batsmen, Adam Hollioake now introduces Saqlain Mushtaq in place of the economical Bicknell (7-0-27-0) and the off-spinner makes a typically tight start, yielding just thirteen runs from his first three overs, and, in partnership with the steady Murtagh, delaying the arrival of the Kent hundred until the start of the nineteenth over.

With the required run rate now up to 8.3 an over, the pressure is building on the fourth-wicket pairing of Smith and Greg Blewett, and, though they keep the score moving with regular singles, they only manage to find the boundary once in the next five overs, when the Australian lofts Saqlain down the ground for four.

There is much relief in the Kent camp, therefore, when Blewett shows signs of taking command by picking Murtagh off for two legside boundaries during the young seamer's seventh over, though the Spitfires' surge is stalled temporarily by an excellent sixth over from Saqlain. After conceding an on-driven single to Smith from the first ball, the Pakistani spin king ties Blewett up for the next three deliveries before sending down a brilliant undetected wrong 'un that spins away to hit the top of the batsman's off stump as he aims towards midwicket. With the newly arrived Matt Walker unable to score from the final ball of the over, the scoreboard is left reading 137-4 after twenty-five overs and Surrey are very much in control of the contest.

Clearly appreciating that they can't allow the asking rate to climb any higher than the current level of 9.3, and that Walker doesn't really have time to play himself in, the fifth-wicket pair launch an immediate offensive, taking thirty-one from the next three overs from the hitherto economical Murtagh and Saqlain. The relatively inexperienced Murtagh suffers especially badly, conceding ten runs, including two elegant drives for four by Smith, from his eighth over, then fifteen from his final over when Walker clips him to the midwicket fence and Smith launches him over long-on for six to complete an impressive half-century from just 47 balls.

Hollioake reacts to this sudden spurt by recalling Bicknell to the attack, thereby leaving two overs from Saqlain up his sleeve, and taking over himself from Murtagh.

More by luck than judgement, the Kent pair manage to scrape together sixteen runs from the wily Bicknell's last two overs, thanks to a combination of leg-byes, edges, miscues and misfields, while Hollioake makes a very poor start at the other end, haemorrhaging twenty runs from his opening two overs. Having conceded a pulled six to Walker in his first over, the Lions' captain is driven over wide long-on by Smith for another 'maximum' in his next over, this stroke bringing up the Spitfires' two-hundred in the thirty-second over, and boosting the visitors' hopes that they could yet win this match.

The rapid ebb and flow of one-day cricket is nicely demonstrated by the next two overs, however, as Rikki Clarke, replacing Bicknell (9-0-41-0) at the Vauxhall end, comes up with an accurate five-run opening over, setting back the Kent cause considerably, before Hollioake delivers a truly awful over - costing no fewer than twenty-three runs, including a pull-driven six and a cover-driven four to Smith, and two successive legside wides that give Batty no chance and zip away to the fine-leg boundary - to send the Spitfires soaring again at 232-4 after thirty-four overs.

Predictably enough, Hollioake takes himself out of the firing line after his 'over horribilis', restoring Azhar to the attack in his stead. With Clarke having meanwhile contributed another decent over and the fifth-wicket partnership now exceeding a hundred, the Pakistani makes a good start to his comeback over before leaking boundaries from the last two deliveries, allowing Walker to complete a fine and feisty fifty from his 38th ball and the Spitfires total to reach 250 from exactly thirty-six overs.

A target of seventy-three from nine overs in perfect batting conditions with six wickets in hand is now looking well within Kent's compass and it is clear that the Lions need a wicket, preferably two, to halt the visitors' charge.

As luck would have it, a chance to break the Smith-Walker stand comes their way in the next over when Smith, on seventy-two, top-edges a pull at Clarke high into the legside, only for Saqlain to misjudge the ball's trajectory so badly that he fails to even get a hand on it as it plummets safely to earth. The disappointment of missing out on securing the vital wicket for his side seems to affect Clarke, since the rest of his over brings Kent three wides and a square-cut boundary to Smith, adding further to Hollioake's problems.

The Surrey skipper therefore decides that he must bring Saqlain back in place of his young all-rounder and, though the spinner can't provide the all-important breakthrough, he does at least manage to put some pressure back on the batsmen with two good overs costing just ten runs, thereby completing his allocation of overs with the very creditable figures of 9-0-40-1.

Looking at the state of the game at this point, the visitors appear to be clear favourites, with thirty-one runs needed from four overs, two well-set batsmen at the wicket, and Surrey's most accurate bowlers having completed their spells. Additionally, Azhar, a key bowler at the death, is about to deliver his final over, leaving just the out-of-sorts Hollioake and the inexperienced Clarke to deliver the last three overs.

Azhar's over therefore has to be a good one from the home side's point of view, and, as Walker secures three runs from the first three deliveries and Smith pulls the fourth ball wide of mid-on for four to take his personal score on to ninety-nine, it looks like Kent will get through it safely enough. No-one expects the stunning yorker that Azhar produces as his penultimate ball, however. A deadly reverse-swinging delivery of impressive pace, it fizzes under the batsman's belated jab and rips out the off stump to give both the Surrey team and their fans renewed hope.

As for poor Smith, he returns to the pavilion to a fine reception for a brilliant 86-ball knock that has taken his side to the brink of a fantastic victory. All his team-mates need to do now is keep their heads and they will surely score the required twenty-three runs from the final three overs.

With Hollioake's options now extremely limited, he re-enters the fray with the gruesome figures of 3-0-43-0 against his name, knowing that he needs, somehow, to produce something special.

The home captain is aided, initially, by the fact that the new batsman, Geraint Jones, is on strike after taking a single from the final ball of Azhar's spell, and manages to restrict the inexperienced wicketkeeper-batsman to just one run from the first two balls of the over. Walker then loses strike immediately by taking a single to extra cover, allowing Hollioake to complete the over at a cost of just three further runs, with a sequence of 0-2-1 leaving Jones on strike once again for the start of the forty-fourth over.

The Spitfires now need eighteen runs to win and they remain favourites as Clarke returns to the bowling crease, though their hopes are immediately dented when Jones thick-edges a drive at the first ball down to third man, where the substitute fielder, Ian Salisbury, takes the catch. We really have a great game on our hands now, though it is to Kent's advantage that Walker is back on strike, the batsmen having crossed while the ball was in the air.

The chunky left-hander appears to be feeling the pressure as much as everyone else, however, as he top-edges a pull at Clarke's next delivery, though he finds luck on his side as the ball lands safely in space at deep backward square leg, allowing the batsmen to hustle back and forth for three runs. Three singles - two of them to Michael Carberry, making his first appearance against his old team - and a leg-bye then complete a good over by Clarke, leaving us with the excitement of a last-over finish.

Hollioake is the bowler and Walker the batsman as the over commences with Kent needing eleven runs to win. It starts well for the Lions as Walker mistimes his drive and can only snatch a single to mid-on, then Carberry drives the next ball straight to the cover sweeper and is unable to get back for a second run.

With nine now needed from four balls, the pressure is growing for all concerned, though Hollioake doesn't show it as he spears a yorker in at Walker's feet. Although the batsman keeps the ball out of his stumps with a hurried jab, it merely dribbles out on the legside via the toe end of the bat, allowing the batsmen to pick up nothing more than a scampered single. Eight runs are now required from three deliveries, and the pendulum appears to have swung back in favour of Surrey.

Any doubt that this is the case is then erased when Carberry edges his drive at the next ball through to Batty and, with Walker stranded at the non-striker's end, the inexperienced James Tredwell has it all to do as he arrives at the crease needing to find the boundary at least once from the final two deliveries.

Almost inevitably, Hollioake's nous wins the day as Tredwell fails to make contact with the penultimate ball of the innings, making the single that accrues from the last delivery irrelevant. It's hard not to feel sorry for Walker, who is left high and dry on eighty from just 62 balls, having faced just six deliveries in the last three overs, though credit must go to the league leaders for staying cool under pressure in a tight situation, and especially to their captain, who has come back from his nightmare opening spell to deliver two overs for just nine runs at the death.

The Surrey players' celebrations are doubtless tinged with relief as they leave the field victorious by six runs at the end of an incredible contest that has seen the record for the highest match aggregate of runs in a Sunday/National League game beaten - the previous best was the 631 runs scored in the aforementioned match when Surrey successfully chased down Nottinghamshire's total of 314 at The Oval in 1993.

MARK RAMPRAKASH'S VIEW FROM THE DRESSING ROOM

I guess you'd have to say that this was an excellent pitch for one-day cricket?
MR - Yes, and there was a short boundary, too, which made it difficult to know what would be a good score. We were very happy with our score of 322 and I didn't really expect Kent to get too close to it, I must admit. But if someone gets in, or someone hits a few sixes over the short boundary then things can change dramatically.

Did you find it strange that Kent were never really in contention at all until Smith and Walker went berserk with the required run-rate at almost ten an over?
MR - We've had several very high-scoring games at The Oval where we've got a lot of runs but people have got quite close, and I think that's because people have really improved in one-day cricket. A big target doesn't necessarily faze them any more - they realise that one boundary an over and a few singles can put them up with the rate. That pair chased the total brilliantly - Ed Smith had a great season and Matt Walker is a very difficult batsman to bowl to in one-day cricket.

Was Azhar's yorker that bowled Ed Smith the key moment of the match?
MR - Yes, I remember it vividly because that was an amazing delivery. At that time they were favourites to win but Azhar is always capable of making things happen when you throw him the ball in that kind of situation. I was off the field at that stage because I'd damaged my hand and I remember watching from the pavilion. I think you'd have to say that it was a match-winning delivery.

Matt Walker faced just six balls in the last three overs. Was that also crucial to the outcome of the game?
MR - Yes, it was very important to keep Walker off strike and put the pressure on the new batsmen, and I think Adam manipulated the bowlers and the field brilliantly… though the guys who bowled those three overs still had to do the job.

SURREY LIONS v KENT SPITFIRES at The Oval
Sunday 18th May — **Surrey Lions won by 6 runs**
Kent Spitfires won the toss and elected to field — **Umpires:- Barry Dudleston & Neil Mallender**

SURREY LIONS

Fall Of Wkt	Batsman	How	Out	Score	Balls	4s	6s
1-78	**I.J. Ward**		**b Trego**	**31**	27	6	0
2-81	**A.D. Brown**		**b Trego**	**44**	24	6	2
	M.R. Ramprakash	**Not**	**Out**	**107**	99	9	2
3-165	**G.P. Thorpe**	**c Trott**	**b Tredwell**	**36**	61	5	0
4-165	**R. Clarke**	**st Jones**	**b Tredwell**	**0**	2	0	0
5-199	**A.J. Hollioake ***	**run**	**out**	**15**	13	1	1
6-314	**Azhar Mahmood**	**c Tredwell**	**b Trego**	**70**	41	6	4
7-322	**J.N. Batty +**	**c Key**	**b Trego**	**8**	3	0	1
	M.P. Bicknell	**did not bat**					
	Saqlain Mushtaq	**did not bat**					
	T.J. Murtagh	**did not bat**					
	Extras	**(6lb, 5w)**		**11**			
	TOTAL	**(45 overs)**	**(for 7 wkts)**	**322**			

Bowler	O	M	R	W	NB	Wd
Saggers	9	0	67	0	-	2
Trott	7	0	67	0	-	1
Ealham	7	1	54	0	-	-
Trego	9	0	66	4	-	2
Blewett	4	0	27	0	-	-
Tredwell	9	0	35	2	-	-

KENT SPITFIRES							
Fall Of Wkt	Batsman	How	Out	Score	Balls	4s	6s
1-14	**M.A. Ealham ***	**c Batty**	**b Azhar**	**4**	7	0	0
3-71	**R.W.T. Key**	**lbw**	**b Murtagh**	**39**	41	7	0
2-62	**P.D. Trego**		**b Murtagh**	**21**	24	3	0
5-299	**E.T. Smith**		**b Azhar**	**99**	86	9	2
4-137	**G.S. Blewett**		**b Saqlain**	**36**	37	4	0
	M.J. Walker	**Not**	**Out**	**80**	62	8	2
6-305	**G.O. Jones +**	**c sub (Salisbury)**	**b Clarke**	**5**	7	0	0
7-315	**M.A. Carberry**	**c Batty**	**b Hollioake**	**3**	4	0	0
	J.C. Tredwell	**Not**	**Out**	**1**	2	0	0
	M.J. Saggers	**did not bat**					
	B.J. Trott	**did not bat**					
	Extras	**(3b, 7lb, 18w)**		**28**			
	TOTAL	**(45 overs)**	**(for 7 wkts)**	**316**			

Bowler	O	M	R	W	NB	Wd
Bicknell	**9**	**0**	**41**	**0**	-	1
Azhar Mahmood	**9**	**0**	**77**	**2**	-	2
Murtagh	**9**	**0**	**68**	**2**	-	-
Saqlain Mushtaq	**9**	**0**	**40**	**1**	-	1
Hollioake	**5**	**0**	**52**	**1**	-	3
Clarke	**4**	**0**	**28**	**1**	-	3

Other NCL Division One Results

At this early stage of the season, the teams were surprisngly spread out, with Surrey, Glamorgan and Essex having built up an eight-point gap between themselves and the rest of the sides, though Worcestershire Royals did have games in hand. The most significant result in this round of matches was the comprehensive victory recorded by the reigning champions, Glamorgan Dragons, over the 2000 champions, Gloucestershire Gladiators. Were Mark Alleyne's side a fading force in the one-day game?

May 10
Chelmsford:- **Essex Eagles (4pts) beat Kent Spitfires by 3 wickets.** Kent 176 (45ov; Napier 3-9); Essex 179-7 (43ov; Trott 3-22).
May 18
Cardiff:- **Glamorgan Dragons (4pts) beat Gloucestershire Gladiators by 10 wickets (D/L method).** Gloucs 133-9 (26ov; Wharf 4-18, Davies 3-31); Glamorgan 135-0 (21.2ov; I.J. Thomas 71*, Croft 60*).
Leicester:- **Leicestershire Foxes (4pts) beat Yorkshire Phoenix by 66 runs**. Leics 247-8 (45ov; Stevens 63, Sehwag 54, Sidebottom 5-42); Yorks 181 (44.2ov; Dagnall 4-41).
Edgbaston:- **Essex Eagles (4pts) beat Warwickshire Bears by 8 wickets**. Warwickshire 143 (18.4ov; Irani 3-21); Essex 146-2 (19.1ov; Jefferson 50, Flower 49*).

NCL DIVISION ONE TABLE AT 18TH MAY

Pos	Prv		P	Pts	W	T	L	A
1	1	Surrey Lions	4	16	4	0	0	0
2	2	Glamorgan Dragons	3	12	3	0	0	0
3	3	Essex Eagles	4	12	3	0	1	0
4	3	Worcestershire Royals	2	4	1	0	1	0
5	3	Gloucestershire Gladiators	3	4	1	0	2	0
=	3	Yorkshire Phoenix	3	4	1	0	2	0
7	3	Kent Spitfires	4	4	1	0	3	0
=	9	Leicestershire Foxes	4	4	1	0	3	0
9	8	Warwickshire Bears	3	0	0	0	3	0

6 Firing On All Fronts

With Surrey now leading the way in both the County Championship and the NCL, things couldn't have been much better for Keith Medlycott's team, though the county's advantage at the top of the Championship table could have been greater had the rain not saved Leicestershire's skin at the end of a game the home side had dominated from start to finish. Having said that, Lancashire had been far and away the most unfortunate team in the competition - rain having denied them clear victory chances in three of their four matches to date - as they continued to confirm the view that they were the side most likely to stop Surrey retaining their title. The other possible contenders, Warwickshire, had meanwhile been devastated by the news that the exciting young Kiwi quickie, Shane Bond, was indeed suffering from a stress fracture to his back and had therefore been forced to pull out of his contract with the Bears.

Surrey had an injury problem of their own, too, with Alex Tudor, having undergone keyhole surgery on his knee, expected to be out for several weeks. In addition, it was confirmed that the Club would be without the services of two further players in the weeks ahead, since the England squad selected for the first Test against Zimbabwe included both Mark Butcher and Alec Stewart. There had been some speculation in the media that Stewart might be omitted in favour of a younger keeper for the series against a pretty weak Zimbabwe side, though this had always seemed unlikely to happen in reality, not least because the Surrey man was in possession of an England contract that took him through till the end of the summer.

With these three players all out of the reckoning for a while, team selection problems were already fast receding for Keith Medlycott and Adam Hollioake as the team prepared for three tough games that lay ahead of them in the course of the next eight days. In the Championship, Surrey were about to take on Essex, who had been something of a bogey side in recent years, with the reigning champions having only recorded one first-class victory over their local rivals since 1991 - when Ali Brown's brilliant century at The Oval in 1999 turned possible defeat into a significant win in the early stages of that memorable title-winning campaign. Two important one-day games were then to follow close on the heels of the Essex match - the team's next NCL fixture, against Gloucestershire Gladiators at Bristol, which was likely to result in another tough, tight scrap for the Lions, and then a trip to Taunton, never a happy hunting ground, to play Somerset in the fourth round of the Cheltenham And Gloucester Trophy.

FRIZZELL COUNTY CHAMPIONSHIP DIVISION ONE - MATCH FIVE

ESSEX versus SURREY
at Chelmsford

First Day - Wednesday 21st May
Surrey 337-8

The Teams And The Toss - *With Mark Butcher and Alec Stewart on England duty,Graham Thorpe and Jon Batty win recalls to Surrey's Championship line-up, while the fit-again James Ormond returns to bolster the seam attack at the expense of the unfortunate Rikki Clarke. Essex welcome back Aftab Habib after a hamstring injury and are only missing the England captain, Nasser Hussain, from their full-strength side, since Ashley Cowan is sidelined for the whole season after the winter reconstruction of a knee. Ormond's return for Surrey appears to be very important, since the pitch looks surprisingly green and grassy as the captains go out to toss up on a cool and overcast morning. Given the prevailing conditions, it is no surprise to see Ronnie Irani put the visitors in to bat after Adam Hollioake again calls incorrectly.*

Despite an indifferent weather forecast, a good-sized crowd is in the ground as Essex make a great start to the game with two wickets in the first four overs - Ian Ward falls to the second ball of the match when he shuffles into line without making any forward or backward movement and is adjudged lbw to Scott Brant, while Jon Batty, perhaps wary of the pitch, pushes tentatively forward to the last delivery of Jon Dakin's second over and edges to James Foster behind the wicket. With Batty out for seven, Surrey are 8-2 and already in trouble.

Mark Ramprakash and Graham Thorpe would appear to be just the men for this situation, however, and they immediately dig in to prevent any further losses. Neither of these experienced batsmen attempts anything too expansive during the opening spells of Brant and Dakin, with the only boundary coming in the eighth over, when Thorpe steers a delivery from the former Leicestershire all-rounder down to third man.

The score has only advanced to 27-2 after thirteen overs, in fact, when Dakin is replaced by Graham Napier, and Brant, after seven excellent overs, gives way to Ronnie Irani, with the first of these changes working wonders for the home side.

Napier's second ball sees Ramprakash fishing uncharacteristically outside the off stump with his bat away from his body and the resultant outside edge is very well snapped up to his right-hand side by the agile Foster to plunge Surrey back into deep water. And things soon get worse for the visitors, as Ali Brown also departs before the end of the over. Having got off the mark with a streaky four, edged just too high and too wide for a leaping third slip to reach, the last ball of the over sees him becoming the second lbw victim of the morning when he plays across the line and pays the ultimate penalty.

With the seamers finding plenty of movement and the Championship leaders struggling badly at 31-4, the scene appears to be set for one of Adam Hollioake's stirring counter-attacks, though it is actually Thorpe who comes up with the boundary strokes - a square cut off Irani and a cover drive off Napier - as the Surrey captain tries to establish himself over the course of the next four overs.

Although Hollioake does eventually break loose after this brief period of reconnaissance - pulling Irani high over wide mid-on for his first four and then driving Napier away in a similar direction for another boundary to raise the Surrey fifty - his attempt to hit his team out of trouble ends in failure as Napier hits back to win his second lbw verdict from umpire Mervyn Kitchen when the visitors' captain fails to make contact with a big hit to leg.

At this point, with the scoreboard reading 51-5, Napier has figures of 4-0-13-3 and it is hard to escape the feeling that the Surrey batsmen just haven't shown the burly former England Under-19 all-rounder sufficient respect, since he has done little more than bowl reasonably straight to a decent length.

While his team-mates have been dropping like flies at the other end, Thorpe has continued to battle away gamely, despite looking some way short of his best form and having been beaten outside the off stump on a number of occasions by the unlucky Irani. He still manages to unfurl the occasional vintage stroke, however, notably when Irani turns back to his opening bowlers in the last forty-five minutes before lunch and Dakin is promptly driven through mid-off and midwicket for successive fours.

The reappearance of the new-ball pair also has an effect on Azhar, since runs begin to flow from his bat, even though they don't all come off the middle. In these conditions the batsmen need some luck, however, and the inside edges and miscued drives that the Pakistani all-rounder occasionally gets away with are more than balanced up by a pair of high-class drives off Dakin, the second of which flies over long-on for six; a pick-up over square leg off Brant that raises the Surrey hundred and the fifty-partnership for the sixth-wicket; and the delicate leg-glance that comes from the following delivery.

With Irani's decision to revert to his opening bowlers having failed to provide him with a further breakthrough, the visitors are at least breathing a little easier at lunch.

Lunch:- Surrey 109-5 (Thorpe 40, Azhar 35*) from 33 overs*

Napier and Irani form Essex's attack in the immediate post-lunch period, though they have no joy in the early stages as Azhar drills the first and last balls of Napier's opening over straight down the ground for four and then cuts the same bowler for another boundary in hustling through to a fine fifty from just 48 balls. It has been a superb knock in adversity on what remains a tricky pitch, as Azhar discovers when his next two fours come via edges to third man from lifting deliveries. Undeterred by these false strokes, he middles both a pull and a pick-up off Irani to claim two further boundaries, raising the Surrey 150 in the process, and at the end of the over the Essex skipper limps from the field, having presumably aggravated the knee injury that has plagued him in recent times.

While Azhar has surged ahead during a partnership that now exceeds a hundred in value, Thorpe has kept a watching brief, though he finally completes his personal half-century in the next over with another of his deft deflections to third man off Napier. A very determined effort, Thorpe's 100-ball innings has been no less valuable than his team-mate's, though, sadly, he has only added a single when the persevering Napier finds his outside edge and has him very well taken, low down in front of first slip, by a diving Foster.

At 162-6 the game looks evenly balanced, with Surrey now needing another partnership to develop as Martin Bicknell arrives in the middle. He loses Azhar almost immediately, however, when Brant, having returned to the attack following his captain's departure, finally gets reward for some good bowling as the Pakistani plays a ball down into the ground and has insufficient time to react as it bounces back onto the stumps.

With Azhar's allocation of luck having finally run out after scoring an excellent seventy-seven from 87 balls, Surrey are now back under the cosh at 168-7, though Ian Salisbury remains calm and collected as he instantly drives the Aussie left-armer through the covers for three. When Bicknell then mirrors his new partner's stroke in the next over from Napier, and Salisbury follows up by finding the rope at deep cover with a repeat performance off Brant, the stand-in Essex captain, Paul Grayson, makes changes to his attack, bringing Dakin back at the Hayes Close end and giving his off-spinner, James Middlebrook, a first taste of the action at the river end.

Neither change bothers Bicknell, however, as he greets the off-spinner with a cover drive to the boundary, before taking twelve runs from Dakin's next over, including top-edged and middled cuts that both bring four runs, to send the score steaming past two-hundred at a rate of knots. The home side's towering former Leicestershire all-rounder suffers further agonies in his next two overs as well. After having Salisbury badly missed at cover - Habib somehow managing to spill an absolute sitter driven to him at waist height with the batsman on fifteen at 208-7 - he is again butchered by Bicknell, who finds the boundary rope with three nicely timed strokes during a fourteen-run over that sees the arrival of the fifty partnership for the eighth wicket.

Bicknell's burst of six fours has rushed him swiftly to the brink of a very valuable half-century and put Surrey within sight of a decent total as Irani returns to the field of play. The home skipper's reappearance doesn't bring any immediate improvement in his team's fortunes, however, as a double bowling change - Napier for Dakin, and Grayson for Middlebrook - sees Bicknell complete his fifty with a single from his seventy-first ball before taking two boundaries off the seamer, and Salisbury driving the spinner over long-on for a six that pushes the score past 250.

With the pitch seemingly becoming easier to bat on, it is looking like the eighth-wicket pair will still be together at tea until an error of judgement from Salisbury with the break four overs away suddenly provides the home side with the breakthrough they have been seeking. Having driven a ball from the newly reintroduced Brant to the left of cover, the Surrey leg-spinner sets off for a single, forgetting that the fielder concerned is the left-handed Grayson, making an already tight run nigh-on suicidal. Bicknell, appreciating the danger, calls 'no' and rightly refuses to budge from the non-striker's end, leaving Salisbury to turn back and make a valiant dive for the crease. Grayson's throw to Foster at the stumps is accurate, however, and an excellent partnership of ninety therefore comes to a disappointing end.

Fortunately for Surrey, Bicknell maintains his concentration after the loss of his partner and by the time the interval arrives he has advanced his score to seventy with the ninth four of his innings, whipped away through midwicket off Grayson.

Tea:- Surrey 266-8 (Bicknell 70, Saqlain 1*) from 72 overs*

If Essex are hoping to wrap up the Surrey innings quickly with the return to the attack of Brant and Dakin then they are soon disappointed. Although the bowlers do find the edge of the bat on a couple of occasions, most notably when Bicknell Chinese-cuts Dakin to the fine-leg boundary, the ninth-wicket pair survive four-over bursts from both bowlers with a fair degree of comfort. Saqlain certainly seems to be settling in well as he drives the former Fox high over long-on into the River Can for six and then glances the Australian for four in the next over.

These are isolated blows, though, and it is largely through the accumulation of singles that the score is moved along to three-hundred - undreamed of riches for Surrey after having been 51-5 - in the eighty-first over. Bicknell does eventually buck this trend, however, with a lovely straight drive for four off Dakin that takes his personal contribution up to eighty-nine.

Since the new ball is now only eight overs away, the Essex spinners are brought back into the attack, presumably in an attempt to hasten its arrival while giving a short breather to the opening bowlers. It seems a strange decision, though, since increasing gloom and drizzle suggest that we are highly unlikely to get through all the remaining twenty-one overs of play.

Bicknell is not to be deflected from his task in any case and, after working his way up to ninety-three with four singles, suddenly advances on Middlebrook and drives him down the ground for six, the stroke having just enough height and power to carry over the head of the 6'4" Dakin at long-on.

One heart-in-mouth moment is then followed by another when Essex appeal loudly for a bat-pad catch as Bicknell pushes forward to the next delivery from the off-spinner and the ball ends up in silly point's hands. Fortunately, umpire Kitchen remains unmoved, allowing the Surrey seamer to push a single to point later in the over, thereby completing a quite superb and most valuable second County Championship century of his career, this one coming from 148 balls and including eleven fours and the six earlier in the over. Although Bicknell's subsequent celebrations are typically understated amidst the applause from the crowd and his team-mates in the pavilion, he does appear to enjoy the sudden release of tension that follows as he sweeps and drives fours in the next two overs on the way to beating his previous best score of 110 not out against Kent at Canterbury on the occasion of his maiden first-class century in 2001.

It isn't long, though, before Bicknell is able to sit down, put his feet up and savour his achievement, since Essex's decision to take the new ball as soon as it becomes due after ninety overs prompts a reassessment of the light by the umpires and the inevitable decision by the batsmen to retire to the pavilion.

Close:- Surrey 337-8 (Bicknell 117, Saqlain 25*) from 90 overs*

Second Day - Thursday 22nd May
Surrey 376 and 7-0; Essex 252

The second day's play starts on time despite overnight rain and early morning drizzle, though it's cool and cloudy as Martin Bicknell continues in the same vein of form that had brought him his third first-class century on the opening day. Four off-side boundaries in the first four overs, three off Brant and one at Napier's expense, take Surrey up to and beyond 350, while Saqlain's unique brand of pull stroke earns him four runs in Brant's following over to make the ninth-wicket partnership worth exactly a hundred.

Only two further runs have been added, however, before Essex's torment ends with Saqlain being bowled via his pads by a legside delivery from the Aussie left-armer. Like his spin twin before him, the Pakistani off-spinner has contributed a useful thirty while Bicknell has dominated the proceedings. Having been 51-5 and then 168-7, it seems incredible that the score is now 360-9, with a haul of maximum batting points not looking totally out of the question.

This turns out to be a bridge too far, however, though they do manage to get as far as 376 before the innings ends with the return of Dakin and the demise of Bicknell, a miscued pull dollying a catch back to the bowler to end a brilliant knock of 141. A repeat of yesterday's close-of-play ovation from the crowd accompanies Bicknell's return to the pavilion to prepare himself for a pre-lunch stint with the ball.

Since he is probably pretty tired after his efforts with the bat, the Surrey hero is doubtless not too unhappy when it starts to rain during the break between innings, allowing him more time to rest before he has to come out and start bowling.

Fortunately for everyone it turns out to be a fairly short shower, though nine overs have been lost by the time play restarts at 12.20pm… and it isn't long before that man Bicknell is again in the thick of the action as Essex get away to the kind of rocky start that their visitors had suffered on day one.

After an initial over from Bicknell that costs six runs, including a clip to the midwicket boundary by Darren Robinson, James Ormond draws first blood for Surrey in his second over when the stocky Essex opener misses a drive and is hit on the back pad, giving umpire Kitchen no choice but to raise his index finger above his head.

A score of 7-1 then rapidly becomes 17-4 as Bicknell skims off the cream of the Essex batting with a spell of three wickets for four runs in just nine balls. Paul Grayson becomes his first victim when he pushes at an outswinger and edges to Jon Batty with the score on eight; Will Jefferson then snicks a drive to the third-man boundary before falling in similar style to Grayson from the next delivery with the total advanced to seventeen; and, finally, the second ball of Bicknell's following over brings the wicket of Aftab Habib, who goes lbw on the drive, in much the same way as Robinson before him, with the total unchanged. Surrey, inevitably, are overjoyed by these successes, and it seems almost impossible that the state of the game can have changed so rapidly in the space of twenty-four hours - this time yesterday, the visitors were well and truly on the rack, yet now they are in a position of great strength.

Lunch:- Essex 29-4 (Flower 5, Irani 7*) from 14 overs*

Having come safely through the morning's final four overs, Andy Flower and Ronnie Irani make a very positive start to the afternoon session as the bowlers almost inevitably fall a little short of the very high standards they had set themselves before lunch. Although there is one edge by Irani off Ormond that flies through a vacant fourth slip position, there are also four boundaries that are nicely middled through the off side during the first four overs of the afternoon and, as a result of these bold strokes, the total rattles past fifty at a fair pace.

Things do quieten down considerably for a while hereafter as the Essex pair go on to complete an important fifty partnership in the twenty-second over, though it arrives in unconvincing style when Irani edges the unfortunate Ormond over the head of second slip and away to the rope at third man.

Having completed lengthy spells either side of lunch, the Surrey opening bowlers now take a well deserved rest - Saqlain Mushtaq relieving Ormond at the river end, and Azhar Mahmood taking over from Bicknell at the Hayes Close end - with the two new bowlers instantly enjoying mixed results.

While Saqlain finds the going tough against Flower when the master of the sweep shot produces two different varieties straight away, both of which bring him four runs, his Pakistani team-mate comes out on top in an all-action three-ball battle with the Essex skipper - Irani pulls and drives Azhar's first two deliveries to the rope at wide mid-on and square cover respectively, but the bowler immediately takes vengeance when the impetuous Mancunian attempts to pull the next ball for another four and ends up miscuing high towards extra cover where Mark Ramprakash takes the catch. It appears that Essex's former England all-rounder has, once again, given his wicket away at an important stage of a match against Surrey, his departure for forty-two leaving his side wobbling badly again at 99-5.

For the home side, much now depends on Flower, who, like Thorpe before him, is not on top of his game yet is battling away gamely and remaining calm, despite being beaten outside the off stump from time to time. He is helped by the fact that his latest ally at the crease, James Foster, offers him solid support in edging the total slowly up towards the 227 that his side need to avoid the follow on.

They have only got as far as 132, however, with Flower having just completed a highly commendable half-century from 88 balls, when Azhar strikes a major blow for his team by having the Zimbabwean taken in the gully by Rikki Clarke, substituting for Ian Ward, from a thick-edged offside forcing stroke. Flower departs disgusted with himself for playing a rather loose shot as Surrey celebrate the fact that they are continuing to turn this game on its head.

Tea is not too far away now as Jon Dakin comes to the wicket and makes an uncomfortable start, top-edging a hook at Azhar into the space between wicketkeeper and long leg, then surviving a confident shout for what looks like a pad-glove catch at silly point off Saqlain. At the other end, though, Foster is starting to play a more expansive game, cutting and on-driving the off-spinner for fours that help to take the total past 150 in the forty-sixth over.

Dakin subsequently appears to draw confidence from his partner, taking two back-foot boundaries from Azhar in the concluding over of the Pakistani's impressive eleven-over spell and forcing Hollioake to turn to Ian Salisbury for the final over of the session.

Tea:- Essex 169-6 (Foster 37, Dakin 15*) from 51 overs*

Surrey open up with Saqlain and Bicknell after tea, though it isn't long before the off-spinner is lofted down the ground by Dakin and replaced by Ormond. By this time the visitors have already captured a seventh wicket, however, with Foster's nicely constructed innings having been ended by the combination of a Bicknell outswinger and an edged forcing stroke to Azhar at second slip in the third over of the session.

Perhaps surprisingly, given that another wicket has just fallen, a flurry of strokes follows, as James Middlebrook opens his account with three offside boundaries off Bicknell, and an increasingly assured Dakin picks the same bowler up over midwicket for a four of his own as the total passes the two-hundred mark.

Hollioake reacts to this sudden spurt by rotating Bicknell, Ormond and Saqlain for the next half-an-hour but the boundaries continue to flow as the eighth-wicket pair belie their positions in the order and Dakin reaches a 71-ball fifty with a swept four off Saqlain that also sees any possibility of being asked to follow on averted. The partnership then extends past the half-century mark as Middlebrook clips and cuts Ormond for successive fours that bring about another Hollioake rethink, with Salisbury being called up in place of Saqlain at the river end.

This turns out to be a good move, since the new Ormond-Salisbury combination captures the last three Essex wickets in the space of just seventeen balls once the big fast bowler has found the edge of Middlebrook's bat with an outswinger with the total on 243. Batty's excellent catch, diving away low in front of first slip, ends the Yorkshireman's brave and largely impressive knock of twenty-nine in the sixty-ninth over and within three overs the hosts are all out. Dakin is the ninth man to go, well taken at head height by Azhar at second slip off Ormond for a spirited fifty-nine at 252, then Napier falls to an astonishing catch by Saqlain off Salisbury from the very next ball bowled. Receiving a low full-toss from the leg-spinner, the Essex number ten drives hard and flat towards deep wide mid-on and sees the off-spinner tumbling away to his right to pull off a brilliant one-handed catch that gives the visitors a 124-run advantage on first innings.

Surrey's hopes of adding significantly to their lead by the close are dashed by two stoppages for bad light, the first after a passage of play lasting just seven balls, during which Scott Brant fails to take a caught-and-bowled chance high to his left-hand side offered by Ward on two, and the second, which ends play for the day, at 6.42pm with a further fifteen balls bowled. Ward's appearance as opener, with Salisbury as his runner, has been rather surprising, since he has been off the field for most of the day after straining his groin attempting to prevent a boundary in the ninth over of Essex's innings.

Close:- Surrey 7-0 (Ward 6, Batty 1*) from 3.4 overs*

Third Day - Friday 23rd May
Surrey 376 and 381-7; Essex 252

Ian Ward continues with his runner at the start of the third day as Jon Dakin and Scott Brant strive to pull their side back into the game with some early wickets. None are forthcoming, however, as the Surrey openers build solid foundations before breaking out with a rash of boundaries between the tenth and fourteenth overs to take the total past fifty.

By this stage, Ronnie Irani has been forced to leave the field, Dakin has given way to Graham Napier, and the reigning champions are nicely placed to push on towards a declaration later in the day. The pitch has certainly eased as the game has progressed and, on what is now a good batting surface, the batsmen gradually assume complete control, especially once James Middlebrook enters the fray and Dakin returns at the Hayes Close end. Jon Batty's strength on the cut shot is fed far too often, allowing him to pepper the cover boundary, and, while Ward falls one short of fifty when Dakin defeats the left-hander's drive with a delivery angled in from round the wicket, the Surrey wicketkeeper makes no mistake in completing his half-century - from 76 balls, no fewer than twelve of which have been hit for four - during the following over.

With the total now into three figures and the lead already extending towards 250, Paul Grayson pairs Middlebrook with Napier, though the former is quickly replaced by Brant after Batty dances down the track to the off-spinner and drives him high over the media centre and beyond the River Can that runs behind it.

Napier, on the other hand, repeats his first-innings trick of taking two wickets in an over by claiming the scalps of Mark Ramprakash and Graham Thorpe in the space of five balls - Ramprakash top-edges a slash at a ball wide of off stump and is very well taken overhead at the second attempt by Andy Flower at first slip, while Thorpe plays three-and-out, driving his first ball beautifully through the covers to pick up three and then edging a good lifting delivery to James Foster as soon as he gets back on strike.

Despite Napier's quick one-two, Surrey are still in a position of great strength at 124-3, though Batty and Ali Brown are careful to ensure that no further losses are incurred before lunch, picking up just fourteen runs in the last five overs of the session as a little rain starts to fall.

Lunch:- Surrey 138-3 (Batty 72, Brown 9*) from 36 overs*

It's 'the Ali Brown show' in the period immediately after lunch as Napier is taken to the cleaners in no uncertain terms, the Essex seamer conceding an incredible thirty-seven runs in three overs to the Surrey middle-order batsman. After taking nine runs from Napier's opening over of the session, Brown then lashes the first four balls of his next over to the fence - enjoying a stroke of luck when the young substitute fielder, Arfan Akram, horribly misjudges a potential catch at deep backward square leg for the first of these - before pulling and driving three further consecutive boundaries in the suffering bowler's third over. In the course of this withering assault, Brown has taken Surrey way beyond the 150 mark, brought up a fourth-wicket fifty partnership, of which he has scored forty-two, and, with a little help from his partner, transformed Napier's figures from 8-0-43-2 to 11-0-83-2. He has also put himself on the brink of a stunning personal half-century, and he duly completes it, from only his thirty-second ball when he turns his attentions to Brant and drives him to the long-off boundary in the next over.

After this incredible Brown blast, things inevitably slow down, largely as a result of the replacement of a shell-shocked Napier by Dakin and the continuation of a decent post-lunch spell from Brant. Although Batty twice cuts Dakin to the rope at backward point, Brown fails to find the boundary again before holing out to the ex-Fox at long-on off the recently introduced James Middlebrook in the fiftieth over. His excellent sixty-four from 57 balls has provided ideal acceleration for his team, though, and the arrival of Adam Hollioake as his replacement in the middle promises further big-hitting entertainment for the crowd.

Predictably enough, the Surrey skipper is soon into his stride with a brace of cover-driven boundaries off Dakin, though the focus quickly switches to Batty who moves to within six runs of his fifth first-class century when he pulls the returning Napier backward of square leg for four before reaching the cherished landmark three overs later, from his 167th ball. The Chesterfield-born wicketkeeper's well-paced innings receives a good hand from the crowd, with the Surrey contingent now expecting fireworks from both batsmen in an attempt to get enough runs on the board to allow a tea-time declaration. Both Batty and Hollioake find boundaries quite hard to come by, however, as Middlebrook bowls thoughtfully to deep-set fields and Napier comes up with a much improved third spell of the innings before being replaced by acting skipper Grayson.

Much to the delight of the visiting supporters, Hollioake does eventually manage a couple of big drives for six in the lead-up to tea, smiting Grayson high onto the roof of one of the houses in Hayes Close and then walloping Middlebrook over the Pearce Stand and the river at wide long-on in the next over. A single in the off-spinner's next over then takes Hollioake through to a 65-ball half-century and at the interval Surrey lead by 426 runs. But is this enough to bring a declaration from the visiting captain?

Tea:- Surrey 302-4 (Batty 128, Hollioake 51*) from 71 overs*

With the Surrey batsmen reappearing after tea, it is clear that the visitors want to put more runs on the board against a side that had chased targets so successfully in the Championship last season. Hollioake is unable to add any runs to his own tally, though, as his lofted drive off Middlebrook's second ball of the session finds the safe hands of Darren Robinson, who runs and slides in from wide long-on to take a fine low catch.

With Brant as his post-tea partner, the former Yorkshire off-spinner continues to do a decent job for his side, bravely giving the ball some air and not conceding his first boundary of the session until his fourth over when Batty succeeds in finding the rope at third man with a reverse sweep. Despite being almost as steady as Middlebrook, Brant remains wicketless, however, and it takes the reintroduction of the all-action Napier to provide Essex with another breakthrough when Azhar Mahmood whips the fourth ball of the bowler's new spell away to deep midwicket where young Akram, subbing for his skipper, this time makes a very awkward catch look easy.

With the lead standing at 463 at this point Surrey would probably like to declare, but there is a problem - with masses of grey clouds overhead, the light is poor and drizzle is in the air. To close the innings now would be tantamount to ending play for the day, since neither the umpires nor Essex would be prepared to start the final innings of the match in the prevailing conditions… so the visitors just keep on batting. This allows Batty to pass both the 150 mark, from 232 balls, and his previous career-best score, last season's 151 against Somerset at Taunton, as well as giving him an opportunity to plunder another couple of fours off the long-suffering Napier. The Essex seamer gains some consolation, though, when he collects a fourth wicket, courtesy of Martin Bicknell's edged drive to James Foster, in his next over.

It's pretty pointless cricket at this stage, really, since Surrey have mountains of runs in the bank now, but it becomes increasingly clear that the light will not improve sufficiently to allow the visitors to bowl at Essex tonight.

Mercifully, rain eventually has the final say, as it begins to fall heavily enough for play to be suspended at 5.48pm with sixteen overs left of the day's allocation and the Championship leaders' advantage standing at 505.

Close:- Surrey 381-7 (Batty 168, Salisbury 9*) from 87 overs*

Fourth Day - Saturday 24th May

Surrey 376 and 381-7dec; Essex 252 and 247
Surrey won by 258 runs
Surrey 21pts, Essex 5

Surrey's inevitable overnight declaration leaves them with ninety-six overs on the final day in which to bowl out their hosts, and they get just the start they need when James Ormond claims his three-hundredth first-class wicket by trapping Will Jefferson lbw with the final ball of the fourth over. The batsman can have no complaints, having barely got half forward to the delivery, and departs for three with the score at sixteen.

With the pitch playing well and showing few signs of wear and tear, further early breakthroughs prove elusive, however, as Martin Bicknell strays too wide of off stump too often, and Ormond is picked off for several fours and threes by the second-wicket pair of Darren Robinson and Paul Grayson, who both take full advantage of Surrey's very attacking field placings.

Since runs are of no concern to the visitors, it's probably not a bad thing to get the batsmen playing strokes, though, and when the second wicket does come, in the tenth over, it is from a rather lazy flick by Grayson at a legside delivery from Ormond. Since Jon Batty has to cover an awful lot of ground away to his left-hand side in order to pick up a brilliant one-handed catch, the batsman can consider himself a little unfortunate as he makes his way back to the pavilion with the scoreboard reading 44-2.

This second wicket clearly does Ormond a power of good as he continues to charge in from the river end, while Azhar Mahmood is introduced at the Hayes Close end for the fifteenth over after Bicknell completes a rather disappointing spell.

Robinson, who has been accompanied by Andy Flower since Grayson's demise, immediately takes a liking to Azhar's bowling by picking up seven runs from the Pakistani's first over, and the match situation is looking just a little brighter for Essex when the Zimbabwean, after a very slow but steady start, finally breaks free from his shackles to drive Ormond to the cover boundary a few overs later.

Unfortunately for the home side, the picture then changes dramatically as both members of the third-wicket union depart in the space of four deliveries with the score on sixty-nine. Flower goes first, undone by a superb lifting delivery from Azhar that he can't get out of the way of and gloves through to Batty, then Robinson departs in a state of high dudgeon when adjudged lbw by umpire Graham Burgess to the second ball of the next over from Ormond. There's no way of knowing whether the batsman feels he has got an inside edge onto his pad or whether he thinks the ball has hit him too high to be given out, but he is clearly not happy as he tears himself away from the crease with his side now in real trouble.

While Robinson has perhaps been unfortunate, his successor at the wicket, James Foster, seemingly gets lucky straight away. Ormond's next ball nips back off the pitch and appears to trap the Essex wicketkeeper right in front of the stumps, prompting an extremely confident appeal from the bowler and his close fielders, but, having disagreed with the batsman on the previous appeal, the umpire disagrees with the fielding side this time, allowing Foster to survive and promptly prosper by clipping the very next ball to the square leg boundary.

In the immediate aftermath of Surrey's double breakthrough, it is understandable that Foster and Aftab Habib should opt to concentrate almost totally on survival, and they are probably relieved when Ormond comes to the end of a fine opening stint after delivering twelve hostile overs that have earned him three wickets.

As the interval approaches, Foster suddenly reveals an inclination to be positive by driving Azhar for three off-side fours in two overs, but nothing can take the gloss off Surrey's morning as the players leave the field in the brightest and best weather of the match.

Lunch:- Essex 106-4 (Habib 7, Foster 23*) from 28 overs*

Having seemingly located a much better line during a couple of overs from the river end just before lunch, Bicknell continues his spell upon the resumption, with Azhar retaining residency at the Hayes Close end.

The impression that Bicknell is bowling a line closer to the stumps is confirmed as he comes up with a couple of decent lbw appeals in his first two overs, while Azhar has a worthwhile shout against Habib rejected shortly afterwards. The bat largely dominates the ball, otherwise, with Habib finding the boundary on five occasions at Azhar's expense in the first half-hour of the afternoon as Hollioake's attacking fields allow the batsmen greater scope for run-scoring than would normally be expected. It is surprising, therefore, that Foster, the principal aggressor before the break, actually takes nine overs to add to his lunch score, but once he is up and running with a glanced boundary off Azhar, followed by a pulled four off Bicknell that raises the Essex two-hundred, he looks in good form again. He even drives Ormond over mid-off's head for three as soon as the sturdy paceman replaces Azhar at the Hayes Close end, though a sliced drive backward of point, again for three runs, in the same bowler's next over is much less convincing.

There is no doubt that the fifth-wicket partnership is becoming quite a concern for Surrey by this stage of the afternoon, and, in an attempt to split the Habib-Foster alliance, Hollioake turns to spin, with Saqlain replacing Bicknell after a good spell either side of lunch from the veteran swing bowler.

This change has no immediate effect, though, and frustration continues to grow for the Championship leaders as Habib's edged cut over the slips off Ormond brings up the hundred partnership and, much to everyone's surprise, prompts the Surrey paceman to test his former Leicestershire team-mate with a few of his off-breaks. This move also proves unsuccessful as Habib completes a battling 85-ball fifty to keep his side very much on course for a draw.

Finally, however, with tea little more than half-an-hour away and the visitors becoming increasingly desperate for a breakthrough, Ormond strikes a major blow for his side by removing Foster with the score at 188 and the fifth-wicket partnership worth 119. Seemingly unsettled by a series of short balls in Ormond's previous couple of overs, Foster is trapped on the crease and rapped on the pads by the first ball of the former England fast bowler's next over and finds umpire Kitchen's upraised digit sending him on his way for forty-two.

This proves to be a particularly vital wicket because it brings further successes in the following two overs, with Ronnie Irani the first to go in the next over from Saqlain. Having struck his first ball from Ormond to the cover boundary and then clipped his first delivery from the Pakistani off-spinner wide of mid-on for another four, the Essex skipper perishes to his seventh ball when Nadeem Shahid, subbing for the injured Ward, picks up a good tumbling bat-pad catch at short leg to reduce the home side to 197-6.

This score then becomes 205-7 by the end of an eventful next over from Ormond that involves three former Leicestershire men. Habib takes the early honours by driving the Surrey paceman's first ball to the long-off boundary, thereby taking the total past two-hundred, but after a single to the former England batsman and an edged three to third man by the new batsman, Jon Dakin, Ormond comes up with a snorter of a delivery that replicates the ball with which Azhar had earlier removed Flower. Like his team-mate before him, Habib is unable to drop his wrists in time as a lifting delivery flicks a glove and flies into the safe hands of Batty, giving Ormond his fifth wicket and putting Surrey back on course for victory.

As Ormond continues to steam in, he almost earns a sixth wicket, too, when James Middlebrook, on four at the time, cuts hard and low to Bicknell at fourth slip. Since the ball is travelling at great speed and going down all the way on its journey to the fielder, it represents an extremely difficult chance, though it could turn out to be a crucial miss as the weather has been changing for the worse during the afternoon and is looking like it could yet deny the Championship leaders their chance of winning the match.

With Dakin and Middlebrook standing firm through the last four overs of the session, Surrey know that they have thirty-nine overs in which to take the remaining three wickets after the interval… weather permitting.

Tea:- Essex 225-7 (Dakin 15, Middlebrook 8*) from 57 overs*

Since there is drizzle in the air, the tea break feels a lot longer than twenty minutes today, and a little light rain is actually falling as play resumes under grey skies.

It is quite possible, given the threat posed by the weather and the somewhat indifferent light, that Adam Hollioake is ready to pair his spinners for the first time in the match anyway, but it becomes increasingly likely that this will happen when Dakin falls to Saqlain's second ball after the break, edging a defensive push low to Azhar in a second slip position.

With his side now two wickets from defeat at 225-8, Graham Napier appears at number ten and immediately shows a surprising degree of aggressive intent, driving his first ball over mid-on for four and then picking up seven further runs, from a pull to the midwicket boundary and a drive wide of mid-on, before the over is out.

This doesn't deter Hollioake from giving Salisbury his first bowl of the innings, however, and it turns out to be a key decision as the leg-spinner quickly wipes away fears that the weather will win the day by finishing the match with the first two balls of his third over. Having pegged back Middlebrook's off stump with an undetected quicker googly, Salisbury disposes of the last man,

Scott Brant, with his next ball when the batsman pushes forward tentatively and dollies up a simple catch to Shahid at short leg.

There is much relief and jubilation in the Surrey camp, especially after rain had robbed the team of certain victory in the previous Championship match, and the points from this game should ensure that the Club's lead at the top of the table will be extended, since it has been a pretty wet week in most areas of the country bar the south-east.

Surrey 376 and 381-7dec; Essex 252 and 247
Surrey won by 258 runs. Surrey 21pts, Essex 5

TALKING POINTS - MARTIN BICKNELL

How did this century compare to your maiden century at Canterbury?
MB - I think they were fairly similar really - I played as well as I can in both games, although I was a bit more adventurous at the start of my innings in the Kent game because we were almost in a do-or-die situation there… so I decided to take a few more risks and then the further I went on the easier it was. With this innings it was difficult at the start because the ball was seaming around a lot, and it was just a case of hanging in there. Then after a while things got a bit easier and it became a case of batting for as long as we could and, being the first innings, making as big a score as we could.

You had a couple of minor scares as you came within sight of your century, with a drive just clearing Jon Dakin at long-on, and an appeal for a bat-pad catch off James Middlebrook when you were on ninety-nine. What do you remember about those nerve-racking moments?
MB - I'd made up my mind that I wasn't going to hang around and wait for things to happen. It didn't appear to be a very long boundary, so I thought I'd take him on but didn't quite get hold of the shot… but it was one of those where I felt the ball was always just going over his head, and fortunately it did. I don't remember too much about the bat-pad appeal, though.

ESSEX v SURREY at Chelmsford — 21st to 24th May

Essex won the toss and elected to field — Umpires:- Graham Burgess and Mervyn Kitchen

SURREY - First Innings

Fall Of Wkt	Batsman	How	Out	Score	Balls	4s	6s
1-0	I.J. Ward	lbw	b Brant	0	2	0	0
2-8	J.N. Batty +	c Foster	b Dakin	7	10	0	0
3-27	M.R. Ramprakash	c Foster	b Napier	10	43	0	0
6-162	G.P. Thorpe	c Foster	b Napier	52	102	9	0
4-31	A.D. Brown	lbw	b Napier	4	4	1	0
5-51	A.J. Hollioake *	lbw	b Napier	10	18	2	0
7-168	Azhar Mahmood		b Brant	77	87	12	1
10-376	M.P. Bicknell	c &	b Dakin	141	196	17	1
8-258	I.D.K. Salisbury	run	out	30	57	2	1
9-360	Saqlain Mushtaq		b Brant	30	65	2	1
	J. Ormond	Not	Out	9	14	1	0
	Extras	(4lb, 2nb)		6			
	TOTAL	(99.3 overs)		376			

Bowler	O	M	R	W	NB	Wd
Brant	29	4	94	3	-	-
Dakin	20.3	5	96	2	-	-
Napier	24	4	82	4	-	-
Irani	9	2	31	0	1	-
Middlebrook	9	0	38	0	-	-
Grayson	8	1	31	0	-	-

ESSEX - First Innings (Needing 227 to avoid the follow-on)							
Fall Of Wkt	Batsman	How	Out	Score	Balls	4s	6s
1-7	**D.D.J. Robinson**	**lbw**	**b Ormond**	**5**	14	1	0
3-17	**W.I. Jefferson**	**c Batty**	**b Bicknell**	**11**	29	1	0
2-8	**A.P. Grayson**	**c Batty**	**b Bicknell**	**1**	11	0	0
6-132	**A. Flower**	**c sub (Clarke)**	**b Azhar**	**51**	98	7	0
4-17	**A. Habib**	**lbw**	**b Bicknell**	**0**	2	0	0
5-99	**R.C. Irani ***	**c Ramprakash**	**b Azhar**	**42**	54	6	0
7-179	**J.S. Foster +**	**c Azhar**	**b Bicknell**	**38**	79	5	0
9-252	**J.M. Dakin**	**c Azhar**	**b Ormond**	**59**	95	9	0
8-243	**J.D. Middlebrook**	**c Batty**	**b Ormond**	**29**	42	5	0
10-252	**G.R. Napier**	**c Saqlain**	**b Salisbury**	**5**	6	1	0
	S.A. Brant	**Not**	**Out**	**0**	0	0	0
	Extras	**(5lb, 6nb)**		**11**			
	TOTAL	**(71.1 overs)**		**252**			

Bowler	O	M	R	W	NB	Wd
Bicknell	**19**	**5**	**67**	**4**	-	-
Ormond	**19**	**3**	**68**	**3**	1	-
Saqlain Mushtaq	**19**	**2**	**65**	**0**	2	-
Azhar Mahmood	**11**	**2**	**39**	**2**	-	-
Salisbury	**3.1**	**1**	**8**	**1**	-	-

SURREY - Second Innings (Leading by 124 runs on first innings)							
Fall Of Wkt	Batsman	How	Out	Score	Balls	4s	6s
1-102	**I.J. Ward**		**b Dakin**	**49**	75	8	0
	J.N. Batty +	**Not**	**Out**	**168**	251	23	1
2-120	**M.R. Ramprakash**	**c Flower**	**b Napier**	**1**	12	0	0
3-124	**G.P. Thorpe**	**c Foster**	**b Napier**	**3**	2	0	0
4-209	**A.D. Brown**	**c Jefferson**	**b Middlebrook**	**64**	57	10	0
5-303	**A.J. Hollioake ***	**c Robinson**	**b Middlebrook**	**51**	69	3	2
6-339	**Azhar Mahmood**	**c sub (Akram)**	**b Napier**	**16**	26	1	0
7-368	**M.P. Bicknell**	**c Foster**	**b Napier**	**13**	21	1	0
	I.D.K. Salisbury	**Not**	**Out**	**9**	9	1	0
	Extras	**(7lb)**		**7**			
	TOTAL	**(87 overs)**	**(for 7 dec)**	**381**			

Bowler	O	M	R	W	NB	Wd
Brant	**19**	**5**	**62**	**0**	-	-
Dakin	**17**	**2**	**55**	**1**	-	-
Napier	**21**	**0**	**124**	**4**	-	-
Middlebrook	**26**	**0**	**117**	**2**	-	-
Grayson	**4**	**0**	**16**	**0**	-	-

ESSEX - Second Innings (Needing 506 to win)							
Fall Of Wkt	Batsman	How	Out	Score	Balls	4s	6s
4-69	**D.D.J. Robinson**	**lbw**	**b Ormond**	**41**	60	2	0
1-16	**W.I. Jefferson**	**lbw**	**b Ormond**	**3**	7	0	0
2-44	**A.P. Grayson**	**c Batty**	**b Ormond**	**19**	19	3	0
3-69	**A. Flower**	**c Batty**	**b Azhar**	**6**	29	1	0
7-205	**A. Habib**	**c Batty**	**b Ormond**	**61**	101	9	0
5-188	**J.S. Foster +**	**lbw**	**b Ormond**	**42**	85	6	0
6-197	**R.C. Irani ***	**c sub (Shahid)**	**b Saqlain**	**9**	7	2	0
8-225	**J.M. Dakin**	**c Azhar**	**b Saqlain**	**15**	22	2	0
9-247	**J.D. Middlebrook**		**b Salisbury**	**13**	31	3	0
	G.R. Napier	**Not**	**Out**	**15**	18	2	0
10-247	**S.A. Brant**	**c sub (Shahid)**	**b Salisbury**	**0**	1	0	0
	Extras	**(11lb, 12nb)**		**23**			
	TOTAL	**(62.2 overs)**		**247**			

Bowler	O	M	R	W	NB	Wd
Bicknell	**15**	**6**	**37**	**0**	-	-
Ormond	**22**	**3**	**82**	**5**	1	-
Azhar Mahmood	**12**	**1**	**72**	**1**	4	-
Saqlain Mushtaq	**11**	**2**	**42**	**2**	1	-
Salisbury	**2.2**	**1**	**3**	**2**	-	-

Other Frizzell Championship Division One Results

Surrey's win saw them extend their lead at the top of the table, since Warwickshire were held to a draw by Kent at a rather wet Edgbaston. Sussex meanwhile moved up to third by beating Nottinghamshire at Horsham, thanks largely to an inspired performance by Mushtaq Ahmed, who claimed twelve wickets in the match.

May 21-24
***Leicester:-* Leicestershire (7pts) drew with Middlesex (8).** Middlesex 201 (Maddy 5-49) & 142-5dec; Leics 198 (Snape 54, Keegan 5-61, Cook 4-42).
***Horsham:-* Sussex (22pts) beat Nottinghamshire (7) by 10 wickets.** Sussex 619-7dec (Prior 133, Montgomerie 105, Innes 103*, Cottey 58, Ambrose 55) & 52-0; Notts 421 (Pietersen 166, Shafayat 71, Welton 50, Mushtaq 6-163) & 247 (Bicknell 61, Mushtaq 6-81, Kirtley 4-74).
***Edgbaston:-* Warwickshire (10pts) drew with Kent (11).** Warwicks 311 (Troughton 120, Smith 57, Saggers 5-62) & 124-2 (Wagh 50*); Kent 376 (Walker 106, Blewett 71, Carberry 58, Brown 5-72).

FRIZZELL CHAMPIONSHIP DIVISION ONE TABLE AT 24TH MAY

Pos	Prv		P	Points	W	D	L	T	Bat	Bwl	Ded
1	1	Surrey	5	72.00	2	3	0	0	19	13	0.00
2	2	Warwickshire	5	59.75	1	2	1	1	19	12	0.25
3	7	Sussex	4	52.00	2	0	2	0	12	12	0.00
4	4	Middlesex	5	49.00	1	4	0	0	6	13	0.00
5	3	Lancashire	4	46.00	0	4	0	0	18	12	0.00
6	5	Essex	5	41.00	0	3	1	1	8	14	0.00
7	6	Nottinghamshire	4	39.00	1	1	2	0	11	11	1.00
8	9	Kent	4	34.00	0	3	1	0	10	12	0.00
9	8	Leicestershire	4	31.00	0	4	0	0	4	11	0.00

NATIONAL CRICKET LEAGUE DIVISION ONE - MATCH FIVE

Gloucestershire Gladiators versus Surrey Lions at Bristol

Sunday 25th May

The keenly anticipated showdown between the teams generally considered to be the nation's finest at one-day cricket (Gloucestershire) and four-day cricket (Surrey) turned out to be a very damp squib. With heavy rain in the morning being followed by an almighty downpour in mid afternoon, the ground was left absolutely saturated and clearly unfit for play. As everyone headed home early, the ability of weather forecasters was being questioned - the previous evening's forecast had promised that it would be 'dry in the west'.

Other NCL Division One Results

The clouds that had deposited so much rain on Bristol were clearly empty by the time they reached Worcester since spectators at New Road witnessed a full game. Kent probably wished that they'd still contained some rain, however, as they crashed to a 139-run defeat. While the abandonment at Bristol had robbed Surrey of their one-hundred percent record, the Glamorgan Dragons maintained theirs with a comfortable win over Yorkshire Phoenix.

May 25
***Worcester:-* Worcestershire Royals (4pts) beat Kent Spitfires by 139 runs.** Worcs 271-4 (45ov; Hick 108, Smith 51); Kent 132 (31.5ov; Leatherdale 5-36).
***Headingley:-* Glamorgan Dragons (4pts) beat Yorkshire Phoenix by 4 wickets (D/L method).** Yorks 153-7 (32ov); Glamorgan 165-6 (27.1ov; Silverwood 4-45).

NCL DIVISION ONE TABLE AT 25TH MAY

Pos	Prv		P	Pts	W	T	L	A
1	1	Surrey Lions	5	18	4	0	0	1
2	2	Glamorgan Dragons	4	16	4	0	0	0
3	3	Essex Eagles	4	12	3	0	1	0
4	4	Worcestershire Royals	3	8	2	0	1	0
5	5	Gloucestershire Gladiators	4	6	1	0	2	1
6	7	Leicestershire Foxes	4	4	1	0	3	0
=	5	Yorkshire Phoenix	4	4	1	0	3	0
8	7	Kent Spitfires	5	4	1	0	4	0
9	9	Warwickshire Bears	3	0	0	0	3	0

C&G Trophy 4th Round - Surrey Battle Back To Win Taunton Cliffhanger

Somerset v Surrey at Taunton. Played on Wednesday 28th May.
Surrey won by 6 runs

Surrey progressed to the fourth round of the C&G Trophy - where they would face Derbyshire at The County Ground, Derby - by winning a thoroughly exciting and entertaining contest against Somerset at Taunton by the slender margin of six runs.

Having lost the toss and been put in to bat while there was some early life and movement in the pitch, the visitors struggled in the opening stages, losing Ali Brown to Nixon McLean with the total at eight and Mark Butcher to Steffan Jones in the eleventh over with the score only advanced as far as thirty-four.

Mark Ramprakash and Graham Thorpe then steadied the ship with a stand of fifty-two in eleven overs before Ramprakash (32) departed to a good catch at cover by Keith Dutch off the Somerset captain, Mike Burns. With Rikki Clarke falling to Keith Parsons for ten shortly afterwards, Surrey were 107-4 after twenty-seven overs and looking likely to fall well short of the par score for the high-scoring County Ground.

Fortunately for the visitors, Thorpe was looking to be back to his very best, reaching his half-century from 64 balls during a 45-ball fifty partnership with his skipper, Adam Hollioake, who contributed a breezy thirty-three at a run a ball before being trapped lbw by the returning Richard Johnson.

When Azhar Mahmood then fell in identical fashion for nought three balls later, Surrey looked to be very much on the ropes at 169-6 after thirty-seven overs, before salvation came in the form of an unbroken seventh-wicket partnership between Thorpe and Jon Batty that was worth 112 runs, ninety-nine of which came from the last ten overs of the innings.

Thorpe was masterful throughout and reached his century from 102 balls by driving a boundary from the penultimate delivery of the fifty overs, while Batty had picked a brilliant time to score his first-ever limited-overs fifty for Surrey, arriving at the mark from just 44 balls earlier in the final over. McLean was clearly the pick of the Somerset bowlers, returning 10-0-29-1 out of a final total of 281-6, though one had to wonder why Burns hadn't given either of his two spinners, Ian Blackwell and Keith Dutch, a single over, particularly once it became clear that his five seamers were unable to contain the seventh-wicket pair.

With their score looking no better than par for the course, it was clear that Surrey needed to capture early Somerset wickets, especially those of the star men, Jamie Cox and Marcus Trescothick. The visitors were delighted, therefore, when Cox went lbw to James Ormond in the second over, and a second wicket followed five overs later when Martin Bicknell bowled James Bryant for nine to reduce the home side to 25-2.

Trescothick remained, however, though he never looked in any sort of form at all before skying a ball at Azhar high to mid-on with the score at fifty-one in the fourteenth over. The England left-hander's struggle was due in no small way to an outstanding spell of 10-2-23-1 from Bicknell, who bowled right through his stint at the start of the Somerset innings.

With the veteran swing bowler out of the equation, a very useful stand developed between Burns and Parsons, who added ninety-seven in eighteen overs before Burns edged Clarke to Batty with the total standing at 148 in the thirty-third over. Somerset were clearly back on course for victory at this stage, and Blackwell further strengthened the home side's position with two successive slog-sweeps for six off Saqlain at the start of over number thirty-six.

At 217-4 with ten overs to go, the home side looked to be hot favourites to win the match but the Surrey off-spinner put the contest back in the melting pot during his last two overs, first luring Blackwell into mishitting to long-off with the total at 223 in the forty-first over after a 30-ball knock of thirty-nine, then having Parsons very well taken low down by Thorpe at cover.

At this point the lower order still only needed to score fifty-one runs at under 6.5 an over, but the belated entry into the attack of the Surrey skipper and the return of Azhar, ever the expert at the death, produced a level of pressure that the batsmen couldn't cope with. By bowling full and straight and varying his pace skilfully, Hollioake claimed Dutch lbw in his first over, bowled Johnson in his second and then 'castled' McLean in his third, the last two batsmen being guilty of unnecessary slogs across the line when singles and twos would still have sufficed for their team.

As a result of this rather unintelligent approach, the last over arrived with Rob Turner and Steffan Jones needing to score twelve off Azhar to win the match. The wily Pakistani all-rounder kept a cool head, however, yielding just five singles to leave Surrey victorious by six runs.

Scores:- Surrey 281-6 (50ov; Thorpe 102*, Batty 55*) beat Somerset 275-9 (50ov; Parsons 83, Burns 47, Hollioake 3-19) by 6 runs.

AZHAR SHINES AT TRENT BRIDGE

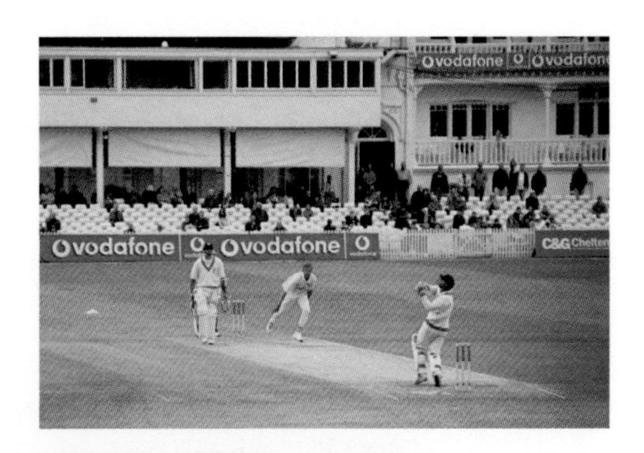

TOP: Azhar Mahmood's excellent innings of ninety-eight is about to end following this miscued pull
MIDDLE: Paul Franks is snapped up by Ali Brown at first slip off Azhar
BOTTOM: A.J. Harris is adjudged lbw to Azhar as Surrey move closer to victory
(All photos by Reg Elliott)

53-YEAR CHELMSFORD DROUGHT ENDS

TOP: Paul Grayson is brilliantly taken down the legside by Jon Batty off James Ormond in Essex's second innings
MIDDLE: Aftab Habib edges a fine Ormond lifter through to Batty
BOTTOM: James Middlebrook is bowled by Ian Salisbury, leaving Essex one wicket from defeat
(All photos by Reg Elliott)

SUSSEX SUCCUMB AT THE OVAL

TOP: Adam Hollioake drives Michael Yardy away wide of mid-on
MIDDLE: Matt Prior is bowled by Saqlain Mushtaq during Sussex's first innings
BOTTOM: Jon Batty launches Mushtaq Ahmed down the ground for four
(All photos by Reg Elliott)

KENT'S RUN CHASE FALLS FLAT

TOP: Dave Fulton loses his off stump to James Ormond as Kent set out to chase 301 in ninety overs at The Oval
MIDDLE: Mark Butcher snaps up a good catch to dismiss Mark Ealham off Saqlain
BOTTOM: Rob Ferley falls lbw to Saqlain as Surrey close in on their unexpected victory
(All photos by Reg Elliott)

LANDMARK MOMENTS

TOP: Martin Bicknell claims his 950th first-class wicket by trapping Ed Joyce lbw at Lord's
MIDDLE: Mark Ramprakash completes a full set of first-class centuries against all eighteen counties with his hundred in the same match
BOTTOM: Alec Stewart takes his final catch for Surrey - Mark Wagh nicely picked up off Adam Hollioake at Edgbaston
(All photos by Reg Elliott)

JIMMY'S JOY

James Ormond's hat-trick at Guildford
TOP: Ben Hutton is very well caught down the legside by Jon Batty
MIDDLE: Ed Joyce goes lbw next ball
BOTTOM: Ormond and his team-mates rejoice as Paul Weekes is bowled to complete the hat-trick
(All photos by Reg Elliott)

RAMPRAKASH & SURREY ENJOY WHITGIFT WEEK

TOP: Mark Ramprakash drives Stuart MacGill down the ground
MIDDLE: Ramprakash cuts for four during his unbeaten 279
BOTTOM: Chris Cairns is well taken at fourth slip by Adam Hollioake off Azhar Mahmood
(All photos by Reg Elliott)

SURREY C.C.C. SQUAD - 2003 SEASON

BACK ROW (left to right):- Keith Booth (Scorer), Dale Naylor (Physio), Neil Walker (Physio), James Benning, Phil Sampson, James Ormond, Rikki Clarke, Scott Newman, Tim Murtagh, Ben Scott, Keith Medlycott (Cricket Manager), Alan Butcher (Coach)
FRONT ROW (left to right):- Mark Ramprakash, Ian Ward, Alex Tudor, Alistair Brown, Martin Bicknell, Alec Stewart OBE, Adam Hollioake (Captain), Mark Butcher, Graham Thorpe, Ian Salisbury, Nadeem Shahid, Jonathan Batty

7 Can't Win 'Em All

The NCL win at Worcester back at the start of the month might have been something of a rarity but it was nothing compared to the Championship victory at Chelmsford, which was Surrey's first in the premier county competition on that ground for fifty-three years! It should be noted that for many years matches between Surrey and Essex were played at Leyton but it was, nevertheless, a considerable achievement and another bogey that had been laid to rest. Many fine individual performances had contributed to the Chelmsford win, with James Ormond's hostile fourth-innings bowling as significant as any, given that the pitch had dried and flattened out into a very good surface by that stage of the game. It was hard to see many other teams winning there without the aid of a declaration or two, and equally easy to see why many matches in 2002 had ended with a final day run chase. The other impressive feature of the Surrey display was the fielding, with some very good catches being taken and only one extremely difficult chance being missed out of fifteen offered by the Essex batsmen in the game.

As well as extending their lead at the top of the Championship table, the side had come through what was potentially their most difficult NCL fixture of the season unscathed, albeit thanks to the dismal Bristol weather, and had progressed to the quarter-finals of the Cheltenham & Gloucester Trophy by winning at Taunton, where victories in one-day cricket had usually proved elusive for Surrey.

All-in-all there didn't seem to be a cloud on the horizon for a confident and unbeaten team, though two members of the squad would be missing for a while in the not-too-distant future as they had been selected for the Nat West Challenge matches and the Nat West Series. It was fantastic to see Rikki Clarke's talent being recognised and rewarded with an England call-up, while Azhar Mahmood's fine form had deservedly earned him a place in the Pakistan squad for the three-match Challenge series against the home nation. Fortunately, Clarke wouldn't miss a huge number of games outside of the two-week Twenty-20 Cup qualifying period, and it was unlikely that Azhar would be away for long, especially if Pakistan were happy for him to continue getting some competitive cricket with Surrey, rather than take up a place in their eleven during their warm-up matches. Of the players who weren't called up, Alec Stewart had, in effect, announced his retirement from One-Day Internationals at the start of the season by stating that he felt the selectors "should be looking at younger options", while no official reason was given for Saqlain's absence from the Pakistan squad… but Surrey wouldn't be complaining!

A former Surrey overseas favourite, Waqar Younis, had meanwhile signed for Warwickshire for the rest of the season. Everyone at Edgbaston hoped this would bring an end to all the problems and bad luck they had suffered with their overseas registrations for the summer, though this was clearly only a stop-gap signing for the Bears. Although the 31-year-old Waqar was still a fine fast bowler, it seemed highly unlikely that he would be able to perform to a high enough level day-in day-out to propel Warwickshire to County Championship success.

This was clearly good news for the current Championship leaders, whose next match was against Sussex, a team who had produced rather erratic form in the competition so far, having won two and lost two of their four fixtures. Many in the media had predicted that they would be relegated come September, while some even felt they were likely to end up at the bottom of the table. With Mushtaq Ahmed and James Kirtley already spearheading their attack to great effect - having accounted for fifty-three of the seventy-three Championship wickets captured by Sussex so far - and some decent batsmen in their ranks, this press pessimism was looking rather foolish, and a mid-table position certainly didn't seem beyond the south coast county's capabilities. Besides, with two wins to their credit they were already halfway to the generally accepted four wins that had, historically, ensured first division survival since the advent of promotion and relegation in

2000. A good contest was expected at The Oval, too, with Surrey keen to gain a revenge victory over one of the two sides who had beaten them during the 2002 Championship-winning campaign.

That game was to be followed by another meeting with Essex, this time in the NCL at The Oval, and a trip to Derby for the C&G Trophy quarter-final. If Surrey could win all these matches then they would be very well placed as we reached the qualifying stages of the Twenty-20 Cup.

FRIZZELL COUNTY CHAMPIONSHIP DIVISION ONE - MATCH SIX

SURREY versus SUSSEX
at The Oval

First Day - Friday 30th May
Surrey 401-8

The Teams And The Toss **-** *With Alec Stewart and Mark Butcher not allowed to play between the first and second Tests against Zimbabwe, and Ian Ward recovered from his groin strain, Surrey go into the match with the same line-up that had vanquished Essex at Chelmsford. Sussex, meanwhile, make two changes from the side that finished their game at Horsham, with Michael Yardy making his first Championship appearance since July 2002 as deputy for the injured Tony Cottey (back), and Kevin Innes preferred to Mark Davis, the off-spinner. Innes had started the Horsham match as a stand-in for James Kirtley, who was in the England squad for the first Zimbabwe Test, and scored his maiden Championship century on the second day, only to be replaced, under a new ruling, by Kirtley for the rest of the match when the Sussex seamer was released by England. For the first time in the 2003 Championship, Adam Hollioake wins the toss and predictably elects to bat first on a fine looking pitch in beautiful weather.*

There appears to be a little more life in this pitch for the bowlers than would normally be expected on the first day of a game at The Oval, and Sussex's opening bowlers, James Kirtley and Billy Taylor, take full advantage by sending down some testing opening overs that yield just a single boundary, edged wide of a diving third slip by Jon Batty.

The shackles appear to be loosening a little when the Surrey wicketkeeper drives Taylor to the rope at long-on in the sixth over and Ian Ward follows up by taking seven runs from the same bowler's following over, but these strokes actually turn out to mark a watershed in the first hour's proceedings.

In the space of nine balls both openers are dismissed - Ward edges a forcing stroke off Kirtley to second slip, where Tim Ambrose picks up a fine catch low to his left, then Batty nibbles at a lifting delivery from Taylor and is caught in the same position by Chris Adams - and three maiden overs then follow as Mark Ramprakash and Graham Thorpe try to re-establish some control following their side's sudden slump from 22-0 to 22-2.

The Surrey total has actually remained unchanged for thirty-three balls when Thorpe finally pushes Taylor to cover to advance it to twenty-three and then cuts Kirtley away for three, much to the relief of the home crowd.

Sussex then suffer an unfortunate setback when Taylor pulls up with a leg injury as he is about to deliver the third ball of his eighth over and has to limp back to the dressing room after a period of on-field treatment, leaving Robin Martin-Jenkins to complete the over. Perhaps caught out by his team-mate's sudden departure, the Sussex all-rounder finds his third and fourth balls being despatched to the rope at long-on and square leg by Thorpe.

With Kevin Innes simultaneously replacing Kirtley, who has contributed an excellent spell of 8-4-10-1, there are a few loose balls on offer as two new bowlers settle in, and Ramprakash is grateful for this as he breaks his duck after forty-five minutes at the crease by pulling the former Northamptonshire all-rounder for four. Although the Surrey number three continues to look rather out of sorts over the course of the next few overs, he has no need to worry because Thorpe is moving along smoothly at the other end, twice driving Martin-Jenkins gloriously down the ground to raise the Surrey fifty.

As lunch approaches, Adams strives to make a further breakthrough by pairing his deadly duo, Kirtley and Mushtaq Ahmed, who now have fifty-four wickets between them in the 2003 Championship as a result of Kirtley claiming Ward's scalp this morning. Oddly enough, however, this move produces runs rather than wickets as four boundaries come from the final five overs of the session - Thorpe, who has looked especially good off his legs throughout the morning, clips both bowlers away through midwicket; Ramprakash cuts Kirtley to fence at backward point to complete a fifty partnership; then Thorpe takes his side through to the interval with a sublime late cut off Mushtaq. It's been a very tough morning for the Championship leaders but they have come through it well, thanks to a very determined Ramprakash and a very much in-form Thorpe.

Lunch:- Surrey 79-2 (Ramprakash 12, Thorpe 40*) from 32 overs*

The Sussex captain draws another blank when he pairs Kirtley and Mushtaq again after lunch, as Thorpe continues to dominate with the bat, cutting and pulling three fours in completing a beautifully constructed fifty from his 83rd ball, before taking the Surrey total into three figures with another cut off Mushtaq.

As Kirtley completes a fairly ordinary post-lunch spell of five overs, Ramprakash suddenly begins to find his touch and timing, driving both the Pakistani leg-spinner and the new bowler, Martin-Jenkins, through the covers with sublime strokes that suggest Sussex could be in for an afternoon of hard graft in the sun. This belief is then strengthened when the former England batsman takes boundaries from three successive Martin-Jenkins deliveries, with two delicate glides to the rope at third man following an extra-cover drive, struck on the up, that completes a century partnership for the third wicket in fine style.

It is therefore fortunate for Sussex that Mushtaq manages to bring Ramprakash to book before he can do any more damage, luring the batsman into a legside push that results in a leading-edge dolly catch to Michael Yardy at cover with the batsman's score on thirty-seven and the total advanced to 132.

The loss of this wicket has no effect on the scoring rate, however, as both Thorpe and the new batsman, Ali Brown, thump Martin-Jenkins for off-side fours in the next over, while Mushtaq yields swept and cut boundaries to Thorpe in the over after that as the Surrey 150 rattles up at a rate of knots.

At this stage, with Kirtley resting and Taylor seemingly unable to bowl again for the rest of the day at least, the Sussex attack is leaning very heavily on their Pakistani leg-spinner, who manages to beat both batsmen from time to time and looks the only likely source of a wicket for his team. At the other end, Martin-Jenkins has been serving up some pretty plain fare and when he rests after a spell of 6-0-34-0, his replacement, Innes, proves even less impressive as Brown plunders three fours and a straight six from three overs costing twenty-four runs.

This Brown-inspired surge, which has seen the completion of a fifty partnership and raised the Surrey two-hundred, has come at an ideal time, since Thorpe is now tiptoeing through the nineties with a succession of singles. The left-hander is still on ninety-five, in fact, when Brown manages to complete his fifty from just 47 balls by driving Mushtaq over mid-off for the ninth boundary of his typically aggressive innings.

With his side wilting under the weight of Surrey runs on a very warm afternoon, Adams has no alternative but to keep his leg-spinner going for as long as possible at the Vauxhall end, while recalling Kirtley at the pavilion end. The captain's prime pair are unable to prevent Thorpe reaching his century, however, as a push to square cover for a single off Mushtaq takes the Farnham-born batsman through to three figures from his 156th ball and prompts an uncharacteristically animated celebration from the Surrey left-hander.

The crowd's applause has not long died away when Thorpe moves back into boundary-hitting mode, pulling Kirtley wide of mid-on for his nineteenth four to herald the arrival of a century partnership that has taken just seventeen overs, largely thanks to Brown's rapid scoring.

This stand has really put the visitors on the back foot and Adams is, by now, reduced to trying to stem the flow of runs by setting ever deeper fields for his bowlers. This does indeed save some boundaries, though he stumbles across an even better method of containment when he introduces Yardy in place of Mushtaq at the Vauxhall end. The left-arm seamer gives up just a single from his two overs before circumstances change with the capture of Brown's wicket by Kirtley at the other end in the penultimate over of the session.

The total has sailed past 250 as a result of the England one-day international bowler conceding three fours in quick succession, but he strikes back by having Brown dropped and then caught from successive deliveries. With the batsman's score on seventy-four, a mortified Montgomerie spills a straightforward slip catch from an edged drive, though he is immediately reprieved and relieved when Brown attempts to force the next ball away to the boundary and sees Murray Goodwin pull off a fine catch diving away to his left at backward point.

Having secured this wicket, Adams sensibly puts Yardy's spell on hold in order to give Mushtaq the final over of the session in the hope that he might make a further breakthrough with a new batsman, Adam Hollioake, at the crease. The vastly experienced Thorpe is wise to this, though, and sensibly blocks out all six balls to save his skipper from having to face the leg-spinner before the break.

Tea:- Surrey 263-4 (Thorpe 121, Hollioake 0*) from 72 overs*

Adams reverts to his support seamers, Innes and Martin-Jenkins, after the break and Surrey take full advantage of another loose spell from the former Northamptonshire player to push the score on at a very healthy rate. Innes only delivers three overs, during which he is battered to the boundary on no fewer than five occasions, before he is predictably replaced by the hard-working Mushtaq.

To accommodate the leg-spinner at the Vauxhall end, Martin-Jenkins is switched to the pavilion end and continues a good post-tea spell, while Mushtaq finds Hollioake almost as hard to bowl to as Innes had before him. Having swept the Pakistani to the midwicket fence for four to take his team's total up to three-hundred in the seventy-eighth over, the Surrey skipper then increases the value of his partnership with Thorpe to fifty-three by driving high and wide of long-on for six shortly afterwards.

Pressed even further back on the defensive, the Sussex captain elects to give Yardy another chance in place of Martin-Jenkins, and, in partnership with Mushtaq, the left-armer again brings some order to the proceedings, with the batsmen reduced to picking up singles for half-a-dozen overs until Hollioake breaks loose with drives to the rope at extra cover and long-on off the leg-spinner that see him through to his personal half-century from just 49 balls. Thorpe then clips Yardy to deep square leg in the next over to secure the single he needs to reach the 150 mark from his 264th ball, while the Surrey 350 clicks up on the scoreboard just a few balls later to complete a landmark treble.

The fifth-wicket partnership is close to giving the scorers yet another milestone to record at this point, but the men with the pencils and laptops are spared a chore when Mushtaq brings the stand to a close four runs short of the hundred mark by capturing the wicket of Thorpe. Having swept a full-toss to the boundary earlier in the Pakistani's thirtieth over, the Surrey left-hander attempts to add another four to his impressive tally of twenty-six by backing away to leg in order to cut through the off side but, unfortunately, finds the ball bouncing higher than expected and only succeeds in top-edging a gentle catch to the Sussex captain at short third man.

With 156 runs to his name after a quite brilliant innings, Thorpe leaves the field to a rousing reception from a crowd estimated in the region of 2,500, most of whom will have thoroughly enjoyed the home side's batting on a very warm and pleasant day. The former, and maybe future, England batsman seems to have put his side firmly in control of the game at 359-5, though the visitors will probably feel they still have a chance if they can snap up further wickets before the close… and they make a good start towards doing that when Kirtley makes an instant return to the attack and dismisses Azhar Mahmood for a fourth-ball duck. For the third time in the innings, Adams is the catcher, this time at second slip, as the Pakistani all-rounder fences at a lifting delivery with his bat away from his body.

With three more overs from Sussex's dream team of Mushtaq and Kirtley yielding no further wickets but three boundaries, two of them to the new batsman, Martin Bicknell, the visiting skipper makes another good decision by taking the new ball, even though only six overs remain for play.

After handing the ball to Martin-Jenkins, Adams sees his move paying dividends almost immediately when Bicknell plays on to the new bowler's fourth delivery with the score at 379, then the tall all-rounder captures an eighth Surrey wicket with the first ball of his next over. Hollioake has just enjoyed a reprieve, surviving a very sharp caught-and-bowled chance to Kirtley after picking off successive boundaries earlier in the same over, but, like Brown before him, he fails to take advantage of his good fortune, falling lbw when hit on the back pad as he aims to leg. The score is 394-8 as Hollioake departs for a typically entertaining seventy-seven and it is left to the Surrey spin twins to shepherd their side past the four-hundred mark in the closing over of an excellent day's cricket.

Close:- Surrey 401-8 (Salisbury 10, Saqlain 2*) from 104 overs*

Second Day - Saturday 31st May
Surrey 480 and 22-0; Sussex 307

With a ball that is only six overs old at his disposal, and Billy Taylor very unlikely to bowl again in the match because of his thigh strain, it is no great surprise that Chris Adams should pair James Kirtley and Robin Martin-Jenkins at the start of day two. Neither bowler looks especially threatening, however, as the overnight pair of Salisbury and Saqlain make a relatively quiet start. Although the Surrey off-spinner does manage to strike Kirtley for a couple of off-side boundaries, it is the more economical Martin-Jenkins who makes way for Mushtaq Ahmed after seven overs of play.

Saqlain and Salisbury versus Mushtaq is an interesting confrontation and it is fascinating to note that the Surrey pair constantly attempt to sweep the Pakistani leg-spinner, presumably in an attempt to unsettle him and disrupt his length. Kirtley meanwhile concedes two boundaries square on the off side to Salisbury and, though he does induce an outside edge from Saqlain which Prior can't quite take low down in front of first slip, a largely unimpressive seven-over spell, costing thirty-two runs, ends with the Surrey off-spinner advancing down the track and driving him straight for six to take the total past 450.

The ninth-wicket partnership, which is now worth fifty-nine and proving immensely irritating for the visitors, then extends further in Mushtaq's next over when the Pakistani's fellow leg-spinner drives him over mid-on for four and then pulls out a slog-sweep that sends the ball soaring away over the midwicket boundary for six. With Saqlain then producing a stroke of his own invention that sees the ball disappearing back over the head of Martin-Jenkins, the new bowler at the pavilion end, it appears that Sussex might be looking at a Surrey total in excess of five-hundred, but, just two balls later, the batsman attempts to repeat his newly developed swat-slog and skies a catch that Richard Montgomerie takes comfortably behind the bowler after running round from deep mid-on.

A score of 469-9 at the fall of Saqlain then becomes 480 all out as Salisbury picks off another couple of fours to advance his score to forty-five before top-edging a cut at Mushtaq and being smartly taken, high to his right-hand side, by Tim Ambrose at slip.

Requiring 331 to avoid the follow on, Sussex are left facing an awkward hour before lunch, and any hopes of coming through this period with all wickets intact are soon dashed by the loss of a wicket in each of James Ormond's first two overs. The Surrey paceman's third delivery brings him the wicket of Montgomerie, who attempts to follow a pulled four with a repeat of the stroke to a faster, fuller ball and unsurprisingly miscues high to Ian Ward at cover, then the left-handed Michael Yardy steers a well-directed delivery tamely to Thorpe at third slip in the bowler's next over and departs for a sixth-ball duck.

With the visitors in turmoil at 13-2, Surrey are ecstatic, though their joy is tempered moments later when Martin Bicknell appears to sustain a leg injury while delivering the fourth ball of his third over and promptly leaves the field after the final delivery.

Incredibly enough, this ends up working, temporarily at least, in the home side's favour since Azhar Mahmood, Bicknell's replacement at the Vauxhall end, picks up the wicket of Chris Adams with his tenth ball.

Having made a very shaky five, courtesy of inside-edges to fine leg, for four and one, off the hostile Ormond, the Sussex captain attempts to locate the middle of his bat with a pull at a short delivery from Azhar but mistimes the stroke horribly, skying the ball high behind the wicket. Jon Batty is required to take just a few steps forward to pouch the catch that reduces Sussex to a sorry 24-3.

Lunch can't come soon enough for the visitors now, though Murray Goodwin and Tim Ambrose manage to find the boundary on three occasions with fine strokes as they repel some more aggressive bowling from Ormond and Azhar and take the total up to forty-six at the interval.

An excellent morning for the home side is only blighted by the reappearance of a limping Bicknell for the last five overs of the session. It remains to be seen whether he will be able to bowl again after lunch.

Lunch:- Sussex 46-3 (Goodwin 21, Ambrose 9*) from 14 overs*

Goodwin looks in sensational form after lunch as a barrage of eight boundaries in seven overs from Ormond and Azhar gives the visitors a welcome fillip. Both Surrey pacemen suffer the indignity of being hit for three fours in an over by the former Zimbabwe batsman as a wide variety of drives, mixed with a pull, a deflection and an edge, bring up three different fifties - first the Sussex total, then the fourth-wicket partnership and, last but not least, Goodwin's personal landmark from 58 balls.

With forty-six runs having haemorrhaged from the forty-two deliveries bowled by the seamers, and Bicknell showing no sign of being able to turn his arm over despite being on the field, the Surrey captain introduces his spinners and enjoys almost immediate success as Saqlain removes Goodwin with his sixth delivery. Having just cut the Pakistani off-spinner for four, the Sussex opener goes onto the back foot again, only to be beaten and bowled through the gate by a big off-break with his score on sixty and the total two shy of the hundred mark.

This wicket brings Robin Martin-Jenkins to the crease and the tall all-rounder makes a very mixed start to his innings. While he looks relatively comfortable against Saqlain as he forces and whips deliveries away to the boundary, he seems totally at sea when faced by Salisbury's leg-spin, edging a drive wide of slip for four and then shouldering arms to a googly, prompting a confident lbw appeal that fails to convince umpire Allan Jones.

Eventually, however, he begins to come to terms with Salisbury as well as Saqlain, taking boundaries through wide mid-on and backward point from the leg-spinner's fifth over as the visitors start to fight back under the warm afternoon sun.

Meanwhile, at the other end, Ambrose, like his partner, has had a couple of edgy moments against the Surrey spin duo, yet he stays nicely composed as he gathers his runs largely in singles before finally breaking out with a square-cut boundary off Salisbury that completes a fifty stand for the fifth wicket.

Despite troubling the batsmen every now and again, the spinners are never really allowed to settle into a rhythm for any length of time and Hollioake acknowledges this by pulling Salisbury out of the attack after seven rather inconsistent overs and recalling Azhar to the bowling crease.

The increasingly confident Martin-Jenkins responds to this change by immediately pulling the Pakistani all-rounder to the midwicket fence, and then collects two further legside boundaries off Saqlain a few overs later to complete a very valuable 58-ball half-century for his side. The last of these fours has quite a dramatic effect on proceedings, in fact, since it sees off not just one, but two, Surrey bowlers - Saqlain is withdrawn from the attack, while Bicknell pulls up in obvious discomfort during his pursuit of the ball and finally admits that his injury has beaten him by leaving the field.

With his options fast receding, Hollioake now brings himself on to bowl and, in partnership with Azhar, sparks off a fascinating period of play where both bowlers strive to make things happen and the batsmen show that they are prepared to take up the challenge.

Although this passage of action doesn't start especially well for Surrey when Hollioake yields a pulled boundary to Martin-Jenkins in an opening over that also includes four leg-byes, a wide and an outside edge to third man, things improve for the home team in the next over when Azhar provides his side with the breakthrough they have been seeking. With his score on sixty-one and the total standing at 189, Martin-Jenkins becomes the fifth man to be dismissed in the Sussex innings, falling lbw to an inswinging delivery which, from the boundary, looks as if it might be doing too much. The man that matters, umpire Roy Palmer, has his finger aloft, however, and Surrey are happy to accept his decision even if the departing batsman looks far from convinced.

Sensing a chance to break through into the visitors' tail, Hollioake now steps up the pressure, sending down a mixture of bouncers and reverse-swinging yorkers that trouble both Ambrose and his new partner, Matt Prior. Miscued hooks and thick edges suddenly become quite commonplace as the total reaches two-hundred, though there is no doubting the quality of the on-driven four off Azhar that takes Ambrose through to a gritty fifty from his 109th ball.

Hard though they try, the Hollioake-Azhar combination fails to find a second breakthrough for the Championship leaders, so, with tea almost upon us, the Surrey captain reverts to spin and hits the jackpot again as Saqlain strikes with his third ball. Having never settled at all during ten overs at the crease, Prior is the man to depart when a beautifully flighted off-break spins wickedly through his defences in the session's penultimate over with the total advanced to 217.

Sussex are back in deep water again as the players leave the field for tea shortly afterwards with the admirable Ambrose undefeated on sixty.

Tea:- Sussex 218-6 (Ambrose 60, Innes 1*) from 54 overs*

Maintaining his all-spin attack after the break, Hollioake soon finds his decision vindicated when Kevin Innes is defeated on the sweep and bowled behind his legs by Salisbury's second delivery with just two runs added to the Sussex total.

This brings Mushtaq Ahmed to the crease and he immediately indicates that he will be looking to get after the spinners by cutting and sweeping his first two balls from his fellow 'leggie' for four. In fact, he adopts the same tactics that the Surrey spin twins had used against him, employing the sweep shot as often as possible to pick up numerous singles and the occasional four, though the stroke with which he takes Sussex through the 250 barrier is a flowing cover drive off Saqlain.

At the other end, Ambrose gets on quietly and efficiently with the business of pushing his side closer to the 331 they need to avoid the follow-on, eschewing the sweep in favour of cuts, pulls and drives. One such cut to the rope at backward point sees off Salisbury, whose four post-tea overs have cost twenty-seven runs, while lovely use of the feet allows him to on-drive Saqlain for the boundary that brings up the fifty partnership for the eighth wicket.

With Surrey in need of another breakthrough, Hollioake's recall of Ormond in place of Salisbury appears sensible, though the big paceman struggles with his line in his first over as Mushtaq picks up three twos on the legside. His second over is much better, however, and the penultimate ball brings him the vital wicket of Ambrose, whose surprisingly loose forcing stroke picks out Mark Ramprakash at gully with his team still fifty-two runs short of averting the possibility of being made to bat again. The young Anglo-Aussie gets a good hand from the crowd for his mature innings of seventy-five, though the home fans are probably hoping that his departure will lead to the rapid folding of the visitors' tail.

Mushtaq certainly doesn't last long, becoming Ormond's fourth victim of the innings in the former Leicestershire fast bowler's next over when adjudged lbw for forty-one to a delivery that perhaps fails to bounce as high as expected, and as the hobbling Billy Taylor, accompanied by Murray Goodwin as his runner, makes his way to the middle to join James Kirtley, Surrey now look likely to earn themselves the option of enforcing the follow-on.

With Sussex still forty-nine runs short of the required mark at this point, Kirtley does his best to reduce the gap between the two sides as he slices, edges and upper-cuts fours off Ormond to earn his side another batting point at three-hundred, though his gallant effort is brought to an end by a good piece of fielding by the Surrey skipper two overs later. When Taylor pushes the first delivery of Ormond's over towards mid-off, Kirtley, looking to steal the strike, backs up too far and is unable to regain his ground as Hollioake picks the ball up cleanly and throws down the stumps at the non-striker's end.

As the players leave the field with ten overs left for play and Surrey having established a first-innings lead of 173 the feeling is that the hosts won't ask their opponents to follow on. Since the weather is apparently set fair for the rest of the match and the bowlers are tired after a very hot day in the field, it doesn't seem unreasonable to suggest that Surrey will bat again, especially if they think that a day's rest and treatment might allow Bicknell to play a part on the final day of the game. And that is what Hollioake, never a big fan of enforcing the follow-on, decides to do.

Ian Ward and Jon Batty are therefore left with a tricky period to survive until the close, but they manage to do so without any real alarms, repelling five overs from Kirtley, four from Martin-Jenkins and one from Mushtaq Ahmed.

Close:- Surrey 22-0 (Ward 16, Batty 6*) from 10 overs*

Third Day - Sunday 1st June
Surrey 480 and 233-3dec; Sussex 307 and 12-0

Tight bowling by James Kirtley and Robin Martin-Jenkins in the opening half-an-hour sees day three getting off to a very slow start, with just thirteen runs coming from the first seven overs. Nobody expects this to last for long, however, since the reigning champions have a match to win.

After such a slow start it seems almost inevitable that the first boundary of the day, driven wide of mid-on by Ian Ward off Kirtley, should be followed by another from the next ball, this time courtesy of a square cut, and when Jon Batty follows his partner's lead by taking two fours off Martin-Jenkins the fifty finally arrives in the twenty-first over. When three further boundaries flow from the Surrey openers' bats in the next two overs, Chris Adams decides, sensibly enough, that his opening bowlers now need a break, so he turns to Kevin Innes at the pavilion end and Mushtaq Ahmed at the Vauxhall end.

Nothing much has changed since the first innings for poor Innes, however, and he again receives rough treatment as Ward, having completed an 81-ball fifty in the previous over, repeats the 'two fours' routine in successive overs from the former Northants man - after pulling two fours in Innes' third over, the left-handed opener reels off a pair of extra-cover drives in the suffering bowler's next over to bring up the Surrey hundred just nine overs after the arrival of the fifty.

Even though the batsmen have been tucking into him, Innes is given another couple of overs, during which Batty cuts twice to the rope at backward point, before Adams decides to spare him further punishment by replacing him with Michael Yardy, though the left-armer also feels the lash of the Batty blade as he is pulled for four almost immediately. Mushtaq, too, finds the going tough as the Surrey keeper continues to move through the gears by lofting the leg-spinner down the ground for a one-bounce four and then slog-sweeping him for six over midwicket to complete his half-century from his 99th ball. 'Mushy' soon takes revenge, however, when the batsman lays back to cut and chops an undetected googly down onto his stumps after advancing his score to fifty-six, though Surrey are already leading by over three-hundred runs at this point.

Having made the breakthrough, Adams reunites Kirtley with Mushtaq, but the new batsman, Mark Ramprakash, soon locates the boundary with a couple of fine strokes after starting his innings with a thick-edged three off his first ball from Mushtaq, while Ward moves into the nineties just before the interval with a slog-sweep for four at the little leg-spinner's expense.

Lunch:- Surrey 165-1 (Ward 93, Ramprakash 16*) from 45 overs*

With the home side ideally placed for a rapid push towards a declaration later in the day it is rather surprising to see Innes back in the attack straight after lunch, though he causes Ward a couple of anxious moments in his first over as the Surrey opener closes in on his century - it's a gloved hook to fine leg that takes Ward on to ninety-six, and he is then forced to dig out a good yorker to progress from ninety-eight to ninety-nine.

Martin-Jenkins presents no such difficulties at the other end, however, as a glorious cover-driven boundary from the tall all-rounder's first ball of the session takes Ward into three figures from his 137th delivery. An immaculate straight drive from the next ball then celebrates the landmark in fine style, with the crowd's applause for a well constructed innings having barely died away.

Thereafter, with very defensive fields in place, runs are harder to come by, and Innes is rewarded for producing his best spell of the match when Ramprakash gets a thin top-edge to an attempted pull and is taken at the wicket by Prior with the total at 192 and Surrey leading by 365.

The biggest threat to the hosts' progress now appears to come from the weather, as rainclouds gather around the ground, though the umpires are guilty of a ludicrous over-reaction when they decide to suspend play, shortly after Ramprakash's dismissal, because of a light drizzle - so light, in fact, that some spectators are left thinking that maybe Surrey have declared as the players leave the field.

Three overs are lost as a result of this ludicrous decision, before the umpires reappear, rather sheepishly, to get the action under way again. Only fourteen deliveries are possible, however, before heavier rain brings play to a halt for a second time with Ward having just taken the total past two-hundred courtesy of a pulled boundary off Martin-Jenkins.

Seven further overs are lopped off the day's allocation before play resumes at 3.13pm with Surrey now clearly in a hurry to reach the point where their captain can declare. Ward signals his intentions by cutting Martin-Jenkins for four, then he plays six-and-out with Innes, hooking one short delivery high over deep backward square leg before finding the safe hands of Murray Goodwin on the boundary at deep midwicket from the next ball.

As Ward returns to the pavilion with 135 runs to his name, Surrey lead by 392 and there is just enough time for that to be extended beyond four-hundred, thanks to Graham Thorpe's assault on Martin-Jenkins which brings him three fours in an over, before light rain returns again, allowing the umpires to take the players off for an early tea.

Tea:- Surrey 233-3 (Thorpe 18, Brown 1*) from 60 overs*

A fairly heavy shower during the interval brings further frustration for Surrey - as well as more cursing of weather forecasters - and the loss of twenty-nine more overs before conditions are playable again at 5.50pm. With so much time lost, Hollioake has declared the Surrey innings closed, leaving Sussex requiring 407 to win from a minimum of 109 overs, thirteen to be bowled tonight and ninety-six tomorrow.

Only twenty-three deliveries are possible, though, before the light closes in sufficiently for umpires Jones and Palmer to consult and then offer the batsmen the chance to retreat to the pavilion. Needless to say, they accept, leaving their hosts to try to pick up ten wickets tomorrow.

Statistical footnote - Sussex didn't concede a single extra in Surrey's second innings... then James Ormond delivered two wides in the opening over of Sussex's second knock.

Close:- Sussex 12-0 (Goodwin 10, Montgomerie 0*) from 3.5 overs*

Fourth Day - Monday 2nd June

Surrey 480 and 233-3dec; Sussex 307 and 293
Surrey won by 113 runs
Surrey 22pts, Sussex 6

After a couple of quiet opening overs on a cool and cloudy morning, the Sussex openers burst into life with a flurry of strokes at the expense of James Ormond and Azhar Mahmood, Surrey's opening bowlers. This sudden spurt starts when Murray Goodwin pulls the final ball of Ormond's second over to the long leg boundary, and continues with Richard Montgomerie taking 4-4-3 from the opening three deliveries of the next over from Azhar, courtesy of a clip to midwicket, a steer to third man and an on-drive. The sequence becomes even more expensive for the Pakistani when Goodwin then adds four from the following ball, but this time Azhar is unlucky as the batsman has profited from an inside edge past his off stump and the diving Jon Batty.

With Sussex having gathered nineteen runs from five consecutive deliveries, the more optimistic of their fans in a fairly small crowd might now be harbouring dreams of a stirring victory, but, after Goodwin adds another boundary to his side's collection with a forcing stroke through backward point from the second ball of the Pakistani's next over, the picture changes with Azhar's revenge. The Surrey all-rounder's following delivery tempts the former Zimbabwe batsman into pulling a ball which isn't quite short enough for the stroke, with the end result being a bottom edge into the stumps. Goodwin is out for twenty-six, the visitors are 45-1, and the Championship leaders have the first of the ten wickets they need to take today if they are to win the match.

The 22-year-old left-hander, Michael Yardy, is the new batsman and he starts confidently enough with a couple of pleasant drives for three off Ormond as the Surrey seamers continue to strive, without any joy, for further successes. Hollioake allows them eight overs apiece before he turns to his spinners - Ian Salisbury at the pavilion end and Saqlain Mushtaq at the Vauxhall end - and things start to happen.

While the spin twins are warming up, Yardy takes advantage of a Salisbury long-hop and Montgomerie punishes a Saqlain half-volley, but ball begins to dominate bat from the moment that the Sussex opener is brilliantly caught at short leg off the Pakistani off-spinner with the total on eighty-three. Having turned the ball firmly to leg, Montgomerie is stunned to see Nadeem Shahid - substituting for hamstring victim Martin Bicknell - diving low to his left to pick up a fabulous one-handed reflex catch.

With the second breakthrough secured, Saqlain is now buzzing, and he follows up with a wicket in each of his next two overs to send Sussex into a spin at 85-4. Chris Adams is his second victim, completing a miserable match with the bat when he makes room to cut and is bowled for a duck by the off-spinner's quicker ball as it scuttles through lower than expected; then Tim Ambrose departs with just a single to his name when he is bowled behind his legs by a fizzing off-break cleverly delivered from wide out on the crease.

Robin Martin-Jenkins reacts to this desperate situation by unleashing a drive to the cover boundary before the over is out, though he is rather lucky not to become Saqlain's fourth victim in four overs when he dances down the track and misses a drive at the off-spinner shortly afterwards, without having added to his score. With the ball squeezing between bat and pad, and maybe even clipping one or the other on the way through, Batty is unable to gather the ball cleanly and effect the stumping.

Incredibly enough, another very difficult chance is then spurned in the Pakistani's next over when Yardy, on twenty-nine, edges a drive at head height to Graham Thorpe at slip and profits by a single when the fielder is unable to hang on to the ball as it flies towards him at speed. The spinners, bowling well as a team, are rampant, and the batsmen are struggling for survival.

An extremely testing morning for the visitors finally comes to a close with another anxious moment shortly after Yardy's escape when Martin-Jenkins is probably only saved by the length of his forward stride as he pads up to a Salisbury googly, just as he had in the first innings.

With the Surrey spin twins having given the batsmen a torrid time since their introduction, it looks like the remaining Sussex batsmen are going to have to bat extremely well if they are to save this match.

Lunch:- Sussex 108-4 (Yardy 30, Martin-Jenkins 14*) from 37 overs*

Adam Hollioake opts to switch to a combination of spin and pace after lunch, as Ormond replaces Salisbury at the pavilion end to link up with Saqlain, whose devastating burst of three wickets for no runs in thirteen balls before lunch would appear to have set Surrey up to push on to victory sometime this afternoon.

Yardy and Martin-Jenkins are clearly not going to give up without a fight, however, though each man adopts a different method to keep the bowlers at bay. While Yardy digs in doggedly, offering a broad defensive bat to anything and everything that he faces, Martin-Jenkins always looks to be positive and isn't afraid to play his shots. Although he does enjoy a couple of lucky moments - when he Chinese-cuts Saqlain to fine leg and then miscues a hook off Ormond just short of Mark Ramprakash at deep square leg - there are a great many more middled strokes to admire from Martin-Jenkins as he plunders boundaries from both bowlers in raising both the fifty partnership for the fifth wicket and the Sussex 150. A pulled four off Ormond in the last over of the paceman's post-lunch spell eventually takes him through to a fine 63-ball half-century and he then greets the replacement bowler, Azhar, with a volley of high-class shots - a straight drive, a hook and a pull - that all rattle the boundary boards in an over costing fourteen.

Runs, of course, are largely irrelevant, since Sussex have no chance at this stage of reaching their target, but overs are being steadily eaten up and, in an attempt to break the stubborn alliance formed by Yardy and Martin-Jenkins, Hollioake turns back to Salisbury in place of Saqlain.

Although the fifth-wicket partnership reaches the century mark when the Surrey leg-spinner is immediately pulled to the rope at midwicket by Martin-Jenkins, the breakthrough that the hosts are seeking with increasing urgency almost comes in Salisbury's next over when the tall all-rounder gets a leading edge while playing to leg and sees the ball lobbing safely over the head of the Surrey skipper at extra cover. Another false stroke, this time a miscued straight drive, by the same batsman off the same bowler, then brings further frustration for the Championship leaders before Martin-Jenkins is finally undone in the following over from Azhar.

The first ball of the over sees something of a mix up between the two batsmen that almost brings about the run out of Yardy at the non-striker's end - Shahid's throw just missing the stumps as the batsman dives for the crease - and it seems possible that this disturbs Martin-Jenkins' concentration sufficiently to render him powerless to keep out a brilliant next delivery from Azhar. It's a superb inswinging yorker that finally brings the breakthrough for Surrey, simultaneously shattering the batsman's stumps and his hopes of a century. The Sussex all-rounder's excellent eighty-eight from 93 balls has included fourteen fours and earns him a good round of applause as he returns to the dressing room with his side now 198-5 and needing to bat for another forty-two overs to secure the draw.

Since Matt Prior is now arriving at the wicket, Hollioake allows Salisbury just one more over before sensibly opting to confront the visitors' wicketkeeper with Saqlain, the bowler who had troubled him, and eventually bowled him, in the first innings. Tea is not that far away at this point, so Surrey are clearly keen to get at least one more wicket in the bag before the interval. They think they might have got it, too, in Saqlain's second over when Yardy pushes very firmly at a ball from the off-spinner and Shahid claims a catch at short leg. The bowler, the catcher and some of the other close fielders seem convinced that it is out, but Yardy is unmoved and unimpressed and so, most importantly, is umpire Jones. The situation clearly gets very heated for a while, with batsman and fielders exchanging words, but, given that there is clear doubt as to whether or not the ball has been jammed into the ground and then caught as it has bounced up again, the correct decision appears to have been made.

As if we haven't already had enough drama for one afternoon, Prior then makes some of his own in the next over by turning blind for a second run that Yardy has no intention of taking on. Realising, belatedly, that his partner hasn't budged from the crease, Prior has to apply the brakes and scramble back to the striker's end as Saqlain returns the ball to Batty. Neither the throw nor the Surrey keeper's gather are good enough, however, allowing Prior to regain his ground.

The Sussex wicketkeeper fails to profit from his good fortune, though, as Azhar earns further reward for an outstandingly hostile and hard-working afternoon spell of eight overs with tea imminent. Taking on a short ball from the Pakistani all-rounder, Prior doesn't quite middle his hook shot and pays the price as Ramprakash runs in from the boundary at deep backward square leg and dives forward to take an excellent catch just inches from the turf.

There has been some brilliantly competitive cricket played in the last forty-five minutes of the session and, as the players leave the field a few minutes after Prior's dismissal for fourteen, Surrey know that they need to secure four more wickets in thirty-three overs after the break to seal victory. If they are to achieve their objective they will probably need to find a way of removing the obdurate Yardy, who has stuck to his task brilliantly, even though he has added just seventeen runs to his score in batting through the entire afternoon session.

Tea:- Sussex 220-6 (Yardy 47, Innes 1*) from 67 overs*

Azhar and Saqlain are paired again upon the resumption, and the off-spinner provides his team with a quick breakthrough when he snares Kevin Innes with a nicely flighted delivery in the fourth over of the session. In attempting to drive what appears to be the wrong 'un, the Sussex all-rounder gets an edge onto his pad and the ball loops up gently to Azhar at second slip to leave the visitors seven down with twenty-nine overs left for play.

The catcher then produces a superb over during which he has no luck at all. It starts with Yardy being beaten twice as he attempts to drive, then, after the sturdy left-hander takes a single to put James Kirtley on strike, the new batsman first edges to third man for four and is then caught at third slip by Hollioake off a no-ball.

Having already delivered eighteen overs today, this represents a great effort by the Pakistani international and it is not too surprising when he gives way to Salisbury after one further over from the pavilion end. Yardy, having just completed a painstaking yet immensely valuable half-century from an incredible 180 balls by glancing Saqlain to the fine-leg boundary, immediately takes advantage of the Surrey leg-spinner's second-ball long-hop to pick up only the sixth boundary of his lengthy vigil, though runs dry up almost completely for some while after this as the eighth-wicket pair eschew all risks and Yardy reverts to blocking mode.

The spinners have sent down four successive maidens, in fact, when Kirtley's ultra defensive approach brings about his downfall as a Salisbury googly bounces up from pad onto glove and provides Shahid with the opportunity to demonstrate his prowess at short leg. The former Essex man pulls off a fine catch as he dives forward to grab the ball just inches from the turf, bringing Kirtley's 33 deliveries of defiance to a close and leaving Sussex in danger of defeat at 242-8.

The decision to promote the outgoing batsman above the incoming Mushtaq Ahmed in the batting order had presumably been made on the basis of Kirtley being more likely to get his head down and defend, yet, as we have just seen, this approach has allowed the spinners to settle into a rhythm and dictate terms with their close fielders clustered around the bat.

It therefore seems unlikely that Mushtaq will play in anything but a positive manner, and so it proves as he pulls his first ball from Salisbury to the rope at midwicket before following up with two further fours in quick succession, the first being swept off his fellow 'leggie' and the second coming from a cut off Saqlain. This last stroke seemingly causes some offence to the Surrey off-spinner since he immediately sends down a bouncer that Mushtaq pulls away to midwicket for two. It is clearly not going to help the home side if 'Mushy' is able to upset their spinners in this way and, as the umpires signal the commencement of the final hour, the pressure to capture Sussex's last two wickets is growing.

As the overs click down one by one, the spinners continue to wheel away, Yardy continues to block and Mushtaq continues to crack any loose offerings from Salisbury to the boundary… but there is no real sign of a wicket.

So, with six of the final sixteen overs completed, and a new ball available to him, Hollioake makes his move… though it is simply to recall Ormond in place of Salisbury, as opposed to switching the ball.

The reintroduction of some pace into the attack causes Mushtaq to play a little more circumspectly, though he does still manage to glance the Surrey seamer to the boundary in the ninth over of the final hour to complete a half-century partnership with Yardy for the ninth wicket.

This vital stand is looking likely to deny the Championship leaders a first home victory in the 2002 competition until Saqlain finally brings thirteen overs of brave resistance to a close in the following over when Mushtaq hits across the line of a faster full-length delivery and is struck on the pads in front of the stumps. Umpire Jones' upraised index finger completes the off-spinner's five-wicket haul and, more importantly, leaves Surrey with thirty-seven deliveries in which to take the last Sussex wicket.

Amidst mounting tension, Saqlain's final ball of the last hour's tenth over is successfully repelled by Billy Taylor, but it takes Ormond just four more deliveries to seal Surrey's victory with a good outswinger that Yardy can only edge low to the left of Azhar at second slip. As soon as everyone sees that the Pakistani has pouched the ball safely, the home team's celebrations begin, both on the pitch and around the ground. The Surrey players form into a joyous huddle, providing a stark contrast to the disconsolate Yardy, who has come so near to denying the reigning champions their victory.

The young left-hander is given plenty of sympathetic applause as he wanders from the field after eighty-six overs of defiant concentration, though the warmest and loudest greeting is obviously reserved for the home team, and in particular Saqlain, whose five-wicket haul is the twenty-ninth of his Surrey career.

Surrey 480 and 233-3dec; Sussex 307 and 293
Surrey won by 113 runs. Surrey 22pts, Sussex 6

TALKING POINTS - ADAM HOLLIOAKE

What was your view of the highly controversial 'catch' given by Michael Yardy to Nadeem Shahid off Saqlain? Did you think it was a clean catch or a bumped ball or what?
AH - I wasn't sure, actually - I didn't know what had happened. Fifty per cent of our side thought it was out and fifty percent thought it wasn't, but I admit that we did use it as an opportunity to unsettle him a bit. But he played well and held it together, and it was particularly sweet to get him out at the end and win the match.

Yardy's innings has to be one of the most dogged and determined I've seen in a long time - an admirable effort of its type, maybe?
AH - I'm not a big fan of that type of innings, to be honest - I always think the best form of defence is attack. I understand there are times when you have to play like that, and he did what he felt he had to do for his team, but it's not an innings I will remember at the end of my career!

As the overs started to run out how tempted were you to take the new ball that was available?
AH - We had the new ball in mind when we declared the previous day - we declared with enough overs left for us to be able to take a new ball if we needed it on the final afternoon. It was good that we had it at our disposal but, fortunately, we didn't need to take it.

SURREY v SUSSEX at The Oval				**30th May to 2nd June**			
Surrey won the toss and elected to bat				Umpires:- Allan Jones and Roy Palmer			
SURREY - First Innings							
Fall Of Wkt	Batsman	How	Out	Score	Balls	4s	6s
1-22	**I.J. Ward**	**c Ambrose**	**b Kirtley**	**9**	29	1	0
2-22	**J.N. Batty +**	**c Adams**	**b Taylor**	**12**	25	2	0
3-132	**M.R. Ramprakash**	**c Yardy**	**b Mushtaq**	**37**	106	7	0
5-359	**G.P. Thorpe**	**c Adams**	**b Mushtaq**	**156**	275	26	0
4-263	**A.D. Brown**	**c Goodwin**	**b Kirtley**	**74**	69	10	1
8-394	**A.J. Hollioake ***	**lbw**	**b Martin-Jenkins**	**77**	78	11	1
6-360	**Azhar Mahmood**	**c Adams**	**b Kirtley**	**0**	4	0	0
7-379	**M.P. Bicknell**		**b Martin-Jenkins**	**11**	18	2	0
10-480	**I.D.K. Salisbury**	**c Ambrose**	**b Mushtaq**	**45**	55	5	2
9-469	**Saqlain Mushtaq**	**c Montgomerie**	**b Martin-Jenkins**	**32**	61	3	1
	J. Ormond	**Not**	**Out**	**1**	1	0	0
	Extras	**(4b, 17lb, 1w, 4nb)**		**26**			
	TOTAL	**(119.5 overs)**		**480**			

Bowler	O	M	R	W	NB	Wd
Kirtley	**33**	**5**	**122**	**3**	2	-
Taylor	**7.2**	**2**	**15**	**1**	-	-
Martin-Jenkins	**23.4**	**8**	**86**	**3**	-	1
Innes	**12**	**4**	**59**	**0**	-	-
Mushtaq Ahmed	**36.5**	**1**	**159**	**3**	-	-
Yardy	**7**	**1**	**18**	**0**	-	-

SUSSEX - First Innings (Needing 331 to avoid the follow-on)

Fall Of Wkt	Batsman	How	Out	Score	Balls	4s	6s
1-5	**R.R. Montgomerie**	**c Ward**	**b Ormond**	**5**	7	1	0
4-98	**M.W. Goodwin**		**b Saqlain**	**60**	66	14	0
2-13	**M.H. Yardy**	**c Thorpe**	**b Ormond**	**0**	6	0	0
3-24	**C.J. Adams ***	**c Batty**	**b Azhar**	**5**	18	1	0
8-279	**T.R. Ambrose**	**c Ramprakash**	**b Ormond**	**75**	152	9	0
5-189	**R.S.C. Martin-Jenkins**	**lbw**	**b Azhar**	**61**	68	10	0
6-217	**M.J. Prior +**		**b Saqlain**	**6**	32	0	0
7-220	**K.J. Innes**		**b Salisbury**	**2**	15	0	0
9-282	**Mushtaq Ahmed**	**lbw**	**b Ormond**	**41**	43	5	0
10-307	**R.J. Kirtley**	**run**	**out**	**21**	27	4	0
	B.V. Taylor	**Not**	**Out**	**4**	14	0	0
	Extras	**(9lb, 2w, 16nb)**		**27**			
	TOTAL	**(73.1 overs)**		**307**			

Bowler	O	M	R	W	NB	Wd
Bicknell	**3**	**1**	**9**	**0**	-	-
Ormond	**15.1**	**2**	**81**	**4**	5	1
Azhar Mahmood	**16**	**1**	**57**	**2**	-	-
Salisbury	**14**	**1**	**67**	**1**	3	-
Saqlain Mushtaq	**21**	**4**	**68**	**2**	-	-
Hollioake	**4**	**0**	**16**	**0**	-	1

SURREY - Second Innings (Leading by 173 runs on first innings)

Fall Of Wkt	Batsman	How	Out	Score	Balls	4s	6s
3-219	**I.J. Ward**	**c Goodwin**	**b Innes**	**135**	166	18	1
1-137	**J.N. Batty +**		**b Mushtaq**	**56**	110	8	1
2-192	**M.R. Ramprakash**	**c Prior**	**b Innes**	**23**	50	3	0
	G.P. Thorpe	**Not**	**Out**	**18**	25	3	0
	A.D. Brown	**Not**	**Out**	**1**	9	0	0
	Extras			**0**			
	TOTAL	**(60 overs)**	**(for 3 dec)**	**233**			

Bowler	O	M	R	W	NB	Wd
Kirtley	**14**	**3**	**49**	**0**	-	-
Martin-Jenkins	**19**	**3**	**66**	**0**	-	-
Mushtaq Ahmed	**11**	**1**	**47**	**1**	-	-
Innes	**14**	**1**	**64**	**2**	-	-
Yardy	**2**	**0**	**7**	**0**	-	-

SUSSEX - Second Innings (Needing 407 to win)

Fall Of Wkt	Batsman	How	Out	Score	Balls	4s	6s
1-45	**M.W. Goodwin**		**b Azhar**	**26**	33	5	0
2-83	**R.R. Montgomerie**	**c sub (Shahid)**	**b Saqlain**	**31**	67	4	0
10-293	**M.H. Yardy**	**c Azhar**	**b Ormond**	**69**	241	7	0
3-83	**C.J. Adams ***		**b Saqlain**	**0**	9	0	0
4-85	**T.R. Ambrose**		**b Saqlain**	**1**	8	0	0
5-198	**R.S.C. Martin-Jenkins**		**b Azhar**	**88**	93	14	0
6-218	**M.J. Prior +**	**c Ramprakash**	**b Azhar**	**14**	20	1	0
7-221	**K.J. Innes**	**c Azhar**	**b Saqlain**	**1**	20	0	0
8-242	**R.J. Kirtley**	**c sub (Shahid)**	**b Salisbury**	**7**	33	1	0
9-293	**Mushtaq Ahmed**	**lbw**	**b Saqlain**	**36**	52	7	0
	B.V. Taylor	**Not**	**Out**	**0**	1	0	0
	Extras	**(9b, 3lb, 2w, 6nb)**		**20**			
	TOTAL	**(95.4 overs)**		**293**			

Bowler	O	M	R	W	NB	Wd
Ormond	**19.4**	**3**	**65**	**1**	-	2
Azhar Mahmood	**21**	**4**	**76**	**3**	2	-
Salisbury	**21**	**5**	**67**	**1**	1	-
Saqlain Mushtaq	**34**	**15**	**73**	**5**	-	-

Other Frizzell Championship Division One Results

Surrey's win over Sussex extended their lead at the top of the table to twenty-eight points, while Lancashire moved up to second place after registering their first win of the season. Essex also got off the mark by trouncing the early Championship leaders, Nottinghamshire, at Trent Bridge.

May 30 - June 1
***Trent Bridge:-* Essex (18pts) beat Nottinghamshire (3) by 268 runs.** Essex 203 (Napier 57, Smith 5-42) & 359 (Habib 151, Foster 85, MacGill 5-118); Notts 79 (Brant 6-45, Dakin 4-22) & 215 (Napier 5-66).
May 30 - June 2
***Canterbury:-* Lancashire (20pts) beat Kent (5) by 75 runs.** Lancashire 347 (Flintoff 154, Chapple 66, Ealham 5-54) & 334 (Loye 86, Law 67, Tredwell 4-112); Kent 267 (Jones 92, Keedy 5-99) & 339 (Ealham 79, Smith 56, Walker 52, Chapple 4-66, Keedy 4-79).

FRIZZELL CHAMPIONSHIP DIVISION ONE TABLE AT 2ND JUNE

Pos	Prv		P	Points	W	D	L	T	Bat	Bwl	Ded
1	1	Surrey	6	94.00	3	3	0	0	24	16	0.00
2	5	Lancashire	5	66.00	1	4	0	0	21	15	0.00
3	2	Warwickshire	5	59.75	1	2	1	1	19	12	0.25
4	6	Essex	6	59.00	1	3	1	1	9	17	0.00
5	3	Sussex	5	58.00	2	0	3	0	15	15	0.00
6	4	Middlesex	5	49.00	1	4	0	0	6	13	0.00
7	7	Nottinghamshire	5	42.00	1	1	3	0	11	14	1.00
8	8	Kent	5	39.00	0	3	2	0	12	15	0.00
9	9	Leicestershire	4	31.00	0	4	0	0	4	11	0.00

Frizzell Championship Division One Results

While Surrey took a break from Championship action, a full programme of matches brought resounding wins for Sussex and Lancashire, with the Red Rose county's 22-point triumph cutting Surrey's advantage at the top of the table to just six points. Sussex advanced to third place after maintaining their no-draw record with another Mushtaq-inspired win, this time over struggling Kent.

June 4-7
***Tunbridge Wells:-* Sussex (20pts) beat Kent (5) by 191 runs**. Sussex 311 (Martin-Jenkins 67, Adams 62, Sheriyar 4-49) & 286 (Martin-Jenkins 84, Goodwin 58, Cottey 52, Sheriyar 4-93); Kent 275 (Symonds 54, Mushtaq 5-70, Kirtley 4-84) & 131 (Mushtaq 4-56).
***Liverpool:-* Lancashire (22pts) beat Leicestershire (5) by 10 wickets.** Lancs 503-6dec (Chilton 108, Law 82, Hooper 74, Flintoff 71*, Sutcliffe 55, Loye 54) & 24-0; Leics 314 (Maddy 85, Stevens 65) & 212 (Hooper 5-52, Keedy 4-61).
***Lord's:-* Middlesex (11pts) drew with Essex (7).** Middx 363 (Hutton 107, Joyce 69, Razzaq 54, Weekes 51*, Dakin 5-86); Essex 166 & 269-8 (Grayson 69, Middlebrook 52, Cook 4-54).
***Edgbaston:-* Warwickshire (9pts) drew with Nottinghamshire (12)**. Warwicks 351 (Trott 63, Wagh 58, Obuya 55, Smith 4-60) & 405 (Knight 146, Bell 64, MacGill 6-117); Notts 646 (Pietersen 221, Cairns 104, Welton 99, Afzaal 72, Franks 62*) & 67-5 (Waqar 4-30).

FRIZZELL CHAMPIONSHIP DIVISION ONE TABLE AT 7TH JUNE

Pos	Prv		P	Points	W	D	L	T	Bat	Bwl	Ded
1	1	Surrey	6	94.00	3	3	0	0	24	16	0.00
2	2	Lancashire	6	88.00	2	4	0	0	26	18	0.00
3	5	Sussex	6	78.00	3	0	3	0	18	18	0.00
4	3	Warwickshire	6	68.75	1	3	1	1	23	13	0.25
5	4	Essex	7	66.00	1	4	1	1	9	20	0.00
6	6	Middlesex	6	60.00	1	5	0	0	10	16	0.00
7	7	Nottinghamshire	6	54.00	1	2	3	0	16	17	1.00
8	8	Kent	6	44.00	0	3	3	0	14	18	0.00
9	9	Leicestershire	5	36.00	0	4	1	0	7	13	0.00

NATIONAL CRICKET LEAGUE DIVISION ONE - MATCH SIX

Surrey Lions versus Essex Eagles at The Oval

Sunday 8th June

Setting The Scene - Ignoring the recent wash-out between Surrey and Gloucestershire at Bristol, this looks to be the biggest game of the NCL season to date, as the first division leaders go head-to-head with the team in third place. With Martin Bicknell having joined Alex Tudor on the injury list, Phil Sampson gets a rare opportunity to shine, while the Lions are also grateful that Pakistan are happy for Azhar Mahmood to stay with his county side until the Nat West Challenge Series gets under way. Essex are meanwhile lacking the services of their injured captain, Ronnie Irani, and therefore give 21-year-old left-arm seamer, Justin Bishop, an outing, while Mark Pettini takes Nasser Hussain's place in the middle-order. There is a surprise at the toss when Adam Hollioake elects to field after Paul Grayson calls incorrectly.

Essex Eagles' Innings

Azhar Mahmood and Phil Sampson share the new ball for the Lions and keep the Essex opening pair of Will Jefferson and Andy Flower very quiet with some tight bowling in the first five overs, conceding just six runs, one of which is a leg-bye. Although Sampson's third over then costs nine, he has the significant consolation of removing the potentially dangerous Jefferson, bowled middle stump, just after the Eagles' giant has looked to be breaking loose with one of his trademark extra-cover drives to the boundary.

Essex then suffer another setback when Flower, too, departs just as he appears to have settled in with a couple of flowing off-side fours, the Zimbabwean's thick-edged drive off Azhar being very well snapped up low to his right by a diving Thorpe in the gully with the score on thirty-five in the ninth over.

The visitors then reveal an interesting change in their batting order as James Foster appears at number four to join Darren Robinson in the middle with his team in some difficulty against the league leaders. To the surprise of many, Adam Hollioake immediately pulls Azhar out of the attack - the Pakistani having bowled just five of his allotted nine overs - though the new bowler at the pavilion end, James Ormond, immediately settles into a testing line and length, starting his spell in fine style with a maiden over.

At the other end, Sampson has become a little more expensive, however, generally leaking one boundary an over, including a square-cut four by Robinson that brings up the Essex fifty in the twelfth over. As a result, Saqlain takes over at the Vauxhall end, though his first over ends up costing nine after Robinson greets him with a lovely on-driven boundary.

With the scoreboard now reading 69-2 after fourteen overs, the Eagles appear to be well on the road to recovery, and Foster confirms this by dancing down the track to Ormond and lofting the ball back down the ground for a handsome straight six. This stroke is an isolated act of violence, however, since the two Surrey bowlers are allowing hardly any liberties at this stage, with the score advancing largely in singles. Foster clearly wants to progress at a faster rate than this, though, and in attempting to attack Saqlain he only succeeds in drilling a drive to midwicket where Ali Brown takes a smart low catch to peg the visitors back to 86-3 in the eighteenth over. With the partnership having just passed fifty, this breakthrough has come at a good time for the hosts, who will now be looking to pressurise the new batsman, Mark Pettini.

Although the highly-promising 19-year-old starts well, striking three fours in the space of four overs and raising the Eagles' hundred at the end of the twentieth over, the Lions quickly hunt down their prey as Ormond finds a good ball to knock back the youngster's off stump with the total having advanced to 114.

Since the loss of wickets at fairly regular intervals is putting Essex in danger of failing to post a decent total, it's no great surprise that the experienced Robinson and Paul Grayson opt for a few overs of re-entrenchment at this stage as Ormond completes an excellent spell of 9-1-33-1 and Hollioake settles in as Saqlain's replacement at the Vauxhall end.

This only serves to strengthen the Lions' position in the short term, however, and when the end of the twenty-eighth over arrives with the scoreboard reading 126-4 it's clear that the visitors must try to get after Hollioake and his new bowling partner, Rikki Clarke.

Robinson does eventually manage a rare boundary when he pulls Clarke over wide mid-on to complete a 72-ball fifty in the thirty-first over, but, though the flow of singles and twos is increasing as the total passes the 150 mark in the next over, it isn't until Saqlain returns in place of Hollioake that the rope is found again, courtesy of Grayson's good footwork and extra-cover drive.

When the Essex skipper repeats both the chassé down the pitch and the stroke against Clarke just seven balls later he completes a fifty partnership with Robinson, and things definitely start to look up for the Eagles when Hollioake again supersedes Saqlain at the Vauxhall end to bowl the thirty-eighth over. Since the off-spinner's seventh over had yielded five singles and a three, the Lions' captain seems justified in making the switch, but then endures a truly torrid over as Robinson boosts both his personal tally and the visitors' total by fifteen runs, including three fours, two driven over wide mid-on and one through extra cover. With the partnership now worth seventy-nine runs and the score looking much healthier from the Essex point of view at 193-4 with seven overs remaining, it would seem that Surrey might well end up chasing a target in excess of 240. But everything is about to change.

By removing both of the established batsmen in his second over after replacing Clarke at the pavilion end, Azhar sparks Surrey celebrations and puts his side back in control of the match. Robinson is the highly-talented all-rounder's first victim, his middle stump ripped out by a magnificent yorker at the start of the over, then Grayson falls to the final ball when he drives a slower delivery to shortish mid-on, where Thorpe plunges forward to take another good low catch.

Although the Eagles' two-hundred has come up during the over - courtesy of an attempted leg-stump yorker which doesn't come out right and ends up as five legside wides instead - the loss of both members of the fifth-wicket partnership is devastating for the visitors, especially as it exposes new batsmen to the skills of two of the game's best 'death' bowlers in Hollioake and Azhar. And Essex fears prove well founded, since their lower-order fails to rise to the challenge.

After a tight four-run over from Hollioake, Azhar is simply irresistible again in his eighth over, first defeating Graham Napier with a full-length delivery and winning an lbw verdict, and then rearranging Jon Dakins stumps with another superb yorker two balls later. Azhar now has five wickets to his name, and his stunning burst of four wickets for twelve runs in eleven balls has seen off Robinson for seventy-eight, Grayson for thirty-seven, Napier for two and Dakin for six, as the Eagles have declined dramatically from 193-4 to 209-8. And he isn't finished yet, either.

With their team's innings now in seemingly terminal decline, James Middlebrook and Justin Bishop try to concentrate their efforts on the accumulation of singles, but they manage only one run off the bat and three leg-byes from ten deliveries before Azhar swoops for his sixth wicket by pinning Bishop leg-before with the fourth ball of his final over. This extends a purple patch of match-winning proportions to five wickets for a dozen runs in sixteen balls and, though he is unable to finish off the Essex innings by claiming a seventh scalp with either of his last two deliveries, he still ends with the stunning figures of 9-1-37-6 and the crowd's applause ringing in his ears.

With just two overs remaining and the Eagles looking to be some way short of the par score for a limited-overs match at The Oval, the last pair now need to perform miracles but can only add another seven runs before Middlebrook drags a drive off the returning Clarke straight to Ali Brown at mid-on, leaving his side all out for 220 with four balls of their forty-five overs unused.

The visitors' total doesn't look anywhere near good enough as a proud Azhar leads his fellow Lions from the field to an extended ovation for a truly outstanding spell of bowling.

Surrey Lions' Innings

Surrey's task of chasing 221 in forty-five overs to maintain their unbeaten record and position at the top of the table doesn't look too daunting as they set out, though the loss of both openers to Scott Brant within the first five overs does put a slightly different complexion on matters.

With the batsman on five and the total standing at eight, Ian Ward is the first Lion to be dismissed when he miscues a pull high to wide mid-on where Grayson takes the catch, then Ali Brown is beaten on the drive and has his middle stump pegged back after making eight out of a total of seventeen.

The Eagles are clearly very much in the match at this point, though Mark Ramprakash and Graham Thorpe soon calm the home fans' nerves by making good starts to their innings - Thorpe drives Brant to the rope at long-on and pulls Jon Dakin to the midwicket fence in successive overs, while his right-handed partner blasts the Australian left-armer high over wide long-on for a sensational six in the very next over. This positive approach leads to the arrival of the fifty after exactly ten overs and, apart from a couple of rather fortunate edged fours off Graham Napier when he replaces Dakin at the Vauxhall end, all seems to be going well for the home side as the third-wicket partnership continues to prosper.

It isn't too long, in fact, before it exceeds fifty in value and, with Justin Bishop having conceded two fours to Ramprakash in his opening two overs after taking over from Brant, it's understandable that Grayson should opt to make another bowling change, withdrawing Napier after just three overs and calling up James Middlebrook to take the pace off the ball with his off-breaks. The in-form Thorpe is not bothered in the slightest by this, however, as he skips down the track to hit Middlebrook's fifth delivery to the long-on boundary and keep Surrey firmly on track for a straightforward victory.

He does lose his third-wicket partner in the next over, though, when Ramprakash misses an attempted sweep at Bishop's slower ball and is adjudged lbw for thirty-eight by umpire Palmer with the total standing at 89. Since the ball was delivered from over the wicket by the left-armer, it would appear to be a somewhat debatable decision, though it seems unlikely to prove too important in the general scheme of things, given the state of the game and the confident start that Rikki Clarke makes by driving Middlebrook for four and sweeping him for two.

The hundred then comes up in the following over, the nineteenth of the innings, and when successive deliveries from Middlebrook and the recalled Napier disappear to the boundary - the first courtesy of a Clarke sweep and the second from a back-foot force through extra cover by Thorpe - Surrey are over halfway to their target with almost twenty-five overs to go.

With the Lions seemingly roaring to victory, Grayson can do little but switch his bowlers around and hope for the best at this stage, though the recall of Napier clearly isn't a success as Clarke pulls the burly seamer for six and Thorpe drives him through the covers for four during an expensive twenty-third over that ends with the home side sitting pretty at 129-3.

It seems to matter little when the first ball of the next over sees Clarke falling lbw to Dakin while attempting an unnecessary big hit to leg after making twenty-one from just seventeen balls, especially as the asking rate is not much over four runs per over with six wickets in hand. Additionally, Thorpe's continued presence offers a comforting sense of security, which is promptly underlined by his completion of a very good half-century from his fifty-sixth ball later in the over of Clarke's dismissal.

There is also no way that the scoring rate will be allowed to flag by the new batsman, Adam Hollioake, and it is no surprise to see the Surrey skipper actually upping the tempo by driving the returning Brant over the rope at long-on within three overs of his arrival at the wicket. Thorpe then almost follows his captain's lead with a lofted straight drive for four off Middlebrook, back in the attack in place of Dakin, to raise the Lions' 150 after 27.2 overs. When three further fours follow by the end of the thirtieth over, at which point the home team are 171-4, it is starting to look like a Surrey stroll, and there is a slightly strange air of inevitability about proceedings, with the visitors seemingly having already accepted their fate. Essex clearly need inspiration... and they need it now.

Having rotated his five main bowlers as much as can be reasonably expected and seen his most potent performer, Brant, complete his nine-over stint, Grayson finally, and belatedly, takes the only other realistic option open to him by bringing himself on to bowl.

The left-arm spinner starts inauspiciously with a legside wide but his first legitimate delivery tempts Hollioake into an impetuous charge down the wicket that leaves the batsman stranded almost in mid-pitch after failing to make contact with a wild swipe to leg. The Surrey captain keeps on walking back to the pavilion as Foster removes the bails to confirm the batsman's dismissal for twenty-six and leave the Lions requiring forty-four runs from almost fourteen overs with five wickets in hand.

Although victory still looks assured for the home side, the wicket has clearly given the visitors a lift as Grayson continues to lead by example, completing the over to Azhar without conceding a run and then following up a four-run over from the recalled Napier by sending down a second over that yields just a single.

Any thought of Surrey playing the game out to a steady and sensible conclusion is quickly dispelled in the space of three balls at the end of the next over, however, as Azhar drives Napier through mid-off for four, lifts his next ball into the pavilion with a towering hit for six, and then pulls the next delivery straight down the throat of the fielder posted at deep backward square leg to depart for fourteen with the scoreboard reading 196-6.

Suddenly, with only four wickets to fall and the hosts' tail looking a little longer than usual with no Bicknell or Salisbury in the team, Essex have a sniff of victory, and the scent grows stronger in the next over from Grayson when Jon Batty misses a sweep at his second ball and is sent on his way by umpire John Hampshire. At 197-7, the tension is rising and a game that Surrey had been completely dominating is possibly back in the balance, even though there is no pressure in terms of the required run-rate, which is currently under three an over.

As Saqlain Mushtaq comes out to bat, many of the home fans are probably wondering which 'Saqi' we are about to see - the sensible and technically-correct batsman that this situation probably demands, or the impulsive inventor of strokes who is almost as likely to hole out with a mishit as he is to smite a towering six.

The answer to this question soon becomes clear as he blocks the last three balls of Grayson's over and then plays out five deliveries in each of the next two overs after Thorpe has taken a 'given' single from the first ball. This approach is absolutely ideal while Thorpe is in occupation as it is clearly much more important to keep wickets intact than worry about an asking rate that is never likely to climb too high. It is still a very tense situation, though, and after Thorpe takes a second-ball single from the thirty-ninth over, bowled by the returning Dakin, Saqlain again concentrates on survival.

Twenty runs are now required from six overs and the senior partner finally shows signs of nerves when he survives a confident lbw shout from Grayson after missing a sweep, and is then beaten on the outside edge by the next delivery. The Lions' left-hander is probably quite relieved to get down to the other end with a single off the fourth ball of the over, and he no doubt feels happier still when Saqlain clips the following delivery to the boundary at backward square leg to simultaneously open his account and break the spell that the bowlers have been casting over the batsmen. With the off-spinner moving his score on to five and the total on to 207 with a single from the final ball of the over, the pressure seems to be lifting at last, and when five runs, including two for a no-ball, accrue from Dakin's final over it looks like Surrey have finally managed to weather the storm.

Still maintaining his studied approach, Saqlain then takes three from Grayson's next over, while Thorpe's pads contribute a leg-bye, and when Bishop returns for the forty-third over the contest is ended in fine style by the Pakistani off-spinner with a lofted drive to the rope at wide mid-on. The Essex team and the umpires seem momentarily unconvinced that the match is actually over, but the celebrating batsmen and Surrey fans soon tell them otherwise and it isn't long before Thorpe and his partner are making their way up to the changing rooms to a joyful reception from the home crowd. The former England left-hander's polished unbeaten seventy-nine has been the major contribution to the Lions' batting effort but Saqlain has remained impressively cool in steering his team through to their fifth NCL win of the season.

JAMES ORMOND'S VIEW FROM THE DRESSING ROOM

When Essex were 193-4 after thirty-eight overs, I guess you must have been expecting us to be chasing something like 240-250 until Azhar struck with his amazing spell of 5-12?
JO - Once you get the momentum going on Sundays you start to think instinctively that you can knock the tail over for next to nothing, especially given the way Azhar and one or two of our other guys can bowl at the death. So I don't think we would have been thinking about them making 250… that's how you lose games, with that sort of attitude.

You seemed to settle in well as a mid-innings bowler during the NCL campaign, usually going straight through your spell. Do you prefer that role in one-day cricket, as opposed to opening the bowling?
JO - I always used to like taking the new ball, but nowadays I don't mind too much when I bowl. Bowling in the middle of the innings is a different prospect to bowling with a new ball, so its just a case of deciding who's best with the new ball for us, which depends on what side we've got out. So, if Bickers is playing for example, he's got to have it because he's a new ball specialist. And Azhar gets fantastic away shape and bounce with the new ball, so we found it worked well if he bowled a spell of four or five overs at the start.

Was this tactic of bowling you straight through your spell due, in part, to your injury problems?
JO - For the last four or five years I've often had to bowl straight through my overs - or certainly a lot of them in one go - in one-day cricket because of my knee. Also, I'm not the best starter when I come back for a second spell, so I think I'm much better when I get settled and my knees are 'oiled' and moving.

Were you surprised that Paul Grayson brought himself on to bowl so late in the innings, with the game almost lost?
JO - He's quite a canny bowler and when he comes on to bowl against our batting line-up they look to try and hit him out of the attack as quickly as possible, I think, but on this occasion he threw the ball up a bit and a few of our lads ran past it! So I guess you could say that it was a decent enough tactic to hold himself back for so long.

From 177-4, we slipped to 197-7. I suppose it was very much to our advantage that we were ahead of the clock, allowing Saqi to come in and play in a very restrained fashion?
JO - Yes, and, with the greatest respect to their bowling attack, it was unlikely to be able to blast decent tailenders away, so we knew we'd be able to stick around. If Thorpey had gone then we might have been just a little more nervous, though.

SURREY LIONS v ESSEX EAGLES at The Oval
Sunday 8th June — **Surrey Lions won by three wickets**
Surrey Lions won the toss and elected to field — **Umpires:- John Hampshire & Roy Palmer**

ESSEX EAGLES

Fall Of Wkt	Batsman	How	Out	Score	Balls	4s	6s
1-15	**W.I. Jefferson**		**b Sampson**	**7**	20	1	0
2-35	**A. Flower**	**c Thorpe**	**b Azhar**	**20**	26	2	0
5-193	**D.D.J. Robinson**		**b Azhar**	**78**	94	9	0
3-86	**J.S. Foster +**	**c Brown**	**b Saqlain**	**26**	25	2	1
4-114	**M.L. Pettini**		**b Ormond**	**17**	13	3	0
6-201	**A.P. Grayson ***	**c Thorpe**	**b Azhar**	**37**	54	3	0
8-209	**J.M. Dakin**		**b Azhar**	**6**	8	0	0
7-208	**G.R. Napier**	**lbw**	**b Azhar**	**2**	4	0	0
10-220	**J.D. Middlebrook**	**c Brown**	**b Clarke**	**2**	11	0	0
9-213	**J.E. Bishop**	**lbw**	**b Azhar**	**1**	5	0	0
	S.A. Brant	**Not**	**Out**	**6**	6	0	0
	Extras	**(7lb, 11w)**		**18**			
	TOTAL	**(44.2 overs)**		**220**			

Bowler	O	M	R	W	NB	Wd
Azhar Mahmood	**9**	**1**	**37**	**6**	-	1
Sampson	**6**	**1**	**30**	**1**	-	-
Ormond	**9**	**1**	**33**	**1**	-	3
Saqlain Mushtaq	**7**	**0**	**45**	**1**	-	-
Hollioake	**9**	**0**	**42**	**0**	-	2
Clarke	**4.2**	**0**	**26**	**1**	-	1

SURREY LIONS

Fall Of Wkt	Batsman	How	Out	Score	Balls	4s	6s
1-8	**I.J. Ward**	**c Grayson**	**b Brant**	**5**	16	0	0
2-17	**A.D. Brown**		**b Brant**	**8**	9	1	0
3-89	**M.R. Ramprakash**	**lbw**	**b Bishop**	**38**	44	4	1
	G.P. Thorpe	**Not**	**Out**	**79**	97	8	0
4-129	**R. Clarke**	**lbw**	**b Dakin**	**21**	17	2	1
5-177	**A.J. Hollioake ***	**c Foster**	**b Grayson**	**26**	25	2	1
6-196	**Azhar Mahmood**	**c Middlebrook**	**b Napier**	**14**	15	1	1
7-197	**J.N. Batty +**	**lbw**	**b Grayson**	**0**	2	0	0
	Saqlain Mushtaq	**Not**	**Out**	**14**	34	2	0
	J. Ormond	**did not bat**					
	P.J. Sampson	**did not bat**					
	Extras	**(4lb, 8w, 4nb)**		**16**			
	TOTAL	**(42.5 overs)**	**(for 7 wkts)**	**221**			

Bowler	O	M	R	W	NB	Wd
Brant	**9**	**0**	**53**	**2**	1	2
Dakin	**9**	**0**	**38**	**1**	1	4
Napier	**9**	**0**	**56**	**1**	-	-
Bishop	**4.5**	**0**	**21**	**1**	-	-
Middlebrook	**5**	**0**	**36**	**0**	-	1
Grayson	**6**	**0**	**13**	**2**	-	1

Other NCL Division One Results

Glamorgan's victory over Worcestershire maintained their one-hundred percent record, while Gloucestershire had recorded two successive wins - first over Leicestershire in the only game played on Sunday 1st June, then over the ailing Warwickshire Bears - to stay in touch with the leading sides.

June 1
***Leicester:-* Gloucestershire Gladiators (4pts) beat Leicestershire Foxes by 3 wickets.** Leics 234-6 (45ov; Hodge 63); Gloucs 235-7 (43.4ov; Windows 76).
June 8
***Swansea:-* Glamorgan Dragons (4pts) beat Worcestershire Royals by 31 runs (D/L method).** Glamorgan 215-9 (39ov; Dale 60, Hemp 59, Kabir Ali 4-38); Worcs 184 (36.2ov; Wharf 4-24, Croft 3-33).
***Gloucester:-* Gloucestershire Gladiators (4pts) beat Warwickshire Bears by 78 runs.** Gloucs 307-8 (45ov; Spearman 153, Weston 61); Warwicks 229 (40.2ov; Knight 70, Troughton 53, Bell 50, Gidman 3-26).
***Tunbridge Wells:-* Kent Spitfires (4pts) beat Yorkshire Phoenix by 22 runs.** Kent 208-7 (45ov; Sidebottom 3-39); Yorks 186-9 (45ov; Lumb 77, Trott 3-19).

NCL DIVISION ONE TABLE AT 8TH JUNE

Pos	Prv		P	Pts	W	T	L	A
1	1	Surrey Lions	6	22	5	0	0	1
2	2	Glamorgan Dragons	5	20	5	0	0	0
3	5	Gloucestershire Gladiators	6	14	3	0	2	1
4	3	Essex Eagles	5	12	3	0	2	0
5	4	Worcestershire Royals	4	8	2	0	2	0
6	8	Kent Spitfires	6	8	2	0	4	0
7	6	Leicestershire Foxes	5	4	1	0	4	0
=	6	Yorkshire Phoenix	5	4	1	0	4	0
9	9	Warwickshire Bears	4	0	0	0	4	0

C&G Trophy Quarter-Final - Derbyshire Bring Surrey Down Again

Derbyshire v Surrey at Derby. Played on Wednesday 11th June.
Derbyshire won by 137 runs

On paper, it had looked a good draw when Surrey were handed a trip to Derby in the C&G Trophy quarter-final, yet there were reasons for believing that this game represented a potential banana skin for the visitors. Derbyshire were, after all, the last team to have beaten Surrey, in the NCL match at The Oval on 18th August 2002, (they had come within an umpire's decision of winning the return encounter at Derby on 2nd September, too) and they had upset the form book, again at The Oval, on the last occasion these sides had met in the premier cup competition, back in 1998. It also had to be noted that they had beaten the reigning NCL champions, Glamorgan, at Cardiff in the previous round of this year's competition.

The fact that the Supporters' Club coach got stuck in a traffic jam, caused by a fatal accident on the M1, on the morning of the match merely added to the sense of foreboding, so it shouldn't have been a great surprise to anyone when Surrey's 21-match unbeaten run in all competitions came grinding to a halt at the County Ground. What was shocking, though, was the margin of victory as Derbyshire emerged triumphant by 137 runs. A combination of Surrey's most recent bogey team and their bogey competition - just one cup-winning campaign in 41 attempts - proved deadly in the extreme.

Fielding the same side that had beaten the Essex Eagles in the NCL, the visitors won the toss, elected to put Derbyshire in to bat on what looked as if it might be a slightly sporty wicket, and got off to a good start by removing Chris Gait - caught behind off Azhar Mahmood for nought - in the third over.

Chris Bassano (33) and Michael DiVenuto then put together an important stand of sixty for the second wicket before James Ormond bowled Bassano to bring Mohammad Kaif, the 22-year-old Indian international, to the crease on his limited-overs debut for the home side.

Fortunately for the visitors, they soon managed to split up Derbyshire's two overseas batsmen when DiVenuto drove James Ormond to mid-off with the score at ninety-nine, but once Saqlain Mushtaq (10-0-24-0, with every run conceded being a single) finished an excellent first spell of seven overs for seventeen, Kaif and Dominic Hewson (34) started to take control.

With Surrey's fielding frequently run ragged by some fantastic running between the wickets and the fourth-wicket pair feasting on some loose overs from Rikki Clarke and the Surrey captain, the partnership eventually added eighty-eight at better than run a ball to set the home side up for a late assault with wickets in hand.

Although Azhar and Hollioake returned to share five wickets and run through the tail in the last three overs, the damage had already been done by a Kaif-inspired charge that saw fifty-nine runs added between overs forty-four and forty-eight before the Indian holed out off Hollioake for a superb eighty-one, scored off 84 balls.

Chasing 272 to win, Surrey were soon in trouble against some excellent new-ball bowling by Kevin Dean (2-26) and Dominic Cork (2-17), subsiding to 26-4 by the end of the eleventh over as the opening bowlers shared the wickets of Ward (6), Brown (first ball duck), Ramprakash (7) and Clarke (first ball duck).

Even at this early stage, the contest looked to be pretty much done-and-dusted, but Derbyshire didn't take their foot off the pedal as they continued to show greater intensity and desire in both their bowling and fielding than their visitors had earlier in the game.

Surrey's hopes were raised briefly by a 40-run stand between their skipper and the in-form Graham Thorpe (37), but once the latter went to a magnificent catch by Luke Sutton standing up to Graeme Welch, the writing was on the wall. The former Warwickshire seamer then cleaned up Hollioake (20) and Azhar (16) in successive overs to ensure there was no way back for the visitors at 97-7, and it was left to Jon Batty (28) to salvage a tiny shred of respectability before being last out with 16.2 overs of the innings left to be bowled.

Since Derbyshire's catching had been every bit as good as their bowling and their batting, no-one could deny that the underdogs had very much deserved their resounding victory. And any dreams Surrey might have harboured of pulling off the 'grand slam' by winning all four major trophies had been dashed in dramatic fashion. Never had the saying "you can't win 'em all" been more appropriate.

Scores:- Derbyshire 271 (50ov; Kaif 81, DiVenuto 51, Azhar 4-49, Ormond 3-53) beat Surrey 134 (33.4ov; Welch 4-26) by 137 runs.

8 Twenty-20's Grand Entrance

Surrey's thrashing at Derby in the C&G Trophy had been a truly humiliating experience, though it was important to remember that this was the team's first defeat of the season, and also that the side's long unbeaten run was bound to end at some point. It was disappointing, however, that the defeat had come in the knockout cup competition where there were no second chances - at this stage of the season a one-game setback in either of the leagues wouldn't have been disastrous, whereas in the C&G Trophy it was fatal. It remained a mystery as to why the premier domestic cup competition had proved such an unhappy tournament for Surrey over the years, with a winner's medal continuing to elude every member of the current squad except Mark Ramprakash, who had tasted success - and indeed won the Man Of The Match award - with Middlesex two days before his 19th birthday in 1988.

There was a new medal for the players to try to add to their collections in 2003, however, with the Twenty-20 Cup about to make its debut just two days after the fourth round C&G matches had been played. Surrey therefore had to put the defeat at Derby out of their minds instantly if they were to get off to a good start in the zonal qualifying matches.

The format for the qualifying tournament, to be played over a period of two weeks, was fairly straightforward. The eighteen counties had been split into three six-team groups - South, North and Midlands/West/Wales - with each county playing the other five sides in their group once, and the best four teams (the three group winners and the second-placed county with the most points/best record) at the end of the qualifying round progressing to Finals Day at Trent Bridge on Saturday 19th July.

Although some of the counties - and their players and supporters - had voiced their reservations about Twenty-20 cricket, it seemed that the ECB and PCA had eventually won the day in persuading most of the doubters that the new competition should be given a chance and fully supported, while the media seemed to find the idea of a fresh format for cricket interesting enough to put greater resources into covering it.

Surrey were about to become one of the first counties to experience this brave new world, too, since they had been allocated a home fixture with London rivals, Middlesex, in the first round of matches taking place on Friday 13th June. It was to be hoped that the date wasn't to prove unlucky for the tournament.

TWENTY-20 CUP SOUTH DIVISION QUALIFYING - MATCH ONE

Surrey Lions versus Middlesex Crusaders

at The Oval on Friday 13th June

On a beautiful mid-summer's evening, Twenty-20 cricket got off to an amazing start with an incredible crowd of around 10,000 packing into The Oval for the showdown between the two London-based counties. The chance to see a complete match in one evening after a day at work clearly appealed to many people, some of whom had undoubtedly been attracted, by the new format and the attendant publicity, to come and witness their first-ever live game of cricket. It was truly awesome to see so many spectators in the ground for a county match and those - myself included - who had felt the competition wouldn't work were already having to think again.

The game itself provided the crowd with all the elements that they would have been hoping for as 39.2 overs of helter-skelter action produced 313 runs, including 2 sixes and 42 fours, sixteen wickets and a last-over finish.

Middlesex Crusaders' Innings

Having been put in to bat, Middlesex's innings was given decent enough foundations by Andy Strauss and Chad Keegan after the first-over loss of Paul Weekes, but once James Ormond entered the attack to bowl the sixth over Surrey took charge. After taking a wicket in each of his opening two overs to peg the Crusaders back to 70-3, the former Leicestershire fast bowler really put the cat amongst the pigeons by removing both Ed Joyce and Simon Cook for first-ball ducks in a third over that had started with the direct-hit run out of Abdul Razzaq by the Lions' debutant, James Benning, from deep mid-off.

With only four wickets standing and ten overs still to bat, the visitors were suddenly unable to take too many risks and were set back even further when Adam Hollioake dismissed Ben Hutton in the thirteenth over with the score on 103.

Although a sensible stand of thirty-six for the eighth wicket by Strauss and Robin Weston eventually enabled the Crusaders to attain some kind of respectability, Ormond then returned to bowl his final over and complete a stunning five-wicket haul by having Strauss caught at deep midwicket in the eighteenth over. Azhar tidied up the innings by taking wickets with the last two balls of Middlesex's twenty overs, leaving the hosts to make 156 for victory.

MIDDLESEX CRUSADERS INNINGS						*********** END-OF-OVER TOTALS ***********					
Ov	Bowler	Runs	Bat 1	Bat 2	Ex	BOWLER	BAT 1	BAT 2	EX	SCORE	OV
1	Bicknell	4	Weekes 4			WEEKES c BATTY b BICKNELL 4					
			Keegan 0	Strauss 0		MB 1-0-4-1	CK 0	AS 0	0	4-1	1
2	Azhar	7	Keegan 0	Strauss 7		AM 1-0-7-0	CK 0	AS 7	0	11-1	2
3	Bicknell	11	Keegan 8	Strauss 1	2lb	MB 2-0-13-1	CK 8	AS 8	2	22-1	3
4	Azhar	9	Keegan 4	Strauss 5		AM 2-0-16-0	CK 12	AS 13	2	31-1	4
5	Bicknell	11	Keegan 4	Strauss 6	1lb	MB 3-0-23-1	CK 16	AS 19	3	42-1	5
6	Ormond	7	Keegan 0			KEEGAN b ORMOND 16					
			Shah 2	Strauss 5		JO 1-0-7-1	OS 2	AS 24	3	49-2	6
7	Sampson	12	Shah 7	Strauss 4	1lb	PS 1-0-11-0	OS 9	AS 28	4	61-2	7
8	Ormond	11	Shah 8			SHAH lbw b ORMOND 17					
			Razzaq 1	Strauss 0	2w	JO 2-0-18-2	AR 1	AS 28	6	72-3	8
9	Sampson	16	Razzaq 16	Strauss 0		PS 2-0-27-0	AR 17	AS 28	6	88-3	9
10	Ormond	2	Razzaq 0			ABDUL RAZZAQ RUN OUT 17					
			Joyce 0			JOYCE c BATTY b ORMOND 0					
			Cook 0			COOK b ORMOND 0					
			Hutton 0	Strauss 2		JO 3-0-20-4	BH 0	AS 30	6	90-6	10
11	Holl'ke	3	Hutton 1	Strauss 2		AH 1-0-3-0	BH 1	AS 32	6	93-6	11
12	Azhar	6	Hutton 1	Strauss 5		AM 3-0-22-0	BH 2	AS 37	6	99-6	12
13	Holl'ke	4	Hutton 1			HUTTON c THORPE b HOLLIOAKE 3					
			Weston 0	Strauss 3		AH 2-0-7-1	RW 0	AS 40	6	103-7	13
14	Benning	6	Weston 5	Strauss 0	1lb	JB 1-0-5-0	RW 5	AS 40	7	109-7	14
15	Holl'ke	6	Weston 3	Strauss 3		AH 3-0-13-1	RW 8	AS 43	7	115-7	15
16	Benning	7	Weston 2	Strauss 5		JB 2-0-12-0	RW 10	AS 48	7	122-7	16
17	Sampson	12	Weston 9	Strauss 1	2w	PS 3-0-39-0	RW 19	AS 49	9	134-7	17
18	Ormond	4		Strauss 3		STRAUSS c WARD b ORMOND 52					
			Weston 2	Alleyne 0	1w	JO 4-0-26-5	RW 21	DA 0	10	140-8	18
19	Holl'ke	9	Weston 4	Alleyne 5		AH 4-0-22-1	RW 25	DA 5	10	149-8	19
20	Azhar	6	Weston 5			WESTON b AZHAR 30					
			Bl'field 0			BLOOMFIELD lbw b AZHAR 0					
				Alleyne 1		AM 4-0-28-2		DA 6	10	155	20

Surrey Lions' Innings

Although no-one was really sure what represented a good score in Twenty-20 cricket, there was a strong feeling that Middlesex hadn't put enough runs on the board, given that the match was being played on a typically good Oval pitch. This appeared to be confirmed when young Benning emerged from the pavilion, after the disappointing early loss of Ali Brown, to hit six fours from just fourteen balls in making a rapid twenty-seven.

Nor did Hollioake hang around after Benning lost his leg stump to Cook with the score at fifty-four in the sixth over, facing the same number of balls as his young team-mate in making twenty-four and putting his side well ahead of the required run-rate at the halfway stage of the innings.

As had been demonstrated earlier, the loss of a cluster of wickets could quickly change the course of an innings, so when Ian Ward, Graham Thorpe and Azhar all departed in the space of five overs for the addition of twenty runs, there was suddenly an element of doubt about the result of the match.

When Jon Batty joined Mark Ramprakash out in the middle, Surrey's target was twenty-nine runs from 28 balls but, fortunately for the Lions and their fans, both batsmen stayed calm to ensure that victory was achieved with four deliveries to spare when the former Middlesex captain drove Cook to the extra-cover boundary.

SURREY LIONS INNINGS						************ END-OF-OVER TOTALS ************					
Ov	Bowler	Runs	Bat 1	Bat 2	Ex	BOWLER	BAT 1	BAT 2	EX	SCORE	OV
1	Bl'field	4	Ward 3	Brown 0	1lb	TB 1-0-3-0	IW 3	AB 0	1	4-0	1
2	Keegan	8	Ward 1	Brown 7		CK 1-0-8-0	IW 4	AB 7	1	12-0	2
3	Bl'field	11		Brown 0		BROWN c STRAUSS b BLOOMFIELD 7					
			Ward 5	Benning 1	6w	TB 2-0-15-1	IW 9	JB 1	7	24-1	3
4	Keegan	11	Ward 0	Benning 9	1b, 1lb	CK 2-0-17-0	IW 9	JB 10	9	35-1	4
5	Bl'field	11	Ward 1	Benning 9	1lb	TB 3-0-25-1	IW 10	JB 19	10	46-1	5
6	Cook	16		Benning 8		BENNING b COOK 27					
			Ward 0	Holl'ke 8		SC 1-0-16-1	IW 10	AH 8	10	62-2	6
7	Razzaq	6	Ward 3	Holl'ke 3		AR 1-0-6-0	IW 13	AH 11	10	68-2	7
8	Weekes	6	Ward 1	Holl'ke 5		PW 1-0-6-0	IW 14	AH 16	10	74-2	8
9	Razzaq	9	Ward 2	Holl'ke 7		AR 2-0-15-0	IW 16	AH 23	10	83-2	9
10	Weekes	6	Ward 5	Holl'ke 1		PW 2-0-12-0	IW 21	AH 24	10	89-2	10
11	Hutton	3		Holl'ke 0		HOLLIOAKE c WESTON b HUTTON 24					
			Ward 9	Thorpe 5		BH 1-0-14-1	IW 30	GT 5	10	103-3	11
12	Weekes	6	Ward 1			WARD RUN OUT 31					
			R'kash 1	Thorpe 4		PW 3-0-18-0	MR 1	GT 9	10	109-4	12
13	Keegan	7	R'kash 1	Thorpe 6		CK 3-0-24-0	MR 2	GT 15	10	116-4	13
14	Razzaq	7	R'kash 0	Thorpe 7		AR 3-0-22-0	MR 2	GT 22	10	123-4	14
15	Keegan	5		Thorpe 1		THORPE c JOYCE b KEEGAN 23					
			R'kash 2	Azhar 1	1b	CK 4-0-28-1	MR 4	AM 1	11	128-5	15
16	Razzaq	3		Azhar 0		AZHAR c STRAUSS b RAZZAQ 1					
			R'kash 1	Batty 0	2nb	AR 4-0-25-1	MR 5	JB 0	13	131-6	16
17	Bl'field	7	R'kash 2	Batty 5		TB 4-0-32-1	MR 7	JB 5	13	138-6	17
18	Cook	11	R'kash 5	Batty 5	1lb	SC 2-0-26-1	MR 12	JB 10	14	149-6	18
19	Weekes	4	R'kash 2	Batty 2		PW 4-0-22-0	MR 14	JB 12	14	153-6	19
20	Cook	5	R'kash 4	Batty 0	1b	SC 2.2-0-30-1	MR 18	JB 12	15	158-6	20

SURREY LIONS v MIDDLESEX CRUSADERS at The Oval							
Friday 13th June			Surrey Lions won by four wickets				
Surrey Lions won the toss and elected to field			Umpires:- Mark Benson & John Steele				
MIDDLESEX CRUSADERS							
Fall Of Wkt	Batsman	How	Out	Score	Balls	4s	6s
1-4	P.N. Weekes	c Batty	b Bicknell	4	5	1	0
8-139	A.J. Strauss *	c Ward	b Ormond	52	48	6	0
2-47	C.B. Keegan		b Ormond	16	11	4	0
3-70	O.A. Shah	lbw	b Ormond	17	8	2	1
4-89	Abdul Razzaq	run	out	17	8	4	0
5-90	E.C. Joyce	c Batty	b Ormond	0	1	0	0
6-90	S.J. Cook		b Ormond	0	1	0	0
7-103	B.L. Hutton	c Thorpe	b Hollioake	3	8	0	0
9-155	R.M.S. Weston		b Azhar	30	24	4	0
	D. Alleyne +	Not	Out	6	4	1	0
10-155	T.F. Bloomfield	lbw	b Azhar	0	1	0	0
	Extras	(5lb, 5w)		10			
	TOTAL	(20 overs)		155			

Bowler	O	M	R	W	NB	Wd
Bicknell	3	0	23	1	-	-
Azhar Mahmood	4	0	28	2	-	-
Ormond	4	0	26	5	-	3
Sampson	3	0	39	0	-	2
Hollioake	4	0	22	1	-	-
Benning	2	0	12	0	-	-

SURREY LIONS							
Fall Of Wkt	Batsman	How	Out	Score	Balls	4s	6s
4-107	**I.J. Ward**	**run**	**out**	**31**	28	4	0
1-22	**A.D. Brown**	**c Strauss**	**b Bloomfield**	**7**	9	1	0
2-54	**J.G.E. Benning**		**b Cook**	**27**	14	6	0
3-89	**A.J. Hollioake ***	**c Weston**	**b Hutton**	**24**	14	2	1
5-123	**G.P. Thorpe**	**c Joyce**	**b Keegan**	**23**	15	3	0
	M.R. Ramprakash	**Not**	**Out**	**18**	16	2	0
6-127	**Azhar Mahmood**	**c Strauss**	**b Abdul Razzaq**	**1**	2	0	0
	J.N. Batty +	**Not**	**Out**	**12**	16	2	0
	M.P. Bicknell	**did not bat**					
	J. Ormond	**did not bat**					
	P.J. Sampson	**did not bat**					
	Extras	**(3b, 4lb, 6w, 2nb)**		**15**			
	TOTAL	**(19.2 overs)**	**(for 6 wkts)**	**158**			

Bowler	O	M	R	W	NB	Wd
Bloomfield	4	0	32	1	-	2
Keegan	4	0	28	1	-	-
Cook	2.2	0	30	1	-	-
Abdul Razzaq	4	0	25	1	1	-
Weekes	4	0	22	0	-	-
Hutton	1	0	14	1	-	-

Other Twenty20 Cup (South Division) Result

In the first-ever televised Twenty-20 contest, Hampshire Hawks claimed a narrow victory over the Sussex Sharks when the visitors to The Rose Bowl were unable to score ten to win from the final over. A crowd of around 9,000 people attended the match, and it was later estimated that the five games played on the opening evening of the tournament - at The Oval, The Rose Bowl, Chester-le-Street, Worcester and Taunton - had attracted a total of well over 30,000 spectators.

June 13
West End:- **Hampshire Hawks (2pts) beat Sussex Sharks by 5 runs.** Hants 153 (19.4ov; Davis 3-13); Sussex 148-7 (20ov; Ambrose 54*).

TWENTY-20 CUP SOUTH DIVISION QUALIFYING - MATCH TWO
Surrey Lions versus Essex Eagles
at Imber Court on Saturday 14th June

Within twenty-four hours of starting their Twenty-20 Cup campaign with a good win at The Oval, Surrey had decamped to Imber Court for their second match, against the Essex Eagles.

Surrey Lions' Innings
With the game again blessed by fine weather, and an excellent crowd in the ground, Surrey made a flying start through Ian Ward and Ali Brown, reaching forty-two by the end of fourth over, before both men fell in the space of three deliveries from Scott Brant and Graham Napier.

When Adam Hollioake then departed quickly to Brant, and James Benning went two overs later to Paul Grayson, much of the openers' good work had been undone at 70-4 in the eighth over and it took five overs of intelligent batting by the experienced Graham Thorpe and Mark Ramprakash to ensure that the Lions wouldn't repeat the mistake made by the Crusaders the previous evening.

Although Ramprakash was bowled when hitting across the line of a slower ball from Ryan ten Doeschate - a Port Elizabeth-born Dutchman who was making his Essex debut - having advanced the total to 106 after thirteen overs, Thorpe went on to record the first Twenty-20 half-century by a Surrey batsman, from 33 balls, before having his stumps similarly rearranged by Jon Dakin.

At 117-6 after fifteen overs, the Lions looked set to fall short of an imposing total on a fast-scoring ground, but Azhar Mahmood, playing his last game for the county before joining up with Pakistan, then proceeded to lash the bowlers all around the park, hitting three mighty sixes and three fours in scoring an unbeaten forty-three from just 18 balls. The last five overs consequently yielded sixty-five runs, allowing the home side to set their visitors a target of 183 to win at a rate of 9.15 runs per over.

SURREY LIONS INNINGS						************ END-OF-OVER TOTALS ************					
Ov	Bowler	Runs	Bat 1	Bat 2	Ex	BOWLER	BAT 1	BAT 2	EX	SCORE	OV
1	Dakin	8	Ward 7	Brown 1		JD 1-0-8-0	IW 7	AB 1	0	8-0	1
2	Brant	12	Ward 7	Brown 4	1lb	SB 1-0-11-0	IW 14	AB 5	1	20-0	2
3	Dakin	16	Ward 11	Brown 5		JD 2-0-24-0	IW 25	AB 10	1	36-0	3
4	Brant	6		Brown 1		BROWN b BRANT 11					
			Ward 5			SB 2-0-17-1	IW 30		1	42-1	4
5	Napier	7	Ward 0			WARD b NAPIER 30					
			Holl'ke 1	Benning 6		GN 1-0-7-1	AH 1	JB 6	1	49-2	5
6	Brant	3	Holl'ke 1			HOLLIOAKE b BRANT 2					
			Thorpe 1	Benning 1		SB 3-0-20-2	GT 1	JB 7	1	52-3	6
7	Napier	13	Thorpe 13	Benning 0		GN 2-0-20-1	GT 14	JB 7	1	65-3	7
8	Grayson	6		Benning 0		BENNING lbw b GRAYSON 7					
			Thorpe 5	R'kash 1		PG 1-0-6-1	GT 19	MR 1	1	71-4	8
9	Ten D'te	5	Thorpe 4	R'kash 1		RT 1-0-5-0	GT 23	MR 2	1	76-4	9
10	Grayson	4	Thorpe 2	R'kash 2		PG 2-0-10-1	GT 25	MR 4	1	80-4	10
11	Ten D'te	7	Thorpe 2	R'kash 5		RT 2-0-12-0	GT 27	MR 9	1	87-4	11
12	Grayson	11	Thorpe 10	R'kash 1		PG 3-0-21-1	GT 37	MR 10	1	98-4	12
13	Ten D'te	8		R'kash 1		RAMPRAKASH b TEN DOESCHATE 11					
			Thorpe 6		1w	RT 3-0-20-1	GT 43		2	106-5	13
14	Napier	9	Thorpe 7	Azhar 2		GN 3-0-29-1	GT 50	AM 2	2	115-5	14
15	Dakin	2	Thorpe 0			THORPE b DAKIN 50					
			Batty 1	Azhar 0	1lb	JD 3-0-25-1	JB 1	AM 2	3	117-6	15
16	Napier	12	Batty 10	Azhar 2		GN 4-0-41-1	JB 11	AM 4	3	129-6	16
17	Ten D'te	7	Batty 5			BATTY c PETTINI b TEN DOESCHATE 16					
				Azhar 1	1w	RT 4-0-27-2		AM 5	4	136-7	17
18	Brant	19	Ormond 2	Azhar 17		SB 4-0-39-2	JO 2	AM 22	4	155-7	18
19	Dakin	11	Ormond 1			ORMOND c TEN DOESCHATE b DAKIN 3					
			Sampson 1	Azhar 7	2nb	JD 4-0-36-2	PS 1	AM 29	6	166-8	19
20	Grayson	16		Azhar 14		AZHAR RUN OUT 43					
			Sampson 2			PG 4-0-37-1	PS 3		6	182-9	20

Essex Eagles' Innings

Chasing what was now a tricky target, Essex got off to a disastrous start, losing both Will Jefferson and James Foster inside the first fourteen balls of their reply as James Ormond and Azhar Mahmood struck early blows for the hosts.

From 12-2, the Eagles then recovered some ground through a stand of forty-one in 28 deliveries between Andy Flower and Ronnie Irani before the Zimbabwean was defeated and bowled by Tim Murtagh when he tried to hit the final ball of the seventh over to leg.

This left the visitors needing to score at exactly ten runs an over for the rest of their innings and, with the next four overs from Murtagh and Phil Sampson bringing just four, five, eight and six runs, Essex fell further and further behind the asking rate, their problems being compounded by Irani holing out to long-on off Murtagh in the last of these overs.

When Sampson then removed the potentially dangerous Dakin two overs later to leave the Eagles 89-5 in the thirteenth over, it was looking an increasingly lost cause for the visitors, especially with the remaining overs in the hands of Messrs Ormond, Hollioake and Mahmood.

Mark Pettini battled hard but neither he nor his colleagues could find the boundary often enough against top-class bowling and the end came quickly, with the Lions' regular 'death' bowlers taking the last four wickets in eleven balls as the visitors subsided to 138 all out, leaving Azhar with four wickets at the end of an impressive all-round match and Surrey victorious by forty-four runs.

ESSEX EAGLES INNINGS						*********** END-OF-OVER TOTALS ***********					
Ov	Bowler	Runs	Bat 1	Bat 2	Ex	BOWLER	BAT 1	BAT 2	EX	SCORE	OV
1	Azhar	4	Jeff'son 4	Flower 0		AM 1-0-4-0	WJ 4	AF 0	0	4-0	1
2	Ormond	7	Jeff'son 0			JEFFERSON b ORMOND 4					
				Flower 7		JO 1-0-7-1		AF 7	0	11-1	2
3	Azhar	4	Foster 0			FOSTER c BATTY b AZHAR 0					
			Irani 2	Flower 2		AM 2-0-8-1	RI 2	AF 9	0	15-2	3
4	Ormond	8	Irani 5	Flower 1	2w	JO 2-0-15-1	RI 7	AF 10	2	23-2	4
5	Murtagh	5	Irani 4	Flower 1		TM 1-0-5-0	RI 11	AF 11	2	28-2	5
6	Sampson	14	Irani 5	Flower 9		PS 1-0-14-0	RI 16	AF 20	2	42-2	6
7	Murtagh	11		Flower 10		FLOWER b MURTAGH 30					
			Irani 1			TM 2-0-16-1	RI 17		2	53-3	7
8	Sampson	4	Irani 2	Pettini 2		PS 2-0-18-0	RI 19	MP 2	2	57-3	8
9	Murtagh	5	Irani 1	Pettini 2	1w, 1lb	TM 3-0-20-1	RI 20	MP 4	4	62-3	9
10	Sampson	12	Irani 6	Pettini 5	1lb	PS 3-0-29-0	RI 26	MP 9	5	74-3	10
11	Murtagh	6	Irani 0			IRANI c AZHAR b MURTAGH 26					
			Dakin 1	Pettini 5		TM 4-0-26-2	JD 1	MP 14	5	80-4	11
12	Holl'ke	4	Dakin 1	Pettini 2	1lb	AH 1-0-3-0	JD 2	MP 16	6	84-4	12
13	Sampson	8	Dakin 4			DAKIN b SAMPSON 6					
			Napier 2	Pettini 2		PS 4-0-37-1	GN 2	MP 18	6	92-5	13
14	Holl'ke	5	Napier 2	Pettini 2	1w	AH 2-0-8-0	GN 4	MP 20	7	97-5	14
15	Ormond	7	Napier 1	Pettini 6		JO 3-0-22-1	GN 5	MP 26	7	104-5	15
16	Azhar	7		Pettini 5		PETTINI b AZHAR 31					
			Napier 1	Grayson 1		AM 3-0-15-2	GN 6	PG 1	7	111-6	16
17	Ormond	10	Napier 0	Grayson 9	1lb	JO 4-0-31-1	GN 6	PG 10	8	121-6	17
18	Holl'ke	12	Napier 0			NAPIER b HOLLIOAKE 6					
			Bopara 0			BOPARA c BROWN b HOLLIOAKE 0					
			Ten D'te 2	Grayson 5	3w, 2lb	AH 3-0-18-2	RT 2	PG 15	13	133-8	18
19	Azhar	5		Grayson 0		GRAYSON b AZHAR 15					
			Ten D'te 4			TEN DOESCHATE b AZHAR 6					
				Brant 1		AM 3.5-0-20-4		SB 1	13	138	19

SURREY LIONS v ESSEX EAGLES at Imber Court							
Saturday 14th June				Surrey Lions won by 44 runs			
Essex Eagles won the toss and elected to field				Umpires:- Graham Burgess & Tony Clarkson			
SURREY LIONS							
Fall Of Wkt	Batsman	How	Out	Score	Balls	4s	6s
2-42	**I.J. Ward**		**b Napier**	**30**	19	4	1
1-42	**A.D. Brown**		**b Brant**	**11**	7	2	0
4-70	**J.G.E. Benning**	**lbw**	**b Grayson**	**7**	6	1	0
3-51	**A.J. Hollioake ***		**b Brant**	**2**	4	0	0
6-115	**G.P. Thorpe**		**b Dakin**	**50**	35	5	2
5-106	**M.R..Ramprakash**		**b ten Doeschate**	**11**	14	1	0
9-182	**Azhar Mahmood**	**run**	**out**	**43**	18	3	3
7-136	**J.N. Batty +**	**c Pettini**	**b ten Doeschate**	**16**	12	3	0
8-164	**J. Ormond**	**c ten Doeschate**	**b Dakin**	**3**	3	0	0
	P.J. Sampson	**Not**	**Out**	**3**	3	0	0
	T.J. Murtagh	**did not bat**					
	Extras	**(2lb, 2w, 2nb)**		**6**			
	TOTAL	**(20 overs)**	**(for 9 wkts)**	**182**			

Bowler	O	M	R	W	NB	Wd
Dakin	**4**	**0**	**36**	**2**	1	-
Brant	**4**	**0**	**39**	**2**	-	-
Napier	**4**	**0**	**41**	**1**	-	-
Grayson	**4**	**0**	**37**	**1**	-	-
ten Doeschate	**4**	**0**	**27**	**2**	-	2

ESSEX EAGLES							
Fall Of Wkt	Batsman	How	Out	Score	Balls	4s	6s
1-11	**W.I. Jefferson**		**b Ormond**	**4**	8	0	0
3-53	**A. Flower**		**b Murtagh**	**30**	18	4	0
2-12	**J.S. Foster +**	**c Batty**	**b Azhar**	**0**	1	0	0
4-75	**R. Irani ***	**c Azhar**	**b Murtagh**	**26**	25	4	0
6-110	**M.L. Pettini**		**b Azhar**	**31**	27	3	0
5-89	**J.M. Dakin**		**b Sampson**	**6**	7	1	0
7-122	**G.R. Napier**		**b Hollioake**	**6**	10	0	0
9-133	**A.P. Grayson**		**b Azhar**	**15**	10	2	0
8-124	**R.S. Bopara**	**c Brown**	**b Hollioake**	**0**	1	0	0
10-138	**R.N. ten Doeschate**		**b Azhar**	**6**	4	1	0
	S.A. Brant	**Not**	**Out**	**1**	2	0	0
	Extras	**(6lb, 7w)**		**13**			
	TOTAL	**(18.5 overs)**		**138**			

Bowler	O	M	R	W	NB	Wd
Azhar Mahmood	**3.5**	**0**	**20**	**4**	-	-
Ormond	**4**	**0**	**31**	**1**	-	2
Murtagh	**4**	**0**	**26**	**2**	-	1
Sampson	**4**	**0**	**37**	**1**	-	-
Hollioake	**3**	**0**	**18**	**2**	-	4

TWENTY-20 CUP SOUTH DIVISION QUALIFYING - MATCH THREE
Surrey Lions versus Sussex Sharks
at Imber Court on Monday 16th June

Returning to Imber Court for the last of their three home matches in the space of four days, Surrey were now up against the Sussex Sharks, who elected to bat on winning the toss.

Sussex Sharks' Innings

Having already been beaten by Hampshire, the visitors couldn't afford to lose to the current group leaders, since they would then be on the brink of going out of the competition after just two games.

This may have accounted for the over-cautious start made by Matt Prior and Bas Zuiderent, who, despite putting on forty-two for the first wicket, failed to take full advantage of the crucial first six overs, during which the usual strict fielding restrictions were in place. To compound this felony, both then fell without ever really cutting loose, Prior to the first ball delivered by a Surrey spinner in the competition so far when he drove Ian Salisbury to long-off.

At the halfway mark, with Zuiderent having just departed to a fine catch by Jon Batty from an inside edge off Phil Sampson, the Sharks were struggling at 64-2, and they then lost two further wickets to the excellent Salisbury and Sampson in successive overs before the score had reached eighty.

Chris Adams and Tim Ambrose rallied their side for a while with a series of boundaries at the expense of Tim Murtagh and Adam Hollioake before the Surrey captain removed his opposite number in the sixteenth over, thanks to another very fine catch by Batty, this time standing up to the wicket.

Although Ambrose went on to strike three more fours in quick succession, the innings completely fizzled out after his departure, with Hollioake and Ormond proving much too good for the Sussex lower order as overs eighteen to twenty yielded the same number of runs as the first three overs of the innings - just fourteen.

Hollioake ended up with four wickets and the Sharks with a score that looked some way below par on this fast-scoring ground.

SUSSEX SHARKS INNINGS						*********** END-OF-OVER TOTALS ***********					
Ov	Bowler	Runs	Bat 1	Bat 2	Ex	BOWLER	BAT 1	BAT 2	EX	SCORE	OV
1	Ormond	5	Prior 5	Zuid'nt 0		JO 1-0-5-0	MP 5	BZ 0	0	5-0	1
2	Murtagh	2	Prior 1	Zuid'nt 1		TM 1-0-2-0	MP 6	BZ 1	0	7-0	2
3	Ormond	7	Prior 4	Zuid'nt 2	1lb	JO 2-0-11-0	MP 10	BZ 3	1	14-0	3
4	Murtagh	12	Prior 3	Zuid'nt 9		TM 2-0-14-0	MP 13	BZ 12	1	26-0	4
5	Ormond	6	Prior 1	Zuid'nt 5		JO 3-0-17-0	MP 14	BZ 17	1	32-0	5
6	Sampson	10	Prior 0	Zuid'nt 10		PS 1-0-10-0	MP 14	BZ 27	1	42-0	6
7	Salisbury	4	Prior 0			PRIOR c BROWN b SALISBURY 14					
			Goodwin 2	Zuid'nt 2		IS 1-0-4-1	MG 2	BZ 29	1	46-1	7
8	Sampson	10	Goodwin 5	Zuid'nt 1	3w, 1lb	PS 2-0-19-0	MG 7	BZ 30	5	56-1	8
9	Salisbury	6	Goodwin 1	Zuid'nt 5		IS 2-0-10-1	MG 8	BZ 35	5	62-1	9
10	Sampson	2		Zuid'nt 0		ZUIDERENT c BATTY b SAMPSON 35					
			Goodwin 1	Adams 1		PS 3-0-21-1	MG 9	CA 1	5	64-2	10
11	Salisbury	5	Goodwin 3	Adams 2		IS 3-0-15-1	MG 12	CA 3	5	69-2	11
12	Sampson	8	Goodwin 4			GOODWIN c MURTAGH b SAMPSON 16					
			M-Jenks 3	Adams 0	1w	PS 4-0-29-2	RMJ 3	CA 3	6	77-3	12
13	Salisbury	5	M-Jenks 0			M-JENKINS c BROWN b SALISBURY 3					
			Amb'se 0	Adams 5		IS 4-0-20-2	TA 0	CA 8	6	82-4	13
14	Holl'ke	9	Amb'se 3	Adams 6		AH 1-0-9-0	TA 3	CA 14	6	91-4	14
15	Murtagh	14	Amb'se 3	Adams 11		TM 3-0-28-0	TA 6	CA 25	6	105-4	15
16	Holl'ke	13		Adams 11		ADAMS c BATTY b HOLLIOAKE 36					
			Amb'se 2			AH 2-0-22-1	TA 8		6	118-5	16
17	Murtagh	11	Amb'se 10	Innes 1		TM 4-0-39-0	TA 18	KI 1	6	129-5	17
18	Holl'ke	6	Amb'se 5			AMBROSE b HOLLIOAKE 23					
			Davis 0	Innes 1		AH 3-0-28-2	MD 0	KI 2	6	135-6	18
19	Ormond	5	Davis 3	Innes 2		JO 4-0-22-0	MD 3	KI 4	6	140-6	19
20	Holl'ke	3		Innes 0		INNES c BROWN b HOLLIOAKE 4					
				Mushtaq 1		MUSHTAQ AHMED b HOLLIOAKE 1					
			Davis 2			AH 4-0-31-4	MD 5		6	143-8	20

Surrey Lions' Innings

With Ian Ward taking seventeen runs off Jason Lewry's third over of the Lions' innings, Sussex were soon appreciating that they had posted an inadequate total, though they went some way towards clawing themselves back into the game by capturing the wickets of both openers by the time the score had reached thirty-eight.

Another promising innings by James Benning, in the company of his captain, soon put the hosts back on top, however, and the Sharks were looking dead in water after nine overs, by which time the score had advanced to 82-2.

Mushtaq Ahmed had other ideas, though, and managed to breathe some life into a dying contest by removing both members of the third-wicket partnership during his second over, demonstrating, as Salisbury had before him, that spinners could most certainly play an important role in Twenty-20 cricket.

The reliable team of Thorpe and Ramprakash then stabilised the innings at a stage when Mushtaq and his spin twin, Mark Davis, were looking dangerous, and, though both eventually fell in the same Davis over, they had left their lower-order colleagues with the reasonably straightforward task of scoring thirty-one from the last five overs.

Only three overs and one ball were required, however, as Batty, with a six and two fours, and Salisbury, with a straight drive for six off Davis, saw their side home to a victory that put the Lions within sight of qualification for Finals Day.

SURREY LIONS INNINGS						*********** END-OF-OVER TOTALS ***********					
Ov	Bowler	Runs	Bat 1	Bat 2	Ex	BOWLER	BAT 1	BAT 2	EX	SCORE	OV
1	Lewry	5	Ward 3	Brown 0	1w, 1lb	JL 1-0-4-0	IW 3	AB 0	2	5-0	1
2	Hutch'n	8	Ward 1	Brown 7		PH 1-0-8-0	IW 4	AB 7	2	13-0	2
3	Lewry	18	Ward 17	Brown 1		JL 2-0-22-0	IW 21	AB 8	2	31-0	3
4	Hutch'n	7		Brown 0		BROWN c AMBROSE b HUTCHISON 8					
			Ward 1	Benning 5	1w	PH 2-0-15-1	IW 22	JB 5	3	38-1	4
5	M-Jenk's	3	Ward 0			WARD c DAVIS b MARTIN-JENKINS 22					
			Holl'ke 1	Benning 2		RMJ 1-0-3-1	AH 1	JB 7	3	41-2	5
6	Hutch'n	9	Holl'ke 8	Benning 1		PH 3-0-24-1	AH 9	JB 8	3	50-2	6
7	M-Jenk's	8	Holl'ke 6	Benning 2		RMJ 2-0-11-1	AH 15	JB 10	3	58-2	7
8	Mushtaq	8	Holl'ke 1	Benning 7		MA 1-0-8-0	AH 16	JB 17	3	66-2	8
9	M-Jenk's	16	Holl'ke 7	Benning 9		RMJ 3-0-27-1	AH 23	JB 26	3	82-2	9
10	Mushtaq	3	Holl'ke 1			HOLLIOAKE c PRIOR b MUSHTAQ 24					
				Benning 1		BENNING c GOODWIN b MUSHTAQ 27					
			Thorpe 0	R'kash 0	1lb	MA 2-0-10-2	GT 0	MR 0	4	85-4	10
11	Davis	5	Thorpe 4	R'kash 1		MD 1-0-5-0	GT 4	MR 1	4	90-4	11
12	Mushtaq	3	Thorpe 2	R'kash 1		MA 3-0-13-2	GT 6	MR 2	4	93-4	12
13	Davis	4	Thorpe 2	R'kash 1	1lb	MD 2-0-8-0	GT 8	MR 3	5	97-4	13
14	Mushtaq	7	Thorpe 2	R'kash 5		MA 4-0-20-2	GT 10	MR 8	5	104-4	14
15	Davis	9		R'kash 0		RAMPRAKASH st AMBROSE b DAVIS 8					
			Thorpe 8			THORPE RUN OUT 18					
			Batty 1			MD 3-0-17-1	JB 1		5	113-6	15
16	Innes	5	Batty 1	Salisbury 3	1lb	KI 1-0-4-0	JB 2	IS 3	6	118-6	16
17	Davis	14	Batty 6	Salisbury 8		MD 4-0-31-1	JB 8	IS 11	6	132-6	17
18	Innes	7	Batty 5	Salisbury 1	1lb	KI 2-0-10-0	JB 13	IS 12	7	139-6	18
19	M-Jenk's	6	Batty 6	Salisbury 0		RMJ 3.1-0-33-1	JB 19	IS 12	7	145-6	19

SURREY LIONS v SUSSEX SHARKS at Imber Court

Monday 16th June — **Surrey Lions won by four wickets**

Sussex Sharks won the toss and elected to bat — Umpires:- Mark Benson & Peter Hartley

SUSSEX SHARKS							
Fall Of Wkt	Batsman	How	Out	Score	Balls	4s	6s
1-42	M.J. Prior	c Brown	b Salisbury	14	14	2	0
2-62	B. Zuiderent	c Batty	b Sampson	35	34	5	0
3-73	M.W. Goodwin	c Murtagh	b Sampson	16	14	2	0
5-118	C.J. Adams *	c Batty	b Hollioake	36	22	5	1
4-77	R.S.C. Martin-Jenkins	c Brown	b Salisbury	3	5	0	0
6-135	T.R. Ambrose +		b Hollioake	23	14	3	0
7-140	K.J. Innes	c Brown	b Hollioake	4	8	0	0
	M.J.G. Davis	Not	Out	5	7	0	0
8-143	Mushtaq Ahmed		b Hollioake	1	2	0	0
	P.M. Hutchison	did not bat					
	J.D. Lewry	did not bat					
	Extras	(2lb, 4w)		6			
	TOTAL	(20 overs)	(for 8 wkts)	143			

Bowler	O	M	R	W	NB	Wd
Ormond	4	0	22	0	-	-
Murtagh	4	0	39	0	-	-
Sampson	4	0	29	2	-	2
Salisbury	4	0	20	2	-	-
Hollioake	4	0	31	4	-	-

SURREY LIONS							
Fall Of Wkt	Batsman	How	Out	Score	Balls	4s	6s
2-38	**I.J. Ward**	**c Davis**	**b Martin-Jenkins**	**22**	12	2	1
1-31	**A.D. Brown**	**c Ambrose**	**b Hutchison**	**8**	9	1	0
4-84	**J.G.E. Benning**	**c Goodwin**	**b Mushtaq**	**27**	22	4	0
3-84	**A.J. Hollioake ***	**c Prior**	**b Mushtaq**	**24**	16	2	1
6-113	**G.P. Thorpe**	**run**	**out**	**18**	16	2	0
5-104	**M.R. Ramprakash**	**st Ambrose**	**b Davis**	**8**	13	0	0
	J.N. Batty +	**Not**	**Out**	**19**	12	2	1
	I.D.K. Salisbury	**Not**	**Out**	**12**	9	0	1
	J. Ormond	**did not bat**					
	T.J. Murtagh	**did not bat**					
	P.J. Sampson	**did not bat**					
	Extras	**(5lb, 2w)**		**7**			
	TOTAL	**(18.1 overs)**	**(for 6 wkts)**	**145**			

Bowler	O	M	R	W	NB	Wd
Lewry	**2**	**0**	**22**	**0**	-	1
Hutchison	**3**	**0**	**24**	**1**	-	1
Martin-Jenkins	**3.1**	**0**	**33**	**1**	-	-
Mushtaq Ahmed	**4**	**0**	**20**	**2**	-	-
Davis	**4**	**0**	**31**	**1**	-	-
Innes	**2**	**0**	**10**	**0**	-	-

Other Twenty20 Cup (South Division) Result

Andrew Symonds' sensational unbeaten innings of ninety-six powered Kent Spitfires to an easy victory over Hampshire Hawks at Beckenham and further strengthened Surrey's position in the South Division.

June 16
***Beckenham:-* Kent Spitfires (2pts) beat Hampshire Hawks by 6 wickets.** Hants 145-6 (20ov; Katich 59*); Kent 147-4 (12ov; Symonds 96*).

TWENTY20 CUP (SOUTH DIVISION) TABLE AT 16TH JUNE

Pos		P	Pts	W	L
1	**Surrey Lions**	**3**	**6**	3	0
2	**Kent Spitfires**	**1**	**2**	1	0
3	**Hampshire Hawks**	**2**	**2**	1	1
4	**Essex Eagles**	**1**	**0**	0	1
5	**Sussex Sharks**	**2**	**0**	0	2
6	**Middlesex Crusaders**	**1**	**0**	0	1

Having played three games in four days, Surrey then had to sit back and watch their rivals contesting five matches over the course of the next week from their lofty perch at the top of the South Division table. By the time the Lions came to play their penultimate game, against Kent at Canterbury, they would have a very good idea about what they needed to do to make Finals Day.

Twenty20 Cup (South Division) Results

With every other side bar Kent having lost at least two matches, Surrey were left in a position of great strength at the end of their one-week break. A win at Canterbury over the Kent Spitfires would now guarantee them top place in the South Division and a trip to Trent Bridge on 19th July. Even if they failed to win that game there would be a second chance to qualify for Finals Day by beating Hampshire Hawks at The Rose Bowl the following day.

June 18
***West End:-* Essex Eagles (2pts) beat Hampshire Hawks by 4 runs.** Essex 155-6 (20ov; Flower 49); Hants 151-3 (20ov; Katich 59*, Kenway 40).

***Hove:-* Sussex Sharks (2pts) beat Middlesex Crusaders by 41 runs.** Sussex 177-9 (20ov; Martin-Jenkins 47*, Prior 46, Keegan 3-34); Middx 136 (19.3ov; Martin-Jenkins 4-20).

June 19

***Richmond:-* Middlesex Crusaders (2pts) beat Kent Spitfires by 7 wickets.** Kent 161-8 (20ov; Noffke 3-29); Middx 165-3 (17.2ov; Strauss 60, Shah 40*).

June 20

***Chelmsford:-* Kent Spitfires (2pts) beat Essex Eagles by 3 wickets.** Essex 116 (18.4ov; Dennington 4-28); Kent 120-7 (16.1ov; Napier 3-20).

June 21

***Hove:-* Sussex Sharks (2pts) beat Essex Eagles by 7 runs.** Sussex 180-6 (20ov; Martin-Jenkins 56*); Essex 173-4 (20ov; Flower 71).

TWENTY20 CUP (SOUTH DIVISION) TABLE AT 21ST JUNE

Pos		P	Pts	W	L
1	**Surrey Lions**	3	6	3	0
2	**Kent Spitfires**	3	4	2	1
3	**Sussex Sharks**	4	4	2	2
4	**Middlesex Crusaders**	3	2	1	2
=	**Hampshire Hawks**	3	2	1	2
6	**Essex Eagles**	4	2	1	3

TWENTY-20 CUP SOUTH DIVISION QUALIFYING - MATCH FOUR
Kent Spitfires versus Surrey Lions
at Canterbury on Monday 23rd June

Surrey Lions' Innings

Having put Surrey in to bat at a very well-populated St. Lawrence Ground, Spitfires' skipper Dave Fulton attempted the interesting ploy of opening the bowling with a combination of raw pace at one end - from their new Pakistani signing, Mohammad Sami - and off-spin, from James Tredwell, at the other.

With Tredwell battered for thirty-six runs in three overs, and the Lions racing to 50-2 at ten runs per over, the experiment wasn't a huge success, though the visitors were immediately pegged back when Andrew Symonds, bowling the sixth over of the innings in his off-spin mode, managed to deliver a wicket-maiden - an incredible feat in Twenty-20 cricket, especially during the first six overs. To everyone's surprise, the Australian all-rounder was immediately withdrawn from the attack, though the visitors still continued to decline somewhat from their flying start, reaching the halfway point at 82-4.

Disaster then loomed for Surrey when Adam Hollioake holed out to long-on off Mark Ealham, leaving the Lions struggling at 93-5 with just eight overs remaining, but Mark Ramprakash and Azhar Mahmood, freshly returned from his participation in the Nat West Challenge, then put together an excellent sixth-wicket partnership of fifty-eight from just 40 balls to turn the tide.

Although Symonds managed to deliver another three restrictive overs when he returned to the attack, Azhar was in good touch from the off, striking two legside sixes within three overs of arriving at the crease and then three more 'maximums' after losing Ramprakash for an excellent fifty-three at the start of the nineteenth over.

Thanks to those three sixes, thirty-five important runs flowed from the final eleven balls of the Surrey innings as Azhar tore into the inexperienced Peter Trego and Matt Dennington to complete a stunning half-century, including 5 sixes and 2 fours, from a mere 29 balls.

A final total of 186 looked good, but not insurmountable, especially with Andy Symonds in the opposition line-up.

SURREY LIONS INNINGS						*********** END-OF-OVER TOTALS ***********					
Ov	Bowler	Runs	Bat 1	Bat 2	Ex	BOWLER	BAT 1	BAT 2	EX	SCORE	OV
1	Tredwell	11	Ward 4			WARD b TREDWELL 4					
			Benning 0	Brown 7		JT 1-0-11-1	JB 0	AB 7	0	11-1	1
2	Sami	12	Benning 0	Brown 8	4lb	MS 1-0-8-0	JB 0	AB 15	4	23-1	2
3	Tredwell	11	Benning 7	Brown 4		JT 2-0-22-1	JB 7	AB 19	4	34-1	3
4	Sami	2		Brown 0		BROWN b SAMI 19					
			Benning 1	Newman 0	1lb	MS 2-0-9-1	JB 8	SN 0	5	36-2	4
5	Tredwell	14	Benning 1	Newman 13		JT 3-0-36-1	JB 9	SN 13	5	50-2	5
6	Symonds	0	Benning 0			BENNING c TREDWELL b SYMONDS 9					
				Newman 0		AS 1-1-0-1		SN 13	5	50-3	6
7	Ealham	6	R'kash 2	Newman 4		ME 1-0-6-0	MR 2	SN 17	5	56-3	7
8	Denn'ton	8	R'kash 6	Newman 2		MD 1-0-8-0	MR 8	SN 19	5	64-3	8
9	Ealham	5		Newman 0		NEWMAN b EALHAM 19					
			R'kash 4	Holl'ke 1		ME 2-0-11-1	MR 12	AH 1	5	69-4	9
10	Denn'ton	13	R'kash 11	Holl'ke 1	1w	MD 2-0-21-0	MR 23	AH 2	6	82-4	10
11	Symonds	5	R'kash 3	Holl'ke 2		AS 2-1-5-1	MR 26	AH 4	6	87-4	11
12	Ealham	7		Holl'ke 5		HOLLIOAKE c SMITH b EALHAM 9					
			R'kash 2	Azhar 0		ME 3-0-18-2	MR 28	AM 0	6	94-5	12
13	Symonds	3	R'kash 2	Azhar 1		AS 3-1-8-1	MR 30	AM 1	6	97-5	13
14	Ealham	13	R'kash 2	Azhar 11		ME 4-0-31-2	MR 32	AM 12	6	110-5	14
15	Symonds	9	R'kash 1	Azhar 7	1w	AS 4-1-17-1	MR 33	AM 19	7	119-5	15
16	Sami	8	R'kash 7	Azhar 1		MS 3-0-17-1	MR 40	AM 20	7	127-5	16
17	Tredwell	10	R'kash 6	Azhar 4		JT 4-0-46-1	MR 46	AM 24	7	137-5	17
18	Sami	14	R'kash 7	Azhar 5	2nb	MS 4-0-31-1	MR 53	AM 29	9	151-5	18
19	Trego	17	R'kash 0			RAMPRAKASH c SYMONDS b TREGO 53					
			Batty 6			BATTY c FULTON b TREGO 6					
			Sal'bury 0	Azhar 11		PT 1-0-17-2	IS 0	AM 40	9	168-7	19
20	Denn'ton	18	Sal'bury 0			SALISBURY b DENNINGTON 0					
			Bicknell 1	Azhar 17		MD 3-0-39-1	MB 1	AM 57	9	186-8	20

Kent Spitfires' Innings

The threat of Symonds was soon highlighted when the big Aussie hit his second, fourth and fifth balls from Tim Murtagh for four, six and four in the second over of the Spitfires' reply, much to the delight of the ever-partisan Canterbury crowd. The young Surrey swing bowler held his nerve well, though, luring the opposition's key batsman into another pull at the next delivery and inducing a mishit that was safely taken by Ali Brown running round behind the bowler.

Players and spectators alike knew that this was a vital wicket, and the mood of despondency amongst the home fans was soon multiplied when Murtagh bowled Kent's other opener, Trego, with his next delivery, and Bicknell had Tredwell taken at point from the fourth ball of the following over.

At 21-3, Kent were in deep trouble and it was only a couple of sixes, blasted away over midwicket by Ealham, and two dropped catches by the normally reliable Benning that kept the home side in the game over the course of the next three overs.

Although Ealham failed to profit from his good fortune by instantly miscuing the newly introduced Azhar to point with the score at forty-four, the Spitfires were brought back into contention by Mat Walker and Ed Smith - Kent's 'nearly men' during the NCL match at The Oval - who added forty-five inside five overs before Walker lofted Salisbury into the hands of Ramprakash at deep midwicket in the eleventh over.

With the asking rate rising above ten, Smith was now the main man for the Spitfires and while he was at the crease victory was always possible for the home side, even after the loss of another wicket Geraint Jones going to Azhar for nine - in the fourteenth over.

The decisive moment of the match therefore came with fifty-eight runs needed from twenty-nin balls when Smith attempted a second leg-bye to Benning at short third man and was run out by brilliant direct-hit throw that easily made up for the youngster's earlier lapses.

When fifteen runs came from the seventeenth over of the innings bowled by Adam Hollioake, Kent' hopes were briefly raised, though they were immediately snuffed out by a superb following over fror

Murtagh that saw just three added to the total and left the home side needing an impossible forty runs from the last two overs. At this point everyone knew the game was up for the Spitfires and that the Lions were roaring on to the Finals Day next month.

KENT SPITFIRES INNINGS						*********** END-OF-OVER TOTALS ***********					
Ov	Bowler	Runs	Bat 1	Bat 2	Ex	BOWLER	BAT 1	BAT 2	EX	SCORE	OV
1	Bicknell	4	Trego 0	Symonds 1	2w, 1lb	MB 1-0-3-0	PT 0	AS 1	3	4-0	1
2	Murtagh	14		Symonds 14		SYMONDS c BROWN b MURTAGH 15					
			Trego 0			TREGO b MURTAGH 0					
				Tredwell 0		TM 1-0-14-2		JT 0	3	18-2	2
3	Bicknell	3		Tredwell 1		TREDWELL c WARD b BICKNELL 1					
			Ealham 1	Walker 0	1w	MB 2-0-6-1	ME 1	MW 0	4	21-3	3
4	Murtagh	13	Ealham 12	Walker 1		TM 2-0-27-2	ME 13	MW 1	4	34-3	4
5	Bicknell	7	Ealham 0	Walker 7		MB 3-0-13-1	ME 13	MW 8	4	41-3	5
6	Azhar	3	Ealham 2			EALHAM c SALISBURY b AZHAR 15					
			Smith 0	Walker 1		AM 1-0-3-1	ES 0	MW 9	4	44-4	6
7	Sal'bury	6	Smith 4	Walker 1	1lb	IS 1-0-5-0	ES 4	MW 10	5	50-4	7
8	Azhar	12	Smith 5	Walker 6	1w	AM 2-0-15-1	ES 9	MW 16	6	62-4	8
9	Sal'bury	9	Smith 7	Walker 2		IS 2-0-14-0	ES 16	MW 18	6	71-4	9
10	Holl'ke	16	Smith 14	Walker 0	1w, 1lb	AH 1-0-15-0	ES 30	MW 18	8	87-4	10
11	Sal'bury	5		Walker 2		WALKER c RAM'KASH b SAL'BURY 20					
			Smith 2	Jones 1		IS 3-0-19-1	ES 32	GJ 1	8	92-5	11
12	Bicknell	14	Smith 13	Jones 1		MB 4-0-27-1	ES 45	GJ 2	8	106-5	12
13	Sal'bury	6	Smith 3	Jones 3		IS 4-0-25-1	ES 48	GJ 5	8	112-5	13
14	Azhar	8		Jones 4		JONES c NEWMAN b AZHAR 9					
			Smith 2	Carberry 0	2w	AM 3-0-23-2	ES 50	MC 0	10	120-6	14
15	Holl'ke	9	Smith 6	Carberry 3		AH 2-0-24-0	ES 56	MC 3	10	129-6	15
16	Azhar	4	Smith 0			SMITH RUN OUT 56					
			Fulton 1	Carberry 1	2lb	AM 4-0-25-2	DF 1	MC 4	12	133-7	16
17	Holl'ke	11		Carberry 6		CARBERRY c BICKNELL b HOLLIOAKE 10					
			Fulton 5	Denn'ton 0		AH 3-0-35-1	DF 6	MD 0	12	144-8	17
18	Murtagh	3	Fulton 1	Denn'ton 1	1lb	TM 3-0-29-2	DF 7	MD 1	13	147-8	18
19	Holl'ke	13	Fulton 2	Denn'ton 11		AH 4-0-48-1	DF 9	MD 12	13	160-8	19
20	Murtagh	8		Denn'ton 0		DENNINGTON b MURTAGH 12					
			Fulton 3	Sami 5		TM 4-0-37-3	DF 12	MS 5	13	168-9	20

KENT SPITFIRES v SURREY LIONS at Canterbury							
Monday 23rd June			Surrey Lions won by 18 runs				
Kent Spitfires won the toss and elected to field			Umpires:- Trevor Jesty & John Steele				
SURREY LIONS							
Fall Of Wkt	Batsman	How	Out	Score	Balls	4s	6s
2-35	**A.D. Brown**		**b Mohammad Sami**	**19**	11	4	0
1-11	**I.J. Ward**		**b Tredwell**	**4**	2	1	0
3-50	**J.G.E. Benning**	**c Tredwell**	**b Symonds**	**9**	10	1	0
4-67	**S.A. Newman**		**b Ealham**	**19**	18	1	1
6-151	**M.R..Ramprakash**	**c Symonds**	**b Trego**	**53**	35	3	3
5-93	**A.J. Hollioake ***	**c Smith**	**b Ealham**	**9**	10	1	0
	Azhar Mahmood	**Not**	**Out**	**57**	31	2	5
7-158	**J.N. Batty +**	**c Fulton**	**b Trego**	**6**	2	0	1
8-168	**I.D.K. Salisbury**		**b Dennington**	**0**	1	0	0
	M.P. Bicknell	**Not**	**Out**	**1**	1	0	0
	T.J. Murtagh	**did not bat**					
	Extras	**(5lb, 2w, 2nb)**		**9**			
	TOTAL	**(20 overs)**	**(for 8 wkts)**	**186**			

Bowler	O	M	R	W	NB	Wd
Tredwell	**4**	**0**	**46**	**1**	-	-
Mohammad Sami	**4**	**0**	**31**	**1**	1	-
Symonds	**4**	**1**	**17**	**1**	-	1
Ealham	**4**	**0**	**31**	**2**	-	-
Dennington	**3**	**0**	**39**	**1**	-	1
Trego	**1**	**0**	**17**	**2**	-	-

KENT SPITFIRES							
Fall Of Wkt	Batsman	How	Out	Score	Balls	4s	6s
2-18	**P.D. Trego**		**b Murtagh**	**0**	6	0	0
1-18	**A. Symonds**	**c Brown**	**b Murtagh**	**15**	6	2	1
3-21	**J.C. Tredwell**	**c Ward**	**b Bicknell**	**1**	2	0	0
4-44	**M.A. Ealham**	**c Salisbury**	**b Azhar**	**15**	11	0	2
5-89	**M.J. Walker**	**c Ramprakash**	**b Salisbury**	**20**	23	2	0
7-130	**E.T. Smith**	**run**	**out**	**56**	33	5	2
6-117	**G.O. Jones +**	**c Newman**	**b Azhar**	**9**	8	1	0
8-140	**M.A. Carberry**	**c Bicknell**	**b Hollioake**	**10**	6	0	1
	D.P. Fulton *	**Not**	**Out**	**12**	12	1	0
9-160	**M.J. Dennington**		**b Murtagh**	**12**	10	1	1
	Mohammad Sami	**Not**	**Out**	**5**	3	1	0
	Extras	**(6lb, 7w)**		**13**			
	TOTAL	**(20 overs)**	**(for 9 wkts)**	**168**			

Bowler	O	M	R	W	NB	Wd
Bicknell	**4**	**0**	**27**	**1**	-	3
Murtagh	**4**	**0**	**37**	**3**	-	-
Azhar Mahmood	**4**	**0**	**25**	**2**	-	3
Salisbury	**4**	**0**	**25**	**1**	-	-
Hollioake	**4**	**0**	**48**	**1**	-	1

Other Twenty20 Cup (South Division) Result

June 23
Uxbridge:- **Middlesex Crusaders (2pts) beat Hampshire Hawks by 8 wickets.** Hants 134-7 (20ov; Cook 3-14, Noffke 3-22); Middx 136-2 (14.5ov; Weekes 56).

TWENTY20 CUP (SOUTH DIVISION) TABLE AT 23RD JUNE

Pos		P	Pts	W	L
1	**Surrey Lions**	4	8	4	0
2	**Kent Spitfires**	4	4	2	2
=	**Middlesex Crusaders**	4	4	2	2
=	**Sussex Sharks**	4	4	2	2
5	**Essex Eagles**	4	2	1	3
=	**Hampshire Hawks**	4	2	1	3

TWENTY-20 CUP SOUTH DIVISION QUALIFYING - MATCH FIVE
Hampshire Hawks versus Surrey Lions
at The Rose Bowl on Tuesday 24th June

Surrey Lions' Innings

A crowd of 6,500 at The Rose Bowl for this 'dead rubber' - Surrey having qualified for the finals and Hampshire out of the competition - emphasised how the public had taken to Twenty-20 Cup cricket.

On a gorgeous evening, typical of those that had blessed just about every match in the tournament, Surrey - fielding a bowler-heavy line-up after electing to rest several players - elected to take first use of what turned out to be a tricky surface that made run-scoring a tough business.

Their total of 140-9 owed almost everything to an excellent opening partnership of seventy-five from 54 balls between Ali Brown and Scott Newman, with Martin Bicknell the only other batsman to get into double figures once the stand was broken and wickets began to tumble on a regular basis to Hampshire's six seamers. Brown's 26-ball innings of thirty-three provided early impetus, while Newman anchored the Lions' effort by batting through to the fourth ball of the nineteenth over in making fifty-nine at exactly a run a ball.

SURREY LIONS INNINGS						*********** END-OF-OVER TOTALS ***********					
Ov	Bowler	Runs	Bat 1	Bat 2	Ex	BOWLER	BAT 1	BAT 2	EX	SCORE	OV
1	Wasim	8	Newman 1	Brown 6	1w	WA 1-0-8-0	SN 1	AB 6	1	8-0	1
2	Giddins	13	Newman 9	Brown 4		EG 1-0-13-0	SN 10	AB 10	1	21-0	2
3	Wasim	4	Newman 3	Brown 1		WA 2-0-12-0	SN 13	AB 11	1	25-0	3
4	Mullally	8	Newman 0	Brown 7	1lb	AM 1-0-7-0	SN 13	AB 18	2	33-0	4
5	Wasim	3	Newman 1	Brown 2		WA 3-0-15-0	SN 14	AB 20	2	36-0	5
6	Mullally	7	Newman 3	Brown 0	4b	AM 2-0-10-0	SN 17	AB 20	6	43-0	6
7	Masc'as	13	Newman 6	Brown 2	5b	DM 1-0-8-0	SN 23	AB 22	11	56-0	7
8	Mullally	7	Newman 5	Brown 1	1w	AM 3-0-17-0	SN 28	AB 23	12	63-0	8
9	Masc'as	13		Brown 10		BROWN b MASCARENHAS 33					
			Newman 0	Benning 1	2nb	DM 2-0-21-1	SN 28	JB 1	14	76-1	9
10	Mullally	5	Newman 4	Benning 1		AM 4-0-22-0	SN 32	JB 2	14	81-1	10
11	Hamblin	7		Benning 1		BENNING b HAMBLIN 3					
			Newman 5		1w	JH 1-0-7-1	SN 37		15	88-2	11
12	Prittipaul	2	Newman 1	R'kash 1		LP 1-0-2-0	SN 38	MR 1	15	90-2	12
13	Hamblin	10	Newman 7	R'kash 2	1w	JH 2-0-17-1	SN 45	MR 3	16	100-2	13
14	Prittipaul	5		R'kash 0		RAMPRAKASH b PRITTIPAUL 3					
			Newman 4	Batty 1		LP 2-0-7-1	SN 49	JB 1	16	105-3	14
15	Hamblin	5		Batty 0		BATTY c KENWAY b HAMBLIN 1					
			Newman 5	Holl'ke 0		JH 3-0-22-2	SN 54	AH 0	16	110-4	15
16	Prittipaul	4		Holl'ke 0		HOLLIOAKE c & b PRITTIPAUL 0					
			Newman 3	Sal'bury 1		LP 3-0-11-2	SN 57	IS 1	16	114-5	16
17	Hamblin	9		Sal'bury 7		SALISBURY c KATICH b HAMBLIN 8					
			Newman 1		1w	JH 4-0-31-3	SN 58		17	123-6	17
18	Prittipaul	6	Newman 1	Bicknell 3	2w	LP 4-0-17-2	SN 59	MB 3	19	129-6	18
19	Wasim	5	Newman 0			NEWMAN b WASIM 59					
			Saqlain 0			SAQLAIN c MASCARENHAS b WASIM 0					
			Murtagh 0	Bicknell 5		WA 4-0-20-2	TM 0	MB 8	19	134-8	19
20	Giddins	6	Murtagh 0			MURTAGH c KENDALL b GIDDINS 0					
			Sampson 4	Bicknell 2		EG 2-0-19-1	PS 4	MB 10	19	140-9	20

Hampshire Hawks' Innings

The home side's reply got off to the worst possible start when Bicknell trapped James Hamblin lbw first ball, though this did at least bring together Hampshire's two most likely match-winners, John Crawley and Simon Katich, early in the piece. They found the going tough, however, when confronted by an inspired opening spell of three overs for six runs from Bicknell that included a rare Twenty-20 maiden over - duly 'celebrated' by the bowler - and then found his replacement at the pavilion end, Phil Sampson, no easier to score off.

A task that was already difficult enough when they reached the halfway point with just fifty-one on the board, then became much harder when Sampson plucked a low hard-hit drive from Crawley out of thin air in his follow-through at the start of the next over, and harder still when they lost the potentially dangerous Wasim Akram to Saqlain Mushtaq in the over after that.

Katich battled on bravely and received excellent support from Derek Kenway in giving the Hawks a glimpse of success at 101-3 after sixteen overs, but Adam Hollioake then took three wickets - including both Kenway and Katich - in the following over to put the Lions back in charge before Bicknell returned to finish an outstanding spell of 4-1-11-2 with a five-run over that killed off Hampshire's hopes.

The tail then crumbled away in the last two overs to leave Hollioake with an impressive return of 5-21 and Surrey victorious by the margin of nineteen runs.

HAMPSHIRE HAWKS INNINGS						*********** END-OF-OVER TOTALS ***********					
Ov	Bowler	Runs	Bat 1	Bat 2	Ex	BOWLER	BAT 1	BAT 2	EX	SCORE	OV
1	Bicknell	4	Hamblin 0			HAMBLIN lbw b ORMOND 0					
			Katich 3	Crawley 0	1w	MB 1-0-4-1	SK 3	JC 0	1	4-1	1
2	Murtagh	3	Katich 2	Crawley 1		TM 1-0-3-0	SK 5	JC 1	1	7-1	2
3	Bicknell	0	Katich 0	Crawley 0		MB 2-1-4-1	SK 5	JC 1	1	7-1	3
4	Murtagh	11	Katich 5	Crawley 6		TM 2-0-14-0	SK 10	JC 7	1	18-1	4
5	Bicknell	2	Katich 0	Crawley 1	1w	MB 3-1-6-1	SK 10	JC 8	2	20-1	5
6	Murtagh	9	Katich 1	Crawley 8		TM 3-0-23-0	SK 11	JC 16	2	29-1	6
7	Sampson	4	Katich 0	Crawley 4		PS 1-0-4-0	SK 11	JC 20	2	33-1	7
8	Salisbury	7	Katich 5	Crawley 1	1lb	IS 1-0-6-0	SK 16	JC 21	3	40-1	8
9	Sampson	2	Katich 1	Crawley 1		PS 2-0-6-0	SK 17	JC 22	3	42-1	9
10	Salisbury	9	Katich 7	Crawley 1	1lb	IS 2-0-14-0	SK 24	JC 23	4	51-1	10
11	Sampson	3		Crawley 0		CRAWLEY c & b SAMPSON 23					
			Katich 2	Wasim 1		PS 3-0-9-1	SK 26	WA 1	4	54-2	11
12	Saqlain	8		Wasim 0		WASIM c SAMPSON b SAQLAIN 1					
			Katich 6	Kenway 2		SM 1-0-8-1	SK 32	DK 2	4	62-3	12
13	Sampson	9	Katich 5	Kenway 3	1w	PS 4-0-18-1	SK 37	DK 5	5	71-3	13
14	Saqlain	8	Katich 5	Kenway 2	1b	SM 2-0-15-1	SK 42	DK 7	6	79-3	14
15	Holl'ke	9	Katich 1	Kenway 8		AH 1-0-9-0	SK 43	DK 15	6	88-3	15
16	Saqlain	13	Katich 1	Kenway 12		SM 3-0-28-1	SK 44	DK 27	6	101-3	16
17	Holl'ke	3		Kenway 0		KENWAY b HOLLIOAKE 27					
				Kendall 1		KENDALL c SALISBURY b HOLLIOAKE 1					
			Katich 1			KATICH c RAMPRAKASH b HOLLIOAKE 45					
			Prittipaul 0	Masc'as 1		AH 2-0-12-3	LP 0	DM 1	6	104-6	17
18	Bicknell	5	Prittipaul 2			PRITTIPAUL c BATTY b BICKNELL 2					
				Masc'as 3		MB 4-1-11-2	LP 2	DM 4	6	109-7	18
19	Holl'ke	9	Pothas 4			POTHAS c RAMPRAKASH b HOLLIOAKE 4					
			Mullally 0			MULLALLY b HOLLIOAKE 0					
			Giddins 0	Masc'as 1	4nb	AH 3-0-21-5	EG 0	DM 5	10	118-9	19
20	Murtagh	3	Giddins 0			GIDDINS c NEWMAN b MURTAGH 0					
				Masc'as 3		TM 4-0-26-1		DM 8	10	121	20

HAMPSHIRE HAWKS v SURREY LIONS at The Rose Bowl

Tuesday 24th June — **Surrey Lions won by 19 runs**

Surrey Lions won the toss and elected to bat — Umpires:- John Holder & Nigel Llong

SURREY LIONS

Fall Of Wkt	Batsman	How	Out	Score	Balls	4s	6s
7-130	**S.A. Newman**		**b Wasim Akram**	**59**	59	7	1
1-75	**A.D. Brown**		**b Mascarenhas**	**33**	26	3	1
2-88	**J.G.E. Benning**		**b Hamblin**	**3**	6	0	0
3-100	**M.R..Ramprakash**		**b Prittipaul**	**3**	6	0	0
4-105	**J.N. Batty +**	**c Kenway**	**b Hamblin**	**1**	4	0	0
5-111	**A.J. Hollioake ***	**c &**	**b Prittipaul**	**0**	2	0	0
6-123	**I.D.K. Salisbury**	**c Katich**	**b Hamblin**	**8**	6	0	0
	M.P. Bicknell	**Not**	**Out**	**10**	7	1	0
8-130	**Saqlain Mushtaq**	**c Mascarenhas**	**b Wasim Akram**	**0**	1	0	0
9-134	**T.J. Murtagh**	**c Kendall**	**b Giddins**	**0**	1	0	0
	P.J. Sampson	**Not**	**Out**	**4**	3	0	0
	Extras	**(9b, 1lb, 7w, 2nb)**		**19**			
	TOTAL	**(20 overs)**	**(for 9 wkts)**	**140**			

Bowler	O	M	R	W	NB	Wd
Wasim Akram	**4**	**0**	**20**	**2**	-	1
Giddins	**2**	**0**	**19**	**1**	-	-
Mullally	**4**	**0**	**22**	**0**	-	1
Mascarenhas	**2**	**0**	**21**	**1**	1	-
Hamblin	**4**	**0**	**31**	**3**	-	3
Prittipaul	**4**	**0**	**17**	**2**	-	2

HAMPSHIRE HAWKS							
Fall Of Wkt	Batsman	How	Out	Score	Balls	4s	6s
1-0	**J.R.C. Hamblin**	**lbw**	**b Bicknell**	**0**	1	0	0
2-52	**J.P. Crawley** *	**c &**	**b Sampson**	**23**	27	3	0
6-103	**S.M. Katich**	**c Ramprakash**	**b Hollioake**	**45**	49	6	0
3-59	**Wasim Akram**	**c Sampson**	**b Saqlain**	**1**	4	0	0
4-101	**D.A. Kenway**		**b Hollioake**	**27**	18	2	1
5-103	**W.S. Kendall**	**c Salisbury**	**b Hollioake**	**1**	2	0	0
	A.D. Mascarenhas	**Not**	**Out**	**8**	9	0	0
7-109	**L.R. Prittipaul**	**c Batty**	**b Bicknell**	**2**	2	0	0
8-114	**N. Pothas** +	**c Ramprakash**	**b Hollioake**	**4**	3	0	0
9-116	**A.D. Mullally**		**b Hollioake**	**0**	2	0	0
10-121	**E.S.H. Giddins**	**c Newman**	**b Murtagh**	**0**	5	0	0
	Extras	**(1b, 2lb, 3w, 4nb)**		**10**			
	TOTAL	**(20 overs)**		**121**			

Bowler	O	M	R	W	NB	Wd
Bicknell	**4**	**1**	**11**	**2**	-	2
Murtagh	**4**	**0**	**26**	**1**	-	-
Sampson	**4**	**0**	**18**	**1**	-	1
Salisbury	**2**	**0**	**14**	**0**	-	-
Saqlain Mushtaq	**3**	**0**	**28**	**1**	-	-
Hollioake	**3**	**0**	**21**	**5**	2	-

Other Twenty20 Cup (South Division) Results

June 24

Chelmsford:- **Essex Eagles (2pts) beat Middlesex Crusaders by 2 runs.** Essex 175-5 (20ov; Flower 83); Middx 173-7 (20ov).

Hove:- **Sussex Sharks (2pts) beat Kent Spitfires by 5 wickets.** Kent 114 (18.5ov; Lewry 3-34); Sussex 115-5 (15.5ov; Zuiderent 42).

FINAL TWENTY20 CUP (SOUTH DIVISION) TABLE

Pos		P	Pts	W	L
1	**Surrey Lions**	5	10	5	0
2	**Sussex Sharks**	5	6	3	2
3	**Essex Eagles**	5	4	2	3
=	**Kent Spitfires**	5	4	2	3
=	**Middlesex Crusaders**	5	4	2	3
6	**Hampshire Hawks**	5	2	1	4

9 Ramps Completes The Set

For two weeks, the Twenty-20 Cup had held sway and received glowing praise in the media, with county cricket attracting more column inches in the Press than it had done for a long time.

Although the new competition's success had been greatly aided by (a) glorious weather; (b) plenty of support from the ECB and their marketing men; and (c) the novelty value of the inaugural tournament, only the most cynical, dyed-in-the-wool traditionalist could have failed to be impressed by the way crowds had flocked to county grounds around the country and, apparently, taken to the shortened version of the great game. It seemed that many people had used Twenty-20 to introduce their children to cricket and, while I personally doubted whether that many of the youngsters would be drawn back to watch the longer formats of the game, I could certainly see a good percentage of them wanting to go out and play cricket, maybe at a local club, after an exciting evening watching stumps flying out of the ground and balls being smashed all around the park for fours and sixes.

It was certainly fair to say that there was rarely time for the pace to slacken in the twenty-overs-a-side format - especially as there were tight regulations about over-rates and the turnaround of batsmen at the fall of a wicket - and more than one person described watching a Twenty-20 contest as like viewing a TV highlights package. With a complete match being condensed into two-and-three-quarter hours, that was indeed quite a good way to describe the experience. Personally, I was pleased to note that the on-field entertainment had spoken for itself, with many of the gimmicks that some counties had employed - such as Jacuzzis, blasts of music to herald boundaries and wickets, and live performances by pop groups - proving to be surplus to the majority of the spectators' requirements. It would be nice to think that counties could save themselves some money by doing without these side 'attractions' in future.

The thing that probably surprised most people, however, was that these twenty-over contests didn't develop into the 'slogfests' that had been predicted. The best batsmen invariably played good cricket strokes - no doubt based on the simple fact that your best chance of making contact is to play down or through the line of the approaching ball! - while the most successful bowlers were those who bowled straight and were able to vary their pace skilfully. The basics of the game were thus preserved, and Twenty-20 wasn't quite the evil that many felt it could be!

Consequently, my pre-season notion that playing standards would be levelled and that we could, therefore, see any old team reaching Finals Day proved to be wide of the mark. The four semi-finalists actually turned out to be Surrey (South Division winners), Gloucestershire (Midlands/West/Wales Division winners), Leicestershire (North Division winners) and Warwickshire (best second-placed team, from Midlands/West/Wales Division). So the two counties generally accepted as the best in the country, Surrey and Gloucestershire, were both there, and the other two sides were also highly respected NCL Division One outfits. July's Finals Day looked nicely set up, therefore, though it was disappointing that the draw for the semi-finals ended up pairing Surrey and Gloucestershire in the second match, with Leicestershire and Warwickshire to clash in the morning game that would launch the big day at Trent Bridge.

Thoughts of that historic day had to be put to the back of the mind for now, though, since the County Championship programme was about to resume after what had been a three-week break for most counties, but four for Surrey, who had sat out the round of matches immediately prior to the start of the Twenty-20 qualifying tournament. With the team leading the way in both the Championship and the NCL, the Twenty-20 'break' hadn't come at the best of times, though it had at least given everyone time to forget the C&G Trophy humiliation at Derby.

Meanwhile, on the international front, it had been a great pleasure to see Rikki Clarke making his first England appearances in the three Nat West Challenge matches against Pakistan, and, even though he hadn't pulled up any trees, there were signs that the Guildford lad was capable of securing a place in the England team on a long-term basis.

As one international career had started, so another one had ended, with Chris Read, as expected, having taken over from Alec Stewart in the Nat West games. Stewart had received ample consolation with some very good news from other quarters, however, since he had been awarded an OBE for services to cricket in the Queen's Birthday Honours List. Having been upgraded from an MBE, he was now the proud possessor of the same honour as his father, Micky.

FRIZZELL COUNTY CHAMPIONSHIP DIVISION ONE - MATCH SEVEN

MIDDLESEX versus SURREY
at Lord's

First Day - Friday 27th June
Middlesex 311-7

The Teams And The Toss - *It has been so long since Surrey's last Championship match that it is no surprise to see their side showing three changes to the line-up that defeated Sussex at The Oval. Mark Butcher and Alec Stewart return to the team as they are not involved in the Nat West Series, displacing Ali Brown - dropped for the first time since 1996, after failing to discover his best form during the first two months of the season - and the unfortunate Jon Batty, while fit-again Alex Tudor is the obvious replacement for Azhar Mahmood who is ruled out by a thigh strain. Middlesex, who appear to be fielding their strongest possible eleven, win the toss and elect to bat.*

On the pitch that had been used for the previous Sunday's England versus Pakistan one-day international, the Middlesex openers, Andrew Strauss and Sven Koenig, make a decent enough start against an accurate Martin Bicknell and a rather inconsistent James Ormond.

Although the batsmen have a little luck with edges that fly through, over and past the slips, they put on fifty-nine for the first wicket in seventeen overs before the deserving Bicknell draws first blood for the visitors. Having just been driven to the cover boundary by Sven Koenig, revenge comes instantly when the batsman miscues a pull to Saqlain Mushtaq at mid-on and becomes Bicknell's nine-hundredth County Championship victim. The crowd offers appropriate applause as this statistic is both announced and flashed up on the scoreboard, though the Surrey swing king is unable to add to his tally before completing a fine opening burst of 10-3-25-1.

Although Alex Tudor beats the left-handed Strauss on a number of occasions during seven largely impressive overs from the pavilion end, it takes the introduction of spin to provide the visitors with a second breakthrough.

Lunch is less than half-an-hour away when Saqlain removes Strauss for forty-seven, thanks to an absolutely breathtaking catch at silly point by Adam Hollioake. As the ball flies at him, he instinctively knocks it up and over his left shoulder with his right hand, and then has to throw himself backwards in order to grab the chance in his left hand just inches off the turf, thereby pegging the hosts back to 92-2.

Owais Shah, who has reeled off the best strokes of the morning in making his way to twenty-five, and Ben Hutton see their side safely through to lunch, though the latter has looked most uncomfortable against the spinners in the closing overs of the session.

Lunch:- Middlesex 100-2 (Shah 25, Hutton 0*) from 36 overs*

Bicknell strikes twice in the third over after the resumption, putting Middlesex in trouble at 110-4 by removing Shah with a fine lifting delivery that the batsman can only nick through to Alec Stewart and then pinning Ed Joyce lbw for a third-ball duck.

After reaching one career milestone during the morning session, the dismissal of Shah has taken Bicknell through to 950 first-class wickets, and it isn't long before the Surrey swing bowler has added another scalp to his career tally. Having blasted his Pakistani team-mate out of the attack with three boundaries in an over, Abdul Razzaq then takes fourteen runs from an over by Saqlain's replacement, Alex Tudor, before becoming Bicknell's fourth victim of the innings when he is adjudged to have been caught at the wicket for a quick-fire twenty-nine.

At 148-5, on what looks to be a blameless pitch, the home side are struggling and, while Hutton battles away in determined fashion, Paul Weekes survives a number of edgy moments against Ormond, who has replaced Tudor at the pavilion end.

Both men manage to survive and prosper, however, after Bicknell finishes his second superb spell of the day with overall figures of 20-5-49-4, and as the sixth-wicket partnership develops during the afternoon Hutton twice breaks loose to smite deliveries for six, the first of these blows being a pull off Mark Butcher, and the second a meaty on-drive at Saqlain's expense.

The grandson of the great Sir Leonard goes on to complete a solid fifty from his 107th ball with a pulled four off Salisbury as tea approaches, and there can be no doubt that his stand with Weekes has evened up the contest by the time the players leave the field three overs later.

Tea:- Middlesex 228-5 (Hutton 54, Weekes 33*) from 72 overs*

Almost immediately after tea, bad light forces the players off the field for five overs, though Hutton is clearly able to see the ball well enough upon the resumption as he notches the third six of his innings, courtesy of a pull over square leg off Bicknell that takes the home team past 250 and raises the hundred partnership for the sixth wicket.

He loses his partner shortly afterwards, however, when Weekes, on thirty-nine, is less successful in trying to pull a short ball from Bicknell, his top edge being brilliantly taken, one-handed, by a leaping Stewart to complete a most worthy five-wicket bag for the bowler.

David Nash therefore comes to the wicket with the game seemingly well balanced again at 256-6 and, in typical style, digs himself in while all the excitement comes at the other end as Hutton presses on towards his century.

After pulling Hollioake for six as soon as the visiting skipper joins the attack in place of the admirable Bicknell, Hutton moves into the nineties with a cover-driven four, before surviving an appeal for a legside catch by Stewart. The left-hander then almost runs himself out in the Surrey captain's next over when taking a very chancy single to Tudor at mid-on that takes his score to ninety-eight, before the newly recalled Ormond causes him further problems in the next over.

With Hutton having moved on to ninety-nine, and Nash having taken the total to three-hundred, Ormond rattles the centurion-elect's helmet with a bouncer and then narrowly misses the off stump with the follow-up yorker.

Hutton deserves a little luck, however, not least for being the only Middlesex batsman to have battled on past fifty, and a single to mid-off in Hollioake's next over takes him through to three figures from his 179th ball. It may not have been a classic innings by the tall left-hander, but no-one can deny that his knock has been extremely valuable to his side, and it takes a lovely piece of bowling to bring it to an end as a competitive day's cricket draws to a close.

Having been largely ignored throughout the day, Salisbury is finally called upon to bowl his seventh over of the innings and soon makes a point when his fifth delivery spins back through Hutton's gate to rattle the batsman's timbers and restore equilibrium to the game.

Close:- Middlesex 311-7 (Nash 22, Noffke 2*) from 99 overs*

Second Day - Saturday 28th June
Middlesex 370; Surrey 274-3

Surrey's hopes of polishing off the Middlesex tail in quick time are boosted by the taking of the new ball at the start of the second day, though Ashley Noffke seems unconcerned by this as he cuts, edges, glances and drives four boundaries in the first six overs from Bicknell and Ormond. The tall Australian is eventually undone by the first delivery of Ormond's fourth over of the day, though, when he plays the ball down onto his stumps after having made twenty-three, then five balls later Simon Cook looks rather unfortunate to be adjudged lbw for nought.

With the home side now 340-9, Surrey appear to have almost got the job done, but Chad Keegan, a very handy man to have coming in at number eleven, shows his batting ability with four lovely front-foot boundaries that take Middlesex through to their highest Championship total of the season so far. It takes a good delivery, too - a leg-stump yorker from Ormond - to finally dismiss Keegan and finish the home side's innings at 370.

The Surrey openers are then fully tested in the early stages of their team's reply as Noffke and Keegan find inside and outside edges without anything going either to hand or onto the stumps.

Ward and Butcher are too experienced to let this worry them, however, and the bat suddenly takes over from the ball as the dominant force when Noffke follows three fine overs with two shockers that cost him twenty-one runs and take all the pressure off the batsmen.

An untidy opening over from Abdul Razzaq, the replacement for Noffke at the pavilion end, subsequently sees the fifty up in the eleventh over, though the Pakistani is unlucky in his second over, with lunch imminent, when Butcher profits by eight runs from two top-edged strokes, the first a cut and the second a hook.

Lunch:- Surrey 71-0 (Ward 36, Butcher 34*) from 16 overs*

While Ward seems to have settled down after his slightly sticky start, Butcher adds another edged boundary to his collection, this time off the newly introduced Simon Cook, before his highly erratic innings ends with a miscued hook off Razzaq that is well caught by Sven Koenig running round from long leg to deep backward square leg.

Although Butcher has fallen six short of his half-century, Ward makes no such mistake, advancing to a 74-ball fifty with his tenth four, a pull off Razzaq, and then profiting handsomely from a number of loose deliveries - one of which he smacks over midwicket for the first six of the Surrey innings - towards the end of Cook's eight-over spell.

Mark Ramprakash has meanwhile made a very slow start and doesn't manage to find the boundary until his twenty-fifth over at the crease when he cracks Keegan to the rope at cover twice in two balls. By this time the total has progressed beyond 150 and Ward, whose share is eighty-nine, has become largely subdued by some good, tight Middlesex bowling, principally from Keegan and Weekes.

As we move ever closer to tea, the Surrey opener moves within sight of his century by driving Weekes to the cover boundary, and then reaches the mark from his 155th ball by pulling Razzaq away wide of mid-on for the fifteenth four of his excellent knock.

Tea:- Surrey 190-1 (Ward 102, Ramprakash 38*) from 53 overs*

The day's final session begins in most turgid fashion with Weekes and Cook stringing together five maiden overs and yielding just three runs from seven overs. It's good, tight stuff from the Middlesex duo and it eventually brings a breakthrough when Ward, possibly frustrated by his inability to break loose, edges a cut at Weekes to slip and departs at the end of a fine innings, having added just two to his tea-time score.

With a new batsman, Graham Thorpe, now at the crease, two further maidens follow, and a run drought that has lasted for a dozen overs is only broken when the Surrey left-hander twice drives Cook to the cover boundary in the seamer's seventh post-tea over.

Even after Keegan replaces Cook at the Nursery end, the war of attrition continues, with Ramprakash's deflection to third man off the new bowler being the only four scored in the next seven overs, before the umpires intervene to change a ball that, although only seventy-four overs old, seems to have gone very soft. One can only assume that Middlesex are unhappy about this, since Weekes' first delivery with the replacement ball is a bouncer to Ramprakash, who evades it comfortably enough and then glances for two later in the over to complete his half-century from 143 balls, making it surely one of the slowest of his long career.

Finally, as we move into the last half-hour of the day and Noffke replaces Keegan, runs start to flow quite freely, with each batsman managing to force Weekes away to the boundary at the end of a very tight and probing spell from the off-spinner, and the tall Australian getting into the bad habit of conceding a four in every over he sends down.

Middlesex do, however, manage to break what has developed into a threatening partnership between Ramprakash and Thorpe in the penultimate over of the day, when Weekes' successor at the pavilion end, Razzaq, has Thorpe very well taken, low to his left, by wicketkeeper Nash from an edged defensive push.

Although the bowlers have stuck to their task well and maintained good control, Surrey remain very much on top as play ends for the day.

Close:- Surrey 274-3 (Ramprakash 68, Saqlain 0*) from 86 overs*

Third Day - Sunday 29th June
Middlesex 370 and 74-0; Surrey 568

Saqlain Mushtaq starts the third day in sensational style with his first two scoring strokes being sixes - the first smashed over extra cover from the fifth ball of the day delivered by Abdul Razzaq, and the second sliced away high over cover in the morning's fourth over from Ashley Noffke. He is then badly missed behind the wicket by David Nash from the next delivery and everything calms down for a while as Middlesex's two overseas bowlers begin to command respect.

Having started his day with a couple of nicely deflected fours, Mark Ramprakash advances his score into the nineties largely by way of singles and twos, while Saqlain still manages to amaze everyone with his strokeplay from time to time, the best example coming when he attempts to hook a short delivery from Noffke at the same time as he is starting to duck underneath it. The entirely predictable miscue that results from this stroke sees the ball lobbing back gently over the astonished bowler's head for a single that brings up the fifty partnership.

Interestingly, the new ball isn't taken until the 103rd over and it is then given to Chad Keegan and Simon Cook. The change of ball and bowlers doesn't present any problems to Ramprakash, however, as the former Middlesex captain soon completes a painstaking 236-ball century, containing just eleven fours, the last of which - an extra-cover drive off Keegan - takes him to the milestone. Although the batsman celebrates in a fairly muted style, this hundred turns out to be quite significant in statistical terms, since it makes Ramprakash the first batsman to have scored first-class centuries against all eighteen first-class counties.

Almost immediately after this record is announced, Ben Hutton misses a chance to end the Surrey number three's innings by spilling a routine catch off Cook at second slip, though he manages to redeem himself in the same bowler's next over when Ramprakash, having moved on from 102 to 110, gives him the opportunity to snap up a more difficult catch in the same position.

Thereafter, Saqlain moves up a gear, with a volley of strokes taking Surrey into the lead and completing the Pakistani's half-century (5 fours, 2 sixes) from 78 balls, while the new batsman,

Alec Stewart, is soon reeling off four handsome legside boundaries to take the visitors beyond four-hundred and bring up a rapid fifty partnership at almost a run a ball.

Lunch:- Surrey 409-4 (Saqlain 65, Stewart 22*) from 120 overs*

Saqlain posts a new career-best score for his adopted county when sweeping Weekes for two shortly after the resumption, though he perishes almost immediately afterwards as he attempts to repeat the stroke and gets a top edge to Keegan at short fine leg.

With Adam Hollioake now joining Stewart in the middle, Surrey are doubtless hoping to push on quickly as possible, though they are stymied in their attempts to do this by Noffke's best spell by far since his opening three overs. Whether or not it is a reaction to being snubbed when the second new ball was taken is impossible to say, but he certainly keeps the batsmen quiet before extracting Hollioake's off stump with a fine delivery that nips back at the visiting skipper.

Stewart, meanwhile, has been progressing nicely at the other end, finding the boundary on several occasions at Weekes' expense and moving on to a 76-ball half-century as Surrey's lead approaches the hundred mark and Noffke's fine spell in the heat of the afternoon comes to a close.

Having reached his fifty in good time, the Surrey keeper becomes rather becalmed for a while thereafter, and it is Alex Tudor who takes on the role of principal aggressor in a stand of fifty-three that ends when the paceman plays on to Razzaq after making thirty.

Fortunately for the visitors, Stewart's response is to move back up a gear, temporarily at least, with a pulled boundary off Keegan that raises the Surrey five-hundred, then he repeats the stroke a few overs later as Razzaq comes towards the end of a decent spell from the pavilion end.

With tea looming, Andy Strauss now recalls Noffke, though it is his surprise choice of bowler at the other end, Ed Joyce, who most impresses and makes another breakthrough for his side. Bowling fast-medium inswingers, the Dublin-born batsman shows that he is more than capable with the ball, as he first restricts the flow of runs and then claims his second first-class wicket by finding Martin Bicknell's outside edge as the Surrey man assays an off-side forcing stroke.

Despite a very good bowling effort and a highly committed fielding performance, Middlesex are 174 runs in the red at the interval.

Tea:- Surrey 544-8 (Stewart 79, Salisbury 4*) from 157 overs*

Although Ian Salisbury manages to locate the boundary on a couple of occasions before having his leg stump knocked back by an inswinging yorker from Cook, Surrey continue to make slow progress against the 26-year-old seamer and the newly discovered bowling talent that is Ed Joyce.

With overs ebbing away fairly pointlessly, it is actually something of a relief when Weekes returns to the attack in place of Joyce but manages to keep his predecessor in the action with a catch on the deep midwicket boundary as Stewart fails to middle his slog-sweep sufficiently well to clear the fielder and the rope. The England wicketkeeper thus falls thirteen short of a century and Surrey end up two runs shy of securing a first-innings lead of two-hundred. The visitors do, however, have nineteen overs tonight in which to try to capture some Middlesex wickets and improve their chances of victory on the final day.

The bowlers know it won't be easy on this very good batting surface, though, and, apart from a couple of rather hopeful appeals for catches by Stewart down the legside, the opening overs suggest that the Championship leaders are going to have to work extremely hard if they are to work their way through what is a strong and long Middlesex batting line-up.

As both Bicknell and Ormond come to the end of rather disappointing spells, a flurry of fours by the impressive Strauss and Koenig prompts Hollioake into bringing Tudor on at the Nursery end, and, a few overs later, Salisbury at the pavilion end. Neither man is able to conjure up a wicket, however, and even Saqlain draws a blank when he is given the last over of the day.

By coming through this important final period of play with all their wickets intact Middlesex look to have greatly improved their chances of denying Surrey victory tomorrow.

Close:- Middlesex 74-0 (Strauss 42, Koenig 29*) from 19 overs*

Fourth Day - Monday 30th June

Middlesex 370 and 218-2; Surrey 568
Match Drawn
Middlesex 10pts, Surrey 12

When heavy overnight rain is followed by a couple of showers during the morning it seems almost certain that the game is destined to end in stalemate.

By the time play is able to get under way at 1.30pm, twenty-nine overs have been lost and it seems highly unlikely that Surrey can take ten wickets - and maybe also knock off some runs - in the sixty-seven overs that are left in the match. Martin Bicknell and James Ormond give it their best shot, however, during opening bursts that lack only in good fortune, but the pitch remains fine for batting as Strauss and Koenig take their partnership into three figures and beyond.

The introduction of Alex Tudor and Ian Salisbury makes little difference to either of the Middlesex left-handers, both of whom complete their personal half-centuries before another shower drives the players from the field at 2.26pm, finally washing away any hopes Surrey might still have harboured of producing something spectacular late in the day.

By taking an early tea at 3.10pm, the umpires salvage a few overs, though everyone knows that we are in for a pointless final session if the weather allows the game to resume after the interval.

Tea:- Middlesex 141-0 (Strauss 73, Koenig 54*) from 33 overs*

After an efficient clean-up operation by the ground staff, play resumes at 3.45pm, with fifteen more overs having been lost.

Surrey use the remaining time to give extended bowls to Tudor, who is short of match fitness after several weeks spent on the sidelines following his knee injury, and Salisbury, who could probably do with getting some more overs under his belt, while interest from the home side's point of view focuses on whether their batsmen can complete centuries.

As it turns out, neither man makes it through to three figures - Salisbury has Strauss (95) taken at leg slip by Mark Butcher after finally extracting some turn and bounce from what has been a pretty docile pitch, while Koenig (89) edges a drive at Hollioake, Tudor's replacement at the pavilion end, to slip, where Thorpe holds a good low catch.

The game then ends in farcical style as the Surrey captain bowls a succession of bouncers at Ben Hutton and Owais Shah, and, after an official warning is followed by three more short-pitched deliveries at the start of his next over, is banned from bowling again in the innings by umpire Graham Burgess… with three balls of the match remaining! Ian Ward duly completes the over for his skipper and everyone leaves the field having shaken hands on the draw.

Middlesex 370 and 218-2; Surrey 568
Match Drawn. Middlesex 10pts, Surrey 12

TALKING POINTS - MARK RAMPRAKASH

You must have been very proud to become the first man to notch a century against all eighteen first-class counties?

MR - Yes, that was a nice feeling. I remember getting the seventeenth - against Glamorgan at Lord's - and that was a very special feeling, too.

I guess it was also special to score a hundred on your first visit back to Lord's to play Middlesex?
MR - People had said to me that you must have been very determined to make a hundred against Middlesex and do well against them, but I don't take any special pleasure in scoring runs against Middlesex, as such. It's more about the pleasure of scoring century for Surrey in a Championship match at Lord's - that's the way I look at it.

Both your fifty (143 balls) and hundred (236 balls) must have been amongst the slowest of your career. They clearly made things very tough for you.
MR - Yes, we had to work very hard for our runs - they went very defensive and bowled in a very disciplined fashion, and there was a period where the ball went ridiculously soft, but the umpires wouldn't change it for a while. So we lost momentum for maybe fifteen overs because we couldn't manage to hit the ball off the square.

TALKING POINTS - MARTIN BICKNELL

I suppose you must have been very pleased with your performance, taking five wickets on a good pitch against a long and strong batting line-up?
MB - Yes, I think this performance was right up there, probably being as well as I bowled the whole year, simply because of the number of overs I had to bowl in the day and the fact that the pitch was dead. The ball did swing around a bit after lunch, which helped, but they had a good long batting line-up so I was pleased to get through it.

You took your 950th first-class wicket in this match. I assume you're counting down to the magical 1,000th and will not need a P.A. announcement to tell you when you've reached that milestone?!
MB - Eighteen to go, I think! Obviously, a thousand first-class wickets is very important to me, but what I'd really like to get is a thousand **Championship** wickets. I think that would be even more of an achievement, as I don't think too many people have got a thousand in the Championship alone.

TALKING POINTS - ADAM HOLLIOAKE

You ended the match by being banned from bowling, following an over that started with three successive bouncers. What was that all about?!
AH - It was basically a bit of fun - I was just trying to liven up what had turned into a boring draw and bring a bit of excitement into things. I couldn't see any other way of doing it. I was also trying to make the point to our bowlers that if we were going to bowl bouncers then they had to be high ones and that even a bowler of my pace could get the ball over the batsman's head.

MIDDLESEX v SURREY at Lord's				**27th to 30th June**			
Middlesex won the toss and elected to bat			Umpires:- Graham Burgess and Nigel Llong				
MIDDLESEX - First Innings							
Fall Of Wkt	Batsman	How	Out	Score	Balls	4s	6s
2-92	**A.J. Strauss** *	**c Hollioake**	**b Saqlain**	**47**	88	6	0
1-59	**S.G. Koenig**	**c Saqlain**	**b Bicknell**	**22**	50	3	0
3-110	**O.A. Shah**	**c Stewart**	**b Bicknell**	**31**	69	5	0
7-305	**B.L. Hutton**		**b Salisbury**	**101**	184	10	4
4-110	**E.C. Joyce**	**lbw**	**b Bicknell**	**0**	3	0	0
5-148	**Abdul Razzaq**	**c Stewart**	**b Bicknell**	**29**	26	6	0
6-256	**P.N. Weekes**	**c Stewart**	**b Bicknell**	**39**	110	4	0
	D.C. Nash +	**Not**	**Out**	**36**	101	2	0
8-340	**A.A. Noffke**		**b Ormond**	**23**	28	4	0
9-340	**S.J. Cook**	**lbw**	**b Ormond**	**0**	5	0	0
10-370	**C.B. Keegan**		**b Ormond**	**20**	29	4	0
	Extras	**(8b, 7lb, 7w)**		**22**			
	TOTAL	**(115.2 overs)**		**370**			

Bowler	O	M	R	W	NB	Wd
Bicknell	35	7	92	5	-	2
Ormond	28.2	3	103	3	-	1
Tudor	13	5	43	0	-	2
Saqlain Mushtaq	24	5	66	1	-	-
Salisbury	9	2	21	1	-	-
Butcher	2	0	12	0	-	-
Hollioake	4	0	18	0	-	2

SURREY - First Innings (Needing 221 to avoid the follow-on)							
Fall Of Wkt	Batsman	How	Out	Score	Balls	4s	6s
2-193	I.J. Ward	c Shah	b Weekes	104	187	15	1
1-89	M.A. Butcher	c Koenig	b Abdul Razzaq	44	66	8	0
4-352	M.R. Ramprakash	c Hutton	b Cook	110	251	12	0
3-270	G.P. Thorpe	c Nash	b Abdul Razzaq	46	88	7	0
5-413	Saqlain Mushtaq	c Keegan	b Weekes	69	104	6	2
10-568	A.J. Stewart +	c Joyce	b Weekes	87	148	10	0
6-444	A.J. Hollioake *		b Noffke	10	24	1	0
7-497	A.J. Tudor		b Abdul Razzaq	30	64	6	0
8-535	M.P. Bicknell	c Nash	b Joyce	10	30	1	0
9-562	I.D.K. Salisbury		b Cook	17	31	3	0
	J. Ormond	Not	Out	1	22	0	0
	Extras	(23lb, 3w, 14nb)		40			
	TOTAL	(168.2 overs)		568			

Bowler	O	M	R	W	NB	Wd
Noffke	37	5	134	1	-	1
Keegan	31	6	102	0	-	-
Abdul Razzaq	29	4	95	3	5	-
Joyce	11	3	25	1	-	-
Cook	28	4	101	2	-	2
Weekes	32.2	7	88	3	1	-

MIDDLESEX - Second Innings (Trailing by 198 runs on first innings)							
Fall Of Wkt	Batsman	How	Out	Score	Balls	4s	6s
1-186	A.J. Strauss *	c Butcher	b Salisbury	95	137	13	0
2-202	S.G. Koenig	c Thorpe	b Hollioake	89	152	6	2
	O.A. Shah	Not	Out	7	39	0	0
	B.L. Hutton	Not	Out	5	26	1	0
	Extras	(10b, 12nb)		22			
	TOTAL	(58 overs)	(for 2 dec)	218			

Bowler	O	M	R	W	NB	Wd
Bicknell	8	0	33	0	-	-
Ormond	12	2	53	0	1	-
Tudor	12	2	45	0	-	-
Salisbury	17	2	60	1	1	-
Saqlain Mushtaq	2	1	1	0	-	-
Hollioake	6.3	1	15	1	4	-
Ward	0.3	0	1	0	-	-

Other Frizzell Championship Division One Results

Sussex moved up to second place in the table - just six points behind Surrey - after hammering Warwickshire at Hove, with Mushtaq (11-140) again very much to the fore.

June 27-29

***Hove:-* Sussex (22pts) beat Warwickshire (3) by an innings and 59 runs.** Sussex 545 (Cottey 188, Prior 100, Montgomerie 66, Ambrose 50, Waqar 5-99); Warwicks 201 (Powell 60, Mushtaq 4-55) & 285 (Powell 80, Knight 64, Mushtaq 7-85).

June 27-30

***Chelmsford:-* Essex (12pts) drew with Kent (10).** Kent 381 (Fulton 93, Jones 84, Carberry 50, Middlebrook 6-123) & 416-8dec (Jones 108*, Ealham 101, Walker 65); Essex 514 (Hussain 206, Habib 77, Sheriyar 4-73).

***Leicester:-* Leicestershire (8pts) drew with Nottinghamshire (10).** Notts 326 (Franks 123*, Pietersen 88, DeFreitas 4-68) & 318-6dec (Pietersen 95, Welton 86, Dagnall 4-61); Leics 243 (Sehwag 137, Smith 4-40) & 5-1.

FRIZZELL CHAMPIONSHIP DIVISION ONE TABLE AT 30TH JUNE

Pos	Prv		P	Points	W	D	L	T	Bat	Bwl	Ded
1	1	**Surrey**	**7**	**106.00**	3	4	0	0	29	19	0.00
2	3	**Sussex**	**7**	**100.00**	4	0	3	0	23	21	0.00
3	2	**Lancashire**	**6**	**88.00**	2	4	0	0	26	18	0.00
4	5	**Essex**	**8**	**78.00**	1	5	1	1	14	23	0.00
5	4	**Warwickshire**	**7**	**71.75**	1	3	2	1	24	15	0.25
6	6	**Middlesex**	**7**	**70.00**	1	6	0	0	14	18	0.00
7	7	**Nottinghamshire**	**7**	**64.00**	1	3	3	0	19	20	1.00
8	8	**Kent**	**7**	**54.00**	0	4	3	0	18	20	0.00
9	9	**Leicestershire**	**6**	**44.00**	0	5	1	0	8	16	0.00

10 Kent Conned, Phoenix Flattened

The draw at Lord's had been something of a disappointment. Both London-based counties remained unbeaten following the stalemate but the result was far more useful for Middlesex, striving to consolidate their first division status, than to a Surrey side chasing the title. Lancashire would certainly have been happy to see the Championship leaders suffer much the same fate as they themselves had at Lord's earlier in the season, since the leaders could now be overhauled if the Red Rose county could win their game in hand. It was also interesting to note that Sussex had sneaked up into second place, courtesy of another victory that had been secured by a fine batting performance followed by a hefty dose of Mushtaq magic. Could they maintain their form into the second half of the season? It looked as if everything would depend on James Kirtley and 'Mushy' staying fit, in form and out of international reckoning, since the rest of the Sussex bowling didn't look capable of winning matches on decent pitches. The bookmakers certainly still had them as clear outsiders, which seemed to be a fair assessment.

Surrey would need to get back on the winning trail, though, if they were to keep their rivals at bay, and, on paper at least, their next match certainly looked to be one they could win. Although they had been unlucky with injuries to some important players, Kent had surprised many with their poor form so far, and they languished in the relegation zone as they travelled to The Oval to play a side who had already beaten them in the NCL and Twenty-20 Cup earlier in the season.

FRIZZELL COUNTY CHAMPIONSHIP DIVISION ONE - MATCH EIGHT

SURREY versus KENT
at The Oval

First Day - Wednesday 2nd July
Surrey 245-3

The Teams And The Toss *- Surrey are forced to make a late change to their side on the morning of the match, with Adam Hollioake pulling out as a result of his father, John, being taken ill. Ali Brown therefore regains his place in the team, and Mark Butcher takes over the captaincy of an otherwise unchanged eleven. Kent, meanwhile, are still without their long-term injury victims, Martin Saggers, Amjad Khan and Min Patel, and lose Alamgir Sheriyar on the eve of the match to a cut hand, apparently sustained while doing the washing up! Since Rob Key is also absent, on duty with England for the Nat West Series, Kent's squad is rather stretched, though they are able to include their recent signing, Mohammad Sami. Rob Ferley, a former England Under-19 left-arm spinner is given his County Championship debut, while Michael Carberry plays against his former colleagues for the first time in the premier domestic competition. As the captains toss up on an overcast morning, the ground is damp following overnight and morning rain, but that doesn't deter Mark Butcher from electing to bat when he wins the toss.*

Surrey are away to a flying start against Mohammad Sami and Ben Trott as Ian Ward and Mark Butcher plunder five boundaries from the morning's first four overs, courtesy of an assortment of cuts, drives and steers. The newly signed Pakistani paceman is certainly sharp in pace, though he soon falls foul of umpire Ian Gould as he consistently follows through into the 'danger area'. Even from the boundary it is possible to see the scuff marks where he is running down the line of middle stump, so it's no surprise when he is issued with a first official warning in the ninth over of the morning.

By this time the Surrey openers have advanced the score to thirty-nine, and when each of them collects a boundary behind point in Sami's next over the total reaches the fifty mark. There have been relatively few alarms so far, though Ward is possibly lucky before the Pakistani's over is out when he shoulders arms and is struck on the pads by a delivery that looks fairly straight. Umpire Gould's cry of 'no-ball' saves him the job of having to uphold or reject the lbw appeal that would otherwise have gone up from the bowler and fielders.

Having now delivered six sparky overs, Sami immediately takes a rest, leaving Butcher and Ward to cope with the much less pacy combination of Ealham and Trott, though it isn't long before everyone has their feet up in the dressing rooms as a shower hits the ground with the score at 67-0 in the seventeenth over.

Fortunately for all concerned, play is able to resume after a loss of around ten minutes - equating to three overs - though the break doesn't seem to have done Ward any good as he soon miscues a pull at Ealham high towards mid-on, where the Kent skipper, Dave Fulton, takes the catch.

With Ward gone for thirty-three and the score standing at 73-1, Mark Ramprakash enters the fray and Sami is immediately recalled in place of Trott at the Vauxhall end. While the new man plays himself in, Butcher, looking very much in form, deals beautifully with everything that comes his way, cutting Ealham for four, forcing Sami backward of point for another boundary, and then advancing down the track to the former England all-rounder and drilling him to the rope at extra cover.

Over-confidence would seem to be Butcher's greatest enemy at this point, so it is perhaps not such a bad thing when a heavy shower sends everyone scurrying for cover at 12.56pm, shortly after the England left-hander has miscued a pull shot at the newly introduced Andrew Symonds just over the head of a retreating midwicket fielder.

Lunch:- Surrey 97-1 (Butcher 42, Ramprakash 6*) from 24.5 overs*

Sami and Symonds continue for Kent once play resumes at 2.30pm, with fourteen overs having been lost, and while Symonds is immediately driven through extra cover for four by Butcher, Sami soon enjoys the sweet taste of success when Ramprakash is surprised by a nasty lifter that he can only fend off to Ealham in the gully.

Butcher then has an edgy moment against Symonds when completing a fine 76-ball fifty in the next over, his defensive snick flying away in the air between the gully and slip fielders for four runs, though this turns out to be a rare lapse from the England left-hander as he proceeds to take three exquisite boundaries from the next two overs, with a cut, a drive through wide mid-on and a back-foot cover drive. The latter stroke is perhaps the pick of the bunch, having come at the end of a very testing four-over spell from Sami. Symonds, meanwhile, continues to be very inconsistent in his seamer mode, mixing good balls with 'four' balls, two of which Graham Thorpe takes advantage of to get his innings moving.

Butcher is proving really hard to contain now as he moves down the track to the returning Trott in order to drive to the rope at long-on, and then crashes Symonds away to the off-side boundary three times in the space of two overs, forcing Fulton to withdraw the big Aussie from the attack as the total speeds past the 150 mark in the thirty-sixth over.

The ever steady Ealham is the bowler chosen to take over at the pavilion end and he does a good job for his captain by sending down five overs that cost just five runs, but Fulton finds it hard to block up the other end as Thorpe sees off Trott with two legside fours in an over and Butcher moves into the nineties with a lovely on-driven boundary off the replacement bowler, James Tredwell. The Kent skipper's problems then continue to pile up as Thorpe gets stuck into the young off-spinner, driving him back over his head when he overpitches and then cutting him for a second four when he drops short, before Butcher moves to ninety-eight with a square-cut boundary of his own.

Perhaps surprisingly, given the treatment Tredwell has received, Fulton decides to stick with his young spinner and replaces the economical Ealham with his second slow bowler, the debutant Rob Ferley, as tea approaches. The 21-year-old left-armer has a tough introduction to Championship cricket as one England left-hander, Thorpe, cuts him for three, then another England southpaw, Butcher, dances down the track and lifts him away over midwicket for a boundary that completes a magnificent century from 142 balls. An innings that has been full of superb strokes shows amazing statistical symmetry, too, since both the first fifty and the second fifty have contained no fewer than ten fours.

Although Butcher fails to find the boundary again in the last seven overs bowled by the young spinners up until tea, Thorpe does manage to locate the rope on three occasions. The first of these fours takes the total past two-hundred, the second raises the century partnership and the last one completes the batsman's own fifty from 75 balls.

Tea:- Surrey 219-2 (Butcher 109, Thorpe 51*) from 55 overs*

Although Ferley is retained in the attack after tea, Tredwell gives way to Symonds, and Thorpe continues to emulate Butcher's fine form by picking up a back-foot boundary off each bowler in the first two overs of the session.

With the fields set deep, the score is then ticked along mainly through the acquisition of singles until, in fading light, Ferley claims his maiden Championship wicket to end the Butcher-Thorpe partnership at 138. Having almost come unstuck in similar style during the left-arm spinner's previous over, Thorpe edges a sweep onto his pad and is caught by wicketkeeper Jones for sixty-eight when the ball pops up into the air.

The batsman can barely be settled back in the dressing room when the umpires decide to offer the light to Butcher and his new partner, Ali Brown, even though two spinners are in action. They accept the chance to retire to the pavilion at 5.12pm, and within a few minutes a thunderstorm breaks over the ground, instantly wiping out any chance of further play.

Close:- Surrey 245-3 (Butcher 117, Brown 0*) from 64 overs*

Second Day - Thursday 3rd July
Surrey 401; Kent 101-2

Although there has been quite a lot of overnight rainfall, play is able to start on time on a cool and cloudy morning with Mohammad Sami and Mark Ealham causing the batsmen a few early problems. Runs are certainly hard to come by and Ali Brown survives a couple of lbw appeals by Ealham before lofting the former England all-rounder down the ground for the day's first boundary in the eighth over.

Since no breakthrough is forthcoming, David Fulton decides to replace his opening bowlers, after five overs apiece, with Ben Trott and Rob Ferley, and this move brings both an increase in the run-rate and two much-needed wickets.

Having pulled Ferley away to the midwicket boundary to bring up a fifty partnership for the fourth wicket, Butcher perishes to Trott in the next over with his score on 144 and the total advanced to 293. Perhaps there is a touch of over-confidence behind his dismissal as he skips down the track and inside-edges a drive that Geraint Jones pouches in an impressively unfussy fashion away to his right-hand side.

Ali Brown then goes in the following over from Ferley, frustratingly just after he has got into his stride with two drives down the ground for six off the left-arm spinner. Although the second of these mighty hits brings up the Surrey three-hundred, it also turns out to be the batsman's last scoring stroke as Ferley takes revenge with a fine piece of bowling, tossing the ball up a little wider of off stump and luring the batsman into a low, skimming drive that is very smartly taken by Andy Symonds at short extra cover.

As Brown makes his way back to the pavilion with twenty-seven runs to his name, passing his replacement, Alex Tudor, as he goes, the drizzle that has been falling since the opening overs of the day gets heavier, prompting the umpires to call a temporary halt to proceedings at 12.10pm.

It turns out to be quite a long break, too, since it is still raining by the time lunch arrives.

Lunch:- Surrey 305-5 (Stewart 1) from 79.5 overs*

By the time play is able to restart at 2.45pm, thirty-one overs have been lost and, consequently, Surrey adopt an even more positive approach to their batting.

They lose Alec Stewart to the first ball he faces upon the resumption when he drives a straightforward return catch to the reintroduced Ealham, but before the over is out Martin Bicknell, the new batsman, has seven runs in the bank, including a square-driven boundary.

The aggressive intent is certainly there for all to see as Tudor drives Ferley through and over extra-cover for fours, while Bicknell edges and forces Ealham away to the boundary before falling for a quick-fire twenty-two to a top-edged slog-sweep off Ferley that Jones scampers across to take in the vicinity of square leg. Surrey are 336-7 at this point and, with a new ball due very soon, it looks as if they could miss out on their fifth batting point. The fourth point is gathered in easily enough, though, when Tudor and his new partner, Ian Salisbury, take a boundary apiece from a Ferley over that costs ten runs and prompts the Kent skipper to reintroduce his opening bowlers.

This turns out to be a very good move, as Trott has Tudor brilliantly taken above his head by a leaping Ealham at gully from a sliced drive at his first delivery then, three balls later, Saqlain, having got off the mark with a deflection to the third-man boundary, charges down the track, misses a drive and loses his leg stump. With Surrey now 359-9, we appear to be witnessing a 'more haste, less points' scenario, though the principle of trying to making up for lost time in an attempt to win the match on the fourth day is entirely laudable.

Since Mohammad Sami is now armed with a new ball, the chances of the last pair making the forty-one runs required to secure the final batting point are fairly slim, though Salisbury quickly knocks eight off the requirement, courtesy of a top-edged hook to fine leg off Sami and a lofted extra-cover drive off Trott. An edged three then follows, and by the time Sami's next over has been negotiated the total is up to 377.

With the Pakistani speedster looking sharp and dangerous, it would seem sensible to try to get after Trott, though no-one can quite believe how successful this tactic turns out to be. In an over that ends up reading 4-1-4-1-2-6, the Surrey duo knock up eighteen runs, with Salisbury's straight-driven four and Ormond's lofted on-drive for six being the highlights.

Just five runs are needed to reach the four-hundred mark as Sami now switches to a more threatening round-the-wicket angle of attack but, fortunately for the home side, Salisbury stays calm and responds with an upper-cut that flies high over the slips for four, followed by a push backward of point for two that sees the Championship leaders through to their initial target of maximum batting points.

It matters little then that Ormond immediately drives the recalled Ferley into the hands of Tredwell at midwicket, thereby ending a partnership of forty-two from just 33 balls and giving the spinner a four-wicket haul on his debut. It also ensures that tea will now be taken between the innings rather than with thirty-two overs remaining for play.

Tea:- Between Innings

Faced by accurate opening spells from Martin Bicknell and James Ormond, Kent's reply gets away to a steady if unspectacular start, and it takes an interesting early bowling change by Mark Butcher to bring the home side an initial breakthrough.

Michael Carberry has just started to get into his stride with an off-driven boundary off Bicknell when the stand-in skipper introduces Saqlain Mushtaq at the Vauxhall end and sees his off-spinner claim the wicket of the former Surrey man with his fifth delivery - as the left-hander pushes forward, the ball pops up into the air on the off-side via bat and pad, allowing Alec Stewart to scurry round from behind the stumps and pick up a very good low catch. With Carberry gone for sixteen the score is now 25-1.

Since the light is proving troublesome again at this late stage of the afternoon, Butcher is then forced to bring his second spinner into the attack. Only three overs are bowled by the spin twins, however, before a combination of bad light and rain brings about the suspension of play with Kent on 39-1, ten of these runs having come from the bat of Ed Smith, who has started confidently with two fours whipped away through the leg side off Saqlain.

Almost half-an-hour is lost as a result of this latest stoppage, though Surrey soon make up for this when Bicknell, returning at the Vauxhall end in place of Saqlain, traps Fulton on the crease with a ball that possibly keeps a little low and wins an lbw verdict from umpire Gould.

With Fulton gone for fourteen and the visitors under pressure at 40-2, the Championship leaders now scent the chance to take a grip on the game, though Smith and the newly arrived Andrew Symonds meet the challenge head-on, especially once Bicknell is again forced out of the attack by indifferent light. Determined that neither spinner should be allowed to settle, Symonds soon gets down the track to the recalled Saqlain and drives him for six over long-on before repeating the stroke, this time for four, in the off-spinner's next over as the third-wicket pair start to fight back. The occasional ball turns enough to suggest that the spinners could be a real threat to Kent on this pitch in the second innings, however, and Salisbury certainly gets a number of his leg-breaks past the outside edge, while also sending down the occasional 'four' ball that both batsmen pounce upon with alacrity and crack to the boundary.

As the day draws towards a close, Symonds has a couple of anxious moments. The first comes when Ramprakash, at short leg, is just unable to scoop up a very difficult chance low to his right off Saqlain when a delivery pops up to take the batsman's glove; then there is a big appeal for a catch at silly point in the last over of the day when the Australian launches into a sweep at the off-spinner, though umpire Gould rules that the ball has come off nothing more than the pad.

With their partnership worth sixty-one and the Kent total into three figures, the two batsmen march off contentedly at the end of the over with a rash of threes showing on the scoreboard and the game evenly balanced, though somewhat behind schedule because of all the interference from the weather.

Close:- Kent 101-2 (Smith 33, Symonds 33*) from 33 overs*

Third Day - Friday 4th July
Surrey 401 and 249-3; Kent 352-5dec

In what are probably the best batting conditions of the match so far, Kent make a fine start against James Ormond and Martin Bicknell, as Ed Smith takes three boundaries from the first four overs of the morning to complete an impressive 76-ball fifty. With Andy Symonds also finding the rope on three occasions, the visitors are away to a flyer, and Mark Butcher is forced to act, pulling Ormond out of the attack after just three overs and replacing him with Saqlain Mushtaq.

To the stand-in captain's delight, the resulting Bicknell-Saqlain combination manages to put the brakes on the Kent juggernaut by delivering three successive maidens, though Smith is soon up and running again with two successive back-foot fours off Saqlain that take his partnership with Symonds past the hundred mark.

Having been becalmed for some while after his good start to the day, the big Aussie finally breaks free with a superb back-foot forcing stroke to the boundary off Bicknell that not only completes his personal half-century from 83 balls but also takes the total beyond 150. He doesn't get any further, however, as the bowler strikes back with the last delivery of his over, a typical outswinger that takes a fairly thick outside edge and flies straight into the hands of Butcher at second slip.

Further breakthroughs would now put Surrey firmly on top, but none are forthcoming as Smith brings Bicknell's seven-over spell to a close with two square-driven boundaries, while the new batsman, Matt Walker, tucks into some ill-directed short stuff from Alex Tudor, the replacement bowler at the Vauxhall end, taking 4-2-4-4 from successive balls in the paceman's second over.

As Ian Salisbury replaces a tidy, but not especially threatening, Saqlain at the pavilion end, Walker again pulls Tudor for four, and the fourth-wicket pair continue to look comfortable despite an impassioned appeal from Salisbury and his close fielders for lbw when Walker pads up to a leg-break. A second consecutive fifty partnership then arrives during the final over of a poor spell of 6-1-34-0 from Tudor when Smith upper-cuts to third man and clips through midwicket for fours that take his personal contribution into the nineties.

Since he is now starting to run out of options, Butcher decides to pair his spinners by recalling Saqlain at the Vauxhall end, though it doesn't prevent Smith from completing a highly impressive 138-ball century by forcing Salisbury to the extra-cover fence and then clipping him to midwicket for a single. Generous applause follows from the ever-sporting Oval crowd.

With lunch not too far away now, Smith gives the impression that he intends to make this a big hundred by eschewing all risks and adding a succession of singles to his score, while Walker adds another couple of boundaries to his tally as the Surrey bowling continues to disappoint right up until the interval, by which time the fourth-wicket stand is worth eighty-nine.

Lunch:- Kent 240-3 (Smith 112, Walker 39*) from 70 overs*

During the interval it has been revealed that Kent have enjoyed a successful morning off the field as well as on it, since the struggling Club has signed Muttiah Muralitharan for the last two months of the season. It is a move that will dramatically enhance their prospects of avoiding relegation in both the Championship and the NCL.

Boosted by this news, the visitors start the afternoon session in stunning style, with Smith battering the recalled Ormond for sixteen runs in the opening over as the Surrey seamer is punished for straying to leg by a sequence of 4-2-4-2-4 that completes a century partnership for the fourth wicket. Walker then joins in the fun by taking a four from each of Salisbury's next two overs, though the Surrey leg-spinner soon has something to celebrate when a perfectly pitched leg-break takes the outside edge of Smith's defensive bat to provide Brown with a regulation slip catch and end the Smith-Walker stand. Having looked the bowler most likely to take a wicket during the morning session, despite his inconsistencies, it is a fitting reward for Salisbury, though most of the crowd's applause is reserved for Smith, whose innings of 135 from 177 balls, including twenty fours, has been a supreme effort and given his side a great chance of building a significant first-innings lead over the reigning County Champions. The loss of so much time to the inclement weather is clearly going to make it difficult for either team to force a victory, but Kent, trailing by just 126 runs with six wickets intact, are surely the better-placed side.

Surrey do manage to even things up a little shortly afterwards, however, when Ormond - sensibly retained in the attack despite his nightmare start to the session - has the recently arrived Mark Ealham edging a defensive stroke low to third slip where Thorpe takes a smart catch.

The Championship leaders still have an outside chance of gaining a first-innings lead if they can pick up another wicket at this stage, since the Kent tail looks rather lacking in experience and quality, but, while Salisbury continues to pose problems for the batsmen during an increasingly impressive spell, Walker and his new partner, Geraint Jones, take full toll of two very loose overs at the other end - Ormond suffers déjà vu as Jones pulls, cuts and drives three fours to take the total beyond three-hundred in the eighty-fifth over, then Saqlain suffers an even worse fate when he replaces the big paceman for the next over at the Vauxhall end, conceding fifteen runs, including a lofted off-drive for four and a slog-sweep for six by Walker.

When Salisbury's period of dominance is then broken by a straight-driven four from Jones and another six from the bat of Walker, this one pulled high over midwicket, Surrey are looking highly likely to concede a first-innings lead again, and Butcher has to seriously consider taking the new ball that is now available.

At this point the players take an unexpected drinks break, during which a group of the home side's more senior players are seen to be having a very serious-looking discussion, which seems reasonable enough, given the rather worrying situation in which they now find themselves.

Having taken the new ball and handed it to Messrs Bicknell and Tudor, the Surrey skipper then leaves the field and makes his way up to the dressing rooms. It is to be hoped that he hasn't sustained an injury, since the home team has already been without Ian Ward throughout their time in the field owing to a recurrence of his groin injury.

Back on the field, Tudor's day shows no sign of improvement as Jones pulls him away over midwicket for six and Walker drills him down the ground for a four to long-off to raise the visitors' 350, though, thankfully for the hosts, Bicknell is meanwhile contributing a few good steady overs at the other end.

Then, completely out of the blue, the players all turn and march off towards the pavilion. Since it isn't raining and the light is perfectly playable, one can only assume that Kent have declared... and suddenly the discussions at the drinks break, plus Butcher's departure from the field, start to make sense. The visitors clearly believe that, given their position near the foot of the table, they need to try to win this match, and that their best chance of doing so is by chasing runs on a decent batting track on the final day. Declaring at 352-5, forty-nine runs behind Surrey, in order to open up the game, appears to be quite a risky strategy, however, since it brings the Championship leaders right back into the contest. Dave Fulton has to do what he believes is best for his own team, of course, but it seems possible that he could be made to regret his decision to ignore the unwritten rule that you don't give a champion individual or team a second chance in sport.

He is clearly prepared to take that chance, however, and, as a result, we can now look forward to a much more interesting and exciting final day tomorrow as the Surrey openers - Mark Butcher and Mark Ramprakash, replacing the injured Ward - come out to bat with around half-an-hour to play before tea.

Thankfully, Kent start with genuine bowlers as Mohammad Sami and Ben Trott take the new ball, and Butcher carries on where he left off in the first innings by instantly blazing Sami away to the fence at cover. Ramprakash later adds an on-driven four off Trott to the list of superb strokes we have seen thus far in the match, before the young spinners, Tredwell and Ferley, come on to bowl the last two overs of the session.

Tea:- Surrey 26-0 (Butcher 17, Ramprakash 9*) from 8 overs*

Everyone in the ground is fully aware that we are about to witness some 'means-to-an-end' cricket in the final session of the day, with Surrey being pretty much allowed to get themselves into a position to declare and set Kent a target tomorrow.

It is to be hoped that the visitors don't resort to too much 'joke' bowling, though most of the Surrey batsmen, especially Butcher, are in such good form that they are capable of scoring quickly enough against proper bowling. This is demonstrated by the stand-in captain hammering thirteen off the first over of the session bowled by Tredwell, who also receives some fearful treatment a couple of overs later when both batsmen smite him for six.

In his current form, against bowling that isn't perhaps fully focused, Butcher has no trouble racing to a 45-ball fifty before losing his partner to a miscued pull off Trott to Symonds at mid-on, and, while Graham Thorpe gets his bearings against a new bowling combination of Carberry's off-breaks and Symonds' seam-up, the home captain continues to find the boundary on a pretty regular basis.

Thanks to Butcher's clean striking, a steady run-rate of five an over is maintained, though the Surrey skipper eventually falls to Carberry when he top-edges a pull to midwicket the ball after moving on to ninety, out of a total of 130, by smashing a full-toss over the legside boundary.

It seems inevitable that Butcher's replacement in the middle, Ali Brown, will enjoy the current bowling, and so it proves as he picks up three fours at Carberry's expense before turning his attention to Ferley, who is on for Symonds at the pavilion end. The left-arm spinner is struck for a four and a six in both his third and fourth overs by Brown, who arrives at his half-century from his fifty-third ball shortly after seeing Thorpe depart for forty-six to a catch at the wicket by Jones off the battered-but-not-beaten Ferley.

With the total now well past two-hundred, runs continue to flow freely as Alec Stewart cracks three back-foot boundaries in an over from Ed Smith, and Brown gets after Ferley again, belting him for another six and a four to leave Surrey 298 runs ahead when stumps are drawn.

Close:- Surrey 249-3 (Brown 64, Stewart 25*) from 44 overs*

Fourth Day - Saturday 5th July

Surrey 401 and 251-3dec; Kent 352-5dec and 114
Surrey won by 186 runs
Surrey 20pts, Kent 7

As play gets under way on the final morning, speculation is rife as to the terms of the deal hammered out by Mark Butcher and David Fulton yesterday afternoon. It's a fair bet that it favours Kent, since Surrey had been in no position to win the match until the collusion had taken place yesterday afternoon, but a general view seems to be that Kent will be chasing something like 320-330 runs in 85-90 overs.

The plot then thickens when just one run is added by the overnight batsmen in the course of the first three overs of the day bowled by James Tredwell and Rob Ferley. It would appear that the target is to be less than 320 and that Surrey are merely blocking out for a while in order to reduce the number of overs that will be left for Kent's chase.

No-one quite expects the declaration to come in the next over, however. After some uncertainty from the batsmen as to whether they are coming off, or staying on for another over, Stewart adds a single to the total and marches off with Ali Brown, leaving the visitors to pursue 301 to win in ninety overs. Given that three-hundred is a far from exceptional total at The Oval and that the match has been moving along at a rate much closer to four runs per over than three, Fulton appears to have negotiated a very good deal for his side. Surrey will clearly have to work very hard, and bowl much better than they did in the first innings, if they are to pull this game out of the fire.

The early indications are that the bowling will indeed be better - Michael Carberry slices and edges to the third-man boundary in James Ormond's first over, while Martin Bicknell barks out two lbw appeals against David Fulton - but as some testing overs go unrewarded the home side must be thinking that perhaps it isn't going to be their day.

By the time we reach the end of the tenth over, we have seen only one further boundary - this one beautifully middled through mid-off by Fulton off Bicknell - but with the required run-rate unlikely to cause them too many problems it matters little for Kent that there are only eighteen runs on the board. The Championship leaders, on the other hand, are already in need of a confidence-boosting wicket.

Further frustration follows almost immediately for Surrey when the visiting skipper slices a drive at Bicknell airily through backward point and profits by three runs, though this stroke turns out to be Fulton's last contribution to his team's cause as the third ball of Ormond's next over jags back to remove the batsman's off stump and send it cartwheeling towards the slips.

This initial breakthrough with the total on twenty-one is then followed by an even more important one when Ormond's third ball does the trick again in his next over. Ed Smith, who is currently in a bizarre run of scores where he is either making a duck or a hundred, follows his first-innings century with a sixth-ball nought when he snicks a drive at the Surrey paceman to second slip, where Butcher does well to cling on to a fast-travelling chance at head height.

Suddenly, the complexion of the game has changed, though Kent's key man, Andrew Symonds, is now taking guard. His first delivery invites the square cut and, inevitably, the Aussie takes it on… and the ball flies off the top edge over the slips and on to the third-man boundary for four. We could be in for a very good contest here.

Butcher is getting to the stage where he needs to rest his opening bowlers, however, and Ormond is the first man out of the attack after Symonds cuts him, this time off the meat of the blade, for a boundary at the end of a fine spell of 9-3-23-2.

The new bowler, Alex Tudor, then suffers the same fate as Ormond when his first ball to Symonds is pitched too short and too wide, while Bicknell's tenth and eleventh overs yield two legside fours to Carberry and a brace of off-side boundaries to Symonds as the total suddenly rushes past fifty in the twenty-first over.

Not surprisingly, Bicknell is promptly withdrawn after a fine opening spell that has gone unrewarded, allowing Saqlain to come into the action at Vauxhall end with lunch looming.

Another wicket before the break would make it Surrey's session, and it only takes the Pakistani off-spinner nine balls to produce the goods with an excellent delivery from round the wicket that takes the outside edge of Carberry's bat as it turns and bounces. With the ball climbing to around throat height, it takes a very good catch by Stewart to complete the job, however, and Carberry can feel a little unfortunate to have fallen to a combination of great delivery and great catch as he returns to the pavilion with the 'honour' of having just become the 700th victim of Saqlain's first-class career and the scoreboard now reading 61-3.

Symonds then comes through the final over of the morning from an improving Tudor… but only just, as he edges an off-side forcing stroke just wide of a diving third slip and picks up four rather fortunate runs.

Lunch:- Kent 65-3 (Symonds 30, Walker 0*) from 26 overs*

With three wickets down and their batting line-up seemingly lacking depth, Kent's task looks considerably more difficult than it had done at 11.30 this morning, though they are always going to be in with a chance while the muscular Symonds is at the crease.

When they lose him to the last ball of the second over after the break, therefore, the balance of power swings dramatically towards Surrey. Having perhaps been unfortunate not to claim the Queenslander's scalp in the last over of the morning, Tudor now gets his man when Symonds middles another cut but fails to keep the ball down, allowing Ian Salisbury to take a fine catch away to his left-hand side in a carefully-set deep gully position. With the trap having been laid and the plan executed to perfection, credit must go to captain, bowler and fielder as Kent slip to 67-4, with the target of 301 now looking a long way off.

The loss of their key man seemingly throws Kent into a state of panic, and the events of the next four overs prove decisive in the outcome of the match.

Having picked up four runs from a slog-sweep at Saqlain, the post-lunch bowler at the Vauxhall end, Matt Walker survives a confident lbw appeal and is then almost run out in the next over from Tudor when confusion arises over whether or not Mark Ealham should take a run for an airy drive that almost carries to Bicknell at mid-on. The chunky left-hander then edges Saqlain just short of Butcher at second slip before a panicky innings of seven is ended by a delivery and a catch that almost exactly mirror those that had accounted for Carberry before lunch.

At 73-5, Kent now appeared to be doomed, and their fate is surely sealed when Ealham falls to another example of good field-placing and another excellent catch, as his genuine leg-glance off Saqlain is very well picked up by Butcher at leg slip. Having probably been unsighted for much of the ball's journey from one end of the pitch to the other, the stand-in skipper does very well to hang on to a sharp chance at chest height that leaves the opposition in all sorts of strife at 78-6.

With both Saqlain and Tudor bowling extremely well after the excellent pre-lunch spells from the opening bowlers, this is a totally different Surrey side from the one that had looked so listless and ineffective with the ball in Kent's first innings, and, had Dave Fulton known just how much the home side were going to lift their game, there is surely no way he would have offered them the second chance that they now look set to take.

Although they are battling a seemingly lost cause, the seventh-wicket pair of Geraint Jones and James Tredwell do manage one very small victory when Tudor is forced to rest after delivering ten good overs either side of lunch, though it is almost predictable, given the excellence of Surrey's performance second time around, that the new bowler, Ian Salisbury, should take a wicket with his first ball. Jones is the man to go, rather foolishly trying to drive a leg-break over mid-on and getting a leading edge that Saqlain does really well to catch at full stretch after chasing back towards the boundary from his position at mid-off.

A sorry score of 92-7 becomes 94-8 a few overs later when Rob Ferley, having looked utterly at sea against Saqlain, plays back to the off-spinner and is pinned leg-before, then Mohammad Sami goes for a first-ball duck two deliveries later after being hit on the back pad by a Salisbury leg-break that straightens from leg stump, leaving the County Champions on the brink of a sensational triumph.

With forty-six of Kent's original ninety overs remaining, the result is now a formality, though Tredwell and Ben Trott do at least manage to lift the score from 95-9 to 114 before Tredwell becomes a third successive lbw victim when Salisbury's googly, delivered from round the wicket, strikes his back pad right in front of the stumps. As umpire Gould's finger rises, the Championship leaders celebrate an almost unbelievable victory at 3.03pm, with an astonishing forty overs to spare.

Surrey's second-innings bowling and catching has been absolutely top-class, and the Kent players can probably not believe what has happened since their captain took the gamble of declaring while in a position of strength. It always looked to be a bold throw of the dice by Fulton, since it offered the champions a chance to redeem themselves after a scruffy first-innings display in the field, and one wonders if this victory over Kent will turn out to be as significant in the race for the title as last year's incredible win at Canterbury was.

Surrey 401 and 251-3dec; Kent 352-5dec and 114
Surrey won by 186 runs. Surrey 20pts, Kent 7

Mohammad Sami looked distinctly sharp in pace. How did he compare with all the other fast bowlers you faced during the season while playing for Surrey and England?
MB - He was very slippery and would easily have been the quickest bowler I faced in the course of the season. It was good for me to face him because facing someone like that gives you the same sort of adrenaline rush as you would get in a Test Match. If he's running in at you then you can't just leap onto the front foot and have a swish, you have to concentrate.

Would it be fair to say that, in Kent's first innings, our performance in the field had fallen below our normal high standards?
MB - Yes, we were absolutely appalling - it was as disappointing a performance from a Surrey team as I can remember. But I guess it worked in our favour in the end - because of the way we'd played, they really fancied their chances of turning us over.

I assume it was Dave Fulton who first mooted the idea of setting up a fourth-innings run chase?
MB - Yes, it was all Dave Fulton's idea, because they were struggling in the Championship and felt they needed a win. Up until that point we were just looking at spending a painful day in the field, with things going from bad to worse, really. Then Dave called me up and we had a chat.

Were you surprised that he was offering us a second chance to win the game?
MB - I think he was only looking at it from Kent's point of view - they felt they needed to win because of their position, and they felt confident they could do that after seeing the way we had bowled and fielded during their first innings.

I assume the negotiations took place when you left the field shortly after an unexpected and rather strangely timed drinks break? And was the exact final-day target agreed at that time?
MB - Yes, that was when it happened, but we'd been talking about it on the field for a while, and the guys had been talking about us giving them about 100 overs to get 340, or something close to that. I then came away from the negotiations thinking "we've set them three-hundred, which no-one has ever got against us to win on the last day at The Oval before… but we've been terrible, the pitch is flat and they've played really well … that's a 50-50." I certainly wasn't confident that we were going to win the game, given the way we'd bowled and fielded … **but**… the one thing I ***was*** confident of was the fact that now the boys thought we could lose the game the strolling around and poor performance would go because they knew the game was on the line. It said something about us… that maybe we were a bit complacent first time around having put four-hundred on the board. But it gave us a huge kick up the backside because they all looked at me like I was mad when I said three-hundred off ninety overs - they thought I was kidding. We sat down on the final morning and I said that I thought this was by no means our game - if we strolled around like we had the previous day then we were going to lose, but if we really wanted to be champions then this was the sort of game we'd got to win.

The agreed target appeared very much in their favour, given that they would be chasing at three-an-over in the final innings of a match that had progressed at pretty much four-an-over. I assume you had decided that beggars couldn't be choosers once Fulton offered us a second bite of the cherry? And you were also banking on the fact that we would almost certainly bowl better second time around, presumably?
MB - Yes, he wanted the whole day to get three-hundred but I said he could only have ninety overs. He still felt he'd got the best side of the deal but history was in the back of my mind - the fact that no-one had ever got that many runs against us on a final day at The Oval. And I felt that

we would improve, yes, what with it being a fresh day and with our boys perhaps stung into action a bit by the thought that we might be in trouble.

I thought the bowling and catching in Kent's second innings was nigh on perfect - fair comment?
MB - Yes, everything was perfect and we looked like a Surrey team again. Whether that was because we'd put ourselves under a bit of pressure, I don't know, but what I **do** know is that the guys were worried that I'd given Kent the game at the end of the third day. And I was worried that I'd done it, too. And so were some of the supporters - when two shots went down to third man for four in the first over and I went to collect the ball I was given some fearful stick by a gentleman who said "they're already going at eight an over, do you want to give them the game?"

SURREY v KENT at The Oval — 2nd to 5th July

Surrey won the toss and elected to bat — Umpires:- David Constant and Ian Gould

SURREY - First Innings							
Fall Of Wkt	Batsman	How	Out	Score	Balls	4s	6s
1-73	**I.J. Ward**	**c Fulton**	**b Trott**	**33**	62	6	0
4-293	**M.A. Butcher ***	**c Jones**	**b Trott**	**144**	243	21	0
2-105	**M.R. Ramprakash**	**c Ealham**	**b Mohammad Sami**	**6**	31	0	0
3-243	**G.P. Thorpe**	**c Jones**	**b Ferley**	**68**	101	11	0
5-305	**A.D. Brown**	**c Symonds**	**b Ferley**	**27**	44	3	2
6-305	**A.J. Stewart +**	**c &**	**b Ealham**	**1**	5	0	0
8-355	**A.J. Tudor**	**c Ealham**	**b Trott**	**18**	29	3	0
7-336	**M.P. Bicknell**	**c Jones**	**b Ferley**	**22**	15	3	0
	I.D.K. Salisbury	**Not**	**Out**	**34**	31	5	0
9-359	**Saqlain Mushtaq**		**b Trott**	**4**	4	1	0
10-401	**J. Ormond**	**c Tredwell**	**b Ferley**	**15**	13	1	1
	Extras	**(5b, 10lb, 2w, 12nb)**		**29**			
	TOTAL	**(95.2 overs)**		**401**			

Bowler	O	M	R	W	NB	Wd
Mohammad Sami	**22**	**3**	**83**	**1**	6	1
Trott	**18**	**5**	**73**	**4**	-	1
Ealham	**21**	**3**	**67**	**1**	-	-
Symonds	**10**	**0**	**55**	**0**	-	-
Tredwell	**8**	**1**	**32**	**0**	-	-
Ferley	**16.2**	**0**	**76**	**4**	-	-

KENT - First Innings (Needing 252 to avoid the follow-on)							
Fall Of Wkt	Batsman	How	Out	Score	Balls	4s	6s
2-40	**D.P. Fulton ***	**lbw**	**b Bicknell**	**14**	55	2	0
1-25	**M.A. Carberry**	**c Stewart**	**b Saqlain**	**16**	31	2	0
4-275	**E.T. Smith**	**c Brown**	**b Salisbury**	**135**	177	20	0
3-151	**A. Symonds**	**c Butcher**	**b Bicknell**	**53**	87	8	1
	M.J. Walker	**Not**	**Out**	**82**	161	10	2
5-286	**M.A. Ealham**	**c Thorpe**	**b Ormond**	**5**	17	1	0
	G.O. Jones +	**Not**	**Out**	**38**	43	5	1
	Extras	**(1b, 5lb, 1w, 2nb)**		**9**			
	TOTAL	**(95 overs)**	**(for 5 dec)**	**352**			

Bowler	O	M	R	W	NB	Wd
Bicknell	**18**	**4**	**65**	**2**	-	-
Ormond	**16**	**4**	**60**	**1**	1	-
Saqlain Mushtaq	**23**	**5**	**63**	**1**	-	-
Salisbury	**29**	**5**	**111**	**1**	-	1
Tudor	**8**	**1**	**47**	**0**	-	-
Butcher	**1**	**1**	**0**	**0**	-	-

SURREY - Second Innings (Leading by 49 runs on first innings)							
Fall Of Wkt	Batsman	How	Out	Score	Balls	4s	6s
2-130	**M.A. Butcher ***	**c Smith**	**b Carberry**	**90**	74	9	4
1-72	**M.R. Ramprakash**	**c Symonds**	**b Trott**	**22**	36	2	1
3-208	**G.P. Thorpe**	**c Jones**	**b Ferley**	**46**	67	3	1
	A.D. Brown	**Not**	**Out**	**64**	74	9	3
	A.J. Stewart +	**Not**	**Out**	**25**	33	5	0
	Extras	**(2b, 2lb)**		**4**			
	TOTAL	**(47.2 overs)**	**(for 3 dec)**	**251**			

Bowler	O	M	R	W	NB	Wd
Mohammad Sami	3	0	10	0	-	-
Trott	7	0	37	1	-	-
Tredwell	6	2	35	0	-	-
Ferley	11.2	2	53	1	-	-
Carberry	8	0	45	1	-	-
Symonds	5	0	28	0	-	-
Walker	4	0	25	0	-	-
Smith	3	1	14	0	-	-

KENT - Second Innings (Needing 301 to win)							
Fall Of Wkt	Batsman	How	Out	Score	Balls	4s	6s
1-21	D.P. Fulton *		b Ormond	11	38	1	0
3-61	M.A. Carberry	c Stewart	b Saqlain	24	78	5	0
2-21	E.T. Smith	c Butcher	b Ormond	0	6	0	0
4-67	A. Symonds	c Salisbury	b Tudor	30	37	6	0
5-73	M.J. Walker	c Stewart	b Saqlain	7	20	1	0
6-78	M.A. Ealham	c Butcher	b Saqlain	5	14	1	0
7-92	G.O. Jones +	c Saqlain	b Salisbury	8	17	0	0
10-114	J.C. Tredwell	lbw	b Salisbury	17	55	3	0
8-94	R.S. Ferley	lbw	b Saqlain	2	14	0	0
9-95	Mohammad Sami	lbw	b Salisbury	0	1	0	0
	B.J. Trott	Not	Out	9	18	1	0
	Extras	(1lb)		1			
	TOTAL	(49.4 overs)		114			

Bowler	O	M	R	W	NB	Wd
Bicknell	11	5	26	0	-	-
Ormond	9	3	23	2	-	-
Tudor	10	2	26	1	-	-
Saqlain Mushtaq	14	5	27	4	-	-
Salisbury	5.4	1	11	3	-	-

Other Frizzell Championship Division One Results

Surrey's win earned them some breathing space at the top of the table, since Sussex weren't in action and Lancashire were much too cautious with a last-day declaration that left them with insufficient time to bowl Essex out. Warwickshire's hopes of mounting a challenge for the title were fading fast after they could only draw with the bottom club, Leicestershire.

July 2-5
***Chelmsford:-* Essex (8pts) drew with Lancashire (8).** Lancs 218 (Law 80, Brant 4-39) & 383-7dec (Chapple 132*, Chilton 70, Hegg 61*, Hooper 50); Essex 208 (Hussain 54, Martin 4-60) & 236-9 (Habib 69, Hooper 6-51).
***Leicester:-* Leicestershire (10pts) drew with Warwickshire (8*).** Warwicks 253 (Knight 66, Waqar 52, Masters 5-53) & 361 (Wagh 138, Bell 93, DeFreitas 6-78); Leics 328 (Maddy 98, Maunders 64, Betts 4-88) & 241-6 (Hodge 128). *** Warwickshire deducted 1pt for their slow over-rate.**

FRIZZELL CHAMPIONSHIP DIVISION ONE TABLE AT 5TH JULY

Pos	Prv		P	Points	W	D	L	T	Bat	Bwl	Ded
1	1	Surrey	8	126.00	4	4	0	0	34	20	0.00
2	2	Sussex	7	100.00	4	0	3	0	23	21	0.00
3	3	Lancashire	7	96.00	2	5	0	0	27	21	0.00
4	4	Essex	9	86.00	1	6	1	1	15	26	0.00
5	5	Warwickshire	8	79.75	1	4	2	1	26	18	1.25
6	6	Middlesex	7	70.00	1	6	0	0	14	18	0.00
7	7	Nottinghamshire	7	64.00	1	3	3	0	19	20	1.00
8	8	Kent	8	61.00	0	4	4	0	22	23	0.00
9	9	Leicestershire	7	54.00	0	6	1	0	11	19	0.00

NATIONAL CRICKET LEAGUE DIVISION ONE - MATCH SEVEN
Surrey Lions versus Yorkshire Phoenix at The Oval
Sunday 6th July

Setting The Scene - It's top versus bottom as Yorkshire Phoenix arrive at The Oval with just one NCL win to their credit and in real danger of being relegated to the second division. Since Surrey are playing their first NCL game for almost a month, it's no surprise to see three changes to the team that played Essex Eagles on 8th June, with Martin Bicknell, Mark Butcher and Ian Salisbury in for Phil Sampson, Ian Ward (groin strain) and Rikki Clarke (with England). Both Butcher and Salisbury are making their first appearance in the competition this year, while Adam Hollioake is able to maintain his ever-present record since his father is, thankfully, on the mend after his health scare. Yorkshire are meanwhile forced to do without Michael Vaughan, Anthony McGrath and Darren Gough (all on England duty), and injured bowlers Matthew Hoggard and Chris Silverwood. Tim Bresnan and Pieter Swanepoel deputise for the missing bowlers, while Andy Gray is preferred to Richard Dawson in the spinner's role. When Matthew Wood - standing in for the regular captain, McGrath - wins the toss he decides to bat.

Yorkshire Phoenix's Innings

Wood is possibly left regretting his decision to bat first when the opening ball of the match, delivered by Martin Bicknell, lifts to the shoulder of his bat and flies away in the direction of fourth slip, where Graham Thorpe running and diving full-length from second slip, pulls off a terrific catch.

Things can only better for Yorkshire after such an awful start and, with their two overseas batsmen, Stephen Fleming and Yuvraj Singh, immediately united at the crease, the visitors do start something of a fightback, with James Ormond the man to suffer. Having twice been pulled to the rope at midwicket by Fleming in his opening over, the Surrey paceman then finds three successive deliveries in his third over being dismissed to the cover boundary by Singh.

Since Bicknell is giving absolutely nothing away at the other end, Adam Hollioake decides to keep faith in Ormond, and this trust is rewarded when the strongly-built seamer unseats Singh with a good short ball that draws a gloved hook from the batsman and provides Jon Batty with a dolly catch behind the wicket. It's 41-2 in the eighth over and honours appear to be fairly even as Michael Lumb comes to the crease at number four.

Luckily for Phoenix, the new batsman soon settles, taking his side past the fifty mark in the tenth over with a leg-glance for three off Ormond in an over that ends up costing nine when Fleming drives the penultimate ball to the cover boundary. With Ormond's first five overs having now yielded forty-one runs, it's no surprise to see him being replaced at the Vauxhall end by Azhar Mahmood, who instantly locates a good line and length.

His Pakistani colleague, Saqlain Mushtaq, doesn't fare so well, however, when he enters the fray in place of Bicknell, whose figures at the end of a fine opening burst are 7-0-22-1. While Azhar surrenders just five runs from his first three overs, the Lions' off-spinner is glanced for three and on-driven for four by Fleming during an opening over that also includes two wides and costs twelve runs.

Since he is a class act, it is no surprise to see Saqlain recover quickly and, despite a sweep by Lumb that finds the rope at midwicket, he concedes just eight runs from his next two overs as the arrival of Yorkshire's hundred is delayed until the first ball of the twentieth over. With eight wickets in hand, the visitors are well placed, though, especially while the dangerous Fleming is around, and it takes a wicket to bring the contest back to a state of equilibrium. The breakthrough that Surrey have been seeking comes in the twenty-first over, with the third-wicket stand worth sixty-five, when Saqlain comes up with a superb quicker ball that straightens from leg and traps Lumb lbw for twenty-nine with the total advanced to 106.

With one of his spinners having achieved success, Hollioake invites the other one, Ian Salisbury, to replace the economical Azhar (5-0-17-0) at the Vauxhall end, though the Lions' 'leggie' gets off to a highly inauspicious start when he sends down a first-ball full-toss that Fleming smashes over the midwicket boundary for six. The Kiwi captain then goes on to complete a fine fifty from his fifty-eighth ball later in Salisbury's over, and it seems that he has found another decent ally in Craig White as the Phoenix duo pick off thirteen singles from the next three overs. The pattern is briefly broken by a lofted extra-cover drive by Fleming off Salisbury that brings two runs, before a return to single-accumulation takes the score up to 139-3 at the end of the twenty-seventh over.

At this point, Yorkshire look capable of posting a very challenging total indeed, but the Tykes' frailty when confronted by Surrey's high-class spin bowlers is suddenly exposed again in dramatic fashion.

Salisbury is the man to make the all-important first breakthrough when White fails to spot a googly and is comprehensively bowled as he attempts to cut, then, six balls later, Saqlain fools Richard Blakey with the off-spinner's version of the wrong 'un. As the batsman aims to leg, the ball loops up into the covers from the leading edge of his bat, giving Mark Ramprakash just enough time to move round smartly to his left and pull off a good diving catch that sends the Phoenix keeper on his way for just two with the score now 142-5.

The loss of these wickets - allied to the fact that Surrey ensure the new batsman, 18-year-old Tim Bresnan, receives most of the strike - seriously stymies the visitors' innings, with only five runs coming from the next three overs. The pressure created by such tight bowling clearly unnerves the Yorkshire youngster and it is not a great surprise when Hollioake, having posted himself at short leg, picks up a bat-pad catch from the first ball of Salisbury's sixth over, thereby reducing Phoenix to 147-6 in the thirty-second over.

Since Saqlain has just completed his stint with the fine figures of 9-0-39-2, the visitors are probably breathing a sigh of relief at the fact that they now only have to face spin at one end... until Ramprakash appears in the Pakistani spin-king's place at the pavilion end. It's an interesting move by Hollioake and it looks to be a good one, too, as the part-time off-spinner gets through three overs for thirteen runs, with the batsmen unable to take too many chances owing to the fact that there is quite a tail to follow them.

Unfortunately for the visiting team, Gray eventually yields to temptation, however, charging down the wicket to the second ball of Salisbury's final over and providing Batty with a routine stumping when a leg-break fizzes past the outside edge of his bat.

Salisbury subsequently delivers four 'dot' balls to Ryan Sidebottom, thereby completing a fine spell with a wicket-maiden and a return of 9-1-40-3, and leaving Phoenix to contemplate a scoreboard that shows they have just seven overs left in which to enhance a score of 175-7.

They make a good start to this run-in period when Sidebottom twice drives Ramprakash over the covers for four to force Hollioake into ending that particular experiment, but with only four runs coming from the next over, delivered by the Lions' captain himself, a total of 230-plus is clearly only going to be feasible now if Fleming can take most of the bowling. Since he has only faced eight deliveries in the last five overs, thanks to clever bowling, good fielding and shrewd captaincy, that might take some doing.

Azhar's return over at the pavilion end does, however, see the New Zealander on strike for four balls, one of which he cuts away backward of point for three and another of which he drives to long-on for a single that takes his score up to eighty-nine.

Unfortunately for Yorkshire, this leaves Sidebottom on strike for the start of the forty-second over, and Hollioake soon proves too good for the long-haired left-hander, deceiving him with a slower ball that is skied to wide mid-on, where Thorpe takes a good over-the-shoulder catch.

Although it's now 196-8, Fleming is at least on strike, with the batsmen having crossed, though he loses it straight away with a single glanced to long leg. He doesn't have to wait long to face the bowling again, however, as a wide and another glanced single, this time to the new batsman, Pieter Swanepoel, follow. Boundaries are now needed if Phoenix are to post a half-decent total and the next delivery, a low full-toss, appears to present Fleming with a good opportunity to hit one. The Kiwi left-hander appears to get caught in two minds as to where to hit the ball, though, and ends up merely poking a catch to Salisbury at a deepish extra cover, thereby handing Hollioake a second wicket. It's a sad way for a fine innings of ninety to end, and the New Zealand captain's lapse turns out to be even more disastrous for Yorkshire when Steve Kirby is immediately pinned lbw in front of his stumps by Hollioake's quicker ball for a first-ball duck. The visitors have therefore lost their last three wickets to the Lions' captain in the space of just five deliveries and end up 199 all out with nineteen balls of their 45-over allocation unused.

Surrey Lions' Innings

Yorkshire get just the start they need if they are to retain any hope of winning the match by picking up a wicket in the second over of the Lions' reply. The successful bowler is Kirby, who nips a ball back at Ali Brown and sees an inside-edged drive very well caught by Blakey diving away to his left behind the wicket. The loss of Brown for two, with the total at eight, is certainly a blow for the league leaders, though the in-form Mark Butcher does his best to make light of it by twice cutting Sidebottom to the point boundary in the next over.

Although both bowlers make life awkward for the batsmen at times during the early overs of the innings, the normally steady Sidebottom proves much easier to score off than the usually erratic Kirby. The flame-haired former Leicestershire bowler actually beats the bat on a number of occasions during an excellent first spell of 6-2-15-1, while his left-arm colleague concedes two further off-side fours to Butcher as twenty-six runs come from his opening five overs.

Sidebottom is convinced that he has gained revenge at the start of his next over, however, when he and his close-catching team-mates appeal for - and indeed celebrate - a catch at the wicket, with the batsman on thirty-two out of a total of thirty six. Both Butcher and umpire Ian Gould remain unmoved, though, allowing the batsman to rub salt into Sidebottom's wound by cutting him away over backward point for another boundary two balls later.

Having so far played an almost totally passive role in seeing off Yorkshire's opening bowlers, Mark Ramprakash takes a four off each of the first-change seamers as soon as they appear, courtesy of a pull at Bresnan's expense followed by an altogether less convincing edge to third man off Swanepoel in the over that sees the arrival of Surrey's fifty.

Butcher has been so dominant that his personal half-century (51 balls) arrives just eleven balls later, at the end of a ten-run over from Bresnan in which the England left-hander has racked up his eighth and ninth fours with a hook and an on-drive from consecutive deliveries that take the score to 66-1 after fifteen overs. Although it's true to say that the Lions are very much on top when nine runs then come from Swanepoel's next over, it seems odd that Wood has no slips in place, since it already appears certain that the only way his team can win this match is by bowling Surrey out.

A slightly more positive move follows when he replaces his ineffective first-change bowlers with Craig White and Andy Gray, though these two are looking no more likely to break the second-wicket partnership than their predecessors as the home side's hundred comes up in unusual circumstances after exactly twenty overs - Butcher's inside edge off Gray results in the ball running away past leg stump and onto the fielders' helmet behind wicketkeeper Blakey, costing the visitors five penalty extras.

The century partnership subsequently arrives in the Yorkshire off-spinner's next over when Ramprakash dances down the track and lofts a drive over mid-on for four, then the same bowler suffers a similar fate at the hands of Butcher two overs later as the Lions continue to charge towards the winning post.

At this stage it seems hard to imagine that things could get any worse for the visitors, but the twenty-fifth over of the innings sees what remains of Yorkshire's spirit crushed. The over starts badly enough when Bresnan misfields Ramprakash's off-drive off White - allowing the batsman to profit by four runs - and Butcher drives over extra-cover for another boundary, but worse follows when the bowler collapses in obvious agony immediately after delivering his next ball, a bouncer. The problem appears to be a recurrence of the former England all-rounder's long-standing rib/side injury and, as he leaves the field to sympathetic applause, it is clear that he is going to be out of action for an awful lot longer than the rest of this match. Yuvraj Singh is forced to complete the over for his stricken team-mate and is then retained in the attack as Kirby, the pick of the Phoenix bowlers by some distance, is sensibly recalled in the hope that he might pick up a couple of wickets.

Sadly for the visitors, the sparky speedster proves a little less effective on his return to the fray, allowing Butcher to register a new career-best limited-overs score with an on-driven four that takes his tally up to ninety-four. A run of singles then moves him on to ninety-eight, before Sidebottom, clearly still smarting from the earlier controversial incident, re-enters the attack at the end of Kirby's fine spell of 9-2-27-1 and is instantly driven to the long-off boundary by a jubilant Butcher. The England left-hander's first-ever limited-overs century, compiled from just 101 balls, has included sixteen fours and put his side on course for an easy victory at 161-1 in the thirty-first over. While Ramprakash congratulates his team-mate out in the middle, and the crowd acknowledge Butcher's achievement with a warm and lengthy round of applause, Sidebottom seems less enthusiastic.

With the game all but over, Gray replaces Yuvraj in the attack and immediately gains a consolation wicket when Butcher drives a catch to the Phoenix skipper at short extra cover with the Lions just thirty-four runs short of victory and departs to a standing ovation with 104 against his name.

The appearance of the Surrey skipper at number four suggests that the league leaders want to get this match over with as quickly as possible, maybe in an attempt to boost their net run-rate, and Hollioake doesn't disappoint.

With the rock-steady Ramprakash at the other end having just completed his half-century from 82 balls, the Lions' captain takes twelve from three balls by Gray, as an on-driven six is followed by a drive for four over mid-off and a delicate late cut for two. He then smashes the recalled Yuvraj over mid-on for another boundary to take his side within six of their victory target in the thirty-seventh over before being caught on the long-on fence at head height by Lumb off Gray while trying to win the game in the grand manner in the following over.

The honour of sealing victory instead falls to Ramprakash who ties up the most convincing of wins, by seven wickets with forty-one deliveries to spare, from the first ball of the thirty-ninth over.

MARK BUTCHER'S VIEW FROM THE DRESSING ROOM

Apart from Stephen Fleming, no-one really batted very well in the Yorkshire innings, did they?
MB - He played really well on what was a belter of a pitch where the par score was around 250-260. I thought we did really well to bowl them out for 200.

How did you rate Steve Kirby's opening spell?

MB - I thought he bowled really well. He's a good bloke to face, actually, because he's aggressive, he's always at you, so it's good fun. But it was a very fine spell and he showed what he can do, even on a flat wicket.

How did it feel to finally reach that elusive maiden limited-overs century?

MB - It's been a weird one, that - I really should have scored a lot more runs in one-day cricket, and I guess I'll look back at the end of my career and think that perhaps I didn't give as much time and attention to scoring the runs that I could have done in all the one-day games I've played in. I know I've done it in some of the bigger games in the past but in the Sunday League I've been awful. So it was fantastic to get there, and it was also nice to make a bit of a point about having been left out of a lot of one-day games by Surrey in the past - there has been this thing about me not being able to play one-day cricket, which I have always thought to be rubbish. So it was a good moment to do it, especially against Yorkshire, and especially at The Oval.

There are many people who feel that your style of play is well suited to the limited-overs form of the game, yet Surrey have often left you out, as you say, while England have never even tried you in a one-day international. I find it difficult to understand. I suppose you must do, too?

MB - I think my chance of playing for England in one-dayers has now gone, but I've still got plenty of time left to show that I can do it in one-day cricket for Surrey and improve on what I've done in the past. When the time comes for me to be playing more games for Surrey, I still think that I've got a real role to play in the one-day side.

SURREY LIONS v YORKSHIRE PHOENIX at The Oval

Sunday 6th July — Surrey Lions won by seven wickets

Yorkshire Phoenix won the toss and elected to bat — Umpires:- David Constant & Ian Gould

YORKSHIRE PHOENIX

Fall Of Wkt	Batsman	How	Out	Score	Balls	4s	6s
1-0	**M.J. Wood ***	**c Thorpe**	**b Bicknell**	**0**	1	0	0
9-199	**S.P. Fleming**	**c Salisbury**	**b Hollioake**	**90**	107	6	1
2-41	**Yuvraj Singh**	**c Batty**	**b Ormond**	**25**	27	5	0
3-106	**M.J. Lumb**	**lbw**	**b Saqlain**	**29**	42	3	0
4-139	**C. White**		**b Salisbury**	**11**	18	0	0
5-142	**R.J. Blakey +**	**c Ramprakash**	**b Saqlain**	**2**	5	0	0
6-147	**T.T. Bresnan**	**c Hollioake**	**b Salisbury**	**4**	11	0	0
7-175	**A.K.D. Gray**	**st Batty**	**b Salisbury**	**12**	21	1	0
8-196	**R.J. Sidebottom**	**c Thorpe**	**b Hollioake**	**13**	16	2	0
	P.J. Swanepoel	**Not**	**Out**	**1**	1	0	0
10-199	**S.P. Kirby**	**lbw**	**b Hollioake**	**0**	1	0	0
	Extras	**(3lb, 9w)**		**12**			
	TOTAL	**(41.5 overs)**		**199**			

Bowler	O	M	R	W	NB	Wd
Bicknell	**7**	**0**	**22**	**1**	-	1
Ormond	**5**	**0**	**41**	**1**	-	1
Azhar Mahmood	**6**	**1**	**24**	**0**	-	4
Saqlain Mushtaq	**9**	**0**	**39**	**2**	-	1
Salisbury	**9**	**1**	**40**	**3**	-	-
Ramprakash	**4**	**0**	**23**	**0**	-	-
Hollioake	**1.5**	**0**	**7**	**3**	-	1

SURREY LIONS							
Fall Of Wkt	Batsman	How	Out	Score	Balls	4s	6s
2-166	**M.A. Butcher**	**c Wood**	**b Gray**	**104**	107	16	0
1-8	**A.D. Brown**	**c Blakey**	**b Kirby**	**2**	6	0	0
	M.R. Ramprakash	**Not**	**Out**	**60**	97	6	0
3-196	**A.J. Hollioake ***	**c Lumb**	**b Gray**	**20**	16	2	1
	G.P. Thorpe	**Not**	**Out**	**2**	3	0	0
	Azhar Mahmood	**did not bat**					
	J.N. Batty +	**did not bat**					
	M.P. Bicknell	**did not bat**					
	I.D.K. Salisbury	**did not bat**					
	Saqlain Mushtaq	**did not bat**					
	J. Ormond	**did not bat**					
	Extras	**(1lb, 6w, 5p)**		**12**			
	TOTAL	**(38.1 overs)**	**(for 3 wkts)**	**200**			

Bowler	O	M	R	W	NB	Wd
Sidebottom	**9**	**0**	**43**	**0**	-	-
Kirby	**9**	**2**	**27**	**1**	-	1
Bresnan	**2**	**0**	**14**	**0**	-	-
Swanepoel	**2**	**0**	**15**	**0**	-	-
White	**4.4**	**0**	**29**	**0**	-	1
Gray	**8**	**0**	**43**	**2**	-	-
Singh	**3.3**	**0**	**23**	**0**	-	-

Other NCL Division One Results

Although Surrey had been one of the few teams to have played no NCL matches during the two weeks set aside for Twenty-20 Cup qualifying matches, little had changed with regard to positions in the table. The Lions' win over the Yorkshire Phoenix had extended their lead to six points, however, following two setbacks for the previously unbeaten Glamorgan Dragons, first at Edgbaston and then at Maidstone.

June 15

Chelmsford:- **Warwickshire Bears (4pts) beat Essex Eagles by 125 runs.** Warwicks 307-5 (45ov; Bell 125, Trott 59); Essex 182 (27.5ov; Napier 52, Bell 5-41).

Beckenham:- **Gloucestershire Gladiators (4pts) beat Kent Spitfires by 6 wickets.** Kent 222-8 (45ov; Jones 74*, Symonds 56); Gloucs 223-4 (41.2ov; Windows 58*, Gidman 49*).

Worcester:- **Leicestershire Foxes (4pts) beat Worcestershire Royals by 2 wickets.** Worcs 193-7 (45ov; Peters 50, Hodge 3-34); Leics 198-8 (42.1ov; DeFreitas 68, Maddy 56, Leatherdale 4-41, Mason 3-26).

June 22

Edgbaston:- **Warwickshire Bears (4pts) beat Glamorgan Dragons by 2 wickets (D/L method).** Glamorgan 193 (44ov; Brown 4-37); Warwicks 179-8 (38.5ov; Knight 75, Kasprowicz 3-20, Wharf 3-27).

Headingley:- **Leicestershire Foxes (4pts) beat Yorkshire Phoenix by 18 runs.** Leics 251-8 (45ov; Hodge 104, Sehwag 65); Yorks 233 (44.4ov; Bresnan 61, Yuvraj Singh 50, DeFreitas 3-33, Masters 3-33).

July 6

Maidstone:- **Kent Spitfires (4pts) beat Glamorgan Dragons by 52 runs.** Kent 291-4 (45ov; Smith 122, Ealham 50*); Glamorgan 239 (41.4ov; Maynard 72, Mohammad Sami 3-30, Ferley 3-59).

Worcester:- **Warwickshire Bears (4pts) beat Worcestershire Royals by 8 wickets.** Worcs 218-8 (45ov; Singh 97); Warwicks 219-2 (41.1ov; Bell 97*, Trott 56*).

NCL DIVISION ONE TABLE AT 6TH JULY

Pos	Prv		P	Pts	W	T	L	A
1	1	Surrey Lions	7	26	6	0	0	1
2	2	Glamorgan Dragons	7	20	5	0	2	0
3	3	Gloucestershire Gladiators	7	18	4	0	2	1
4	4	Essex Eagles	6	12	3	0	3	0
5	7	Leicestershire Foxes	7	12	3	0	4	0
=	9	Warwickshire Bears	7	12	3	0	4	0
7	6	Kent Spitfires	8	12	3	0	5	0
8	5	Worcestershire Royals	6	8	2	0	4	0
9	7	Yorkshire Phoenix	7	4	1	0	6	0

11 The Taming Of The Lions

Things could hardly have been better for Surrey at this stage of the season with the team having developed decent, though not significant, leads at the top of both tables. It had to be conceded, however, that the victory over Kent was rather fortunate in the way it had come about, since the match had looked to be on course for a draw until David Fulton had intervened. I still couldn't quite understand why he had felt the need to open the game up in pursuit of victory, even allowing for Kent's plight near the foot of the table. They had, after all, still got eight matches - half a season, in other words - to play after the game at The Oval, where they were on course for a twelve-point draw, which would have represented a very good return. There was still plenty of time, therefore, to make up the dozen or so points by which they trailed the sixth-placed side. Additionally, while the figures appeared to add up in favour of Fulton's decision - he was gambling five points (one more batting point and four for the draw) in order to try and gain fourteen for the win - sides had historically struggled to chase fourth-innings totals of any magnitude at The Oval since Surrey had signed Ian Salisbury and Saqlain Mushtaq.

Another, perhaps even more significant, reason why there was no need for Kent to be panicking was the signing of Muttiah Muralitharan. Only a fool would have bet against the Sri Lankan almost single-handedly securing at least two or three of the four wins his new employers required to retain first division status.

When all was said and done, however, Mark Butcher had been pretty brave to accept the deal of 301 in ninety overs, and fortune had gone on to favour him. Surrey certainly weren't complaining… though, apparently, Sussex and Lancashire were, with Chris Adams said to have been particularly unhappy that Fulton had let the Championship leaders back into the game.

Edgbaston was now the next stop for Surrey, with their opponents, Warwickshire, having failed to live up to expectations in both the Championship and the NCL. Although the Bears had been hit hard by the problems they had encountered with their overseas registrations, the results still didn't seem to match the talent in the squad. Could they lift their game for Surrey's visit or would they continue to underperform?

FRIZZELL COUNTY CHAMPIONSHIP DIVISION ONE - MATCH NINE

WARWICKSHIRE versus SURREY
at Edgbaston

First Day - Wednesday 9th July
Surrey 355; Warwickshire 85-1

The Teams And The Toss - *Surrey make two changes to the side that beat Kent, with Adam Hollioake returning in place of Ali Brown and the fit-again AzharMahmood replacing Alex Tudor. Warwickshire are meanwhile deprived of the services of Ashley Giles and Jim Troughton, who are both taking part in the Nat West Series, while Alan Richardson and Melvyn Betts are both injured. Surprisingly, the veteran off-spinner, Neil Smith, is preferred to their Kenyan leg-spinner, Collins Obuya. When Adam Hollioake wins the toss he elects to bat.*

The performances of Warwickshire's opening bowlers are like chalk and cheese as the Championship leaders get away to a good start on what appears to be a decent pitch. While Waqar Younis is right on the spot during three opening maidens, Neil Carter, making his first Championship appearance of the season, finds no fewer than five of his deliveries disappearing to the boundary in his first three overs, with Mark Butcher plundering three successive off-side fours from a particularly undistinguished second over. When Ian Ward then hooks the big left-armer to the rope at the end of an eight-run fourth over, Michael Powell is forced to remove Carter from the attack with the less than impressive figures of 4-0-27-0.

The South African-born paceman's replacement at the city end, Graham Wagg, makes an equally uninspiring start, however, as Ward pulls and clips him to the legside boundary, and things are looking far from promising for the Bears when Waqar yields ten runs to Butcher - including two off-side fours - in his sixth over after giving up just two singles from his first five.

Luckily for the home side, Waqar then strikes back with an important breakthrough, thanks to some good field-setting and a great catch. Although Powell has posted four fielders in the arc between backward point and short extra cover, the confident and in-form Butcher takes on a cover drive in the Pakistani paceman's next over, but lifts the ball slightly off the deck, allowing Jonathan Trott to dive away to his left and pluck it out of the air quite brilliantly. This fine piece of planning and execution terminates a bright and breezy knock of twenty-eight with the total at forty-seven, and only nine runs have been added when Surrey's other opener follows his partner back to the pavilion. Wagg is the wicket-taker this time when a good delivery from the young left-armer takes the outside edge of Ward's bat and flies at a comfortable height into the safe hands of Nick Knight at first slip. With Surrey now 56-2, and Ward gone for twenty-three, the home side look to have got their noses in front.

This doesn't seem to worry Graham Thorpe, however, as he clips the next ball of the innings through square leg for four and further spoils Wagg's wicket-taking over with a glance to the rope at fine leg from the final delivery. The Surrey left-hander then hooks Waqar for successive boundaries in the next over to bring an intelligent and thoughtful ten-over spell from the former Oval favourite to a close and reassert the visitors' authority.

After a typically quiet period of reconnaissance, Mark Ramprakash finally joins his partner on the attack with a back-foot forcing stroke for four during the rather variable Wagg over that follows, before Dougie Brown takes over from Waqar at the pavilion end and almost brings Thorpe to book immediately. Having induced a thick edge early in the over, Brown then lures the former England batsman into a mistimed pull that results in the ball lobbing just over the head of Waqar at mid-on.

Despite these minor scares, Thorpe demonstrates that he is still happy to hook and pull by cracking Wagg to the fence at midwicket as the promising 20-year-old reaches the end of a decent eight-over spell and gives way to Carter with lunch not too far away.

The recall of one left-armer for another turns out to be a good move by the Warwickshire skipper, as both batsmen fall in the space of three balls during the returning bowler's second over.

Although Carter's second burst of the morning starts with Thorpe driving gloriously through mid-off to take the score to 99-2, the bowler gains almost instant revenge in his next over when he captures two wickets in three balls - the left-hander falls lbw for thirty while aiming to hit the third ball to leg, and then, after Alec Stewart has got off the mark with a single from his first delivery, Ramprakash is adjudged to have nicked the fifth ball through to Frost behind the stumps. The former Middlesex man is clearly convinced that umpire Mike 'Pasty' Harris is wrong to have given him out as he leaves the field in a state of high dudgeon with his side now struggling a little at 103-4 and, though a couple of high-class boundaries by Stewart help to calm the nerves, it's probably fair to say that Surrey are on the back foot at the interval.

Lunch:- Surrey 115-4 (Stewart 11, Hollioake 2*) from 31 overs*

Luck is very much on Surrey's side in the first two overs after the break as both batsmen survive chances, Hollioake on two with the total on 116 in Wagg's opening over, then Stewart on eleven with the score advanced to 124-4 in the following over from Waqar.

The Hollioake miss is quite incredible. The batsman skies a miscued pull to a shortish mid-off position, square with the non-striker's stumps, and is amazed to hear and see Brown, from extra cover, calling for the catch, despite being in a far inferior position to take it than either the bowler or Carter at mid-off. Since the Scotsman seems so sure of himself, his colleagues leave him to complete the dismissal - a decision they instantly regret as he fails to hang on to the ball despite a last-ditch dive that enables him to get both hands to it. The chance that Stewart then offers shortly afterwards falls to Knight at first slip when the Surrey wicketkeeper edges a defensive push at Waqar. In this case, the fielder is due some sympathy, however, since he is clearly distracted by Frost, who makes an initial move to dive across in front of slip before deciding against it at the last moment.

Having survived these scares that could have seen Surrey in all sorts of trouble at 124-6, the batsmen launch a sustained assault on Waqar that brings seven superb boundaries in a four-over spell that takes the total past 150 and transforms their former team-mate's figures from 10-6-24-1 to 14-6-54-1. Needless to say, the Pakistani paceman is immediately pulled out of the attack, while Wagg, whose first four overs of the afternoon have cost just ten runs and been largely impressive, starts to take some flack from Hollioake. In an over that sees the total leap forward by fifteen runs, the Surrey skipper drives fours over extra cover, over mid-on and through backward point as the fifth-wicket partnership begins to put the visitors back on track.

Waqar's replacement at the pavilion end turns out to be Carter, and, after an opening wide, the sturdy seamer almost claims the wicket of Stewart when the batsman mistimes a pull and offers the bowler an awkward caught-and-bowled chance high to his right-hand side. Carter just fails to hang on to the catch with Stewart's score on twenty-one and the stand with Hollioake worth sixty-nine, and is instantly punished for this latest lapse when the former Surrey captain reels off a lovely extra-cover drive for four.

Wagg then attracts further attention from Hollioake, who takes vengeance for being hit on the glove earlier in the over by launching a drive straight down the ground for six, before completing a quite astonishing 41-ball half-century with a late-cut single to third man at the end of the over. Although his figures (14-2-73-1) don't look too great as he is withdrawn from the attack, Wagg has bowled pretty well in the innings so far and, with a bit of luck, could have had another wicket or two.

The bowler who replaces the young left-armer at the city end is Neil Smith, with the Warwickshire captain doubtless hoping that his opposite number might attempt something rash against the veteran off-spinner and self-destruct. Smith has to bowl to Stewart first, though, and he doesn't have the best of starts as the England wicketkeeper picks off successive fours, driven and then cut through the covers. As the batsmen continue to dominate, Hollioake then slashes Carter over backward point to raise his team's two-hundred in the forty-fifth over, simultaneously completing a century partnership.

Although the balance of power has now shifted towards the visitors, the Carter-Smith combination does at least give Powell a little more control for a while, until Carter gives way to Brown after a decent spell of five overs for twenty-one.

Once he recovers from the shock of having the first ball of his new spell driven over mid-off for four by Hollioake, the former England one-day international all-rounder also proves capable of keeping things reasonably tight, while Smith, bowling largely to Stewart, doesn't fare too badly, even though the Surrey wicketkeeper does eventually drive him to the rope at extra cover to go through to a nicely compiled fifty from his eighty-second delivery. On a very warm afternoon, the Championship leaders appear to be turning the heat up on the Bears and, just before drinks are taken, Hollioake confirms this feeling by taking ten runs from an over by Smith to push his team's total beyond 250.

The drinks break proves to be a real watershed in the Surrey innings, however, as the visitors soon lose their captain, and then, just a few overs later, subside in the face of an inspired burst from the Bears.

Hollioake has advanced his score to eighty-eight, and the fifth-wicket partnership to exactly 150, when Brown strikes at the start of his second over after the resumption, tempting his former England one-day international captain into a drive that comes off a very thick inside edge and finds the hands of Mark Wagh in a shortish midwicket position.

Fortunately for the reigning champions, Stewart is seemingly unaffected by the loss of his team-mate as he drives Brown wide of mid-on for four and then takes two boundaries from the medium-pace of Ian Bell, who has been given an opportunity as a partnership-breaker at the city end in place of Smith.

Since Bell has looked pretty ordinary during his three overs, and Brown is now through seven successive overs in the heat, Powell opts for a double bowling change at this point… and it has a devastating effect on the course of the innings.

All seems well for Surrey, initially, as Stewart and Azhar Mahmood take thirteen runs from the first five balls sent down by the returning Wagg, but in trying to pull the final delivery of a ropey over for another four, Azhar gloves the ball through to Frost, who takes a good tumbling catch away to his left to make the score 288-6 and bring the Bears back into the game.

An incredible over from Carter then follows, and, by the time it is complete, Warwickshire are not just back in contention, they are well on top.

The left-armer's first ball of his third spell brings a pull from Stewart that results in a thin top edge to Frost, then the next delivery sees another snick flying through to the keeper as Ian Salisbury pushes forward defensively. Three wickets have fallen in three balls, with Frost completing a wicketkeeper's hat-trick, and Surrey have suddenly slumped to 288-8. And Carter is now on a hat-trick himself, of course.

One can only imagine the panic and chaos that this clatter of wickets has created in the visitors' dressing room, though it's obvious that Saqlain Mushtaq, the next man in, hasn't been prepared for anything like this, since he takes a lot longer than the allowed two minutes to appear on the field to face the music. Luckily, and sportingly, Warwickshire don't appeal for a 'timed out' dismissal, and when he finally faces his first ball the new batsman manages to dig out a fine hat-trick delivery that is straight and full of length. The next ball, however, clips inside edge and pad, and dollies up to Trott at short leg to give Carter three wickets in four balls, and five in total, while the home team has captured four wickets in five deliveries. Surrey have crashed to 288-9, a score that looks well below par on what seems to be a decent pitch, and the Bears are now in charge.

James Ormond, who probably can't believe that he is suddenly standing at the crease with bat in hand, averts the possibility of Carter causing any more damage for the moment with a push to square leg for two, thereby getting his team off the dreaded 288, while an equally bemused Martin Bicknell stands at the other end waiting to receive his first ball after watching both Surrey spinners depart since his arrival in the middle.

While Hollioake and Stewart had been going so well, a full hand of five batting points had looked more than likely, so it seems incredible that the last pair are now together and need to find another ten runs if they are to secure a third point.

Fortunately, after taking a few overs to steady the heavily listing Surrey ship, Bicknell forces Wagg to the cover boundary and drives Carter backward of point for two to bring up the three-hundred, though further runs are needed if the visitors are to record an acceptable total. Ormond certainly does his bit towards this goal, helping the score along nicely with an inside edge to the rope at fine leg off the unfortunate Wagg, and two much more convincing fours off Brown when the 33-year-old all-rounder comes on to relieve his young colleague at the city end.

At this point, tea should be taken but, since nine wickets are down, the laws of the game decree that play should continue for half-an-hour or until the innings ends, whichever is the sooner.

It turns out to be the close of the innings, though not before the last-wicket pair have boosted the total to 355, claiming another batting point along the way. Both Ormond and Bicknell produce some fine strokes during a very valuable stand of sixty-seven, with the latter's two successive cover drives for four off Waqar when the Pakistani returns to the attack in place of Carter, and Ormond's drive for six over long-off at Brown's expense, standing out. This last stroke is the one that clinches the fourth point, and is followed, somewhat ironically, by a classic shouldering of arms to the next ball that results in the Surrey number eleven's off stump going AWOL.

As the players leave the field for tea - with the five-wicket man, Carter, leading the way - we can all finally relax after what has been a quite sensational session.

Tea:- Between Innings

With tea having been taken so late, the final session is a short one of just twenty-four overs, giving Surrey a good chance to throw everything at Warwickshire before the close.

Nothing much happens for the visitors early on, though, as Michael Powell gets away confidently with cover-driven and leg-glanced boundaries in Martin Bicknell's opening over, while Nick Knight deflects Ormond to the rope at third man in the second.

The bowlers tighten up a little thereafter, though the ball doesn't beat the bat on too many occasions and Bicknell ends a below-par first spell of six overs by being driven over cover for four and through extra cover for three by the Warwickshire captain.

Ormond subsequently switches to the pavilion end previously occupied by Bicknell, while Azhar joins the attack at the city end, though there doesn't seem to be an awful lot to trouble the batsmen, apart from the occasional inconsistent bounce that has been evident all day, as the total moves past fifty in the fourteenth over.

With his seamers having made little headway, Hollioake turns to spin, in the shape of Ian Salisbury, for the seventeenth over, and this move is rewarded with a wicket from the leg-spinner's second delivery when Powell's defensive push at a leg-break results in an outside edge that Azhar, at slip, picks up brilliantly with a full-length dive away to his right-hand side.

As Powell departs for twenty-seven at 62-1, the visitors are hoping for further breakthroughs in the last seven overs of the day, but Knight and Mark Wagh hold on comfortably enough, even when Saqlain joins his spin twin for the last four overs of the day with fielders clustered around the bat. There are signs of turn, however, which is encouraging for the Championship leaders as play ends at 7.15pm after a long but eventful day that has ended with little to choose between the two sides.

Close:- Warwickshire 85-1 (Knight 37, Wagh 9*) from 24 overs*

Second Day - Thursday 10th July
Surrey 355 and 282-3; Warwickshire 245

After a single exploratory over from Saqlain Mushtaq at the city end, it's Azhar Mahmood who joins Martin Bicknell in the attack as the overnight batsmen make wildly contrasting starts to the new day.

While Nick Knight struggles to re-establish himself, Mark Wagh finds the boundary on five occasions in the first six overs, including a cover drive and a back-foot forcing stroke through point in an over from Azhar that costs ten and takes the Bears past the hundred mark in style. So dominant is Wagh in these early overs that his personal tally has moved on by twenty-three before Knight adds to his overnight score with an upper-cut off Bicknell that races away to the rope at third man to complete a fifty partnership for the second Warwickshire wicket.

The former England left-hander has only advanced his score by a single, however, when he elects to take on an Azhar bouncer and only succeeds in miscuing high towards deep backward square leg, where James Ormond picks up a good catch after running fifteen yards around the boundary in the direction of long leg.

With the batsmen having crossed, Wagh pushes the next delivery to deep midwicket for two before Azhar, delivering the following ball from wide on the crease, traps the former Oxford University captain lbw for thirty-four. A score of 114-1 has therefore been transformed into 116-3 in the space of just three deliveries... and there's more to come, as Warwickshire do a passable impression of Surrey's first-day collapse.

The new batsman is Ian Bell, who must be feeling a little nervous as he starts out, since he has failed to score in the first innings of each of his two previous Championship matches.

He must, therefore, be a relieved man when both he and his partner, Jonathan Trott, get off the mark at the start of Azhar's next over, though the latter doesn't make it past the third ball as he falls leg-before in almost identical style to Wagh in the previous over. Surrey's overseas all rounder has captured three wickets in eight balls and the home side are now under pressure at 120-4.

Two consecutive maidens then follow as Tony Frost tries to steady the ship with Bell, but the Bears hit the rocks again in the following over from Bicknell when the former England Academy batsman extends his run of first-innings failures by edging a drive at an outswinger to Alec Stewart, who takes a fine catch low down in front of first slip. As Bell trudges disconsolately back to the pavilion with just a single to his name, Surrey are in with a chance of taking a tight grip on the game, since their hosts are now 120-5, still trailing by 235 runs.

It is perhaps fortunate for Warwickshire that both Bicknell and Azhar are now coming to the end of top-class spells and, indeed, after two further overs apiece, Adam Hollioake is forced to turn to Saqlain at the city end and Ormond at the pavilion end.

Although neither of the new men bowls poorly, the Bears now have two real battlers at the crease in Frost and Dougie Brown, and, in their very different styles, they rise to the challenge that now faces their side. The Warwickshire wicketkeeper is steady and unyielding, while the Scottish all-rounder bristles with aggression and counter-attacks effectively, taking successive fours off Saqlain in the forty-sixth over and shepherding his team past 150 by steering an Ormond delivery to the third-man boundary three overs later.

Worryingly for the home side, there are one or two examples of uneven bounce during Ormond's spell, though neither batsman is distracted by this as a burst of four boundaries in the space of three overs takes the sixth-wicket partnership past fifty. This sudden surge encourages Hollioake to withdraw Ormond from the attack in favour of Ian Salisbury, thereby creating an all-spin attack in the lead-up to lunch.

It seems like a reasonable idea, but, unfortunately for the Surrey skipper, Saqlain continues to look a little below par, while Salisbury's indifferent opening over yields two fours to Brown, courtesy of an on-drive and a pull.

Having been very much on top earlier in the morning, Surrey find that they have been dragged back to a position of equality as the players leave the field for lunch.

Lunch:- Warwickshire 190-5 (Frost 24, Brown 45*) from 57 overs*

With Adam Hollioake nursing a hand injury sustained at short leg during the morning session, Mark Butcher leads the Surrey side after lunch, and the stand-in skipper predictably opts to use Bicknell and Azhar as his first pair of bowlers.

Although Azhar starts with a wild legside delivery that costs him five wides, he is soon back on the mark, and his third legitimate ball of the session brings him the important wicket of Frost, comfortably taken at second slip by Butcher when the batsman fails to find any answer to a fine lifting delivery that shapes away from the bat. The removal of Frost without addition to his lunchtime score is terrific news for the Championship leaders, though Brown continues to play his strokes, pulling Azhar away to the midwicket boundary in the third over to simultaneously raise the two-hundred and complete a fighting 56-ball personal fifty that has included eight fours.

His new partner, Graham Wagg, is not one to play passively either, as he shows by twice driving the Pakistani all-rounder to the rope at long-on two overs later, and it would appear that a dangerous partnership might be about to develop when Brown follows up by driving Bicknell for four and three in the following over to advance the score to 222-6.

The game then takes another one of its dramatic twists, however, as Ormond replaces Azhar at the city end and immediately strikes a crucial blow with a delivery that beats the unfortunate Brown all ends up as it shoots through low and pins him lbw for a very well played sixty-one.

For the third time in the match, one wicket then results in a cluster of dismissals as the Warwickshire innings falls away in the space of five overs.

Four balls after Brown's departure, Wagg wafts at Bicknell and is caught at the wicket by Stewart for eleven with the total on 224, then a brief period of belligerence from Neil Carter - during which he plunders three fours off Ormond and one off Bicknell - ends with the loss of the last two Warwickshire wickets in the space of three deliveries. Carter goes first, with the total on 245, when he top-edges a cut at Ormond and is very well taken at shoulder height by Thorpe at first slip, then Neil Smith is last out, without addition to the score, when he carves Bicknell straight to a well-positioned substitute fielder, Ali Brown, on the cover boundary.

Having established a first-innings lead of 110, Surrey then set off like a train at the start of their second knock, with two woeful overs from Wagg receiving heavy punishment - Ward hooks and on-drives fours in the left-armer's first over, then Butcher picks up a brace of boundaries in his next over, courtesy of a pull and a straight drive.

Waqar is a somewhat different proposition at the other end, though, and when Ward tries to hook the Pakistani paceman in the fifth over he gets a thick top-edge that soars high into the sky towards fine leg. For a few seconds it looks like he might get away with his mistake, but Frost, having turned and sprinted towards the boundary, reaches the ball just in time as it drops over his shoulder to complete an excellent catch about ten yards inside the rope.

The loss of Ward for nine, with the total at twenty, looks unlikely to prove a significant blow since Butcher is still in sublime form, as he demonstrates by taking five fours from Waqar's next four overs with a wide variety of well-timed strokes - a glorious straight drive is followed by a square cut, a late cut, an off-drive and a pull.

With Mark Ramprakash starting confidently against Wagg's replacement, Carter, at the other end by collecting four equally varied boundaries in as many overs, the total rushes past fifty at a rate of knots, causing a few Warwickshire heads to drop and Powell to make a double bowling change.

The introduction of Wagg and Brown does nothing to staunch the flow of runs, however, as both bowlers stray far too often to leg. Of the eight fours that they concede in the next four overs - during which Butcher races through to a 51-ball half-century and the total soars into three figures in only the eighteenth over - no fewer than six come from legside strokes.

With their brief spell in harness having yielded the small matter of thirty-nine runs, Wagg and Brown are unsurprisingly expelled from the attack and replaced by Carter, enjoying a rapid recall at the pavilion end, and Smith.

These two restore a degree of order to proceedings from the Bears' point of view, though the Butcher-Ramprakash partnership extends beyond a hundred when the left-hander sweeps Smith for two in the penultimate over before tea.

As the players leave the field, it would seem that we have just witnessed the decisive session of the match, with Surrey having claimed the last five Warwickshire wickets for just fifty-five runs and then extended a lead of 110 to 231 with nine second-innings wickets still in hand. There appears to be no way back for the home side from here, even allowing for the unpredictable nature of this match so far.

Tea:- Surrey 121-1 (Butcher 71, Ramprakash 40*) from 25 overs*

Starting the day's final session with his two most economical bowlers to date - Waqar and Smith - seems like a sensible idea by the Warwickshire skipper and, with largely defensive fields in place, these two very experienced bowlers do manage to keep things fairly quiet for the first five overs. Although Ramprakash still manages to find the boundary rope on three occasions in advancing to his fifty from 77 balls during this period of relative calm, Butcher is restricted to just a handful of singles.

All this soon changes, however, as another glut of boundaries, including a straight six by Butcher off Smith, sees thirty runs coming from the next five overs, taking Surrey past the 150 mark and their left-handed opener into the nineties. Butcher doesn't waste any time there, though, as he immediately lofts the off-spinner away over wide mid-on for four and then slog-sweeps for six to complete a magnificent 102-ball ton in an entirely appropriate style.

With the opposition's lead already approaching three-hundred, Powell is now running out of options, though his decision to replace Waqar with Carter at this point is a good one, since it brings about a slight slackening of the tempo. The new bowler also manages to expose the rather capricious nature of the pitch again, as one delivery lifts more sharply than expected, cracking Butcher on the glove and necessitating a period of on-field treatment for the England left-hander.

Once it has been confirmed that no serious damage has been done, the Surrey opener reacts positively by crashing Carter's next delivery over point for four and hitting further boundaries from the first two balls of the following over from Smith, before top-edging a cut at the third delivery and departing, for 118, to a catch at the wicket with the total on 207.

As he leaves the field, Butcher is warmly applauded for a top-class innings, and the home crowd must be expecting to witness the continued destruction of their team's bowling as Graham Thorpe comes to the wicket.

Their fears prove totally unfounded, however, as the new batsman struggles for twenty-one balls, during which time he is dropped on nought - an absolute sitter to Trott off Smith at deepish mid-on - and three - an awkward chance to Wagh's left at slip off Carter - before the Warwickshire off-spinner gets his man just a few balls later. As a leading edge loops back gently down the track for Smith to claim what is probably the easiest caught-and-bowled of his career, Thorpe trudges off at the end of what must be the worst innings of four that he has played in his life. He can at least console himself with the thought that it has come at a good time, since his team are already leading by 329 runs and are in total control of the game.

With nigh-on eleven overs left in the day's play, Alec Stewart now arrives at the crease and immediately makes an impact by blasting Smith for four boundaries in two overs. Despite this, Powell keeps his off-spinner going, though he does rest Carter after six very good overs in trying circumstances, turning to his other southpaw seamer, Wagg, in his stead. Ramprakash has no objections to this, since he is nearing a century and, after a square-cut four off the newly returned seamer takes him to ninety-five, he duly arrives at the three-figure mark, from his 144th ball, in Smith's next over with a back-foot forcing stroke to the cover boundary.

As well as completing a fine century that draws a generous ovation from the crowd, this shot raises the Surrey 250 in just the fifty-second over of the visitors' second innings and extends their lead to 360.

This advantage is then increased to 392 by the time stumps are drawn five overs later, with a late burst of five boundaries from the fourth-wicket pair including a slog-swept six by the rampant Ramprakash off the persevering Smith.

At the end of day two, the match is already in the sort of position you would expect at the close of the third day and, unless poor weather intervenes, which looks highly unlikely, Surrey are nicely set up to claim their fifth Championship victory of the season.

Close:- Surrey 282-3 (Ramprakash 121, Stewart 29*) from 57 overs*

Third Day - Friday 11th July
Surrey 355 and 450-5dec; Warwickshire 245 and 304-5

Since the home side's fate is already pretty much sealed, Surrey have no real need to hurry as the third day's play starts in warm and sunny weather with Mark Ramprakash and Alec Stewart facing Dougie Brown and Neil Carter. It's really just a case of how many runs Adam Hollioake wants in the bank before he declares and begins the process of attempting to capture the ten wickets that will win the match.

Faced by understandably defensive fields, singles are the norm and boundaries something of a rarity in the early stages of the day, though Stewart does manage to find the rope with an extra-cover drive off Brown and a pull off Carter before playing on to Brown for forty-five in the ninth over of the morning. The fourth-wicket partnership has added exactly a hundred and, with Surrey leading by 429, Hollioake has 'licence to thrill' as he comes out to bat.

With Wagg now replacing Carter at the pavilion end, the visiting captain takes a few overs to set his sights before lofting Brown over mid-on for four and then crashing the young left-armer for two sixes, the first sailing over the rope at long-off and the second landing on the roof of the Hollies Stand at wide long-on. The young Bear quickly takes revenge, however, by trapping Hollioake lbw with a full-length delivery in his next over.

While the fireworks have been going off at the other end, Ramprakash has made his way to 150 from his 206th ball and clearly appreciates that all he really needs to do is feed the strike to his master-blaster middle-order colleagues, the next of whom, Azhar Mahmood, has just arrived at the crease.

As was the case with his captain before him, the Pakistani all-rounder takes three overs to have a look at the bowling and then goes on the rampage, smashing Wagg into the Hollies Stand for six, and then adding two fours later in the same over, with the last of these boundary strokes taking the Surrey total to four-hundred in the seventy-seventh over.

Unlike his skipper, however, Azhar manages to sustain his assault, and undoubtedly enjoys his contest with Waqar Younis when his former Pakistani team-mate enters the fray, rather belatedly, at the pavilion end. Azhar clearly comes out on top as he picks Waqar up over midwicket for a 'maximum' and then drives the next ball straight back down the ground for four, though he is a little lucky in the next over from his compatriot when he top-edges a hook over Frost's head to the rope at long-stop. A single from the following delivery completes a whirlwind half-century from just 25 balls in thirty minutes, and there is just time for Ramprakash to add to Waqar's misery with a couple of boundaries of his own before Hollioake finally calls it a day with the score at 450-5. Warwickshire are therefore left to chase a theoretical target of 561 in a minimum of 173 overs.

With about half-an-hour to go until lunch, Bicknell and Ormond are set loose on Powell and Knight, in the hope that they might be able to secure a wicket, or maybe even two, before the break. Powell starts well, however, repeating his first-innings feat of taking two fine fours from

Bicknell's opening over, and there are no real alarms as the interval approaches. Having endured a very difficult time in the field, Powell is at last enjoying himself a little as he drives Ormond for two off-side boundaries in the penultimate over and walks off to lunch unbeaten on twenty.

Lunch:- Warwickshire 27-0 (Powell 20, Knight 6*) from 9 overs*

After Ormond starts the afternoon with a loose over, containing two no-balls and a leg-glanced four to Powell, Bicknell makes an important first breakthrough for Surrey when his fifth delivery nips back and keeps a little low to trap Knight lbw for eight. Bearing in mind the former England left-hander's heroics earlier in the season at The Oval, it's understandable that the Championship leaders are delighted to see the back of him with the total at thirty-nine.

The new batsman, Mark Wagh, has also enjoyed recent success against Surrey, of course, and he is well tested by Bicknell in the early stages of his innings, while Powell finds the boundary rope behind point on four occasions when facing Ormond, though there is an element of luck about a couple of the strokes he plays. It's a much more convincing shot, forced away off the back foot to the fence at square cover, that takes him through to a battling 73-ball fifty, including ten fours, in the twentieth over, before Wagh suddenly wrests the initiative from Bicknell at the pavilion end by picking off two successive legside boundaries in an over costing twelve.

Hollioake takes this as a sign to replace both his opening bowlers, with Ormond's figures of 10-2-51-0 fairly reflecting his erratic burst and Bicknell's 11-5-31-1 not really doing him justice.

While Azhar's introduction at the pavilion end is entirely predictable, the appearance of the Surrey skipper at the city end most certainly isn't, with everyone having been expecting an early dose of spin. It's an interesting decision and it looks to be a good one, too, during a second over that sees Wagh snicking a low-bouncing delivery along the ground between wicketkeeper and first slip to raise the fifty partnership for the second wicket, then thick-edging a drive just wide of gully. Azhar follows up by inducing another thick edge from the same batsman in the next over, though there is again no joy for the bowler as Wagh profits by four runs, bringing up the Warwickshire hundred in the process.

These two bowlers certainly keep the batsmen guessing by adopting the familiar tactics of mixing up bouncers with yorkers and slower balls, though the Bears' pair don't have too many scares as they take advantage of the occasional leg stump delivery to maintain a good scoring rate with a drive through mid-on or midwicket. One such stroke takes Wagh to his fifty, from 69 balls, in Hollioake's sixth over, though it turns out to be his last contribution to the match as the Surrey captain gets him driving outside the off stump later in the same over and the resultant outside edge is very well snaffled up by the ever alert Stewart diving away in front of first slip.

This breakthrough, with the score standing at 138, is just what the visitors need, having gone twenty-one overs without success since Knight's dismissal, and hopes of further joy are raised slightly when Bell - whose recent second-innings form in Championship cricket has been good - edges another near-shooter to the third-man boundary. Even though we are seeing these occasional variations in bounce, the pitch remains basically pretty good to bat on, so Hollioake decides that a bit of spin is needed in the lead-up to tea and introduces Ian Salisbury at the pavilion end and Saqlain Mushtaq at the city end.

Although Saqlain starts poorly when Bell lifts the off-spinner's first delivery away over wide mid-on for four and then drives him through extra cover for another boundary later in the over, Salisbury soon slips into a decent rhythm and almost has Powell playing on in his third over.

Having survived this heart-in-mouth moment, the home captain goes on to reach his highest Championship score of the season when he cuts the leg-spinner to deep cover for a single in the last over of the session.

Tea:- Warwickshire 173-2 (Powell 81, Bell 19*) from 45 overs*

The visitors are hit by an unfortunate blow immediately after the break when Bicknell chases after Powell's cover drive from Saqlain's first ball and injures himself while saving a run with a slide into the boundary boards. He limps back to the dressing room with Neil Walker, the Surrey physio, leaving Ormond to deliver the spell that the veteran swing bowler was probably about to embark upon from the pavilion end.

This turns out to be a twist of fate, however, since the big paceman dismisses Powell with the second delivery of his second over… though he does get some help from the pitch. Having driven the first ball of the over to the point boundary, thereby completing a fifty partnership with Bell and moving his own personal score on to ninety-one, the Warwickshire skipper is undone by a wicked delivery that cuts back and keeps low, sending the middle stump spinning away on a jig of delight towards wicketkeeper Stewart.

With the hosts now 188-3, the Championship leaders have just taken another sizeable step towards victory, though the new batsman, the South African-born Jonathan Trott, appears totally unfazed as he whips Saqlain away on the legside for two boundaries during his second over at the crease. The Pakistani off-spinner has been disappointing in this match so far, and, with Ormond not on top of his game either, runs begin to flow quite freely - Bell cuts and on-drives the paceman for fours in consecutive overs, while Trott treats the spinner with similar disdain as successive overs yield straight-driven and swept boundaries.

Bell does offer the bowlers hope, however, since his concentration appears to waver from time to time. Having miscued a pull off Ormond just short of mid-on with his score on forty, he edges the same bowler low to the right of Butcher at third slip two overs later, with his score advanced by a single, and lives to tell the tale as the ball fails to stick in the fielder's hands. A thick-edged boundary then follows later in the same over, though there is nothing wrong with the square-driven four that takes him to fifty from his eighty-fourth ball before the over is complete.

Since Ormond's luck seems to have run out, Hollioake now recalls Azhar at the pavilion end, while Saqlain also looks like he needs to be replaced as Trott drives and cuts fours that leave the off-spinner nursing the very undistinguished figures of 11-0-56-0.

With the score zipping past the 250 mark in Azhar's first over, courtesy of a lovely on-driven boundary by Bell, the Surrey captain clearly has some thinking to do, though he allows his Pakistani pairing to hold sway for half-a-dozen overs before turning to the under-used Salisbury - surprisingly in place of Azhar rather than Saqlain - for the sixty-seventh over of the innings. The off-spinner is soon removed from the firing line, however, when his next over includes a lofted on-drive for four by Bell and a swept boundary to Trott that sees the 22-year-old arriving at an impressive half-century from 67 balls and also completes a 100-run partnership between the two young batsmen.

This stand has taken the Bears to 289-3, within 272 runs of their theoretical target, though any hopes their most optimistic fans might have of the home side pulling off an amazing victory are soon to be dashed.

Although Bell has another narrow escape when his pull off Salisbury just evades the upstretched hands of Saqlain at deepish mid-on, Trott is the batsman who departs when Hollioake makes a successful return to the attack. The Surrey skipper's first delivery is full of length and swings in to the young South African, pinning him lbw as he aims to leg across a firmly planted front pad. It's taken a great piece of captaincy and a fine delivery to end a really good innings at fifty-one, and the Championship leaders are clearly relieved to have made such an important breakthrough as the day draws towards a close.

Having done what his frontline bowlers had been unable to do, Hollioake then makes another interesting move by taking himself off after just the one over and bringing Saqlain back at the city end. It seems an odd decision, yet it pays off handsomely as Bell dances down the track to the off-spinner's second ball, and drags a mistimed on-drive to Salisbury at deepish wide mid-on to provide Surrey with what is surely the decisive wicket. As the former England Academy batsman departs, justifiably disgusted with himself, for seventy-one at 296-5, the visitors' celebrations betray their belief that the game can now be finished off quickly sometime tomorrow morning.

Tony Frost and Dougie Brown come safely through the last five overs of the day but, with the warm and sunny mid-summer weather set to continue, there is no prospect of the reigning champions being denied their fifth victory of the 2003 campaign.

Close:- Warwickshire 304-5 (Frost 6, Brown 2*) from 77 overs*

Fourth Day - Saturday 12th July

Surrey 355 and 450-5dec; Warwickshire 245 and 425
Surrey won by 135 runs
Surrey 21pts, Warwickshire 4

Adam Hollioake hands his spinners the ball on a gloriously sunny morning and both men slip into a good line and length right from the start. Saqlain begins with a maiden, while Salisbury has Dougie Brown missed from his third ball, after the first two have gone past the outside edge. The difficult catching chance falls to Saqlain when Brown, still on his overnight score of two, top-edges a slog-sweep high and wide of mid-on yet survives when the ball drops to safety through the retreating fielder's outstretched hands.

Thereafter, Brown and Frost dig in doggedly, scoring exclusively in singles until they are parted when Frost drives over a faster delivery of full length from Saqlain and has his off stump removed. As the Warwickshire wicketkeeper departs for twelve in the ninth over of the morning the total has only advanced as far as 321.

The next man in, Graham Wagg, certainly doesn't hang around - in any sense - advancing on Saqlain to lift the ball over wide mid-on for the first four of the day during his second over at the crease, before edging a defensive push to the substitute fielder, Ali Brown, at slip two deliveries later. This dismissal leaves Surrey just three wickets from victory, and there would now seem to be a strong possibility of the match being sewn up before lunch, especially as Saqlain is bowling much more impressively than on the third day and Salisbury is regularly beating the bat.

As a result, the game hits the buffers for a while, with the normally aggressive pairing of Brown and Neil Smith concentrating almost entirely on defence, futile though it surely is.

Smith takes six overs to get off the mark, and then another half-a-dozen pass before he finds the boundary with a slog-sweep at Saqlain's expense to take the total up to 351. This shot clearly goes to his head, though, as the Surrey off-spinner lures him into attempting a next-ball repeat that sends the ball sailing skywards off a top edge in the direction of deep wide mid-on. Salisbury gives chase from mid-on, possibly more in hope than expectation, but is within range as the ball drops over his shoulder and puts in a last-gasp dive that enables him to complete a very fine catch. As every member of the Surrey team races over to congratulate Salisbury, the visitors are now on the verge of victory, and the battling Brown seems to acknowledge that fact when he next faces the Pakistani spin king. Adopting a much more positive approach, the former England one-day international clobbers Saqlain for three boundaries in four balls before surviving a pretty straightforward stumping chance from the last delivery of the over with his score on forty-two.

Brown's revised approach is soon shown to be the correct way to go, since Neil Carter falls lbw to Salisbury's googly when he misses a pull three overs later, giving the leg-spinner a richly-deserved first scalp of the innings and leaving the hosts just one wicket from defeat.

Luckily for Brown, there is still time for him to complete a fighting 116-ball fifty two overs later, while Waqar Younis, a decent number eleven, immediately shows his intentions with a few bold strokes, some of which come off the middle of the bat and some of which definitely don't.

To everyone's surprise, the last-wicket pair are still together at lunch, having taken the total past four-hundred and added thirty-five runs.

Lunch:- Warwickshire 422-9 (Brown 54, Waqar 29*) from 112 overs*

It takes Surrey just seven balls to wrap up the Warwickshire innings after the break. Saqlain's first ball of the second over tempts Brown into a slog-sweep and the ball pops up into the air in front of the batsman via bat and pad for Thorpe to collect a simple catch. Brown immediately turns to shake hands with Stewart and goes on to offer his congratulations to all the other Surrey players as everyone returns to the pavilion. Saqlain, with another five-wicket haul to his credit, is invited to lead the victorious team off the field but generously acknowledges the fact that Salisbury has outbowled him by insisting that his spin twin accompanies him in doing so.

It has to be said that it's been a brave effort by Warwickshire to compile 425, their highest-ever second-innings total in first-class cricket, though they will reflect ruefully on a poor display with the bat in the first innings and a dismal effort with the ball in the second innings when they sit down and analyse their performance.

Surrey have no such worries, however, having retained their position at the top of the Championship table with a comfortable victory.

Surrey 355 and 450-5dec; Warwickshire 245 and 425
Surrey won by 135 runs. Surrey 21pts, Warwickshire 4

TALKING POINTS - ADAM HOLLIOAKE

I was a little surprised to see you bringing yourself into the attack ahead of our spinners on the third afternoon - for quite a long spell, too. What was the thinking behind that move?
AH - The ball was reverse-swinging a little bit, so I felt that I could prove to be quite difficult for the batsmen on what was a pretty docile wicket. Then I came back later for an over because I fancied my chances of getting Trott out - he was falling over to the off-side and I felt I could get him out lbw, bowling wicket-to-wicket... and I got him straight away, according to plan.

This pitch was typical of many this season, in that it hardly changed in nature over the course of the game - it didn't seem to break up at all. Do you have any idea why this should have been, and could it go some way to explaining why our spinners were less effective this year?
AH - There was a little bit in the pitch at the start, but then it went very flat. I think there's an argument that this new Surrey loam they are putting down gives you pitches that last longer... but I'm not sure, so I'd like to reserve judgement and see what happens next year really. It's easy to blame pitches but, personally, I don't think our spinners bowled as well this season as they have done for us over the years, and I think they would admit that.

How about the pitches at The Oval? To my eyes, there are some that appear to have become a bit slower and lower. Do we need to consider re-laying any yet?
AH - No, I think they are good enough pitches. I just don't think we've bowled that well this year, to be perfectly honest. I think we went away from some of the basics of the game and perhaps tried to be too clever at times - I just don't think we put the ball in the right areas often enough. I have a simple theory about bowling. The first thing you have to do is keep your foot behind the line, then you've got the ball in play. Once you've done that you've got to hit a line and length, and then you are halfway there - anything from there, whether it spins or seams, is a bonus. Too many times this year we were over the front line or we weren't on a line and length. The basics of the game haven't changed for a hundred-odd years and, at the end of the day, we didn't bowl as well as some of the other sides.

WARWICKSHIRE v SURREY at Edgbaston — 9th to 12th July

Surrey won the toss and elected to bat — Umpires:- John Hampshire and Mike Harris

SURREY - First Innings

Fall Of Wkt	Batsman	How	Out	Score	Balls	4s	6s
2-56	**I.J. Ward**	**c Knight**	**b Wagg**	**23**	47	5	0
1-47	**M.A. Butcher**	**c Trott**	**b Waqar**	**28**	37	6	0
4-103	**M.R. Ramprakash**	**c Frost**	**b Carter**	**18**	44	4	0
3-102	**G.P. Thorpe**	**lbw**	**b Carter**	**30**	39	6	0
7-288	**A.J. Stewart +**	**c Frost**	**b Carter**	**74**	115	13	0
5-253	**A.J. Hollioake ***	**c Wagh**	**b Brown**	**88**	89	14	1
6-288	**Azhar Mahmood**	**c Frost**	**b Wagg**	**13**	18	2	0
	M.P. Bicknell	**Not**	**Out**	**25**	43	4	0
8-288	**I.D.K. Salisbury**	**c Frost**	**b Carter**	**0**	1	0	0
9-288	**Saqlain Mushtaq**	**c Trott**	**b Carter**	**0**	2	0	0
10-355	**J. Ormond**		**b Brown**	**33**	47	4	1
	Extras	**(4b, 3lb, 4w, 12nb)**		**23**			
	TOTAL	**(79.2 overs)**		**355**			

Bowler	O	M	R	W	NB	Wd
Waqar Younis	**17**	**7**	**65**	**1**	-	-
Carter	**17**	**0**	**75**	**5**	-	1
Wagg	**18**	**2**	**101**	**2**	6	3
Brown	**17.2**	**4**	**59**	**2**	-	-
Smith	**7**	**0**	**34**	**0**	-	-
Bell	**3**	**0**	**14**	**0**	-	-

WARWICKSHIRE - First Innings (Needing 206 to avoid the follow-on)

Fall Of Wkt	Batsman	How	Out	Score	Balls	4s	6s
1-62	**M.J. Powell ***	**c Azhar**	**b Salisbury**	**27**	50	5	0
2-114	**N.V. Knight**	**c Ormond**	**b Azhar**	**42**	106	7	0
3-116	**M.A. Wagh**	**lbw**	**b Azhar**	**34**	52	6	0
5-120	**I.R. Bell**	**c Stewart**	**b Bicknell**	**1**	16	0	0
4-120	**I.J.L. Trott**	**lbw**	**b Azhar**	**1**	4	0	0
6-195	**T. Frost +**	**c Butcher**	**b Azhar**	**24**	70	3	0
7-224	**D.R. Brown**	**lbw**	**b Ormond**	**61**	70	9	0
8-224	**G.G. Wagg**	**c Stewart**	**b Bicknell**	**11**	25	2	0
10-245	**N.M.K. Smith**	**c sub (Brown)**	**b Bicknell**	**1**	7	0	0
9-245	**N.M. Carter**	**c Thorpe**	**b Ormond**	**20**	17	4	0
	Waqar Younis	**Not**	**Out**	**0**	0	0	0
	Extras	**(4lb, 5w, 14nb)**		**23**			
	TOTAL	**(68.2 overs)**		**245**			

Bowler	O	M	R	W	NB	Wd
Bicknell	**21.2**	**4**	**62**	**3**	1	-
Ormond	**15**	**3**	**57**	**2**	4	-
Azhar Mahmood	**16**	**4**	**61**	**4**	2	1
Salisbury	**6**	**2**	**20**	**1**	-	-
Saqlain Mushtaq	**10**	**0**	**41**	**0**	-	-

SURREY - Second Innings (Leading by 110 runs on first innings)

Fall Of Wkt	Batsman	How	Out	Score	Balls	4s	6s
1-20	**I.J. Ward**	**c Frost**	**b Waqar**	**9**	13	2	0
2-207	**M.A. Butcher**	**c Frost**	**b Smith**	**118**	116	20	2
	M.R. Ramprakash	**Not**	**Out**	**182**	236	25	1
3-219	**G.P. Thorpe**	**c &**	**b Smith**	**4**	21	0	0
4-319	**A.J. Stewart +**		**b Brown**	**45**	56	8	0
5-364	**A.J. Hollioake ***	**lbw**	**b Wagg**	**30**	25	1	2
	Azhar Mahmood	**Not**	**Out**	**50**	26	4	2
	Extras	**(3b, 7lb, 2nb)**		**12**			
	TOTAL	**(82 overs)**	**(for 5 dec)**	**450**			

Bowler	O	M	R	W	NB	Wd
Waqar Younis	**14**	**1**	**81**	**1**	-	-
Wagg	**13**	**0**	**88**	**1**	-	-
Carter	**20**	**3**	**81**	**0**	1	-
Brown	**12**	**0**	**74**	**1**	-	-
Smith	**22**	**1**	**111**	**2**	-	-
Bell	**1**	**0**	**5**	**0**	-	-

WARWICKSHIRE - Second Innings (Needing 561 to win)							
Fall Of Wkt	Batsman	How	Out	Score	Balls	4s	6s
3-188	**M.J. Powell ***		**b Ormond**	**91**	147	13	0
1-39	**N.V. Knight**	**lbw**	**b Bicknell**	**8**	26	0	0
2-138	**M.A. Wagh**	**c Stewart**	**b Hollioake**	**51**	71	10	0
5-296	**I.R. Bell**	**c Salisbury**	**b Saqlain**	**71**	112	11	0
4-293	**I.J.L. Trott**	**lbw**	**b Hollioake**	**51**	69	9	0
6-321	**T. Frost +**		**b Saqlain**	**12**	51	1	0
10-425	**D.R. Brown**	**c Thorpe**	**b Saqlain**	**56**	131	5	0
7-327	**G.G. Wagg**	**c sub (Brown)**	**b Saqlain**	**4**	5	1	0
8-351	**N.M.K. Smith**	**c Salisbury**	**b Saqlain**	**8**	26	1	0
9-387	**N.M. Carter**	**lbw**	**b Salisbury**	**11**	12	1	0
	Waqar Younis	**Not**	**Out**	**30**	34	4	0
	Extras	**(8b, 14lb, 10nb)**		**32**			
	TOTAL	**(113.1 overs)**		**425**			

Bowler	O	M	R	W	NB	Wd
Bicknell	**11**	**5**	**31**	**1**	-	-
Ormond	**17**	**3**	**83**	**1**	3	-
Hollioake	**11**	**2**	**32**	**2**	-	-
Azhar Mahmood	**10**	**0**	**53**	**0**	2	-
Salisbury	**29**	**2**	**70**	**1**	-	-
Saqlain Mushtaq	**35.1**	**3**	**134**	**5**	-	-

Other Frizzell Championship Division One Results

Since Surrey's victory had been matched by Sussex's win at Arundel - where Jason Lewry was to the fore with ten wickets - the only real change at the top of the table concerned the gap that was developing. With Lancashire again sitting out a round of matches, the top two had managed to pull away quite dramatically and it was clear that the Red Rose county would have to win their games in hand if they were to retain any hope of staying in touch. It was already looking highly unlikely that any other side could now mount a challenge for the title. At the wrong end of the table, Kent did their chances of survival a power of good by thrashing Nottinghamshire at Maidstone, largely thanks to a stunning performance by Mohammad Sami, who took 15-114 in the match.

July 9-11
***Maidstone:-* Kent (21pts) beat Nottinghamshire (3) by 287 runs.** Kent 362 (Smith 149, Jones 82) & 418-3dec (Key 140, Smith 113, Symonds 103*); Notts 156 (Gallian 51, Mohammad Sami 8-64) & 337 (Gallian 106, Pietersen 62, Cairns 58, Mohammad Sami 7-50).
July 9-12
***Southgate:-* Middlesex (22pts) beat Leicestershire (7) by 8 wickets.** Middx 620-7dec (Strauss 147, Nash 103*, Joyce 102) & 166-2 (Strauss 73); Leics 447 (Sehwag 130, Maunders 55, Nixon 52*, Hodge 52, Keegan 6-114) & 335 (Hodge 112, Maddy 94).
***Arundel:-* Sussex (21pts) beat Essex (6) by 6 wickets.** Essex 340 (Hussain 95, Napier 89*, Lewry 5-72) & 274 (Grayson 71, Flower 54, Habib 53, Lewry 5-52); Sussex 359 (Cottey 107, Ambrose 88) & 257-4 (Cottey 98, Ambrose 93*).

FRIZZELL CHAMPIONSHIP DIVISION ONE TABLE AT 12TH JULY

Pos	Prv		P	Points	W	D	L	T	Bat	Bwl	Ded
1	1	**Surrey**	**9**	**147.00**	5	4	0	0	38	23	0.00
2	2	**Sussex**	**8**	**121.00**	5	0	3	0	27	24	0.00
3	3	**Lancashire**	**7**	**96.00**	2	5	0	0	27	21	0.00
4	6	**Middlesex**	**8**	**92.00**	2	6	0	0	19	21	0.00
5	4	**Essex**	**10**	**92.00**	1	6	2	1	18	29	0.00
6	5	**Warwickshire**	**9**	**83.75**	1	4	3	1	27	21	1.25
7	8	**Kent**	**9**	**82.00**	1	4	4	0	26	26	0.00
8	7	**Nottinghamshire**	**8**	**67.00**	1	3	4	0	19	23	1.00
9	9	**Leicestershire**	**8**	**61.00**	0	6	2	0	16	21	0.00

NATIONAL CRICKET LEAGUE DIVISION ONE - MATCH EIGHT
Warwickshire Bears versus Surrey Lions at Edgbaston
Sunday 13th July

Setting The Scene - This match sees the NCL Division One's two 'form' sides going head-to-head, since the Lions are still unbeaten, while the Bears have won their last three matches after a wretched start to the campaign. Warwickshire make three changes to the side that lost in the Championship, with Jim Troughton, Trevor Penney and Collins Obuya taking the places of Mark Wagh, Tony Frost and Graham Wagg. Penney, having stood in as wicketkeeper for a number of Twenty-20 and NCL matches, is the designated gloveman since Frost has an injured finger, while Wagh's omission is explained by the fact that he is nursing a sore shoulder. Even though the Nat West Series is now over - with an England side that included Rikki Clarke having thrashed South Africa in yesterday's final - Ashley Giles is not permitted to play for the Bears. The Surrey team meanwhile shows just one change from the eleven that took on Yorkshire Phoenix, with Ian Ward replacing Saqlain Mushtaq, who has a finger injury. After winning the toss Surrey elect to bat.

Surrey Lions' Innings

Although Ian Ward is back in the Lions' line-up, it is last week's centurion, Mark Butcher, who is chosen to open with Ali Brown... though he only gets to face six balls, the last of which sees him falling lbw to Waqar Younis for a duck as he aims across the line. It's a bad blow to lose a man in such good form to the fourth delivery of the second over, with the score on eight, but the unbeaten Lions know they will have to deal with such setbacks if they are to maintain their coveted place at the top of the table.

Fortunately, Brown looks in decent touch as he supplements a pulled four in Neil Carter's opening over of the match with two further boundaries from Waqar's second over to give the innings some early impetus. He then follows up by driving his former team-mate away over cover for a fourth four in the sixth over, but perishes to the next delivery when he snicks another drive and sees Nick Knight pull off a fine head-high catch at slip, despite the fact that the ball is travelling at great speed and the stand-in wicketkeeper has made an initial move to go for the catch.

At 28-2, the wind has been taken out of the visitors' sails and, as a result, Mark Ramprakash and Graham Thorpe are forced to take stock of the situation, with just two fours - a glance by Ramprakash and a drive by Thorpe - and a handful of singles coming from the next five overs.

Carter, at the city end, has been very much on the spot throughout the innings so far, though he remains wicketless as Waqar strikes another blow for the Bears in the twelfth over, claiming his third scalp when Thorpe is adjudged to have got a thin edge through to Penney after scoring seven out of a total of forty-five.

Ian Ward now comes to the wicket in the unaccustomed position of number five and promptly brings up the Lions' fifty with an extra-cover drive to the boundary off Waqar in the fourteenth over, at the end of which both opening bowlers take a rest after contributing fine spells that have put the league leaders in real trouble.

The new bowlers are Neil Smith, at the city end, and Dougie Brown, at the pavilion end, and, even though Ramprakash forces Smith's second delivery through the covers for four, a score of 58-3 at the end of the first fifteen overs looks well below par.

As they continue to re-establish the innings, the fourth-wicket pair manage to keep the scoreboard ticking over against the veteran off-spinner and the other new bowler, Dougie Brown, with twelve most welcome runs coming from the twentieth over, during which each batsman contributes a back-foot boundary to the Surrey cause.

Alas, a promising stand is cut off at forty-two in the next over when Ward dances down the track to Smith and is defeated by turn, leaving Penney to complete a routine stumping with the batsman yards from home. The visitors are committing the cardinal sin of losing wickets at regular intervals as Ward departs for twenty-one at 87-4.

Ramprakash clearly needs someone who can contribute a sustained positive knock at the other end, and his latest partner, Adam Hollioake, soon looks like he could be the man for the job as he cleverly deflects a ball from Brown to the fine third-man boundary and then sweeps Smith to the rope at midwicket to raise the Lions' hundred in the twenty-fifth over. The run-rate is almost as much of a worry as the wickets lost at this period of the game, since the pitch looks to be a decent one, and any total below 230 will leave Warwickshire strong favourites to win.

With Brown through five overs from the pavilion end, Michael Powell now makes an interesting move by bringing on the Kenyan leg-spinner, Collins Obuya, thereby creating an all-spin attack, and the Surrey skipper responds by blasting the new bowler's first delivery over long-off for six. The over ends up costing nine, and is then followed by a ten-run over from Smith, as momentum looks to be building again.

The spinners quickly put those loose overs behind them, though, and, by bowling to the fields that have been set for them, they prevent the batsmen from finding the boundary and, as a consequence, gain reward for their efforts. After a few overs of being restricted to singles, Hollioake clearly decides that he must set his sights higher, but in aiming a huge heave to leg he is bowled for twenty-five by a good, quicker leg-break from Obuya, who has seemingly read the batsman's mind. This is the last thing the visitors need - another batsman failing to go on after getting into the twenties and another partnership sawn off before it can really hurt the opposition.

At least Ramprakash is still there to offer hope, and he reaches a 79-ball fifty, two deliveries after Hollioake's departure, from the final ball of the thirtieth over, at which point the Lions are 139-5. Just to underline the fact that the league leaders are feeling the pressure and know that they can't afford to lose another wicket for a while, Smith is able to deliver a maiden to Azhar Mahmood of all people, thereby completing an excellent spell with figures of 9-1-37-1.

Unfortunately for Surrey, their position becomes even more precarious two overs later when Brown, returning to the attack in place of Smith, unseats Ramprakash with the total at 150 in the thirty-third over. The Surrey number three has just cut the Warwickshire all-rounder for four to move his score on to fifty-seven when he attempts another off-side forcing stroke and chops the ball down onto his stumps, much to the delight of the Bears' players and an Edgbaston crowd of around 6,000 on a hot and sunny afternoon. The Warwickshire faithful are fully aware that the Lions are now in desperate trouble… and their position is soon to deteriorate further.

Following a maiden from Obuya to the new batsman, Jon Batty, the Surrey total suddenly leaps forward when fifteen runs - including pulled and straight-driven boundaries from Azhar -come from the next over delivered by Brown, but the visitors' joy is short-lived as the third delivery of the leg-spinner's sixth over brings about the downfall of Azhar for seventeen with the total on 166. In attempting to launch a leg-break straight down the ground, the Pakistani all-rounder miscues high towards deep mid-off where Jim Troughton takes a very good catch after running in from the long-off boundary.

Since spin is proving so successful for him, Powell immediately brings the catcher into the attack to replace Brown, and the league leaders' eighth-wicket pair of Batty and Martin Bicknell do a decent damage-limitation job over the course of the next five overs, adding thirty-two valuable runs. With Bicknell content to hold his end up and pick off the occasional single, Batty is very much to the fore, sweeping Troughton's left-arm spin for four and cutting Obuya to the rope at backward point, before taking full advantage of two more loose deliveries in the leg-spinner's eighth over - a full-toss is smashed high into the Hollies Stand, then a long-hop is cut through square cover for another four.

Unfortunately for the Lions, Waqar then returns to the fray in place of Troughton and cleans up Batty with a fine inswinging yorker that extracts middle stump, pegging the visitors back to 198-8 in the forty-first over and maintaining the Bears' firm grip on the game.

With Carter making a predictable reappearance in place of Obuya at the pavilion end, the experienced pair of Bicknell and Ian Salisbury take the total beyond two-hundred while seeing off the last over from Waqar, who completes an impressive return of 9-1-35-4. They then scrape together another nine runs from the last over of Carter's fine spell (9-0-35-0), thanks largely to Salisbury's square-driven four from the third delivery, leaving the scoreboard reading 219-8 at the start of the final over.

Since Waqar, Carter and Smith have all delivered their allotted stints, Powell now has to choose between Brown and Obuya to complete the innings and opts for his leg-spinner, who, despite a couple of expensive overs, has the very respectable figures of 8-1-42-2.

The over starts well for the Kenyan when Bicknell drives to long-off for a single, but it quickly turns sour for him when Salisbury takes 6-4-6-6 from the next four deliveries, with a drive over the rope at long-off being followed by an extra-cover drive, a pull over midwicket and another drive, this time high over wide long-on. Although Obuya extracts a degree of revenge when his fellow leg-spinner backs away and top-edges a cut at the last ball of the innings into the safe hands of Troughton at point, Salisbury has given his team hope with his ultra-positive knock of thirty-three from just 17 balls. Surrey have, in fact, added ninety-one runs from their last eleven overs... though this probably only goes to show that batting on this track is rather easier than they have made it look at times. This is not to take any credit away from Warwickshire, who have bowled and fielded very well for the greater part of the Lions' innings.

Warwickshire Bears' Innings

Surrey's unbeaten run of eleven NCL games - four to close the 2002 season and seven so far this term - is clearly on the line as their first-choice pair of opening bowlers in this competition, Martin Bicknell and Azhar Mahmood, send down the opening overs to Nick Knight and Neil Carter.

Although the sturdy Carter - regularly promoted to the open the innings in one-day cricket - does manage to find the boundary on three occasions in the first five overs, he is greatly helped by the fact that he faces twenty-three balls to Knight's seven in this time. When he then departs to the first ball of the sixth over - very well caught low down at slip by Ali Brown off Azhar - having scored eighteen from twenty-four balls and starved Knight of the strike during an important phase of the game, one has to question his elevation up the order. Not that the visitors are complaining, of course, as Jonathan Trott plays out the rest of the over to leave the Bears on 21-1 after six overs.

Knight needs to take a little more control now that Carter has gone, and he does exactly that by taking eight from Bicknell's fourth over, while Trott sensibly beds himself in at the other end. The former England opener then contents himself with ones and twos for a few overs, nudging the total up to 39-1 after ten overs, at which point Trott has just three singles to his credit.

By the end of the next over, the South African youngster has moved on to sixteen, however, after cutting loose at Bicknell's expense with a lofted extra-cover drive and two successive pulls that race to the boundary and bring up the home side's fifty from 10.5 overs. He then follows up by whipping Azhar away wide of mid-on for another four in the twelfth over, prompting Hollioake to make a double bowling change that sees the Surrey skipper replacing the rather disappointing Bicknell (6-0-39-0), and James Ormond taking over from the impressive Azhar (6-0-21-1).

The new pair of bowlers get off to a good start, conceding just six singles and a couple of twos from their first three overs in harness, and, though Trott clips Ormond to the rope at square leg in the next over and Knight follows up with a cover-driven boundary off Hollioake, the Lions are still in the hunt as Warwickshire reach 89-1 after eighteen overs. They do need to break the Knight-Trott partnership, however, and Hollioake attempts to do this by asking Ian Salisbury to take over at the city end.

The leg-spinner is immediately unlucky when Knight top-edges a cut to the rope at third man, but there is nothing wrong with the two boundaries that the Bears' opener picks up in Ormond's next over to take the total into three figures and his personal contribution to forty-seven. He duly completes a intelligently-compiled half-century from his fifty-eighth delivery two overs later, and it is now looking vital for Surrey's chances that he doesn't stick around much longer.

Since the Bears know that they have the Lions at their mercy, they are happy to push singles around at this stage, especially when facing the excellent Salisbury, whose third and fourth overs cost a total of just four runs, in addition to producing a very difficult catching chance to Batty from a top-edged sweep by Trott with the batsman on forty-one.

With twenty-five overs gone, the home side have made steady progress to 123-1 and, while the league leaders desperately need a couple of wickets to get back into the match, the in-form Bears probably only need a couple of good overs to break the opposition's resolve.

Unfortunately for Surrey, the next over from Ormond is, therefore, something of a nightmare, since Knight drives the first delivery over long-off for six, edges the second just wide of a diving Batty for four, and then sees the Lions' keeper only just fail to hang on to what would have been a brilliant one-handed catch from a genuine leg-glance. Thirteen runs come from the over, and the feeling that it just isn't going to be Surrey's day is confirmed when Knight top-edges a sweep off Salisbury into space backward of square leg in the same over that Trott completes an impressive fifty from 62 balls.

With Warwickshire now needing 101 from eighteen overs with nine wickets in hand, Hollioake turns back to Bicknell in place of Ormond at the pavilion end, and sees his senior bowler get off to a dreadful start, with a no-ball being followed by Knight's drive to the extra-cover boundary from the free-hit delivery. Further agony is in store when the former England batsman edges the next ball through the vacant slip area for two to take his team to the 150 mark after 27.2 overs, though it is at this point, when they are seemingly down and out, that the Lions suddenly start to roar.

The deserving Salisbury first puts a smile back on the faces of the visiting supporters when he has Knight (74) caught at short fine leg from another top-edged sweep, and he then changes the smiles to grins by removing the other half of the second-wicket partnership three balls later when Trott, on fifty-one, carelessly miscues a pull to Azhar at long-on.

Two wickets in four balls then becomes three in seven when Bicknell goes round the wicket to the newly arrived Jim Troughton and has the left-hander lbw, playing no real stroke to a delivery that is angled into him, for a second-ball duck. This wicket is Bicknell's 235th for Surrey in the Sunday/National League and takes him past Robin Jackman's Club record for wickets in the one-day league, though at this moment in time it is of greater importance that it has pulled his team back into the match. The state of play has changed dramatically, with Warwickshire declining from 151-1, with two well-set batsmen at the crease, to 152-4, with two new men, Ian Bell and Mike Powell, at the wicket.

It is important now that the league leaders keep these two quiet for a while in order to build some run-rate pressure and maybe capture another wicket, but, unfortunately for the Lions, Bell gets away to a fine start, driving Bicknell through wide mid-on for a boundary in his third over at the crease, reverse-sweeping Salisbury for another four in the following over, and then smashing

Ormond - replacing the bowled-out Bicknell - over mid-off for a third boundary in as many overs. With the former England Academy batsman looking so much more confident than he had done during the Championship match, twenty-five runs have come from overs thirty-two to thirty-four, putting Warwickshire right back on course for victory.

Captain Hollioake - replacing Salisbury, even though the leg-spinner has one over left to bowl - is then lofted over wide mid-on by captain Powell for a boundary during a nine-run thirty-fifth over, reducing the Bears' target to fifty-four runs from ten overs, and, once Ormond has completed nine erratic overs at a cost of sixty-one runs, Azhar is recalled to the attack for over number thirty-eight.

Surrey need another match-turning performance from the talented Pakistani at this stage, but there appears to be too much to do as the batsmen bide their time and wait for a loose ball to come along. Bell's square-cut boundary off Hollioake in the next over keeps his team firmly in control, and when Powell picks Azhar up over midwicket for six shortly afterwards, during an over that yields twelve runs, the end of the Lions' long unbeaten run is nigh.

The league leaders' fate is then sealed by successive off-side fours by Bell during the Hollioake over in which he reaches a splendid 42-ball half-century that brings a warm round of applause and cheering from home fans who have been baking under a hot sun all afternoon.

Salisbury's return, with just ten runs needed by the Bears, is nothing more than a token gesture, and Bell's seventh four, a pull off Hollioake, wraps things up with seventeen balls to spare.

IAN SALISBURY'S VIEW FROM THE DRESSING ROOM

How did we view our final total of 242 on that pitch? Roughly a par score?
IS - No, I thought it was plenty - in fact, I thought we'd got about thirty runs too many for them. When I was scoring my runs late on, I thought they were just bonus runs really, because I knew, from facing Waqar when I first came in, how difficult it was to score runs on that pitch if you bowled properly.

You seemed to find it pretty easy to get after Collins Obuya at the end of the innings. Is he perhaps lacking in a bit of variety in his bowling at this stage of his career?
IS - I feel a bit sorry for the guy, really. He did well in the World Cup, but then all of a sudden he was thrust into county cricket. He'd never played four-day cricket before in his life, and all of a sudden he was having to learn a different game in different conditions with a different type of ball. He did alright for Warwickshire in the one-dayers, but he's only 21, and there was a lot of pressure on him without him having much experience.

Ian Bell looked more at home in this format of the game than in the Championship, where he has rarely shone against us. Could that be down to the weight of expectation that has been placed upon him?
IS - Sometimes one-day cricket can be a form of release - you are able to free yourself up and show your true colours because there's no slips or gully, which is where you'd fancy getting him out. He's obviously a talented player, but sometimes you can try too hard in the four-day game - he's expected to do this, that and the other by a lot of people.

Was there just a glimmer of hope when you and Bickers took three wickets in two overs?
IS - There was, but, realistically, we didn't bowl very well in this game - we should have defended that total. I think we were over-confident going into the match and would have won comfortably if we'd bowled properly.

WARWICKSHIRE BEARS v SURREY LIONS at Edgbaston	
Sunday 13th July	Warwickshire Bears won by six wickets
Surrey Lions won the toss and elected to bat	Umpires:- John Hampshire & Mike Harris

SURREY LIONS

Fall Of Wkt	Batsman	How	Out	Score	Balls	4s	6s
1-8	**M.A. Butcher**	**lbw**	**b Waqar**	**0**	6	0	0
2-28	**A.D. Brown**	**c Knight**	**b Waqar**	**20**	14	4	0
6-150	**M.R. Ramprakash**		**b Brown**	**57**	84	7	0
3-45	**G.P. Thorpe**	**c Penney**	**b Waqar**	**7**	20	1	0
4-87	**I.J. Ward**	**st Penney**	**b Smith**	**21**	27	3	0
5-134	**A.J. Hollioake ***		**b Obuya**	**25**	33	2	1
7-166	**Azhar Mahmood**	**c Troughton**	**b Obuya**	**17**	20	3	0
8-198	**J.N. Batty +**		**b Waqar**	**28**	25	4	1
	M.P. Bicknell	**Not**	**Out**	**14**	24	1	0
9-242	**I.D.K. Salisbury**	**c Troughton**	**b Obuya**	**33**	17	2	3
	J. Ormond	**did not bat**					
	Extras	**(5b, 5lb, 10w)**		**20**			
	TOTAL	**(45 overs)**	**(for 9 wkts)**	**242**			

Bowler	O	M	R	W	NB	Wd
Carter	**9**	**0**	**35**	**0**	-	3
Waqar Younis	**9**	**1**	**35**	**4**	-	-
Smith	**9**	**1**	**37**	**1**	-	1
Brown	**7**	**0**	**47**	**1**	-	-
Obuya	**9**	**1**	**65**	**3**	-	-
Troughton	**2**	**0**	**13**	**0**	-	1

WARWICKSHIRE BEARS

Fall Of Wkt	Batsman	How	Out	Score	Balls	4s	6s
1-20	**N.M. Carter**	**c Brown**	**b Azhar**	**18**	24	3	0
2-151	**N.V. Knight**	**c Thorpe**	**b Salisbury**	**74**	84	7	1
3-152	**I.J.L. Trott**	**c Azhar**	**b Salisbury**	**51**	65	5	0
	I.R. Bell	**Not**	**Out**	**59**	47	7	0
4-152	**J.O. Troughton**	**lbw**	**b Bicknell**	**0**	2	0	0
	M.J. Powell *	**Not**	**Out**	**26**	32	1	1
	T.L. Penney +	**did not bat**					
	D.R. Brown	**did not bat**					
	C.O. Obuya	**did not bat**					
	N.M.K. Smith	**did not bat**					
	Waqar Younis	**did not bat**					
	Extras	**(1b, 5lb, 8w, 2nb)**		**16**			
	TOTAL	**(42.1 overs)**	**(for 4 wkts)**	**244**			

Bowler	O	M	R	W	NB	Wd
Bicknell	**9**	**1**	**54**	**1**	1	1
Azhar Mahmood	**8**	**0**	**34**	**1**	-	3
Hollioake	**7.1**	**0**	**47**	**0**	-	-
Ormond	**9**	**0**	**61**	**0**	-	4
Salisbury	**9**	**0**	**42**	**2**	-	-

Other NCL Division One Results

With the Dragons having taken advantage of Surrey's slip-up at Edgbaston by recording a stunning victory over the Eagles at Cardiff they were now back within two points of the Lions.

July 13

Cardiff:- **Glamorgan Dragons (4pts) beat Essex Eagles by 8 wickets.** Essex 267-6 (45ov; Hussain 144, Irani 63); Glamorgan 269-2 (38.1ov; Maher 142, Croft 64).

Oakham School:- **Leicestershire Foxes (4pts) beat Worcestershire Royals by 76 runs.** Leics 295-7 (45ov; Sehwag 76, Ward 68, Maddy 58); Worcs 219 (41.5ov; Peters 82).

NCL DIVISION ONE TABLE AT 13TH JULY

Pos	Prv		P	Pts	W	T	L	A	NRR
1	1	Surrey Lions	8	26	6	0	1	1	5.65
2	2	Glamorgan Dragons	8	24	6	0	2	0	9.10
3	3	Gloucestershire Gladiators	7	18	4	0	2	1	7.44
4	5	Leicestershire Foxes	8	16	4	0	4	0	0.79
5	5	Warwickshire Bears	8	16	4	0	4	0	0.76
6	4	Essex Eagles	7	12	3	0	4	0	-0.67
7	7	Kent Spitfires	8	12	3	0	5	0	-4.60
8	8	Worcestershire Royals	7	8	2	0	5	0	0.46
9	9	Yorkshire Phoenix	7	4	1	0	6	0	-16.35

First-Class Friendly - Surrey Youngsters Given Stern Examination By India 'A'

By all accounts this was a pretty woeful performance from Surrey, who were perhaps guilty of not taking a fairly high-profile friendly as seriously as they might have done, though there were extenuating circumstances. It was understandable that many first-team players should be rested ahead of Twenty-20 Cup Finals Day, so it was a young Surrey side that took the field, with a record five players (James Benning, Ben Scott, Matthew Todd, Neil Saker and Jade Dernbach) making their first-class debut. A third-day washout probably spared the hosts' blushes after India 'A' had amassed their runs at almost five an over, with Clarke's return of 18-5-36-2 standing out like a beacon amongst some truly horrific Surrey bowling figures.

Scores:- Surrey 173 (Bhandari 5-54) and 39-0 drew with India 'A' 462-4dec (Gambhir 130*, Sriram 115, Rayadu 101*, Das 74)

Frizzell Championship Division One Results

While Surrey were playing India 'A', Sussex were beating Leicestershire - with Mushtaq claiming yet another ten-wicket match haul - to move themselves back within five points of the leaders. Lancashire meanwhile lost further ground after being under the cosh for the whole of the drawn game with Kent at Blackpool.

July 15-18
***Blackpool:-* Lancashire (9pts) drew with Kent (12).** Kent 602-6dec (Smith 203, Walker 150, Ealham 95, Jones 66*); Lancs 365 (Chilton 114, Schofield 66, Hooper 60) & 244-6 (Hooper 128*).
***Leicester:-* Sussex (21pts) beat Leicestershire (5) by 5 wickets.** Leics 320 (DeFreitas 103, Stevens 50, Mushtaq 5-93) & 258 (Stevens 51, Ward 50, Mushtaq 5-96); Sussex 416 (Cottey 147, Prior 96, Montgomerie 52, DeFreitas 5-55) & 166-5 (Cottey 58).
***Southgate:-* Middlesex (8pts) drew with Warwickshire (12).** Warwicks 496 (Brown 113, Giles 96, Frost 84); Middx 260 & 281-3 (Hutton 102*, Koenig 96).

FRIZZELL CHAMPIONSHIP DIVISION ONE TABLE AT 18TH JULY

Pos	Prv		P	Points	W	D	L	T	Bat	Bwl	Ded
1	1	Surrey	9	147.00	5	4	0	0	38	23	0.00
2	2	Sussex	9	142.00	6	0	3	0	31	27	0.00
3	3	Lancashire	8	105.00	2	6	0	0	31	22	0.00
4	4	Middlesex	9	100.00	2	7	0	0	21	23	0.00
5	6	Warwickshire	10	95.75	1	5	3	1	32	24	1.25
6	7	Kent	10	94.00	1	5	4	0	31	29	0.00
7	5	Essex	10	92.00	1	6	2	1	18	29	0.00
8	8	Nottinghamshire	8	67.00	1	3	4	0	19	23	1.00
9	9	Leicestershire	9	66.00	0	6	3	0	19	23	0.00

12 Twenty-20 Triumph

Some four weeks after the completion of the highly successful qualifying rounds, we arrived at Twenty-20 Finals Day, with one of Gloucestershire Gladiators, Leicestershire Foxes, Surrey Lions or Warwickshire Bears to be crowned as the inaugural winners of the new tournament.

By now, all the statistics for the matches played back in June had been compiled, and it was revealed that the forty-five Divisional matches had been watched by over 240,000 spectators, giving an average attendance of 5,300 per match. Impressive stuff, especially when you considered that there were a number of 'dead' matches towards the end of the two-week qualification period.

The highest total was the 221-7 that Gloucestershire had compiled against Glamorgan, while Lancashire's 91 all out against Derbyshire had been the lowest score recorded. Somewhere in the middle of those two totals lay the generally accepted par score, given decent conditions for batting. As far as individuals were concerned, Adam Hollioake was the leading wicket-taker to date, with thirteen victims, while Martin Bicknell shared the current record for the most economical analysis, courtesy of his spell of 4-1-11-2 at The Rose Bowl. On the batting front, Azhar Mahmood rated second in the strike-rate table, having scored his runs at the rate of 198.04 per hundred balls, with Andrew Symonds leading the way with a phenomenal rate of 226.67. Azhar was also ranked third-equal in the six-hitting chart with eight to his name, behind Yorkshire's Michael Lumb, on thirteen, and Gloucestershire's Craig Spearman, on eleven.

In front of a near-capacity crowd of 15,000 on a lovely day at Trent Bridge, the action began with the first semi-final, which pitted the Leicestershire Foxes against the Warwickshire Bears in a match that started at 11am.

Having elected to bat, the Foxes were greatly indebted to an excellent innings of sixty-six from 50 balls by Brad Hodge as they compiled 162-7, with the only significant support coming from Darren Maddy with twenty-six.

Warwickshire then set off in pursuit at a cracking pace, with Nick Knight (32) and Neil Carter (35) taking full toll of some woeful early Leicestershire bowling to score sixty-one off the first five overs.

The Foxes did eventually manage to haul the Bears back from 67-0 to 99-3, thanks to some good bowling from the part-time off-spinners, Virender Sehwag (4-0-17-1) and Hodge (4-0-27-1), but Warwickshire always seemed to be in control and were seen home, with four balls to spare, by Trevor Penney (43 not out) and Jim Troughton (33 not out).

With one of the finalists now known, there was an increased buzz around the ground as we waited for the match that many people had wanted to see as the final.... the one-day kings, Gloucestershire Gladiators, against the County Champions, Surrey.

TWENTY-20 CUP SEMI-FINAL
Gloucestershire Gladiators versus Surrey Lions
at Trent Bridge on Saturday 19th July (2.45pm)

The Teams And The Toss - Since they wish to play both their spinners on a dry and grassless pitch against a Gloucestershire side that has tended to struggle against top-quality slow bowlers in recent times, Surrey are forced to make a choice between Martin Bicknell and James Ormond, and opt for the latter. Bicknell is not the only unlucky player, though, since the promising James Benning is displaced by Rikki Clarke, who had been with England during the qualifying campaign, and is therefore making his Twenty-20 Cup debut for the Lions. Gloucestershire meanwhile have to do without the services of the injured Mark Alleyne and Jack Russell, so Mark Hardinges and Stephen Pope deputise, with Craig Spearman taking over the captaincy. When Adam Hollioake wins the toss he elects to bat.

Surrey Lions' Innings

The canny Mike Smith is, as ever, a tough opponent at the start of the innings, yielding just two singles and a leg-bye from the opening over, though Jon Lewis is, fortunately for the Lions, a different proposition as both the first and third balls he bowls to Ali Brown disappear back over his head for sixes. Ian Ward then drives a rare loose delivery from Smith over mid-off for four at the start of the next over before normal service is resumed, with the left-arm swing bowler conceding just two singles from the rest of the over, which ends with Surrey on 22-0.

Brown, who has yet to catch fire in the competition that many people thought was made for him, starts the fourth over by cracking Lewis away to the rope at point but then skies the next delivery to deep backward square leg off the top edge and is caught by Matt Windows for eighteen. With Rikki Clarke taking Brown's place in the middle, four singles complete the over, leaving honours pretty even at 30-1 after four overs.

Smith then tilts things back in favour of the Gladiators with another superb over that yields just a single to the Surrey score, before Lewis again undoes his partner's great work with a pretty ragged thirteen-run over that sees Clarke lifting the second ball over wide mid-on for four and Ward driving the last delivery high over long-on for six.

Utilising a combination of swing, changes of pace and slight variations in length, Smith again confounds Clarke in the final over of his spell, with the batsman able to score from just one delivery - a leg-glance for two - leaving Surrey a little off the pace at 46-1 with more than a third of their innings gone. Having conceded just eleven runs from his outstanding stint, thereby equalling the competition record, the veteran left-armer retires to the outfield with the crowd's applause ringing in his ears.

The Lions' rather precarious position then deteriorates further when Lewis - bowling straight through his allotted overs, like his team-mate - turns out to have saved his best till last, with just three runs and a leg-bye coming from an over that sees the Surrey fifty finally clicking up from the final delivery. Since eight of the final twelve overs are to be bowled by a combination of the dependable off-spinner, Martyn Ball, and Ian Harvey, justifiably reckoned to be one of the best limited-overs bowlers in the world, the Lions already look to have quite a struggle on their hands if they are to post a decent total.

The one bowler they really must get after is Mark Hardinges, who is now coming on to bowl at the pavilion end. A couple of wides and three singles get the over off to an acceptable start from the Surrey point of view, before Clarke, having struggled to fifteen from 23 balls, makes ground down the track to the fourth delivery and is comfortably stumped by Pope when his drive is defeated on the outside edge.

This dismissal brings Adam Hollioake to the wicket with his team in need of one of his most explosive innings. Just six singles are garnered from the remainder of Hardinges' over and the first over from Ball, however, leaving the Lions very much second best at the halfway stage of their innings with the scoreboard showing 61-2.

With some high-scoring overs clearly needed, the eleventh over is something of a godsend as Ward twice locates the boundary rope - with a late cut and an extra-cover drive - as thirteen runs are added to the total. When ten runs then result from the following over by Ball, thanks to a last-ball on-drive for four by Hollioake, things are continuing to look up for Surrey, though over number thirteen turns out to be a mixed one for the South Division winners.

It starts well enough, with Ward's fortunate inside-edged boundary largely responsible for seven runs coming from the first three balls, but the Lions lose their captain to the next delivery when he gets a thick edge as he aims towards mid-on, and the ball flies down to Alex Gidman at third man for a straightforward catch.

The loss of Hollioake for fifteen makes the score 91-3, though the sight of Azhar Mahmood coming out to bat is a comforting one for Surrey eyes - if anyone can supply the rapid acceleration that the team needs then it is him. A no-ball and two singles complete the thirteenth over, at which point the Lions are 95-3, and, though the run-rate is now back above seven an over, Hardinges, the man considered to be the weakest link, is now through three-quarters of his spell. Worse still, Ian Harvey is just about to enter the attack to bowl four of the last seven overs.

Although the batsmen are unable to get any delivery away for more than two runs, Surrey probably consider the nine runs that accrue from Harvey's first over to be a decent result, though they have been helped by a no-ball just after the arrival of the hundred from the fourth delivery. The Gladiators coach, John Bracewell, will surely be unhappy that his bowlers have overstepped the crease twice in the last two overs and also by a fielding display that has been rather mixed so far, with the honourable exception of Jonty Rhodes.

We now arrive at Hardinges' final over but, again, it doesn't yield as many runs as Surrey would have hoped for. Only four runs come from the first four deliveries, before Azhar cuts to the point boundary from the fifth and then skies the sixth behind the bowler, allowing Rhodes to run in from long-on and complete a good catch that further dents the Lions' hopes. Hardinges has done a great job for his side as he finishes with 4-0-37-3, leaving the NCL first division leaders still struggling at 112-4 with just five overs left.

That score then becomes 116-5 two balls into Harvey's next over when Graham Thorpe - on strike because the batsmen had crossed while Azhar was being caught from Hardinges' final delivery - drives his first ball wide of mid-on for four before having his stumps rearranged by the yorker that immediately follows. Unsurprisingly, the rest of the over is pretty quiet with three singles taking the total to 119-5.

Over number seventeen then sees the return of Ball, who is again right on the mark, allowing only one stroke worth more than a single, when Ward reverse-sweeps to the boundary from the fifth ball in an over worth eight runs.

Double-figure overs are what Surrey need now, though, but they don't even get close to that mark in either of the next two overs as their last remaining hopes of achieving a big total disappear out of sight.

Three wickets fall over the course of overs eighteen and nineteen, in fact, with Ward the first to go in Harvey's third over for a very good, battling forty-nine. Attempting to make some room to hit through the off-side, the left-handed opener becomes another victim of the Australian's yorker with the total at 129 then, seven balls and eight runs later, Ball picks up wickets with the final two deliveries of a very good spell, Mark Ramprakash to a return catch at head height and Ian Salisbury bowled off-stump after advancing down the track to drive.

Gloucestershire seem to hold all the aces now, with Surrey 137-8 as we go into the final over, though Jon Batty does his best to give the total a late boost by cutting over backward point for a first-ball boundary. A single to cover from the next delivery leaves Saqlain Mushtaq on strike, and the Lions' off-spinner manages twos from balls three and five - though the second two results from a dropped skier at straight long-on by Gidman - before being run out off the final delivery of the innings when attempting an implausible second run to Windows at deep midwicket. It is understandable that Saqlain takes the run on, however, since Surrey's total of 147-9 looks below par, even on a Trent Bridge pitch that is not perhaps the easiest to bat on.

During the interval it comes to light that the Lions' score is the highest made by a side batting first against Gloucestershire in this season's Twenty-20 Cup, with none of the four previous teams to have taken first knock against the Gladiators having got past 134. It's a very revealing and interesting statistic, though it doesn't make Surrey's 147 look any bigger.

SURREY LIONS INNINGS						*********** END-OF-OVER TOTALS ***********					
Ov	Bowler	Runs	Bat 1	Bat 2	Ex	BOWLER	BAT 1	BAT 2	EX	SCORE	OV
1	Smith	3	Ward 1	Brown 1	1lb	MS 1-0-2-0	IW 1	AB 1	1	3-0	1
2	Lewis	13	Ward 1	Brown 12		JL 1-0-13-0	IW 2	AB 13	1	16-0	2
3	Smith	6	Ward 5	Brown 1		MS 2-0-8-0	IW 7	AB 14	1	22-0	3
4	Lewis	8		Brown 4		BROWN c WINDOWS b LEWIS 18					
			Ward 2	Clarke 2		JL 2-0-21-1	IW 9	RC 2	1	30-1	4
5	Smith	1	Ward 0	Clarke 1		MS 3-0-9-0	IW 9	RC 3	1	31-1	5
6	Lewis	13	Ward 6	Clarke 7		JL 3-0-34-1	IW 15	RC 10	1	44-1	6
7	Smith	2	Ward 0	Clarke 2		MS 4-0-11-0	IW 15	RC 12	1	46-1	7
8	Lewis	4	Ward 1	Clarke 2	1lb	JL 4-0-37-1	IW 16	RC 14	2	50-1	8
9	H'dinges	7		Clarke 1	2w	CLARKE st POPE b HARDINGES 15					
			Ward 3	Holl'ke 1		MH 1-0-7-1	IW 19	AH 1	4	57-2	9
10	Ball	4	Ward 2	Holl'ke 2		MB 1-0-4-0	IW 21	AH 3	4	61-2	10
11	H'dinges	13	Ward 9	Holl'ke 2	2b	MH 2-0-18-1	IW 30	AH 5	6	74-2	11
12	Ball	10	Ward 2	Holl'ke 8		MB 2-0-14-0	IW 32	AH 13	6	84-2	12
13	H'dinges	11		Holl'ke 2		HOLLIOAKE c GIDMAN b HARDINGES 15					
			Ward 6	Azhar 1	2nb	MH 3-0-29-2	IW 38	AM 1	8	95-3	13
14	Harvey	9	Ward 2	Azhar 4	2nb	IH 1-0-9-0	IW 40	AM 5	10	104-3	14
15	H'dinges	8		Azhar 7		AZHAR c RHODES b HARDINGES 13					
			Ward 1			MH 4-0-37-3	IW 41		10	112-4	15
16	Harvey	7		Thorpe 4		THORPE b HARVEY 4					
			Ward 1	R'kash 2		IH 2-0-16-1	IW 42	MR 2	10	119-5	16
17	Ball	8	Ward 6	R'kash 2		MB 3-0-22-0	IW 48	MR 4	10	127-5	17
18	Harvey	6	Ward 1			WARD b HARVEY 49					
			Batty 3	R'kash 2		IH 3-0-22-2	JB 3	MR 6	10	133-6	18
19	Ball	4		R'kash 2		RAMPRAKASH c & b BALL 8					
				Salisbury 0		SALISBURY b BALL 0					
			Batty 2			MB 4-0-26-2	JB 5		10	137-8	19
20	Harvey	10		Saqlain 5		SAQLAIN RUN OUT 5					
			Batty 5			IH 4-0-32-2	JB 10		10	147-9	20

Gloucestershire Gladiators' Innings

Since it seems unlikely that there is a more destructive pair of opening batsmen in Twenty-20 cricket than Craig Spearman and Ian Harvey, it is obvious that Surrey must remove at least one, or preferably both, of them early in the Gladiators' reply.

It is, therefore, a huge relief to the Lions' players and supporters when James Ormond nips the final ball of the first over back at Spearman and rattles the batsman's stumps as he aims an ambitious drive over mid-on. It's 4-1, with the very dangerous Spearman gone for just a single.

Surrey then strike another important blow in the second over of the innings, bowled by Azhar when Jonty Rhodes nibbles at his first ball, a good lifting delivery just outside off stump, and edges to Batty, thereby reducing the Gladiators to 5-2. Suddenly, the Lions' total is looking bigger and better!

They still have to contend with Harvey, however, and also the promising Alex Gidman, who gets off to a confident start by driving the fifth ball of Azhar's successful opening over to the rope at extra cover.

The same stroke, with the same result, is then played by Harvey from the opening delivery o Ormond's second over, though the last five balls bring just a single and a leg-bye as the bowle recovers well to keep Gloucestershire under the Surrey thumb at 15-2 after three overs.

The advantage that the Lions hold is then increased dramatically three balls into Azhar's nex over when Harvey miscues an attempted pull and sees Saqlain run in from mid-on to hold routine, yet crucial, catch that sees the back of the Australian for seven and the Gladiators slippin further into trouble at 17-3. Surrey joy is unconfined, with the three main dangermen all back i the pavilion and Gloucestershire still 131 runs short of their target.

With neither of the Gladiators' vastly experienced middle-order men, Mark Alleyne and Jack Russell, in the side today, much now depends on the new batsman, Matt Windows, and he gets off to an unusual start when, following a no-ball from Azhar, he skies a hook at the free-hit delivery and is called through for the first run of his innings as the ball soars into the air behind the wicket before landing in Batty's gloves.

Hollioake is really going for the kill at this point, with three slips in place, though he is forced to reconsider this move by the end of the fifth over as Gidman takes 2-4-4 from the final three deliveries with a pull, an on-drive and a leg-glance. At 31-3, Gloucestershire are still in a sickly state, however, and their condition becomes critical over the next three overs as they add just five runs to their score and lose another wicket.

Saqlain's opening over as the replacement for Azhar at the pavilion end yields just two singles, then Ormond follows up with another two-run over to complete a fine spell of 4-0-21-1 that has justified his selection. The first ball of Saqlain's second over then brings the wicket of Windows, whose desperate attempt to cut a ball that hits off stump has surely resulted from the pressure that has been built up by the previous two economical overs. With just a single coming from the remainder of the eighth over, the Gladiators are now in grave danger of sinking to a humiliating defeat at 36-4.

Since Ormond has completed his stint and Saqlain is proving so effective, it's no surprise that Hollioake elects to pair his spinners by introducing Ian Salisbury at the Radcliffe Road end for the ninth over. The leg-spinner makes an inauspicious start when Gidman cuts his second ball for four, but the over ends up costing just seven runs in total, which is satisfactory for Surrey, since Gloucestershire already need to score at nine-an-over to win the match.

The Gladiators exceed that target by three in the next Saqlain over, however, largely thanks to Hardinges' lofted straight drive for four and Gidman's slog-sweep for six that takes his side's total beyond fifty, though Salisbury immediately negates his spin twin's expensive over by delivering the next one at a cost of just six runs.

Hardinges then regains the lost ground by cutting the first ball of Saqlain's final over to the rope at point but, with just five singles coming from the rest of the over, the off-spinner finishes a good spell of 4-0-24-1 on a high note to keep Surrey on top.

With eight overs now remaining, and the Lions' skipper joining the attack at the Radcliffe Road end, Gloucestershire need seventy-eight to win, which is still very much a possibility given the volatile nature of twenty-overs-a-side cricket.

Hollioake immediately makes things a little harder for his opponents by giving up just three singles and a wide from his first five balls, though he spoils his opening over a little by giving Gidman enough room to slash the last delivery away to the backward point boundary and thereby prevent the asking rate from climbing any higher.

The next over from Salisbury, following a switch of ends, sees it rise from exactly ten-an-over to 11.17, though, as the leg-spinner sends down five fine deliveries that yield just a leg-bye after a first-ball on-drive for two by Hardinges. Although they appear to be coming off second-best at this stage, the Gladiators can at least take heart from the fact that they have two well-set batsmen at the crease and enough wickets in hand for them to launch a late attack.

This plan takes a hit in the following over from Hollioake, however, when Hardinges' knock of twenty-four is terminated by a full-length delivery that cannons into the stumps via the batsman's pads with the total at eighty-seven. Despite the loss of this wicket, the over isn't a total disaster for Gloucestershire, as it produces ten runs, thanks to Hardinges' edge to the third-man boundary from the opening delivery, and the newly arrived Chris Taylor's top-edged hook to the rope at fine leg from the final ball.

Much is clearly resting on the shoulders of young Gidman now, with fifty-seven needed from thirty balls, though he appears to be relishing the challenge as he slog-sweeps the no-ball with which Salisbury starts his final over for a huge six over midwicket to progress to a brave and well-played 41-ball half-century. Fortunately for Surrey, the free-hit delivery only yields a single, though their experienced leg-spinner concedes a wide and another slog-swept six - this one coming more off the top edge of the bat than off the middle - before the over is complete. With nineteen runs having been racked up in total, it looks as if this over could be expensive in more ways than one, since the Gladiators' task has now been scaled down to thirty-eight from twenty-four balls.

In keeping with the wild shifts in fortunes that seem to be part of Twenty-20 cricket, the balance then swings back very much in favour of the Lions when their captain comes up with a magnificent seventeenth over of the innings that brings just three singles, one of which comes from a complete miscue and another from an inside edge.

Thirty-five off eighteen looks to be a tough task now, especially against 'death' bowlers as skilled and experienced as Hollioake and the returning Azhar, though Taylor appears to be keeping his cool as he clips the Pakistani's first ball to the square leg boundary, much to the delight of the Gloucestershire fans in the crowd. A single to Taylor and pull to long-on for two to Gidman follow from the next two deliveries, before Azhar serves up one of his specials - the inswinging yorker - to shatter Gidman's stumps and, almost certainly, the Gladiators' hopes as well. As the young batsman returns to the pavilion to a fine reception for his gallant knock of sixty-one, his side needs twenty-eight runs from fourteen deliveries... and by the end of Azhar's successful over the requirement has become twenty-six from twelve.

All hope is not lost, though, as Taylor promptly launches Hollioake's opening delivery of the nineteenth over for six over midwicket to restore a little balance to the contest and raise doubts in the minds of the Surrey faithful. Their leader is unfazed by this stroke, however, and, after Taylor manages just a single from the next two balls, almost bowls Martyn Ball with each of the next two deliveries before the off-spinner drives the final ball wide of long-off for two.

The second semi-final therefore reaches the last over with Gloucestershire needing seventeen to win as Taylor faces Azhar.

A leg-bye from the first delivery gives the Lions a big advantage, before Ball keeps his team's hopes alive with a straight-driven two and a lofted extra-cover drive to the boundary from the next two balls. Ten runs are now needed from three deliveries if the men from the west country are to win outright, though nine will suffice, since the Gladiators have lost fewer wickets than the Lions. A single for a pull to long leg by Ball then leaves Taylor needing to find the boundary, but the inevitable leg-stump yorker that Azhar fires in with such accuracy enables the batsmen to garner nothing more than a leg-bye from the penultimate delivery of the match. The game is now up for Gloucestershire, and the two runs that Ball takes following his straight drive from the last ball of an excellent spell by Azhar prove purely academic. Surrey Lions will be playing Warwickshire Bears in the first-ever Twenty-20 Cup final.

Man Of The Match - Azhar Mahmood

GLOUCS GLADIATORS INNINGS						*********** END-OF-OVER TOTALS ***********					
Ov	Bowler	Runs	Bat 1	Bat 2	Ex	BOWLER	BAT 1	BAT 2	EX	SCORE	OV
1	Ormond	4	Spearm'n 1		2nb	SPEARMAN b ORMOND 1					
				Harvey 1		JO 1-0-4-1		IH 1	2	4-1	1
2	Azhar	5	Rhodes 0			RHODES c BATTY b AZHAR 0					
			Gidman 4	Harvey 1		AM 1-0-5-1	AG 4	IH 2	2	9-2	2
3	Ormond	6	Gidman 0	Harvey 5	1lb	JO 2-0-9-1	AG 4	IH 7	3	15-2	3
4	Azhar	6		Harvey 0	1w	HARVEY c SAQLAIN b AZHAR 7					
			Gidman 2	Windows 1	2nb	AM 2-0-11-2	AG 6	MW 1	6	21-3	4
5	Ormond	10	Gidman 10	Windows 0		JO 3-0-19-1	AG 16	MW 1	6	31-3	5
6	Saqlain	2	Gidman 1	Windows 1		SM 1-0-2-0	AG 17	MW 2	6	33-3	6
7	Ormond	2	Gidman 1	Windows 1		JO 4-0-21-1	AG 18	MW 3	6	35-3	7
8	Saqlain	1		Windows 0		WINDOWS b SAQLAIN 3					
			Gidman 0	H'dinges 1		SM 2-0-3-1	AG 18	MH 1	6	36-4	8
9	Salisbury	7	Gidman 5	H'dinges 2		IS 1-0-7-0	AG 23	MH 3	6	43-4	9
10	Saqlain	12	Gidman 7	H'dinges 5		SM 3-0-15-1	AG 30	MH 8	6	55-4	10
11	Salisbury	6	Gidman 6	H'dinges 0		IS 2-0-13-0	AG 36	MH 8	6	61-4	11
12	Saqlain	9	Gidman 2	H'dinges 7		SM 4-0-24-1	AG 38	MH 15	6	70-4	12
13	Holl'ke	8	Gidman 5	H'dinges 2	1w	AH 1-0-8-0	AG 43	MH 17	7	78-4	13
14	Salisbury	3	Gidman 0	H'dinges 2	1lb	IS 3-0-15-0	AG 43	MH 19	8	81-4	14
15	Holl'ke	10		H'dinges 5		HARDINGES b HOLLIOAKE 24					
			Gidman 1	Taylor 4		AH 2-0-18-1	AG 44	CT 4	8	91-5	15
16	Salisbury	19	Gidman 14	Taylor 2	2nb, 1w	IS 4-0-34-0	AG 58	CT 6	11	110-5	16
17	Holl'ke	3	Gidman 1	Taylor 2		AH 3-0-21-1	AG 59	CT 8	11	113-5	17
18	Azhar	9	Gidman 2			GIDMAN b AZHAR 61					
			Ball 0	Taylor 6	1lb	AM 3-0-19-3	MB 0	CT 14	12	122-6	18
19	Holl'ke	9	Ball 2	Taylor 7		AH 4-0-30-1	MB 2	CT 21	12	131-6	19
20	Azhar	11	Ball 9	Taylor 0	2lb	AM 4-0-28-3	MB 11	CT 21	14	142-6	20

TWENTY-20 CUP SEMI-FINAL
GLOUCESTERSHIRE GLADIATORS v SURREY LIONS at Trent Bridge
Saturday 19th July (2.45pm) **Surrey Lions won by 5 runs**

Surrey Lions won the toss and elected to bat — Umpires:- Barry Dudleston & George Sharp

SURREY LIONS

Fall Of Wkt	Batsman	How	Out	Score	Balls	4s	6s
6-129	**I.J. Ward**		**b Harvey**	**49**	48	5	1
1-26	**A.D. Brown**	**c Windows**	**b Lewis**	**18**	7	1	2
2-55	**R. Clarke**	**st Pope**	**b Hardinges**	**15**	23	1	0
3-91	**A.J. Hollioake ***	**c Gidman**	**b Hardinges**	**15**	11	1	0
4-112	**Azhar Mahmood**	**c Rhodes**	**b Hardinges**	**13**	9	1	0
5-116	**G.P. Thorpe**		**b Harvey**	**4**	2	1	0
7-137	**M.R. Ramprakash**	**c &**	**b Ball**	**8**	11	0	0
	J.N. Batty +	**Not**	**Out**	**10**	6	1	0
8-137	**I.D.K. Salisbury**		**b Ball**	**0**	1	0	0
9-147	**Saqlain Mushtaq**	**run**	**out**	**5**	4	0	0
	J. Ormond	**did not bat**					
	Extras	**(2b, 2lb, 2w, 4nb)**		**10**			
	TOTAL	**(20 overs)**	**(for 9 wkts)**	**147**			

Bowler	O	M	R	W	NB	Wd
Smith	**4**	**0**	**11**	**0**	-	-
Lewis	**4**	**0**	**37**	**1**	-	-
Hardinges	**4**	**0**	**37**	**3**	1	1
Ball	**4**	**0**	**26**	**2**	-	-
Harvey	**4**	**0**	**32**	**2**	1	-

GLOUCESTERSHIRE GLADIATORS							
Fall Of Wkt	Batsman	How	Out	Score	Balls	4s	6s
1-4	**C.M. Spearman ***		**b Ormond**	**1**	5	0	0
3-17	**I.J. Harvey**	**c Saqlain**	**b Azhar**	**7**	8	1	0
2-5	**J.N. Rhodes**	**c Batty**	**b Azhar**	**0**	1	0	0
6-120	**A.P.R. Gidman**		**b Azhar**	**61**	49	6	3
4-35	**M.G.N. Windows**		**b Saqlain**	**3**	11	0	0
5-87	**M.A. Hardinges**		**b Hollioake**	**24**	26	3	0
	C.G. Taylor	**Not**	**Out**	**21**	15	2	1
	M.C.J. Ball	**Not**	**Out**	**11**	8	1	0
	S.P. Pope +	**did not bat**					
	J. Lewis	**did not bat**					
	A.M. Smith	**did not bat**					
	Extras	**(5lb, 3w, 6nb)**		**14**			
	TOTAL	**(20 overs)**	**(for 6 wkts)**	**142**			

Bowler	O	M	R	W	NB	Wd
Ormond	**4**	**0**	**21**	**1**	1	-
Azhar Mahmood	**4**	**0**	**28**	**3**	1	1
Saqlain Mushtaq	**4**	**0**	**24**	**1**	-	-
Salisbury	**4**	**0**	**34**	**0**	1	1
Hollioake	**4**	**0**	**30**	**1**	-	1

TWENTY-20 CUP FINAL
Surrey Lions versus Warwickshire Bears
at Trent Bridge on Saturday 19th July (7.15pm)

The Teams And The Toss - Just six days after these two teams had clashed in the NCL, they come face-to-face again, giving the Lions an early chance to avenge the six-wicket defeat that had ended their unbeaten run in that competition. For this inaugural Twenty-20 Cup final, Surrey field the side that had beaten Gloucestershire, with Azhar Mahmood taking his place in the team despite being inconvenienced by a thigh strain picked up in the semi-final. Warwickshire meanwhile make one change to their eleven that had beaten Leicestershire, replacing Jonathan Trott with Tony Frost, since they feel a specialist wicketkeeper is needed on this pitch against a side as strong as Surrey. Nick Knight, the Bears' captain for the Twenty-20 Cup, wins the toss and elects to bat first, partly because he expects batting to be a more hazardous occupation later in the evening when the floodlights come into play.

Warwickshire Bears' Innings

The final starts with an interesting over from James Ormond to Neil Carter, that sees the Warwickshire left-hander offering a hard-hit chance to Ian Salisbury at cover from the fourth delivery and then pulling a mighty six over midwicket from the last ball.

When Knight then takes seven runs from the first three deliveries sent down by Azhar, thirteen runs have come from the last four balls bowled, and it is looking like Surrey are in for another tough contest until their bowlers hit back well to turn the tables on the Bears over the course of the next five overs.

Ormond's second over brings him the first wicket of the final when Carter, perhaps frustrated by going scoreless for the first three balls, charges recklessly down the wicket to the next delivery and chops the ball onto his stumps with the total on sixteen.

The new batsman, Ian Bell, gets off the mark immediately with a single to backward point off Ormond, and then profits by two when Mark Ramprakash just fails to pull off a right-handed diving catch from a lofted off-drive during a tight next over from Azhar.

Having clawed the Bears back to 20-1 after four overs, Ormond then comes up with a two-wicket over that puts the Lions firmly in charge. Knight goes to the first delivery, edging the ball onto his middle-and-off stumps after making room to hit through the off-side, then Jim Troughton falls to the fifth ball when he snicks a good, lifting delivery to the left of first slip and sees Ali Brown pull off a good catch. Warwickshire are now 22-3... and things are just about to get worse for them.

Although Trevor Penney upper-cuts the fourth delivery of Azhar's third over for six just over the head of a back-pedalling Adam Hollioake at third man, the Pakistani all-rounder picks up the wicket of Bell two balls later when a nasty lifter takes the shoulder of the 21-year-old's bat and loops gently to Rikki Clarke at backward point, leaving the Bears with sore heads at 32-4.

Surrey have now taken complete control of the final, and you get the feeling that the game is almost over as a contest when Ormond picks up his fourth wicket in his final over. After Penney takes a single from the first ball, Dougie Brown is beaten by balls two and three before edging the fourth delivery - another good one, lifting and leaving the bat - through to Batty behind the stumps. At 33-5, Warwickshire need to produce a performance worthy of Harry Houdini, and Ormond is given three slips by Hollioake as he completes his stint with the outstanding figures of 4-0-11-4, thereby equalling the economy record held by Martin Bicknell, Mike Smith and Martyn Ball.

While Ormond enjoys the applause of the crowd, Saqlain Mushtaq takes over from Azhar at the pavilion end, and this move is much appreciated by Penney in particular as he sweeps the off-spinner's second ball for four and contributes eight runs to the total of eleven that are plundered from the over.

Rikki Clarke, given his first bowl of Finals Day as Ormond's replacement at the Radcliffe Road end, then comes up with a tight over that costs just two runs, before Saqlain again suffers at the hands of Penney, with a one-run over suddenly costing seven when the batsman pulls out his slog-sweep and earns himself six runs from the last ball.

The picture is still very gloomy for Bears' fans, however, with the scoreboard reading 53-5 at the halfway mark, though the pitch gives them a little encouragement as Clarke extracts some exaggerated bounce during another good over that yields just four singles.

Since the pitch seems to have been more treacherous when the seamers have been bowling, the appearance of Adam Hollioake in place of Saqlain for the twelfth over makes perfect sense, and it's a move that brings further joy for the Lions when Penney perishes to the new bowler's fourth ball, having lofted the previous two down the ground for two and four. Aiming more towards midwicket on this occasion, the 35-year-old is beaten by an inswinger and has his leg stump knocked back. As Penney departs for thirty-three, the score is now 63-6 and another nail has just been hammered into the Warwickshire coffin.

With eight overs remaining to be bowled, the depth of their batting still gives the Bears hope of making a half-decent total, though the talented all-rounder, Graham Wagg, doesn't last very long. Having scored five runs from his first five balls - two at the end of Hollioake's successful over and three during another respectable Clarke over that costs eight runs in total - Wagg reveals his inexperience in the Surrey captain's following over. With Frost having already taken nine runs from the first four deliveries, there is no real need for the 20-year-old to try to drive the next ball away to the legside boundary, though he undoubtedly only appreciates this fact as he is on his way back to the pavilion having been bowled by Hollioake's slower inswinging yorker.

Learning from his team-mate's mistake, Collins Obuya's approach is more measured as he sensibly deflects the final ball of the over to the rope at third man, leaving his side with six overs in which to add to a rather sorry looking score of 87-7.

Further restrained batting brings six more runs from the final over of Clarke's impressive spell of 4-0-20-0, before Obuya raises the Warwickshire hundred by smashing the recalled Saqlain away over 'cow corner' for the fourth six of his team's innings. With ten runs coming from the off-spinner's over, the Bears are still in with a chance of totalling around 130-140 if all goes well for them over the course of the final twenty-four deliveries of the innings.

Alas, they are only able to muster five from Hollioake's comeback over at the Radcliffe Road end, and then disaster strikes as the innings crumbles away in the space of just five deliveries.

Having taken the score along to 112-7 after the first two balls of Saqlain's last over, Frost's valiant innings of thirty-one ends when he holes out to Ormond at long-off, then Obuya slog-sweeps the penultimate delivery of the off-spinner's spell to Ian Ward at deep midwicket in equally panic-stricken fashion. Warwickshire therefore end the over at 115-9 and are in danger of failing to bat out their twenty overs.

As it happens, they waste no fewer than eleven deliveries, since Waqar Younis hits the first ball of the nineteenth over to cover, calls Neil Smith for a single and then changes his mind, leaving the veteran off-spinner with no chance of regaining his ground at the non-striker's end before the throw comes in from Clarke to Hollioake. The last three wickets have therefore gone down for the addition of just three runs and Surrey have one hand on the Twenty-20 Cup, thanks to a terrific display in the field.

WARWICKSHIRE BEARS INNINGS						************ END-OF-OVER TOTALS ************					
Ov	Bowler	Runs	Bat 1	Bat 2	Ex	BOWLER	BAT 1	BAT 2	EX	SCORE	OV
1	Ormond	6	Carter 6	Knight 0		JO 1-0-6-0	NC 6	NK 0	0	6-0	1
2	Azhar	10	Carter 2	Knight 8		AM 1-0-10-0	NC 8	NK 8	0	16-0	2
3	Ormond	1	Carter 0			CARTER b ORMOND 8					
			Bell 1	Knight 0		JO 2-0-7-1	IB 1	NK 8	0	17-1	3
4	Azhar	3	Bell 2	Knight 0	1w	AM 2-0-13-0	IB 3	NK 8	1	20-1	4
5	Ormond	3		Knight 0		KNIGHT b ORMOND 8					
				Trought'n 1		TROUGHTON c BROWN b ORMOND 1					
			Bell 1	Penney 1		JO 3-0-10-3	IB 4	TP 1	1	23-3	5
6	Azhar	9	Bell 1			BELL c CLARKE b AZHAR 5					
				Penney 8		AM 3-0-22-1		TP 9	1	32-4	6
7	Ormond	1	Brown 0			BROWN c BATTY b ORMOND 0					
			Frost 0	Penney 1		JO 4-0-11-4	TF 0	TP 10	1	33-5	7
8	Saqlain	11	Frost 3	Penney 8		SM 1-0-11-0	TF 3	TP 18	1	44-5	8
9	Clarke	2	Frost 1	Penney 1		RC 1-0-2-0	TF 4	TP 19	1	46-5	9
10	Saqlain	7	Frost 1	Penney 6		SM 2-0-18-0	TF 5	TP 25	1	53-5	10
11	Clarke	4	Frost 2	Penney 2		RC 2-0-6-0	TF 7	TP 27	1	57-5	11
12	Holl'ke	9		Penney 6		PENNEY b HOLLIOAKE 33					
			Frost 0	Wagg 3		AH 1-0-9-1	TF 7	GW 3	1	66-6	12
13	Clarke	8	Frost 4	Wagg 2	2nb	RC 3-0-14-0	TF 11	GW 5	3	74-6	13
14	Holl'ke	13		Wagg 0		WAGG b HOLLIOAKE 5					
			Frost 9	Obuya 4		AH 2-0-22-2	TF 20	CO 4	3	87-7	14
15	Clarke	6	Frost 4	Obuya 2		RC 4-0-20-0	TF 24	CO 6	3	93-7	15
16	Saqlain	10	Frost 2	Obuya 8		SM 3-0-28-0	TF 26	CO 14	3	103-7	16
17	Holl'ke	5	Frost 4	Obuya 1		AH 3-0-27-2	TF 30	CO 15	3	108-7	17
18	Saqlain	7	Frost 1		2nb	FROST c ORMOND b SAQLAIN 31					
				Obuya 2	1w	OBUYA c WARD b SAQLAIN 17					
			Smith 1	Waqar 0		SM 4-0-35-2	NS 1	WY 0	6	115-9	18
19	Holl'ke	0	Smith 0			SMITH RUN OUT 1					
				Waqar 0		AH 3.1-0-27-2		WY 0	6	115	19

Surrey Lions' Innings

It's Neil Carter bowling to Ian Ward at the start of the Lions' reply and, after the opening delivery flicks off the batsman's pad and runs away to fine leg for four leg-byes, the Surrey opener proceeds to take boundaries from the last four balls of the over with beautifully executed strokes - a cut is followed by an extra-cover drive, a square drive and a pull over mid-on. The scoreboard consequently reads 20-0 after the opening over and any chance of Warwickshire getting back into the game has surely already been erased. Their inadequate total now looks utterly insignificant and it would seem that only a major miracle can save them from humiliation, since a required run-rate that started at 5.8 per over has already been reduced to 5.05 per over.

Misery then piles upon misery for the Bears when Ali Brown cuts his first ball from Waqar Younis over backward point for another boundary, though the former Surrey bowler does at least bring a little respectability to proceedings by allowing just three singles from the rest of the over.

Carter redeems himself very slightly with a four-run third over that sees Brown almost playing-on to the first delivery, then Waqar finds an outside edge when bowling to the same batsman in the next over but concedes four runs because there is no third slip in place. It seems strange that the fields aren't more aggressive since the only way Warwickshire can possibly retain even the faintest hope of winning the match is by taking wickets… ten of them… very quickly.

With thirty-seven runs on the board after just four overs, Dougie Brown replaces Carter at the Radcliffe Road end and, though Ward almost runs himself out in taking on a risky single from the third ball, an otherwise accurate over ends perfectly for Surrey when the bowler's namesake pulls for six over wide long-on.

It is interesting to note that Knight now has a third slip in position as Waqar bowls his third over, but the horse has already bolted and Brown brings up the Lions' fifty with a pulled four in the midst of a tidy over costing just five.

Everyone knows that we have already reached a 'game over' scenario, but it is still surprising how rapidly the match is surrendered from this point. Sixteen runs flood from Dougie Brown's next over as Ali Brown, with a straight six, and Ward, with pulled and on-driven fours, add to Warwickshire's distress, then Waqar ends his spell by conceding pulled fours to both batsmen during an over that sees eleven added to the Surrey total.

With the scoreboard showing 77-0 after just eight overs, the Lions are cruising home with embarrassing ease, and they continue to hurtle towards victory by taking eighteen from the next over delivered by Collins Obuya, replacing the hapless Brown, whose two overs have yielded twenty-four runs. As well as three singles, and a leg-glance for three by Ward, there's a six apiece for the two Surrey batsmen, with Brown's coming from a pull-drive over wide long-on and Ward's resulting from a pull over midwicket.

It's clear that the Bears are now happy for the game to end as soon as possible, though they do salvage a sliver of respect in the tenth over when Wagg replaces Waqar at the pavilion end. The left-arm seamer has Ward caught at mid-on from a miscued pull two balls after the Lions' opener has reached an excellent 26-ball fifty with a magnificent on-driven boundary that has brought up only the third century partnership so far recorded in the Twenty-20 Cup.

This one small bright spot for the Bears is then followed by a further sharp descent towards defeat, however, as a wide, a no-ball, and two back-foot fours by Brown - the second of which takes him to a fine 32-ball half-century - complete a truly erratic Wagg over.

With the scores level at the end of the tenth over, the honour of scoring the winning runs in the first-ever Twenty-20 Cup final falls to Mark Ramprakash when he crashes Knight's fifth delivery to the extra-cover boundary, sparking Surrey celebrations both on the pitch and amongst their disappointingly small contingent of supporters in the stands.

After the presentation of the cup to Adam Hollioake by David Morgan, chairman of the ECB, the champagne corks pop, the cameras flash and the players complete a lap of honour around the outfield. The Twenty-20 Cup has become the seventh major title won by Surrey since 1996, and there is a chance of one or two more being added to the list before the season is out.

Man Of The Match - James Ormond

SURREY LIONS INNINGS						*********** END-OF-OVER TOTALS ***********					
Ov	Bowler	Runs	Bat 1	Bat 2	Ex	BOWLER	BAT 1	BAT 2	EX	SCORE	OV
1	Carter	20	Ward 16	Brown 0	4lb	NC 1-0-16-0	IW 16	AB 0	4	20-0	1
2	Waqar	7	Ward 1	Brown 6		WY 1-0-7-0	IW 17	AB 6	4	27-0	2
3	Carter	4	Ward 1	Brown 3		NC 2-0-20-0	IW 18	AB 9	4	31-0	3
4	Waqar	6	Ward 1	Brown 5		WY 2-0-13-0	IW 19	AB 14	4	37-0	4
5	Brown	8	Ward 1	Brown 7		DB 1-0-8-0	IW 20	AB 21	4	45-0	5
6	Waqar	5	Ward 1	Brown 4		WY 3-0-18-0	IW 21	AB 25	4	50-0	6
7	Brown	16	Ward 9	Brown 7		DB 2-0-24-0	IW 30	AB 32	4	66-0	7
8	Waqar	11	Ward 6	Brown 5		WY 4-0-29-0	IW 36	AB 37	4	77-0	8
9	Obuya	18	Ward 10	Brown 8		CO 1-0-18-0	IW 46	AB 45	4	95-0	9
10	Wagg	18	Ward 4			WARD c WAQAR b WAGG 50					
			R'kash 0	Brown 10	2w, 2nb	GW 1-0-18-1	MR 0	AB 55	8	113-1	10
11	Knight	4	R'kash 4	Brown 0		NK 0.5-0-4-0	MR 4	AB 55	8	117-1	11

TWENTY-20 CUP FINAL
SURREY LIONS v WARWICKSHIRE BEARS at Trent Bridge
Saturday 19th July (7.15pm) Surrey Lions won by nine wickets

Warwickshire Bears won the toss and elected to bat. Umpires:- Barry Dudleston & John Holder

WARWICKSHIRE BEARS

Fall Of Wkt	Batsman	How	Out	Score	Balls	4s	6s
1-16	N.M. Carter		b Ormond	8	12	0	1
2-20	N.V. Knight *		b Ormond	8	6	1	0
4-32	I.R. Bell	c Clarke	b Azhar	5	11	0	0
3-22	J.O. Troughton	c Brown	b Ormond	1	3	0	0
6-63	T.L. Penney		b Hollioake	33	21	2	2
5-33	D.R. Brown	c Batty	b Ormond	0	3	0	0
8-112	T. Frost +	c Ormond	b Saqlain	31	35	1	0
7-83	G.G. Wagg		b Hollioake	5	6	0	0
9-115	C.O. Obuya	c Ward	b Saqlain	17	11	1	1
10-115	N.M.K. Smith	run	out	1	2	0	0
	Waqar Younis	Not	Out	0	1	0	0
	Extras	(2w, 4nb)		6			
	TOTAL	(18.1 overs)		115			

Bowler	O	M	R	W	NB	Wd
Ormond	4	0	11	4	-	-
Azhar Mahmood	3	0	22	1	-	1
Saqlain Mushtaq	4	0	35	2	1	1
Clarke	4	0	20	0	1	-
Hollioake	3.1	0	27	2	-	-

SURREY LIONS

Fall Of Wkt	Batsman	How	Out	Score	Balls	4s	6s
1-100	I.J. Ward	c Waqar	b Wagg	50	28	8	1
	A.D. Brown	Not	Out	55	34	6	3
	M.R. Ramprakash	Not	Out	4	5	1	0
	R. Clarke	did not bat					
	A.J. Hollioake *	did not bat					
	Azhar Mahmood	did not bat					
	G.P. Thorpe	did not bat					
	J.N. Batty +	did not bat					
	I.D.K. Salisbury	did not bat					
	Saqlain Mushtaq	did not bat					
	J. Ormond	did not bat					
	Extras	(4lb, 2w, 2nb)		8			
	TOTAL	(10.5 overs)	(for 1 wkt)	117			

Bowler	O	M	R	W	NB	Wd
Carter	2	0	20	0	-	-
Waqar Younis	4	0	29	0	-	-
Brown	2	0	24	0	-	-
Obuya	1	0	18	0	-	-
Wagg	1	0	18	1	1	2
Knight	0.5	0	4	0	-	-

FINAL QUOTES

ADAM HOLLIOAKE
"That was really enjoyable - the other games have been so close, so it was nice to get everything right in the one game."
"It makes us all very proud to go out and nail it in the way we did. It may not be the biggest one (trophy) out there, but at this moment it is, and we'll be celebrating it like any other."

IAN WARD
"I got off to a flier and then Browny followed me. When you're chasing down a target like that, it sometimes pays to be ultra-positive and try and take a big chunk out of it as early as you can."

JAMES ORMOND
"I am a Warwickshire fan and there is always something special about playing against them because I feel as though I have to do well. They gave us a real drubbing last Sunday so it was nice to return the favour."

NICK KNIGHT
"We had the advantage of winning the toss, but to be honest we were outplayed. It's as simple as that. You have to hold your hands up sometimes and I have to say that I thought Jimmy's spell was awesome. He had conditions that helped him and he got the ball in the right areas and exploited it. It was a match winning performance."
"Looking at the bigger picture, there were 15,000 people out there today and they have all had a bloody good time and enjoyed themselves. This is what cricket needs."

ADAM HOLLIOAKE (on the Twenty-20 experience)
"Don't ask us, you just have to look at the crowds - they are the judge of whether something is a good product or not."

13 Foiled At The Fortress

Having secured one trophy, Surrey now had to turn their attention back to the other two that they were continuing to chase, with both the NCL and the Championship title races seemingly down to three contenders apiece at this stage of the season.

In the NCL, the Glamorgan Dragons and the Gloucestershire Gladiators were the Lions' rivals, with the latter perhaps the bigger threat since they had embarked on a good run after making a slow start to the campaign. Since Surrey had yet to play Glamorgan home or away, and had a floodlit match with Gloucestershire on the horizon, there were a lot of important 'eight-pointer' games to come, so it was all to play for in that league.

In the Championship, meanwhile, it was impossible to see any county other than Lancashire or Sussex being able to keep pace with Surrey. Although Lancashire were unbeaten, they clearly had to turn more draws into wins if they were to challenge, and Warren Hegg's timid declaration in the match with Essex at Chelmsford, coupled with a really disappointing display against Kent at Blackpool, suggested that they might still be lacking in self-belief if they came within range of a first outright Championship triumph since 1934. Sussex, one of five sides who had never won the Championship since it was formally organised in 1890, faced a similar problem, though they now had to be considered genuine contenders for the 2003 title. While much still depended on the continuing fitness and form of a handful of key players, particularly Mushtaq Ahmed, the recent victory over Essex at Arundel had been significant, since the little Pakistani leg-spinner had contributed relatively little to a success that had seen Jason Lewry take over the match-winner's mantle by taking ten wickets. Clearly, they weren't quite the one-man team that everyone had thought they were, and if other players could keep on chipping in with good performances to support Mushtaq then there was no reason why they couldn't sustain their most unexpected Championship challenge. It was fair to say that Surrey remained hot favourites, though, and they would certainly be hoping to enjoy continued success in both leagues as they headed to 'fortress Guildford' for a Championship match against Middlesex and an NCL game with Worcestershire Royals.

Alec Stewart Announces His Retirement From Test Cricket

It wasn't totally unexpected when, on 22nd July, just two days before the first Test against South Africa, Alec Stewart announced his decision to retire from Test cricket at the end of the summer. "There has been a lot of speculation in the media and, having made up my mind, I felt it was right to get it out in the open now, so the selectors are aware of my thoughts and we can get on with the series," he said. "It's not something you take lightly, but after thirteen years as an international cricketer I believe this should be my last series," Stewart added, while suggesting that he would like to continue to play first-class cricket with Surrey for one more year. No-one could have disagreed with his assertion that "the body is fine and I feel I'm still performing well" after his performances with Surrey and England during the summer, and it was to be hoped that Stewart would be allowed to retain his Test place and therefore end his international career by playing in the final game of the South African series at The Oval in September.

FRIZZELL COUNTY CHAMPIONSHIP DIVISION ONE - MATCH TEN

SURREY versus MIDDLESEX
at Guildford

First Day - Wednesday 23rd July
Surrey 375-9

The Teams And The Toss - *Having won their last eight Championship encounters at the Woodbridge Road ground, Surrey are clearly in confident mood as they prepare to take on Middlesex, though their line-up is lacking both Adam Hollioake and Azhar Mahmood, who are nursing injuries, while Alec Stewart and Mark Butcher have returned to international duty since the last Championship match at Edgbaston. Ali Brown, Alex Tudor, Jon Batty and Rikki Clarke therefore return to the Championship leaders' line-up in place of the absent four, while Ian Ward stands in as captain. Middlesex, meanwhile, are fortunate enough to be at full strength, and they are further boosted when Andy Strauss wins the toss and elects to field.*

Since batting conditions are usually at their toughest on the first morning at Guildford, Strauss looks to have made a good decision, though the opportunity to test his theory is delayed until 11.18am by a burst of showery rain that hits the ground at 10.30am.

When play does get under way, Ashley Noffke and Chad Keegan prove to be quite a handful, with the tall Australian finding some quite extreme bounce at times and the ball beating the bat with some regularity.

Although Ian Ward manages to locate the boundary backward of point from successive Noffke deliveries in the fifth over, both he and Jon Batty are back in the pavilion by the end of the seventh. The Surrey keeper goes first, with the total at sixteen, when he is beaten on the drive by Keegan and bowled off his pads, then Ward plays on to Noffke in the next over with just four runs added to the score.

Mark Ramprakash and Graham Thorpe are therefore thrown together in something of a crisis at 20-2, but both cope admirably well, adding forty-seven in eight overs, almost entirely through nicely-timed drives off the front foot, before a short but heavy shower leads to the suspension of play at 12.20pm.

Seven overs are lost - to add to the five that had been lopped off at the start of the day - before play resumes at 12.45pm with Abdul Razzaq and Simon Cook taking over the bowling duties. Thorpe immediately completes a very valuable fifty partnership by driving the Pakistani to the extra-cover boundary, though his partner has a stroke of luck, on seventeen at 76-2, when he is dropped by Paul Weekes at second slip off the same bowler.

Although the rain has eaten into the morning's play, there is still time for each batsman to take a boundary off Cook before lunch is taken with Surrey in a decent position, thanks to the efforts of their vastly experienced third-wicket pair in testing conditions.

Lunch:- Surrey 95-2 (Ramprakash 22, Thorpe 40*) from 25 overs*

Strauss pairs Keegan and Cook after the break, and in the sixth over of the session Cook removes Ramprakash for thirty-three with a fine lifting delivery that takes the batsman's outside edge on its way through to David Nash behind the stumps.

Inspired by this wicket in his seventh over, Cook then goes on to capture further scalps in his ninth and tenth overs as Surrey fall away from 113-2 to 131-5.

Having reached an excellent fifty from 76 balls with a pulled six off Keegan in the over after the loss of Ramprakash, Thorpe becomes a controversial second victim for Cook when he jabs down on a full-length delivery and is adjudged to be caught by Weekes at second slip - though the batsman clearly thinks he has squeezed the ball into the ground - then Ali Brown mistimes a lofted off-drive and is well taken by Strauss running back from mid-off.

Fortunately for the home side, Rikki Clarke and Alex Tudor respond positively to this crisis, with the Guildford lad taking ten runs from the rest of the over in which Cook has removed Brown, and Tudor picking up successive fours from Ben Hutton's first over as Keegan's replacement at the railway end.

With Razzaq having not reappeared since lunch, and Cook having completed a good ten-over spell either side of lunch, Noffke now returns to the attack, only for Clarke to cut him for three fours in two overs, while Tudor again takes consecutive boundaries off Hutton at the other end.

These thrilling strokes from the Surrey pair send the scoreboard into a frenzy for a while, though Noffke and the newly introduced Weekes regain a little control once the partnership passes fifty. Although the occasional ball is still getting past the outside edge at this stage, the pitch does appear to have flattened out to some degree, which is par for the course at Woodbridge Road.

The total has passed two-hundred, courtesy of Clarke's superb drive to the rope at extra cover off Weekes, and the partnership has extended to seventy-nine, before Middlesex finally make another breakthrough when Keegan is recalled to the fray and serves up a well-disguised slower ball that loops to gully off a leading edge as Tudor aims to drive through midwicket.

Clarke, on forty-nine at the time of his partner's dismissal for twenty-seven, duly completes a very valuable fifty in the next over from the impressive Weekes, but loses another colleague as tea approaches when Bicknell has his off stump extracted while assaying a drive at Keegan.

At the interval, Surrey are still struggling somewhat at 237-7, though their chances of converting this into a really good total are improved by the news that Razzaq has injured his ankle and is therefore unlikely to bowl again in the match.

Tea:- Surrey 237-7 (Clarke 59, Salisbury 5*) from 61 overs*

Clarke and Salisbury both look in fine fettle after the break, comfortably repelling everything that Cook and Weekes have to offer while taking the total past 250, before gradually extending their partnership towards fifty with a mix of sensible single-accumulation and fine strokeplay.

Since this bowling combination is unable to provide him with the wicket he requires, Strauss reverts to Noffke and Keegan, with almost immediate results. Having secured the single that completes the half-century stand at the start of the tall Australian's first over, Clarke falls, in unfortunate fashion, to the last ball as it cuts back at him and runs back onto the stumps via inside edge and boot. The young all-rounder is warmly applauded by his home crowd as he returns to the pavilion with eighty-five well-played runs to his name and Surrey in a much healthier state, at 283-8, than when he arrived at the crease.

The Championship leaders could still do with more runs on the board, however, and the new batsman, Saqlain Mushtaq, certainly seems in a hurry to add to the total as he cracks successive deliveries from Noffke to the extra-cover boundary within minutes of taking guard. The first of these fours comes from a conventional stroke, while the other is courtesy of a 'Saqi speciality' shot that is most certainly not in any text book and ires the bowler sufficiently for him to send down a fiery next over during which he hits both Surrey spinners with short-pitched deliveries.

The ninth-wicket pair respond positively to this, however, rattling off five superb boundaries in four overs before Noffke tempts Salisbury into a pull that sends the ball spiralling almost vertically up in the air for Nash to catch as he jogs in from his position behind the wicket.

With Salisbury gone for an attractive and valuable forty at 322-9, the Middlesex openers are probably starting to wonder how long they might have to bat for tonight, though James Ormond soon reminds them that he's a much better batsman than his position at number eleven in the order suggests. During his first full over at the crease, he lofts Keegan over extra-cover, mid-on and mid-off for three magnificent fours from consecutive deliveries, to the delight of the Guildford crowd, before both he and Saqlain settle down to ease their team up to and beyond the 350 mark. This sort of score - and the four batting points that go with it - had appeared to be almost out of reach at 131-5, but this Surrey side possesses such phenomenal strength and depth of batting that just about anything seems possible.

As the day draws to a close, Strauss turns back to Weekes and Cook, possibly with a view to keeping things quiet until the close of play, since a new ball is almost due. If this is indeed his plan then it fails dismally, since Saqlain twice deflects Cook to the third-man boundary, while Ormond on-drives Weekes first for four and then, from the day's final delivery, for a towering six that completes a marvellous half-century stand by the tenth-wicket pair. This stroke tops off a great Surrey recovery and it's interesting to note that Ormond has turned around and is on his way back to the pavilion by the time the ball comes to earth somewhere way beyond the boundary.

Close:- Surrey 375-9 (Saqlain 40, Ormond 32*) from 92 overs*

Second Day - Thursday 24th July
Surrey 411; Middlesex 346-8

Predictably enough, Middlesex take the new ball at the start of day two, though it doesn't bring the visitors the final wicket that they desire. Instead, it produces a welter of boundaries and landmarks in the first five overs as Saqlain leg-glances Cook for four in the first over; Ormond spanks Keegan through the off-side for two boundaries in the second; Saqlain drives Cook through the covers for the four that completes an 87-ball fifty in the next over; then Ormond clips Keegan for four backward of square leg to take him through to a new highest first-class score for Surrey of forty-four. When Saqlain then plunders the home side's sixth boundary of the morning, courtesy of a clip to midwicket off Cook in the fifth over, he brings up the Championship leaders' four-hundred and deposits the final batting point in the bank.

After this flurry of strokeplay, just eight further runs are added in five overs before Keegan denies Ormond a half-century by inducing a top-edged hook that Weekes pouches safely after trotting in the direction of third man from his position at second slip. With the big paceman having fallen for forty-seven, the home side's final total is a very satisfactory 411, and they will now be hoping to capture a few wickets before lunch.

Things don't start too promisingly for the county champions, however, as a highly impressive Strauss reels off a succession of fine strokes all around the wicket in finding the boundary rope five times during the opening six overs from Bicknell and Ormond.

Although the pitch is now much easier to bat on than it had been twenty-four hours previously, the bowlers get surprisingly few balls past the bat, and when Sven Koenig begins to expand his repertoire sufficiently to collect clipped and hooked fours off Ormond, it's looking like Surrey could be in for a hard day with the ball.

With the score having raced along to sixty at a rate of five runs per over, it is, surprisingly, the less flamboyant of the Middlesex openers who is now taking charge - he pulls a Bicknell no-ball to the square leg boundary to end the senior bowler's opening spell at 7-0-39-0, and then blasts Ormond out of the attack shortly afterwards with a cut for four and a pull for six that leave the Surrey seamer nursing figures of 8-1-44-0. Without taking anything away from either of the visitors' opening batsmen, it has to be said that the home side's opening bowlers have been rather disappointing this morning, and it's only when Alex Tudor - operating off a shortened run at a reduced pace - and Rikki Clarke take over in the last half-hour before lunch that the scoring rate is dragged back towards four.

Although they are unable to stop Strauss completing a classy fifty from his seventieth ball, or prevent Koenig from taking the partnership into three figures with two deflections and a thick edge to the rope at third man, Tudor does provide his side with a much-needed breakthrough as lunch comes into view, luring Koenig into a drive that results in an outside edge to Jon Batty behind the wicket.

Lunch:- Middlesex 105-1 (Strauss 57, Shah 0*) from 25 overs*

Bicknell and Clarke are Ian Ward's chosen bowlers upon the resumption, though batting continues to look easy as Strauss cuts and drives consecutive Bicknell deliveries for four in the sixth over after the restart, while Owais Shah tucks into some loose stuff from Clarke that hastens the return of Ormond at the railway end.

This doesn't help matters, initially, as Strauss cuts the former Fox to the rope at point to raise the Middlesex 150 in the thirty-fourth over, then Shah forces Bicknell away through square cover to bring up a fifty partnership for the second wicket in the thirty-fifth.

The Championship leaders are becoming desperate for a wicket at this stage, yet the runs keep flowing as both batsmen pick up a boundary in Ormond's next over to take the total up to 162-1. Then, after Bicknell has contributed a good one-run over, the game takes an incredible twist that is totally out of context with everything that has gone before it.

The drama begins when Ormond traps Strauss lbw on the back foot for an excellent eighty-seven with the opening delivery of his eleventh over of the innings, thereby providing his team with the breakthrough they have been craving.

Ben Hutton, arriving at number four, is then quickly away with a push past gully for two before falling to his third delivery when he gloves Ormond's well-directed short ball down the legside and sees Batty make up a lot of ground to his right to hold a fantastic diving catch just above the turf. As they celebrate with their bowler and wicketkeeper, the Surrey players are clearly thrilled by this double strike that has brought them right back into the match… and further excitement is imminent.

Having been dismissed for a third-ball duck in the recent Championship match at Lord's, and for a first-ball zero in the Twenty-20 Cup game at The Oval, Ed Joyce, the new batsman, must have bad memories of matches against Surrey, and he soon has another one to add to his list. Rapped on the pads by a first delivery that swings back into him, he sees umpire Mark Benson's finger raised in response to the justifiably confident appeal that goes up from the bowler and his close fielders. Ormond is therefore on a hat-trick as the disconsolate batsman heads for the pavilion after failing to score against Surrey once again. The home fans, like their team, have suddenly come to life and there is understandable excitement and tension around the ground as Paul Weekes, having no doubt had quite a rush to get his pads on, comes out to bat.

After taking his time to mark his guard, Weekes eventually settles over his bat and Ormond runs in from the railway end, accompanied by the crowd's inevitable buzz of expectancy. In the seat behind me, Mark Church of BBC London 94.9 is commentating for listeners on the Internet and there is obvious excitement in his voice… 'Ormond comes in to bowl to Weekes on a hat-trick… he's up to the stumps… he bowls… and he's bowled him! James Ormond has taken a hat-trick!' Weekes' tentative defensive push has proved to be no match for the former England fast bowler's fine delivery that has held its line to clip the top of the off stump, sending the bails flying and everyone with Surrey connections into a state of pure ecstasy. The triumphant bowler runs away in the direction of backward point, arms aloft, and he is instantly engulfed by a swarm of jubilant team-mates as the crowd erupts and rises as one to applaud a fantastic achievement. Ormond not only has his maiden first-class hat-trick, he has taken four wickets in the over and sent Middlesex into free-fall from 163-1 to 165-5. At the start of the over his figures were

10-1-56-0, yet here he is, six balls later, boasting an analysis of 11-1-58-4. Incredible! The crowd are still on their feet and continuing to applaud as poor Weekes reaches the pavilion, which makes for a strange scene, since it appears that he is receiving an extended standing ovation for a first-ball duck!

Even though they have just enjoyed an incredible ten minutes, the home side show that they aren't about to let up now as Bicknell re-ignites the crowd almost immediately by having Shah taken at the wicket from an edged defensive stroke at an outswinger with the third ball of his next over. As the Surrey players celebrate in a joyous huddle, the visitors are probably unable to believe that they have lost five wickets in nine balls, and that they have gone from a pretty strong position to one where they are going to have to fight hard to reach the follow-on figure of 262.

With all the excitement, there are probably many in the crowd who aren't aware which batsmen are out in the middle now, though it is, in fact, Abdul Razzaq, with Sven Koenig as his runner because of his injured ankle, and the doughty David Nash. The first mission facing these two is to calm the crowd, and they do this with some very positive batting as both Bicknell and Ormond come to the end of their spells - Nash steers and clips fours off successive Bicknell deliveries, while Razzaq drives Ormond through extra cover for four and then upper-cuts him for six, before a lofted cover drive convinces Ward that he should make a double bowling change.

Tudor and Clarke are, initially, on the receiving end of the same rough treatment, however, as Razzaq picks Tudor up over midwicket for six to raise the Middlesex two-hundred, and Nash drives a Clarke full-toss to the long-on boundary. Another Razzaq drive to the rope at Tudor's expense then continues the visitors' revival, though the tall paceman almost has his revenge later in the over when Ian Salisbury in the gully fails to hang on to a catch that arrives at a comfortable height but an uncomfortable pace. With Razzaq on twenty-six at the time and the score 210-6, Surrey can only hope that this doesn't turn out to be a significant moment.

Having survived this scare, the Pakistani all-rounder rather retreats into his shell, and it's Nash who takes over the lead role as Ward switches Clarke to the pavilion end and brings Saqlain into the attack for his first bowl of the innings in the fifty-second over.

It seems that nothing can dislodge either batsman, however, as the partnership extends well beyond fifty, and, during the last over of the session, Razzaq finally cuts loose again, with two successive off-driven fours off Saqlain pushing the total past the 250 mark and almost wiping out any chance of his side having to follow on.

A bizarre session ends with Surrey having taken five wickets in nine balls, yet no wickets in the seventy-three balls that preceded that most purple of patches, and none either in the 130 balls that had followed it - I guess you could say that it had been 'a session of three thirds'!

Tea:- Middlesex 256-6 (Razzaq 49, Nash 38*) from 60 overs*

After Razzaq completes his fifty, from his eighty-first delivery, during Ormond's opening over after the break, Ian Salisbury is given his first chance to bowl in the innings, succeeding Clarke at the river end.

Although the leg-spinner doesn't really establish any rhythm as the visitors pass the follow-on mark of 262 with plenty to spare, he does have Razzaq missed at slip by Brown - a top-edged cut high to the fielder's right-hand side - with the batsman's score on sixty-three and the total at 277-6.

The Pakistani enjoys another moment of good fortune, too, when Ormond, in the middle of a really good fiery spell, has him fending a short ball away just over the head of Clarke at second slip, though Razzaq responds well to the bouncer that follows by hooking for four.

After a largely disappointing spell of five overs, Salisbury then gives way to his spin twin, while Ormond is simultaneously replaced by Bicknell after an impressive, yet sadly fruitless, burst of 6-4-10-0.

Nash is certainly not unsettled by these changes, though, as he clips Saqlain to midwicket for the single that completes a very determined half-century from 84 balls, and then repeats the stroke, this time for four, to raise the Middlesex three-hundred.

With the pitch now looking very good to bat on, neither side seems capable of seizing the initiative, though the Championship leaders do miss another chance - albeit a very difficult one - to secure an advantage when a diving Salisbury just fails to hang on to a sliced drive by Nash off Bicknell with the batsman on sixty and the score 309-6.

Fortunately for the aggrieved bowler, he gets some recompense two overs later when he claims the scalp of Razzaq for seventy-eight with the seventh-wicket partnership worth 155, a record for this wicket in County Championship cricket on this ground. It's a fine catch by Ward, diving away high to his left at extra-cover, that finally brings the breakthrough with the total advanced to 320, and there is clearly much relief in the Surrey camp that an opportunity has finally been taken to end a really good knock by the Pakistani all-rounder.

On a day of difficult chances that haven't stuck in fielders' hands, there is, unfortunately, another one to catalogue shortly after Razzaq's departure - Ashley Noffke, having just taken two fours off Bicknell, drives uppishly to the right of Ormond at mid-on and survives when the big paceman's full-length dive sees him gather the ball in, only for it to jog out as he hits the turf.

Luckily for the home team, the Aussie fast bowler doesn't profit greatly from this miss with his score on ten at 330-7, as he skies a top-edged slog-sweep back to Saqlain half-a-dozen overs later with the day's play drawing to a close.

As the players leave the field at 'stumps', the match is very evenly balanced, which seems incredible, bearing in mind that Surrey had captured five wickets in nine balls at one stage earlier in the day. This burst of wickets, and especially "Ormond's over", will doubtless be remembered for years to come. Now we need the match to catch fire over the course of the next two days.

Statistical footnote - Ormond's hat-trick was only the third by a Surrey bowler in first-class cricket at Guildford, with Jim Laker and Pat Pocock the others to achieve the feat. It was also a unique hat-trick in County Championship cricket since all three victims were left-handers... as was Andrew Strauss, Ormond's fourth victim in that never-to-be-forgotten over.

Close:- Middlesex 346-8 (Nash 69, Cook 1*) from 92 overs*

Third Day - Friday 25th July
Surrey 411; Middlesex 346-8
(No play - rain)

Persistent rain, heavy at times, leads to the first completely washed-out day at Guildford since 1985, with the umpires eventually giving up hope and calling off play for the day at around 2pm.

The loss of a whole day has killed the game stone dead and we are almost certainly going to suffer our second dull Surrey versus Middlesex stalemate of the season tomorrow.

Fourth Day - Saturday 26th July

Surrey 411 and 94-0; Middlesex 385
Match Drawn
Surrey 12pts, Middlesex 11

There is drizzle in the air as play starts with Martin Bicknell and James Ormond attempting to polish off the Middlesex innings with the new ball. There's only time for five overs, however - during which time Ian Ward, at third slip, misses a chance offered to him by Simon Cook off Ormond on three at 356-8 - before rain leads to a twenty-minute suspension of play.

When the action resumes, David Nash advances, in a somewhat panicky fashion, to ninety-three with a boundary off each bowler before he loses Cook, adjudged lbw to Bicknell for four with the total on 377. This doesn't help Nash's nerves as he frets over his chances of reaching his century, though his concerns appear justified as his new partner, Chad Keegan, looks like he could be dismissed at any moment. Having been dropped before he has scored by Rikki Clarke at second slip off the unlucky Ormond - an extremely difficult chance, one-handed low to his left, diving in front of first slip - the Middlesex seamer then edges the next ball to the third-man boundary.

Having witnessed these near misses from the other end, it's surprising that Nash takes a single at the start of Bicknell's next over, and he is soon left to rue his decision when the hapless Keegan misses a drive and loses his off bail. Nash gets a sympathetic round of applause from the very small crowd as he leaves the field undefeated on ninety-six, while Keegan slinks off shamefaced after a dismal attempt to help his partner through to his ton.

Surrey have at least managed to secure their final bonus point this morning, but they now face a fairly pointless afternoon's batting, which starts in the lightest of drizzle.

Although Jon Batty provides a degree of entertainment with some elegant strokeplay, it's not unfair to say that the only noteworthy incident before lunch comes when Ashley Noffke strikes the Surrey keeper on the helmet with two successive short deliveries during what turns out to be the last over of the morning. On the second occasion Batty requires lengthy on-field treatment as the physio checks to see that both the batsman and his battered helmet are still in reasonable shape.

Lunch:- Surrey 41-0 (Ward 12, Batty 25*) from 11 overs*

Batty fails to reappear after the break, which seems to be an eminently sensible decision. In the course of two periods of play, split by a half-hour break for rain, Ward and Ramprakash have few problems in extending the Surrey score to 94-0, before a further shower sends the players off for an early tea at 3.20pm.

Mercifully for all concerned, umpires Hartley and Benson elect to abandon the game at 4.20pm with rain still falling. This is therefore the first drawn County Championship match at Guildford since 1992, and the first since the full introduction of four-day cricket.

Tea:- Surrey 94-0 (Ward 33, Ramprakash 28*) from 26 overs*

Surrey 411 and 94-0; Middlesex 385
Match Drawn. Surrey 12pts, Middlesex 11

TALKING POINTS - JAMES ORMOND

From 163-1, everything went crazy for a while during that incredible over. Looking back, what stood out most for you about that over and the hat-trick?

JO - That it didn't have any real effect on the game, basically. If you get a hat-trick and it changes the game from that position and you then end up winning the game then that's brilliant, but if the game peters out into a draw then it's not very rewarding. On a personal level it was great, though, and it's one of those things you can tell the grandkids about, I suppose.

What was going through your head as you ran up to bowl the hat-trick ball?

JO - I think you just have to concentrate on the delivery itself, and nothing else, in that situation. As soon as you start thinking about being on a hat-trick and bowling the 'magic' ball you just end up bowling a leg stump full toss. I'd taken one hat-trick before, when I was playing Grade cricket in Sydney, and I remembered that on that occasion I'd decided not to put any more pressure on myself by thinking about the hat-trick too much, so I just did the same again here.

I assume it must have helped you that all your victims in the over were left-handers, which meant that you didn't need to adjust your line?
JO - People say it's difficult bowling to left-handers, but that doesn't really apply with Middlesex because they've got so many of them, so you can get into a groove easily enough. I was in that kind of groove at the time so, yes, it was quite good that a right hander didn't come in.

SURREY v MIDDLESEX at Guildford				**23rd to 26th July (No play 25th - rain)**			
Middlesex won the toss and elected to field				Umpires:- Mark Benson and Peter Hartley			
SURREY - First Innings							
Fall Of Wkt	Batsman	How	Out	Score	Balls	4s	6s
2-20	**I.J. Ward ***		**b Noffke**	**10**	25	2	0
1-16	**J.N. Batty +**		**b Keegan**	**2**	14	0	0
3-113	**M.R. Ramprakash**	**c Nash**	**b Cook**	**33**	76	5	0
4-126	**G.P. Thorpe**	**c Weekes**	**b Cook**	**51**	87	7	1
5-131	**A.D. Brown**	**c Strauss**	**b Cook**	**8**	18	1	0
8-283	**R. Clarke**		**b Noffke**	**85**	110	13	0
6-210	**A.J. Tudor**	**c Strauss**	**b Keegan**	**27**	47	5	0
7-232	**M.P. Bicknell**		**b Keegan**	**11**	22	2	0
9-322	**I.D.K. Salisbury**	**c Nash**	**b Noffke**	**40**	48	7	0
	Saqlain Mushtaq	**Not**	**Out**	**61**	111	10	0
10-411	**J. Ormond**	**c Weekes**	**b Keegan**	**47**	60	7	1
	Extras	**(7b, 15lb, 14nb)**		**36**			
	TOTAL	**(101.5 overs)**		**411**			

Bowler	O	M	R	W	NB	Wd
Noffke	**24**	**3**	**91**	**3**	4	0
Keegan	**28.5**	**3**	**114**	**4**	-	-
Abdul Razzaq	**5**	**1**	**17**	**0**	2	-
Cook	**22**	**4**	**77**	**3**	1	-
Hutton	**3**	**0**	**18**	**0**	-	-
Weekes	**19**	**3**	**72**	**0**	-	-

MIDDLESEX - First Innings (Needing 262 to avoid the follow-on)							
Fall Of Wkt	Batsman	How	Out	Score	Balls	4s	6s
2-163	**A.J. Strauss ***	**lbw**	**b Ormond**	**87**	122	15	0
1-101	**S.G. Koenig**	**c Batty**	**b Tudor**	**42**	59	6	1
6-165	**O.A. Shah**	**c Batty**	**b Bicknell**	**22**	50	5	0
3-165	**B.L. Hutton**	**c Batty**	**b Ormond**	**2**	3	0	0
4-165	**E.C. Joyce**	**lbw**	**b Ormond**	**0**	1	0	0
5=165	**P.N. Weekes**		**b Ormond**	**0**	1	0	0
7-320	**Abdul Razzaq**	**c Ward**	**b Bicknell**	**78**	140	10	2
	D.C. Nash +	**Not**	**Out**	**96**	178	10	0
8-343	**A.A. Noffke**	**c &**	**b Saqlain**	**18**	35	2	0
9-377	**S.J. Cook**	**lbw**	**b Bicknell**	**4**	35	0	0
10-385	**C.B. Keegan**		**b Bicknell**	**4**	12	1	0
	Extras	**(8b, 10lb, 14nb)**		**32**			
	TOTAL	**(104.3 overs)**		**385**			

Bowler	O	M	R	W	NB	Wd
Bicknell	**29.3**	**3**	**102**	**4**	2	-
Ormond	**26**	**5**	**106**	**4**	2	-
Tudor	**11**	**4**	**28**	**1**	-	-
Clarke	**17**	**2**	**74**	**0**	2	-
Saqlain Mushtaq	**16**	**3**	**33**	**1**	1	-
Salisbury	**5**	**0**	**24**	**0**	-	-

SURREY - Second Innings (Leading by 26 runs on first innings)							
Fall Of Wkt	Batsman	How	Out	Score	Balls	4s	6s
	I.J. Ward *	Not	Out	33	71	5	0
	J.N. Batty +	retired	hurt	25	39	6	0
	M.R. Ramprakash	Not	Out	28	51	6	0
	Extras	(8nb)		8			
	TOTAL	(26 overs)	(for 0 wkt)	94			

Bowler	O	M	R	W	NB	Wd
Noffke	6	1	21	0	2	-
Keegan	8	1	29	0	-	-
Cook	6	1	21	0	1	-
Hutton	5	0	20	0	1	-
Joyce	1	0	3	0	-	-

Other Frizzell Championship Division One Results

With the top three sides all held to 12-point draws, the leading positions remained unchanged. Kent dropped back into the relegation zone only because they were the team sitting out this round of matches.

July 23-26

***Southend:-* Essex (9pts) drew with Leicestershire (12).** Leics 600-7dec (Ward 168, Stevens 149, Hodge 74, Snape 52*); Essex 351 (Flower 127, Middlebrook 82, Foster 50, Maddy 4-42) & 111-1 (Jefferson 54).

***Old Trafford:-* Lancashire (12pts) drew with Warwickshire (7.75).** Lancs 575-6dec (Law 236*, Chapple 132, Sutcliffe 86); Warwicks 255 (Brown 52, Chapple 4-82) & 211-4 (Wagh 76*, Knight 56).

July 25-28

***Trent Bridge:-* Nottinghamshire (8pts) drew with Sussex (12).** Sussex 497-6dec (Goodwin 148, Martin-Jenkins 121*); Notts 296 (Pietersen 139, Kirtley 5-60) & 291-4 (Warren 114*).

FRIZZELL CHAMPIONSHIP DIVISION ONE TABLE AT 28TH JULY

Pos	Prv		P	Points	W	D	L	T	Bat	Bwl	Ded
1	1	Surrey	10	159.00	5	5	0	0	43	26	0.00
2	2	Sussex	10	154.00	6	1	3	0	36	30	0.00
3	3	Lancashire	9	117.00	2	7	0	0	36	25	0.00
4	4	Middlesex	10	111.00	2	8	0	0	25	26	0.00
5	5	Warwickshire	11	103.50	1	6	3	1	34	26	1.50
6	7	Essex	11	101.00	1	7	2	1	22	30	0.00
7	6	Kent	10	94.00	1	5	4	0	31	29	0.00
8	9	Leicestershire	10	78.00	0	7	3	0	24	26	0.00
9	8	Nottinghamshire	9	75.00	1	4	4	0	21	25	1.00

NATIONAL CRICKET LEAGUE DIVISION ONE - MATCH NINE

Surrey Lions versus Worcestershire Royals at Guildford

Sunday 27th July

Setting The Scene - Having lost their last four games in the NCL, the Worcestershire Royals languish in eighth place in the table coming into this match against the league leaders at Guildford, though their chances of springing a surprise are improved by the fact that Surrey have a number of players out injured. With Ian Ward and Graham Thorpe joining Azhar Mahmood on the sidelines, the Lions bring in Scott Newman and James Benning for their first NCL appearances of the season, while Adam Hollioake returns to the side after missing the Championship match with a back problem. One other change sees Tim Murtagh being preferred to Ian Salisbury on a pitch that is certain to be damp after being exposed to a lot of rain during the four-day game. The Royals meanwhile appear to have a full-strength eleven at their disposal, with Stephen Peters losing out to Anurag Singh at the top of the order. Given the nature of the pitch, it is no surprise at all when Hollioake elects to field after winning the toss.

Worcestershire Royals' Innings

It would appear that the Lions have won a good toss as Martin Bicknell and James Ormond find early movement and a couple of equally early wickets to go with it. Anurag Singh has yet to get off the mark after ten balls when he edges a drive at Bicknell down to Ormond at third man with the score on seven at the end of the third over, then Vikram Solanki departs in the sixth over when he plays on to Ormond for just four. The total is eighteen at this point, thanks to pulled and cut boundaries by Graeme Hick, who then continues his confident start by pulling Bicknell for two further fours in over number seven.

It is already obvious that the ball has to be kept up to the bat on this rain-affected track, and this is underlined in Ormond's next over when a good-length delivery takes the outside edge of Ben Smith's bat, earning the Royals' captain four fortunate runs to third man, while a shorter delivery at the end of the over is cut away to the rope with some ease by Hick.

After a fine over from Bicknell, during which he has two confident appeals for lbw against Smith turned down by umpire Peter Hartley, Ormond errs in length once again and is punished by another rapier-like cut from the blade of Hick, though it is, ironically, another short delivery that brings about the former England batsman's dismissal two balls later. Attempting to pull yet again, Hick finds the ball on him sooner than expected and miscues a dolly catch to Scott Newman at mid-on with the total on forty in the tenth over.

With both Surrey bowlers now in a good groove, the fourth-wicket pair of Smith and Andrew Hall, the South African all-rounder, really have to battle for survival, and just six runs come from the next five overs. The Lions' ground fielding, led by Rikki Clarke, is very impressive at this stage, though the batsmen are not helping themselves by failing to find any singles to keep the scoreboard moving.

It is finally jolted into action at the start of the eighteenth over, however, when Tim Murtagh comes on to replace Ormond, who is through seven overs with figures of 2-25. The young seamer's first two deliveries are short and promptly seized upon by Hall, who pulls both balls to the boundary, taking the score past fifty in the process.

Although the league leaders seem to be very well placed at this moment in time, the fact that Ormond has only two overs left to bowl and Bicknell is just about to complete his spell is something of a worry.

As if to show his team-mates what they will soon be missing, Surrey's senior bowler finishes on a high note, conceding just a single - only the sixth of the innings in the seventeenth over, illustrating the poor nature of the Royals' running - to finish his allotted overs with the highly impressive figures of 9-4-17-1.

As Bicknell retires to the outfield to a well-deserved round of applause, the visitors are really under pressure at 55-3, but the fears of the Lions' fans appear to be well founded as thirty-seven runs gush from the next six overs delivered by Murtagh and Rikki Clarke, Bicknell's replacement at the pavilion end. During this period of Royals' rule, the fifty partnership between Smith and Hall comes up in fine style when Hall drives Clarke down the ground to the boundary, just before Hollioake opts for a change by bringing himself on in place of Murtagh.

While the Surrey skipper makes an impressive start, conceding just seven runs from his first three overs, Clarke is forced out of the attack and replaced by Saqlain Mushtaq after a disappointing fifth over from the local lad yields two pulled boundaries to Smith.

With the fourth-wicket partnership increasing in magnitude and the run-rate rising steadily, the Lions are clearly in need of a wicket, and it finally comes their way in the thirty-first over, thanks to a brilliant catch on the midwicket boundary by James Benning. For most of its journey off the bat Hall's slog-sweep looks sure to carry for six, but Benning times his jump perfectly to take the ball above his head, in the style of a goalkeeper claiming a cross, to send the South African packing for thirty-two out of a score of 127-4.

This is an important breakthrough for Surrey, though they need to build on it, since two-hundred could well be a good score on this pitch unless it eases before Worcestershire's impressive hand of seamers - Hall, Kabir Ali, Nantie Hayward, Matt Mason and David Leatherdale - get to work on it. Smith remains the key man, therefore, as he moves through to a skilfully compiled fifty from eighty balls in the over following Hall's demise.

David Leatherdale, the new batsman, soon makes it clear that he is determined to push on in support of his captain, though he has a lucky escape on six when Ali Brown is unable to hang on to a reasonably straightforward catch high to his right-hand side at midwicket off Hollioake. Fortunately for the home side, it doesn't prove terribly expensive, since the veteran all-rounder is never able to come to grips with Saqlain, and has his off stump knocked out by Murtagh immediately after contributing his sole boundary, a slogged six over midwicket off the young seamer, who has returned to the attack in place of his captain.

At 161-5 after thirty-eight overs, Worcestershire still appear to have the edge, though the Lions can clearly shift the balance of power if they can remove the well-established Smith or keep chipping away with wickets at the other end. They are unable to do either, however, as the Surrey 'old boy', Gareth Batty, follows his skipper's lead by taking whatever singles he can, while making sure than the occasional loose ball is despatched to the boundary.

Although the league leaders continue to come up with some top-class ground fielding, the sixth-wicket pair plough on in steady but unspectacular fashion until Batty raises the Royals' two-hundred with a mighty six driven over long-off during an expensive return over from Ormond that also includes a cover-driven four to Smith and costs thirteen runs in total.

The last two overs of the innings then yield seventeen runs in singles, twos and extras - despite Batty holing out to Brown at deep cover off Ormond with three balls of the innings remaining - to push the visitors' total up to a highly respectable 219-6. Smith finishes unbeaten on ninety-three, having played the ideal knock in the prevailing conditions, and no doubt realises that the Royals are in with a chance of upsetting the form book if the pitch continues to offer help to his seamers after the break.

As the Surrey players leave the field for tea, James Ormond is awarded his county cap on the outfield and receives a fine round of applause from a home crowd that appreciates this is a richly-deserved reward for the big paceman's efforts since his move from Leicestershire at the end of the 2001 season.

Surrey Lions' Innings

The Lions' reply gets off to a poor start when Kabir Ali claims the wicket of Ali Brown with his fifth delivery. Having picked the Royals' opening bowler up over midwicket for a boundary from the fourth ball of the innings, Brown edges a drive at the next delivery to Leatherdale at first slip, to the obvious delight of the visiting team.

Worcestershire's total of 219 then continues to look above-par when their 22-year-old paceman induces another edged drive in his next over, this time from Mark Ramprakash, and sees Steve Rhodes take the catch that reduces the league leaders to 14-2.

Since their line-up is so lacking in experience today, the loss of the two batsmen who had destroyed the Worcestershire attack in the match at New Road earlier in the season is particularly devastating for the Lions… and Kabir hasn't finished yet.

With the total having advanced to twenty-eight in the eighth over, he strikes again when Scott Newman attempts to drive through the on-side and gets a leading edge that dollies up a simple catch to Leatherdale at cover. As Newman drags himself back to the pavilion, Surrey are in all sorts of trouble on a pitch that is clearly still doing plenty for the bowlers.

This is underlined in the next over, delivered by Nantie Hayward, when Rikki Clarke is beaten by three successive deliveries, and also in Kabir's fifth over, when James Benning miscues a drive to Smith at backward point and becomes the young seamer's fourth victim. It's now 34-4 and the Lions' unbeaten record is about to go up in smoke unless their captain, coming in at number six, can produce one of his most inspirational innings.

As things work out, he doesn't get to face his first ball for almost three overs as Clarke picks up singles from the last ball of successive overs from Matt Mason, replacing Hayward at the railway end, and Kabir. The young Surrey all-rounder adds ten further runs to his personal tally, courtesy of an off-driven four and a pull over midwicket for six, both off Mason, during this spell to give his side something of a fillip in their hour of need.

Unfortunately for the home team and their fans, Mason then hits back in style by first delivering a maiden to Clarke and then having him very well caught, from a top-edged pull, by Gareth Batty at short fine leg, the former Lion running round from square leg to take the ball over his shoulder and plunge his old employers into deeper trouble at 55-5.

At this point, Hollioake has still only faced eight deliveries during six-and-a-half overs in the middle, so he is obviously keen to get some runs under his belt when he finally gets to face a full over from Hall, who has replaced Kabir at the pavilion end after a potentially match-winning spell of 7-1-23-4 from the highly-rated young paceman. The home skipper plunders thirteen from the South African's over, including three nicely struck boundaries in the arc between straight mid-on and cover, and then lofts Mason over mid-off for another four in the following over.

Hopes of a dramatic turnaround then increase further when Jon Batty takes ten from Hall's next over, though Mason quickly terminates the Surrey keeper's innings by having him caught behind in the next over, leaving the Lions in a pretty hopeless mess at 86-6.

Things then go from bad to worse nine balls later when Bicknell is bowled on the drive by Mason for one to make it 90-7, before the same bowler grabs his fourth wicket, the all-important one of Hollioake, to put the final nail in the league leaders' coffin two overs later. Having just been pulled for six by the Surrey captain, the strapping West Australian has Hollioake caught at deepish cover by Solanki from a mistimed off-side slash. The game is certainly all over bar the shouting now, with the hosts having subsided to a pitiful 99-8 in only the twenty-fourth over.

Mason completes his devastating spell with figures of 9-1-34-4 soon afterwards, leaving Saqlain and Ormond to try to salvage some pride and ensure that their team's net run-rate doesn't take too much of a battering. A handful of fours, including two extra-cover drives in the space of three balls by Saqlain off Hall, hint briefly at a possible repeat of this pair's brilliant last-wicket stand in the Championship match earlier in the week, until Batty enters the attack for the thirty-first over and sneaks a delivery through Ormond's drive as the Lions' paceman goes on the charge.

From the depths of 126-9, the final pair of Saqlain and Murtagh manage to slowly nudge the total up to 140 over the course of six overs before the latter runs himself out in attempting a suicidal single to mid-on, leaving the relegation-haunted Royals victorious by 79 runs.

While the Worcestershire players enjoy their well-deserved success, Surrey are left to reflect on a sub-standard display that has seen them bowled out for their lowest total in a one-day match at Guildford since 1982.

MARTIN BICKNELL'S VIEW FROM THE DRESSING ROOM

The pitch obviously started pretty damp. Why hadn't it been covered with matting during the Championship match against Middlesex?

MB - I don't know really, though the matting is really only put down to stop scuffing, so I'm not sure it would have prevented the pitch from getting damp. It had sweated under the flat sheets for the best part of two days, though, so it was always likely to be a fairly fruity wicket.

This was a disappointing performance in many ways, I felt. Would it be fair to say that we were totally outplayed?
MB - Yes, Ben Smith played very well and got them to an above-par score mainly because we didn't bowl as well as we should have done on a pitch that helped the seam bowlers throughout the match. They had a perfect attack for the conditions and bowled very well, but we were pretty poor with the bat, too. Once Ramps got out, people were playing big shots all the time and it was a bit of a kamikaze effort, really.

I guess the track wouldn't have been too dissimilar from a typical New Road surface?
MB - Yes, that's absolutely right - they actually thought it was a good wicket! That tells you what New Road can be like at times!

There was a curious last-wicket partnership by Saqlain Mushtaq and Tim Murtagh, where they used up a lot of overs without really going anywhere. Was that simply a damage limitation exercise as far as our net run-rate was concerned?
MB - Quite possibly, yes - we were very aware of the net run-rate throughout the whole year because we knew everything could come down to that at the end of the season. At that time we were behind our rivals in that respect, so we were conscious about scoring as many runs as we could.

We'd now lost two NCL games in a row. Were you worried that we were about to throw away the advantage we'd built up at the top of the table or did you regard these losses as mere blips?
MB - You always know that you are going to lose a couple of games along the way in the one-day league, so it's all about hanging in there - it's not going to be plain sailing all the way through. We were aware that we'd played fairly poorly in both these games and that we had to get back on track as soon as possible.

SURREY LIONS v WORCESTERSHIRE ROYALS at Guildford
Sunday 27th July — Worcestershire Royals won by 79 runs
Surrey Lions won the toss and elected to field — Umpires:- Mark Benson & Peter Hartley

WORCESTERSHIRE ROYALS

Fall Of Wkt	Batsman	How	Out	Score	Balls	4s	6s
2-18	**V.S. Solanki**		**b Ormond**	**4**	13	0	0
1-7	**A. Singh**	**c Ormond**	**b Bicknell**	**0**	10	0	0
3-40	**G.A. Hick**	**c Newman**	**b Ormond**	**25**	22	6	0
	B.F. Smith *	**Not**	**Out**	**93**	122	10	0
4-127	**A.J. Hall**	**c Benning**	**b Saqlain**	**32**	58	5	0
5-161	**D.A. Leatherdale**		**b Murtagh**	**18**	26	0	1
6-216	**G.J. Batty**	**c Brown**	**b Ormond**	**23**	20	1	1
	Kabir Ali	**Not**	**Out**	**0**	0	0	0
	S.J. Rhodes +	**did not bat**					
	M.S. Mason	**did not bat**					
	M. Hayward	**did not bat**					
	Extras	**(13lb, 9w, 2nb)**		**24**			
	TOTAL	**(45 overs)**	**(for 6 wkts)**	**219**			

Bowler	O	M	R	W	NB	Wd
Bicknell	**9**	**4**	**17**	**1**	-	-
Ormond	**9**	**2**	**46**	**3**	1	2
Murtagh	**9**	**0**	**54**	**1**	-	-
Clarke	**5**	**0**	**30**	**0**	-	1
Hollioake	**6**	**0**	**21**	**0**	-	1
Saqlain Mushtaq	**7**	**0**	**38**	**1**	-	1

SURREY LIONS							
Fall Of Wkt	Batsman	How	Out	Score	Balls	4s	6s
3-28	**S.A. Newman**	**c Leatherdale**	**b Kabir Ali**	**15**	14	2	0
1-5	**A.D. Brown**	**c Solanki**	**b Kabir Ali**	**4**	4	1	0
2-14	**M.R. Ramprakash**	**c Rhodes**	**b Kabir Ali**	**4**	6	1	0
5-55	**R. Clarke**	**c Batty**	**b Mason**	**15**	47	1	1
4-34	**J.G.E. Benning**	**c Smith**	**b Kabir Ali**	**6**	9	1	0
8-99	**A.J. Hollioake ***	**c Solanki**	**b Mason**	**33**	40	5	1
6-86	**J.N. Batty +**	**c Rhodes**	**b Mason**	**10**	9	2	0
7-90	**M.P. Bicknell**		**b Mason**	**1**	5	0	0
	Saqlain Mushtaq	**Not**	**Out**	**27**	50	4	0
9-126	**J. Ormond**		**b Batty**	**6**	15	0	0
10-140	**T.J. Murtagh**	**run**	**our**	**6**	24	0	0
	Extras	**(2b, 6lb, 5w)**		**13**			
	TOTAL	**(37.1 overs)**		**140**			

Bowler	O	M	R	W	NB	Wd
Kabir Ali	**9**	**1**	**30**	**4**	-	-
Hayward	**9**	**1**	**20**	**0**	-	2
Mason	**9**	**1**	**34**	**4**	-	1
Hall	**7**	**1**	**39**	**0**	-	2
Batty	**3.1**	**0**	**9**	**1**	-	-

Other NCL Division One Results

With Gloucestershire having won an isolated floodlit match on 17th July and then beaten the reigning champions, Glamorgan, at Cheltenham, they were suddenly level on points with the Lions at the top of the table. Net run-rate would be used to split sides who were tied on points and wins at the end of the season, and, after their two recent crushing victories, the Gladiators were significantly better off than the Lions in this respect.

July 17
***Chelmsford:-* Gloucestershire Gladiators (4pts) beat Essex Eagles by 7 wickets.** Essex 252 (45ov; Hussain 98); Gloucs 255-3 (35ov; Spearman 101, Harvey 91).
July 27
***Southend:-* Essex Eagles (4pts) beat Leicestershire Foxes by 37 runs.** Essex 203-6 (45ov; Jefferson 61, Snape 3-14); Leics 166 (42.2ov).
***Cheltenham:-* Gloucestershire Gladiators (4pts) beat Glamorgan Dragons by 7 wickets.** Glamorgan 197 (37.2ov; Averis 3-34, Hardinges 3-43); Gloucs 199-3 (36.5ov; Windows 54*, Gidman 49).
***Scarborough:-* Yorkshire Phoenix (4pts) beat Kent Spitfires by 18 runs.** Yorks 197-8 (45ov; Trott 3-39); Kent 179 (43.5ov; Craven 4-22).

NCL DIVISION ONE TABLE AT 27TH JULY

Pos	Prv		P	Pts	W	T	L	A	NRR
1	3	**Gloucestershire Gladiators**	**9**	**26**	6	0	2	1	9.21
2	1	**Surrey Lions**	**9**	**26**	6	0	2	1	1.09
3	2	**Glamorgan Dragons**	**9**	**24**	6	0	3	0	7.68
4	5	**Warwickshire Bears**	**8**	**16**	4	0	4	0	0.76
5	4	**Leicestershire Foxes**	**9**	**16**	4	0	5	0	-0.84
6	6	**Essex Eagles**	**9**	**16**	4	0	5	0	-1.29
7	8	**Worcestershire Royals**	**8**	**12**	3	0	5	0	4.47
8	7	**Kent Spitfires**	**9**	**12**	3	0	6	0	-4.77
9	9	**Yorkshire Phoenix**	**8**	**8**	2	0	6	0	-13.24

14 Staying On Course For The Treble

After a disappointing Guildford Festival week, the team now faced their biggest seven days of the campaign to date, with matches against their nearest rivals in both the Frizzell Championship and the NCL. The first of these potentially pivotal clashes was with Sussex at Hove in the four-day competition, while the second, under lights at The Oval three days later, was with the Gloucestershire Gladiators, who now led the NCL table on net run-rate. Wins in both of these matches would bring dreams of a treble one step closer to reality, though it was clear that nothing would actually be decided, by any stretch of the imagination, whatever happened in these key contests. There were psychological points to be scored, however, and as far as the Championship was concerned there was a feeling that a Surrey victory at Hove could badly damage a Sussex side who had already lost to the reigning County Champions at The Oval and still faced two very tough matches against Lancashire.

FRIZZELL COUNTY CHAMPIONSHIP DIVISION ONE - MATCH ELEVEN

SUSSEX versus SURREY
at Hove

First Day - Wednesday 30th July
Sussex 362-4

The Teams And The Toss - *Surrey are still without their England pair, Alec Stewart and Mark Butcher, for this vital clash on the south coast, and have also lost the services of Alex Tudor, whose old hip injury had flared up again during the match at Guildford. Since Adam Hollioake and Azhar Mahmood are fit again, the Surrey eleven shows two changes to the line-up that took on Middlesex, with Ali Brown and Tudor the men to be displaced. For Sussex, Jason Lewry (side) and Kevin Innes (groin) are ruled out by injury, but Tim Ambrose passes a late fitness test on a troublesome knee, allowing the home side to field an eleven that is pretty much at full strength, with Mark Davis playing as a second spinner. When Chris Adams wins the toss he elects to bat.*

Sussex's openers, Murray Goodwin and Richard Montgomerie, make hugely contrasting starts to their innings as the big match gets under way with Martin Bicknell bowling down the hill from the Cromwell Road end and James Ormond coming up it from the sea end. While Goodwin latches on to three wide long-hops from Ormond to get his favoured square cut into the action early on, the out-of-form Montgomerie edges three fours off Bicknell, unerringly picking out the gap in the slips cordon, wherever it happens to be at the time.

The pattern then changes, temporarily, as Montgomerie finally locates the middle of his bat with an off-drive for two and an on-drive that results in an all-run four in Bicknell's fourth over, while Goodwin uses a straight bat, rather than a cross bat, to find the boundary backward of point in the following over from Ormond. It is, however, the familiar Goodwin square cut, this time played against Bicknell, that brings up the home side's fifty in the eleventh over.

Apart from Bicknell's early moral victories, the Surrey opening bowlers have really struggled to get the ball in the right areas so far, and they have, if anything, fed the strengths of the Sussex batsmen during largely unimpressive spells. As Bicknell finishes his first stint by conceding a pulled four to Goodwin, and Ormond is driven to the rope by both openers during the next over, the hosts have established a very good base of 70-0 after fourteen overs.

Ormond's eighth over is, thankfully, rather better, bringing Montgomerie's outside edge into the action again to earn the batsman another four rather fortunate runs, while Hollioake, Bicknell's replacement at the Cromwell Road end, starts with a maiden, and then induces an edged boundary from Goodwin in his second over.

Unfortunately for the visitors, things go downhill again from this point as Goodwin takes three runs off each bowler with much more convincing strokes, before tucking into Azhar Mahmood's first over as Ormond's replacement, pulling a four that takes him to a fine fifty from 57 balls and then cutting to the rope at backward point to raise the Sussex hundred in just the twentieth over.

At this stage, with very few deliveries beating the bat, Surrey can at least draw some comfort from the five largely very economical overs that follow, though it's clearly a breakthrough that the Championship leaders crave more than anything else. It isn't forthcoming, however, and when Hollioake signs off with a seventh over that yields cut and driven boundaries that take Montgomerie through to a valuable, if patchy, fifty from 84 balls, Sussex are very much on top.

By recalling Bicknell in his stead as lunch comes into sight, Hollioake at least makes a move that drags the scoring rate back a little further, though the nearest Surrey come to a wicket is when Montgomerie gloves a pull at Azhar just wide of the diving Jon Batty and profits by four runs.

Even Saqlain, introduced for the penultimate over before the interval, falls into the 'short-and-wide' trap, allowing Montgomerie to cut his second delivery to the boundary and take the home side to lunch in a powerful position, largely thanks to a really ragged performance by the normally reliable Surrey bowlers.

Lunch:- Sussex 148-0 (Montgomerie 67, Goodwin 74*) from 35 overs*

By taking two wickets in the first three overs after the resumption, Surrey finally make a mark on the game and serve notice to Sussex that they might have put this morning's woes behind them.

Goodwin is the first man dismissed, with the opening partnership worth 149, when he pushes forward to Ormond's first post-lunch delivery and loses his off stump in spectacular style after a fine knock of seventy-five, then the final ball of the session's third over sees Tony Cottey beaten on the crease by a Saqlain off-break and adjudged lbw by umpire Mike Harris.

There is now a real prospect of Surrey making further breakthroughs, since the Sussex captain, Chris Adams, is arriving at the crease with a 2003 Championship record of 318 runs at an average of 18.70, which is even worse than the 456 at 26.82 recorded by Montgomerie coming into this game.

Things are therefore very edgy for a while, and it's the eighth over of the afternoon that turns out to be something of a watershed in proceedings. Ormond starts the over by having a big lbw appeal against Adams turned down by umpire Mark Benson, and then hits the home skipper on the helmet when the batsman ducks into a next-ball bouncer. Sussex profit by four leg-byes as the ball flies away to the boundary, then another twelve runs come the way of their captain before the over is complete, as Adams cuts the next two balls to the rope; swishes and misses at ball five; and then ends an action-packed over with another cut for four.

Although Ormond is unfortunate again when Montgomerie adds another thick-edged four to his collection in the big paceman's next over, Adams ultimately wins his battle with Ormond when another square-cut boundary shortly afterwards prompts Hollioake to bring Azhar Mahmood back into the attack in place of his former Leicestershire bowler.

The feeling that Adams is just as likely to enjoy a no-holds-barred encounter with the Pakistani all-rounder as he did with Ormond is soon confirmed, with the Sussex skipper again coming out on top by picking off a couple of boundaries square of the wicket in Azhar's first three overs.

After a rather uncertain start, Adams is now looking anything but a man out of form, while Montgomerie, who has added just twelve runs to his score in twenty-one overs since lunch, is looking woefully out of touch, despite his lengthy stay at the wicket. He does briefly break free when he glances Azhar to the rope at fine leg at the end of the over in which Adams has taken his side to the two-hundred mark with a rather streaky inside edge to long leg for a single, but, thereafter, he retreats into his shell again as Bicknell rejoins the fray opposite the exceedingly steady Saqlain. It seems bizarre that Ian Salisbury has yet to be given an over, but one can only assume that Hollioake wishes to attack with seam at the Cromwell Road end while his off-spinner - conceding no more than 1.5 runs per over - continues to do a holding job from the sea end.

With ten overs to be bowled before tea, Adams briefly cuts loose again with a cover-driven boundary off Bicknell and a lofted on-drive for four off Saqlain in the off-spinner's sixteenth over. Incredibly enough, this is the first boundary Saqlain has conceded since the second delivery of his lengthy spell, though, fortunately, it doesn't deter the Surrey captain from finally introducing the patient Salisbury in place of Bicknell at the Cromwell Road end to deliver the sixty-seventh over.

Adams immediately picks the leg-spinner off for a single to midwicket that takes him through to an impressive 85-ball half-century, though he loses his partner to a fine piece of bowling two overs later with the total advanced to 232. Montgomerie's resistance is finally ended ten runs short of a century when he pushes forward to a Salisbury googly that knocks back his off stump after finding a gap between bat and pad.

Although Tim Ambrose cuts the next delivery for four, and Adams drives Saqlain to the rope at extra cover in the final over of the session, we have undoubtedly witnessed a much better bowling display by the visitors since lunch, though they will need to capture further wickets upon the resumption if they are to get themselves back into the match.

Tea:- Sussex 246-3 (Adams 56, Ambrose 6*) from 72 overs*

To the surprise of many, Salisbury is replaced by Ormond at the Cromwell Road end immediately after tea, even though he had delivered three good overs before the break.

This decision looks fair enough when the paceman starts with a couple of tight overs, but then begins to appear flawed as Adams, with yet another square-cut boundary that takes him on to a season's best Championship score of sixty-three, and Ambrose, with two classy strokes through square cover, rattle up thirteen runs from a wayward third over.

Despite this, Hollioake allows Ormond two more overs, costing ten runs and seeing the arrival of the fifty partnership for the fourth wicket, before reverting to Salisbury and, therefore, an all-spin attack.

Although Saqlain is maintaining decent control as he continues to wheel away from the sea end, the batsman are, by now, finding it easy to 'milk' him away for a stream of singles in the square leg area, which keeps the scoreboard ticking over and means that they don't need to take any undue risks against either spinner. As a consequence of this, only one boundary - a clip through midwicket by Adams off Saqlain - is scored between the eighty-second and the ninety-sixth over, yet the total moves smoothly beyond the three-hundred mark and the Sussex captain progresses into the nineties.

He has reached ninety-three, in a score of 330-3, before Surrey finally secure their next, much-needed, breakthrough with the capture of Ambrose's scalp for forty-three. Having looked much the most dangerous bowler in the visitors' attack, Salisbury is the worthy wicket-taker when his near-perfect leg-break, delivered from round the wicket, takes the outside edge of Ambrose's defensive bat and ends in the safe hands of Azhar at slip.

Further wickets must now be taken before the close of play if the Championship leaders are to retrieve more of the ground lost earlier in the day, and Robin Martin-Jenkins offers the visitors hope of achieving this during a typically nervy start against the Surrey spinners. Salisbury causes him particular discomfort, but he hangs on gamely as his captain advances slowly but surely to a well-constructed century from 169 balls in the one-hundredth over of the day, reaching the cherished mark with a push to cover for a single off Saqlain. The Hove faithful rise to their skipper, who has come good with his first Championship ton for fifteen months in this most important of matches and thereby given his side a platform from which they could go on to win the game and leapfrog over their opponents to the top of the table.

Their first priority is to build a very large first-innings total, however, and, by surviving the last four overs of the day without any real alarms, Adams and Martin-Jenkins greatly improve their side's chances of doing just that when play resumes tomorrow.

For Surrey, on the other hand, it has been a truly wretched day - all the seamers have been guilty of bowling too short and/or too wide on a flat pitch; their champion off-spinner has been tight yet lacking in penetration; and their best bowler on the day, Salisbury, has been kept out of the action for far too long.

Close:- Sussex 362-4 (Adams 107, Martin-Jenkins 12*) from 104 overs*

Second Day - Thursday 31st July
Sussex 429; Surrey 212-6

Although he had rejected the opportunity to take the new ball yesterday evening while his spinners were bowling well, Adam Hollioake is clearly more than happy to accept it this morning, and it proves to be an important factor in a revival by the Championship leaders as James Ormond picks up a wicket in each of his first three overs of the day.

With the overnight score having increased by just a leg-bye from the opening ball of the morning, Chris Adams departs to the next delivery, which is short of a length and gloved by the batsman down the legside, producing a wonderful one-handed diving catch by Jon Batty. Umpire Benson seems unconvinced that the ball has hit the glove and looks unlikely to give Adams out, but, to his great credit, the Sussex captain 'walks' once he has ascertained that Batty has caught the ball cleanly.

The capture of Adams' wicket without addition to his overnight score is obviously a great fillip to the Surrey side, and they then claim Matt Prior's scalp two overs later when the young wicketkeeper-batsman edges a drive to Graham Thorpe at first slip and departs for a nine-ball duck with the total still at 363.

The bowling at this point is certainly better than anything we had seen yesterday, with Bicknell particularly unlucky not to remove Martin-Jenkins in his next over when he goes past the outside edge three times. Ormond makes up for this, though, by taking his third wicket in the space of thirteen deliveries - thanks to a good, instinctive piece of captaincy - during his third over of the day. Having moved Rikki Clarke in at third slip to strengthen the cordon at the start of the over, Hollioake is understandably delighted when Mark Davis tries to force the second ball away through the off-side and nicks it straight into the hands of the newly arrived fielder. With Davis gone for nought, Sussex have subsided from 363-4 to 367-7 and the game is suddenly much more evenly balanced.

It is entirely predictable that the new batsman, Mushtaq Ahmed, will adopt a very positive approach, and he doesn't disappoint, slicing Bicknell away high over backward point for four during his second over at the wicket, and then picking him up over midwicket for a mighty six that clears the scoreboard and results in a replacement ball being pressed into operation for the rest of the over until the original one is located. Perhaps inspired by his partner, Martin-Jenkins then cuts and hooks Ormond for fours that take the total beyond four-hundred, before clipping Bicknell to the rope at midwicket in the next over.

Although Ormond is replaced by Azhar Mahmood at this juncture, after a fine spell of 5-2-19-3, Bicknell is retained in the attack and immediately wreaks vengeance on Martin-Jenkins with a fine delivery that nips back to remove the batsman's off bail and send him back to the pavilion with forty to his name at 415-8.

The newly dismissed batsman is then joined in the pavilion by all the other players after six more deliveries have been bowled, as light rain sweeps across the ground with the clock reading 12.05pm. Sussex aren't too upset by this stoppage, however, since James Kirtley is still making his way back from Lord's where he has been on standby for England on the first morning of the second Test against South Africa. He seems sure to make it to Hove in time to bat, even though the umpires eventually decide to take lunch at 1pm, with play to resume, hopefully, at 1.40pm.

Lunch:- Sussex 420-8 (Mushtaq 25, Hutchison 0*) from 116.3 overs*

Play does indeed restart at 1.40pm, with fourteen overs wiped off the day's allocation, and Surrey soon pick up a ninth Sussex wicket when Mushtaq attempts to steer an Azhar delivery to third man but only succeeds in edging a catch to Batty behind the wicket.

The tenth-wicket pair of James Kirtley - back in Hove after his drive from London - and Paul Hutchison are not expected to last too long, though they hang around for seven overs, adding just six runs, before Hutchison flays a Bicknell delivery away square on the off-side and is stunned to see Ian Ward diving away to his right to pluck a splendid catch out of the air at backward point. Sussex are all out for 429, with the last seven wickets having therefore added a meagre ninety-nine runs, thanks to a much-improved Surrey performance in slightly more bowler-friendly conditions today. The worry for the visitors is that the damage might already have been done by the events of the first day.

Sussex are certainly determined to show Surrey how pumped-up they are for this match as the Championship leaders start their reply. The best example of this comes when Kirtley produces a spitting cobra of a delivery for Ward that prompts an almighty appeal for a catch at the wicket, though it is clear that the ball has bounced far too much for it to have flicked either the bat or the glove.

Hutchison is equally fired up at the sea end, and, as both bowlers receive loud vocal encouragement from their colleagues, Ward and Batty benefit from a couple of over-enthusiastic short deliveries that they pull to the boundary to get the innings away to a decent start. The Sussex seamers are still creating wicket-taking chances, though - Ward edges, at catchable height, through the gap that has been left between second and fourth slips, while both batsmen come close to giving a catch to gully, Batty off Kirtley and Ward off Hutchison.

The intensity of the home side's bowling and fielding is evident even from the boundary and you have to wonder what will happen if the Surrey openers can weather the early storm that is being whipped up by Adams and his men.

Alas for the visitors, we never get to find out, since Ward and Batty depart in the space of six balls, the former being adjudged lbw to Kirtley by umpire Benson, and the latter failing to get enough bat on an attempted upper-cut off Hutchison and being brilliantly caught above his head by wicketkeeper Ambrose.

With 32-0 having become 32-2, there is much work for Mark Ramprakash and Graham Thorpe to do, though they manage to strike three pleasing boundaries between them while seeing off the last few overs of each bowler's opening burst. The left-armer, Hutchison, has probably outbowled his team-mate, who had yet again come close to an England Test cap earlier in the day, though both spells have certainly been very impressive.

And now the batsmen have to contend with Mushtaq Ahmed. Supported at the Cromwell Road end by Robin Martin-Jenkins, the little wrist spinner is soon into his stride after Thorpe cuts him for an early boundary to take Surrey beyond fifty, though the third-wicket pair seem to be dousing the Sussex fire as Ramprakash drives and deflects Martin-Jenkins for three fours in the space of two overs.

Unfortunately for the batsman and his team, Thorpe then suffers an apparent lapse of concentration when he clips a delivery from the Sussex all-rounder to backward square leg, where a carefully positioned Mark Davis takes a good low catch. You have to give full marks to the captain, bowler and fielder for what seems to have been a well-planned dismissal, but 'nul points' to the batsman for a careless stroke that has put his side back in trouble at 75-3.

Fortunately for the Championship leaders, their new man at the crease, Rikki Clarke, is soon up and running by driving the last ball of Martin-Jenkins' successful over straight down the ground in classical style, before adding two further boundaries to his collection with a cover drive off Mushtaq and an extra-cover drive 'on the up' off Martin-Jenkins. Regrettably, however, he follows this last stroke with a hook that sends the ball flying straight down the throat of Mushtaq at deep backward square leg. Another wicket has been rather tossed away, and, with the visitors now struggling at 89-4, Sussex are very much in control. This is fully appreciated by the crowd, too, as 'Championship fever' grips the supporters of the south coast county… and understandably so, given that the Club has finished as runners-up in the premier competition on no fewer than seven occasions in their history.

The champions of 2002 are certainly aware that they have a tough game on their hands now, as Mushtaq squeezes a couple of sharp chances out of Adam Hollioake shortly after the Surrey captain arrives at the wicket. With his score on one, at 98-4, Hollioake is reprieved when Ambrose can't quite hang on to a defensive outside edge, then he survives another tough chance, with his tally increased by four and the total by eight, when Tony Cottey at slip fails to grab hold of a low-flying edge from another defensive push at a leg-break. These misses don't prove costly, however, since Mushtaq gets his man in the last over before tea, trapping Hollioake lbw on the back foot just a couple of balls after the visiting skipper has swept the leg-spinner for a boundary.

Tea:- Surrey 116-5 (Ramprakash 35) from 33.5 overs*

Chris Adams sensibly pairs Mushtaq and Kirtley immediately after the break, in the hope that a couple of quick wickets could prove decisive to the outcome of the game.

He doesn't have to wait long for his first breakthrough, either, as Azhar Mahmood falls to his compatriot in the fourth full over of the session. Having inside-edged the remaining delivery of Mushtaq's incomplete over past his leg stump upon the resumption, the Surrey all-rounder looks to be settling down as he cuts and drives boundaries in successive Kirtley overs, but he then pushes only half-forward to the leg-spinner and is adjudged lbw by umpire Harris for nine to plunge the visitors into desperate trouble at 126-6.

Consequently, the seventh-wicket pair batten down the hatches, blocking out three maiden overs before Martin Bicknell briefly cuts loose with a cover-driven four off Mushtaq and a clip to square leg off Kirtley that earns him three more runs. Ramprakash meanwhile battles on in ever more determined fashion, picking off nothing more than an occasional single, while Mushtaq screams out appeals at regular intervals. It is interesting to note that the Sussex fans who had taken such offence at the little leg-spinner's appealing last summer when Mushtaq was playing the first of his two games for Surrey are seemingly quite happy about it this year!

Eventually, Bicknell breaks free again by taking two successive fours in a Kirtley over that not only costs eleven and brings up the league leaders' 150 but also results in Adams resting his leading seam bowler in favour of Hutchison at the Cromwell Road end.

Having put in an impressive opening burst at the start of the innings, the left-arm paceman's second spell of four overs turns out to be quite a disappointment from the Sussex point of view, and it is no great surprise when he gives way to Martin-Jenkins. Meanwhile, at the other end, Ramprakash notches his first boundary of the session with a slog-sweep off Mushtaq to take his contribution to the visitors' cause up to forty-six.

Ramprakash's fifty then arrives four overs later when he dances down the track to the leg-spinner and lofts him high over mid-on for the eighth boundary of a gutsy 130-ball innings that looks increasingly likely to hold the key to his team's destiny in this match. Hearts are in mouths a few seconds later, therefore, when the Surrey number three inside-edges the next delivery, a googly, just past his leg stump and wicketkeeper Ambrose to add four lucky runs to his tally.

By now, the Ramprakash-Bicknell alliance has calmed both the crowd and the home team somewhat, and it becomes worth fifty priceless runs in the next over when Bicknell clips Martin-Jenkins to midwicket for two. Given that there are just seven overs remaining for play at this point, you would expect the batsmen to start playing for stumps, yet that is certainly not the case with this duo, as Ramprakash drives Mushtaq to the rope at extra-cover and Bicknell forces Martin-Jenkins away for a four of his own in the following over.

This last stroke convinces Adams that he should give Mark Davis, his off-spinner, a taste of the action at the Cromwell Road end for the sixty-third and sixty-fifth overs of the innings before close of play. The resultant all-spin combination fails to produce a further breakthrough for Sussex, however, as Surrey cruise past two-hundred, with three boundaries, and twenty-one runs in total, coming from the day's last four overs.

As the players leave the field at the end of a day that has seen a lot of good, competitive cricket played, Sussex are still in control, though the eighty-six runs that Ramprakash and Bicknell have added with some excellent batting do at least give the Championship leaders hope for tomorrow.

Close:- Surrey 212-6 (Ramprakash 74, Bicknell 42*) from 66 overs*

Third Day - Friday 1st August
Sussex 429 and 69-2; Surrey 355

As Surrey start day three still needing another sixty-eight runs to avoid the follow-on, Adams surprises everyone by giving Mark Davis the first over of the day. His motive for doing this soon becomes clear, however, when James Kirtley bowls the next over, allowing Mushtaq Ahmed to switch to the Cromwell Road end from the sea end that had been his virtual home for the greater part of the second day's play.

Mushtaq's change of ends proves highly effective, too, as he snaps up the wickets of Martin Bicknell and Ian Salisbury in the space of three deliveries to dump Surrey back in the mire at 217-8. Bicknell goes to the final ball of the leg-spinner's first over when he is beaten on the back foot by what appears to be a flipper, then Salisbury is smartly stumped by Ambrose when his drive is defeated by a googly, causing him to overbalance out of his crease.

The pressure is really on again now, and, as Mark Ramprakash and his new partner, Saqlain Mushtaq, battle for survival, the total advances largely in singles. While his top-order partner looks as composed and technically correct as ever, Saqlain endures some nervy moments against Mushtaq, though he does manage to register the only two boundaries of the first hour's play by lofting the leg-spinner back over his head and snicking a Kirtley delivery all along the ground through the slips.

With the Sussex paceman having been unable to break this partnership despite putting in a decent spell, Hutchison takes over at the sea end, shortly after Ramprakash has moved into the nineties with a sweep for two off Mushtaq. Another stroke for two, this time off the left-arm seamer, then leads to a moment of controversy, and disappointment for Sussex, when Mushtaq's brilliant throw from long leg hits the stumps at the non-striker's end with Saqlain seemingly struggling to make his ground. The home fielders in the vicinity feel sure that the batsman is out, but the man whose decision matters, umpire Harris, rules 'not out'. With Saqlain on fourteen, and Surrey still thirty-two runs short of avoiding the follow-on at the time, it's no surprise that Sussex are unhappy that the verdict has gone against them.

This incident does, however, spark off some exciting and dramatic action during the remainder of the session, starting with Saqlain blazing Hutchison away over long-off for six just a few balls after his narrow escape and then lifting the ball back over Mushtaq's head for four in the next over.

Ramprakash is now facing Hutchison with his score on ninety-seven, and when the former Yorkshire bowler bangs a ball in short the batsman sees a chance to move straight through to his hundred with a boundary. His attempted pull only results in a top edge, however, and, as he runs around the boundary from long leg towards fine leg, Mushtaq seems to be homing in on a possible catch. He appears to have judged it almost perfectly, in fact, as he arrives with the ball coming down at around waist height, yet he somehow fails to get a hand to it, leaving Ramprakash to celebrate a superb and most timely century, and umpire Harris to enquire whether he should be signalling four or six. By confirming that the ball has landed inside the rope, Mushtaq effectively admits to having missed an opportunity to rid his side of Ramprakash, who has otherwise given the opposition scarcely a sniff of capturing his wicket during an excellent 211-ball innings that receives a very good round of applause from another decent-sized crowd at the County Ground.

The master technician's knock has certainly given his side a great chance of avoiding the follow-on, and Saqlain ensures that the visitors won't suffer this embarrassment in the very next over when he blasts Mushtaq down the ground for two sixes in three balls, boosting the value of the ninth-wicket partnership to sixty-four in the process.

With the new ball due in three overs time, the Surrey off-spinner then runs amok, sweeping Mushtaq for four and then taking three boundaries from what turns out, unsurprisingly, to be the final over of Hutchison's spell from the sea end. The second of these fours off the left-armer completes Saqlain's third fifty in his last five Championship innings, this one from 61 balls, while the final boundary brings up the visitors' three-hundred - riches indeed after having been 126-6.

Predictably enough, Adams doesn't waste any time taking the new ball… and nor does the recalled Kirtley waste any time in making good use of it, since he snares Ramprakash with his first delivery, an outswinger that the batsman can only nick through to Ambrose.

As the former England batsman departs to a thoroughly well deserved ovation from the crowd for his 104, compiled out of a total of 301-9, the home side still have a chance to secure a very significant first-innings lead, though James Ormond immediately clears four further runs from Surrey's deficit with a cover-driven boundary from the second ball he faces.

The last-wicket pair rather enjoy their contest with the new ball, in fact, as eighteen runs come from the next two overs, courtesy of a series of aerial strokes down the ground and over the slips, before Ormond ends the session with two classy boundaries - a clip through midwicket and an off-drive - from the final two deliveries sent down by Kirtley.

Lunch:- Surrey 337-9 (Saqlain 66, Ormond 26*) from 98 overs*

To the disbelief of almost everyone, the Sussex skipper spurns two chances to finish the Surrey innings off, and thereby deny them a fourth batting point, within three overs of the restart. The lucky batsman and the suffering bowler are the same on both occasions as Ormond's two snicks off Martin-Jenkins to Sussex's one and only slip fielder - the first a regulation catch with the batsman on twenty-six, and the second a tricky chance low to the left with Ormond having added a single - fail to stick in Adams' hands. Insult is then added to injury for poor Martin-Jenkins when Ormond edges the ball that follows his second reprieve through the vacant second slip position for four runs, before cutting crisply for another boundary at the end of the over.

At 348-9, Surrey are now on the threshold of what could turn out to be an important batting point, and Ormond carries his side over it in style during Kirtley's next over with a lofted extra-cover drive to the fence that also completes a fifty stand for the last wicket. Any dreams the visitors might harbour of stealing a fifth point are soon scotched, however, when Martin-Jenkins finally gets his third wicket, plucking out Saqlain's off stump with a superlative delivery that shapes away to defeat the batsman's defensive push.

Sussex therefore have a first-innings lead of seventy-four and almost five sessions in which to build on it and push for victory.

Their second innings doesn't get away to a good start, though, as Richard Montgomerie falls lbw for two to the final delivery of Martin Bicknell's second over with the total on seven. They find Surrey's opening bowlers far less accommodating than they had been on the first day, too, with a number of balls beating the bat, and only one boundary - a back-foot forcing stroke through point by Tony Cottey off Bicknell - coming in the nine overs following Montgomerie's departure. Starved of balls to pull and cut, Murray Goodwin is rendered virtually strokeless, leaving Cottey to keep the score moving, which he manages to do with a mixture of outside edges and nicely middled shots, mostly off the front foot and principally at Bicknell's expense. The diminutive Welshman actually takes fifteen runs from the last two overs of an otherwise very good spell from Surrey's senior bowler, before Saqlain Mushtaq takes over at the sea end.

The Pakistani off-spinner is then paired with Azhar Mahmood shortly after the total passes fifty in the nineteenth over at the end of Ormond's impressive stint of 10-3-17-0, and, as the new bowlers come up with a series of testing overs, the run-rate takes another dive.

After six overs operating in tandem, reward then comes the way of Azhar when Cottey mistimes a pull at a delivery that is on to him much quicker than he expects and, consequently, provides Ramprakash with an absolute dolly catch at square leg after making forty-one out of a total of sixty-seven. Cottey might have a valid excuse for an apparently wretched stroke, however, since the light has been steadily deteriorating on a grey afternoon and, after one more over from Saqlain, the umpires offer Goodwin and the newly arrived Sussex skipper, Chris Adams, the opportunity to retire to the pavilion. Although the hosts are in a very strong position, leading by 143 runs, their batsmen elect to accept the offer.

With thirty-seven overs left for play, the umpires make the sensible decision to take tea straight away, in the hope that the light might be better in twenty minutes time.

Tea:- Sussex 69-2 (Goodwin 21, Adams 1*) from 28 overs*

With banks of slate grey cloud having settled over the ground, the light just doesn't improve at any stage and the umpires eventually call play off for the day at 6.15pm. With so many overs lost, it is now hard to see either side forcing a victory unless tomorrow morning's opening session brings a glut of wicket or a flood of runs. Since Surrey's run-in looks slightly easier than Sussex's, it would seem that a draw might suit the reigning champions more than it would the pretenders to their throne. Having said that, it isn't in Surrey's nature to play for a draw if a win is even remotely possible.

Close:- Sussex 69-2 (Goodwin 21, Adams 1*) from 28 overs*

Fourth Day - Saturday 2nd August

Sussex 429 and 302-5dec; Surrey 355 and 114-1
Match Drawn
Sussex 12pts, Surrey 11

Adam Hollioake chooses Martin Bicknell and Saqlain Mushtaq to launch Surrey's assault on the Sussex batting as the final day's play starts in glorious sunshine. Early wickets are clearly needed if the Championship leaders are to retain realistic hopes of winning the match, while the home side's approach during the morning session should indicate whether or not they believe they can press on fast enough to declare and then bowl Surrey out later in the day.

It is disappointing, therefore, that there is little real action to speak of in the first half-hour, other than a clip to the square leg boundary by Chris Adams off Bicknell in the first over of the day and a sweep for four by Murray Goodwin at Saqlain's expense five overs later.

There are stirrings of life soon after this second boundary, however, when the former Zimbabwe batsman attempts to pull the Surrey off-spinner away over midwicket only to see Ian Ward timing his leap perfectly to pull in a fine overhead catch. With Goodwin - apparently handicapped by a damaged thumb - gone for a painstaking twenty-nine, Sussex are now, effectively, 163-3, with eighty-eight overs left in the contest.

Apart from another couple of boundaries to Adams off Bicknell - the second of which brings up the Sussex hundred and prompts the replacement of Surrey's senior bowler with Ian Salisbury at the sea end - the hosts do nothing in the course of the next seven overs to suggest that they have any desire to press on, especially against Saqlain who has settled into a nice rhythm at the Cromwell Road end.

Having troubled the batsmen on a number of occasions, it is good to see the Pakistani off-spinner getting some reward for his efforts as we approach the mid-point of the morning session, though Adams is clearly very unhappy to be adjudged lbw by umpire Harris when Saqlain's quicker delivery thuds into his pads with the total advanced to 108. It's hard to fathom the exact nature of his grievance as he delays his departure from the crease and glares at the umpire, though an inside-edge, or a belief that the ball was heading down the legside, would appear to be the most likely reasons for his dissatisfaction at having had his innings terminated at forty-one.

Surrey now need to maintain this momentum by capturing further wickets almost immediately, but they are unable to manage this as Salisbury takes a while to settle, and is picked off for two fours and a three by Tim Ambrose, while Saqlain can't find a way to unseat Martin-Jenkins, even though the tall all-rounder makes his usual nervy start against the spinners.

The fifth-wicket pair have been together for a dozen overs when, with lunch approaching, Ambrose again finds the boundary at Salisbury's expense, taking the Sussex total beyond 150 in the process, and the chances of the reigning champions pulling off a victory by dismissing their hosts is out of the question by the time lunch arrives with the partnership worth fifty-nine. Will Adams now be prepared to set the opposition a target later in the afternoon on what is a pretty flat pitch or will he be happy to take the draw and thereby reduce Surrey's lead at the top of the table by just one point? The latter option would seem to be favoured, given that his batsmen have shown no great desire to get on with things this morning while adding just ninety-eight runs in thirty-four overs.

Lunch:- Sussex 167-4 (Ambrose 37, Martin-Jenkins 15*) from 62 overs*

When Martin-Jenkins pulls and cuts boundaries during Salisbury's opening over, and twenty-seven runs come from the first four overs delivered by the spinners after lunch, there is just a flicker of hope that Sussex might be looking to set up a run-chase later in the day - a move that would certainly go down well with a decent-sized crowd basking in the Hove sunshine.

Alas, this sudden surge turns out to be short-lived, and it becomes a gentle stream of singles as Ambrose completes both his personal fifty, from 114 balls, and a century partnership with Martin-Jenkins during the same Saqlain over.

With Hollioake happy to plug away relentlessly with his spinners, and the batsmen showing no real attacking ambition, it's clear that Adams is not prepared to set Surrey any sort of target on what is, admittedly, a batsman-friendly pitch. To give his side any chance of winning he would have to dangle a reasonably tasty carrot in front of the Championship leaders and hope that they self-destructed in the pursuit of victory, which is a risk that he is, unsurprisingly, unwilling to take.

Although the visitors do capture another wicket when Salisbury bowls Martin-Jenkins behind his legs with the batsman on forty-five and Sussex's advantage standing at 302, the game rather degenerates as the afternoon wears on and everyone realises that the home team will not be declaring. Ambrose, with two sixes off Salisbury, and Matt Prior, with one off Saqlain, gradually take advantage of the spinners' increasing weariness and disenchantment, with things reaching a head when both bowlers deliver an over of medium-pace seamers.

We are then 'treated' to the sight of Hollioake sending down five of his pretty unimpressive leg-breaks, allowing Prior to register a fifty from 49 balls and Adams to declare, for no apparent reason, at 3.25pm, leaving himself thirty-six overs after tea in which to bowl at Surrey. The visitors have achieved some amazing feats with the bat in recent years, but chasing 377 at more than ten runs per over is a challenge that they clearly won't be taking on.

As the two unbeaten batsmen leave the field there is a nice touch as they are each awarded their county cap. It seems unlikely that Sussex will be able to keep these two equally impressive young wicketkeeper-batsmen happy in the longer term, but for the moment all is well as they soak up the applause of the crowd on their way back to the dressing room.

Tea:- Between Innings

Having decided to declare, it's incredible to see just two slips, a gully and a short leg posted for the Surrey openers as they face up to James Kirtley and Paul Hutchison - surely Adams doesn't believe that the Championship leaders are going to have a stab at this target?

For Kirtley, he does eventually make a change by moving the short leg to third slip, but it's a fourth slip that he needs as both batsmen edge at catchable height through that very position within the space of a few balls during the seventh and eighth overs. Although the Sussex skipper is guilty of showing an almost total lack of attacking ambition with regard to his field placings, it must be said that the Surrey openers make batting look very easy as they find the boundary with some regularity in raising the fifty during the fourteenth over.

The bowlers do manage to capture one wicket, when an unhappy Ian Ward is adjudged lbw to Mark Davis' fifth delivery by umpire Harris, but even Mushtaq is dealt with quite easily as Jon Batty completes a good half-century from 58 balls and the match ends in the inevitable stalemate at 5.30pm.

It's a disappointing end to the game after some excellent cricket had been played on the first two-and-a-half days, with the net swing of one point to Sussex unlikely to prove significant come the end of the season. Surrey lead the table by four points and it's all to play for.

Sussex 429 and 302-5dec; Surrey 355 and 114-1
Match Drawn. Sussex 12pts, Surrey 11

TALKING POINTS - MARTIN BICKNELL

Personally, I felt that our first morning display in the field was the worst I'd seen from us in a very long time. Am I being unfair? Were there any excuses for what I thought was a pretty dismal performance?

MB - No, you are absolutely spot-on - nobody bowled well. We were hyped-up enough for the game…it wasn't as if we'd been caught asleep or anything like that… we knew how big a game it was and we were desperate to stamp our authority on it, but things just didn't go our way and the harder we tried the worse it got. The whole of the first day was poor for us - a real damp squib, very disappointing.

Were you surprised that they accepted the offer of bad light at 69-2 on the third afternoon?
MB - Yes, very much so, and I thought that it would turn out to be a major point in the season. You don't win Championships by sitting back and waiting for the opposition to hand it to you, you've got to take it by the scruff of the neck. They were in the box seats, they were ahead of the game, and it was ridiculous that they could even contemplate losing the game from that position.

I guess you had a good idea that Chris Adams wouldn't be looking to set a target on the final day, no matter how well Sussex batted in the morning?
MB - The events of the previous afternoon had given us a clear indication of what was going to happen. We knew that we had to bowl really well in the morning and have a good hard go at bowling them out within a couple of hours if we were to have any chance of winning the game. We stuck at it and played some decent cricket after the first day, but they clearly had no thoughts about winning the game, which was very surprising.

I guess they would turn round and say that they had got their tactics right, though, seeing as they went on to win the title?
MB - Yes, absolutely, they had the last laugh by winning the Championship.

All our bowlers, bar you, struggled badly when bowling from the sea end. Is there any reason why this should be? Surely it shouldn't be an insurmountable problem for experienced bowlers to bowl up the slope at Hove?
MB - It shouldn't be a problem, no, and it's difficult to pinpoint why we've had this problem in recent years. I've always had a problem bowling downhill, especially at Hove, and I can't remember very many occasions when I've bowled really well down the hill there, apart from in 1999. In this game it took me all of the first day to realise I'd be better off coming up the hill. If you are struggling to bowl either up or down a hill, I think it indicates that you might have a problem with your rhythm as a bowler - when things are clicking, you can bowl anywhere, but when you are not on top of your game it can affect you. So, in this case, it might suggest that our bowlers weren't on top of their game.

TALKING POINTS - MARK RAMPRAKASH

I was impressed by the desire and intensity of Sussex bowling and fielding at the start of our first innings, and I felt it compared favourably to ours. Were you aware of how fired-up they were during your innings?
MR - Yes, very much so. It was like two different games - I thought we were very flat when we fielded and we got put to the sword on the first morning because we put up a very poor performance. Then if you compare that to when we batted… they had got a good score on the board and came out really fired up, knowing that they had a great chance to put us under pressure. They backed up accurate bowling with good fielding and created even more pressure by their intensity in the field.

All things considered, I guess you must regard your century in this match as one of the best backs-to-the-wall innings of your career?
MR - Definitely, considering the quality of their attack and the intensity that they played with combined with the importance of the game and the situation we were in. With Mushtaq in their attack, the guys at the other end know that all they've got to do is rock up, hit the wicket hard and bowl line and length, which made it very hard for us. I think there was a period after tea where I only scored about four runs and stayed up at Mushtaq's end quite a lot to try and blunt him a little

bit and give the batters a chance to get in at the other end, and in the end it was Bickers who did brilliantly well to hang around.

I thought the games against Sussex and Lancashire this year were a credit to first division domestic cricket - from the boundary, they appeared to be like Test Matches in terms of competitiveness and intensity. Does it feel that way to you as a player?

MR - Yes, the games were played on good wickets and the players had a Test Match type of mentality, where batsmen had to work hard for their runs and bowlers had to maintain their discipline to keep the batsmen under pressure. I think county cricket at the moment is very good - I don't agree with successive England captains criticising it because I think the standard is high and you really have to work hard for your wins. It's good cricket played on good pitches, with some of the best overseas players in the world playing in it. I think Division One cricket is very tough and a very good stepping stone to Test cricket.

SUSSEX v SURREY at Hove — **30th July to 2nd August**

Sussex won the toss and elected to bat — Umpires:- Mark Benson and Mike Harris

SUSSEX - First Innings

Fall Of Wkt	Batsman	How	Out	Score	Balls	4s	6s
3-232	**R.R. Montgomerie**		**b Salisbury**	**90**	201	13	0
1-149	**M.W. Goodwin**		**b Ormond**	**75**	114	12	0
2-150	**P.A. Cottey**	**lbw**	**b Saqlain**	**1**	8	0	0
5-363	**C.J. Adams ***	**c Batty**	**b Ormond**	**107**	184	12	0
4-330	**T.R. Ambrose +**	**c Azhar**	**b Salisbury**	**43**	96	4	0
8-415	**R.S.C. Martin-Jenkins**		**b Bicknell**	**40**	68	6	0
6-363	**M.J. Prior**	**c Thorpe**	**b Ormond**	**0**	9	0	0
7-367	**M.J.G. Davis**	**c Clarke**	**b Ormond**	**0**	3	0	0
9-423	**Mushtaq Ahmed**	**c Batty**	**b Azhar**	**26**	27	2	1
10-429	**P.M. Hutchison**	**c Ward**	**b Bicknell**	**5**	34	1	0
	R.J. Kirtley	**Not**	**Out**	**1**	23	0	0
	Extras	**(6b, 13lb, 22nb)**		**41**			
	TOTAL	**(126 overs)**		**429**			

Bowler	O	M	R	W	NB	Wd
Bicknell	**26**	**5**	**94**	**2**	3	-
Ormond	**25**	**6**	**106**	**4**	-	-
Hollioake	**7**	**3**	**23**	**0**	-	-
Azhar Mahmood	**18**	**5**	**61**	**1**	3	-
Saqlain Mushtaq	**36**	**5**	**84**	**1**	5	-
Salisbury	**14**	**0**	**42**	**2**	-	-

SURREY - First Innings (Needing 280 to avoid the follow-on)

Fall Of Wkt	Batsman	How	Out	Score	Balls	4s	6s
1-32	**I.J. Ward**	**lbw**	**b Kirtley**	**20**	36	4	0
2-32	**J.N. Batty +**	**c Ambrose**	**b Hutchison**	**12**	23	2	0
9-301	**M.R. Ramprakash**	**c Ambrose**	**b Kirtley**	**104**	225	13	0
3-75	**G.P. Thorpe**	**c Davis**	**b Martin-Jenkins**	**23**	45	3	0
4-89	**R. Clarke**	**c Mushtaq**	**b Martin-Jenkins**	**12**	17	3	0
5-116	**A.J. Hollioake ***	**lbw**	**b Mushtaq**	**13**	19	3	0
6-126	**Azhar Mahmood**	**lbw**	**b Mushtaq**	**9**	14	2	0
7-215	**M.P. Bicknell**	**lbw**	**b Mushtaq**	**42**	97	5	0
8-217	**I.D.K. Salisbury**	**st Ambrose**	**b Mushtaq**	**1**	7	0	0
10-355	**Saqlain Mushtaq**		**b Martin-Jenkins**	**68**	92	8	3
	J. Ormond	**Not**	**Out**	**42**	41	8	0
	Extras	**(1b, 6lb, 2nb)**		**9**			
	TOTAL	**(102.3 overs)**		**355**			

Bowler	O	M	R	W	NB	Wd
Kirtley	**28**	**4**	**90**	**2**	-	-
Hutchison	**16**	**2**	**58**	**1**	1	-
Mushtaq Ahmed	**38**	**7**	**123**	**4**	-	-
Martin-Jenkins	**17.3**	**3**	**67**	**3**	-	-
Davis	**3**	**0**	**10**	**0**	-	-

SUSSEX - Second Innings (Leading by 74 runs on first innings)							
Fall Of Wkt	Batsman	How	Out	Score	Balls	4s	6s
3-89	**M.W. Goodwin**	**c Ward**	**b Saqlain**	**29**	103	3	0
1-7	**R.R. Montgomerie**	**lbw**	**b Bicknell**	**2**	8	0	0
2-67	**P.A. Cottey**	**c Ramprakash**	**b Azhar**	**41**	75	5	0
4-108	**C.J. Adams ***	**lbw**	**b Saqlain**	**23**	49	4	0
	T.R. Ambrose +	**Not**	**Out**	**76**	162	5	0
5-228	**R.S.C. Martin-Jenkins**		**b Salisbury**	**45**	88	3	0
	M.J. Prior	**Not**	**Out**	**50**	49	4	2
	Extras	**(9b, 8lb, 14nb, 5p)**		**36**			
	TOTAL	**(87.5 overs)**	**(for 5 dec)**	**302**			

Bowler	O	M	R	W	NB	Wd
Bicknell	**16**	**5**	**54**	**1**	2	-
Ormond	**10**	**3**	**17**	**0**	-	-
Saqlain Mushtaq	**35**	**7**	**97**	**2**	4	-
Azhar Mahmood	**4**	**1**	**3**	**1**	-	-
Salisbury	**22**	**0**	**98**	**1**	-	-
Hollioake	**0.5**	**0**	**11**	**0**	1	-

SURREY - Second Innings (Needing 377 to win)							
Fall Of Wkt	Batsman	How	Out	Score	Balls	4s	6s
1-82	**I.J. Ward**	**lbw**	**b Davis**	**33**	59	5	0
	J.N. Batty +	**Not**	**Out**	**65**	83	12	0
	M.R. Ramprakash	**Not**	**Out**	**14**	14	1	1
	Extras	**(2lb)**		**2**			
	TOTAL	**(26 overs)**	**(for 1 wkt)**	**114**			

Bowler	O	M	R	W	NB	Wd
Kirtley	**6**	**1**	**23**	**0**	-	-
Hutchison	**7**	**1**	**30**	**0**	-	-
Martin-Jenkins	**3**	**0**	**17**	**0**	-	-
Mushtaq Ahmed	**6**	**1**	**26**	**0**	-	-
Davis	**4**	**1**	**16**	**1**	-	-

Other Frizzell Championship Division One Results

With the Sussex versus Surrey clash having ended in stalemate, Lancashire moved back into contention for the title by beating Leicestershire at Grace Road. Wins for Kent and Middlesex moved both sides into safe mid-table positions, while the teams they beat, Essex and Nottinghamshire, slipped deeper into relegation trouble.

July 30 - August 1
***Canterbury:-* Kent (17pts) beat Essex (3) by 55 runs.** Kent 189 (Smith 108, Palladino 6-41) & 284 (Fulton 94); Essex 183 (Irani 52, Ealham 4-65) & 235 (Flower 83, Muralitharan 6-61).
July 30 - August 2
***Leicester:-* Lancashire (22pts) beat Leicestershire (4) by 7 wickets.** Leics 259 (DeFreitas 57, Stevens 54) & 287 (Maunders 75, Stevens 50); Lancs 479 (Law 186, Hooper 117, DeFreitas 6-88) & 68-3.
***Trent Bridge:-* Middlesex (19pts) beat Nottinghamshire (5) by 4 wickets.** Notts 254 (Pietersen 67, Noffke 5-52) & 169 (Welton 69, Dawes 5-46); Middx 278 (Koenig 75) & 146-6.

FRIZZELL CHAMPIONSHIP DIVISION ONE TABLE AT 2ND AUGUST

Pos	Prv		P	Points	W	D	L	T	Bat	Bwl	Ded
1	1	Surrey	11	170.00	5	6	0	0	47	29	0.00
2	2	Sussex	11	166.00	6	2	3	0	41	33	0.00
3	3	Lancashire	10	139.00	3	7	0	0	41	28	0.00
4	4	Middlesex	11	130.00	3	8	0	0	27	29	0.00
5	7	Kent	11	111.00	2	5	4	0	31	32	0.00
6	6	Essex	12	104.00	1	7	3	1	22	33	0.00
7	5	Warwickshire	11	103.50	1	6	3	1	34	26	1.50
8	8	Leicestershire	11	82.00	0	7	4	0	26	28	0.00
9	9	Nottinghamshire	10	80.00	1	4	5	0	23	28	1.00

NATIONAL CRICKET LEAGUE DIVISION ONE - MATCH TEN
Surrey Lions versus Gloucestershire Gladiators at The Oval
Tuesday 5th August

Setting The Scene - Surrey's second top-of-the-table clash inside a week sees them taking on the Gloucestershire Gladiators under lights at The Oval and, after successive defeats at the hands of Warwickshire Bears and Worcestershire Royals, they will obviously be desperately keen to get their NCL title challenge back on track. It is therefore good news for the Lions that they are able to field what is, arguably, their strongest NCL eleven, with Ian Ward, Graham Thorpe and Azhar Mahmood returning to the side after missing out through injury at Guildford. Gloucestershire, on the other hand, are without three key men, since Jonty Rhodes (hamstring) and Mike Smith (back) are both injured, while Ian Harvey is on one-day international duty for Australia against Bangladesh. The loss of Harvey is partially balanced by the inclusion of the Gladiators' stand-in overseas player, Shoaib Malik, the Pakistani all-rounder. Gloucestershire, regarded as the nation's one-day kings, have a surprisingly poor record against Surrey as they come into this match, with the Lions having emerged triumphant in five of the last six contests between the two counties since the B&H Super Cup quarter-final in 1999. The home side could do with extending that impressive record tonight, and they make a good start when Adam Hollioake wins the toss on a lovely summer's afternoon. With conditions looking perfect for batting, he unhesitatingly elects to take first use of what appears to be a typically excellent Oval pitch.

Surrey Lions' Innings

Ian Ward and Ali Brown get Surrey away to a typically rapid start against Jon Lewis and James Averis, with the opening four overs bringing five well-struck boundaries and thirty-one runs in all.

Although the Gladiators are already missing the consistently economical Mike Smith, they do manage to claim their first wicket in the next over, with the score advanced to thirty-four, when Ward badly miscues a pull at Lewis to provide the visiting skipper, Mark Alleyne, with a pretty simple catch at mid-off.

The loss of this wicket is followed by a three-over period of calm as Mark Ramprakash settles in, Brown plays out six 'dot' balls from Lewis, and just three runs, two of them extras, are added to the total.

This does, however, turn out to be the proverbial calm before the storm, since twenty-seven runs flood from the following two overs, fourteen from over number nine, when Brown cuts, edges and pulls Lewis for boundaries that take the total past fifty, and thirteen from the tenth over, when Averis is twice lifted high over long-on for six by Surrey's master-blaster.

Predictably enough, Averis is immediately pulled out of the firing line by captain Alleyne, who takes over at the Vauxhall end and starts with a very steady over - during which Brown's under-edge brings him four fortunate runs as the ball flies away between Jack Russell's legs - while Lewis keeps going for two further overs. While the first of these Lewis overs is on the spot and costs the bowler just two runs, the second is much less successful, as each batsman retreats to leg in order to blast the ball over the off-side ring of fielders for four. Brown's boundary completes a stunning 37-ball half-century, including two sixes and eight fours, that has propelled his team to a commanding 83-1 after thirteen overs.

The next two overs then echo the ninth and tenth of the innings, as twenty-seven runs again haemorrhage from the twelve balls delivered by the Gladiators bowlers. Eleven come from Alleyne's second over as the batsmen celebrate the arrival of a fifty partnership by notching a boundary apiece, then Alex Gidman suffers a nightmare introduction into the attack, conceding sixteen runs to Brown, including a skimming drive over extra cover for six and a brace of cuts for four.

With Alleyne pushing his fielders as deep as possible, the tempo drops for the following couple of overs, and singles become the order of the day until Brown gets back on the boundary trail in the eighteenth over with an off-drive at the Gloucestershire skipper's expense. Much to the visitors' relief, this turns out to be the Surrey opener's last boundary, as the introduction of Martyn Ball in place of Gidman at the pavilion end brings about Brown's demise… though only thanks to a brilliant catch, taken one-handed above his head by a jumping Lewis at long-off.

It's a great pity that Brown has fallen sixteen short of a century, though the home crowd, building steadily in number as people finish work, are still hugely appreciative of a terrific 61-ball knock that has put the Lions in a very strong position at 130-2 in the nineteenth over.

Brown's innings has certainly set things up nicely for those expert accumulators, Ramprakash and Thorpe, to do what they do best against Ball and Shoaib Malik - the latter having just joined the attack to form an accurate off-spinning liaison - and it is therefore no surprise to see runs coming almost exclusively in singles for the next eight overs. Thirty-seven runs are, nevertheless, added to the total in that time, giving Surrey a great base of 167-2 after twenty-seven overs from which to build an imposing total.

The batsmen start to crank things up a little almost immediately, in fact, as Thorpe paddle-sweeps Alleyne - returning to the fray in place of Shoaib - for the first boundary of his innings in the following over, before Ramprakash secures the first four off Ball's bowling with an extra-cover drive that completes a fifty partnership for the third wicket, as well as his personal half-century from his sixty-eighth ball.

After two further wicketless overs, during which the batsman add another thirteen runs, Alleyne makes a double bowling change by recalling first Averis, and then Shaoib, in an attempt to split up the third-wicket pair. Although this move doesn't instantly bear fruit, as Averis is pulled to the midwicket fence by Ramprakash and sliced away over backward point for six by Thorpe two overs later, Shoaib does eventually make the breakthrough for his captain by drawing the Lions' left-hander down the track and having him stumped by Russell when the ball spins past the outside edge.

As Thorpe departs for thirty-six at 215-3 in the thirty-fifth over, Rikki Clarke comes out to the middle and the runs dry up for a couple of overs as Ball replaces Averis at the Vauxhall end to finish his spell. The 33-year-old off-spinner has his figures dented by Ramprakash's lofted on-drive for six at the start of his final over, but still returns creditable figures of 9-1-46-1 before retiring to the outfield to watch Clarke cut loose by taking eight runs from three deliveries in Shoaib's next over.

With six overs now remaining, Surrey look set for a total in the region of 280-290, though this projection soon has to be reassessed when both Ramprakash and Adam Hollioake fall in the space of three balls at the end of Alleyne's latest comeback over at Vauxhall end. Having made an excellent eighty-three from 102 balls, the former Middlesex batsman misses a pull and is bowled with the total at 242, then the Lions' captain attempts to steal a single for Clarke's dab to short third man but fails to beat Shoaib's throw to Russell.

If the Gladiators harbour any hopes that these two quick wickets might disrupt Surrey's progress towards a daunting total they are quickly dashed, as Clarke and Azhar Mahmood blast three sixes while taking twenty-eight from the next two overs from Shoaib and Alleyne. These highly productive overs take the Lions past 250 after 40.2 overs, and then on to a new record highest score for Surrey against Gloucestershire in the Sunday/National League, forcing Alleyne to recall Averis and Lewis to bowl the last three overs of the innings with the score already standing at 271-5.

It's a pretty thankless task that faces the two seamers, though they don't cope too badly. Averis' eighth over yields ten, including a swept four to Clarke before the young all-rounder is run out at the non-striker's end in attempting a second run for Azhar's straight drive; the next over from

Lewis again brings just one boundary - an upper-cut by Azhar - and also costs ten; then Averis manages to keep the home side's total below three-hundred by conceding just six runs during a good final over.

With 297 runs on the board, the Lions should be confident of victory, however, especially as the Gladiators will be batting under the lights for the second half of their innings.

Gloucestershire Gladiators' Innings

The current league leaders - albeit only on net run-rate - clearly have to take full advantage of the first fifteen overs, during which the fielding restrictions are in place, if they are to challenge Surrey's total in front of a crowd that has built to something like 7,500 on a fine August evening.

It's 'advantage Surrey' for the first three overs as only thirteen runs are posted, despite Philip Weston's off-driven four at Martin Bicknell's expense, and Craig Spearman's superb straight six off Azhar, though the picture changes dramatically during the Pakistani's second over from the Vauxhall end as Spearman demonstrates why he is such a dangerous customer. Starting the over with a pull for six over backward square leg, the former New Zealand batsman goes on to strike the next four deliveries for four - one of them off a no-ball - with three of the strokes coming in the mid-off/extra-cover arc and the fourth being a sweep from the free-hit delivery. With the bowler throwing in a wide for good measure, the over ends up costing twenty-five runs, and suddenly a required run-rate of 6.62 per over doesn't seem quite so bad.

Things then get worse for the Lions as a score of 38-0 after four overs becomes 52-0 after five, with Bicknell being cut for four by Spearman and driven over wide long-on for a six by Weston that brings up the fifty from just 4.4 overs.

James Ormond, who has, not surprisingly, been called upon to take over from Azhar, restores a little sanity to proceedings with an opening over that yields just five runs, then Bicknell follows suit, despite Weston's lofted off-drive for four. The left-handed former Worcestershire opener goes on to notch the third four of his innings with a cover drive in Ormond's next over, before top-edging a cut at Bicknell and being well taken by Jon Batty standing up to the stumps with the total on seventy in the ninth over.

This breakthrough obviously comes as some relief to the home side, though Spearman soon reminds them that Gloucestershire are very much in this game by driving the final ball of Bicknell's successful over for a 'maximum' over extra cover.

The balance of power is swinging back and forth rapidly at this early stage of the innings, and this is nicely illustrated during the next two overs. After Ormond's tight one-run over to Gidman, ten runs come from Bicknell's following over - during which Spearman strikes two further boundaries to reach a muscular fifty, including three sixes and seven fours, from a mere 33 balls - prompting Hollioake to call a halt to his senior bowler's opening spell after six overs.

By the time the new bowler, Saqlain Mushtaq, comes to deliver his first ball, another twelve runs have been added to the Gladiators' score, courtesy of cover-driven, pulled and edged fours by Gidman off Ormond, with the last of these three boundaries having brought up the visitors' hundred from exactly twelve overs. As a result, the asking rate has been reduced to exactly six runs per over for the final thirty-three overs of the contest, and we appear to have a really good game on our hands.

The Surrey captain is no doubt pinning his hopes on a tight spell from Saqlain at this point, though he certainly doesn't get a good opening over from his off-spinner, as a top-edged reverse-sweep for four by Spearman is followed by a legside wide that hurries away to the boundary rope in an over that ends up adding thirteen to the total.

Luckily for the home side, Ormond comes to the rescue again with another fine over that costs just one run and, as a very nice bonus, also brings the wicket of Gidman from the final delivery, though it comes in the form of a run out, rather than a well-deserved scalp for the bowler. The credit for the dismissal actually goes to Rikki Clarke, who throws down the stumps at the non-striker's end when Gidman pushes the ball into the backward point region but fails to respond quickly enough to Spearman's call for a slightly risky single.

With Gidman gone for fifteen at 114-2, the Lions are back in business, and it isn't long before everyone is watching a replay of the dismissal… not the one on the big screen that we have on the ground today for this televised game, but a real-life re-run, with Windows playing the role of Gidman. Just three runs have been added to the total during a tight Saqlain over when the carbon-copy run out - same shot, same fielder, same deadly direct-hit throw - sees the back of Windows for just a single and leaves everyone rubbing their eyes in disbelief.

It's now 117-3 and, with Ormond and Saqlain keeping a tighter grip on the batsmen, Surrey are fighting back impressively. They don't really need any more help from the Gladiators but they get some anyway, as Spearman again plays an important role in the run out of another unfortunate team-mate, this time Shoaib Malik, with the total having advanced to 125 after seventeen overs. Strangely enough, Ormond is again the bowler when Spearman pushes to midwicket and calls his partner for a single, only to change his mind when he sees Thorpe moving swiftly on to the ball. The Gloucestershire opener attempts to send his partner back, but he is too late, as the fielder turns and throws down the non-striker's stumps with Shoaib still short of his ground.

The needless loss of these three wickets with the visitors well ahead of the required run-rate and with plenty of overs still to bat, certainly changes the pattern of the game dramatically, since Spearman and his new partner, Tim Hancock, now have to adopt a more cautious approach against continued impressive bowling from Ormond and Saqlain. Ormond concedes just a single in each of his last two overs, in fact, to complete a fine spell of 9-0-37-0, while Saqlain has now contributed five overs for twenty-three at the other end since the nightmare of his thirteen-run opening over. As a result, the Gladiators reach the end of the twenty-third over at 149-4, exactly halfway to their target.

Hollioake now has to find a successor to Ormond at the Vauxhall end and opts for Clarke, who concedes just five, including a pulled four by Hancock, in a good first over. The Lions' captain then makes another change straight away by replacing Saqlain with Azhar, and he is no doubt delighted, though not surprised, when the Pakistani shows no ill effects from his earlier battering by turning in a fine two-run over.

A potentially decisive moment then arrives when Clarke delivers the first ball of his second over to Spearman. To be honest, it's not a great delivery - a leg-stump full-toss, in fact - but it brings about the downfall of Spearman, nevertheless, as the Kiwi flips it away behind square on the legside and is horrified to see James Benning, the substitute fielder, running in a few paces from the fence to take a good catch.

With Spearman gone for a bold 73-ball eighty-five, Surrey seize the chance to squeeze their opponents with a few more tight overs, thereby pushing the asking rate back up beyond seven, and then towards eight, runs per over. Consequently, the pressure on the batsmen increases and, eventually, the Gladiators crack again, losing yet another wicket to a run out. The victim this time is Hancock, who digs out an Azhar yorker in the direction of mid-on and sets off for a run without noticing that Mark Alleyne, at the non-striker's end, is not budging. Unlike on the previous three occasions, when the run-out verdict has been left to the third umpire, this decision is a straightforward one for umpire Gould as Ramprakash's throw to Batty sees Hancock hopelessly stranded and the visitors running - in more ways than one - into serious difficulties at 172-6 at the end of the twenty-ninth over.

Much now clearly depends on the very experienced pair of Alleyne and Jack Russell, though they now have a major task on their hands against Clarke and Azhar, who are both bowling really well. After his earlier traumas, Azhar's second spell reads 4-0-12-0, at which point he is saved for the last overs of the innings, with Hollioake coming on in his place for his first bowl of the match.

Since Clarke has conceded nine runs, including a drive to the rope at extra cover by Alleyne, in the previous over, the Surrey skipper needs to start well, and he doesn't disappoint the home fans, giving away just five runs and almost having Russell very well caught, high to the fielder's left, by Thorpe at midwicket.

Even though they still need 103 runs from twelve overs, Gloucestershire are battling hard, and their captain raises the league leaders' hopes by picking Clarke up over backward square leg for six to raise his team's two-hundred during the next over.

He and Russell can only muster four from Hollioake's excellent second over, however, and a very difficult task then becomes almost impossible for the visitors when Alleyne has his stumps rearranged by a fine Clarke yorker at the start of the thirty-sixth over.

As the Gladiators' skipper departs for a battling twenty-nine, leaving his lower order to score ninety runs from fifty-nine balls, the Lions appear to be on course to join their visitors on thirty points at the top of the NCL.

This feeling continues to grow as Gloucestershire's eighth-wicket pair scrape together just eight singles and a two from the next seventeen deliveries, sending the asking rate soaring to 11.43 per over, and we then reach a 'game over' situation during the thirty-ninth over when two more wickets fall in the space of four balls. Having carved the first ball of the over away to the fence at backward point, Russell goes to the next delivery when his crude smear to leg is defeated by Hollioake's slower ball, then Martyn Ball becomes the fifth run-out victim of the innings when Ward's brilliant pick up and throw from deep midwicket to the bowler's end sees the Gladiators' off-spinner unable to complete a second run for James Averis' legside heave.

With the opposition now 225-9, Surrey clearly want to polish off the innings quickly in order to secure the biggest possible margin of victory, thereby maximising the reduction in the net run-rate advantage that Gloucestershire currently hold over them. Luckily, they only have to wait seven balls to complete a win by sixty-six runs, as Jon Lewis follows a pulled boundary off Clarke with a horrible miscue that the Lions' second substitute fielder, Tim Murtagh, pouches safely as he runs round behind the bowler.

Clarke's third wicket completes a tremendous all-round match for him and, Gloucestershire players and supporters apart, everyone leaves The Oval in high spirits at the end of a hugely entertaining match that has boosted Surrey's hopes of claiming the NCL title.

ALI BROWN'S VIEW FROM THE DRESSING ROOM

Gloucestershire were without Ian Harvey, Jonty Rhodes and Mike Smith for this game. I guess those would be the three players who you would most like to be missing from their line-up if you were playing them in a one-day match?
AB - Yes, Ian Harvey, in particular, has been a big player for them and I think he'll be sorely missed this year. But even though they were big players to be missing, you've still got to make sure that you take full advantage of the situation, which is what we did here.

You've faced Mike Smith many times. What makes him so hard to get away?
AB - He's very consistent, he's very accurate... and he's very short! He bowls at the stumps a lot and, given the general shape he gets into a right-hander, if you get rapped on the pads the ball tends not to be going over the top of the stumps, and there's a fair chance that it's going to be out. He's been very consistent for them over the years, but I've always felt that if you can get after their front two of Smith and Harvey, then the rest of their bowlers tend to struggle a bit.

There was some electrifying fielding by Rikki Clarke in this game. Would you say that he's up there with the best fielders in world cricket.

AB - I wouldn't go that far… he's certainly our best fielder at Surrey but because we're all getting old and he's young we make him look better than he really is! I wouldn't yet have him in the top five in the world - he's not a Jonty Rhodes - but he's not far off being as good as Ben (Hollioake)… and Ben was probably the best fielder we've had at Surrey for quite some time.

There was a very good restrictive nine-over spell in the middle of their innings by James Ormond. Do you see him filling that mid-innings role on a regular basis?

AB - I think Jimmy's the sort of bowler who will bowl well wherever he bowls in the innings. He's good at the start of the innings, too, as he proved in the Twenty-20 Cup, but he'd be up to the task wherever you used him. When he's fully fit, I'd say he's our most destructive bowler in all forms of cricket.

SURREY LIONS v GLOUCESTERSHIRE GLADIATORS at The Oval

Tuesday 5th August — Surrey Lions won by 66 runs

Surrey Lions won the toss and elected to bat — Umpires:- Ian Gould & Roy Palmer

SURREY LIONS

Fall Of Wkt	Batsman	How	Out	Score	Balls	4s	6s
1-34	**I.J. Ward**	**c Alleyne**	**b Lewis**	**13**	15	2	0
2-130	**A.D. Brown**	**c Lewis**	**b Ball**	**84**	61	12	3
4-242	**M.R. Ramprakash**		**b Alleyne**	**83**	102	6	1
3-215	**G.P. Thorpe**	**st Russell**	**b Shoaib**	**36**	46	2	1
6-281	**R. Clarke**	**run**	**out**	**36**	26	2	2
5-243	**A.J. Hollioake ***	**run**	**out**	**1**	2	0	0
	Azhar Mahmood	**Not**	**Out**	**21**	13	1	1
	J.N. Batty +	**Not**	**Out**	**8**	6	0	0
	M.P. Bicknell	**did not bat**					
	Saqlain Mushtaq	**did not bat**					
	J. Ormond	**did not bat**					
	Extras	**(5lb, 10w)**		**15**			
	TOTAL	**(45 overs)**	**(for 6 wkts)**	**297**			

Bowler	O	M	R	W	NB	Wd
Lewis	**8**	**0**	**53**	**1**	-	5
Averis	**9**	**1**	**64**	**0**	-	-
Alleyne	**8**	**0**	**64**	**1**	-	3
Gidman	**2**	**0**	**20**	**0**	-	-
Ball	**9**	**1**	**46**	**1**	-	-
Shoaib Malik	**9**	**0**	**45**	**1**	-	1

GLOUCESTERSHIRE GLADIATORS

Fall Of Wkt	Batsman	How	Out	Score	Balls	4s	6s
5-156	**C.M. Spearman**	**c sub (Benning)**	**b Clarke**	**85**	73	10	3
1-70	**W.P.C. Weston**	**c Batty**	**b Bicknell**	**25**	24	3	1
2-114	**A.P.R. Gidman**	**run**	**out**	**15**	19	3	0
3-117	**M.G.N. Windows**	**run**	**out**	**1**	6	0	0
4-125	**Shoaib Malik**	**run**	**out**	**3**	5	0	0
6-172	**T.H.C. Hancock**	**run**	**out**	**22**	36	3	0
7-208	**M.W. Alleyne ***		**b Clarke**	**29**	36	1	1
8-222	**R.C. Russell +**		**b Hollioake**	**17**	20	1	0
9-225	**M.C.J. Ball**	**run**	**out**	**7**	12	0	0
	J.M.M. Averis	**Not**	**Out**	**3**	4	0	0
10-231	**J. Lewis**	**c sub (Murtagh)**	**b Clarke**	**5**	5	1	0
	Extras	**(3b, 14w, 2nb)**		**19**			
	TOTAL	**(40 overs)**		**231**			

Bowler	O	M	R	W	NB	Wd
Bicknell	**6**	**0**	**44**	**1**	-	-
Azhar Mahmood	**6**	**0**	**43**	**0**	1	2
Ormond	**9**	**0**	**37**	**0**	-	1
Saqlain Mushtaq	**6**	**0**	**36**	**0**	-	3
Clarke	**9**	**0**	**48**	**3**	-	1
Hollioake	**4**	**0**	**20**	**1**	-	1

Other NCL Division One Results

The Lions' victory saw them back level on points with Gloucestershire after the Gladiators had gone four points ahead following a very easy win over Yorkshire Phoenix at Cheltenham two days earlier. Surrey's impressive winning margin at The Oval had made quite a difference to the net run-rate of both sides, with the gap between the teams having closed from 8.12 to 3.55.

July 30
***Worcester:-* Worcestershire Royals (4pts) beat Glamorgan Dragons by 3 runs (D/L method).** Worcs 117-6 (18ov; Kasprowicz 3-23); Glamorgan 122-7 (18ov).
August 3
***Cheltenham:-* Gloucestershire Gladiators (4pts) beat Yorkshire Phoenix by 8 wickets.** Yorks 183 (41.5ov; Averis 4-50); Gloucs 184-2 (32.4ov; Spearman 93, Weston 62).
***Canterbury:-* Kent Spitfires (2pts) tied with Essex Eagles (2pts).** Kent 254-9 (45ov; Ealham 73, Jones 58); Essex 254-9 (45ov; Flower 100, Jefferson 58, Saggers 4-36).
***Leicester:-* Warwickshire Bears (4pts) beat Leicestershire Foxes by 4 wickets.** Leics 172 (45ov; Nixon 51, Waqar 4-37); Warwicks 173-6 (41.5ov; Knight 50).
August 5
***Chelmsford:-* Essex Eagles (4pts) beat Glamorgan Dragons by 143 runs.** Essex 298-5 (45ov; Hussain 161*, Flower 57, Cosker 5-54); Glamorgan 153 (26.1ov; Maynard 50, Napier 4-26).

NCL DIVISION ONE TABLE AT 5TH AUGUST

Pos	Prv		P	Pts	W	T	L	A	NRR
1	1	**Gloucestershire Gladiators**	**11**	**30**	7	0	3	1	7.31
2	2	**Surrey Lions**	**10**	**30**	7	0	2	1	3.76
3	3	**Glamorgan Dragons**	**11**	**24**	6	0	5	0	0.39
4	6	**Essex Eagles**	**11**	**22**	5	1	5	0	4.20
5	4	**Warwickshire Bears**	**9**	**20**	5	0	4	0	1.49
6	7	**Worcestershire Royals**	**9**	**16**	4	0	5	0	4.33
7	5	**Leicestershire Foxes**	**10**	**16**	4	0	6	0	-1.39
8	8	**Kent Spitfires**	**10**	**14**	3	1	6	0	-4.32
9	9	**Yorkshire Phoenix**	**9**	**8**	2	0	7	0	-14.39

15 Ramps Revels In Whitgift Week

Having maintained their lead at the top of the Frizzell Championship table with their draw at Hove, and then ended Gloucestershire's seven-match unbeaten run in the NCL to secure an advantage in that competition - level on points but with a game in hand - everything was still looking good for Surrey as the first Whitgift Festival week arrived. Every single game from now until the end of the season was going to be a big one, however, and the outcome of those matches would decide whether the Club ended the season with one, two or three trophies in their cabinet. So there was no time to relax.

It had been amply demonstrated at Hove that a single bad session or day could make the world of difference in a four-day match. Two pretty horrific sessions - the first one of the game, and the middle one on day two - had put paid to any chance of beating Sussex and, potentially, denting their confidence badly enough to put them out of contention for the title. It was interesting to note that most of the broadsheet reporters had condemned Sussex's ultra-cautious approach, and some had even suggested that Chris Adams had virtually handed the title to Surrey. A lot of Hove regulars had seemed to concur with this view, too, and had been particularly disenchanted with the decision to go off for bad light on the third afternoon. Adams' comments in the local *Argus* newspaper at the conclusion of the match had, therefore, been interesting, with his assertion that "People who criticise us for coming off on Friday don't understand the game, I'm afraid," unlikely to win him too many friends. Personally, I found it hard to agree with his views and, though he was obviously going to be 'talking-up' his own team during the interview, thought he was talking utter rubbish when he suggested that his side had "dominated Surrey for four days".

There were other reasons, apart from the fact that Sussex had appeared to be running scared at Hove, why most people felt Surrey were still hot favourites to win a fourth Championship crown in five years. The fact that the reigning champions had been there before and knew all about winning titles was not the least of them, though the run-in fixtures also looked to favour Surrey. The Championship leaders had highly winnable matches to come, against Nottinghamshire, Leicestershire and Essex, the three sides currently in the relegation zone; a tricky looking fixture against Kent at Canterbury; and a potentially hazardous game with Lancashire at Old Trafford. Sussex's run-in consisted of two matches against relegation-threatened sides, Essex and Leicestershire; a fixture with hard-to-beat Middlesex; and two games against Lancashire. On paper, you simply had to favour Surrey.

In the NCL, the situation was less clear-cut. Surrey appeared to have a more testing set of fixtures than Gloucestershire but had one extra game to play, which possibly tilted the balance in their favour. The volatile nature of one-day cricket meant that predictions could easily be made to look foolish, however, so it was probably best just to say that the top two were very unlikely to be challenged by any other team at this stage of the campaign.

We were certainly in for an exciting final five weeks of the season, whatever happened in the two leagues, and it was likely that the cliché about 'taking one match at a time' would, justifiably, be trotted out many times before the end of the summer.

The first fixture for Surrey to concentrate their minds on was the Championship encounter with Nottinghamshire, which was to be the first-ever four-day match played by the county at Whitgift School's ground in South Croydon. I think it would be both true and fair to say that many people were concerned about whether the pitch would be good enough for a game of this standard and duration, since the tracks used for NCL games in the past had occasionally been a little uneven in the bounce. Everyone therefore had their fingers crossed as the big day approached - the last thing the Club needed was a dodgy pitch that could, at best, make the game a lottery, or, at worst, bring a points deduction.

SURREY versus NOTTINGHAMSHIRE
at Whitgift School

First Day - Wednesday 13th August
Surrey 488-8

The Teams And The Toss *- Nottinghamshire, who haven't recorded a win in the Championship since the opening round of matches back in April, face a stiff task as they take on the Championship leaders at Whitgift - their last victory over Surrey in the premier domestic competition came in 1992, since when the men from London SE11 have won seven of the eight contests between the sides. They are further handicapped by the absence of Jason Gallian (broken thumb) and Bilal Shafayat (captaining England Under-19's), though they are able to field a much stronger eleven than they put out at Trent Bridge in May, with Kevin Pietersen, Russell Warren, Stuart MacGill and Chris Cairns - who captains the side in place of Gallian - all available this time around. Surrey meanwhile have to make do without the services of their two England men, Butcher and Stewart, plus James Ormond, who has a knee injury, though there is better news about Martin Bicknell and Graham Thorpe, who both pass late fitness tests and take their places in the side. Adam Hollioake wins the toss and not surprisingly elects to bat since the pitch is something of an unknown quantity.*

Whitgift's County Championship debut is blessed by glorious weather as the Surrey openers get their side away to a fine start with a rash of boundaries, mostly off the front foot, at the expense of Charlie Shreck. Jon Batty, in particular, looks in tremendous form as he takes four fours from the giant Cornishman's first two overs, but he finds life much more difficult when he gets to the other end for the first time at the start of the seventh over. After playing out a maiden from the impressive left-armer, Greg Smith, he then falls to the first delivery of the South African's next over when he fences at a lifting delivery and edges to Russell Warren at first slip.

Batty's departure for seventeen at 33-1 is then followed by the loss of Ian Ward for the same score, with the total advanced by eight, in the next over of the innings delivered by Shreck. Having just taken his third four in three overs from the Nottinghamshire paceman, courtesy of a square drive, the Surrey opener attempts to force the next ball away in the same area off the back foot but only succeeds in getting an inside edge onto his stumps.

While the game has been progressing at breakneck speed, everyone has had one eye on the pitch, and the most noticeable thing so far has been that it seems to possess good pace and carry. This almost brings about the downfall of the new batsman, Graham Thorpe, during his second over at the crease, in fact, as he top-edges a hook at Shreck and sees the ball land just about five yards in front of Darren Bicknell as the former Surrey man runs in from long leg.

Perhaps surprised by the degree of bounce the bowlers are able to extract from the surface, Thorpe continues to struggle in the early stages of his innings, though his partner, Mark Ramprakash, looks in no trouble at all as he drives Shreck to the long-on boundary to take the home side past fifty.

After one further maiden, Smith takes a well-earned breather at the end of a very fine spell of 7-4-10-1, and is replaced at the School House end of the ground by Paul Franks, who immediately strays to leg and is glanced to the rope by Ramprakash.

Shreck, meanwhile, is given another over at the Nottingham Road end and helps Thorpe get his innings properly under way by delivering a leg stump half-volley that is driven to the boundary at wide mid-on. Having conceded nine fours during an erratic eight-over spell that has cost him forty-five runs in return for the wicket of Ward, the 6' 7" paceman then retires to the outfield, allowing Chris Cairns to bring himself into the attack.

It is immediately noticeable that the Kiwi all-rounder looks distinctly medium-pace in comparison to his predecessor, though he starts with two accurate maidens as the visitors gain a measure of control for the first time since the start of play. This doesn't last for long, though, as Ramprakash picks off a boundary in each of the next two overs before being felled by a Cairns delivery that somehow evades the pad and cracks the Surrey number three on the inside of the knee.

The injured Ramprakash is treated on the pitch for some while by the physio before electing to continue his innings, though his running between the wickets makes it clear that he is in some pain. With his strokeplay seemingly also inhibited, it is just as well for Surrey that Thorpe is finally starting to flow. The Farnham-born left-hander takes four boundaries from Cairns' next three extremely innocuous overs as the third-wicket partnership extends beyond fifty and the home team's hundred arrives in the thirtieth over.

Shreck subsequently replaces his captain for another brief burst before lunch, during which Ramprakash strikes an on-drive to the boundary, while Thorpe glances Franks for four in the penultimate over of the session to move his score ahead of his partner's at the interval.

Lunch:- Surrey 118-2 (Ramprakash 31, Thorpe 32*) from 33 overs*

Cairns and Smith form Nottinghamshire's attack immediately after the break, though this pairing is soon broken up when Thorpe pulls and on-drives boundaries in the left-armer's second over to complete a century partnership for the third-wicket.

Although Stuart MacGill, Smith's replacement at the School House end, starts with a couple of decent overs, Cairns is clearly struggling to find a consistent line and length at the Nottingham Road end, and, having conceded a boundary in all but one of his five overs since the restart, gives way to his South African left-armer, who has therefore switched ends.

The final boundary off Cairns, an exquisite off-drive, had taken Ramprakash to fifty from his 107th ball, and he is soon followed to this landmark by Thorpe, who drives MacGill wide of mid-on for four to complete his half-century from 106 deliveries. With two top-class batsmen now very well set, this stand is looking rather ominous for the team that are currently propping up the Championship table, especially as the combination of their best two bowlers seems unable to provide a breakthrough.

Having been less impressive with an older ball than he was at the start of the day, Smith is again withdrawn from the fray following hooked and straight-driven fours by Thorpe, while MacGill lasts for one more over before Ramprakash batters him out of the attack with three boundaries in an over - two square-cuts and a majestic extra-cover drive that brings up the Surrey two-hundred in the fifty-first over.

Since he is running out of options, Cairns now entrusts Paul Franks and Kevin Pietersen with the ball, and, while the paceman initially looks as tidy and generally impressive as he had during his pre-lunch stint, the part-time off-spinner really doesn't seem up to the task, conceding two fours to each batsman during an utterly ineffective four-over spell. When Franks is then picked off for a boundary by both Ramprakash and Thorpe during an expensive final over of an otherwise decent burst, we suddenly have a race on our hands between the batsmen to see who will reach three figures first.

As MacGill and Shreck return to the attack, Ramprakash moves ahead by ninety-six to ninety-one with a cover-driven boundary off the leg-spinner that also completes a 200-run partnership, though Thorpe slowly closes the gap during a five-over period of uncharacteristically accurate bowling by the visitors.

Finally, however, Ramprakash drives MacGill to the rope at midwicket to complete an absolutely flawless century from 168 balls, and promptly celebrates with successive boundaries in Shreck's next over, and a glorious straight six off the Australian that, fittingly, takes the former England batsman past 1,000 first-class runs for the season. A rather disappointing - but certainly not disappointed - crowd applaud Ramprakash's achievements, and prepare themselves to offer up a similar ovation for Thorpe's century, as the left-hander is now on ninety-eight... though the consistently unreliable scoreboard says ninety-seven.

Unfortunately, they only end up applauding Thorpe as he returns to the pavilion at the conclusion of a fine knock of ninety-nine, since Cairns, replacing Shreck at the School House end, brings the Surrey southpaw to book with his fifth delivery, having conceded the batsman's ninety-ninth run from his first ball back. Frustratingly, the scoreboard is still a run behind as Thorpe attempts to cut the Kiwi away through point and gets a top edge to Chris Read behind the stumps with the total standing at 282 and the third-wicket partnership having added 241 runs.

This wicket is a blessed relief to the beleaguered visitors but, instead of building on this success during the last five overs of the session, they serve up some pretty poor fare that allows the hosts to add twenty-eight runs to their score. Rikki Clarke gets away to a flying start with an extra-cover drive to the rope off MacGill and a pulled four off Cairns, while Ramprakash takes three consecutive boundaries from the Aussie leg-spinner in the session's final over with beautiful strokes down the ground, through backward point and through extra cover.

Tea:- Surrey 310-3 (Ramprakash 130, Clarke 11*) from 72 overs*

It's Clarke, rather than Ramprakash, who leads the way for Surrey after the break as Cairns and MacGill continue in harness and feel the weight of the young all-rounder's blade. After cutting the New Zealander to the point boundary in the opening over of the session, Clarke takes fourteen from the Australian's first two post-tea overs, with a drive to the rope at extra-cover being followed by a slog-sweep for six and a paddle-sweep for four.

Although the Guildford lad adds another boundary to his collection with a square cut when he next faces MacGill, the hyped-up leg-spinner takes vengeance later in the same over when Clarke drags his back foot out of the crease in attempting a drive and falls prey to Read's smart stumping.

As the 21-year-old departs, after an entertaining knock of thirty-six, at 345-4, Nottinghamshire are probably less than thrilled to see the potentially destructive Ali Brown coming to the wicket, though a new batsman gives them more hope of achieving further success than the seemingly immovable Ramprakash at the other end.

While Brown acquaints himself with the pitch and the bowling for a few overs, the former Middlesex batsman hooks Cairns to the fine-leg boundary for the runs that take Surrey past 350, bringing to a close another pretty ordinary spell from the visiting skipper.

His replacement at the School House end is Franks, who instantly discovers that Brown is getting into his stride when he drops short outside the off stump and gets cut for four. Surrey's middle-order maestro then brings up MacGill's hundred in style with a chassé down the pitch and a straight drive for six, before taking another four in the leg-spinner's next over, courtesy of an on-drive. Sandwiched between these strokes by Brown off MacGill is a cut to the boundary by Ramprakash off Franks that takes the batsman through to 150 from 230 balls, a milestone that receives another warm ovation from the crowd as they bask in the late afternoon sunshine.

The visitors have certainly been roasted by both the sun and the home batsmen today, though they suddenly find some relief during the eighty-seventh over of the day, delivered by Franks. Just as things had been getting completely out of control for Nottinghamshire, with Brown driving MacGill for another six and upper-cutting Franks for four, the visitors' former England one-day international strikes back with successive deliveries, as both Brown and Adam Hollioake top-edge cuts through to Read. With 392-4 having therefore become 392-6, the Championship's bottom team has at least managed to pick up a second bowling point, as well as removing two very dangerous batsmen in the space of two balls.

They still need to deal with the potential menace of Azhar Mahmood, however, and that point is underlined immediately when the Pakistani all-rounder drives and cuts Franks for two fours to bring up the Surrey 400 and thereby bank the final batting point.

The new ball is now imminent, and, if Cairns is in any doubt about whether or not he should take it, his mind is probably made up by the events of the ninetieth over, during which Ramprakash drives MacGill straight down the ground for six and then watches Azhar smite the 'leggie' over mid-off for four.

Even with the new ball in their hands, Franks and the recalled Smith are unable to prevent four boundaries - two to each batsman - leaking from the next four overs, though things even out very slightly when the left-armer removes Azhar a couple of overs later, courtesy of an edged drive that Pietersen, at second slip, takes well at chest height.

It's 442-7 as the batsman makes his way back to the pavilion, and within three overs Martin Bicknell is making the same journey with the score advanced to 457-8, having contributed two fours to the Surrey total before falling caught-and-bowled to Cairns, who has replaced Franks at the School House end.

With five overs left for play, Nottinghamshire might now have hopes of dismissing their hosts before the close, but it is not to be, as Ramprakash and his new partner, Ian Salisbury, rather enjoy themselves at the expense of MacGill when the Aussie is recalled to deliver two of the day's last three overs. The visitors' leg-spinner probably wishes he had been left grazing in the outfield as he is battered for eighteen runs, including thirteen in the final over of play. While Surrey finish on a high note, with Ramprakash's drives to the long-on and extra-cover boundaries supplemented by a square-cut four from Salisbury, MacGill ends a day to forget with the gruesome figures of 26-3-146-1.

As the players leave the field, Whitgift and Ramprakash have both had a fantastic day, with the school's pitch having played almost as well as the batsman who has amassed 191 unbeaten runs - including thirty-two fours and two sixes - on it.

Close:- Surrey 488-8 (Ramprakash 191, Salisbury 13*) from 104 overs*

Second Day - Thursday 14th August
Surrey 693; Nottinghamshire 224-8

The weather is again beautiful, and the attendance is again disappointing, as Mark Ramprakash and Ian Salisbury resume their innings, with Greg Smith, the visitors' best performer on day one, and Charlie Shreck opening the bowling.

Neither man is able to provide Nottinghamshire with an early breakthrough, however, as each batsman thumps Smith to the cover boundary and total passes five-hundred. Having not put a foot wrong during his immaculate 'coaching video' display yesterday, Ramprakash looks surprisingly vulnerable during the opening half-an-hour but gets away with a couple of edges that drop short of the slips before steering his 311th delivery to third man for the single that takes him through to the ninth double-century of his career. The ovation that follows is very well deserved.

While Ramprakash has been struggling a little, Salisbury has looked to be fine form, locating the boundary rope on three occasions while adding sixteen to his overnight score, and then continuing in the same vein once Ramprakash has secured his double-ton. Pulling and driving three fours in the same number of overs, the Surrey leg-spinner sees off Smith, who has been much less impressive than he had been twenty-four hours ago, and then lays into the replacement bowler, Stuart MacGill, driving a flat six over long-on and then despatching his fellow 'leggie' through midwicket for four to complete both a personal fifty at exactly a run a ball and a century partnership for the ninth wicket.

Shreck then becomes the third bowler to complete an unwanted ton when Ramprakash drives him to the long-off boundary, before the Surrey pair become record-breakers during MacGill's following over when they overtake the existing ninth-wicket partnership record for Surrey against Nottinghamshire of 109 by Fender and Brooks at Trent Bridge in 1933.

Ramprakash then registers a new career-best first-class score for Surrey when he passes the 218 he made at Taunton in 2002, while Salisbury greets Paul Franks, replacing Shreck at the Nottingham Road end, with a square-driven boundary in the next over as both the Championship leaders' total and Cairns' problems continue to mount.

He doesn't have to wait too much longer for a desperately needed breakthrough, however, as Salisbury follows a square-cut four off Franks with an upper-cut that is well picked up, low down, by Smith at third man. As the batsman returns to the pavilion to warm applause for an entertaining knock of sixty-five in a partnership of 129, the scoreboard now reads 586-9 and the visitors must be hoping that their ordeal will soon be over.

As Saqlain Mushtaq, as good a number eleven as you could find anywhere, comes out to bat, Cairns exercises his captain's prerogative by bringing himself into the attack in place of MacGill, and very nearly brings the innings to a close on two separate occasions in his second over. Strangely enough, though, it's Ramprakash, not Saqlain, who is the fortunate batsman as, first, a top-edged hook lands safely over the rope after interesting a back-pedalling fielder at deep backward square leg for most of its journey from the bat, then an inside edge just misses leg stump on its way to the fine-leg boundary.

A single from the next delivery then takes Ramprakash's score up to 236, which not only beats his previous career-best score of 235 for Middlesex against Yorkshire at Headingley in 1995 but also sets a new record for the highest score by a Surrey batsman against Nottinghamshire… with the man whose mark he has just surpassed being none other than Darren Bicknell, whose 235 not out had been scored at Trent Bridge in 1994.

The scorers and statisticians are kept busy for another over, too, as Ramprakash's single off Franks brings up the Surrey six-hundred and also takes him past William Gunn's unbeaten 236, making this innings the highest recorded by any batsman in matches between Surrey and Nottinghamshire.

With the stats out of the way, the batsmen continue on their merry way, as Saqlain drives Franks over mid-off for four at the end of another good spell by the former England one-day international, while Ramprakash drives Cairns to the rope at extra cover an over later.

MacGill now returns at the Nottingham Road end to pair up with his skipper in the attack, though neither overseas player is able to keep the batsmen quiet, let alone polish off the innings. Saqlain takes a boundary off paceman and leg-spinner alike, before Ramprakash completes his maiden 250 from his 372nd ball with a straight six off MacGill that increases his boundary count to four sixes and thirty-seven fours.

When the fifty partnership comes up shortly afterwards, Cairns gives way to Smith and sees his premier opening bowler edged, slogged and slashed by Saqlain for a four and two sixes in the space of two overs, with the second six creating yet another record. Having now added eighty-eight for the tenth-wicket, Ramprakash and Saqlain replace Bryson and Boiling as the holders of the highest partnership for this wicket by either side in matches between Surrey and Nottinghamshire.

The new record is soon extending past the hundred mark when Ramprakash profits by four from a Chinese-cut off the returning Shreck - MacGill having been replaced in the attack with his runs-conceded tally standing at 196 - and Saqlain lifts Smith over extra cover for four, but, with the off-spinner having just completed his third successive Championship fifty from 54 balls, and the record total for Surrey against Nottinghamshire (706-4dec) in sight, the visitors' suffering is finally brought to an end. Saqlain is the man dismissed, with lunch imminent and the total on 693, when he flicks at a legside delivery from Smith and is very well caught by wicketkeeper Read tumbling away to his left behind the stumps. It must be admitted that this slightly fortunate 'strangle' is owed to the visitors, since they have had no luck at all while Surrey have been piling on the runs this morning.

Nottinghamshire now have an almighty fight on their hands when they come out to bat after the break, since they need the small matter of 544 runs to avoid the follow-on. That is due principally, of course, to Mark Ramprakash, who receives a thoroughly well deserved standing ovation for his magnificent unbeaten 279 as he leads the players off the field. Whitgift's debut County Championship match has witnessed a phenomenal innings, spanning exactly four-hundred balls and including forty fours and four sixes, that will be remembered forever by everyone who has been lucky enough to see it. And it has certainly laid to rest those fears about the quality of the pitch!

Lunch:- Between Innings

The visitors must be feeling pretty weary after four extremely hard sessions in the field in very warm weather, though their top-order batsmen are soon able to go and put their feet up as Martin Bicknell strikes three early blows.

Guy Welton is the first to go, for a six-ball duck, at the start of the third over, when he plays back to the Surrey swing king and edges to Graham Thorpe at third slip, then Usman Afzaal - restored to the Notts side after being omitted from the last four matches - departs in Bicknell's next over, with just eleven runs on the board. Having found the extra-cover boundary with a beautifully timed forward push from the third ball of the over, the former England left-hander then offers a limp bat to the next delivery and sees the resultant outside edge very well snapped up by Azhar Mahmood low to his right at second slip.

At the other end, Darren Bicknell has had problems of his own in between watching the dismissals of his colleagues, with Azhar inducing both an inside edge past leg stump in the fourth over and an outside edge that drops just short of fourth slip two overs later. It is beginning to look as if it might be his lucky day, in fact, when he gloves a pull at his brother in the next over and sees the ball spin up in the air before bouncing over the stumps, though he appears convinced that his luck has run out when he is struck on the back pad by Martin's next delivery and is adjudged lbw by umpire Vanburn Holder. As the former Surrey opener departs for a very scratchy fourteen, Nottinghamshire are in desperate trouble at 20-3.

The fourth-wicket pair of Russell Warren and Kevin Pietersen approach the enormous task that now lies ahead of them in very different ways. While Warren scores just two runs during his first eleven overs at the crease, Pietersen quickly takes advantage of the home side's ultra-attacking fields to pull and drive four boundaries in reaching twenty within seven overs of arriving in the middle.

The first major goal that these two achieve is seeing off Bicknell, after a top-class spell of 9-3-20-3, and Azhar, whose impressive eight-over burst has gone unrewarded, and it seems possible that Surrey's lack of a specialist third seamer could now count against them… though they are clearly going to be well buffered by the enormous total they have put on the board.

As it happens, Saqlain Mushtaq and Rikki Clarke, the new bowlers at the School House end and the Nottingham Road end respectively, both make decent starts, with Saqlain the more economical of the two, and Clarke the more dangerous of the pair, as he induces a couple of outside edges and a top-edged hook from Pietersen that soars away over Jon Batty's head for six to give a further indication of the pace and carry in this pitch.

Two further Pietersen boundaries, in the twenty-third and twenty-fourth overs, then complete a fifty partnership for the fourth-wicket, and, though Warren's share is just nine, his contribution in terms of crease occupation is proving vital.

Although the former Northamptonshire batsman finally manages to notch the second boundary of his innings four overs later, with a sliced drive backward of point off Saqlain, he still doesn't look especially comfortable and appears to be missed by Batty from a top-edged cut at Saqlain with his score on eighteen as tea approaches. Since Pietersen has survived a caught-and-bowled chance to Clarke in the previous over, before pulling and deflecting fours to complete an impressive 64-ball fifty and take his side's total into three figures, it seems that the visitors are now definitely receiving a fairer share of the luck.

The Nottinghamshire pair even go to tea with a flourish after Ian Salisbury joins up with Saqlain in the attack. Warren is responsible for initiating this late spurt by driving Saqlain away to the rope wide of mid-on, then Pietersen continues it with a straight-driven four in Salisbury's opening over, followed by a 4-4-6 sequence of sweeps and slog-sweeps off Saqlain that take the partnership beyond the century mark in the penultimate over the session.

Tea:- Nottinghamshire 129-3 (Warren 26, Pietersen 75*) from 35 overs*

Saqlain and Pietersen go head-to-head again immediately after tea, with the Surrey off-spinner winning the war after losing the earlier battles. The young South African looks, initially, like he might continue to hold sway as he sweeps the session's first ball for another four, but the canny Saqlain tempts him into repeating the shot two balls later against a delivery that is not quite there for the stroke, with disastrous consequences for the batsman and his team - the ball sails skywards off the top edge, allowing Clarke to run round behind the wicketkeeper from his position at short fine leg and pouch a comfortable catch. This is clearly a huge blow for a team that is already struggling badly, and they are now in desperate need of another substantial partnership.

With Salisbury again joining his spin twin in the attack, Warren and the new batsman, Chris Cairns, are faced with a tricky dilemma - they aren't in a position to take too many chances, yet they know that it would be fatal to let the spinners dominate. These two experienced batsmen handle the situation well, though, as Warren adopts a more aggressive approach in whipping Saqlain away to the rope at midwicket and then twice sweeping Salisbury for four, while Cairns relies on his renowned ability to hit straight down the ground, picking up three boundaries in this way, before adding another four runs to the total with a more subtle leg-glance.

With the partnership closing in on fifty, Hollioake replaces Salisbury with Bicknell at the Nottingham Road end, and, though Warren immediately drives the Surrey seamer to the cover boundary, the switch turns out to be a very good one for the Championship leaders. Having just reached a painstaking yet valuable fifty from his 144th ball with a single off Saqlain, Warren can only watch helplessly from the other end as another two of his colleagues are blown away by Bicknell in the space of two fine overs.

Cairns is the first man to depart, with his score on twenty-six and the total standing at 186, when his rather indeterminate back-foot stroke is defeated by a ball that appears to nip back at him, then Chris Read falls to his eighth ball when he flashes indiscriminately at a delivery wide of off stump and sees his edge well taken by Batty to his right-hand side at chest height.

With the loss of these two important wickets, there is clearly no prospect at all of Nottinghamshire averting the follow-on, especially as Bicknell is following yesterday's batting masterclass from Ramprakash with a masterclass in fast-medium swing bowling, and Salisbury, having been moved to the School House end in place of Saqlain, is instantly causing problems for Paul Franks, the new man at the crease.

Warren continues to battle on bravely, however, finding the rope with another sweep off the leg-spinner to steer his side past the two-hundred mark and then, to everyone's surprise, taking ten - including two lovely back-foot boundaries - from what turns out to be the last over of Bicknell's fairly brief but very significant spell.

Azhar returns in Bicknell's place and looks set to bowl through to the close with Salisbury, until the former England 'leggie' ends Warren's brave knock of seventy-six in the day's penultimate over with a googly that traps the former Northamptonshire batsman on the crease and wins an lbw verdict from umpire Nigel Llong.

Eight balls now remain to be bowled today, and, after Greg Smith has blocked out Salisbury's last two balls, Hollioake pulls a rabbit out of the hat by replacing Azhar with Saqlain for the day's final over. It looks to be a good move, since the man on strike, Franks, has looked much more comfortable against seam than he has against spin, and it takes Saqlain just two deliveries to vindicate his skipper's decision by having the left-hander taken by Thorpe at slip from an edged defensive push at an off-break.

With the visitors' innings having been steadily dismantled by some very good bowling, especially by Bicknell, who finishes the day with figures of 15-3-42-5, Surrey are already on course for victory.

Close:- Nottinghamshire 224-8 (Smith 0) from 66.2 overs*

Third Day - Friday 15th August

Surrey 693; Nottinghamshire 240 and 242
Surrey won by an innings and 211 runs
Surrey 22pts, Nottinghamshire 4

The third day of the match gets away to a lively start when Stuart MacGill slog-sweeps the second ball from Saqlain for six, though, sadly for Nottinghamshire, it's all downhill for them from this point onwards.

Their first innings is certainly polished off in double-quick time by the Surrey spinners, as Greg Smith skies a drive off Saqlain to Rikki Clarke at deep mid-on in the morning's fourth full over, then MacGill charges recklessly down the pitch to the final ball of the next over from Ian Salisbury and is virtually shaking hands with the bowler as Jon Batty completes a simple stumping. Without taking anything away from the Surrey bowlers, the visitors have performed pretty dismally to be dismissed for 240 on what is still a very good pitch, and no-one could argue that only Pietersen and Warren have performed to an acceptable standard.

Since Nottinghamshire are promptly invited to follow on, the batsmen do at least have an early chance to redeem themselves... or not, as the case may be.

Having recorded scores of nought and four in the match against Surrey at Trent Bridge in May, poor Guy Welton completes a pair in this game when he pushes at the first delivery of the second over, bowled by Azhar Mahmood, and edges straight to Clarke at second slip. As he wanders back to the pavilion, past a scoreboard reading 0-1, with a golden duck to his name, he must be reflecting that cricket can be a very cruel game at times.

After showing Welton no mercy, Surrey are soon spoiling Usman Afzaal's day, too, as the former England left-hander reprises his first-innings performance by getting off the mark with a lovely off-side boundary and then falling to Martin Bicknell almost immediately afterwards. Although the four comes off Azhar this time, and the mode of dismissal is lbw rather than caught, it all adds up to further disappointment for Afzaal and his team as he departs, for five on this occasion, at 6-2.

Having got well used to this pitch during his first knock, Russell Warren starts very positively second time around, on-driving and cutting fours in Azhar's second over, though he is soon back in the familiar position of watching a team-mate depart at the other end. This time it's Darren Bicknell, who is clearly surprised by a short delivery in Azhar's next over and fends the ball off to short leg where the young substitute fielder, Sam Woodward, takes the simplest of catches. A desperately disappointed Darren drags himself off the field with just three to his name and his team in all sorts of strife at 18-3, still a massive 435 runs in arrears.

You have to feel sympathy for Warren, though he now appears to adopt an "If you can't beat 'em, join 'em… back in the pavilion" attitude when he flails at a delivery wide of off stump later in the same Azhar over and falls to a very fine catch by Batty diving away in front of first slip. We are almost back to the days of Twenty-20 again as Azhar finishes the over with figures of 3-0-17-3, though very few teams in that competition were ever in as much trouble as Nottinghamshire are here, at 19-4.

Kevin Pietersen and Chris Cairns now face a pretty hopeless task, confronted as they are by two fine bowlers putting the ball in testing areas and beating the bat time after time. Pietersen does manage to find the cover boundary with a drive off Bicknell, and then picks up three for an on-drive at Azhar's expense, but Cairns only thrives for a short while before becoming a fourth victim for the Pakistani all-rounder in the tenth over of the innings. Having picked up two fours through point earlier in the over, the Nottinghamshire skipper sees his defensive push at Azhar end in a very good catch, low to his left, by his opposite number at fourth slip. It's hard to believe, but the visitors are 35-5 and hurtling towards a crushing defeat with lunch still nearly an hour away.

Surrey are obviously cock-a-hoop at this point… and things get even better for them three overs later when Pietersen falls to the deserving Bicknell with his score on sixteen and the total standing at forty-five. Having pulled the first delivery of Bicknell's seventh over to the midwicket boundary, the tall South African looks to attack the next delivery as well, but his seemingly premeditated advance down the pitch only results in a mistimed drive to Clarke at extra-cover.

As Paul Franks joins Chris Read in the middle, Notts are staring into the abyss and facing one of the biggest defeats in their history, unless the lower-order can offer much sterner resistance than they had in the first innings. Read does at least take his side past fifty with a pleasant extra-cover drive off Bicknell, who retires to the outfield at the end of the over with figures of 8-2-19-2 that really don't do justice to an outstanding spell. Azhar then follows his new-ball partner out of the attack shortly afterwards when Read drives and pulls fours that slightly spoil the Surrey all-rounder's excellent opening-spell return of 9-1-45-4, though it's clearly the wickets that count in this situation, not the runs conceded.

Although Bicknell's replacement at the Nottingham Road end, Rikki Clarke, is a little unlucky when Read, on twenty-two, escapes a very tough chance to Woodward at short leg, neither he nor the other new bowler, Saqlain, can create the same kind of pressure as their predecessors, and, consequently, both Nottinghamshire batsmen find the going a little easier in the lead-up to lunch. With Read, the dominant partner in the seventh-wicket alliance, taking two fours from Clarke's fourth over, the score begins to develop just the slightest hint of respectability, and the stand reaches fifty when Franks takes a single off Saqlain in the penultimate over of the session.

Lunch:- Nottinghamshire 96-6 (Read 34, Franks 10*) from 25 overs*

Having delivered the last over before lunch, Adam Hollioake retains himself in the attack at the Nottingham Road end upon the resumption, with Saqlain continuing to occupy the School House end.

One thing that has changed since lunch, however, is the approach of Franks. Having taken thirteen overs to score ten before the break, he looks a different player in the first four overs after returning to the field as he cuts, drives, edges and pulls fours that suggest we might be about to witness a do-or-die effort from the tall left-hander.

Unfortunately for the visitors, it turns out to be the latter, as he adds just a single to his score before Hollioake goes round the wicket and penetrates a loose drive with a delivery that knocks back the middle stump. With their feeble-looking tail of Smith, MacGill and Shreck to follow, the writing now looks well and truly on the wall as Franks returns to the pavilion with twenty-seven to his name and Nottinghamshire reeling at 129-7.

Read consequently ups the tempo of his innings as soon as he reaches a game fifty, from 74 balls, two overs after Franks' departure. At this point, Salisbury replaces a slightly disappointing Saqlain in the attack, though it is Hollioake who Read initially targets for punishment, taking three fours from successive balls at the end of the Surrey skipper's sixth over, before adding another from the first ball of his seventh. With three of the boundaries coming from pulls it's clear that Hollioake is trying to 'buy' the England one-day international keeper's wicket. He doesn't succeed, however, so the home captain reverts to an all-spin attack, with Saqlain now appearing at the Nottingham Road end.

With neither spinner seemingly on top form, both Read and Smith are able to pick off the occasional boundary, and before long they have a fifty stand to celebrate. Smith, in particular, gains noticeably in confidence the longer he sticks around and, as his partner moves into the nineties, the South African drives Saqlain down the ground for three fours, taking the total past two-hundred in the process.

There is a surprisingly end-of-term feel to the cricket at this stage, with Saqlain wearing his headband vertically, rather than horizontally (i.e. over the top of his head and under his chin) and it appears as if everyone has accepted the inevitable Surrey win and doesn't really want the game to end just yet. Smith is happy enough with this, since it enables him to both raise a century partnership for the eighth wicket and also equal his highest first-class score for his adopted English county.

The party is soon over, however, as Salisbury sparks a final Nottinghamshire slump by denying Read a century, while Saqlain dashes Smith's hopes of setting a new career-best mark. In both cases the bowler's cunning - a change of angle in the first instance, and the subtle movement of a fielder in the second - brings about the batsman's downfall.

Read is on ninety-three when he attempts to sweep the leg-spinner, who has switched to bowling round the wicket, but is cramped for room as the ball spins back at him and only succeeds in gloving a catch to Azhar at slip with the total on 233 and the eighth-wicket partnership having added 104.

By the time he has got his pads off, after receiving a good ovation from the crowd for a gutsy knock, Stuart MacGill has got off the mark with a slog-sweep for six for the second time in the day - though this time off Salisbury - and Smith has driven a flat catch to Ali Brown, who has only just been pushed deeper at mid-off by Saqlain.

With MacGill and Shreck now together it's just a case of which spinner takes the final wicket, and it turns out to be Saqlain when MacGill miscues a drive high to Brown in that deep mid-off position again with Nottinghamshire's second-innings effort having surpassed their first by just two runs.

The jubilant Surrey players therefore leave the field victorious by an innings and 211 runs, with just over four sessions of play to spare. There will doubtless be tougher tasks ahead if the

Championship title is to be retained, though this 22-point win will do nicely for the moment, as it puts increased pressure on Sussex and Lancashire, who are currently engaged in a battle at Hove that is due to end on Sunday. Anything but a Sussex win would do very nicely for the reigning champions.

Surrey 693; Nottinghamshire 240 and 242
Surrey won by an innings and 211 runs. Surrey 22pts, Nottinghamshire 4

TALKING POINTS - MARK RAMPRAKASH

On the Internet radio coverage, Mark Church and I described your innings - on the first day, at least - as a batting masterclass, in terms of how to build an innings. Would you say it was one of your best knocks in terms of technical perfection and absence of errors?
MR - Yes, I was really pleased with the way I played in this innings. It was certainly my most fluent innings of the year, maybe along with the second innings at Edgbaston. I was really happy with my judgement - what to leave, what to attack - and I'd definitely rate it as my best innings of the season.

Chris Read is clearly a good keeper-batsman, as we saw during this game, but Jon Batty seems very unlucky to have been ignored for the England job. I've always felt that wicket-keepers, like spin bowlers, don't reach their peak until their late twenties or early thirties, yet it seems to me that England are only really looking at those keepers who are under twenty-five. Do you think it's his age that is counting against 'JB', or something else?
MR - I think Jon Batty is very unlucky, and I would certainly hope that the England team isn't being selected on age, because that's nonsense - it should always be picked on merit. I think it should carry a lot of weight that he has averaged over fifty while opening the batting in Division One. I certainly think he's got as good a batting technique as any of the other keepers, his figures stand out head-and-shoulders above everybody else's, and he's scored good runs, especially the innings at Old Trafford, which I thought was a very fine knock. In this match, I think Read played some nice shots, but, in terms of building and playing an innings at the highest level, I don't think he's found his game yet. I think Jon, on the other hand, has found his game, he's shown maturity in his batting - he can bat time; he can play against good bowling; and he can be patient when he has to, and then hit the bad ball when it comes along. I think Chris Read is a very good cricketer and obviously has a lot of potential - he has all the shots to work with, but it's all about putting it together in an innings.

TALKING POINTS - MARTIN BICKNELL

There was much speculation before this game about whether the pitch would be good enough. As it turned out, from the boundary, it looked to be one of the best cricket wickets of the season, with plenty of pace and bounce in it. What did you think of the surface?
MB - We all shared that feeling and felt it might be turning square by the end of the first day. But it didn't, and we were really surprised by the pace of the pitch. The ball went through really well and it was one of the quickest pitches we'd played on for a long long time - it was a bit like Trent Bridge in that regard.

You got Darren out again, though he didn't look very impressed with the umpire's decision. It seemed to hit him on the back pad, but might he have had a reason to feel aggrieved in terms of height or an inside edge?
MB - I thought it was stone dead! And I saw the replay afterwards, and it still looked out to me!

SURREY v NOTTINGHAMSHIRE at Whitgift School 13th to 15th August

Surrey won the toss and elected to bat — Umpires:- Vanburn Holder and Nigel Llong

SURREY - First Innings

Fall Of Wkt	Batsman	How	Out	Score	Balls	4s	6s
2-41	**I.J. Ward**		**b Shreck**	**17**	31	4	0
1-33	**J.N. Batty +**	**c Warren**	**b Smith**	**17**	24	4	0
	M.R. Ramprakash	**Not**	**Out**	**279**	400	40	4
3-282	**G.P. Thorpe**	**c Read**	**b Cairns**	**99**	162	17	0
4-345	**R. Clarke**	**st Read**	**b MacGill**	**36**	38	6	1
5-392	**A.D. Brown**	**c Read**	**b Franks**	**32**	35	3	2
6-392	**A.J. Hollioake ***	**c Read**	**b Franks**	**0**	1	0	0
7-442	**Azhar Mahmood**	**c Pietersen**	**b Smith**	**25**	30	6	0
8-457	**M.P. Bicknell**	**c &**	**b Cairns**	**9**	13	2	0
9-586	**I.D.K. Salisbury**	**c Smith**	**b Franks**	**65**	66	11	1
10-693	**Saqlain Mushtaq**	**c Read**	**b Smith**	**50**	57	6	2
	Extras	**(16b, 13lb, 5w, 30nb)**		**64**			
	TOTAL	**(140.3 overs)**		**693**			

Bowler	O	M	R	W	NB	Wd
Smith	**27.3**	**7**	**110**	**3**	3	-
Shreck	**25**	**4**	**112**	**1**	5	3
Franks	**22**	**2**	**91**	**3**	-	-
Cairns	**27**	**3**	**133**	**2**	7	2
MacGill	**35**	**3**	**196**	**1**	-	-
Pietersen	**4**	**0**	**22**	**0**	-	-

NOTTINGHAMSHIRE - First Innings (Needing 544 to avoid the follow-on)

Fall Of Wkt	Batsman	How	Out	Score	Balls	4s	6s
3-20	**D.J. Bicknell**	**lbw**	**b Bicknell**	**14**	27	2	0
1-1	**G.E. Welton**	**c Thorpe**	**b Bicknell**	**0**	6	0	0
2-11	**U. Afzaal**	**c Azhar**	**b Bicknell**	**4**	9	1	0
7-224	**R.J. Warren**	**lbw**	**b Salisbury**	**76**	189	11	0
4-133	**K.P. Pietersen**	**c Clarke**	**b Saqlain**	**79**	80	13	2
5-186	**C.L. Cairns ***		**b Bicknell**	**26**	49	4	0
6-196	**C.M.W. Read +**	**c Batty**	**b Bicknell**	**4**	8	1	0
8-224	**P.J. Franks**	**c Thorpe**	**b Saqlain**	**8**	30	1	0
9-237	**G.J. Smith**	**c Clarke**	**b Saqlain**	**6**	16	1	0
10-240	**S.C.G. MacGill**	**st Batty**	**b Salisbury**	**9**	15	0	1
	C.E. Shreck	**Not**	**Out**	**0**	5	0	0
	Extras	**(5b, 5lb, 4nb)**		**14**			
	TOTAL	**(72 overs)**		**240**			

Bowler	O	M	R	W	NB	Wd
Bicknell	**15**	**3**	**42**	**5**	1	-
Azhar Mahmood	**11**	**3**	**32**	**0**	-	-
Saqlain Mushtaq	**21**	**4**	**80**	**3**	1	-
Clarke	**7**	**0**	**32**	**0**	-	-
Salisbury	**18**	**6**	**44**	**2**	-	-

NOTTINGHAMSHIRE - Second Innings (Following on, 453 runs in arrears)

Fall Of Wkt	Batsman	How	Out	Score	Balls	4s	6s
3-18	**D.J. Bicknell**	**c sub (Woodward)**	**b Azhar**	**3**	17	0	0
1-0	**G.E. Welton**	**c Clarke**	**b Azhar**	**0**	1	0	0
2-6	**U. Afzaal**	**lbw**	**b Bicknell**	**5**	6	1	0
4-19	**R.J. Warren**	**c Batty**	**b Azhar**	**9**	9	2	0
6-45	**K.P. Pietersen**	**c Clarke**	**b Bicknell**	**16**	23	3	0
5-35	**C.L. Cairns ***	**c Hollioake**	**b Azhar**	**9**	11	2	0
8-233	**C.M.W. Read +**	**c Azhar**	**b Salisbury**	**93**	111	17	0
7-129	**P.J. Franks**		**b Hollioake**	**27**	54	5	0
9-239	**G.J. Smith**	**c Brown**	**b Saqlain**	**42**	78	8	0
10-242	**S.C.G. MacGill**	**c Brown**	**b Saqlain**	**7**	11	0	1
	C.E. Shreck	**Not**	**Out**	**2**	11	0	0
	Extras	**(16b, 8lb, 1w, 4nb)**		**29**			
	TOTAL	**(55 overs)**		**242**			

Bowler	O	M	R	W	NB	Wd
Bicknell	8	2	19	2	-	-
Azhar Mahmood	9	1	45	4	1	1
Clarke	4	0	22	0	-	-
Saqlain Mushtaq	15	1	49	2	1	-
Hollioake	8	0	41	1	-	-
Salisbury	11	2	42	1	-	-

Other Frizzell Championship Division One Results

Sussex's surprising victory over Lancashire, by the crushing margin of 252 runs, achieved late on the final day with just twelve minutes remaining until 'stumps', enabled them to stay hot on Surrey's heels and, effectively, reduced the title race to a straight contest between the top two teams.

August 13-16
***Lord's:-* Kent (22pts) beat Middlesex (7) by 8 wickets.** Middx 407 (Nash 113, Cook 65, Koenig 57, Muralitharan 5-103) & 165 (Weekes 51, Muralitharan 4-38); Kent 477 (Fulton 86, Khan 78, Symonds 71, Ealham 58) & 96-2.

August 14-17
***Hove:-* Sussex (21pts) beat Lancashire (7) by 252 runs.** Sussex 385 (Adams 140, Montgomerie 72, Mushtaq 60) & 383-7dec (Adams 190, Montgomerie 70); Lancs 377 (Law 96, Chilton 65, Chapple 54, Mushtaq 6-124) & 139 (Mushtaq 5-49, Taylor 4-42).

***Edgbaston:-* Warwickshire (19pts) beat Leicestershire (5.5*) by 8 wickets.** Leics 346 (Hodge 70, Sadler 59*, Maddy 51) & 195 (Wagh 4-20, Waqar 4-37); Warwicks 277 (Waqar 61, Brown 56*) & 267-2 (Knight 122*, Wagh 58, Troughton 55*). *** Leicestershire deducted 0.5pt for their slow over-rate.**

FRIZZELL CHAMPIONSHIP DIVISION ONE TABLE AT 17TH AUGUST

Pos	Prv		P	Points	W	D	L	T	Bat	Bwl	Ded
1	1	**Surrey**	12	**192.00**	6	6	0	0	52	32	0.00
2	2	**Sussex**	12	**187.00**	7	2	3	0	45	36	0.00
3	3	**Lancashire**	11	**146.00**	3	7	1	0	45	31	0.00
4	4	**Middlesex**	12	**137.00**	3	8	1	0	32	31	0.00
5	5	**Kent**	12	**133.00**	3	5	4	0	36	35	0.00
6	7	**Warwickshire**	12	**122.50**	2	6	3	1	36	29	1.50
7	6	**Essex**	12	**104.00**	1	7	3	1	22	33	0.00
8	8	**Leicestershire**	12	**87.50**	0	7	5	0	29	31	0.50
9	9	**Nottinghamshire**	11	**84.00**	1	4	6	0	24	31	1.00

NATIONAL CRICKET LEAGUE DIVISION ONE - MATCH ELEVEN

Surrey Lions versus Glamorgan Dragons at Whitgift School

Sunday 17th August

Setting The Scene - Having lost three of their last four games in the competition, the Glamorgan Dragons come to Whitgift knowing that they simply have to win to retain any hope at all of retaining their NCL title. It's a tough task for them, especially as Surrey are able to field what would appear to be their full-strength side - the same eleven that had beaten the Gloucestershire Gladiators. The visitors are without long-term injury victims, Steve James and Darren Thomas, but otherwise appear to have their best possible team at their disposal. Adam Hollioake wins the toss for the Lions and opts to take first use of the Whitgift wicket.

Surrey Lions' Innings

In fine conditions for batting, the Lions' start is stunted by the excellent Michael Kasprowicz, who concedes just three runs from his opening three overs from the School House end as the total struggles up to 15-0 after the first five overs. It's only thanks to a couple of slightly loose deliveries from Andrew Davies at the Nottingham Road end that the score has got this far, in fact, though the Neath-born seamer turns out to be the man who draws first blood for the Welshmen when Ali Brown chops the last ball of the sixth over down onto his stumps, having despatched the previous delivery to the rope at backward point. With Brown gone for fourteen, Surrey are 23-1.

Although Ian Ward then puts the first real dents in Kasprowicz's bowling analysis by pulling and cover-driving fours in the big Aussie's fourth over, the next twelve balls of the innings bring just five runs, four of those from an edge by Mark Ramprakash off Kasprowicz that drops short of a diving slip fielder and races away to the boundary. A score of 36-1 from the first nine overs is clearly below par for this ground, though each batsman manages to locate the rope at extra-cover as ten runs are gathered in from overs ten and eleven.

At this point, the Dragons start to lose their grip on proceedings, as Kasprowicz is withdrawn from the attack after a fine spell of 6-2-20-0, and the hitherto steady Davies finds Ward taking two fours from his sixth over and Ramprakash plundering two more from his seventh, to boost the score to 70-1 after fourteen overs. In between these two expensive Davies overs that bring the 26-year-old's spell to a halt at 7-0-44-1, Alex Wharf has found his first delivery of the match being pulled to the fine-leg boundary by Ramprakash, though the former Yorkshire and Nottinghamshire bowler comes back really well to deliver a second-over maiden to Ward.

With the new bowler at the Nottingham Road end, Adrian Dale, yielding just a single from the sixteenth over, it looks as if the league leaders have hit another sticky patch, though they snap out of it with a boundary in each of the next two overs, as Ramprakash glances Wharf to fine leg and Ward drives Dale over long-on for a towering six.

You have to give the Glamorgan seamers credit, though, as they bounce back again, taking the wicket of Ward - who inside-edges a drive at Dale into his stumps after making forty-four out of a total of ninety-three - in the midst of a series of six tight overs that produce just nineteen runs for the Lions, seventeen of them in singles.

Since Ramprakash knows the pitch intimately after his knock in the Championship, and Thorpe is gradually becoming more established, it would seem that containment won't be enough for the Dragons, and there are signs that Wharf might be about to suffer a backlash from the batsmen as each of them takes a boundary from his nine-run seventh over.

Reading the signs well, Robert Croft, the Glamorgan skipper, switches immediately to an all-spin attack, with Dean Cosker taking the Nottingham Road end and delivering a very respectable opening over that costs just three runs. Croft's appearance at the School House end isn't quite as successful, however, as Ramprakash cuts the off-spinner for four runs backward of point to complete a good half-century in the surprisingly quick time of 57 balls.

With the scoreboard now reading 123-2 after twenty-seven overs, the batsmen show that they are aware of the need for further acceleration as Thorpe drives the first ball of Cosker's second over for six over long-on and Ramprakash then follows suit by sweeping the first ball of Croft's second over out of the ground at square leg. These two overs not only see nineteen runs added to the Surrey score, but also include the first misfield of what has been an outstanding fielding display to date, a quite remarkable effort on a ground with a rather undulating outfield.

With the batsmen now well set and in six-hitting mood, two more 'maximums' follow in the course of the next three overs, as Ramprakash drives Cosker high over long-off and Thorpe lifts the same bowler over wide long-on. These strokes, along with a late-cut four by Ramprakash off Croft, see the score rushing up to 168-2 at the end of the thirty-second over, and clearly convince the Dragons' captain that this is not a ground for spin bowlers, since he immediately reverts to seam bowling at both ends.

The reintroduction of Kasprowicz at the School House end is clearly an attempt to break up an increasingly dangerous partnership but the experienced Surrey pair are wise to this and, apart from a clip for four over midwicket by Ramprakash, content themselves with picking up singles from the Queenslander's seventh and eight overs.

At this stage, with Dale's return at the other end having yielded just eight runs from two overs, Croft has to decide whether he continues to attack with Kasprowicz or save his strike bowler's last over until the end of the innings. With the score now 188-2 after thirty-six overs and his need for a breakthrough increasingly desperate, he probably takes the best option by asking the Australian to complete his spell, though the gamble doesn't pay off as Ramprakash picks the first ball of Kasprowicz's final over up over wide mid-on for six runs to complete a century partnership with Thorpe from just 97 deliveries and move his personal tally on to ninety-five. The last five balls of the over are then safely negotiated for the addition of four runs - three of which take Ramprakash up to ninety-eight - and, as Kasprowicz retires to the outfield with very good final figures on this fast-scoring ground of 9-2-42-0, the Lions are now well placed to run amok during the last eight overs of their innings.

Having got through seven overs for thirty-one runs so far, Dale suddenly finds the going much tougher - Thorpe drives the first two balls of the medium-pacer's eighth over to the boundary as Surrey's score sails past the two-hundred barrier, before Ramprakash secures singles to long-off and fine-leg that complete an excellent century from just 91 deliveries. As the crowd rises to him he must almost be wishing that he could play at Whitgift every week.

The Surrey number three's aggregate for the week has risen to an amazing 380 runs before he is finally dismissed by the most unlikely of bowlers, Jimmy Maher, who has been brought on, almost in desperation, to bowl a few overs of his very occasional medium-pace seamers. It's a top-edged sweep to Davies at short fine leg that finally unseats Ramprakash with the total on 213 in the thirty-ninth over, though the jubilant Australian soon discovers that bowling has a down side, too, when Thorpe, having just completed his half-century from 56 balls, drives him away to the rope at extra-cover before the over is out.

With Azhar Mahmood having been sensibly promoted up the order, Dale's final over turns out to be even more expensive than his eighth over, as the Pakistani all-rounder drives wide of mid-on for four and then launches the next ball for a straight six, before handing over to Thorpe, who picks off a boundary to midwicket at the end of a sixteen-run over.

At 235-3 after forty overs, the Lions are now set to post a massive total, though Azhar is unable to inflict any more pain on the Dragons as he provides Maher with a second wicket by miscuing a legside hit high to Croft at cover. The rest of the over yields an acceptable nine runs, including a square-cut boundary to Thorpe, though the forty-second over turns out to be a good one for Glamorgan as the recalled Davies restricts the Surrey left-hander and his new partner, Adam Hollioake, to six singles.

It's obvious that the Lions' captain won't be happy to settle for singles in the last three overs, however, and it's no surprise when the return of Wharf at the School House end sees Hollioake moving into top gear. Having driven the first delivery to the rope at extra cover and then failed to score from the next two balls, the Surrey skipper blasts the following two deliveries for six over extra cover and long-off before finishing a twenty-run over with a lofted off-drive for four that takes the score to 270-4 with two overs remaining.

Having started the penultimate over with three good deliveries that only permit singles, Davies then gets his come-uppance from Hollioake when his next two balls disappear into the distance back over his head for the third and fourth sixes of the batsman's brief but violent innings.

Since Croft chooses to entrust the final over to Maher rather than Wharf, further fireworks might be expected, but, incredibly enough, the Aussie picks up a third scalp when Hollioake skies the second ball of the over to Matt Maynard at deep midwicket and retires to the pavilion to rapturous applause for a stunning cameo of forty-one runs from just sixteen balls.

With Thorpe and Rikki Clarke managing a boundary apiece from the last four balls of the innings, the Lions end up just shy of the three-hundred mark at 298-5, having added a quite incredible 110 runs from the last nine overs of their innings. Thorpe earns further Surrey cheers as he leaves the field with an unbeaten seventy-seven to his name and his side in pole position in the match.

Maher meanwhile ends with an amazing Twenty-20-style analysis of 3-0-29-3 as a set of rather shell-shocked Glamorgan players traipse from the park having produced an excellent fielding display and bowled well for the greater part of the innings... yet Surrey have still amassed a very impressive total.

Glamorgan Dragons' Innings

It's a fair bet that the Glamorgan team mention their outstanding, if ultimately failed, attempt to chase Surrey's record-breaking total of 438-5 in last year's C&G Trophy match at The Oval during the tea interval. They will need to adopt the same positive mental attitude that they displayed on that day if they are to win this game and keep their slender title hopes alive.

On 19th June 2002, Robert Croft had hit Martin Bicknell's first five deliveries to the boundary, but things are very different today as just two singles - one to Croft and one to his opening partner, Jimmy Maher - accrue from the Surrey swing bowler's opening over. When Azhar Mahmood then follows up with a one-run second over, the league leaders have laid a few ghosts from that C&G game, where Glamorgan's stunning start was the key to their brilliant chase, as well as adding to the pressure that the batsmen must already be feeling.

Maher finally sparks the visitors' innings into life, however, by driving the first ball of Bicknell's second over straight down the ground for four, though Welsh joy is short-lived as he drills the next delivery straight into the hands of that man Ramprakash at cover.

Having witnessed the loss of one of their key batsmen with the total on just seven, the Dragons' fans in the crowd are immediately lifted by the sight of Mike Powell driving his first ball to the rope at cover, and Croft lofting the final delivery of an eventful Bicknell over away to the same boundary.

With the third over having cost thirteen runs, Glamorgan then add seven to their total from the first two balls of Azhar's second over, thanks to a no-ball and a clubbed legside four by Croft from the free-hit delivery, though the Lions' bowlers regain control for a short while hereafter as the Dragons' skipper's six over long-off at Bicknell's expense in the fifth over is surrounded by a cluster of dots in the scorebook.

Having reached 36-1 by the end of the seventh over, the visitors are then briefly boosted by a burst of three boundaries in six balls by Croft, with the last of these fours coming off James Ormond, who has replaced Bicknell at the Nottingham Road end. This change turns out to be a good one by Adam Hollioake, since the Glamorgan captain perishes to the penultimate delivery of Ormond's opening over when he advances down the track and edges a drive through to Jon Batty after contributing thirty-one to a total of fifty.

Surrey look to be holding the whip hand now, though Powell soon reminds everyone how quickly things can change in one-day cricket by plundering a total of five fours from overs ten and eleven to put the Dragons in a much more promising position at 73-2.

With Azhar having delivered five good overs from the School House end, Hollioake now recalls Bicknell to the attack, and, while his senior bowler comes up with a decent over costing just five runs, Ormond presents him with a bit of a poser by conceding nine from his third over, including a pulled six by the recently arrived Matt Maynard.

This proves sufficient to persuade the Lions' captain to introduce Saqlain Mushtaq in place of Ormond at the Nottingham Road end, and the off-spinner starts reasonably enough with a six-run opening over, during which both the Glamorgan hundred and the fifty partnership click up.

Since fifteen overs have now been bowled, the fielding restrictions are lifted, though this doesn't seem to help Bicknell very much - Maynard pulls him to the rope backward of square leg, and then Powell drives him for fours wide of mid-on and through extra cover to complete an excellent half-century, including ten boundaries, from just 37 balls.

With his veteran seamer having conceded fifty-two runs from seven overs, and the score having raced up to 114-2 after sixteen overs, Hollioake is grateful for the tight two-run over from Saqlain that follows, and not too unhappy with the six-run opening over that Rikki Clarke comes up with after replacing Bicknell at the School House end.

The game looks really well balanced at this stage, and nothing much changes as a total of thirteen runs are added to the Dragons' total during the nineteenth and twentieth overs, at the end of which the visitors stand at 135-2.

Glamorgan must know that if they can keep wickets in hand they will be favourites going into the last ten overs on this fast-scoring ground, so it is surprising to see Powell selling his wicket rather cheaply in Saqlain's next over. Having looked in no trouble at all while reaching sixty at better than a run a ball, the talented 26-year-old dances down the track, misses a drive and is bowled, much to the delight of the Surrey off-spinner and his team-mates.

Possibly as a result of the capture of this wicket, Hollioake immediately relieves Clarke of his bowling duties, despite the fact that the youngster has delivered two pretty decent overs, and recalls Ormond to the attack to bowl the twenty-second over.

This proves to be another inspired decision, since Maynard and the new batsman, David Hemp, find this revised bowling combination almost impossible to get away, and the flow of boundaries dries up completely. With the Lions' fielders giving Saqlain and Ormond top-class support, just twenty-two runs - every one a single - are added from the next seven overs, and, as the balance of power shifts markedly towards the league leaders, Maynard, having been afflicted by an attack of cramp, finally loses patience, pushing back a firm caught-and-bowled chance that Ormond snaps up gleefully at head height.

With their former skipper gone for forty-one, the Dragons are 159-4 at the end of the twenty-eighth over, and, as Adrian Dale comes to the middle, the asking rate is not too much above eight-an-over, which is certainly attainable on this ground.

Two more accurate overs from Ormond and Saqlain - who is then surprisingly rested in favour of Clarke after a superb spell has produced figures of 8-0-28-1 - build a little more pressure on the batsmen, though the fifth-wicket pair manage to regain some of the lost ground by taking seven from Clarke's comeback over and six from the final over of Ormond's stint. The former Leicestershire seamer's second spell of 6-0-17-1 has been quite outstanding and there is no doubt that he and Saqlain have tilted the game back in Surrey's favour.

There is still work to be done, however, and the batsmen demonstrate that the reigning NCL champions are not ready to give up their crown just yet by notching ten runs from the thirty-third over, delivered by Clarke, thanks largely to a magnificent straight-driven six by Hemp from the last delivery.

With 110 now needed from twelve overs, the Lions' captain makes a double bowling change, as Bicknell returns at the School House end in place of Ormond, while Hollioake himself makes a belated entrance into the attack by taking over from Clarke at the Nottingham Road end.

Bicknell certainly wastes no time in making an impact, claiming the scalp of Dale with his first delivery when the batsman lifts his back foot, allowing Batty to pull off a smart stumping that pegs Glamorgan back to 189-5. As a result, the thirty-fourth over belongs to Surrey, despite the fact that Mark Wallace and Hemp garner seven runs from the last five balls.

You can chalk up the thirty-fifth to the home side, too, since Hollioake emulates Bicknell by striking a blow for his team in his first over, when a slower delivery deceives and bowls Wallace as the young keeper gives the Lions' skipper the charge.

These two quick wickets look to have put the league leaders firmly on course for their eighth NCL victory of the campaign, even though the Dragons manage to raise their two-hundred from the final ball of the thirty-fifth over, leaving ninety-nine runs to be scored from the last ten overs. With six or seven wickets in hand, you would probably make the chasing side favourites on this ground, but Glamorgan are now down to four as a result of some rather panicky batting.

The visitors are then further undermined by some careless running, and, since the batsman concerned is Hemp, it looks like it could be a decisive dismissal. The 32-year-old left-hander pushes the fourth ball of Bicknell's final over towards mid-on and ambles down the pitch for a single, failing to appreciate, until it is too late, that Ali Brown's sharp throw is going to reach the non-striker's stumps before he can reach the safety of the crease. As the Lions celebrate, Hemp trudges off the field with thirty to his name and the scoreboard reading 203-7, knowing that his sloppy running will almost certainly turn out to be the final act of surrender for the Welshmen.

The new batsman, Alex Wharf, is capable of scoring quickly, but he doesn't last long, taking legside fours from the first two balls of Hollioake's next over, before an attempt to repeat the dose from the following delivery results in a set of rearranged stumps.

Although it's now looking like a lost cause, Michael Kasprowicz battles bravely, driving boundaries at the end of Hollioake's over and from the penultimate ball of the returning Saqlain's brilliant stint, but Andrew Davies struggles to get the ball away at the other end before popping a simple return catch back to the Surrey captain in the thirty-ninth over with the total at 225.

Hollioake then raises a few eyebrows around the ground by asking Brown to take over from Saqlain at the School House end, but, as with just about every other decision today, it turns up trumps. Kasprowicz drives the occasional off-spinner's first two balls through the covers and down the ground for boundaries, but, as soon as the big Aussie loses the strike, Dean Cosker flicks a catch to Clarke at deep backward square leg to confirm the Lions' victory by a margin of fifty-eight runs.

Although Surrey are delighted with this win that moves them four points clear of Gloucestershire Gladiators at the top of the NCL, celebrations are slightly muted by the shock news from the Championship match at Hove that Sussex have beaten Lancashire by 252 runs late in the day.

MARK RAMPRAKASH'S VIEW FROM THE DRESSING ROOM

You were phenomenally consistent in the NCL in 2003 and your century in this match was your seventh score above fifty. Which of your innings in the competition gave you most pleasure?
MR - Well, it's always nice to score a one-day hundred because I don't have a lot of those to my credit, but I probably put greater value on those innings where the game is close and the runs are really needed by your team. So, although I didn't particularly enjoy it, and it was hard work, I would say it would be the fifty I got in the match against Glamorgan at Cardiff to seal the title.

Mike Powell played very well and his partnership with Matt Maynard looked threatening at one stage. Would you say that Powell's dismissal was the crucial moment of the match?
MR - He certainly looked in very good form, so it was an important dismissal, yes. All through the season we were in positions where teams were chasing and seemed to be going well, but we always knew that, when the pressure builds, all you need is one or two reasonable overs and a breakthrough, then you can put a lot of pressure on the incoming batsman.

Are you surprised that Powell hasn't yet put himself in the frame for higher honours?
MR - Yes, I'm surprised he hasn't really gone on because Duncan Fletcher was obviously down at Glamorgan and would know all about him, and I've always rated him highly when I've seen him.

TWENTY-20's GRAND ENTRANCE

TOP: The crowd packed into the Peter May Stand for the first Twenty-20 Cup match at The Oval
MIDDLE: Mushtaq Ahmed is bowled by Adam Hollioake at Imber Court
BOTTOM: Mark Ramprakash narrowly escapes being run out in the same match against Sussex Sharks
(All photos courtesy of Surrey C.C.C.)

TWENTY-20 SEMI-FINAL ACTION

TOP: Man Of The Match, Azhar Mahmood, hits the ball away on the legside during his innings
MIDDLE: Matt Windows is bowled by Saqlain Mushtaq
BOTTOM: Azhar celebrates the capture of the wicket of Jonty Rhodes
(All photos courtesy of Surrey C.C.C.)

TWENTY-20 FINAL ACTION

TOP: Graham Wagg is bowled by Adam Hollioake
MIDDLE: Ali Brown pulls to the boundary
BOTTOM: Ian Ward, sporting the revolutionary 'helmet cam', pulls through mid-on
(All photos courtesy of Surrey C.C.C.)

NCL SNAPSHOTS

TOP: Martin Bicknell appeals for lbw against Ben Smith at Guildford
MIDDLE: James Ormond receives his county cap from Adam Hollioake
BOTTOM: Mark Ramprakash drives through the legside against Gloucestershire at The Oval
(Middle photo by Steve Porter of The Surrey Advertiser; Other photos courtesy of Surrey C.C.C.)

NCL SNAPSHOTS 2

TOP: Peter Trego of the Kent Spitfires is bowled by Tim Murtagh at The Oval
MIDDLE: Yorkshire's Michael Lumb falls lbw to Saqlain Mushtaq at The Oval
BOTTOM: The wait is over! Mark Butcher celebrates reaching his first-ever limited-overs century
(All photos courtesy of Surrey C.C.C.)

NCL - LIONS SLAY DRAGONS AT WHITGIFT

(1) Graham Thorpe drives to leg; (2) Mike Powell is bowled as he charges at Saqlain;
(3) The batsmen steal a tight single despite the efforts of James Ormond;
(4) David Hemp survives Ali Brown's run-out attempt - he was less fortunate later.
(All photos courtesy of Surrey C.C.C.)

CELEBRATIONS

TOP: All smiles at Trent Bridge as the Twenty-20 Cup is celebrated
MIDDLE: Adam Hollioake shows off the spoils of the season
BOTTOM: Keith Medlycott and Adam Hollioake celebrate at the end of an era
(All photos courtesy of Surrey C.C.C.)

STEWIE'S OVAL TEST FAREWELL

TOP: Alec Stewart is chaired off by Steve Harmison and Andrew Flintoff at the end of the match
BOTTOM: The Surrey four who played such a major role in England's victory
(Both photos courtesy of Surrey C.C.C.)

I felt that Glamorgan threw away too many wickets with panicky batting, perhaps not appreciating that ten runs an over is possible from the last ten overs at Whitgift if you've got five or six wickets in hand. How did you see it?

MR - I think that they would probably look back at this game and realise that on a small ground like Whitgift they could have hit a boundary every over and maybe had one really big over somewhere. So I'm happy that they panicked! But, having said that, we have a number of very good bowlers to bowl at the end of an innings - people like Saqlain, Adam and Azhar - and these guys are brilliant bowlers at the 'death' with their slower balls and yorkers, and they held their nerve time and time again under pressure through the season.

SURREY LIONS v GLAMORGAN DRAGONS at Whitgift School
Sunday 17th August — Surrey Lions won by 58 runs
Surrey Lions won the toss and elected to bat — Umpires:- Vanburn Holder & Nigel Llong

SURREY LIONS

Fall Of Wkt	Batsman	How	Out	Score	Balls	4s	6s
2-93	I.J. Ward		b Dale	44	64	6	1
1-23	A.D. Brown		b Davies	14	18	2	0
3-213	M.R. Ramprakash	c Davies	b Maher	101	93	11	3
	G.P. Thorpe	Not	Out	77	72	8	2
4-235	Azhar Mahmood	c Croft	b Maher	12	5	1	1
5-288	A.J. Hollioake *	c Maynard	b Maher	41	16	2	4
	R. Clarke	Not	Out	5	2	1	0
	J.N. Batty +	did not bat					
	M.P. Bicknell	did not bat					
	Saqlain Mushtaq	did not bat					
	J. Ormond	did not bat					
	Extras	(4w)		4			
	TOTAL	(45 overs)	(for 5 wkts)	298			

Bowler	O	M	R	W	NB	Wd
Kasprowicz	9	2	42	0	-	-
Davies	9	0	67	1	-	2
Wharf	8	1	47	0	-	-
Dale	9	0	59	1	-	-
Cosker	4	0	32	0	-	-
Croft	3	0	22	0	-	1
Maher	3	0	29	3	-	1

GLAMORGAN DRAGONS

Fall Of Wkt	Batsman	How	Out	Score	Balls	4s	6s
2-50	R.D.B. Croft *	c Batty	b Ormond	31	32	6	1
1-7	J.P. Maher	c Ramprakash	b Bicknell	6	10	1	0
3-137	M.J. Powell		b Saqlain	60	57	11	0
4-159	M.P. Maynard	c &	b Ormond	41	48	2	1
7-203	D.L. Hemp	run	out	30	41	1	1
5-189	A. Dale	st Batty	b Bicknell	12	18	1	0
6-199	M.A. Wallace +		b Hollioake	6	5	1	0
8-212	A.G. Wharf		b Hollioake	11	9	2	0
	M.S. Kasprowicz	Not	Out	18	8	4	0
9-225	A.P. Davies	c &	b Hollioake	3	7	0	0
10-240	D.A. Cosker	c Clarke	b Brown	5	4	1	0
	Extras	(11lb, 2w, 4nb)		17			
	TOTAL	(39.4 overs)		240			

Bowler	O	M	R	W	NB	Wd
Bicknell	9	0	63	2	-	-
Azhar Mahmood	5	0	25	0	1	-
Ormond	9	0	45	2	1	-
Saqlain Mushtaq	9	0	36	1	-	1
Clarke	4	0	29	0	-	-
Hollioake	3	0	22	3	-	1
Brown	0.4	0	9	1	-	-

Other NCL Division One Results

The Lions' triumph over the Dragons saw them move back to the top of the table with a four-point advantage over the Gladiators, who had not been in NCL action since their defeat at The Oval. Additionally, the gap between the top two sides' net run-rates had been further reduced, thanks to Surrey's convincing margin of victory.

August 6
***Headingley:-* Yorkshire Phoenix (4pts) beat Warwickshire Bears by 7 wickets.** Warwicks 273-6 (45ov; Knight 95, Troughton 77); Yorks 274-3 (38.2ov; Fleming 139, Wood 65).
August 10
***Cardiff:-* Glamorgan Dragons (4pts) beat Warwickshire Bears by 7 wickets.** Warwicks 196 (43.5ov; Penney 64*); Glamorgan 198-3 (40.5ov; Croft 70).
***Leicester:-* Leicestershire Foxes (4pts) beat Essex Eagles by 6 wickets (D/L method).** Essex 212-6 (43.3ov; Flower 103); Leics 90-4 (15.4ov).
August 11
***Canterbury:-* Kent Spitfires (4pts) beat Worcestershire Royals by 8 wickets.** Worcs 225-8 (45ov; Solanki 70); Kent 226-2 (36.2ov; Symonds 93*, Carberry 79).
August 13
***Edgbaston:-* Warwickshire Bears (4pts) beat Leicestershire Foxes by 8 wickets.** Leics 178 (40.4ov; Hodge 55); Warwicks 182-2 (30.5ov; Carter 75, Bell 54).
August 17
***Scarborough:-* Yorkshire Phoenix (4pts) beat Worcestershire Royals by 3 wickets.** Worcs 170 (44.5ov; Smith 54); Yorks 171-7 (42ov; Wood 60).

NCL DIVISION ONE TABLE AT 17TH AUGUST

Pos	Prv		P	Pts	W	T	L	A	NRR
1	2	**Surrey Lions**	**11**	**34**	8	0	2	1	5.58
2	1	**Gloucestershire Gladiators**	**11**	**30**	7	0	3	1	7.31
3	3	**Glamorgan Dragons**	**13**	**28**	7	0	6	0	-0.83
4	5	**Warwickshire Bears**	**12**	**24**	6	0	6	0	1.75
5	4	**Essex Eagles**	**12**	**22**	5	1	6	0	3.92
6	7	**Leicestershire Foxes**	**12**	**20**	5	0	7	0	-3.62
7	8	**Kent Spitfires**	**11**	**18**	4	1	6	0	-2.41
8	6	**Worcestershire Royals**	**11**	**16**	4	0	7	0	1.23
9	9	**Yorkshire Phoenix**	**11**	**16**	4	0	7	0	-10.10

16 Mixed Emotions

After Sussex's surprise win over Lancashire at Hove there could now be little or no doubt that the Championship was a two-horse race. Even if the Red Rose county won their game in hand with maximum points, there seemed very little chance of them closing the gap on the leading pair unless they beat them both at Old Trafford in the last few weeks of the season - a tall order indeed.

Going into the final day at Hove, the most likely result had looked to be a draw, and when Chris Adams eventually declared 'setting' Lancashire 392 to win in a minimum of seventy-five overs, stalemate looked certain, since the pitch had apparently played very well throughout. Billy Taylor had removed the top four during an inspired opening spell, however, allowing Mushtaq to work his way through the rest of the batting and secure a victory that few had expected, in the seventy-fourth over, with twelve minutes left until 'stumps'.

Both Sussex and Surrey were likely to have to do without a key bowler for some of their remaining matches as the title race came to the boil, however, since England had been hit by a crop of injuries to their pacemen, in addition to the sudden retirement of Darren Gough after the Lord's Test. Having recently turned to one of county cricket's most consistent performers, with excellent results, they were just about to make a surprise call to another.

The first of these call-ups had seen James Kirtley making a sensational debut in the Trent Bridge Test - which England had won by seventy runs to level the series at 1-1 - taking 6-34 in the second innings and thereby, one would assume, securing his place in the national side for the rest of the summer. This would obviously be a blow to Sussex's Championship prospects, even though Billy Taylor had stepped into Kirtley's shoes so admirably against Lancashire.

If Sussex fans had been left with mixed emotions by Kirtley's success, then Surrey supporters were soon in the same boat when a certain M.P. Bicknell, at the ripe old age of thirty-four, was named in a squad of thirteen for the fourth Test at Headingley. If Bickers were to play for England again after a ten-year period in the wilderness then it would maybe hit his county's title hopes, yet it was a fair bet that every single Surrey fan would be hoping that this most deserving cricketer would make the final eleven at Leeds. Even allowing for the fact that the likes of Hoggard, Johnson, Jones and Harmison were incapacitated, it seemed odd that the selectors had finally seen the error of their ways in ignoring Bicknell's claims for so long, but maybe he was now to get another chance as he moved towards the twilight of his career.

Returning to the domestic situation, both Sussex and Surrey now faced matches against sides in the relegation zone, with the reigning champions heading up to Grace Road, while their unexpected Championship rivals were making the trip to Colchester. Both title contenders would be expecting to win against struggling opposition, so there was every chance that the top of the table might not look too different at the end of this round of matches. Sussex's game started one day earlier, however, since Surrey had a floodlit NCL encounter with Leicestershire to fit in before their Championship fixture. This NCL match was also very important, of course, since victory over the relegation-threatened Foxes would enable the Lions to open up an eight-point lead at the top of the table, putting greater pressure on the Gloucestershire Gladiators, whose next game was a tricky looking visit to New Road to play the Worcestershire Royals.

NATIONAL CRICKET LEAGUE DIVISION ONE - MATCH TWELVE

Leicestershire Foxes versus Surrey Lions at Leicester

Wednesday 20th August

Setting The Scene - With things so tight at the bottom of the table, and the sixth-placed Foxes having played one game more than the sides currently in the relegation zone, this looks to be a key match for both sides. Since Martin Bicknell is in Leeds with the England squad, the Lions are forced to make one change to the side that had beaten Glamorgan Dragons at Whitgift, with Ian Salisbury the man coming into their eleven. Leicestershire are meanwhile without the injured Trevor Ward and Darren Stevens, though they have the consolation of winning the toss when Adam Hollioake calls incorrectly. Phillip DeFreitas elects to bat first, in the hope that Surrey might find batting under the lights tricky later in the evening.

Leicestershire Foxes' Innings

James Ormond, back on his old stomping ground, and Azhar Mahmood get Surrey away to a good start by conceding just nine runs in the first three overs, with four of those coming from an outside edge by DeFreitas off Ormond that flies at a catchable height between wicketkeeper and slip in the third over.

DeFreitas quickly adds three well-struck fours to this lucky boundary, however, while Ormond soon has a wicket to his name on his twenty-sixth birthday when John Maunders pays the price for aiming across the line, falling lbw for three in the fifth over with the total on twenty-four.

Top-class bowling by the Lions' new-ball operators, coupled with what appears to be a rather conservative approach by the Foxes' skipper and his new partner, Brad Hodge, sees the scoring stagnate between the fifth and tenth overs, however, as just fifteen runs are added.

With the situation becoming rather serious for the home team, the next over from Ormond provides some welcome relief, since it brings twelve runs, thanks largely to an inaccurate shy at the stumps that turns Hodge's fourth-ball single into a five, and an on-driven four by DeFreitas from the final delivery that takes the total beyond fifty.

Although his sixth over has been a costly one, Ormond continues his spell at the pavilion end, while Saqlain Mushtaq takes over from Azhar at the Bennett end, and, as in the Glamorgan match at Whitgift, this combination works wonders for the league leaders, with just twenty-four runs coming from the next seven overs, along with the wicket of DeFreitas for thirty-nine from the last ball of Ormond's stint. The Foxes are 73-2 after seventeen overs when their skipper edges a drive to Ali Brown, who has been sensibly retained at slip, leaving Ormond to retire to the outfield with figures of 9-0-38-2 at the end of a fine spell, and Rikki Clarke to take over the bowling at the pavilion end.

The Guildford youngster doesn't fare too well, though, as two overs cost seventeen runs, including three pulls to the boundary, the last of which Darren Maddy, the new batsman, nails for a 'maximum' to send the total rocketing into three figures at the end of the twenty-first over.

With the run-rate rising and Saqlain's fifth over of a good spell having yielded seven runs, Hollioake opts for a double bowling change at this point, pairing himself with Ian Salisbury and immediately applying the brakes to Leicestershire's progress.

After just thirteen runs have been added from the first four overs delivered by the new bowlers, the loss of Hodge to the last ball of the twenty-fifth over - bowled by a Hollioake inswinger that ricochets off the batsman's pad onto his off stump - comes as an especially bad blow to the home side's prospects of making a challenging total.

Nor do things get any easier for Maddy and the new batsman, Paul Nixon, as more brilliant bowling keeps the Foxes on a very tight leash. With Nixon's performance confirming recent reports that he is desperately out of form, a mere twenty-six runs trickle from the nine overs following Hodge's dismissal, before Hollioake takes a break with the impressive figures of 6-0-18-1 and recalls Saqlain in his place with the score 139-3 after thirty-four overs.

The off-spinner's return sees Maddy making a move to increase the run-rate with a straight-driven boundary, though, from Leicestershire's point of view, Salisbury's dismissal of Nixon with a perfectly pitched googly that the left-hander edges to Jon Batty, might actually be more significant. Having struggled to score ten from twenty-four deliveries it's almost a blessed relief for the Foxes' keeper that Salisbury has earned some reward for his excellent bowling, and it's true to say that the home team's innings perks up almost instantly, with Maddy driving the Surrey leg-spinner through extra cover for four, and John Sadler, Nixon's replacement, immediately cracking Saqlain away to the point boundary.

Maddy then progresses to a 69-ball half-century by taking a square-cut four from the penultimate ball of Salisbury's impressive spell of 9-1-37-1 and, with nine runs coming from the following Saqlain over, Leicestershire, at 176-4 after thirty-nine overs, are finally showing signs of pushing on towards a respectable total.

With Salisbury finished, and Saqlain withdrawn from the attack, the Foxes still have their work cut out if they are to score heavily in the final stages, though, as the last six overs are to be bowled by two cunning 'death' bowlers in Hollioake and Azhar.

And so it proves. Although Sadler finds the rope at extra cover with a lofted drive in Azhar's first over back, the first three of these run-in overs yield just fifteen runs, leaving Leicestershire nine short of the two-hundred mark with only eighteen deliveries left to be bowled.

Consequently, there's never a dull moment for the rest of the innings, with the forty-third over setting the tone, as Maddy pulls a four off Hollioake and raises a 48-ball fifty partnership, before Sadler brings up the two-hundred and then holes out to Graham Thorpe at long-on from the Lions' skipper's slower ball for a breezy twenty-seven.

Maddy then falls to another slower delivery, in unusual circumstances, during the penultimate over of the innings - he advances on Azhar and misses his drive but cannot regain his ground before Batty moves in and hits the wicket with an underarm throw to complete a stumping that ends the former England man's well-played knock on sixty-six at 202-6.

Eight runs then come from the rest of Azhar's over, including a lofted off-drive to the boundary by Jeremy Snape, before the final over turns out to be a serious disappointment for the Foxes and their fans in a crowd that has built up nicely during the latter stages of the afternoon.

After the first four deliveries bring seven runs, courtesy of three singles and four byes, Hollioake ends an excellent day's work with the ball by having Vasbert Drakes safely taken by Brown at long-on from a massive skier from the penultimate delivery, and Snape caught at long-off by Ward from the last ball. The Surrey captain therefore ends up with very well-deserved figures of 4-35 as Leicestershire's innings fizzles out - having never really exploded, to be honest - at a rather inadequate-looking 217-8. The home side will be fighting tooth-and-nail to defend this total, however, since their first division future will be in the balance if they lose tonight.

Surrey Lions' Innings

Leicestershire's hopes of victory are badly hit before they even step onto the field for the Lions' innings, with the news that Phillip DeFreitas will play no further part in the match because of a toe injury inflicted by an Ormond yorker during the home captain's innings. The loss of arguably their best bowler is a huge blow for the Foxes, and there must now be serious doubts as to whether he will be able to play in the Championship match starting tomorrow.

The absence of their skipper isn't felt at all during three excellent opening overs from Charlie Dagnall and Vasbert Drakes, however, as Dagnall follows an opening maiden with an inspired over, during which Ali Brown, on one at the time, is badly missed by the stand-in captain, Darren Maddy, at slip from an edged drive that reaches the fielder at a perfect height.

Missing any chance offered by the potentially lethal Brown can be expensive, so when the Surrey opener takes nine from Drakes' next over, including a fine forcing stroke to the rope at cover, Foxes' fans are already fearing the worst.

Dagnall is still proving almost unplayable at the other end, however, and for the first four deliveries of the fifth over, Brown, who has almost totally monopolised the strike since the second over, can scarcely lay a bat on the ball. That situation changes dramatically, though, when the

Lions' batsman forces the fifth delivery to the cover boundary and then drives the final ball over long-on for a towering six.

Suddenly, the bowlers' hold over the batsmen is broken and it's a totally different game as eleven runs come from the following over, with Brown adding two further fours to his collection, courtesy of a whip through midwicket and a lofted straight drive.

A score of 35-0 after six overs then becomes 45-0 after seven as Ward moves his score from two to six with a flick off his hip to the square leg boundary and then pushes to cover for a single that allows the rampant Brown to pick Dagnall up over midwicket for four.

Although Drakes then manages five 'dot' balls to the Surrey master-blaster after seeing the first ball of his fourth over disappear to the fence at cover, DeFreitas' absence is starting to be felt as Ward finally gets to face a full over and bursts into life with a sequence of 4-2-2-4-4 at the expense of Dagnall, whose early dominance is now a distant memory. To be fair to the bowler, two of these five scoring strokes from Ward do come off the edge, though this is no consolation to either Dagnall or a team whose 217-8 is looking increasingly feeble in the face of a Surrey assault that has taken the score to 65-0 after nine overs. The worst is yet to come, though.

A change of bowling at this point sees David Masters enter the fray and receive a terrible mauling from the Lions' batsmen. During an opening over that costs no fewer than twenty-three runs, Brown pulls to midwicket and cuts to backward point for fours before pulling again, this time for six, to complete an amazing fifty from thirty-seven balls. The half-centurion then takes a single to third man, allowing Ward to get in on the act with a magnificent six of his own over long-off from the last ball of a traumatic over for Masters.

Surprisingly, after a four-run over from Drakes, who has switched to the Bennett end, Masters is retained in the attack and suffers further misery when Ward's pulls for four and three are followed by Brown's pull to the boundary and lofted extra-cover drive for three. With the truly gruesome figures of 2-0-37-0 to his name, Masters is probably safe to assume that his spell is now over, while everyone in the ground is probably safe to assume that, with Surrey 106-0 after twelve overs, the match is also, effectively, over.

Although the persevering Drakes does his best to haul things back a little with an over that again contains just a solitary loose ball - a full-toss glanced to the fine-leg boundary by Brown - Maddy, replacing the shell-shocked Masters at the pavilion end, soon undoes the good work with an opening over that sees the right-handed Lions' opener registering the twelfth, thirteenth and fourteenth fours of his innings with a pick-up over backward square leg, a cut through extra cover and a lofted straight drive. This volley of strokes has not only taken Brown to eighty-four out of a total of 123-0 after just fourteen overs, but also made victory a formality, and, perhaps just as importantly, given Surrey's net run-rate a massive boost.

It is something of a blow for the visitors and their crowd-pleasing opening batsman, therefore, when Brown falls eleven runs short of what would have been a breathtaking century during the first over bowled by Brad Hodge, who has succeeded his stand-in captain at the pavilion end. Having dropped the Lions' opener at the start of the innings, and then delivered a distinctly unimpressive twelve-run over, Maddy finally makes a positive contribution to the Foxes' fielding effort by diving away to his left at midwicket to snap up a fine catch from Brown's well-struck pull at the part-time off-spinner's third delivery.

As the batsman returns to the pavilion to a good hand from a decent-sized crowd for his thrilling 65-ball knock, which has included fourteen fours and two sixes, Surrey make a sound tactical decision by sending in Azhar Mahmood, with the clear intention of maintaining the stunning tempo that has been set by the opening partnership of 131 from 15.3 overs.

This move isn't hugely successful, however, as just five runs come from the next twelve deliveries from Hodge and Jeremy Snape - Drakes' replacement at the Bennett end - during which time Ward, on thirty-nine, is badly dropped by Dagnall at deep midwicket from a slog-sweep off Snape at 134-1.

Although Azhar does then break free with a big six over wide long-on off Hodge, he has only progressed as far as eleven from ten balls when he holes out to Drakes in a similar position off Snape with the total on 147 in the nineteenth over.

Rightly maintaining their positive policy, Adam Hollioake strides out to replace Azhar and, following a brief period of reconnaissance, during which the score moves on to 156-2 after twenty-one overs, the Lions' leader drives Hodge for a straight six before repeating the dose in Snape's next over, four balls after Ward has completed a very good fifty from 47 deliveries.

When eleven runs then come from Hodge's fifth over, taking the visitors within thirty-three of victory with twenty-one overs remaining, Maddy elects to recall Masters to the attack, presumably in the hope that the former Kent seamer will be able to get through a couple of confidence-restoring overs after his earlier battering. The stand-in skipper's move produces mixed results, however, as Hollioake drives successive deliveries for two, four and two, before being yorked when making room to crash the last ball of the over through the off side.

The visiting captain's 21-ball knock of twenty-eight has taken his team to the brink of victory at 199-3, allowing Rikki Clarke to come in and deflect boundaries off Masters and Snape that take the Lions home to victory by seven wickets with exactly one-hundred balls to spare.

Ward ends undefeated on seventy, from just sixty-five balls, having faced a great deal less than half of the strike, as the players leave the field with Leicestershire now looking increasingly likely to be relegated and Surrey having moved another step closer to winning the Sunday/National League title for only the second time in their history.

ALI BROWN'S VIEW FROM THE DRESSING ROOM

Although all the Surrey bowlers performed well, I wasn't alone in thinking that Ian Salisbury was the pick of the attack. Is he a bit unlucky not to play in more one-day games for Surrey?

AB - Yes, I think he's very unlucky not to play in more of our one-dayers and I think he's very underused, not just in one-day cricket, but in the Championship as well. I'd certainly like to see him play more in limited-overs cricket because he's a good all-round cricketer - he can swing the bat effectively and he fields well. You regularly see a barrage of seamers in that form of the game, but I believe you've got to have variation in your bowling in all forms of cricket, and he definitely gives you that. Certainly on a slow wicket I would always try to play two spinners if possible, because there aren't too many batsmen out there who have the guts to come out and play shots straight away against spin. I was disappointed that he wasn't even considered for the first Twenty-20 game because people thought spinners would be smashed around the ground. But, as we saw throughout the competition, that wasn't the case.

I felt that Leicestershire's early batsmen played too conservatively. Would you agree with that?

AB - I'm not sure that they were necessarily conservative, no. When we came in at the end of their innings we thought it was going to be a pretty straightforward target to reach, and we fancied ourselves strongly, but when Wardy and I got out to bat on that pitch we changed our view a bit. It was certainly the sort of wicket that did a bit when the bowlers put the ball in the right areas.

The first three overs of our innings were a real struggle, with the bowlers looking in complete control. Then you suddenly produced an incredible flurry of strokes. What happened?

AB - Once we'd seen what the wicket was like, we decided that perhaps we should try to take the bull by the horns and be positive. So we came down the wicket a few times, we didn't back off, and we put together a good opening partnership. On wickets like that, you've got to take a bit of a chance and not let the bowlers dominate.

It was a smart move to change the batting order and blast away selflessly in an obvious attempt to boost our net run-rate. At what point was that decision made, and who made it?
AB - It was pretty much a team decision, I think. We were very well aware of the possible importance of net run-rate from the early stages of the competition, and we were a bit behind Gloucestershire going into this game, so I think we took that decision quite early on. Obviously we couldn't decide to do it before we went out to bat, but, once Wardy and I had got us off to a good start, the game was as good as won and it became clear that every time we lost a wicket we wanted to keep bringing in the players who were going to maintain or increase that run rate. It clearly worked very well, and at the end of that game we felt like we'd just gained eight points, rather than four, because of the way we'd gone ahead of Gloucestershire on run-rate.

LEICESTERSHIRE FOXES v SURREY LIONS at Leicester
Wednesday 20th August — Surrey Lions won by seven wickets
Leicestershire Foxes won the toss and elected to bat — Umpires:- David Constant & Jeff Evans

LEICESTERSHIRE FOXES

Fall Of Wkt	Batsman	How	Out	Score	Balls	4s	6s
1-24	**J.K. Maunders**	**lbw**	**b Ormond**	**3**	9	0	0
2-73	**P.A.J. DeFreitas ***	**c Brown**	**b Ormond**	**39**	51	7	0
3-113	**B.J. Hodge**		**b Hollioake**	**46**	65	5	0
6-202	**D.L. Maddy**	**st Batty**	**b Azhar**	**66**	87	6	1
4-147	**P.A. Nixon +**	**c Batty**	**b Salisbury**	**10**	24	0	0
5-201	**J.L. Sadler**	**c Thorpe**	**b Hollioake**	**27**	23	3	0
8-217	**J.N. Snape**	**c Ward**	**b Hollioake**	**10**	8	1	0
7-217	**V.C. Drakes**	**c Brown**	**b Hollioake**	**2**	3	0	0
	D.G. Brandy	**Not**	**Out**	**0**	0	0	0
	D.D. Masters	**did not bat**					
	C.E. Dagnall	**did not bat**					
	Extras	**(4b, 4lb, 6w)**		**14**			
	TOTAL	**(45 overs)**	**(for 8 wkts)**	**217**			

Bowler	O	M	R	W	NB	Wd
Ormond	**9**	**0**	**38**	**2**	-	1
Azhar Mahmood	**8**	**1**	**39**	**1**	-	-
Saqlain Mushtaq	**8**	**0**	**43**	**0**	-	-
Clarke	**2**	**0**	**17**	**0**	-	1
Salisbury	**9**	**1**	**37**	**1**	-	2
Hollioake	**9**	**0**	**35**	**4**	-	2

SURREY LIONS

Fall Of Wkt	Batsman	How	Out	Score	Balls	4s	6s
	I.J. Ward	**Not**	**Out**	**70**	65	6	1
1-131	**A.D. Brown**	**c Maddy**	**b Hodge**	**89**	65	14	2
2-147	**Azhar Mahmood**	**c Drakes**	**b Snape**	**11**	10	0	1
3-199	**A.J. Hollioake ***		**b Masters**	**28**	21	1	2
	R. Clarke	**Not**	**Out**	**14**	9	2	0
	M.R. Ramprakash	**did not bat**					
	G.P. Thorpe	**did not bat**					
	J.N. Batty +	**did not bat**					
	I.D.K. Salisbury	**did not bat**					
	Saqlain Mushtaq	**did not bat**					
	J. Ormond	**did not bat**					
	Extras	**(2lb, 4w)**		**6**			
	TOTAL	**(28.2 overs)**	**(for 3 wkts)**	**218**			

Bowler	O	M	R	W	NB	Wd
Dagnall	**5**	**1**	**40**	**0**	-	3
Drakes	**7**	**0**	**39**	**0**	-	-
Masters	**4**	**0**	**55**	**1**	-	-
Maddy	**1**	**0**	**12**	**0**	-	-
Hodge	**5**	**0**	**38**	**1**	-	1
Snape	**6.2**	**0**	**32**	**1**	-	-

NCL DIVISION ONE TABLE AT 20TH AUGUST

Pos	Prv		P	Pts	W	T	L	A	NRR
1	1	Surrey Lions	12	38	9	0	2	1	8.45
2	2	Gloucestershire Gladiators	11	30	7	0	3	1	7.31
3	3	Glamorgan Dragons	13	28	7	0	6	0	-0.83
4	4	Warwickshire Bears	12	24	6	0	6	0	1.75
5	5	Essex Eagles	12	22	5	1	6	0	3.92
6	6	Leicestershire Foxes	13	20	5	0	8	0	-6.07
7	7	Kent Spitfires	11	18	4	1	6	0	-2.41
8	8	Worcestershire Royals	11	16	4	0	7	0	1.23
9	9	Yorkshire Phoenix	11	16	4	0	7	0	-10.10

FRIZZELL COUNTY CHAMPIONSHIP DIVISION ONE - MATCH THIRTEEN

LEICESTERSHIRE versus SURREY
at Leicester

First Day - Thursday 21st August
Surrey 349-4

The Teams And The Toss *- Team selection at Headingley is almost as important as at Grace Road today, and everyone with Surrey connections is delighted to learn that Martin Bicknell has been included in the England team this morning, thereby making his first Test appearance for ten years and setting a new record by reappearing for his country after an absence of 114 Tests. Strangely enough, the previous record holder - with a 104-Test gap - had been another Surrey man, Younis Ahmed, the left-handed Pakistani batsman. Back at Leicester, Ali Brown is unlucky to be omitted from Surrey's eleven after his excellent NCL knock, with James Ormond returning to the Championship side in place of Bicknell, and an extra bowler, Tim Murtagh, being preferred to Brown. Leicestershire are meanwhile delighted that Phillip DeFreitas has declared himself fit enough to play despite his toe injury and, therefore, field exactly the same team that had been beaten last night. Adam Hollioake calls correctly at the toss and elects to bat first.*

With the start of play delayed until 11.30am because of last night's floodlit contest, everyone with Surrey leanings finds a television in the ground and settles down to watch Martin Bicknell dismiss Herschelle Gibbs - caught behind by Alec Stewart - with the second ball of his return to the national side, and then remove Jacques Kallis, courtesy of a catch at short cover by Michael Vaughan, in his sixth over.

Although it has been terrific to see Bickers in the England shirt again, and even better to see him taking early wickets, attention switches back to Grace Road once the Leicestershire team and the Surrey batsmen emerge from the pavilion.

On a rather cool and cloudy morning, it's almost like the NCL game revisited as Ian Ward cuts Phil DeFreitas' first delivery to the cover boundary and then forces the fifth ball away for four runs backward of point. Jon Batty then follows up with a cover-driven boundary in Vasbert Drakes' opening over before everyone settles into a more normal tempo for Championship cricket.

One can only assume that Drakes isn't happy about bowling from the pavilion end, since he is removed from the attack after just two overs and replaced by Charlie Dagnall, though nothing seems to disturb the batsmen as they make comfortable progress over the course of the next forty-five minutes, scoring almost exclusively in boundaries. The statisticians in the ground must be delighted to note that the first forty-seven runs of the innings come from eleven fours and a three, with the first single - which takes the score up to forty-eight - not being scored until the seventeenth over, when Batty pulls Drakes, who has just taken over from DeFreitas at the Bennett end, to long leg.

At this point, Darren Maddy replaces Dagnall at the pavilion end, and Batty promptly drives the new bowler to the rope at cover, thereby raising the Surrey fifty in fine style. The first extras of the innings then arrive in the following over when Drakes oversteps the crease, and, having contributed just three overs in his second spell, the West Indian is pulled out of the attack again and replaced by David Masters.

The former Kent seamer must surely have been plagued by nightmares when he went to bed last night, following his stint of 4-0-55-1 in the NCL match, and he starts today's spell with an attack of déjà vu as Batty steers and cover-drives fours in an opening over costing nine runs, before recovering well in the lead-up to lunch with three inexpensive overs.

At the other end, meanwhile, Jeremy Snape - ignored for so long in the Championship match at The Oval in May - has been introduced in the twenty-fourth over in place of Maddy, but looks no more likely to make a breakthrough than his team-mates as each batsman takes a boundary off him in a three-over spell.

At lunch, Surrey are very well placed, having made steady and sensible progress against respectable bowling on what looks to be a good pitch.

Lunch:- Surrey 88-0 (Ward 38, Batty 48*) from 28 overs*

Defying obvious pain from his injured toe, DeFreitas returns at the Bennett end after lunch with an amazingly defensive field in place - cover sweeper, just one slip and a gully - and, with Snape retained at the pavilion end, it appears that containment is, at the moment anyway, the height of Leicestershire's ambitions.

This seems extremely negative, but, when Batty cuts loosely to Maddy at backward point in the fifth over of the session with just five runs added to the lunch score - including the single that had completed the Surrey keeper's fine fifty from 103 balls - DeFreitas' tactics appear to have been vindicated.

The former England seamer then becomes even more defensive with the appearance of Mark Ramprakash, setting eight-one off-side fields for both batsmen and sending down a succession of deliveries appropriately wide of the off stump. As a result, DeFreitas strings together four successive maidens, though his efforts are completely negated by Snape at the other end, as the off-spinner is twice driven for straight sixes by Ramprakash, who then adds a back-foot forcing stroke to the rope at cover for good measure.

Ward has meanwhile been very quiet since lunch, and it is only when Dagnall replaces Snape that the Surrey opener rediscovers the boundary, after a twenty-over hiatus, with a pull that takes him through to a solid 116-ball half-century.

While Ramprakash continues to look in imperious form, following up an amazing slog-sweep for six off Dagnall with a glorious cover-drive that penetrates DeFreitas' off-side cordon, Ward's innings is brought to a close as soon as Maddy replaces Dagnall at the pavilion end. Having just raised the fifty partnership for the second wicket with a clip to the square-leg boundary, the former England left-hander pads up to an inswinger and is sent on his way by the upraised digit of umpire David Constant.

With the scoreboard reading 145-2 as Graham Thorpe takes guard, Surrey are still very much in control, and Ramprakash keeps his side on course for a big total as he wins his long-running battle with DeFreitas. After finding a way through the packed off-side ring again with an extra-cover drive that takes the total past 150, he confounds the Leicestershire captain by producing a cheeky sweep for four in each of the bowler's next two overs, with the second of these boundaries completing a superb fifty from just 62 deliveries.

Having made a sticky start, Thorpe now begins to find his timing, and the outlook is rather bleak for the home team as the left-hander takes successive fours off Maddy and then glances DeFreitas to the rope at fine leg to convince the Foxes' skipper that he has outstayed his welcome at the bowling crease after a brave fourteen-over effort.

As tea approaches they receive a welcome boost, however, when Ramprakash surprisingly chips Maddy tamely to mid-on, where the young substitute fielder, Luke Wright, takes a good tumbling catch low to his left-hand side. The former England batsman returns to the pavilion with the score standing at 178-3 and, like Batty and Ward before him, he must be very disappointed to have got himself out in the fifties when a century was clearly there for the taking.

Rikki Clarke, the new batsman, now has a tricky period to survive until the interval, though he shows no nerves whatsoever as he immediately clips Maddy to the fence at square leg and then off-drives Masters - DeFreitas' replacement at the Bennett end - for another boundary in the next over.

With Maddy completing a good seven-over spell that has brought him two wickets, and Masters conceding eleven runs from his next over, including two off-side fours to Thorpe, the home side turn to spin for the last three overs of the session. Neither Snape nor Brad Hodge cause any problems, however, as Thorpe takes his side up to the two-hundred mark and adds another four to his collection with a sweep to fine leg off Hodge.

As the players leave the field for tea, one has to wonder why Vasbert Drakes, Leicestershire's second overseas player and, supposedly, their main strike bowler, has been completely unemployed despite being on the field throughout. It seems ludicrous that he has bowled just five overs out of a total of sixty-four delivered to date.

Tea:- Surrey 206-3 (Thorpe 32, Clarke 8*) from 64 overs*

The suspicion that an extreme reluctance, or even refusal, to bowl from the pavilion end has been the principal reason behind Drakes being so sparingly used thus far would appear to be confirmed when he opens the bowling from the Bennett end after tea. With the West Indian bowling to seven-two off-side fields, in the style of DeFreitas, and Snape continuing to occupy the pavilion end, it seems that Leicestershire still feel they can contain at one end and then force mistakes, born of frustration, at the other end.

They are wrong. Clarke is the first to prove this when he finds the boundary three times in the first three overs of the session, then Thorpe joins in with a leg-glanced four off Drakes that completes a fifty partnership inside twelve overs. Surrey's 21-year-old all-rounder then shows his tremendous ability and versatility on the drive by first crashing Drakes to the long-on boundary, then drilling Snape along the ground through mid-off for four and back over his head into the pavilion for a glorious six. He also demonstrates that he has the more delicate strokes in his repertoire when he late-cuts the off-spinner to the rope at third man to bring up Surrey's 250 in the seventy-second over.

While Clarke has been peppering the boundary boards, Thorpe has been restricted to singles at the other end, so it is no surprise that the left-hander has been left behind in the forties by the time his junior partner reaches an excellent fifty from just 55 balls with an on-driven single off Snape.

With neither Leicestershire bowler having shown any sign of being able to break the Thorpe-Clarke partnership, DeFreitas now opts for a double change that sees Dagnall and Maddy returning to the fray, and Thorpe soon drives Dagnall to the extra-cover boundary to become the fifth Surrey batsman out of five to register a half-century in the innings. Having taken seventy-seven balls to reach the mark, he ranks third-fastest behind Clarke and Ramprakash.

Dagnall then misses an opportunity to end the fourth-wicket partnership in his next over when Clarke thumps back a hard caught-and-bowled chance that doesn't stick in the bowler's outstretched right hand... and the former Warwickshire man is instantly punished as the batsman pulls the next delivery to midwicket for the four runs that make the stand worth a hundred.

Although Leicestershire are really struggling now, their ground fielding remains pretty good, which is just as well because Surrey's running between the wickets has been excellent since tea. Even when Dagnall and Maddy string together a series of accurate overs at this stage of the day, the total is kept moving by a sequence of well-taken singles.

Thorpe eventually breaks this run of six boundary-free overs, however, when he drives each bowler to the extra-cover fence, with the second of these strokes taking the visitors past the three-hundred mark and prompting another double bowling change that sees Masters and Snape paired for the first time.

This combination doesn't look as if it's going to be any more successful than those that have gone before it, however, as Clarke takes a liking to Masters' bowling by driving him to the long-off boundary - taking the fourth-wicket partnership past 150 - and then cracking successive deliveries to the midwicket fence in the tall seamer's next over, while Thorpe takes advantage of a couple of loose deliveries from Snape to cut and drive fours of his own.

The Surrey left-hander falls, in rather unfortunate circumstances, during Snape's penultimate over of the day, however, when umpire Constant adjudges him to have tickled a legside delivery through to Nixon behind the stumps with the batsman's score on eighty-seven and the total at 347. It's a sad way for a fine innings and an excellent stand of 169 with Clarke to have ended, though the visitors' very strong position at the end of the day no doubt compensates to some extent.

Close:- Surrey 349-4 (Clarke 90, Saqlain 0*) from 96 overs*

Second Day - Friday 22nd August
Surrey 501; Leicestershire 127-7

Phil DeFreitas and Vasbert Drakes have a new ball in their hands at the start of day two, though this clearly doesn't bother the batsmen too much - Rikki Clarke drives Drakes straight down the ground for a boundary in the second over, and then watches in admiration from the other end as Saqlain Mushtaq, Surrey's nightwatchman, thrashes DeFreitas through extra cover and over mid-on for fours in the following over.

Having progressed to ninety-eight with a thick-edged single to third man in Drakes' second over of the morning, Clarke then drives DeFreitas to the rope at cover to complete a splendid century from 133 balls and receives a good hand from the Grace Road regulars and the sprinkling of travelling Surrey fans. His knock almost comes to an end later in the same over, however, when a top-edged cut is put down at first slip by Brad Hodge with the batsman's score still on 102 and the total 369-4.

With Drakes looking much more like a Test bowler this morning, after his poor display yesterday, the going soon becomes more difficult and, having edged the West Indian just wide of a diving second slip in the eighth over of the morning, Saqlain falls lbw for thirteen just two overs later when he is trapped on the crease by a ball that Drakes nips back at him off the pitch.

It's clear that we are now witnessing the best Leicestershire bowling of the game so far, though the hosts still have an awful lot to do if they are to get back into the match. DeFreitas and Drakes continue to send down some testing overs, though, and, while Clarke is kept very quiet for just about the first time in his innings, the new batsman, Adam Hollioake, is beaten on a number of occasions as he makes a very uncertain start.

Clarke does eventually break free, however, driving DeFreitas to the cover boundary and then picking off successive legside fours off Drakes to take the total past four-hundred, and this seemingly inspires Hollioake to do likewise when David Masters replaces the Foxes' skipper for the next over at the Bennett end. The Surrey skipper's taste of freedom, which brings him three beautifully driven off-side boundaries off the former Kent paceman, is only fleeting, though, as an attempt to square-cut Drakes in the following over results in a bottom edge onto the stumps that pegs Surrey back just a little at 420-6.

The Barbadian fast bowler has deserved his two successes this morning, though it is clear that he is running out of steam after ten overs when Clarke clips a full-toss through square leg for four. Since Masters has shown that he continues to be allergic to Surrey batsmen during a third over that sees him driven to the boundary by both Clarke and the newly arrived Azhar Mahmood, the home skipper is left with no option but to make another of his double bowling changes by calling up Charlie Dagnall at the pavilion end and Jeremy Snape at the Bennett end.

This switch almost brings instant success, too, since Azhar, on eleven, edges Snape's first delivery low to the left of Hodge at slip but survives when the Aussie fails to hang on to a catch for the second time in the morning.

The unlucky bowler is soon celebrating his second wicket of the innings, however, when Clarke gets a thin edge to a drive a few overs later and is picked up by Paul Nixon behind the stumps with the total standing at 456. A disappointed Clarke seems unconvinced that he has touched the ball, but drags himself from the crease and receives a warm welcome as he returns to the pavilion having scored 139 from 199 balls, twenty-one of which he has struck for four and one of which he has hit for six.

The loss of this wicket, with lunch around half-an-hour away, sparks a brief period of explosive cricket, with Azhar and his new partner, Ian Salisbury, plundering five boundaries - including a straight-driven six by the leg-spinner off Snape - in the space of three overs.

Everything quietens down very suddenly, though, when Azhar, having swapped his helmet for a sunhat, top-edges a sweep at Snape into his face and requires lengthy on-field treatment for what appears to be a very nasty injury to his nose.

With the Pakistani having shed a fair bit of blood, and in no fit state to continue his innings, James Ormond takes his place in the middle and promptly edges his fifth ball from the off-spinner to Nixon, leaving Salisbury and Tim Murtagh to bat out the last three overs before the break.

Lunch:- Surrey 486-8 (Salisbury 15, Murtagh 4*) from 132 overs*

After a couple of boundaries from Salisbury, the second of which takes the total past the five-hundred mark, Murtagh snicks an off-side forcing stroke off Drakes and is well picked up, away to his left-hand side, by Maddy at second slip to end the Surrey innings.

With Ali Brown already on the field as a substitute for the injured Azhar at the start of Leicestershire's reply, the visitors look like they might have another problem straight away as John Maunders clips Ormond's first delivery through midwicket and Adam Hollioake can only manage a very laboured chase as the ball runs on to the boundary

Ormond then has an interesting battle with Maunders during his second over, with two big lbw appeals from the bowler being followed by a clip to the rope at square leg by the former Middlesex left-hander, and a missed chance by Brown, low down at first slip, with the batsman's score on eight, and the total on ten.

Just to rub salt in the wound, Maunders then adds another boundary to his collection in the former Leicestershire paceman's next over, courtesy of a fine on-drive, while Maddy notches his first four with an off-drive at the expense of the other opening bowler, Tim Murtagh.

At this point, the visitors lose their captain, who is clearly struggling with some kind of injury as he retires to the pavilion and is replaced by Phil Sampson. Ian Ward therefore takes over as skipper and enjoys almost instant success as Surrey remove both openers in the space of three overs.

Maunders goes first, when he edges a drive at Ormond through to Jon Batty with the total on twenty-four, then Maddy plays all around a straight full-length delivery from the impressive Murtagh and falls plumb lbw with just six runs added to the score.

Since they are now struggling at 30-2, it is fortunate for the Foxes that the new batsmen, Brad Hodge and John Sadler, start confidently with a boundary apiece off Murtagh at the end of a very good seven-over spell from the 22-year-old seamer.

Saqlain Mushtaq is the man to take over from Murtagh at the pavilion end, while Ormond continues his fine stint from the Bennett end and almost claims the wicket of Sadler when the former Yorkshire left-hander misses a pull and watches the ball land perilously close to the stumps as it drops down off his body. Another short delivery later in the over, this time to Hodge, only brings pain to Ramprakash at short leg, however, as a full-blooded pull crashes into the fielder's upper torso. With Azhar and Hollioake having already been forced out of the action, it's turning out to be a bad day for Surrey on the injuries front, though Ramprakash, fortunately, is able to continue, despite looking to be in some discomfort.

At least the match position is more encouraging for the Championship leaders, and they take a tighter grip on the game once Rikki Clarke replaces Ormond at the Bennett end. Having been driven to the extra-cover boundary by Hodge in his first over, the England all-rounder is then forced away to the rope backward of point by the same batsman in his following over, before taking spectacular revenge with his next ball, which turns out to be an excellent yorker that flattens the Australian's off stump.

At 58-3, Leicestershire are now really up against it, especially as the new batsman, Jeremy Snape, is surely too high up the order at number five. With Clarke extracting some surprising lift from the pitch to trouble the former Northamptonshire and Gloucestershire all-rounder from the outset, and Sadler looking uncomfortable at times when faced by Saqlain at the other end, it seems that another wicket is just around the corner at this stage.

Sadler appears to be a fast learner, though, as he eventually manages to get the Pakistani off-spinner away for a couple of pleasant boundaries, before driving him back down the ground for a rather unexpected straight six that prompts Ward to make a change at the pavilion end.

It's at the Bennett end where the most significant action takes place in the last couple of overs before tea, however, as Clarke picks up two late wickets to further strengthen his team's hold on the match. Having switched to a round-the-wicket attack against Sadler, he immediately nips a ball back through an indeterminate stroke to clip the top of the off stump with the total on eighty-nine, then, with just nine runs added, he claims the scalp of the distinctly unimpressive Snape with a low right-handed catch in his follow-through.

Tea:- Leicestershire 98-5 (Nixon 4) from 34.2 overs*

The tea-time news concerning Surrey's walking wounded isn't too promising, with Azhar having sustained a badly broken nose and Hollioake said to be laid low with a rather unpleasant viral infection, while Ramprakash hopes to soldier on despite suffering pain in his shoulder from the blow he took at short leg.

The resumption of play is delayed for twenty minutes by bad light, and once we get under way again the sixth-wicket pair edge the score up to and beyond a hundred with a series of singles off Clarke and Salisbury.

Nixon does eventually manage to pull Clarke for a boundary backward of square leg - thereby bringing to an end the Surrey all-rounder's excellent fourteen-over occupation of the Bennett end - but then loses two partners in the space of three balls from the new bowler, Tim Murtagh. After an uncomfortable stay of twenty-seven balls for four runs, Brandy loses his off stump as he pushes forward defensively, then DeFreitas has the same stump extracted when he assays a drive at his second ball, having driven his first to the long-off boundary.

To be fair to the batsmen, one has to wonder if indifferent light has played a part in these dismissals, since the umpires confer again before the start of Murtagh's next over and find their offer of a retreat to the pavilion gratefully accepted by Nixon and Drakes.

Surprisingly, the light improves sufficiently for the players to return to the middle at 6.12pm, and Drakes immediately suggests that he can see the ball well enough by driving Murtagh's first two deliveries to the boundary. After another eleven balls, the umpires decree that the light has closed in again, however, and play finally ends for the day at 6.22pm with Leicestershire in deep trouble at 127-7.

It's just as well that Surrey are holding all the aces in this match, since Sussex have already walloped Essex by an innings and 120 runs at Colchester, with the game ending at 3.50pm on the third day. The reigning champions now know that they must go on to win this contest if they are to retain top spot in the Championship.

Close:- Leicestershire 127-7 (Nixon 16, Drakes 9*) from 46.1 overs*

Third Day - Saturday 23rd August
Surrey 501; Leicestershire 166 and 348-2

Since their position is already extremely precarious, Leicestershire need to make sure that Surrey have to work really hard for every wicket from here on in, so it's something of a disaster for them when they lose Vasbert Drakes to a run out from the tenth ball of the morning.

The Barbadian is clearly surprised to be called through for a single when a Salisbury leg-break hits him on the pad and bobbles out on the legside, and, as a result, he is slow out of the blocks and still stretching for the crease at the non-striker's end when Jon Batty's throw hits the stumps. It looks to be a pretty tight call, but umpire Constant decides that the West Indian international is out, leaving the home side in deeper disarray at 129-8.

Although Nixon partially atones for his part in the dismissal by twice driving Salisbury to the off-side boundary, and Charlie Dagnall pushes the score up to 150 with edged and clipped fours off Tim Murtagh, the hosts are now absolutely certain to be following on and their sole objective is to minimise the first-innings deficit that they will be facing.

There is still a huge gap of 348 runs between the sides when they lose their ninth wicket at 153, however, with Nixon the man to depart as he misses a sweep at Salisbury and falls lbw for thirty.

Dagnall then takes a couple of nice fours off Murtagh, first through square leg and then through backward point, prompting Hollioake - who has recovered sufficiently to take his place on the field this morning - to turn to Rikki Clarke at the Bennett end.

The 21-year-old immediately justifies his captain's faith in him, and returns new career-best figures of 4-31 in the process, when David Masters attempts to turn a hip-high full-toss loosener away on the leg side and only succeeds in getting a leading edge straight to Ian Ward in the gully. The batsman seems highly aggrieved about his dismissal and stands his ground, presumably feeling that the delivery should have been deemed a no-ball on height, but the umpires are unimpressed and Leicestershire are all out for a dismal 166.

With the opposition 335 runs in arrears, Hollioake asks them to follow on, and both Maunders and Maddy make a rather nervous start against Ormond, with the first boundary of the innings coming from Maunders' edge, on the bounce, through the slips. Murtagh is again sharing the new ball with Ormond in the continued absence of Azhar Mahmood, who has now been joined on the injured list by Mark Ramprakash, with substitute fielder duties being carried out by Ali Brown and Phil Sampson.

Clearly determined to make a better fist of their second innings, the Foxes' openers battle gamely, with their former colleague providing the main threat and having one particularly confident lbw appeal against Maunders turned down by umpire Constant in the fifteenth over, just after Saqlain Mushtaq has replaced Murtagh at the pavilion end.

After nine testing overs, Ormond joins his new-ball partner in taking a break, with Clarke taking over and sending down three eventful overs in the lead-up to lunch.

While Saqlain is studiously blocked out at the other end, Clarke enjoys an interesting contest with Maddy, which he wins in the final over of the session. Having had a big appeal for leg-before rejected by umpire Cowley, and then been pulled to the boundary, he makes an important first breakthrough by having the former England man taken at the wicket by Batty from an edged defensive stroke at a good lifting delivery with the total standing at forty-nine.

Brad Hodge then brings up the Foxes' fifty from the next ball with an uppish drive that earns him a single as it falls just short and wide of mid-on, before Maunders takes the home side to lunch on a more positive note with a clip for four behind square on the legside.

Lunch:- Leicestershire 56-1 (Maunders 19, Hodge 2*) from 23 overs*

While the weather has changed dramatically during the break, with the sun bursting through the clouds to give us a glorious afternoon, Hollioake makes no changes to his attack, as Saqlain and Clarke remain his bowlers of choice and start the session with three maidens.

Although Hodge is the batsman to break the spell, with an on-driven four off Saqlain, it's his left-handed partner who then develops the aggressive theme by finding the off-side boundary three times in four overs, prompting the replacement of Saqlain with Salisbury at the pavilion end.

When Clarke then concedes deflected, cut and glanced fours to Hodge in the course of his next over, he, too, is replaced, with Ormond the man to take over at the Bennett end. The total has zipped into three figures during Hodge's sequence of boundaries, while the partnership has passed fifty, with Maunders having grown in confidence as it has developed.

For now, though, it's Hodge who is playing the leading role as he notches a back-foot four in each of Salisbury's next two overs and then forces Ormond away to the rope backward of point in the following over.

Although the score is already moving on quite nicely for Leicestershire at this stage, it receives a massive boost when the batsmen take seventeen runs from the fourth over of Ormond's spell, bringing up a whole host of milestones in the process - Maunders' extra-cover drive for four from the first delivery completes a solid fifty, from 134 balls, for the former Middlesex batsman, while a square-cut boundary by Hodge three balls later takes the Victorian to a rapid half-century from his fifty-second delivery, as well as raising the Foxes' 150 and the century partnership for the second wicket. The Australian then finishes the over with a straight drive for two and an extra-cover drive to the rope at extra cover, much to Ormond's chagrin.

With the sun now beating down quite fiercely, a drinks break is taken, and, while Ormond, initially, comes back well from his battering, Salisbury suddenly finds the batsmen getting after him, as Hodge plunders a back-foot boundary on each side of the wicket before Maunders dances down the track and lofts the leg-spinner down the ground for the over's third four. Suddenly, Surrey are not having everything their own way, the ground fielding is becoming a little ragged and Azhar's absence is being felt for the first time in the match.

Hollioake immediately signals for Saqlain to return to the attack in place of Salisbury, though Ormond very nearly makes the breakthrough that the visitors are seeking in the over before this change takes place… but not by taking a wicket. A nasty, spitting delivery at the start of the forty-seventh over of the innings cracks Hodge on the hand, and, for a while, it appears as if he might be forced to retire hurt. Fortunately for the home side, the gritty Victorian eventually decides that he is able to continue, and he shows no obvious signs of discomfort as he cuts the next ball to the boundary and follows it with a square-driven four, before Ormond finds the same spot on the wicket again to rap the batsman's knuckles for a second time.

While Saqlain wheels away fairly economically at the other end, Hollioake perseveres with Ormond in the hope that he has sown some seeds of doubt in the batsmen's minds about the state of the pitch. Hodge responds brilliantly, however, by taking five fours from the former England fast bowler's next two overs, with only the last of these - a top-edged cut over the slips - not coming right out of the meat of the bat.

As a result of his stirring counter-attack, Hodge's score has advanced to ninety-six; the total has raced past two-hundred; and the second-wicket partnership has not only exceeded the 150 mark, it has also become the biggest for Leicestershire versus Surrey at Grace Road. It has also seen Ormond out of the attack at the end of a hard-working but rather erratic spell, with Clarke nominated as his replacement.

Once Maunders has welcomed the Surrey all-rounder back into the attack with an off-side forcing stroke for four, Hodge takes centre stage again, moving elegantly to an outstanding century by advancing on Saqlain and driving him to the rope at extra cover. The Australian's amazing innings has taken just 87 balls and included no fewer than twenty fours, and, as an added bonus, it is announced that this is the one-thousandth first-class century recorded by a Leicestershire batsman.

Maunders then reaches a far more modest milestone in the following over from Clarke when he whips the ball away to the midwicket boundary to post a new career-best first-class score of seventy-seven, and promptly celebrates by taking ten from the same bowler's next over.

With tea looming, Hollioake has now seen enough, and brings himself into the attack, as well as giving Murtagh his first opportunity to bowl since the twelfth over of the innings.

From the Surrey point of view, these two not only offer a little more control, they also come close to splitting the second-wicket pair, with Hollioake inducing an outside edge from Hodge that flies through the vacant second/third slip area, and Murtagh preying on Maunders' arrival in the anxious eighties to beat him three times outside the off stump in a single over.

A very dispiriting session for the visitors ends soon afterwards with the Leicestershire pair having batted quite brilliantly to add an unbeaten 201 runs since lunch, which therefore makes their partnership worth 208 at this stage. The reigning champions have clearly lost control under the hot sun, though they remain in a strong position in the match, with their hosts still trailing by seventy-eight runs. If they can break this stand and pick up another couple of wickets during the final session of the day then they should be back on track for victory.

Tea:- Leicestershire 257-1 (Maunders 90, Hodge 118*) from 62 overs*

The appearance of Azhar Mahmood after tea suggests that the visitors are more than a little concerned about the situation in which they now find themselves, since it had been said that he was unlikely to play any further part in the match. It's very brave of the Pakistani all-rounder to attempt to help his team out in this way, and he is immediately pressed into the attack opposite Murtagh, who had bowled tidily before the break and has certainly earned a longer spell.

With these two bowlers in tandem, the flood of runs that we had witnessed during the middle session becomes more of a trickle, with Hodge largely becalmed and Maunders following the softly-softly route towards a maiden first-class century by picking off a succession of singles. Before the Foxes' opener can reach that mark, however, his partner equals his career-best first-class score of 140 and puts the duo's partnership, which is now worth 241 runs, into the record books as the highest for the second wicket for Leicestershire against Surrey at any venue.

Maunders' magical moment then follows two overs later when he clips Murtagh through midwicket for two to reach 101 from his 219th delivery, and celebrates in understandably joyous style, having made his maiden ton in very difficult circumstances against the team generally considered to be the best in the land.

Although his post-tea bowlers have both delivered decent spells, Hollioake knows that he must capture some wickets before the close, so he recalls Salisbury to the attack at the pavilion end and gives himself another go at the Bennett end.

Salisbury almost makes the breakthrough straight away, when Maunders inside-edges a drive past his leg stump and profits by four runs, thereby increasing the value of the partnership to 250, though the rest of the over yields singles that take the total to three-hundred and Hodge on to his new career-best score. By way of celebration, the Victorian then gets back on the boundary trail, with an extra-cover drive off Hollioake being followed by a straight drive and a cut off Salisbury that take him through to his maiden first-class 150 from his 161st ball.

At this point, Saqlain replaces Hollioake at the Bennett end, and it is beginning to look as if Surrey have forgotten what it's like to take a wicket as Maunders sweeps the off-spinner for two boundaries. It has been sixty-one overs since the visitors' last success, in fact, when a Salisbury leg-break, delivered into the rough from round the wicket, spits up to Hodge's glove and is very well caught by Batty as he scurries away in the direction of short backward square leg and puts in a last-ditch dive. Umpire Cowley, who is clearly not sure that the ball has come off the glove, remains unmoved as Surrey appeal for the catch but, fortunately, the Australian sportingly 'walks' once Batty has confirmed that he has taken the ball cleanly. Hodge duly receives a well deserved standing ovation for a special innings of 157, which has included no fewer than twenty-nine fours and given his side a fighting chance of escaping from this game with a draw, though they still have much to do, despite the fact that they have reduced the deficit to just five runs at 330-2.

Now that the visitors can see a chink of light at the end of the tunnel they apply pressure with a close-set field for their two spinners for the last ten overs of the day. Maunders and his new partner, John Sadler, hang on grimly, though, despite a few inside edges, plus appeals for lbw and a catch at short leg, and slowly but surely move their team into a lead of thirteen runs by the close.

Although the final session has seen a much improved Surrey bowling display, the damage may already have been done by the events of the post-lunch session. They can console themselves with the fact that Leicestershire start out tomorrow with their two best batsmen already dismissed, and, if the worst comes to the worst, there must be a possibility that their relegation-threatened hosts might be prepared to do a deal with regard to a declaration and run chase.

Close:- Leicestershire 348-2 (Maunders 126, Sadler 6*) from 94 overs*

Fourth Day - Sunday 24th August
Surrey 501 and 117-2; Leicestershire 166 and 636-4dec
Match Drawn
Leicestershire 6pts, Surrey 12

With a new ball in the hands of Azhar Mahmood and James Ormond, and overcast conditions prevailing at the start of play, Surrey have a realistic chance of claiming some early wickets, working their way through the home side's fragile-looking batting line-up, and then knocking off whatever runs are required to win the game towards the end of the day. Well, that's the plan anyway.

The two inexperienced left-handers, John Maunders and John Sadler, make an appropriately watchful start for a side who are effectively 13-2, though each of them is beaten by an occasional good delivery from a nicely fired-up Ormond.

Having failed to add to his score during the first three overs, Sadler registers the first boundaries of the day, courtesy of a leg-glance off Ormond and an extra-cover drive off Azhar, before things quieten down again, with neither side able to take the initiative.

Maunders, seemingly not the best of starters, shows that he is growing in confidence as we come towards the end of the first hour's play, however, by hooking Azhar to the fence and then lofting Ormond straight back down the ground off the back foot. These strokes also demonstrate how dead the pitch has become, and, with neither bowler able to locate the spot from which Ormond had made balls rear at Hodge yesterday afternoon, Surrey's task is looking more difficult than anyone had expected.

Having contributed good but luckless spells, Azhar and Ormond are replaced by Rikki Clarke and Saqlain Mushtaq at around the same time as the total moves past four-hundred and Maunders reaches his 150 from his 355th delivery.

Saqlain, who had frequently bowled with his cap on back-to-front yesterday, decides that he will do so again today, though if it's meant to bring him good fortune it isn't working, as Maunders soon miscues into space at extra cover.

Sadler also enjoys a slice of luck at this stage, when he edges Clarke low to the left of Ali Brown at first slip, but, unfortunately for the bowler and Surrey, the fielder is barely able to get a hand to a chance that Batty might have gone for, and the ball races away to the boundary.

Apart from these isolated anxious moments, the batsmen look pretty much at ease against these two bowlers, so Hollioake makes a double switch that allows Ian Salisbury and Tim Murtagh brief spells before lunch. Neither man is able to create a chance, though, as Maunders takes the third-wicket partnership into three figures with a lofted on-drive for four off Salisbury, while Sadler picks off two impressive off-side boundaries during Murtagh's final over of the session to progress to a 129-ball half-century and take the total past 450.

As the players depart for lunch, it's clear that Surrey's inability to take a wicket this morning has probably cost them the chance of winning the match by conventional means, and, given the docile nature of the pitch, one has to wonder whether Phil DeFreitas will be prepared to enter into any discussions regarding a fourth-innings run-chase, even though his team's desperate position in the relegation zone suggests that he really ought to.

Lunch:- Leicestershire 454-2 (Maunders 169, Sadler 57*) from 125 overs*

The word around the ground during the interval is that the two captains have had a discussion about contriving a run chase and that it is quite possible something will be set up during the afternoon.

There is no immediate suggestion of any collusion, however, as Salisbury and Hollioake open the bowling after lunch, with Sadler passing his previous career-best first-class score of fifty-nine during the leg-spinner's first over.

With the two young Leicestershire batsmen having extended their partnership to 135 runs, Surrey do at least manage to claim their third wicket of the innings two overs later when Maunders attempts to sweep Salisbury and only succeeds in gloving the simplest of catches to Batty. The 22-year-old receives a fine reception as he returns to the pavilion, having put together a most determined innings of 171 that has spanned eight-and-a-half hours and dug his side out of a very deep hole… and possibly put a large dent in Surrey's Championship hopes, too.

Paul Nixon is the new batsman, and he shows further signs of his wretched current form as he scratches around unproductively for half-a-dozen overs while Sadler plays the lead role in advancing the total from 465, at the point of Maunders' dismissal, to 483.

With the Leicestershire advantage standing at 148 at this point, and nothing very positive happening, the dreaded switch to 'joke' bowling takes place, as Ian Ward and Graham Thorpe are chosen by Hollioake to send down some extremely innocuous slow offerings in order to donate some easy runs to their hosts.

Nixon's timing is so poor, however, that he immediately offers Ward a caught-and-bowled chance off a leading edge with his score on two but, thereafter, the batsmen help themselves to whatever runs they fancy, with Sadler taking advantage of the situation to cruise through to a maiden first-class century by thrashing a Ward full-toss straight back down the ground for six. Since most of his runs in a 186-ball innings have come against genuine bowling, these late 'freebies' shouldn't detract from a fine effort that has now given his team the advantage in this contest - DeFreitas will clearly have held the whip hand in discussions with Hollioake, since Surrey's need to win the game is greater than Leicestershire's. The reigning champions have a title to chase and wish to regain their place at the top of the table, after all, while the Foxes would have nothing more than an outside chance of avoiding filling one of the three relegation slots even if they were to win here.

As runs continue to flow freely, speculation concerning the eventual target that the visitors might be set turns to speculation about whether or not DeFreitas is planning to dangle any carrot at all. The total meanwhile builds beyond 550, and, once we reach 586, Leicestershire record their highest-ever total against Surrey, surpassing the 585-6 declared that they compiled in the Championship decider at The Oval in 1998.

By the time Sadler, on 145, cuts Thorpe straight into Hollioake's hands at extra cover in the 152nd over of the innings, the home side are 588-4 and leading by 253 runs, with approximately forty-five overs left for play, and hopes of a potentially exciting final session are receding rapidly.

The new batsman, Damien Brandy, then takes advantage of a dropped catch at deep mid-on by Ramprakash - briefly on the field as a substitute, and clearly struggling with his shoulder injury - off Thorpe, to rush his side to the six-hundred mark and beyond with two sixes and a four at the expense of the same bowler.

Finally, as Hollioake returns at the pavilion end in place of Thorpe, DeFreitas calls his batsmen in, leaving Surrey an entirely notional 'target' of 302 in eighty-five minutes plus sixteen overs.

Since Ward and Batty show no inclination to play any expansive strokes during the seven overs delivered by DeFreitas and Drakes before tea, it is clear that the visitors are resigned to the draw and the fact that Sussex are the leaders of the Championship.

Tea:- Surrey 19-0 (Ward 10, Batty 6*) from 7 overs*

A surprising burst of five boundaries in the first two overs after the break leaves everyone wondering if Surrey might just have a dart at the target, though the fact that they have lost Ward in the process - he attempts an almost impossible single to mid-off, and fails to beat Masters' direct-hit throw at the non-striker's end - probably puts the lid on this fanciful idea straight away.

This is indeed the case, and the game heads towards its inevitable conclusion with only some pleasant strokeplay from Batty and Thorpe to brighten the way. Although the Surrey keeper falls lbw to DeFreitas for thirty when missing a pull in the twentieth over, Thorpe manages to complete a 55-ball half-century before stumps are drawn.

Surrey 501 and 117-2; Leicestershire 166 and 636-4dec
Match Drawn. Leicestershire 6pts, Surrey 12

TALKING POINTS - RIKKI CLARKE

Would you say that this was your best performance with the ball in the Championship so far?
RC - Yes, definitely. I felt I bowled with good rhythm, I hit good areas and I found a little bit of pace on a slow wicket.

Would you consider consistency to be the main thing missing from your bowling at the moment? And how do you go about improving in that area? Is it a case of 'grooving' your action?
RC - Yes, consistency is definitely the main thing. I need to train my brain to repeat an action, and once I've got that sorted out then that should bring greater consistency. I've worked very hard on my bowling and it seems to be going in the right direction and getting better year-by-year.

After we bowled Leics out 335 in arrears early on day three it all seemed to go wrong for us. What happened?
RC - It wasn't an easy pitch to bowl on because it got flatter, and they batted well, so you can't take anything away from them. Hodge played wonderfully well and John Maunders gave him good support to score his century, and that partnership put us out of reach of winning the game.

TALKING POINTS - ADAM HOLLIOAKE

What happened with regard to the proposed declaration and run-chase?
AH - It was bizarre. I'd never come across a situation like that before, where we'd come to an agreement on a declaration, we started sending down declaration bowling, and then they changed their minds halfway through. I don't know why - you can't rationalise that sort of thinking. But in both games their fear of losing was shown from an early stage. They employed incredibly negative tactics and that's probably why they now find themselves in the second division.

I'm rather surprised at a positive cricketer like Phil DeFreitas changing his mind like that.
AH - Well, I'm not sure how much of it was his decision - I know the coach was involved. I know Phil quite well, and he assured me that he wanted to declare but the rest of the side wasn't necessarily so keen.

LEICESTERSHIRE v SURREY at Leicester — 21st to 24th August

Surrey won the toss and elected to bat — Umpires:- David Constant and Nigel Cowley

SURREY - First Innings

Fall Of Wkt	Batsman	How	Out	Score	Balls	4s	6s
2-145	**I.J. Ward**	**lbw**	**b Maddy**	**59**	133	10	0
1-93	**J.N. Batty +**	**c Maddy**	**b DeFreitas**	**50**	112	9	0
3-178	**M.R. Ramprakash**	**c sub (Wright)**	**b Maddy**	**55**	70	6	3
4-347	**G.P. Thorpe**	**c Nixon**	**b Snape**	**87**	133	12	0
7-456	**R. Clarke**	**c Nixon**	**b Snape**	**139**	199	21	1
5-378	**Saqlain Mushtaq**	**lbw**	**b Drakes**	**13**	33	3	0
6-420	**A.J. Hollioake ***		**b Drakes**	**21**	28	3	0
	Azhar Mahmood	**retired**	**hurt**	**30**	46	4	0
	I.D.K. Salisbury	**Not**	**Out**	**24**	36	4	1
8-481	**J. Ormond**	**c Nixon**	**b Snape**	**0**	5	0	0
9-501	**T.J. Murtagh**	**c Maddy**	**b Drakes**	**6**	13	1	0
	Extras	**(8b, 2lb, 1w, 6nb)**		**17**			
	TOTAL	**(134.1 overs)**		**501**			

Bowler	O	M	R	W	NB	Wd
DeFreitas	**29**	**10**	**87**	**1**	-	1
Drakes	**21.1**	**2**	**85**	**3**	3	-
Dagnall	**23**	**3**	**88**	**0**	-	-
Maddy	**14**	**1**	**40**	**2**	-	-
Masters	**16**	**0**	**78**	**0**	-	-
Snape	**30**	**6**	**108**	**3**	-	-
Hodge	**1**	**0**	**5**	**0**	-	-

LEICESTERSHIRE - First Innings (Needing 352 to avoid the follow-on)							
Fall Of Wkt	Batsman	How	Out	Score	Balls	4s	6s
1-24	**J.K. Maunders**	**c Batty**	**b Ormond**	**12**	17	3	0
2-30	**D.L. Maddy**	**lbw**	**b Murtagh**	**12**	29	1	0
3-58	**B.J. Hodge**		**b Clarke**	**20**	39	4	0
4-89	**J.L. Sadler**		**b Clarke**	**31**	77	4	1
5-98	**J.N. Snape**	**c &**	**b Clarke**	**10**	39	1	0
9-153	**P.A. Nixon +**	**lbw**	**b Salisbury**	**30**	59	4	0
6-108	**D.G. Brandy**		**b Murtagh**	**4**	27	0	0
7-112	**P.A.J. DeFreitas ***		**b Murtagh**	**4**	2	1	0
8-129	**V.C. Drakes**	**run**	**out**	**10**	16	2	0
	C.E. Dagnall	**Not**	**Out**	**22**	30	4	0
10-166	**D.D. Masters**	**c Ward**	**b Clarke**	**1**	15	0	0
	Extras	**(4b, 4lb, 2nb)**		**10**			
	TOTAL	**(58.1 overs)**		**166**			

Bowler	O	M	R	W	NB	Wd
Ormond	**9**	**1**	**30**	**1**	1	-
Murtagh	**16**	**2**	**68**	**3**	-	-
Saqlain Mushtaq	**8**	**4**	**18**	**0**	-	-
Clarke	**12.1**	**4**	**21**	**4**	-	-
Salisbury	**13**	**5**	**21**	**1**	-	-

LEICESTERSHIRE - Second Innings (Following on, 335 runs in arrears)							
Fall Of Wkt	Batsman	How	Out	Score	Balls	4s	6s
3-465	**J.K. Maunders**	**c Batty**	**b Salisbury**	**171**	390	20	0
1-49	**D.L. Maddy**	**c Batty**	**b Clarke**	**20**	73	3	0
2-330	**B.J. Hodge**	**c Batty**	**b Salisbury**	**157**	169	29	0
4-588	**J.L. Sadler**	**c Hollioake**	**b Thorpe**	**145**	235	20	1
	P.A. Nixon +	**Not**	**Out**	**44**	72	5	0
	D.G. Brandy	**Not**	**Out**	**31**	23	3	2
	Extras	**(18b, 21lb, 29nb)**		**68**			
	TOTAL	**(158 overs)**	**(for 4 dec)**	**636**			

Bowler	O	M	R	W	NB	Wd
Ormond	**25**	**5**	**91**	**0**	4	-
Murtagh	**18**	**2**	**62**	**0**	1	-
Saqlain Mushtaq	**26**	**8**	**57**	**0**	4	-
Clarke	**18**	**3**	**82**	**1**	-	-
Salisbury	**25**	**5**	**92**	**2**	3	-
Hollioake	**9**	**0**	**39**	**0**	1	-
Azhar Mahmood	**14**	**3**	**37**	**0**	-	-
Ward	**12**	**0**	**64**	**0**	-	-
Thorpe	**11**	**1**	**73**	**1**	1	-

SURREY - Second Innings (Needing 302 to win)							
Fall Of Wkt	Batsman	How	Out	Score	Balls	4s	6s
1-32	**I.J. Ward**	**run**	**out**	**23**	28	5	0
2-89	**J.N. Batty +**	**lbw**	**b DeFreitas**	**30**	60	6	0
	G.P. Thorpe	**Not**	**Out**	**52**	60	9	0
	R. Clarke	**Not**	**Out**	**3**	21	0	0
	Extras	**(7lb, 2nb)**		**9**			
	TOTAL	**(28 overs)**	**(for 2 wkts)**	**117**			

Bowler	O	M	R	W	NB	Wd
DeFreitas	**9**	**2**	**31**	**1**	1	-
Drakes	**8**	**1**	**41**	**0**	-	-
Masters	**6**	**1**	**19**	**0**	-	-
Dagnall	**3**	**0**	**14**	**0**	-	-
Brandy	**2**	**1**	**5**	**0**	-	-

Other Frizzell Championship Division One Results

Surrey paid a heavy price for their inability to beat Leicestershire, as Sussex moved to the top of the table following their comprehensive demolition of Essex at Colchester. Lancashire had meanwhile blown their chances of getting back into contention by drawing with Middlesex on a featherbed of a pitch at Old Trafford. At the other end of the table, Essex, Nottinghamshire and Leicestershire were looking increasingly doomed to relegation.

August 20-21

***Trent Bridge:-* Kent (18pts) beat Nottinghamshire (3) by 9 wickets.** Notts 177 (Pietersen 100, Saggers 5-42) & 126 (Muralitharan 6-36); Kent 242 (Ealham 83) & 65-1.

August 20-23

***Colchester:-* Sussex (22pts) beat Essex (5) by an innings and 120 runs.** Sussex 612 (Goodwin 210, Prior 153*, Montgomerie 97, Lewry 70, Akram 5-130); Essex 283 (Robinson 64, Jefferson 55, Flower 50, Mushtaq 4-87) & 209 (Jefferson 59, Taylor 4-50).

August 21-24

***Old Trafford:-* Lancashire (10pts) drew with Middlesex (10).** Lancs 734-5dec (Hooper 201, Law 144, Loye 137, Chilton 125, Schofield 58*); Middx 544 (Strauss 155, Shah 147, Hutton 107, Keedy 5-188) & 237-7 (Strauss 63).

FRIZZELL CHAMPIONSHIP DIVISION ONE TABLE AT 24TH AUGUST

Pos	Prv		P	Points	W	D	L	T	Bat	Bwl	Ded
1	2	**Sussex**	**13**	**209.00**	8	2	3	0	50	39	0.00
2	1	**Surrey**	**13**	**204.00**	6	7	0	0	57	35	0.00
3	3	**Lancashire**	**12**	**156.00**	3	8	1	0	50	32	0.00
4	5	**Kent**	**13**	**151.00**	4	5	4	0	37	38	0.00
5	4	**Middlesex**	**13**	**147.00**	3	9	1	0	37	32	0.00
6	6	**Warwickshire**	**12**	**122.50**	2	6	3	1	36	29	1.50
7	7	**Essex**	**13**	**109.00**	1	7	4	1	24	36	0.00
8	8	**Leicestershire**	**13**	**93.50**	0	8	5	0	29	33	0.50
9	9	**Nottinghamshire**	**12**	**87.00**	1	4	7	0	24	34	1.00

NCL Division One Results

With Surrey have won at Leicester, Gloucestershire needed to respond with a victory at Worcester, and they duly managed to achieve this in a low-scoring game. The Lions' quick-fire triumph had seen them overtake the Gladiators in the net run-rate stakes, however, giving them an added advantage at this stage of the campaign.

August 24

***Colwyn Bay:-* Glamorgan Dragons (4pts) beat Yorkshire Phoenix by 1 run.** Glamorgan 238-8 (45ov; Powell 61, Maher 53); Yorks 237 (45ov; Lumb 92).

***Edgbaston:-* Warwickshire Bears (4pts) beat Kent Spitfires by 4 wickets.** Kent 212 (44.5ov; Walker 72, Waqar 4-20); Warwicks 213-6 (42.2ov; Wagh 66).

***Worcester:-* Gloucestershire Gladiators (4pts) beat Worcestershire Royals by 4 wickets.** Worcs 146 (44.2ov; Kemp 50); Gloucs 148-6 (40.5ov; Gidman 67*).

NCL DIVISION ONE TABLE AT 24TH AUGUST

Pos	Prv		P	Pts	W	T	L	A	NRR
1	1	**Surrey Lions**	**12**	**38**	9	0	2	1	8.45
2	2	**Gloucestershire Gladiators**	**12**	**34**	8	0	3	1	7.32
3	3	**Glamorgan Dragons**	**14**	**32**	8	0	6	0	-0.74
4	4	**Warwickshire Bears**	**13**	**28**	7	0	6	0	2.07
5	5	**Essex Eagles**	**12**	**22**	5	1	6	0	3.92
6	6	**Leicestershire Foxes**	**13**	**20**	5	0	8	0	-6.07
7	7	**Kent Spitfires**	**12**	**18**	4	1	7	0	-2.67
8	8	**Worcestershire Royals**	**12**	**16**	4	0	8	0	0.45
9	9	**Yorkshire Phoenix**	**12**	**16**	4	0	8	0	-9.25

17 The Crown Slips

For three days everything had gone to plan at Grace Road, with the NCL points safely secured - and the net run-rate boosted - to strengthen Surrey's position in that competition, followed by two days of domination in the Championship match. Then it had all gone horribly wrong. As at Hove, a couple of very poor sessions had proved costly, with the second session on the third day, when Hodge and Maunders had added 201 unbeaten runs, having probably been the pivotal period of the contest, since it had given the home side a massive boost as well as undoing a lot of the good work Surrey had done earlier in the match. It was probably fair to say that the bowling had been rather disappointing, even after taking into account the loss of Azhar to injury until the sixty-third over of Leicestershire's second innings and a pitch that seemed to get slower and lower as the game progressed. Without taking anything away from John Maunders and John Sadler, the fact that two inexperienced young batsmen were both able to record a maiden first-class century suggested that Surrey's high-class attack had not been functioning at its peak. Perhaps the greatest worry for the reigning champions at this time was the fact that two key bowlers, James Ormond and Saqlain Mushtaq, were suddenly experiencing something of a wicket drought, with the normally penetrative pair having claimed just eight victims from 174 overs in the last two away games, at Hove and Leicester. Saqlain's zero-return from thirty-four overs at Grace Road had certainly come as something of a shock as it was the first time he had gone wicketless in a Championship game in which he had bowled since July 2001 at Guildford - but on that occasion he had delivered only eight overs.

The Leicestershire game was now history, however, and everyone had to accept that Sussex had taken their chance to move to the top of the table. It would be interesting to see how they would react to their new lofty position. Would they feel under greater pressure now they were the Championship leaders? Would the weight of expectation prove too great for them as they closed in on a first-ever Championship title? Time alone would tell, and, for now, Surrey had to concentrate on their next fixture, a tough one against Lancashire at Old Trafford, starting approximately forty hours after the match had finished at Grace Road. Lancashire were in the same boat, though they were, at least, spared the travelling, since the game they had just completed against Middlesex had also been at Old Trafford. A ludicrous piece of fixture scheduling was made worse by the fact that both teams had just spent two solid days in the field, so there were likely to be twenty-two very tired cricketers on parade on Tuesday morning. You could also be sure that there would be any number of players carrying injuries, with Surrey having obvious doubts over Azhar Mahmood, Mark Ramprakash and their virus victim, Adam Hollioake.

Martin Bicknell was another man with a 'niggle', apparently, after the Headingley Test, though he wouldn't be considered for the Old Trafford match in any case, tight hamstring or not. Sadly, England had lost Bickers' comeback Test by 191 runs, though the Surrey veteran had performed pretty well, returning 27-11-50-2 in the first innings and 22-3-75-2 in the second. Mark Butcher had, incidentally, been England's top-scoring batsman in both innings, with knocks of seventy-seven and sixty-one. It was to be hoped that Bicknell would be fit for the final Test of the series at The Oval, and that he would be given another chance by the selectors. No-one deserved that more than Bickers.

FRIZZELL COUNTY CHAMPIONSHIP DIVISION ONE - MATCH FOURTEEN

LANCASHIRE versus SURREY
at Old Trafford

First Day - Tuesday 26th August
Surrey 330-9

The Teams And The Toss *- There's bad news for Surrey on the morning of the match as Mark Ramprakash is ruled out by his shoulder injury, though this allows Ali Brown to return to a team that is otherwise unchanged following the draw at Leicester. Lancashire also lose a key batsman in Mal Loye, who misses out because of back spasms, and they replace him with Mark Currie, a 23-year-old who has been playing for Cheshire and is now about to make his County Championship debut. With all England players rested between the fourth and fifth Tests, the nominated elevens are close to full available strength. Since both teams are still recovering from having spent two days in the field, the toss is an important one, and when Adam Hollioake calls correctly it is entirely predictable that he should elect to bat. Warren Hegg's reaction to the loss of this toss is amazing - he drop-kicks the offending coin into the back of beyond!*

Surrey look to have got away to a great start when Ian Ward drives and pulls two boundaries in Peter Martin's opening over from the Statham end but, unfortunately for the left-handed opener, umpire Tony Clarkson adjudges him to have been caught behind by Hegg from the first ball of Martin's second over, with the score at ten.

This brings Graham Thorpe to the crease at number three in the absence of Mark Ramprakash and he makes a good early impression by driving his third ball to the rope at wide long-on.

With Martin tending to overpitch slightly, allowing the batsmen to drive through the covers, and Glen Chapple at the Stretford end bowling too short, giving Jon Batty regular opportunities to force and cut through point, the visitors' fifty arrives in the twelfth over, during a sequence of three boundaries by the Surrey wicketkeeper.

This very positive strokeplay, albeit against some understandably weary-looking bowling, forces Hegg into a double change that sees John Wood - one of three Yorkshire-born bowlers in the Lancashire attack - entering the fray at the Statham end and, surprisingly, Carl Hooper at the Stretford end.

With these two new bowlers delivering three maidens between them during their first five overs in tandem, the Lancashire captain at last has some control. Hooper, who soon elects to come round the wicket to both batsmen, is steadiness personified, while Wood does spoil some of his good work with a couple of loose overs, during which Thorpe gets after him - in his fourth over, the former Durham seamer is cut and pulled for boundaries, while in his sixth he is twice driven to the rope at extra cover as the former England batsman completes an excellent 79-ball half-century.

Although Wood slips back into a better line and length during his next over, a no-ball sees the arrival of the Surrey hundred and the departure from the attack of the thickset seamer, with Chapple taking his place for a first bowl from the Statham end.

This change works well for the home side, since it soon brings to an end a second-wicket partnership that has just surged into three figures, courtesy of Batty's bold chassé and lofted straight drive for four in Hooper's ninth over. Having been glanced to the fine-leg boundary by Thorpe earlier in his second over back in the attack, Chapple takes swift revenge with a full-length delivery that traps the left-hander lbw for fifty-seven as he aims to leg.

Surrey are still well placed at 114-2, however, and their position has improved further by the time lunch arrives twenty minutes later, thanks to Rikki Clarke's two legside fours off Chapple, and Batty's square-driven boundary off Hooper and sweep to the rope at fine leg in Gary Keedy's final over of the session as replacement for the West Indian at the Stretford end. This last stroke completes a very impressive fifty by the Surrey keeper from his ninety-seventh ball.

Lunch:- Surrey 132-2 (Batty 51, Clarke 8*) from 36 overs*

Warren Hegg decides to pair Glen Chapple and Gary Keedy after lunch, with impressive results. While the right-arm seamer is much more accurate and threatening than he had been during the morning session, it's the left-arm spinner who really casts a spell over the batsmen, before picking up two well-deserved wickets to bring Lancashire right back into the match.

Although Batty manages to cut and drive isolated fours off Chapple, five of the afternoon's first eight overs are maidens, and, as a result, a frustrated Clarke, who has added just three singles to his lunch score, charges at Keedy and is defeated by spin to provide Hegg with a routine stumping that pegs Surrey back to 143-3.

Then, with the total having advanced by just four runs in the next three overs, Keedy strikes again with the first ball of his eighth over, having Ali Brown well taken off bat and pad by Iain Sutcliffe at short leg for one at 147-4.

With Lancashire having completely tied up their opponents at this stage, another barren spell of one run from four overs prefaces the capture of a fifth Surrey wicket as soon as Chapple, after a much-improved post-lunch spell of 8-2-13-0, gives way to Martin at the Statham end. Adam Hollioake becomes the veteran swing bowler's second victim of the innings when he fails to make any positive movement, forward or backward, to a delivery that maybe keeps a touch low and is bowled neck-and-crop for a nineteen-ball nought - a stat that speaks volumes about the accuracy of the bowling.

At this point, with the visitors having slumped to 148-5, a paltry sixteen runs have accrued from almost nineteen post-lunch overs, and the figures for Keedy's mesmeric spell during that period are 9-7-3-2.

It's absolutely certain that the new batsman, Azhar Mahmood, will relish the challenge that this situation presents, and, sure enough, he is soon cutting the left-arm spinner for four and driving Martin through extra-cover for three. And suddenly the shackles are off, as three singles come from Keedy's next over; Batty cuts Martin to the boundary; and Azhar takes consecutive fours off the left-arm spinner, with a lofted on-drive being followed by a late cut. When Batty then adds a superb off-driven six and a slog-swept four in Keedy's next two overs, Hegg opts for a double bowling change, recalling Wood at the Statham end and Hooper at the Stretford end.

These two manage to restore some order for a while, though Batty does find the rope at extra-cover off the burly seamer to register a very valuable fifty partnership, while Azhar steers to third man later in the same over to bring up the Surrey two-hundred.

The visitors are certainly back on track now, and, as tea approaches, Azhar takes a further boundary off each bowler, while his partner progresses to ninety-five by whipping Hooper away through midwicket for three.

In an attempt to break this increasingly dangerous partnership, the Lancashire captain turns to Chris Schofield for the final over of the session, but there is no joy for the 24-year-old leg-spinner as Azhar pulls him away wide of mid-on for the seventh four of his innings.

Tea:- Surrey 222-5 (Batty 95, Azhar 41*) from 73 overs*

Hegg reverts to Chapple and Keedy upon the resumption, though they are unable to recapture the magic of their post-lunch spell as Batty completes a truly excellent century in the second over by chopping the 205th delivery of his innings to the third-man boundary. Having scored a ton in last year's Championship match on this ground, it's a fair bet that Old Trafford would feature high on the Surrey keeper's list of favourite venues.

Azhar seems to quite like the surroundings, too, as he arrives at his personal half-century from 73 balls just four overs later by pulling and glancing successive deliveries from Chapple for four. When Batty then takes a third boundary from the over to bring up the Surrey 250 and the hundred partnership, Hegg concedes that his flame-haired seamer has come up with a third unimpressive spell out of four today, and signals to him that he should take a break.

The Lancashire skipper is then faced with something of a dilemma at the other end after Azhar despatches Keedy to the rope at midwicket twice in the course of the following over. Having given the matter some thought, Hegg elects to retain the Wakefield-born left-arm spinner in the attack at the Stretford end, opposite the newly introduced Schofield, and he turns out to be absolutely correct to have made this choice as Azhar immediately top-edges a cut at a shorter, quicker delivery into the keeper's gloves. It's been a fine innings of sixty-three by the Pakistani all-rounder, whose partnership of 113 with Batty has equalled the sixth-wicket record for Surrey versus Lancashire at Old Trafford and restored parity to the game, with the visitors on 261-6.

Since he is clearly aware that the loss of further wickets at this stage would hand the advantage to the opposition, Ian Salisbury, the new man at the crease, makes a very circumspect start against the Lancashire spinners, with Batty doing all the scoring, principally against Keedy, who he is now playing with great confidence. This is demonstrated when he twice dances down the track to drive deliveries to the boundary, with the second of these fours being immediately followed by a sweep to the rope at fine leg.

Batty's increasingly fluent strokeplay against the left-armer results in Hegg replacing Keedy with Hooper shortly afterwards, though it seems nothing can stop the Surrey keeper at the moment as he immediately cuts the West Indian backward of point for the twenty-third four of his innings. Unfortunately, his partner has been unable to make any headway against Schofield at the other end and, in trying to break free, Salisbury leans back on a drive and holes out to Mark Currie at square cover for five, giving his fellow leg-spinner a first wicket that reduces the visitors to 298-7.

It is now important for the new pair of Batty and Saqlain Mushtaq to survive the final nine overs of the day, since the last thing a weary Lancashire side will want is to be kept in the field for any length of time tomorrow. Having almost completed three full days in the field in the course of the last four days, another session or two could prove to be the straw that breaks the camel's back.

At least the fielding side hasn't had to contend with any Manchester sun on what has been a day of overcast skies, and, as the light begins to fade a little, Hegg makes an interesting move by replacing his spinners, including the very recently successful Schofield, with Wood and Martin.

This decision appears to suit Surrey, as Wood's opening over of his new spell sees Batty cutting for four and Saqlain pulling high over midwicket for six, though the Yorkshireman is to have the last laugh in his next over, after Batty has completed an outstanding 150 from his 276th ball with a leg-glanced single off Martin.

The third ball of Wood's second over tempts Saqlain into another almighty pull-cum-drive that sends the ball almost into orbit behind the wicket on the off-side, and, after what seems like an eternity, the ball finally lands in Hegg's gloves to the obvious delight of the whole Lancashire team.

Their joy is then doubled two balls later. Having regained the strike by crossing while Saqlain's satellite was returning to earth, Batty, perhaps unwisely, takes a leg-bye from the next delivery, exposing James Ormond to the bowling in what is now indifferent light. Consequently, the new man pushes forward, perhaps more in hope than anything else, at his first delivery and has his off stump unceremoniously uprooted.

Before Tim Murtagh can reach the middle, the umpires have offered the light to Batty and he has, not surprisingly, accepted. Having played immaculately from the start of the day until the close, the Surrey wicketkeeper leaves the field to a thoroughly well deserved ovation for a brilliant knock that has given his team a decent looking total.

Close:- Surrey 330-9 (Batty 152) from 99.5 overs*

Second Day - Wednesday 27th August
Surrey 337; Lancashire 341

Surrey would clearly like another twenty runs at least, in order to secure a fourth batting point, as the last-wicket pair come out to bat at the start of day two. They only manage to add another seven, however, before Tim Murtagh's unconvincing innings of five is terminated by Peter Martin, who promptly plucks out the left-hander's off stump as soon as he switches to a round-the-wicket attack during the third complete over of the morning. Jon Batty is therefore left high and dry on 154 and becomes the first Surrey batsman to carry his bat against Lancashire since Tom Hayward in 1907, and the first player from the county to do so at Old Trafford since Harry Jupp in 1870.

Having amassed a total of 337 that looks about par for the course on a pitch that has offered decent pace and bounce to the bowlers, the visiting side could be forgiven for thinking that the elements are conspiring against them as they come out to field, since the sun is just breaking through the clouds for the first time in the match.

As Lancashire's reply gets under way, James Ormond and Azhar Mahmood immediately cause problems for Mark Chilton, who almost plays on to Azhar in the second over, and then edges Ormond just wide of a diving third slip in the next. It's hugely ironic, therefore, that Iain Sutcliffe is the man to depart when Surrey strike their first blow of the innings in the eighth over. Pushing a delivery from Azhar firmly to leg, the former Leicestershire batsman is stunned to see Adam Hollioake cling on to a very sharp catch at short leg, though it's debatable how much the fielder knows about it, judging by the players' delayed reaction to what has happened. It provides the visitors with one of the early wickets that they crave, however, and also brings the debutant batsman, Mark Currie, to the crease in a high-pressure situation at 18-1.

Stuart Law would have been the obvious man to come in at this point, though Currie doesn't look at all fazed as he starts with a couple of pleasant strokes into the legside for two runs apiece off Azhar, followed by a forcing stroke backward of point off Ormond that brings his first boundary in Championship cricket. At this point, with Chilton reeling off a series of handsome fours at the other end, Currie must be thinking that county cricket is pretty easy, but Azhar soon changes that perception by working him over with a series of bouncers and yorkers, several of which very nearly squeeze under the 23-year-old's bat.

Having endured a few extremely testing overs and survived some other close calls with lbw appeals and inside edges, Currie must be delighted to see both opening bowlers - but Azhar in particular - taking a rest and being replaced by Tim Murtagh and Saqlain Mushtaq.

These changes might well be to Currie's liking, but they produce a second breakthrough for the visitors when Chilton suddenly attempts to whip a straight delivery from Murtagh through midwicket and loses his middle stump with his score on twenty-seven and the total having advanced to sixty in the twenty-first over.

Stuart Law now arrives at number four, and he looks in ominously good touch as he deflects his second delivery to the rope at third man, clips his third through midwicket for another four, and then steals the strike with a single from the final ball of Murtagh's over. Alarm bells are already starting to ring for Surrey when the Queenslander then proceeds to cut his first delivery from Saqlain to the cover boundary, though over-confidence almost brings about his departure towards the end of the over, when he checks a drive and pops the ball up just short of a scrambling Ali Brown at mid-on.

Having survived this anxious moment, Law helps Currie to take thirteen runs off a disappointing fourth over from Murtagh before both batsmen settle down for the last three overs of a morning that ends with honours just about even.

Lunch:- Lancashire 88-2 (Currie 27, Law 20*) from 26 overs*

Adam Hollioake fails to return to the field after lunch, having been struck down by the return of his virus, so Ian Ward assumes the role of captain and employs his two Pakistani internationals as his first pair of bowlers.

With Azhar again troubling Currie, it's Law who does most of the scoring in the immediate post-lunch period, delighting a good-sized crowd with a couple of lovely cover-driven boundaries off Saqlain, before advancing down the track to lift the off-spinner straight down the ground for a third four in three overs.

Surrey spurn opportunities to break the partnership during the first forty minutes of the session, however, as Clarke's throw misses the stumps at the non-striker's end when Law takes on an almost suicidal single to complete a fifty partnership, while Batty fails to hang on to an edge offered by Currie off Saqlain with the batsman on forty.

Another chance then goes begging soon after Clarke replaces the unlucky Azhar at the Statham end. Having been put through the wringer again by the Pakistani all-rounder, Currie - on forty-five, at 137-2 - edges the new bowler to his tormentor at second slip and lives to tell the tale as the sharp chance, at a good height to the fielder's left, goes down. These missed opportunities are starting to become very frustrating and could yet be very damaging, not only in the context of this match, but also in terms of the Championship race.

Salt is then rubbed in the visitors' wounds as both batsmen complete their fifties within a few balls of each other, Law with a glorious straight-driven boundary off Clarke, from his fifty-seventh delivery, and Currie with an equally impressive drive, through extra cover off Saqlain, from his 121st ball. As the crowd offers up its applause for the Australian's sparkling knock and the debutant's gutsy performance, Ward is clearly mulling over his next move, which is to make a double bowling change that sees the introduction of Ian Salisbury at the Stretford end and the return of James Ormond at the Statham end.

Neither bowler makes the most promising of starts, however, as Law cuts the leg-spinner's first delivery to the rope at extra cover, while Currie forces the paceman away for an off-side boundary that brings up the hundred partnership for the third wicket.

Surrey's position is now starting to give cause for concern to their supporters, so it is just as well that Law possibly becomes a victim of his own confidence a few overs later. Having driven the first ball of Salisbury's third over through straight mid-on for the tenth four of his innings, the Queenslander tries to pull the next delivery for another boundary but miscues slightly and ends up providing Brown at deep mid-on with a comfortable catch.

Having seen the back of Law for sixty-seven to peg Lancashire back a little at 169-3, the reigning champions then come close to further successes when Carl Hooper inside-edges the very next ball from Salisbury just past his leg stump, and then plays a significant role in a mix-up that sees Surrey making an awful mess of a great opportunity to complete the run out of a hopelessly stranded Currie for fifty-five.

Fortunately for the fielding side, the Cheshire batsman has only added a single to his score when he becomes a well-deserved first victim for Ormond four overs later with the total standing at 175. Edging a drive at an outswinger, the Lancashire debutant is well snapped up at second slip by Azhar, who thereby partially atones for his earlier miss.

The hosts still hold a slight advantage at this point, but that is soon wiped out as two further wickets fall in the next two overs - 'leg-spinner takes leg-spinner' for the second time in the match when Chris Schofield falls lbw on the back foot to Salisbury for a duck, then Glen Chapple, on one, virtually steers an Ormond delivery to second slip, where Azhar picks up another good low catch. Suddenly, the Red Rose county are 183-6 and it's 'advantage Surrey' as Warren Hegg makes his way out to the middle.

The very experienced seventh-wicket pair take the first step to stabilising the innings again by seeing off the rest of Ormond's good spell from the Statham end, though they both enjoy an identical stroke of good fortune against his replacement, Azhar, in the lead-up to tea. After Hegg top-edges a hook over the head of Batty for the four runs that raise his team's two-hundred in the sixty-third over, Hooper replicates his captain's shot in the final over of the session, by which time Lancashire have restored equilibrium to the contest.

Tea:- Lancashire 218-6 (Hooper 26, Hegg 19*) from 67 overs*

The visitors make a good start to the final session, with Azhar securing a hard-earned second wicket in the second over, courtesy of Hegg's hook to deep backward square leg, where Ormond takes a good catch low down as he runs in a few paces from the boundary.

Hooper immediately cancels out the slight edge that Surrey have just gained, however, as he glances Salisbury away to fine leg for four and then advances on the leg-spinner's next delivery to drive high over long-off for six. The former West Indian skipper then finds the Gods smiling kindly on him when a mistimed pull only just clears the fielder at shortish midwicket to bring him two further runs.

This sudden ultra-positive approach either suggests that Hooper doesn't have a lot of faith in his team's tail, or it could be designed to unsettle Salisbury, who had bowled very well before the break. If it's because he is concerned about the ability of the lower-order then he might just be right, since Peter Martin's lovely cover-driven four off Azhar during his second over at the crease is followed by a tame edge to fourth slip in the Pakistani's next over with the score at 250.

Ward might be thinking along the same lines as Hooper, it seems, since he starts to push all his fielders back for the former Kent batsman, in order to get the new arrival, John Wood, on strike as much as possible. This causes some initial confusion between the batsmen, however, as both men have a lucky escape from the same delivery in Azhar's next over. Having been rather fortunate to see his hook land just short of Ormond at deep backward square leg, Hooper turns down the single that is on offer, only to see that Wood is happy to take it and has come rushing down the track. As he turns to head back to the non-striker's end, the former Durham seamer doesn't appear to be in any great danger, but the fielder's fine throw scores a direct hit on the stumps, catching umpire Clarkson unawares. As the Surrey team appeal, it looks like the verdict should be 'out', but Wood escapes, since Clarkson is not in a position - in more ways than one - to make the judgement. This scenario mirrors the one we had seen at Hove, where Mushtaq Ahmed was the fielder and Saqlain Mushtaq the batsman, so it's quite possible that things have just evened themselves out here.

Surrey don't have to wait long to get their man in any case, as Wood goes in the next over from Salisbury, following a fine piece of bowling from the leg-spinner. Coming round the wicket, Salisbury floats up an undetected googly that 'gates' and bowls the rather naïve batsman as he accepts the invitation to launch into an off-drive. The bowler and his team-mates are understandably cock-a-hoop, not only because they have reduced Lancashire to 262-9, still seventy-five runs in arrears, but also because this wicket has just earned the bowling point that takes them back to the top of the Championship table.

Hooper responds to the loss of Wood by going on to the offensive against Azhar, top-edging one hook for four to complete a 71-ball half-century, before middling another for six to gee up a crowd that has been swollen by a contingent of Manchester United fans who have dropped in for a while en route to a match at the other Old Trafford later this evening.

All the while, the visitors are attempting to get the Lancashire number eleven, Gary Keedy, on strike, though Hooper is proving very adept at stealing singles at the appropriate times, as well as finding the boundary much too frequently for Surrey's liking. Although he has a little luck when two pulled fours off Salisbury are followed by a towering drive off the same bowler that only just clears Clarke at long-off, you have to admire Hooper's skill in manipulating the strike to make a mockery of the opposition's tactics.

Ward responds to the assaults on Azhar and Salisbury by recalling Ormond and Saqlain to the attack, and, though this move sees the arrival of the hosts' three-hundred when Hooper drives Ormond to the wide long-on boundary, it also comes close to bringing about the Guyanese batsman's downfall when he pulls Saqlain straight to Murtagh at square leg with his score on eighty-eight and the total at 307. Sadly for Surrey, the fielder fails to accept the hard-hit head-high chance, though there is a small degree of consolation in the fact that, with no run accruing from Murtagh's miss, Keedy is left on strike at the start of an over for the first time since he arrived in the middle nine overs ago.

Ormond promptly strikes the left-hander on the pads with his opening delivery, only to find his confident appeal for lbw turned down by umpire Clarkson, adding to the champions' frustration and the baying home crowd's delight. They are clearly enjoying Surrey's suffering, and it isn't long before they are applauding a fifty partnership and preparing to acclaim a super Hooper hundred as the batsman pulls Ormond away to the midwicket fence to move on to ninety-six.

A push to square leg for a single off Saqlain takes him to the magical mark in the next over, in fact, triggering a well-deserved standing ovation all around the ground for a masterful 124-ball knock that has included three sixes and eleven fours, in addition to a number of very important strike-stealing singles during this last-wicket stand.

Since Lancashire are now rapidly closing in on his team's total, Ward is forced to act again, bringing Clarke into the attack for one over and then recalling Salisbury for a single over at Keedy before reverting to the young all-rounder.

Hooper reacts to this last change by blasting Clarke high over long-on for successive sixes, thereby taking the Red Rose county into the lead amidst escalating jubilation from an increasingly raucous crowd that becomes even more volatile when both the bowler and the Surrey captain react angrily to a highly contentious umpiring decision. In attempting to prevent Hooper from stealing a single at the end of his over, Clarke fires in a short legside delivery that umpire Clarkson calls as a wide. It would be a fair enough decision in a one-day game but, in the heat of the moment, the official appears to have forgotten that this is a Championship match.

At this point, with feelings running high, it's probably just as well that Ward belatedly takes the new ball, gives it to Azhar, and sees Hooper carve the second delivery with it straight down the throat of Salisbury at third man.

This well-warranted fourth success for Azhar therefore brings Hooper's breathtakingly brilliant knock to an end at 114, with Lancashire having secured a narrow first-innings lead of four runs. Although the West Indian certainly deserves the rousing reception he receives as he returns to the pavilion, the gritty and extremely valuable efforts of Keedy - undefeated on one from 36 balls - should not be forgotten.

Since the light has faded badly in the latter stages of the home side's innings, Surrey are spared the potentially hazardous task of having to face a couple of overs tonight. That is at least one consolation for the visitors at the end of an exciting and fascinating day that has ended with Lancashire holding the most slender of advantages.

Close:- End of the Lancashire innings

Third Day - Thursday 28th August
Surrey 337 and 137-8; Lancashire 341

Surrey's day starts on a high, since they have moved a step closer to clinching the NCL Division One title without even playing, thanks to Kent's 36-run victory over Gloucestershire under the lights at Bristol last night. The Lions are now four points ahead of their rivals, and also have a game in hand, so things are looking very promising in that competition.

A Championship win here is much more important, however, though a combination of overnight rain and morning drizzle puts the game on hold until 11.45am, when the umpires decide play can get under way, with twelve of the day's 104 overs lost.

Unfortunately for Surrey, conditions look ideal for seam and swing bowling, so it's no great surprise that Peter Martin and Glen Chapple are a handful right from the start. Jon Batty has already survived an appeal for lbw, in fact, when he pushes defensively at Martin in the third over and edges low to the left of first slip, where Stuart Law picks up a very good catch. As he departs with his team 1-1, Batty has, therefore, repeated the unusual feat he achieved at Taunton in 2002 of recording a duck and a score of 150-plus in the same match.

The quality of the bowling is so good at this stage that it takes Surrey almost five overs to clear their first-innings deficit of four runs, and they are only six runs to the good when the impressive Martin strikes again as Ian Ward snicks a defensive stroke to Mark Chilton at third slip.

Since they are now under real pressure at 10-2, the visitors are pleased to see Graham Thorpe in good touch early in his innings as he picks up five runs from Chapple's next over and then glances Martin to the rope at fine leg. In the absence of Mark Ramprakash, who would surely have relished this situation, they need a long innings from the left-hander.

This point is then underscored in the next over when Rikki Clarke falls to his fourth ball, Chapple claiming him lbw for a single to reduce the visitors to 23-3 and spark further celebrations from the Lancashire team.

They know that they now have Surrey on the run, and their belief that they can topple the champions is further boosted when Martin appears to pick up another wicket in the very next over. As Ali Brown sways away from a short ball that clips something on its way through to Hegg, the home side appeal, and umpire Barrie Leadbeater raises his finger. The batsman, clearly shocked by the whole business, points towards his helmet and stands his ground, however, prompting the umpire to walk down the pitch and curtail the Lancashire celebrations, after seemingly changing his mind about his decision.

The vast majority of the crowd are undoubtedly unsure about what has happened as Brown continues his innings, in understandably subdued mode for a while, and Thorpe continues to take the attack to the opposition wherever possible, cracking Chapple to the cover boundary in successive overs. This, amazingly, prompts Hegg to post a cover sweeper and, less surprisingly, also leads to the replacement of Chapple with Gary Keedy at the Stretford end. In turn, this brings about a sudden burst of activity from Brown, who hooks Martin for four, drives the first ball he faces from Keedy straight down the ground for six, and then despatches the next delivery to the midwicket boundary with a slog-sweep that raises Surrey's fifty and sees Hegg dropping three men - at long-off, long-on and cover sweeper - out on to the fence. This again seems to be something of an over-reaction from the Lancashire captain, though it does at least ensure that only four more singles are added in the last three overs before the interval.

Lunch:- Surrey 57-3 (Thorpe 32, Brown 20*) from 21 overs*

During the lunch interval it has emerged that umpire Leadbeater had indeed reversed his initial decision to give Ali Brown out off Peter Martin and had been brave enough to explain what had happened to the Press, saying "My initial thought was that it came off the bat handle, so I gave him out, but I realised that the sound was wrong. I told the batsman and the Lancashire fielders that I was changing the decision." He had added that Brown's reluctance to walk had no bearing on his thinking.

With that all sorted out, Surrey have a match to turn around, hopefully with the assistance of a long innings from the reprieved batsman, who needs a century against these opponents if he is to complete a full set of hundreds against all the other counties. Needless to say, today would be a great day to do it.

Strangely, Hegg is again employing his ultra-conservative fields for both of his selected bowlers, Gary Keedy and John Wood - the left-arm spinner has five men back on the boundary, while the paceman operates with just one slip. This seemingly takes all the pressure off the batsmen, allowing them to gather singles almost as they wish on the way to completing a fifty partnership in the third over of the afternoon.

Brown is still inclined to play his natural game, though, and enjoys mixed results, with a cut off Keedy and a pull off Wood earning him genuine boundaries, while an edged drive at the spinner, and a gloved hook at the seamer that loops the ball over Hegg's head, add rather more fortunate runs to his account. He progresses to his fifty, nevertheless, from his seventieth ball, at which point things are looking a little rosier for Surrey, who are now 93-3. It only takes one wicket to shift the balance of power, however, so when Thorpe edges a cut at Wood in the same over and is well taken by Hegg away to his left-hand side the visitors are back in real trouble at 93-4.

Despite their precarious position and the deep-set fields, Surrey clearly have no intention of taking their foot off the gas as Brown pulls Keedy away to the rope at deep square leg, and the newly arrived Azhar Mahmood lofts Wood over mid-off to open his account with two runs that take the total into three figures. It's a puzzling approach, given that there are so many fielders back on the fence, but it's clear that nothing will deter the batsmen from their bold approach as Azhar follows up by driving Keedy straight for six.

To give credit to the left-arm spinner, he continues to give the ball plenty of air, and he gets his reward for this later in the over when Azhar's attempt to repeat the six-hit treatment results in a miscue towards long-off, where Martin pouches the catch after running in about ten yards from the rope. The Pakistani all-rounder is obviously angry with himself - as well he should be - since his team are now in real danger at 108-5, with his ailing skipper coming in to bat at number seven.

Adam Hollioake's state of health clearly won't have been helped by the state of the game at this moment in time, though neither of these things seems to inhibit him as he takes cover-driven and hooked boundaries from Wood during his first over at the crease.

Sadly, as things rapidly go from bad to worse for the visitors, he doesn't get to see out the next over… and nor does Ian Salisbury. Hollioake falls to the fifth delivery of Keedy's tenth over when he aims a push into the leg side and edges to Law at slip as the ball spins away from the bat, then Salisbury finds his first ball turning and bouncing wickedly to flick his glove on the way through to an ecstatic Hegg, who hangs on well to a very awkward catch behind the stumps. At 119-7, Surrey's position in both the match and the Championship race is looking dire, with all their hopes now resting on Brown producing something utterly sensational.

But it isn't to be, as Keedy brings Brown to book for sixty-one in his next over. When the batsman backs away to leg in an attempt to cut, and is comprehensively beaten and bowled by a faster arm-ball, the Lancashire spinner has taken four wickets for as many runs in the space of twelve balls and the champions' innings is in tatters at 122-8.

Although Saqlain Mushtaq and James Ormond battle through six more overs from Keedy and Carl Hooper - replacing Wood at the Statham end - before rain sends the players off for an early tea, there seems no way back for Surrey from this position.

Tea:- Surrey 137-8 (Saqlain 11, Ormond 6*) from 42 overs*

Although it never becomes very heavy, the rain continues unabated until the umpires decide, at 5.50pm, that there is no chance of any further play today. Unless there is rain tomorrow, this looks unlikely to affect the outcome of the match, since the contest has moved forward at pace during the forty-two overs that have been possible today, largely thanks to some grossly indisciplined Surrey batting and some excellent bowling, first by Peter Martin and then by the vastly improved Gary Keedy. Surrey are staring down the barrel, and rain will be of no use to them now as they really needed to win this game in order to put pressure back on Sussex.

Close:- Surrey 137-8 (Saqlain 11, Ormond 6*) from 42 overs*

Fourth Day - Friday 29th August

Surrey 337 and 138; Lancashire 341 and 135-2
Lancashire won by eight wickets
Lancashire 20pts, Surrey 6

Any faint hopes Surrey might have harboured of producing something spectacular are obliterated in the space of seven deliveries, as Saqlain Mushtaq slices a drive at Peter Martin's third ball of the morning to provide Gary Keedy with a very comfortable catch at point, then James Ormond runs himself out from the first ball of the next over. Having top-edged a sweep to short fine leg, the sturdy paceman calls for a highly ambitious second run and is well beaten by Stuart Law's throw to the wicketkeeper. A dismal score of 137-8 has therefore been transformed into a disastrous 138 all out, leaving Lancashire to score a paltry 135 to win.

Early wickets - and plenty of them - might just make things interesting, but they aren't forthcoming as Mark Chilton and Iain Sutcliffe rattle off three well-struck boundaries in the first two overs from Ormond and Azhar.

Adam Hollioake immediately turns to Saqlain to deliver the fourth over of the innings, but the Pakistani off-spinner isn't able to extract the degree of turn from the surface that Keedy had during the visitors' innings. He does, initially, manage to restrict the run-flow at the Stretford end, though this is of little use, since Sutcliffe is keeping the score moving at the other end by reeling off a succession of attractive drives at Ormond's expense.

It would seem to make more sense to utilise Salisbury, who has been outbowling his spin twin in recent Championship games, but, instead, the Surrey captain keeps his largely impotent off-spinner going, and replaces Ormond with Azhar at the Statham end. As a result, the score races past fifty in the twelfth over, and Chilton, after a very slow start, breaks free with two well-timed boundaries in Saqlain's sixth over.

By the time Sutcliffe perishes for a well-played forty-seven, when he nicks Azhar to Jon Batty in the seventeenth over, the game is all but over at 69-1, and it is only when Saqlain is glanced and driven for further fours that Salisbury is given an opportunity.

Within twelve deliveries the leg-spinner has claimed the wicket of Mark Currie, courtesy of a comfortable return catch, but it does nothing more than make a point to the skipper as Stuart Law comes in to hasten the end of the game. In the course of five overs at the crease before lunch, the Australian picks up three boundaries from the suffering Saqlain, leaving Surrey teetering on the brink of inevitable defeat.

Lunch:- Lancashire 116-2 (Chilton 31, Law 19*) from 29 overs*

Thankfully, the mercy killing comes soon after the resumption, with Law driving Salisbury over mid-off for four, and then ending the game in style with a late-cut four and a slog-swept six off Ali Brown. After two tight days, when it was impossible to separate the teams, Lancashire have run away with the game and completed a very comfortable victory by eight wickets with almost two sessions to spare. While this win looks to have come too late for Lancashire to mount a challenge themselves - even though they have yet to play Sussex at Old Trafford - they have almost certainly dealt a fatal blow to Surrey's hopes of retaining the title. The crown hasn't fallen off the King's head yet, but it has slipped very badly indeed.

Surrey 337 and 138; Lancashire 341 and 135-2
Lancashire won by eight wickets. Lancashire 20pts, Surrey 6

TALKING POINTS - JON BATTY

This looked to be a very good toss to win, as both sides had just spent a couple of days in the field. I assume everyone was delighted when Adam called correctly?
JB - Yes, there were a lot of happy faces in our dressing room. One of the problems with playing so much cricket is the fatigue factor. Even if the wicket had been appalling and we should have bowled first, I think we would still have batted, which is obviously a far from ideal situation.

Given how tired the Lancashire players must have been, I felt that we could have broken them if we had managed to bat well into the second day and got to 450. How significant do you think it was that our lower order wasn't able to stick around with you, as it usually would do?
JB - I think it was crucial. If we had managed to bat even until halfway through the second day then I'm convinced they would have been blown out of the water. Full credit to them, though, for the way they came at us hard, even though they were knackered, on the first evening and second morning. I think they probably realised that if we got away and got through the first session or session-and-a-half of the second day then they would have been gone.

Do you think we went astray tactically during the last-wicket partnership? In my view, the tactic of pushing the field back for the main batsman and concentrating all your efforts on one or two balls an over at the number eleven doesn't seem to work especially well.
JB - No, I think most teams would have gone exactly the same way that we did, and I think we tried everything we could - we had the field up, we pushed it back - but we just couldn't contain him. We tried mixing it up, but whatever we tried didn't work, so I think we got it about right… it was a masterful innings.

How significant was that stand in changing the course of the game?
JB - I think it was very significant. If we could have broken that partnership and come away with a decent first-innings lead then I still think they would have been broken in much the same way as if we'd have been able to bat for longer. I think the combination of their opening attack and Hooper's innings turned the game in their favour.

TALKING POINTS - IAN SALISBURY

Was that the best innings you've seen from Jon Batty?
IS - Definitely. We were pretty knackered coming into this game after the Leicestershire match, and I think it showed in how the other ten batsmen got out, but 'JB' just played brilliantly - though he was dead on his feet for the next three days! He got a really good hundred at Old Trafford the year before and played really well then, but this was his best innings as an opening batsman.

Gary Keedy looks a much-improved bowler to me. How do you rate him?
IS - He was the best non-overseas spinner we played against all year. He got into a great rhythm and bowled beautifully. In fact, I'd say that was the best bowling I've seen from an English finger-spinner for a long time.

LANCASHIRE v SURREY at Old Trafford 26th to 29th August

Surrey won the toss and elected to bat Umpires:- Tony Clarkson and Barrie Leadbeater

SURREY - First Innings

Fall Of Wkt	Batsman	How	Out	Score	Balls	4s	6s
1-10	**I.J. Ward**	**c Hegg**	**b Martin**	**10**	7	2	0
	J.N. Batty +	**Not**	**Out**	**154**	283	24	1
2-114	**G.P. Thorpe**	**lbw**	**b Chapple**	**57**	97	10	0
3-143	**R. Clarke**	**st Hegg**	**b Keedy**	**11**	45	2	0
4-147	**A.D. Brown**	**c Sutcliffe**	**b Keedy**	**1**	9	0	0
5-148	**A.J. Hollioake ***		**b Martin**	**0**	19	0	0
6-261	**Azhar Mahmood**	**c Hegg**	**b Keedy**	**63**	89	11	0
7-298	**I.D.K. Salisbury**	**c Currie**	**b Schofield**	**5**	39	0	0
8-329	**Saqlain Mushtaq**	**c Hegg**	**b Wood**	**11**	17	0	1
9-330	**J. Ormond**		**b Wood**	**0**	1	0	0
10-337	**T.J. Murtagh**		**b Martin**	**5**	13	1	0
	Extras	**(8b, 6lb, 6nb)**		**20**			
	TOTAL	**(102.4 overs)**		**337**			

Bowler	O	M	R	W	NB	Wd
Martin	**14.4**	**2**	**54**	**3**	-	-
Chapple	**21**	**4**	**87**	**1**	-	-
Hooper	**18**	**6**	**38**	**0**	-	-
Wood	**15**	**4**	**64**	**2**	3	-
Keedy	**24**	**9**	**62**	**3**	-	-
Schofield	**10**	**2**	**18**	**1**	-	-

LANCASHIRE - First Innings (Needing 188 to avoid the follow-on)

Fall Of Wkt	Batsman	How	Out	Score	Balls	4s	6s
2-60	**M.J. Chilton**		**b Murtagh**	**27**	64	5	0
1-18	**I.J. Sutcliffe**	**c Hollioake**	**b Azhar**	**8**	23	1	0
4-175	**M.R. Currie**	**c Azhar**	**b Ormond**	**56**	152	6	0
3-169	**S.G. Law**	**c Brown**	**b Salisbury**	**67**	75	10	0
10-341	**C.L. Hooper**	**c Salisbury**	**b Azhar**	**114**	147	11	5
5-178	**C.P. Schofield**	**lbw**	**b Salisbury**	**0**	4	0	0
6-183	**G. Chapple**	**c Azhar**	**b Ormond**	**1**	6	0	0
7-221	**W.K. Hegg *+**	**c Ormond**	**b Azhar**	**19**	41	3	0
8-251	**P.J. Martin**	**c Clarke**	**b Azhar**	**8**	12	1	0
9-262	**J. Wood**		**b Salisbury**	**6**	14	1	0
	G. Keedy	**Not**	**Out**	**1**	36	0	0
	Extras	**(8b, 7lb, 3w, 16nb)**		**34**			
	TOTAL	**(94.2 overs)**		**341**			

Bowler	O	M	R	W	NB	Wd
Ormond	**20**	**3**	**70**	**2**	3	1
Azhar Mahmood	**24.2**	**3**	**76**	**4**	2	1
Murtagh	**5**	**1**	**26**	**1**	-	-
Saqlain Mushtaq	**20**	**2**	**58**	**0**	2	-
Clarke	**6**	**0**	**26**	**0**	-	1
Salisbury	**19**	**2**	**70**	**3**	1	-

SURREY - Second Innings (Trailing by 4 runs on first innings)

Fall Of Wkt	Batsman	How	Out	Score	Balls	4s	6s
2-10	**I.J. Ward**	**c Chilton**	**b Martin**	**3**	21	0	0
1-1	**J.N. Batty +**	**c Law**	**b Martin**	**0**	9	0	0
4-93	**G.P. Thorpe**	**c Hegg**	**b Wood**	**38**	69	4	0
3-23	**R. Clarke**	**lbw**	**b Chapple**	**1**	4	0	0
8-122	**A.D. Brown**		**b Keedy**	**61**	89	6	1
5-108	**Azhar Mahmood**	**c Martin**	**b Keedy**	**8**	10	0	1
6-119	**A.J. Hollioake ***	**c Law**	**b Keedy**	**8**	8	2	0
7-119	**I.D.K. Salisbury**	**c Hegg**	**b Keedy**	**0**	1	0	0
9-137	**Saqlain Mushtaq**	**c Keedy**	**b Martin**	**11**	30	0	0
10-138	**J. Ormond**	**run**	**out**	**7**	15	1	0
	T.J. Murtagh	**Not**	**Out**	**0**	3	0	0
	Extras	**(1lb)**		**1**			
	TOTAL	**(43.1 overs)**		**138**			

Bowler	O	M	R	W	NB	Wd
Martin	**12**	**5**	**20**	**3**	-	-
Chapple	**7**	**1**	**24**	**1**	-	-
Keedy	**14.1**	**1**	**57**	**4**	-	-
Wood	**7**	**0**	**29**	**1**	-	-
Hooper	**3**	**0**	**7**	**0**	-	-

LANCASHIRE - Second Innings (Needing 135 to win)							
Fall Of Wkt	Batsman	How	Out	Score	Balls	4s	6s
	M.J. Chilton	**Not**	**Out**	**33**	77	4	0
1-69	**I.J. Sutcliffe**	**c Batty**	**b Azhar**	**47**	62	9	0
2-92	**M.R. Currie**	**c &**	**b Salisbury**	**13**	25	2	0
	S.G. Law	**Not**	**Out**	**35**	22	5	1
	Extras	**(2b, 1lb, 4nb)**		**7**			
	TOTAL	**(30.4 overs)**	**(for 2 wkts)**	**135**			

Bowler	O	M	R	W	NB	Wd
Ormond	**5**	**1**	**25**	**0**	2	-
Azhar Mahmood	**7**	**1**	**28**	**1**	-	-
Saqlain Mushtaq	**13**	**3**	**49**	**0**	-	-
Salisbury	**5**	**0**	**19**	**1**	-	-
Brown	**0.4**	**0**	**11**	**0**	-	-

Other Frizzell Championship Division One Results

Surrey's defeat had seriously damaged their hopes of retaining their Championship crown, with Sussex now looking on course for their first-ever title if they could hold their nerve. The reigning champions needed to win their final two matches to retain any chance of edging Sussex out.

August 26-29
***Trent Bridge:-* Nottinghamshire (8pts) drew with Leicestershire (12).** Notts 290 (Shafayat 68, Welton 60, Bicknell 59, DeFreitas 7-51) & 241-7dec (Cairns 75, Read 65); Leics 523-7dec (Hodge 302*, Nixon 65, Shreck 5-100).
***Edgbaston:-* Warwickshire (18pts*) beat Middlesex (5) by 31 runs.** Warwicks 290 (Powell 73, Brown 71, Wagh 62) & 198 (Troughton 64, Bloomfield 4-57, Keegan 4-67); Middx 286 (Joyce 107, Shah 54, Waqar 4-69) & 171 (Strauss 61, Waqar 5-40). *** Warwickshire deducted 1pt for their slow over-rate.**

FRIZZELL CHAMPIONSHIP DIVISION ONE TABLE AT 29TH AUGUST

Pos	Prv		P	Points	W	D	L	T	Bat	Bwl	Ded
1	2	Surrey	14	210.00	6	7	1	0	60	38	0.00
2	1	Sussex	13	209.00	8	2	3	0	50	39	0.00
3	3	Lancashire	13	176.00	4	8	1	0	53	35	0.00
4	5	Middlesex	14	152.00	3	9	2	0	39	35	0.00
5	4	Kent	13	151.00	4	5	4	0	37	38	0.00
6	6	Warwickshire	13	140.50	3	6	3	1	38	32	2.50
7	7	Essex	13	109.00	1	7	4	1	24	36	0.00
8	8	Leicestershire	14	105.50	0	9	5	0	34	36	0.50
9	9	Nottinghamshire	13	95.00	1	5	7	0	26	36	1.00

18 Two Wins And A Hand On The Trophy

Defeat at Old Trafford was clearly a huge blow, though it had to be put into context. It was, after all, Surrey's first defeat in the Championship since they lost to Sussex at Hove on 11th August 2002, over a year ago, and only their fourth reverse in their last fifty-five matches in the competition. Additionally, it was only the Club's fourth defeat of the season, following the two successive setbacks in the NCL and that shocker at Derby in the C&G Trophy. It was unfortunate, however, that it had come at the worst possible time, and there was no doubt that minor miracles were now needed if the Championship was to be retained. Lancashire certainly had to beat Sussex at Old Trafford, since the men from Hove seemed unlikely to lose to Middlesex, and it was very hard to see them failing to win their final game against a Leicestershire side who would surely be relegated by the time that match came around. Above all else, the reigning champions simply **had** to win their final two games against Kent and Essex… and then hope.

Strangely, despite recent indifferent form that had seen him go four Championship innings without a wicket, Saqlain Mushtaq had been called up at short notice by Pakistan to play in the final Test of their three-match series against Bangladesh, and, if he was then retained for the one-day series that followed, he was unlikely to play for Surrey again this season. Although there was no doubt that he would be missed, I suppose it spoke volumes that this didn't seem to be the massive blow that it might once have done. People had almost started to believe that the spin wizard could never hit a bad run of form or suffer from a lack of confidence, but he was only human, after all, and he did look short in both of these areas for the first time in his superb career. It seemed odd that the Pakistani selectors had turned to Saqlain, bearing in mind that they had a leg-spinner available to them who was very much amongst the wickets, in brilliant form and extremely confident. Sussex must have been dreading the announcement of every Pakistan squad as the season progressed!

In addition to Saqlain, Surrey were set to lose Graham Thorpe for both of the forthcoming matches against Kent, since his status of '**former** England batsman' now had to be amended to simply 'England batsman', following his recall to the side in place of the injured Nasser Hussain for the final Test against South Africa at The Oval, starting on 4th September. It was also great to see that Martin Bicknell had been retained in the squad, even though he, perhaps more than any of the others on international duty, would be sorely missed at Canterbury.

The missing bowlers would clearly be hard to replace, but at least there were in-form batsmen who could step into the team, since Nadeem Shahid and Scott Newman had put on an astonishing 552 for the first wicket in a second eleven game against Derbyshire at The Oval on 14th August. Surrey had started their reply to the visitors' 580-7declared not long before lunch on the second day, but by the close of play they had raced along to an incredible 547-0, with both batsmen on 266. Unfortunately, Shahid fell early on the second day, without adding to his score, though Newman had gone on to reach 284, thereby recording the fifth-highest individual score in the history of the second eleven championship. Shahid had then followed his 266 with scores of 272 against Sussex at Hove and 125 versus Middlesex at Uxbridge.

The team's Championship woes had to be forgotten for a while now, though, since two potentially vital NCL games were on the agenda in the next four days. Gloucestershire's defeat at the hands of Kent had been a great fillip for the Surrey team, but the Lions now had to make sure they took full advantage by winning at least one of the forthcoming games at Headingley and Canterbury. This would be no easy task, not only because these venues were unhappy hunting grounds for Surrey, but also because both opponents were scrapping hard to avoid relegation.

NATIONAL CRICKET LEAGUE DIVISION ONE - MATCH THIRTEEN
Yorkshire Phoenix versus Surrey Lions at Headingley
Sunday 31st August

Setting The Scene - It's top versus bottom as the Lions hit Headingley in the hope of erasing some of the disappointment felt after the defeat at Old Trafford. Surrey are forced to make two changes to the side that had won at Leicester in their last NCL outing, with Mark Ramprakash ruled out by his shoulder injury and Saqlain Mushtaq away with Pakistan. The replacements are handy, though, as Mark Butcher and Martin Bicknell step in for a run out ahead of the Oval Test. Yorkshire are meanwhile unlucky when plans to give a debut to Damien Martyn - recently signed as a replacement overseas player for the last few weeks of the season - are scuppered by illness at the eleventh hour, but, with the exception of the injured Craig White, they are otherwise pretty much at full strength. When the Phoenix skipper, Anthony McGrath, wins the toss he elects to put the Lions in to bat... isn't that always the way of things when Surrey play at Headingley?

Surrey Lions' Innings

Darren Gough and Matthew Hoggard represent a useful new-ball pairing for the struggling Phoenix, and they make life tough for Ian Ward and Ali Brown after the left-hander has cut Gough's first delivery of the match to the boundary. Only three other runs - two of them wides - come from the remainder of the first three overs, though Ward makes up for this by taking seven from the opening two deliveries of Hoggard's second over and then repeating his cut for four off Gough in over number five. There is certainly something in the pitch for the seamers, as is often the case at Headingley, but both batsmen avoid trouble by showing good judgement of where their off stump is in these early overs.

Having failed to score from his first fourteen balls, Brown then demonstrates fine awareness of where the midwicket boundary is, too, by hoisting Hoggard over it for a huge six to get off the mark in style, and then follows up by driving Gough high over long-on in the following over to move his tally on to twelve and the Lions' score on to 31-0 after seven overs.

Given the conditions, and the bowlers, this appears to be a good start, though Yorkshire manage to peg their visitors back a little in the next over when Hoggard claims the wicket of Ward. Having just guided the previous delivery backward of point for four, the left-hander aims a hook at the 26-year-old England paceman and is adjudged to have got a top edge onto his helmet as the ball steeples into the air behind the wicket and is taken by Richard Blakey.

In the absence of Mark Ramprakash, it's Mark Butcher who comes in at number three to play something of an anchoring role, it seems, as Brown continues his run of boundaries with a square cut and a cover drive that take the score up to 44-1 at the end of Hoggard's next over.

Having delivered five tidy overs for eighteen from the rugby stand end, Gough is now replaced by Steve Kirby, who is soon being cut to the rope at point by Brown. Then, with his score on twenty-five, the Surrey opener drives the next delivery hard and flat to deep cover, where Michael Lumb grasses what is really a fairly routine catch. Having positioned the fielder perfectly, it's a huge disappointment for both the bowler and the captain that the chance has gone begging, and, to add insult to injury, the single that results from the spillage brings up the Lions' fifty.

Kirby then has further reasons to rue this missed chance as Brown and Butcher boost the visitors' total by thirty-three runs in just three overs. Eight come from over number thirteen as Brown drives the flame-haired seamer to the long-off boundary and then pops up a dolly catch to cover from a slower ball that also happens to be a no-ball; the next over yields eleven as Butcher gets into the action with two off-side boundaries from the last over of Hoggard's opening spell;

then Brown runs riot in the fifteenth over by pulling and driving two fours and a six to complete a fifty partnership with Butcher and leave Kirby close to tearing his hair out.

Having pushed the score up to an impressive 88-1 with this assault on the Yorkshire fast bowler, Brown then completes a fine 49-ball fifty with a forcing stroke through the off-side for two in the first over from Anthony McGrath, the new bowler at the Kirkstall Lane end, only to fall to the next delivery when he misses a pull and is bowled.

The Phoenix team and their fans are obviously pleased to see the back of Brown, and even more delighted when this wicket quickly brings two more as Surrey complete a sudden slide from 91-1 to 96-4 in the space of fourteen deliveries. McGrath is rewarded for keeping faith in Kirby when Butcher checks a drive at a slower ball and pops up a catch to Vic Craven at mid-off in the over after Brown's departure, then Graham Thorpe cuts loosely at McGrath nine balls later, giving Matthew Wood a comfortable catch at backward point.

Suddenly, the whole complexion of the game has changed, with the Lions limping, rather than roaring, to the hundred mark, courtesy of a wide by Kirby in the nineteenth over, as Rikki Clarke and Adam Hollioake try to re-establish the innings. Having conceded twenty-eight runs from his first three overs, the former Leicestershire paceman yields just five from his next three before being replaced by Richard Dawson, while McGrath's gentle seamers are proving impossible to get away at the Kirkstall Lane end. This probably brings about the dismissal of Hollioake in the twenty-fourth over, since the sight of a rare short delivery tempts the Surrey skipper into a pull that he top-edges straight down the throat of Kirby at long leg. As Hollioake departs at the end of a totally untypical innings of two from twenty-three balls, the scoreboard reads 107-5 and the visitors are now in deep trouble.

With Dawson starting very tidily, the pressure on the batsmen continues to grow, even though Azhar Mahmood manages to notch Surrey's first boundary for eleven overs with an on-drive off McGrath in the twenty-sixth over. The Yorkshire skipper then offers a little assistance to his opponents by slipping the first ball of his next over down the legside to add five wides to the total, but makes amends a few balls later when Azhar falls in identical style to his captain - same ball, same shot, same fielder, same result. At 126-6 in the twenty-eighth over, the league leaders' situation is now critical, with much resting on the young shoulders of Clarke.

Fortunately for the Lions, their latest England one-day international doesn't freeze in the glare of the spotlight, unfurling a lovely straight-driven boundary in the Phoenix captain's penultimate over before securing the first four from Dawson with a square cut in the off-spinner's fifth over. Surprisingly, this proves sufficient for the former England spinner to be removed from the attack, despite having conceded just seventeen runs.

Before Gough can return to the fray in Dawson's place, however, McGrath has one more over to deliver, and it turns out to be a good one for Surrey, as the medium-pacer finds an analysis of 8.5-1-32-4 becoming 9-1-41-4 when he slides another ball down the legside to donate a further five wides to the visitors' cause and then ends with a half-volley that Jon Batty drives crisply to the rope at extra cover. Although the Yorkshire skipper has bowled really well and returned career-best one-day figures, the fourteen runs he has conceded in extras - twelve in wides and two from a no-ball - could yet prove expensive in what looks like being a fairly low-scoring match.

Having passed the 150 mark during McGrath's final over, things are looking just a shade more promising for the Lions, though they soon receive another blow when Kirby's return in place of his skipper brings the downfall of Batty, who slices a drive to Wood at backward point and departs for eleven at 159-7.

At this stage, since almost twelve overs remain in the innings, there would appear to be a real possibility of the Phoenix dismissing their opponents inside the distance, so it's not too surprising that Clarke and Ian Salisbury take no chances against the potentially dangerous pairing of Gough and Kirby during the next couple of overs.

Rather than go for the kill with Gough, who has two overs left, McGrath then makes a surprise move by introducing Craven's medium pace at the rugby stand end for the thirty-seventh over. Although this causes a few raised eyebrows around the ground, the Yorkshire captain turns out to have made a good decision as Salisbury shuffles across his stumps, misses a flick to leg, and falls lbw for seven to the new bowler's fourth delivery, thereby plunging Surrey deeper into the mire at 170-8.

Luckily, the Lions' renowned depth of batting is illustrated by the appearance of Martin Bicknell at number ten, and he plays the same kind of supporting role as Batty and Salisbury, while Clarke on-drives the last ball of Kirby's stint to the boundary and then chips the returning Hoggard over midwicket for another very valuable four towards the end of the fortieth over.

The fact that Bicknell is then beaten by the first three balls of Gough's first over back in place of Craven at least proves that there is always going to be help for the bowlers from this pitch and offers a degree of comfort to the visitors as they struggle towards the two-hundred mark. Their hopes of reaching that score receive a setback, however, when Bicknell snicks the last ball of Gough's over to Fleming at slip, reducing Surrey to 190-9.

As McGrath finally goes for the jugular by allowing Hoggard and Gough to complete their spells, James Ormond off-drives for four to complete a pretty poor stint by Hoggard, while Clarke manages to supply the three runs that his team needs to reach two-hundred during the last over of Gough's fine spell of 9-0-28-1.

With the last two overs of the Lions' innings having now been left to Craven and Dawson, Surrey must be hoping to finish with a flourish but, unfortunately, the medium-pacer adds a tight two-run over to the two good ones he had sent down in his previous spell, and then it takes the off-spinner just two balls to penetrate Ormond's drive with a full-length delivery, leaving the league leaders all out for 202. They are clearly going to have to bowl and field well if they are to defend what appears to be a slightly below-par total, though they will certainly hope to do better than the home side on the extras front. In a total of 202, Yorkshire's contribution of thirty-one sundries looks excessive and could prove costly.

Yorkshire Phoenix's Innings

Yorkshire make an unconvincing start to their reply, with Matthew Wood - taking most of the strike during the first four overs from Martin Bicknell and Azhar Mahmood - progressing to seven with a couple of edges and a forcing stroke backward of point that only just evades the leaping Rikki Clarke. It's no surprise, therefore, when he nicks another loose attacking shot at Azhar through to Jon Batty in the sixth over with the total at sixteen.

Michael Vaughan then appears at number three and edges his first delivery through the slips on the bounce to get off the mark with a boundary, before forcing Bicknell away through point to earn a second four in the next over.

With the ball seemingly moving around even more for the Lions than it had for the Phoenix, the early signs are encouraging for the visitors, though Vaughan and his partner, Stephen Fleming, soon begin to settle down and look dangerous - Vaughan's clip to the rope at midwicket off Azhar is followed by Fleming's square-driven four off Bicknell and a very expensive tenth over of the innings from the Pakistani that sees the arrival of the Yorkshire fifty. During this over, the Kiwi skipper enjoys a stroke of good fortune when his top-edged pull flies over third man for six, though there is nothing lucky about the middled pull and the lofted on-drive that follow in what turns out to be a fifteen-run over.

Surrey obviously can't afford any more overs like that, though they are soon in a position where they don't have to worry about Fleming any more, as the New Zealander advances on Bicknell and miscues a drive high in the air behind square on the off-side where the safe hands of Clarke eventually get to complete an important dismissal.

At this point, James Ormond takes over from Azhar at the Kirkstall Lane end and, after being pulled for four by Vaughan in his first over, strikes another blow for the Lions in his next over by inducing a horribly miscued pull from Michael Lumb that results in the simplest of catches to Ian Salisbury at mid-on. As the young left-hander departs for a ten-ball duck and is replaced in the middle by Anthony McGrath, Surrey now appear to hold the advantage, with their hosts floundering slightly at 60-3 after fourteen overs.

Yorkshire's position is then made even more uncomfortable by a maiden from the admirable Bicknell and a testing four-run over from Ormond, before the visitors' senior bowler tightens the screws still further by completing a superb stint of 9-2-21-1 with an over costing just three runs.

These three consecutive economical overs have piled further pressure on the fourth-wicket pair, and Ormond's next over proves even more damaging to their cause as McGrath emulates Lumb by pulling without due care and attention. Even allowing for the fact that the pitch is tricky to bat on, we have seen some poor strokes played in the match so far, but this one possibly edges out Lumb's as the worst, since the Phoenix skipper fails to get into any sort of position to execute the shot properly and only succeeds in getting a very thick top edge that sends the ball on a gentle arc to Hollioake at mid-on. As Surrey celebrate this fourth wicket, with the score on sixty-eight in the eighteenth over, there is no doubt that they hold the whip hand, especially as the rest of Yorkshire's batting line-up doesn't look too strong.

Vaughan remains the key man, though Vic Craven, coming in at six, starts well by taking cut and pulled fours from the first two overs delivered by Clarke, the replacement for Bicknell at the rugby stand end. Fortunately for Surrey, a maiden from Ormond has separated the new bowler's rather costly first two overs, and the ball is quickly back on top of the bat as the hosts make their way to the hundred mark from the last delivery of the twenty-fourth over.

As if things aren't already bad enough for the home team, Adam Hollioake now enters the fray in place of Clarke and helps Ormond to squeeze a little more life out of the Phoenix with successive maidens that push the required run-rate up above five for the first time. Vaughan senses that the game is slowly drifting away from his side, however, and responds with a straight-driven boundary from the first ball of Ormond's next over, though the big paceman still finishes with the impressive return of 9-2-28-2.

Salisbury is the man to take over from Ormond at the Kirkstall Lane end, and the England captain immediately cuts the Surrey leg-spinner for two to reach a very good 72-ball fifty as eight runs come in total from the over, making it the most productive for the home side since the nineteenth of the innings.

The Lions' captain consequently makes an instant change, reintroducing Azhar in place of Salisbury, though neither the new bowler nor Hollioake himself are able to separate the fifth-wicket pair over the course of the next few overs as the stand starts to develop match-winning potential for the hosts. Having endured a lengthy spell in the doldrums after his impressive start, Craven finally gets some reward for sticking to his task when he breaks free with drives for four in consecutive Hollioake overs, at the end of which Yorkshire's requirement is down to fifty-four runs from ten overs with six wickets in hand.

The Surrey skipper is forced into a double bowling change at this point, since he clearly wishes to retain overs from himself and Azhar for the latter stages of the contest. He therefore recalls Clarke at the Kirkstall Lane end and Salisbury at the rugby stand end, in the hope that one or other of his new pair can break up a partnership that now looks capable of seeing the Phoenix through to a rare and extremely valuable NCL victory.

Since the batsmen don't need to take any major risks, the next five overs are very frustrating for the visitors as twenty-four runs accrue without there being any real sign of the bowlers making a breakthrough. Consequently, Hollioake opts to take over from Salisbury after a decent four-run over from Clarke, during which the ball is changed by the umpires, probably because it has become dirty and difficult to see in light that is starting to fade. With six wickets in hand and two well-set batsmen at the crease it has to be conceded that Yorkshire are now favourites to score the required thirty runs from the last five overs.

Their position is then further strengthened when the Lions' captain's comeback over turns out to be pretty disastrous. Twelve vital runs leak from it, including a wide, a leg-bye, and a boundary glanced to the rope at fine leg by Vaughan, leaving just eighteen to be scored from four overs. It seems that we may have just witnessed the decisive over.

The plan had almost certainly been for the Surrey captain and Azhar to see out the rest of the match, but, following his disappointing last over, Hollioake is forced into a rethink and discusses his options with some of his team-mates. Although the visitors are up with the required over-rate, the crowd view this as an attempt to slow things down and take advantage of the gathering gloom. The umpires are more understanding, however, and the Lions' skipper does eventually settle on a change of plan, allowing Clarke, who appears to be in a good rhythm, to continue at the Kirkstall Lane end. And it proves to be an inspired move.

After a couple of wides early in Clarke's over, the visitors finally get the breakthrough they have been seeking when Vaughan drops the ball down short on the legside and Craven calls his partner through for a quick single, only to be defeated by the bowler's direct-hit on the striker's stumps, courtesy of an impressive right-foot 'shot'. It's an unfortunate way for Craven to be dismissed, three runs short of his half-century, and it certainly gives the league leaders hope again, with the home side now needing fifteen runs from nineteen balls. While Vaughan is in occupation Yorkshire remain clear favourites, though, and if he is still there at the end, then the home side will win, of that there can be no doubt.

With Richard Blakey having taken a single from the last ball of Clarke's over, Phoenix need fourteen from three overs as Azhar returns in place of Hollioake at the rugby stand end to deliver the forty-third over. Unfortunately for Surrey, their overseas all-rounder's attempt at a leg stump yorker to Vaughan from the second ball of the over ends up as a low full-toss that the England captain clips away backward of square on the legside for four precious runs. This looks like it could be the killer blow as, with three singles coming from the rest of the over, the hosts' task is reduced to scoring a mere six runs from the last two overs with five wickets still in hand.

Not surprisingly, further discussions then take place among the Lions' players, much to the displeasure of the home fans, before Clarke starts the penultimate over with a leg stump delivery that Vaughan clips away in the direction of deep midwicket. As Ian Ward races in from the rope, the batsmen have the option of either settling for a straightforward single or pushing for a tight two, and Vaughan decides to take the latter course, probably because he wishes to retain the strike. Unluckily for him, the fielder's pick-up and throw are both absolutely immaculate and, as the ball fizzes towards Batty's gloves over the top of the stumps, the England skipper is struggling to make his ground. Having taken Ward's pinpoint return cleanly, the Lions' keeper then whips the bails off with the minimum of fuss, the appeal goes up, and Vaughan, to his obvious dismay, is adjudged run out by umpire John Holder.

Although the Surrey team are understandably very excited about this wicket, Yorkshire still hold all the aces as a disappointed Vaughan makes his way from the field at the end of a fine knock of ninety. With one run having been completed before the run out occurred, the Phoenix requirement is down to just five runs from eleven deliveries, so the league leaders are still going to have to produce something very special if they are to pull this game out of the fire.

They make a good start towards achieving this, however, when the new batsman, Richard Dawson, fails to score from any of the next four balls delivered by Clarke, and then finds his desperate heave to leg defeated by a fine slower ball that knocks back his middle stump. Suddenly, we are looking at a grandstand finish to this game. The Lions' lads are absolutely cock-a-hoop at the end of a great over from their young all-rounder, and you can sense that there is now a real chance that the league leaders' confidence could take them through to triumph over a bottom-placed team racked with self-doubt.

With five runs still needed by the home side, it's all to play for as Azhar bowls to Blakey and beats the Yorkshireman's flailing bat with two fine outswingers at the start of the final over. It looks like the home batsmen see one big hit as their best chance of winning the game, but, unfortunately for them, Blakey again fails to connect as Azhar's superb inswinging yorker crashes into his stumps, leaving the Phoenix struggling at 198-8.

As Steve Kirby joins Darren Gough in the middle, Surrey continue to take their time getting their field-settings correct, and the crowd get very agitated again, though they are probably more frustrated by their own team's incompetence than anything else. When everyone is settled, Azhar races in to Kirby and strikes him on the pad with an low inswinging full-toss. The bad news for the Lions is that it is adjudged 'not out', while the bad news for the Phoenix is that they are unable to steal a leg-bye, so the home side's total remains exactly where it was when Vaughan was dismissed ten balls ago, at 198.

They finally move on to 199 from the penultimate ball of the match - though only just - when Hollioake, at backward point, gets both hands to Kirby's looping leading edge but can't hold on to a potentially decisive catch as he tumbles backwards.

Darren Gough is therefore left to face the last ball - which is also **his** first ball - needing four to win the game for his team. Without taking anything away from the Surrey bowlers, it seems incredible that Yorkshire have got themselves into this situation, though it probably explains why they are likely to be relegated. They desperately need Gough to find the rope as Azhar delivers a low full-toss, but the former England fast bowler is only able to drive the ball away for a single on the off-side, leaving a happy huddle of Lions' players celebrating a quite astonishing two-run victory that has taken them closer still to NCL glory.

RIKKI CLARKE'S VIEW FROM THE DRESSING ROOM

Although the Vaughan-Craven partnership kept growing, I always felt that we were in with a chance. Were you thinking along the same lines?
RC - In one-day cricket you are always in the game, though I must admit that even when we broke that partnership and got into their tail they were still very much in control. I don't think they played it very well, though - they looked to hit out when all they really needed to do was look for the singles. That's probably where they went wrong.

Towards the end of that partnership the ball was changed. Did Yorkshire request the change because the ball was getting dirty and, therefore, difficult to see? Or did the umpires prompt the ball change?
RC - I think it was down to the umpires. It was certainly getting darker and they were the ones who asked to have a look at the ball, so I think it must have been their decision to replace it.

Your right boot broke the stand when you ran out Craven in your follow-through. A bit of a fluke or do you have faith in your footballing skills in that situation?!
RC - It's just down to luck, really. But it goes to show that all the football warm-ups we have in the mornings pay off eventually!

Michael Vaughan looked a little upset when he was adjudged to be run out. Do you know if that was because he felt he'd made his ground or because he feared that his dismissal could be a turning point in the game?
RC - I think he felt he'd made his ground, actually, but it was difficult for the umpire as there were no television replays and he had to make the decision in the gloom.

Despite the fact that we were ahead of the required over-rate, the crowd started giving us a lot of stick for slowing the game down a little. But we were entitled to do that, weren't we, especially as the game was so tight and we needed to make sure we got our field settings spot-on?
RC - Definitely. I think the crowd were looking for an excuse for what was happening so they decided to turn it on us. But they pay their money, so they are entitled to their opinion, I suppose. We weren't concerned about it, though - we knew we weren't behind on the over-rate.

YORKSHIRE PHOENIX v SURREY LIONS at Headingley
Sunday 31st August — **Surrey Lions won by 2 runs**

Yorkshire Phoenix won the toss and elected to field — **Umpires:- John Holder & Neil Mallender**

SURREY LIONS

Fall Of Wkt	Batsman	How	Out	Score	Balls	4s	6s
1-35	**I.J. Ward**	**c Blakey**	**b Hoggard**	**21**	26	4	0
2-91	**A.D. Brown**		**b McGrath**	**50**	50	6	3
3-93	**M.A. Butcher**	**c Craven**	**b Kirby**	**12**	21	2	0
4-96	**G.P. Thorpe**	**c Wood**	**b McGrath**	**2**	5	0	0
	R. Clarke	**Not**	**Out**	**46**	72	4	0
5-107	**A.J. Hollioake ***	**c Kirby**	**b McGrath**	**2**	23	0	0
6-126	**Azhar Mahmood**	**c Kirby**	**b McGrath**	**8**	13	1	0
7-159	**J.N. Batty +**	**c Wood**	**b Kirby**	**11**	17	1	0
8-170	**I.D.K. Salisbury**	**lbw**	**b Craven**	**7**	15	1	0
9-190	**M.P. Bicknell**	**c Fleming**	**b Gough**	**6**	17	0	0
10-202	**J. Ormond**		**b Dawson**	**6**	10	1	0
	Extras	**(5lb, 20w, 6nb)**		**31**			
	TOTAL	**(44.2 overs)**		**202**			

Bowler	O	M	R	W	NB	Wd
Gough	**9**	**0**	**28**	**1**	-	1
Hoggard	**9**	**0**	**57**	**1**	1	3
Kirby	**9**	**0**	**47**	**2**	1	4
McGrath	**9**	**1**	**41**	**4**	1	4
Dawson	**5.2**	**0**	**17**	**1**	-	-
Craven	**3**	**0**	**7**	**1**	-	-

YORKSHIRE PHOENIX

Fall Of Wkt	Batsman	How	Out	Score	Balls	4s	6s
1-16	**M.J. Wood**	**c Batty**	**b Azhar**	**8**	23	1	0
2-50	**S.P. Fleming**	**c Clarke**	**b Bicknell**	**27**	31	4	1
6-198	**M.P. Vaughan**	**run**	**out**	**90**	112	7	0
3-60	**M.J. Lumb**	**c Salisbury**	**b Ormond**	**0**	10	0	0
4-68	**A. McGrath ***	**c Hollioake**	**b Ormond**	**1**	5	0	0
5-188	**V.J. Craven**	**run**	**out**	**47**	75	6	0
8-198	**R.J. Blakey +**		**b Azhar**	**3**	6	0	0
7-198	**R.K.J. Dawson**		**b Clarke**	**0**	5	0	0
	D. Gough	**Not**	**Out**	**1**	1	0	0
	S.P. Kirby	**Not**	**Out**	**1**	2	0	0
	M.J. Hoggard	**did not bat**					
	Extras	**(12lb, 10w)**		**22**			
	TOTAL	**(45 overs)**	**(for 8 wkts)**	**200**			

Bowler	O	M	R	W	NB	Wd
Bicknell	**9**	**2**	**21**	**1**	-	-
Azhar Mahmood	**9**	**1**	**49**	**2**	-	1
Ormond	**9**	**2**	**28**	**2**	-	1
Clarke	**8**	**0**	**33**	**1**	-	4
Hollioake	**7**	**1**	**37**	**0**	-	4
Salisbury	**3**	**0**	**20**	**0**	-	-

Other NCL Division One Results

With the Lions' sensational win coming on top of the Gladiators' midweek defeat at the hands of the Spitfires, they now appeared to have one hand on the trophy - one win from three games might now be sufficient to secure the title, while two would make it absolutely certain. Gloucestershire had meanwhile picked up some silverware the previous day when they had thrashed Worcestershire by seven wickets in the C&G Trophy final at Lord's. As a result of their participation in the final, they were to play a rearranged fixture against the Warwickshire Bears at Edgbaston the next day, and all Surrey eyes would be on that match, since defeat for the Gladiators would bring NCL glory closer still for the Lions.

August 27
***Bristol:-* Kent Spitfires (4pts) beat Gloucestershire Gladiators by 36 runs.** Kent 251-7 (45ov; Walker 101, Smith 59, Harvey 4-55); Gloucs 215 (43ov; Muralitharan 5-34).
August 28
***Colchester:-* Essex Eagles (4pts) beat Worcestershire Royals by 2 wickets (D/L method).** Worcs 141-3 (25ov); Essex 86-8 (9.5ov).

NCL DIVISION ONE TABLE AT 31ST AUGUST

Pos	Prv		P	Pts	W	T	L	A	NRR
1	1	**Surrey Lions**	13	42	10	0	2	1	7.71
2	2	**Gloucestershire Gladiators**	13	34	8	0	4	1	5.35
3	3	**Glamorgan Dragons**	14	32	8	0	6	0	-0.74
4	4	**Warwickshire Bears**	13	28	7	0	6	0	2.07
5	5	**Essex Eagles**	13	26	6	1	6	0	3.97
6	7	**Kent Spitfires**	13	22	5	1	7	0	-1.41
7	6	**Leicestershire Foxes**	13	20	5	0	8	0	-6.07
8	8	**Worcestershire Royals**	13	16	4	0	9	0	0.21
9	9	**Yorkshire Phoenix**	13	16	4	0	9	0	-8.54

NCL Division One Result

Despite a furious late Trevor Penney-inspired onslaught that produced an incredible thirty-seven runs from the last two overs, Gloucestershire hung on to win by just two runs and therefore kept alive their slender hopes of catching Surrey at the top of the table.
September 1
***Edgbaston:-* Gloucestershire Gladiators (4pts) beat Warwickshire Bears by 2 runs.** Gloucs 246-6 (45ov; Gidman 73); Warwicks 244-7 (45ov; Penney 88*).

NCL DIVISION ONE TABLE AT 1ST SEPTEMBER

Pos	Prv		P	Pts	W	T	L	A	NRR
1	1	**Surrey Lions**	13	42	10	0	2	1	7.71
2	2	**Gloucestershire Gladiators**	14	38	9	0	4	1	4.97
3	3	**Glamorgan Dragons**	14	32	8	0	6	0	-0.74
4	4	**Warwickshire Bears**	14	28	7	0	7	0	1.86
5	5	**Essex Eagles**	13	26	6	1	6	0	3.97
6	6	**Kent Spitfires**	13	22	5	1	7	0	-1.41
7	7	**Leicestershire Foxes**	13	20	5	0	8	0	-6.07
8	8	**Worcestershire Royals**	13	16	4	0	9	0	0.21
9	9	**Yorkshire Phoenix**	13	16	4	0	9	0	-8.54

NATIONAL CRICKET LEAGUE DIVISION ONE - MATCH FOURTEEN

Kent Spitfires versus Surrey Lions at Canterbury

Wednesday 3rd September

Setting The Scene - Three days after their sensational victory over the Yorkshire Phoenix, Surrey face Kent under the lights at Canterbury in another contest that is of vital importance to both sides for very different reasons. Having recently beaten the Gloucestershire Gladiators, the Spitfires will feel optimistic about their chances of overcoming the other title contenders, especially given Surrey's dismal record in Sunday/National League matches on Kent soil - just two wins in fifteen matches. The Lions are not helped by the loss of three players from the eleven that won at Headingley, with Mark Butcher, Graham Thorpe and Martin Bicknell now all on England duty. Their replacements are Mark Ramprakash, Nadeem Shahid and the 31-year-old former West Indian fast bowler, Franklyn Rose, who has been signed, late in the day, as an overseas replacement for Saqlain Mushtaq. Kent are without Ed Smith, who is also away with England, but otherwise appear to be pretty much at full strength. When Dave Fulton wins the toss for Kent he makes the predictable decision to bat first.

Kent Spitfires' Innings

After Michael Carberry pulls the fourth ball of the match for four, Surrey's new-ball bowlers, Azhar Mahmood and Franklyn Rose, utterly dominate the opening exchanges, with the former Lion and his partner, Rob Key, tied down and then dismissed within the first seven overs. Key goes with the total on twelve when his slightly mistimed pull off Rose is brilliantly caught right-handed above his head by a leaping Mark Ramprakash at midwicket, then Carberry follows him back to the pavilion four balls later when he top-edges a cut at Azhar through to Jon Batty, who takes a good catch high to his left-hand side. The loss of Carberry, with the score on fourteen, is bad news for Kent, but things could have been worse - Ian Ward had been unable to cling on to Andrew Symonds' fierce square cut from the previous delivery, and had profited by a single rather than returning to the pavilion with a duck to his name.

It has already been evident that there is decent pace and bounce in the pitch for the seamers, and Surrey's overseas duo take full advantage of this, keeping both the big Aussie and Matt Walker completely bottled up as the total crawls ever so slowly up to nineteen after eleven overs, at which point the league leaders suffer their first setback of the afternoon when Azhar leaves the field with what appears to be an injured left hamstring. Thankfully, he is already through six of his nine overs, with fine figures of 1-13, though Adam Hollioake will still have some serious thinking to do towards the end of the innings if his star 'death' bowler is unable to rejoin the action.

Having delivered 5.5 overs for just six runs, Surrey's other opening bowler now suffers a similar downturn in fortunes as twenty runs flow from his next seven balls - after Walker cuts the last delivery of Rose's sixth over and the first ball of his seventh over for four, each batsman pulls to the rope at midwicket, with Symonds' boundary coming from a free-hit delivery following a no-ball.

When the Australian then carves the opening ball of the next over from Ormond away over point for yet another four, and then raises the Spitfires' fifty with a deflection to third man for two, the hosts seem to be restoring balance to the contest, though the Lions soon regain their advantage when Walker falls to Rikki Clarke's second delivery after replacing Rose at the Nackington Road end. Aiming to drive wide of mid-on, the diminutive left-hander loses his off stump to a fine yorker and departs for nineteen with the total standing at fifty-two in the sixteenth over.

Surrey are then lifted further by Azhar's return to the field, while Kent receive a boost of their own as Clarke comes up with a rather wayward second over that costs him seventeen runs, including a superb off-driven six by Symonds and two legside fours to the recently arrived Dave Fulton.

It's just as well that Ormond has settled into a good accurate spell at the pavilion end, since Clarke's replacement, Ian Salisbury, also finds the going tough during his opening two overs, with Symonds locating the extra-cover boundary on three occasions, once with a cut and twice with drives. The first of these fours brings up the Kent hundred from 21.2 overs, while the third boundary completes a marvellous half-century for the Queenslander from just 37 balls.

With the game seemingly back in the balance, Hollioake promptly relieves Salisbury of his duties at the Nackington Road end and makes a grand entrance that tips the match firmly back in favour of his side.

Having taken just three balls to lure his opposite number into a loose stroke outside the off stump that results in an edge to Batty with the total on 109, Hollioake then picks up the prize scalp of Symonds with the final delivery of a possibly pivotal opening over as the Queenslander is trapped lbw by a ball that nips back a little. The capture of this key wicket clearly means a lot to the Surrey players as they celebrate joyfully, while a 6,000-strong Canterbury crowd has, by way of contrast, fallen silent, with Kent having slipped to a sorry 110-5 after twenty-four overs.

The Spitfires desperately need to rebuild through the two new batsmen, Geraint Jones and Mark Ealham, but the Kent wicketkeeper never looks comfortable as he twice edges to the third-man boundary before driving Hollioake's slower ball to Nadeem Shahid at mid-off in the twenty-eighth over with the total advanced to 124.

It would seem that things can't get much worse for the home side now, but they most certainly do, as they lose three more wickets in the space of four balls to subside to a woeful 126-9. The deserving Ormond starts the slide by hitting James Tredwell's off stump with the final ball of his fine stint of 9-1-35-1, then the Lions' skipper dismisses both Amjad Khan and Martin Saggers for first-ball ducks with the second and third deliveries of the next over. While Khan is another leg-before victim, Saggers is yorked by a delivery that somehow turns him around and passes between his feet en route to the stumps.

Muttiah Muralitharan is therefore left to face Hollioake's hat-trick ball, and he comes pretty close to nicking it through to Batty, before slightly denting the bowler's figures with an almighty slog for four over cow corner from the next delivery and a much more elegant off-driven two from the final ball of the over.

Moving in for the final kill, Hollioake now recalls Rose at the pavilion end as Ormond's replacement, though the West Indian is unable to complete the job during an over in which Murali drives over mid-off for another boundary.

It is therefore left to the Surrey captain to finish what he had started by claiming a third lbw victim, and his sixth wicket, when Ealham aims to hit the fourth ball of the thirty-second over through midwicket and misses.

Incredible though it seems, Kent are all out for 142 at 6.18pm, with no fewer than eighty deliveries of their forty-five overs unused, while Hollioake has returned the astonishing figures of 4.4-0-17-6. Most importantly, though, his team are in with a great chance of virtually sewing up the NCL title here at Canterbury.

Surrey Lions' Innings

The statisticians have been busy during the interval and have revealed that Adam Hollioake's figures are, not surprisingly, the best of his career, as well as being the best ever recorded by any bowler from either side in the history of Kent versus Surrey games in the Sunday/National League. Additionally, Kent's 142 is their lowest total against Surrey in the history of fixtures between the two sides in that competition.

Although their target of 143 doesn't look too demanding, the Lions' pursuit of those runs - and the four points that will almost put them beyond Gloucestershire's reach - gets away to a bad start when Ward falls to the fifth ball of the innings with the total on two. Calling his partner, Ali Brown, through for a leg-bye when the ball bounces away towards point off Brown's pads, Ward seems to have reached the striker's end just ahead of Matt Walker's direct-hit underarm throw, but the television replay tells a different story and he has to depart for the pavilion.

This brings Mark Ramprakash to the crease rather earlier than he might have hoped. He had appeared to be struggling in the field with his injured shoulder, though he doesn't look to be too badly inconvenienced in the opening stages of his innings as he and Brown make steady progress to 20-1 after five very respectable overs from Martin Saggers and Amjad Khan.

At this point, it is apparent that one set of the temporary floodlights has failed, though this isn't an immediate problem, with the game ahead of schedule and the natural light still holding up well enough. The umpires discuss the situation with the batsmen and David Fulton before play continues and, thankfully, power is restored to the offending set of lights within a couple of overs.

Unfortunately for Surrey, the lights go out on Brown's innings at about the same time, as a sortie down the track to Saggers results in a missed drive and an extracted leg stump. The visitors are 22-2 and the Canterbury faithful are starting to come alive.

The last thing the Lions need at this stage is a partisan crowd reviving Kent's spirits, so it's just as well that the new batsman, Nadeem Shahid, and Ramprakash manage to pick up four nicely-timed boundaries, and twenty-five runs in total, in the course of the next four overs to take the score up to 47-2 after eleven overs.

Any hopes that it might all be plain sailing from here for Surrey are rapidly dashed, however, when Andrew Symonds enters the attack in place of Khan and accounts for Shahid with his third delivery as the batsman flirts outside the off stump and edges through to Geraint Jones. As the batsman makes his way back to the pavilion past a scoreboard reading 48-3, the Spitfires are still very much in the match, with the Lions really needing a stand of forty or fifty runs in order to subdue the home team and their typically vociferous fans.

Since Rikki Clarke, the new man in the middle, has often batted well with Ramprakash, hopes are high that such a partnership can be formed, and it looks promising when the youngster starts impressively with a square-cut boundary in the second over from Mark Ealham - Saggers' replacement at the pavilion end - and a pulled four in the former England all-rounder's third over.

This prompts the rather belated appearance of Muttiah Muralitharan to deliver the seventeenth over - with Kent clearly needing to bowl Surrey out if they are to pull this game out of the fire, everyone had been expecting to see the Sri Lankan spin wizard in action much earlier.

The combination of Symonds and Muralitharan looks to be a good one from the home side's point of view, and so it proves as the flow of runs slows to little more than a trickle. Consequently, the score has only advanced as far as seventy-three in the twenty-first over when Clarke misses a slog-sweep at Muralitharan and, having dragged his back foot out of his crease, is stumped by Jones.

Although the league leaders are over halfway towards their target, and only need to score at a rate of around three-an-over, Kent are bringing a little bit of pressure to bear on them as Adam Hollioake makes his way to the middle. It is utterly baffling, therefore, to see Fulton removing both Symonds (7-1-17-1) and Muralitharan (4-1-6-1) from the attack, in favour of Ealham and Saggers, within three overs of Hollioake's arrival.

Although the new bowlers start reasonably well by yielding just seven runs from their first three overs, Saggers' second over then costs ten, as the Lions' captain drives and pulls to the midwicket boundary, taking his team's total into three figures in the process.

The most predictable move of the match then sees Muralitharan making an immediate reappearance at the pavilion end to bowl the next over, with Ealham switching to the Nackington Road end, but it seems the damage has already been done. With Ramprakash looking as solid as ever as he continues to pick off the occasional single, Hollioake virtually seals Kent's fate with three boundaries in the course of the thirty-first and thirty-second overs, cutting Muralitharan through point, before adding a drive and a pull at Ealham's expense. A very cool and sensible partnership then reaches the fifty mark two overs later when Hollioake takes a single from the returning Khan, who is picked up over midwicket for the seventh four of the Lions' skipper's innings shortly afterwards as victory comes into sight for Surrey.

Although the Danish paceman takes revenge almost immediately by having the visiting captain caught on the cover boundary by Saggers, thereby ending a perfectly judged knock of thirty-eight, it counts for nothing, as Ramprakash collects only the second four of his measured innings with a force through the covers off Murali before Azhar Mahmood completes the Lions' triumph with a cover-driven four from the final delivery of the Sri Lankan's allotted nine overs.

A very professional display by the visitors has seen them closing in on their second title of the season, while the Spitfires remain in serious danger of relegation.

ADAM HOLLIOAKE'S VIEW FROM THE DRESSING ROOM

You came on to bowl at 108-3, halfway through their innings, with Andrew Symonds going really well. At that point, what target were you realistically expecting us to be chasing?
AH - At that stage I probably would have taken a score of 240, though it wasn't a great wicket, to be honest - it was quite sporty, so I think we'd bowled quite badly for them to have reached 108-3.

Would it be fair to say that the over in which you took the wickets of Symonds and Fulton completely changed the course of the match?
AH - Whenever you get two wickets in an over you are changing the course of a game, but when you are getting out two batsmen who are well set then you are changing it even more… and when one of those batsmen is Andrew Symonds then it's more significant still.

You ended up taking six wickets in 4.4 overs. Given that it all happened so quickly, were you really able to appreciate what you'd done, or did it take a while to sink in?
AH - At that stage of the season I was so tired, and wanted to win these games so much, that I didn't really think about it, to be honest. Once their innings was over, I immediately turned my attentions to trying to make sure that we got home with the bat, because I always felt it was going to be a hard little chase.

Did you have any worries as you walked out to bat at 75-4, or were you still happy enough while Ramps was out there in the middle?
AH - I was genuinely concerned, because I knew that if we lost a couple of quick wickets at that stage it would have been an almost impossible chase from there on. So we had to treat the bowling with respect and I think we started off very cautiously. Then we had a bit of a chat and decided that he'd just try and stay there, while I tried to put a bit more pressure back on to them.

KENT SPITFIRES v SURREY LIONS at Canterbury
Wednesday 3rd September — Surrey Lions won by five wickets
Kent Spitfires won the toss and elected to bat — Umpires:- Ian Gould & George Sharp

KENT SPITFIRES

Fall Of Wkt	Batsman	How	Out	Score	Balls	4s	6s
2-14	M.A. Carberry	c Batty	b Azhar	6	17	1	0
1-12	R.W.T. Key	c Ramprakash	b Rose	5	21	0	0
5-110	A. Symonds	lbw	b Hollioake	53	42	7	1
3-52	M.J. Walker		b Clarke	19	34	3	0
4-109	D.P. Fulton *	c Batty	b Hollioake	19	29	2	0
6-124	G.O. Jones +	c Shahid	b Hollioake	12	17	2	0
10-142	M.A. Ealham	lbw	b Hollioake	6	16	0	0
7-125	J.C. Tredwell		b Ormond	0	5	0	0
8-126	A. Khan	lbw	b Hollioake	0	1	0	0
9-126	M.J. Saggers		b Hollioake	0	1	0	0
	M. Muralitharan	Not	Out	11	8	2	0
	Extras	(3lb, 6w, 2nb)		11			
	TOTAL	(31.4 overs)		142			

Bowler	O	M	R	W	NB	Wd
Azhar Mahmood	6	0	13	1	-	1
Rose	8	1	33	1	1	2
Ormond	9	1	35	1	-	1
Clarke	2	0	22	1	-	2
Salisbury	2	0	19	0	-	-
Hollioake	4.4	0	17	6	-	-

SURREY LIONS							
Fall Of Wkt	Batsman	How	Out	Score	Balls	4s	6s
1-2	**I.J. Ward**	**run**	**out**	**1**	2	0	0
2-22	**A.D. Brown**		**b Saggers**	**10**	20	1	0
	M.R. Ramprakash	**Not**	**Out**	**42**	95	2	0
3-48	**N. Shahid**	**c Jones**	**b Symonds**	**19**	20	3	0
4-73	**R. Clarke**	**st Jones**	**b Muralitharan**	**14**	32	2	0
5-133	**A.J. Hollioake ***	**c Saggers**	**b Khan**	**38**	51	7	0
	Azhar Mahmood	**Not**	**Out**	**4**	2	1	0
	J.N. Batty +	**did not bat**					
	I.D.K. Salisbury	**did not bat**					
	J. Ormond	**did not bat**					
	F.A. Rose	**did not bat**					
	Extras	**(4b, 2lb, 9w)**		**15**			
	TOTAL	**(37 overs)**	**(for 5 wkts)**	**143**			

Bowler	O	M	R	W	NB	Wd
Saggers	**7**	**0**	**29**	**1**	-	4
Khan	**7**	**0**	**33**	**1**	-	4
Ealham	**7**	**0**	**32**	**0**	-	-
Symonds	**7**	**1**	**17**	**1**	-	-
Muralitharan	**9**	**1**	**26**	**1**	-	1

Other NCL Division One Result

Surrey were now on the brink of success, requiring to win just one of their last two games to secure the title. Given the advantage they held over Gloucestershire in terms of net run-rate it was possible that they might actually have enough points already, though they clearly wouldn't be taking any chances on that score!

September 2
Cardiff:- **Leicestershire Foxes (4pts) beat Glamorgan Dragons by 3 wickets.** Glamorgan 226-7 (45ov; Powell 91*); Leics 227-7 (45ov; Ward 104, Nixon 67*).

NCL DIVISION ONE TABLE AT 3RD SEPTEMBER

Pos	Prv		P	Pts	W	T	L	A	NRR
1	1	**Surrey Lions**	**14**	**46**	11	0	2	1	8.33
2	2	**Gloucestershire Gladiators**	**14**	**38**	9	0	4	1	4.97
3	3	**Glamorgan Dragons**	**15**	**32**	8	0	7	0	-0.73
4	4	**Warwickshire Bears**	**14**	**28**	7	0	7	0	1.86
5	5	**Essex Eagles**	**13**	**26**	6	1	6	0	3.97
6	7	**Leicestershire Foxes**	**14**	**24**	6	0	8	0	-5.56
7	6	**Kent Spitfires**	**14**	**22**	5	1	8	0	-2.41
8	8	**Worcestershire Royals**	**13**	**16**	4	0	9	0	0.21
9	9	**Yorkshire Phoenix**	**13**	**16**	4	0	9	0	-8.54

19 Title Surrender

With a second trophy almost in the bag, Surrey now needed a superhuman effort in their last two Championship matches if they were to retain any hope at all of matching the trebles achieved by Warwickshire and Gloucestershire. Since their team was possibly going to be lacking up to five players - Azhar, Bicknell, Ramprakash, Saqlain and Thorpe - who had been regulars in the Championship side for the greater part of the season, Surrey's task of winning the game against Kent was bordering on Herculean. To make matters worse, Kent had been revitalised in the Championship since the signing of Muttiah Muralitharan and the return from injury of Martin Saggers and Amjad Khan. Matters were, in any case, now out of Surrey's hands to a large extent, so eyes - and ears - would have to be kept on news of Sussex's progress against Middlesex at Hove in a game that started one day later, on Friday 5th September.

Surrey fans at Canterbury would also be keen to know what was going on at The Oval where an England team containing four of their county's players - Alec Stewart, Mark Butcher, Graham Thorpe and Martin Bicknell - were starting out on their attempt to level the Test series against South Africa. The profile of what was already an important match had been raised by the fact that it was to be Alec Stewart's final appearance for England… and quite possibly his last appearance in first-class cricket, since there was no guarantee that he would play for Surrey in any of their final three matches of the season. In fact, given that he hadn't played in any one-day games, it seemed that the match against Essex in the Championship represented the only realistic chance of a Surrey swansong for Stewie.

FRIZZELL COUNTY CHAMPIONSHIP DIVISION ONE - MATCH FIFTEEN

KENT versus SURREY
at Canterbury

First Day - Thursday 4th September
Kent 435-5

The Teams And The Toss *- With four players on duty with England, one away with Pakistan, and Azhar Mahmood failing a late fitness test, Surrey are very much below full strength and are forced into three changes from the side that played at Old Trafford - Azhar, Graham Thorpe and Saqlain Mushtaq are replaced by Franklyn Rose, who is making his Championship debut for the county, Nadeem Shahid, who is making a first Championship appearance of the season, and Mark Ramprakash, who takes his place in the side even though he is still struggling with his shoulder injury. Kent are short of two batsmen for this contest, since Ed Smith is also involved in the Test at The Oval, and Rob Key is nursing a suspected broken finger, sustained during last night's NCL match. On a glorious morning, David Fulton wins the toss and elects to bat.*

In excellent batting conditions, the Kent openers are clearly delighted to have first use of the wicket and set about taking advantage of their good fortune.

Although Franklyn Rose comes up with an excellent opening burst of seven overs, during which he beats the bat on numerous occasions, James Ormond appears to be struggling right from the start with his troublesome knee and leaves the field as soon as he has completed six fairly innocuous overs, during which Michael Carberry has impressed with a couple of wristy whips through midwicket.

After Murtagh takes over from Ormond, and sees Fulton, on fifteen, put down by Ali Brown at first slip, the Kent fifty arrives from the first ball of Rikki Clarke's opening over as Rose's replacement at the Nackington Road end when Carberry cuts to the rope at backward point.

Although there are a few too many 'four balls' flying around from the young Surrey bowlers, it has to be said that neither of them enjoys any luck at all as the total climbs and Carberry reels off further impressive strokes. The 22-year-old left-hander eventually completes a fine 70-ball fifty by taking three fours from the seventh over of Murtagh's spell, which has otherwise been impressive, as evidenced by Fulton edging two boundaries in the young swing bowler's next over to raise the Kent hundred.

The reigning champions' spirits are then dampened, first when Ormond returns to the field but goes straight into second slip, suggesting that he is not going to be fit enough to bowl too many more overs, and then when Clarke yields two fours in the final over of his spell, the first of which brings Carberry his highest Championship score of the summer, and the second of which heralds the arrival of Fulton's fifty from 87 balls.

As lunch approaches, Adam Hollioake and Ian Salisbury take a turn in the attack, though neither man proves able to provide the breakthrough that Surrey desperately crave. The visiting skipper's second over does, however, see Carberry passing his career-best Championship score of eighty-four with the second of two back-foot fours, while Fulton takes his side beyond 150 with a boundary of his own.

By the time the interval arrives Carberry is just nine away from a century and Kent are in total command at 158-0, though Surrey have undoubtedly bowled better than the score suggests and are probably wondering how they haven't got a wicket to their credit.

Lunch:- Kent 158-0 (Fulton 64, Carberry 91*) from 35 overs*

Carberry falls eight short of his maiden County Championship century when Rose gets reward for his very good morning spell by inducing an outside edge to Jon Batty in the first over after the interval. It's been a fine knock by the former Surrey man and he fully deserves the ovation he receives from a fair-sized crowd at the St. Lawrence ground as he returns to the pavilion.

With Salisbury posing problems at the other end, the visitors enjoy a spell in the ascendancy, during which the former West Indies paceman strikes again when Fulton edges a drive to provide Batty with another catch that sets the home side back a little at 175-2.

After three successive maidens and a very circumspect start by Andrew Symonds, hopes of Surrey continuing their revival take a dive as the Queenslander sees off Salisbury with three well-struck boundaries, before rising again when Murtagh, the leg-spinner's replacement, gets due reward for his earlier bowling by claiming Alex Loudon lbw as the batsman pads up to a ball nipping back at him. Unfortunately for the visitors, this turns out to be another false dawn, since Symonds is soon hammering Rose out of the attack with three glorious drives that take the score past two-hundred and bring another good spell by the 6' 5" Jamaican to a close.

The big Australian then takes a back seat for a short while as Matt Walker starts impressively, before racing through to an exhilarating half-century from 45 balls during a period in which he plunders five boundaries from three Murtagh overs.

Clarke has meanwhile cranked up his pace a notch at the Nackington Road end and gets some tangible reward for a good burst when Walker provides him with his first wicket of the innings by edging to Brown at first slip with the total at 262.

In an attempt to secure further wickets before tea, Hollioake pairs a clearly unfit Ormond with a recalled Salisbury but, despite their best efforts, they can neither make the breakthrough nor stem the flow of runs. Symonds takes full toll of a couple of long-hops from Ormond before launching the paceman over long-on for a six that takes the total past three-hundred, while Mark

Ealham recovers from a rather edgy start to pull Salisbury over midwicket for six, and then completes a fifty partnership for the fifth wicket with a drive for two off the same bowler on the stroke of tea.

Tea:- Kent 312-4 (Symonds 86, Ealham 22*) from 72 overs*

After cutting Salisbury to the rope at extra cover in the first over of the session, Symonds is, thankfully, subdued for a few overs by deep-set fields and his own desire to complete a century, though he duly reaches the magic mark, from his ninety-ninth ball, in the sixth post-tea over when he cuts Rose to the backward point boundary. This is the seventeenth four of an excellent knock, which has also included one six.

With Rose turning in his least impressive spell of the day, and Ealham starting to find his form with the bat, the score soon climbs past the 350 mark, and the hundred partnership arrives two overs later when Symonds sweeps Salisbury to fine leg for two.

It's actually becoming difficult to see where the next wicket is coming from when the Surrey leg-spinner suddenly produces a fine delivery to remove the big Queenslander for 121 with the score standing at 368-4. Tempted down the track by a well flighted delivery, Symonds is beaten through the gate by a googly and, luckily for the bowler and wicketkeeper, is far enough down the track for Batty to complete the stumping at the second attempt, after fumbling the initial take.

The Surrey stumper is not so lucky four overs later, however, when Geraint Jones, on two at the time, charges at a Salisbury leg-break and misses, only for Batty to fluff what appears to be a straightforward take. To add insult to injury for the former England leg-spinner, Jones then miscues a drive just over the head of mid-off for two, before middling a sweep that sends the ball soaring over the square leg boundary for six.

Ealham then completes his fifty from his eighty-seventh delivery with a leg-glance for four off Clarke, who has returned for another sparky spell at the Nackington Road end, before underlining his increasing confidence with successive boundaries off Salisbury that raise the hosts' four-hundred.

The fourth fifty-plus partnership of the innings then clicks up as Salisbury finishes his unlucky spell and Clarke comes to the end of another whole-hearted burst, allowing Murtagh and Hollioake to deliver the final eight overs of the day at a cost of just twelve runs. While Murtagh impresses again with a fine spell, Hollioake bangs in plenty of bouncers, most of which fail to interest, or bother, the batsmen.

As stumps are drawn, Surrey's Championship hopes look to be dead and buried, though the bowlers have stuck to their task well for the greater part of the day and have probably deserved better than they have got.

Close:- Kent 435-5 (Ealham 80, Jones 26*) from 104 overs*

Second Day - Friday 5th September

Kent 535; Surrey 125 and 169-7

Surrey take the new ball straight away at the start of day two and enjoy a couple of early successes, though they do come at a price. Mark Ealham, for example, has already taken two fours off Tim Murtagh before he falls lbw for ninety-three in the third over of the morning, while fifteen runs have come from Franklyn Rose's opening two overs before he claims the wicket of Rob Ferley, thanks to a brilliant catch by Rikki Clarke diving in from gully when the batsman hopelessly miscues an attempted upper-cut.

The main reason why runs have flowed so freely as Kent have progressed to 472-7 is that the bowlers have tended to pitch too short, a point that is promptly emphasised when Geraint Jones pulls Murtagh for four and Amjad Khan hooks Rose for six.

While the Jamaican continues to disappoint, eventually being driven over extra cover by Khan for another six, Murtagh learns his lesson and, as a result, removes Jones with a fine outswinger that the Kent keeper nicks to his Surrey counterpart shortly after completing a 77-ball fifty.

Once Rose has conceded a couple of fours to Martin Saggers and been replaced by Clarke, the end comes swiftly for the home side. The Guildford all-rounder provides Jon Batty with a fifth victim when Khan gloves a pull, then Murtagh picks up his fourth wicket when Muttiah Muralitharan miscues a slog to point, where Mark Ramprakash takes the catch that ends the innings at 535. This turns out to be Kent's highest total against Surrey at Canterbury, and it has undoubtedly snuffed out the County Champions' last hopes of retaining their title.

Anyone with Surrey connections who remains unconvinced about this is soon having to pull out their white flag, as the events of the next forty minutes leading up to lunch prove utterly decisive.

We are only in the third over when Saggers rips out Ian Ward's off stump with a ball that snakes back between bat and pad as the left-handed opener drives, then the same bowler strikes again in his fourth over, claiming his fiftieth first-class wicket of the season when he extracts Ramprakash's middle stump with a fine late inswinger.

With Surrey's two most important batsmen in this kind of situation having been so brilliantly removed so early in the piece, it's not a great surprise that there are then further casualties before the interval. Nadeem Shahid is comprehensively beaten on the crease and pinned lbw in Saggers' next over, while Ali Brown clips the final ball of the session from Khan straight to David Fulton, who has only just stationed himself at leg gully. Terrific cricket by Kent, of course, but rather shabby stuff from Surrey, too. Will there be - indeed, **can** there be - any response this afternoon?

Lunch:- Surrey 30-4 (Batty 12) from 10 overs*

The answer to that question is a most definite 'no'. Although Batty picks off three classy boundaries in Saggers' opening over of the afternoon, and then collects another off Khan to raise his team's fifty, he departs shortly afterwards when Saggers takes vengeance with a superb outswinger that glides past the edge of the visiting keeper's defensive push and sends the off stump flying.

Having played a rather frenetic innings since arriving at crease immediately after lunch, Clarke is the next man to join the sad Surrey procession, with the total at seventy-eight, when he top-edges a cut at Khan through to Jones, then the visitors slip further into despair at 79-7 two overs later when Hollioake, having never really settled, is rapped on the back pad by a ball from the Danish paceman that keeps low, leaving umpire Ian Gould with no option but to raise his finger.

At this point, Saggers rests with figures of 4-40 after an excellent spell of ten overs either side of lunch, allowing Muralitharan to enter the attack. That's all Surrey need at this stage of proceedings!

Perhaps sensing that the end could be nigh - or maybe he is just caught up in the fever of the innings - Ian Salisbury slashes Khan away for two boundaries, and then looks on from the other end as Andrew Symonds replaces the Dane in the attack and takes Surrey's eighth wicket with his third ball. James Ormond is the Australian's victim as he pushes forward stylishly but unfortunately only succeeds in getting an inside edge onto his off stump, which follows the trend of the innings by flying out of the ground.

With the visitors now 99-8, it is entirely predictable that Franklyn Rose will adopt an aggressive approach, and his debut innings for Surrey lasts exactly five balls before he middles a sweep off Muralitharan very nicely... but, unfortunately, straight to deep backward square leg, where Ferley picks up a good low catch.

Tim Murtagh, arriving at number eleven, then edges Symonds at catchable height between the first and second slip fielders during his first full over at the crease, before reeling off three authentic boundaries, including an excellent straight drive off Muralitharan. Salisbury is less successful when pitted against the Sri Lankan two overs later, however, as he falls to a catch by Matt Walker at silly point, leaving Surrey all out for an abysmal 125, which includes twenty-one extras. They therefore trail by 410 runs on first innings, and not a soul in the ground is surprised to hear that Kent will now enforce the follow-on.

With Symonds opening the bowling alongside Saggers, the visitors get away to a slightly better start second time around, though the first bowling change - Ealham for Saggers in the ninth over - soon brings a breakthrough for Kent.

Having just guided the first two balls from the new bowler down to the rope at third man, Batty presumably decides he should be more circumspect when playing deliveries around off stump, and pads up to the next delivery, which turns out to be an inswinger from the wily Ealham. This fine piece of bowling is rewarded by umpire Gould's upraised finger, leaving Surrey in further disarray at 23-1 in their second innings.

Thankfully, the second-wicket pair of Ward and Ramprakash manage to repel the final thirteen overs leading up to the interval, including a short fiery burst from Khan and a solitary pre-tea over from Muralitharan.

Although he has only played for Kent for around five weeks, the little Sri Lankan is awarded his county cap as he leaves the field.

Tea:- Surrey 57-1 (Ward 22, Ramprakash 14*) from 22 overs*

Fulton pairs his two most dangerous bowlers, Saggers and Muralitharan, upon the resumption and, as a result, soon has two more wickets in the bag.

Ramprakash, who goes in the fourth over with just five added to the tea score, looks rather unlucky to be adjudged lbw by a trigger-fingered umpire Sharp, since his pad appears to have been struck outside the line of off stump by Saggers, though Shahid can have no complaints two overs later when he mishits a pull at the same bowler into the hands of Fulton, who has moved himself back into that leg gully position that had brought success earlier in the day.

The batsman who had been undone by that field placing, Brown, is then almost the victim of another soft dismissal when he hooks Saggers to Loudon at long leg with his score on just five and sees the youngster spill a low chance that would have been made easier by taking a couple of steps forward.

At this point, Ward seemingly decides to go on the attack, taking boundaries off Saggers, Muralitharan and Symonds - Saggers' successor at the Nackington Road end - in the space of four overs. The boundary off Murali, with Surrey's total not long into three figures, is a pull over deep backward square leg for six that takes Ward through to a well constructed 118-ball half-century, though the batsmen isn't able to savour his achievement for long as the Sri Lankan defeats his attempted cut with a quicker ball that knocks back the off stump later in the same over.

With the light now starting to fade, and Symonds having just been hit for three boundaries in two overs by the fifth-wicket pair of Brown and Clarke, the Kent skipper brings Ferley into the attack opposite Muralitharan, and the all-spin combination soon brings the wicket of the junior member of the batting partnership. Clarke is unfortunate, however, since he receives a nasty delivery from the Sri Lankan that spits up to his glove and is beautifully snapped up low down by Loudon as he dives in from short leg.

This dismissal leaves the visitors at 144-5, and it only takes five overs for that to become 155-6 when Hollioake charges rashly at Ferley in very poor light and is comfortably stumped by Jones. Like Ramprakash (34) before him, the Surrey skipper (32) has therefore been dismissed twice on his birthday.

To cap a truly awful day for Hollioake's team, Brown then falls for a battling forty in the penultimate scheduled over of the day when Muralitharan cleverly tosses up an off-break wide of off stump, drawing the Surrey batsman into a cover drive and bowling him through the gate as the ball spins back sharply.

Salisbury and Ormond subsequently play out the final eight deliveries, only to find the umpires allowing Kent to take the extra half-hour in dreadful light at 6.40pm.

Ormond appears to be missed by Walker at silly point off Murali in the third over of the extra period, before Messrs Gould and Sharp finally accept that conditions really are too bad for play to continue at 6.53pm, with five extra overs having been delivered.

Surrey live to fight another day… though probably not for too long.

Close:- Surrey 169-7 (Salisbury 3, Ormond 0*) from 59 overs*

Third Day - Saturday 6th September

Kent 535; Surrey 125 and 255
Kent won by an innings and 155 runs
Kent 22pts, Surrey 3

Surrey's lower-order batsmen keep this one-sided contest going for exactly eleven overs on the third morning, though they do at least offer the light sprinkling of spectators some highly entertaining fare before they succumb to their inevitable defeat.

Although Salisbury departs in the day's third over, when he shuffles across his stumps and is palpably lbw to Saggers, Ormond plunders two fours and a six - picked up beautifully over midwicket - off Muralitharan to take the score beyond two-hundred before making his exit for thirty-two when he pops up a simple catch to Walker at silly point off the Sri Lankan.

With Ferley having replaced Saggers in the attack, Murtagh and Rose then make merry during a last-wicket stand of forty from just twenty-one balls. While Murtagh reels off a few classy strokes that showcase his ability with the willow, Rose delights the spectators with a towering on-driven six off each Kent spinner before miscuing a drive at Ferley that Saggers takes nicely as he runs back from extra cover.

Kent therefore emerge victorious by an innings and 155 runs to extinguish Surrey's Championship aspirations, barring sensational events at Hove, where Sussex had dismissed Middlesex for 392 on the first day, thereby equalling the number of points that the current champions have obtained from this match.

Statistical Footnote - This was Surrey's first defeat at the hands of Kent in county cricket's premier competition since September 1997, and their first defeat by an innings in the competition since that traumatic match against Leicestershire at The Oval at the end of 1998. Additionally, history had repeated itself, since Surrey's last back-to-back Championship defeats had come against Lancashire and Kent at the end of 1997.

Kent 535; Surrey 125 and 255
Kent won by an innings and 155 runs. Kent 22pts, Surrey 3

KENT v SURREY at Canterbury — 4th to 6th September

Kent won the toss and elected to bat — Umpires:- Ian Gould and George Sharp

KENT - First Innings

Fall Of Wkt	Batsman	How	Out	Score	Balls	4s	6s
2-175	**D.P. Fulton ***	**c Batty**	**b Rose**	**71**	121	11	0
1-160	**M.A. Carberry**	**c Batty**	**b Rose**	**92**	112	16	1
3-191	**A.G.R. Loudon**	**lbw**	**b Murtagh**	**9**	38	2	0
5-368	**A. Symonds**	**st Batty**	**b Salisbury**	**121**	123	18	1
4-262	**M.J. Walker**	**c Brown**	**b Clarke**	**25**	45	3	1
6-451	**M.A. Ealham**	**lbw**	**b Murtagh**	**93**	148	11	1
8-506	**G.O. Jones +**	**c Batty**	**b Murtagh**	**53**	80	6	1
7-472	**R.S. Ferley**	**c Clarke**	**b Rose**	**4**	9	0	0
9-528	**A. Khan**	**c Batty**	**b Clarke**	**25**	34	0	2
	M.J. Saggers	**Not**	**Out**	**10**	16	2	0
10-535	**M. Muralitharan**	**c Ramprakash**	**b Murtagh**	**5**	4	1	0
	Extras	**(11lb, 16nb)**		**27**			
	TOTAL	**(120.2 overs)**		**535**			

Bowler	O	M	R	W	NB	Wd
Ormond	**10**	**0**	**48**	**0**	-	-
Rose	**28**	**8**	**101**	**3**	4	-
Murtagh	**27.2**	**2**	**130**	**4**	-	-
Clarke	**21**	**1**	**95**	**2**	4	-
Hollioake	**7**	**1**	**35**	**0**	-	-
Salisbury	**27**	**4**	**115**	**1**	-	-

SURREY - First Innings (Needing 386 to avoid the follow-on)

Fall Of Wkt	Batsman	How	Out	Score	Balls	4s	6s
1-6	**I.J. Ward**		**b Saggers**	**2**	7	0	0
5-64	**J.N. Batty +**		**b Saggers**	**28**	39	6	0
2-19	**M.R. Ramprakash**		**b Saggers**	**4**	16	1	0
3-27	**N. Shahid**	**lbw**	**b Saggers**	**4**	9	1	0
4-30	**A.D. Brown**	**c Fulton**	**b Khan**	**2**	6	0	0
6-78	**R. Clarke**	**c Jones**	**b Khan**	**26**	22	3	0
7-79	**A.J. Hollioake ***	**lbw**	**b Khan**	**3**	11	0	0
10-125	**I.D.K. Salisbury**	**c Walker**	**b Muralitharan**	**16**	30	3	0
8-99	**J. Ormond**		**b Symonds**	**1**	15	0	0
9-100	**F.A. Rose**	**c Ferley**	**b Muralitharan**	**1**	5	0	0
	T.J. Murtagh	**Not**	**Out**	**17**	18	4	0
	Extras	**(5b, 5lb, 1w, 10nb)**		**21**			
	TOTAL	**(28.5 overs)**		**125**			

Bowler	O	M	R	W	NB	Wd
Saggers	**10**	**1**	**40**	**4**	1	1
Khan	**11**	**0**	**50**	**3**	4	-
Muralitharan	**4.5**	**2**	**11**	**2**	-	-
Symonds	**3**	**0**	**14**	**1**	-	-

SURREY - Second Innings (Following on, 410 runs in arrears)

Fall Of Wkt	Batsman	How	Out	Score	Balls	4s	6s
4-112	**I.J. Ward**		**b Muralitharan**	**53**	120	8	1
1-23	**J.N. Batty +**	**lbw**	**b Ealham**	**17**	19	4	0
2-62	**M.R. Ramprakash**	**lbw**	**b Saggers**	**15**	55	1	0
3-68	**N. Shahid**	**c Fulton**	**b Saggers**	**1**	5	0	0
7-159	**A.D. Brown**		**b Muralitharan**	**40**	70	7	0
5-144	**R. Clarke**	**c Loudon**	**b Muralitharan**	**13**	28	2	0
6-155	**A.J. Hollioake ***	**st Jones**	**b Ferley**	**6**	13	1	0
8-183	**I.D.K. Salisbury**	**lbw**	**b Saggers**	**7**	36	1	0
9-215	**J. Ormond**	**c Walker**	**b Muralitharan**	**32**	40	5	1
10-255	**F.A. Rose**	**c Saggers**	**b Ferley**	**36**	26	5	2
	T.J. Murtagh	**Not**	**Out**	**12**	9	2	0
	Extras	**(8b, 13lb, 2nb)**		**23**			
	TOTAL	**(70 overs)**		**255**			

Bowler	O	M	R	W	NB	Wd
Saggers	**14**	**5**	**37**	**3**	-	-
Symonds	**10**	**3**	**36**	**0**	-	-
Ealham	**6**	**1**	**17**	**1**	-	-
Khan	**4**	**0**	**11**	**0**	1	-
Muralitharan	**25**	**5**	**90**	**4**	-	-
Ferley	**11**	**2**	**43**	**2**	-	-

Other Frizzell Championship Division One Results

It was all over for Surrey, with Sussex looking odds-on to secure their first-ever County Championship title unless something extraordinary happened during the last two rounds of matches. Nottinghamshire were definitely relegated after being hammered by Essex, while Leicestershire were all but mathematically certain to join the men from Trent Bridge in Division Two next season.

September 3-5
***Chelmsford:-* Essex (20pts) beat Notts (5) by 9 wickets.** Notts 284 (Cairns 70, Gallian 65, Dakin 4-53) & 204 (Gallian 79, Clarke 4-34); Essex 335 (Foster 58, Flower 53, Irani 51, McMahon 4-59) & 154-1 (Cook 69*).
***Edgbaston:-* Lancashire (21pts) beat Warwickshire (6) by an innings and 145 runs.** Warwicks 449 (Brown 140*, Trott 126, Betts 73) & 187 (Chapple 5-86); Lancs 781 (Hooper 177, Law 168, Chilton 121, Loye 102, Chapple 60, Wagh 7-222).
September 5-8
***Hove:-* Sussex (22pts) beat Middlesex (7) by 7 wickets.** Middx 392 (Shah 140, Strauss 138, Mushtaq 6-145) & 250 (Weekes 65, Mushtaq 4-80); Sussex 537 (Davis 168, Prior 148, Mushtaq 57, Keegan 4-120) & 108-3 (Montgomerie 54).

FRIZZELL CHAMPIONSHIP DIVISION ONE TABLE AT 8TH SEPTEMBER

Pos	Prv		P	Points	W	D	L	T	Bat	Bwl	Ded
1	2	**Sussex**	**14**	**231.00**	9	2	3	0	55	42	0.00
2	1	**Surrey**	**15**	**213.00**	6	7	2	0	60	41	0.00
3	3	**Lancashire**	**14**	**197.00**	5	8	1	0	58	37	0.00
4	5	**Kent**	**14**	**173.00**	5	5	4	0	42	41	0.00
5	4	**Middlesex**	**15**	**159.00**	3	9	3	0	43	38	0.00
6	6	**Warwickshire**	**14**	**146.50**	3	6	4	1	43	33	2.50
7	7	**Essex**	**14**	**129.00**	2	7	4	1	27	39	0.00
8	8	**Leicestershire**	**14**	**105.50**	0	9	5	0	34	36	0.50
9	9	**Nottinghamshire**	**14**	**100.00**	1	5	8	0	28	39	1.00

Surrey Stars Shine In Stewie's Final Test As England Level The Series

While Surrey were slipping to defeat at Canterbury, England were staging an amazing fightback at The Oval to emerge victorious by nine wickets and level the series with South Africa at 2-2, with both Graham Thorpe, in his comeback Test, and Martin Bicknell very much to the fore on a typically excellent pitch.

At the end of the first day, South Africa had looked in complete control at 362-4, even though they had slipped slightly from a high point of 290-1, but Bicknell struck two important blows at the start of the second day to finish with the best bowling return of the innings (20-4-71-2) as England gradually worked their way through the rest of the batting.

The home side still had it all to do if they were to square the series from this point, but a magnificent record-breaking stand of 268 for the third wicket between Trescothick and Thorpe enabled them to reach 346-2, before Flintoff came up with a tremendous 104-ball knock from number seven in the order to prevent his side from frittering away a good position, eventually earning them 120-run lead on first innings.

Harmison and Bicknell then chipped away at the South African second innings on their way to Test-best figures, leaving England requiring just 110 to win. These were knocked off easily enough, for the loss of Vaughan, in front of a happy, cheering crowd.

Although he had fallen lbw to Pollock for thirty-eight in his final Test innings it was terrific for Alec Stewart to end his 133-match England career on his home ground as part of a match-winning and series-levelling team.

Scores:- South Africa 484 (Gibbs 183, Kirsten 90, Pollock 66*, Kallis 66) and 229 (Harmison 4-33, Bicknell 4-84) lost to England 604-9dec (Trescothick 219, Thorpe 124, Flintoff 95, Pollock 3-111) and 110-1 (Trescothick 69*) by nine wickets.

NCL Division One Results

The Gladiators kept the title race open by beating the Eagles at Bristol, though their narrow margin of victory hadn't helped their net run-rate. At the bottom, Worcestershire Royals were relegated, and would be joined in the second division by Yorkshire Phoenix, since Kent Spitfires and Leicestershire Foxes were due to meet in the next round of matches.

September 7
***Bristol:-* Gloucestershire Gladiators (4pts) beat Essex Eagles by 5 runs.** Gloucs 232-7 (45ov; Windows 83*, Napier 3-40); Essex 227 (45ov; Flower 90, Irani 61, Harvey 5-38).
***Worcester:-* Yorkshire Phoenix (4pts) beat Worcestershire Royals by 7 wickets.** Worcs 223-7 (45ov; Hick 52, Hoggard 3-29); Yorks 227-3 (43.4ov; Wood 91, Lumb 62*).
September 9
***Edgbaston:-* Warwickshire Bears (4pts) beat Worcestershire Royals by 18 runs (D/L method).** Warwicks 250-4 (45ov; Knight 122, Trott 51*); Worcs 173-6 (35.3ov).
September 10
***Chelmsford:-* Essex Eagles (4pts) beat Yorkshire Phoenix by 4 wickets.** Yorks 174 (43.5ov; Clarke 4-28); Essex 177-6 (42.5ov; Pettini 59).

NCL DIVISION ONE TABLE AT 10TH SEPTEMBER

Pos	Prv		P	Pts	W	T	L	A	NRR
1	1	Surrey Lions	14	46	11	0	2	1	8.33
2	2	Gloucestershire Gladiators	15	42	10	0	4	1	4.71
3	3	Glamorgan Dragons	15	32	8	0	7	0	-0.73
4	4	Warwickshire Bears	15	32	8	0	7	0	1.93
5	5	Essex Eagles	15	30	7	1	7	0	4.02
6	6	Leicestershire Foxes	14	24	6	0	8	0	-5.56
7	7	Kent Spitfires	14	22	5	1	8	0	-2.41
8	9	Yorkshire Phoenix	15	20	5	0	10	0	-8.07
9	8	Worcestershire Royals	15	16	4	0	11	0	-0.18

Frizzell Championship Division One Results

By destroying Sussex at Old Trafford, Lancashire had pushed Surrey down into third place and suddenly given themselves just an outside chance of stealing up on the blind side to win the title. It was no more than that, though, since the leaders were up against relegated Leicestershire in their final game and needed just six points. Essex had meanwhile blown their remaining chance of avoiding the drop by losing at Edgbaston.

September 10-12
***Leicester:-* Leicestershire (19pts) beat Kent (3) by 10 wickets.** Leics 295 (Maunders 129, Muralitharan 6-51) & 5-0; Kent 130 & 169
September 10-13
***Old Trafford:-* Lancashire (22pts) beat Sussex (4) by an innings & 19 runs.** Lancs 450-6dec (Law 163*, Loye 144); Sussex 251 (Goodwin 118*, Mushtaq 54, Keedy 5-106) & 180 (Goodwin 57, Keedy 5-61).
***Lord's:-* Middlesex (10pts) drew with Nottinghamshire (11).** Notts 361 (Warren 123, Gallian 73, Pietersen 70) & 407-5dec (Gallian 116, Warren 113*, Pietersen 68); Middx 326 (Shah 87, Nash 53*, MacGill 4-98).
September 11-14
***Chelmsford:-* Warwickshire (22pts) beat Essex (5) by 9 wickets.** Essex 256 (Stephenson 75*) & 302 (Pettini 78, Jefferson 62, Cook 55, Waqar 5-77, Wagh 4-111); Warwicks 503 (Wagh 116, Brown 77, Trott 65, Knight 64, Middlebrook 5-154) & 61-1.

FRIZZELL CHAMPIONSHIP DIVISION ONE TABLE AT 14TH SEPTEMBER											
Pos	**Prv**		**P**	**Points**	W	D	L	T	Bat	Bwl	Ded
1	**1**	**Sussex**	**15**	**235.00**	9	2	4	0	57	44	0.00
2	**3**	**Lancashire**	**15**	**219.00**	6	8	1	0	63	40	0.00
3	**2**	**Surrey**	**15**	**213.00**	6	7	2	0	60	41	0.00
4	**4**	**Kent**	**15**	**176.00**	5	5	5	0	42	44	0.00
5	**5**	**Middlesex**	**16**	**169.00**	3	10	3	0	46	41	0.00
6	**6**	**Warwickshire**	**15**	**168.50**	4	6	4	1	48	36	2.50
7	**7**	**Essex**	**15**	**134.00**	2	7	5	1	29	42	0.00
8	**8**	**Leicestershire**	**15**	**124.50**	1	9	5	0	36	39	0.50
9	**9**	**Nottinghamshire**	**15**	**111.00**	1	6	8	0	32	42	1.00

20 Two Out Of Four Ain't Bad

With the chance of a treble now gone, Surrey had to make sure that the sense of disappointment that they were so clearly feeling didn't lead to them slipping up in the NCL. After a fine season that had so far yielded twenty-six wins and just five defeats, two trophies would seem to represent a fair return... one trophy would most certainly not. No-one was under any illusions that the forthcoming game against Glamorgan Dragons at Cardiff would be anything other than a hard battle, however, so it was comforting to know that there was always the home game against the Leicestershire Foxes in which to secure the title-clinching win, if necessary. Everyone clearly wanted to sew things up as soon as possible, though, with a victory over the reigning NCL champions on their own patch being as good a way as any to seal the triumph.

Since the defeat at Canterbury there had been plenty of news to digest. On September 10th the England winter touring squads had been revealed, and there was good news for three Surrey players, with Mark Butcher, Graham Thorpe and Rikki Clarke all being selected to tour Bangladesh and Sri Lanka before Christmas. Additionally, Scott Newman had been awarded a place in the England Academy squad, after Keith Medlycott seemingly persuaded the selectors that Newman's very limited number of first-team opportunities shouldn't count against him.

More parochial news on September 12th concerned the resignation of Paul Brind, who had been Ground Manager at The Oval since succeeding his father, Harry, in 1994. Brind, who was twice voted Groundsman Of The Year, cited ill health as the principal reason for his departure, adding "I feel that now is the right time to take the opportunity of changing my career path and moving on to other things." Everyone certainly wished both him and his successor, Bill Gordon - who had been standing in for Brind for part of the season - all the best for the future.

Little did Surrey fans know that this was to be the first of many changes that would be announced in the weeks and months ahead, with two major revelations coming on the morning of the match at Cardiff - Alec Stewart had announced that he was retiring from first-class cricket, while Ian Ward would be leaving Surrey at the end of the season. Keith Medlycott was quoted as saying that financial restraints had forced the Club's hand. "We are part of a bigger industry, and that is the business itself, and we have to deal with what is put in front of us," he said. "We have to abide by certain rules and, as much as we've tried to bend those and eke out extra money, we weren't able to do that. It's an unfortunate scenario but players' worth in recent years has gone up in astronomical amounts but income has not followed suit." While Ward was set to move on to another county, despite rumours that he had been considering going full-time as a presenter with Sky Sports, it was suggested that Stewart might well be remaining with the Club in some capacity, with the former Surrey and England captain hinting at this himself in the last sentence of a statement he made to the Press, which read as follows:- "Playing for Surrey throughout my career has been a fantastic privilege. I have been lucky enough to play with some great players and particularly to be a part of the huge success the Club has achieved over the last eight years. I look forward to contributing to Surrey's continued success, both on and off the pitch, in years to come." The news of Ward's departure, which had come as something of an unexpected bombshell, was accompanied by the following statement - "Surrey and I have decided to part company. I am desperate to resurrect my England career. I feel a move away with new ideas and new drive is what I need. I will definitely be playing cricket elsewhere next year but nothing has been finalised yet."

These announcements were not ideally timed, coming just a matter of hours before the players took to the field in an attempt to secure the NCL title, and it was rather disappointing to hear that Ward would not be taking his place in the Lions' line-up for what was, after all, a very significant game. He would, instead, be spending his afternoon in the Sky commentary box. Whether that was Ward's decision or the Club's decision, it seemed to be at odds with the player's declaration that the split with Surrey was entirely amicable. The left-handed opener's final knock for the Club had, therefore, been his battling fifty-three in the annihilation at Canterbury, while Stewart's Surrey swansong had been - unbeknown to any of us at the time - the Championship victory at Edgbaston in July, during which he scored seventy-four and forty-five.

NATIONAL CRICKET LEAGUE DIVISION ONE - MATCH FIFTEEN

Glamorgan Dragons versus Surrey Lions at Cardiff

Sunday 14th September

Setting The Scene - Surrey go into this match on the back of five straight NCL wins, while the 2002 champions are on a poor run that has seen them lose seven of their last ten games in the competition. The Lions replace Ian Ward with Scott Newman, while Tim Murtagh comes in for the injured James Ormond, and the returning England pair, Graham Thorpe and Martin Bicknell, step into the shoes of Nadeem Shahid (omitted) and Azhar Mahmood (injured). The Dragons' line-up shows two changes from the side that had played at Whitgift School, with Ian Thomas and David Harrison replacing Matt Maynard and Andrew Davies, though they are still very close to being at a full strength. When Adam Hollioake wins the toss he elects to take first use of a pretty poor looking pitch that might deteriorate as the game progresses.

Surrey Lions' Innings

Surrey nearly lose a very early wicket in this potential title-decider when Scott Newman plays the second ball of the innings from Michael Kasprowicz down into the ground and it trickles back onto the stumps without dislodging a bail.

At the other end, by way of contrast, David Harrison most certainly doesn't threaten the timbers in the course of an opening over that yields five separate wides, as well as a cut to the rope at extra cover by Ali Brown that helps the Lions' score along to 11-0 after the first two overs.

When Newman then cracks two off-side boundaries off the Australian, and Brown takes two fours from the first four deliveries of Harrison's following over, it looks like the visitors are building up a good head of steam, but they are suddenly halted in their tracks when Brown misses an unattractive heave to leg and has his off stump pegged back by the young Glamorgan seamer's next ball.

Surrey's position is then further weakened by Kasprowicz, whose next three overs cost just one run and also bring the wicket of Newman, who is beaten by a ball swinging back into his pads and departs lbw for ten with the score at thirty-one.

From a position of 35-2 at the end of the ninth over, the Lions bite back briefly as Mark Ramprakash drives Harrison over cover for four and Graham Thorpe drills Kasprowicz to the rope at long-off, before the Queenslander lures the England left-hander into driving a catch to Jimmy Maher, who has only just moved from second slip to short extra cover.

The loss of Thorpe for nine with the total advanced to forty-nine, brings Rikki Clarke to the crease at a testing time, with Kasprowicz just finishing an excellent opening burst of 7-2-20-2 and the first-change seamers, Adrian Dale and Alex Wharf, hitting their straps right from the start.

Just seven runs have come from the first twenty-three balls sent down by the new bowlers, in fact, when Wharf penetrates a loose drive from Clarke with a good delivery that nips back a little to knock back the off stump and leave Surrey struggling at 61-4 after seventeen overs.

It is therefore fortunate for the Lions that their captain soon finds the extra-cover boundary with a fine stroke off the successful Glamorgan bowler, though it's already clear that it is going to remain difficult to score quickly on this pitch throughout the contest, with the spinners possibly most likely to hold the key. This would seem to be the way that Robert Croft is thinking anyway, since he removes Dale from the attack after three good overs for just eight runs and introduces Dean Cosker in his place at the river end to bowl the twentieth over, at which point the NCL champions-elect are 71-4.

Hollioake responds positively to this move by launching the left-arm spinner's fourth ball over mid-off for four, though the fact that batting remains a largely hazardous business is underlined in the next over from the unlucky Wharf when an inside edge to fine leg earns a boundary for Ramprakash, and an outside edge to fine third man adds four to the Surrey skipper's score.

Croft's immediate reaction is to join Cosker in an all-spin attack, thus taking the pace off the ball at both ends of the ground, and the tactic works well as the fifth-wicket pair are made to fight hard for every run. The score advances only by way of singles and an occasional two as the hundred finally clicks up from the first ball of the twenty-eighth over, and a 79-ball fifty partnership arrives exactly three overs later, at which point the scoreboard reads 111-4.

With the Dragons' spinners having not conceded a boundary during their ten overs in tandem, it seems clear that something has to give soon and that we are at a crossroads in the game. At this rate of scoring, the league leaders are unlikely to post a winning total, yet the loss of a couple of wickets at this juncture would be disastrous for them.

Step forward - almost literally - Adam Hollioake. Advancing down the track to the first ball of Cosker's seventh over, he drives the left-arm spinner straight down the ground for a towering six, and then sweeps the next delivery to fine leg for four, before adding another six and a further four to the total with lofted straight drives from the third and fourth balls of the over. A single to long-on from ball number five then completes a very impressive 49-ball half-century for Hollioake and leaves the Lions in a much more promising position at 135-4 with thirty-two overs completed. There is a definite feeling that, in the context of the game, we have just witnessed a very significant over, and, though the Surrey skipper is bowled by Croft in the next over when he plays back and is defeated by a faster delivery that shoots through rather low, he may have already made an important mark on the match.

With the battered Cosker now replaced by Dale, and Hollioake replaced by Jon Batty, the visitors' approach instantly reverts to one of steady accumulation, and it is entirely appropriate that Ramprakash should reach a highly valuable fifty with a drive to mid-off for a single from his ninety-first ball, having hit just two fours in the course of his knock.

He does become slightly more adventurous when lifting Croft away over wide mid-on for three in the next over, though an attempt at something similar on the off-side from the bowling of Dale shortly afterwards results in his dismissal to a very good low catch by Wharf at mid-off.

As Ramprakash makes his way back to the pavilion with fifty-three hard-earned runs to his name, the Lions' score is 159-6, with 7.2 overs left in the innings. Two-hundred would seem to be a fair score in the conditions, though Jon Batty and Ian Salisbury suggest that something better might be attainable as the Surrey keeper reverse-sweeps Croft for a boundary at the end of tight spell from the Glamorgan captain, and the leg-spinner thick-edges Dale to the rope at third man.

Unfortunately for the champions-elect, Batty then drives Dale straight to Maher at extra cover, and things quieten down again until Salisbury clips a legside full-toss from the medium-pacer to the backward square leg boundary a couple of overs later.

With the recalled Cosker contributing two tight overs from the Cathedral Road end, the Lions reach the final two overs with 189-7 on the board and two-hundred still looking an achievable target, though the picture rapidly changes as Dale strikes twice, having Salisbury well taken over his shoulder at deep mid-off by Maher following a miscued drive, and Franklyn Rose caught by Wharf at long-off from a toe-ended heave at a low full-toss.

Having secured just three singles from the last over of Dale's fine stint of 9-1-35-4, the last-wicket pair of Bicknell and Tim Murtagh are left to face a final-over salvo from Kasprowicz.

and manage to scrape together six further runs to take the league leaders up to a final score of 198-9. Will this be enough to secure victory and the 2003 NCL Division One title?

Glamorgan Dragons' Innings

After an opening maiden by Bicknell to Maher, overs two and three cost ten runs apiece as the Australian and his opening partner, Ian Thomas, notch three boundaries in what appears to be an attempt to put early runs on the board while the ball is still hard. The Dragons are obviously aware that a combination of this slow pitch and a soft ball could make run-scoring very difficult later in the match.

Following a rather erratic first over, Franklyn Rose comes up with a much better second over, from which just one run accrues, before the fifth over of the innings brings first pain, and then pleasure, to Surrey. It starts badly for the visitors when Maher's push for two runs backward of square leg is followed by a superb pick-up over midwicket for six, then it improves markedly as the Lions capture a wicket from each of the next two deliveries. Maher goes first, when he cuts half-heartedly and is taken at the wicket by Batty off the top edge, then Alex Wharf, promoted to number three in the hope that he might score some quick runs, proceeds to run himself out from the first delivery he faces. Pushing the ball out square on the off-side, he sets off for a single, despite Clarke making a decent stop, and is unable to beat the fielder's sensible throw to Batty when Thomas rightly sends him back.

At 29-2, Glamorgan are suddenly on the back foot, and the Surrey new-ball bowlers make life increasingly difficult for them over the course of the next three overs as just eight runs are added to the total, with seven of these coming to third man as the batsmen find loose deliveries very few and far between.

Thomas eventually manages to break the spell in style during the ninth over, when he advances on Bicknell and strikes a mighty drive over long-on for six, though Rose instantly negates this with a fine one-run over to Mike Powell, who has made a very slow start after coming in at number four. He has scored just five singles from eighteen balls, in fact, when he manages to pick up his first two with a glance off Bicknell, then his opening boundary comes from the following delivery when a miscued drive over cover takes the Dragons beyond the fifty mark.

It would probably be fair to say that honours are still fairly even at this stage, though the first ball of the next over sees the Lions stealing an advantage, thanks to a brilliant catch by Batty, diving full-length away to his right, as the left-handed Thomas glances Rose towards fine leg. This is a well-deserved wicket for the Jamaican, even though it has come from one of his least impressive deliveries.

With the Welsh county having just lost a third wicket, this seems to be a good time for Tim Murtagh to enter the attack, though he doesn't get away to the best of starts as Powell suddenly finds his touch and timing, taking boundaries from the young swing bowler's first two balls with a clip to midwicket and a forcing stroke backward of point. The 26-year-old middle-order batsman then confirms that he could pose a real threat to Surrey's chances by picking up another four with an on-drive off a Rose no-ball that brings the West Indian's spell to a close at 7-0-33-1.

The concession of seventeen runs from the last two overs is clearly not acceptable for the league leaders, since it has boosted Glamorgan's run-rate beyond five-an-over when they only require a rate of 4.42 to win. It's just as well, therefore, that Murtagh bounces back impressively with a maiden, and that Clarke immediately hits an ideal line and length as Rose's replacement at the Cathedral Road end, yielding just four runs from his first three overs.

Having pegged the reigning NCL champions back to 87-3 from twenty overs, it's disappointing for Surrey that Murtagh then sends down another loose over that includes a no-ball and ends up costing eleven runs, including four from a glorious straight drive by Powell.

Although Clarke immediately repairs some of the damage with a tight over in which he concedes just two singles, the second of which takes the Dragons' total into three figures, it's a surprise to see Hollioake entrusting Murtagh with another over, especially with Powell now looking so dangerous.

As is so often the case, though, the Lions' captain turns out to have made the right decision, as the young Surrey seamer finds some late inswing with the first ball of his over to defeat Powell's drive, knock back his off stump and send him on his way for forty. The visitors are clearly delighted to have captured this scalp, perhaps believing that, as at Whitgift, Powell is the key man.

This certainly looks to be the case as Glamorgan lose two further wickets in the next three overs to subside to 114-6 after twenty-six overs. The left-handed David Hemp becomes a second victim for Murtagh in the space of ten deliveries when a fine late outswinger takes the outside edge of a defensive bat and brings another brilliant diving catch out of Batty, then Clarke gets due reward for his excellent spell to date when Mark Wallace nicks a drive and becomes the Surrey keeper's fourth victim of the innings.

With Adrian Dale and Robert Croft now at the crease, the Dragons are most certainly still in the game as Hollioake replaces Murtagh at the river end, and, following another economical over, Clarke gives way to Rose at the Cathedral Road end with figures of 7-0-15-1 to his name.

Although Rose's final two overs cost fourteen runs, which is rather too expensive in the context of this game, Hollioake more than justifies his decision to bring himself into the attack at this stage, since he dismisses Dale in his third over when the batsman mistimes a clip to leg from a slower delivery and pops up a straightforward catch to Graham Thorpe at midwicket.

At 130-7, the NCL champions are looking increasingly likely to be handing over their crown to the opposition later today, though it's fair to say that neither Croft nor the new batsman, Michael Kasprowicz, will be giving up without a fight.

With Ian Salisbury being finally brought into the fray in place of Rose to bowl the thirty-fourth over on a pitch that should make him a difficult proposition, the home side have a fair bit to do, however, even after they have managed to take eight runs from the leg-spinner's opening over to move the score on to 150-7 with eleven overs remaining.

Although the required run-rate isn't excessive, the batsmen find themselves restricted to a diet of singles over the course of the next three overs and, though this is acceptable in the circumstances, Croft clearly feels the need to locate the boundary rope as he takes a swing at the final ball of Hollioake's sixth over… with fatal results. Having picked on one of the Lions' captain's slower deliveries and, consequently, skied the ball high towards deep wide mid-on, Croft can only wait and watch as Bicknell makes good ground from long-on to take a fine plunging catch and put his side within sight of the title. As a dejected Glamorgan skipper departs for twenty, the scoreboard is reading 161-8 after thirty-seven overs, leaving the champions-elect just two wickets from glory.

The ninth-wicket pair manage to keep the contest alive, however, as Kasprowicz's lofted on-drive for four off Hollioake ensures that a more-than-adequate eleven runs come from the next two overs.

At this stage, the Lions' leader elects to recall Murtagh at the Cathedral Road end, even though Salisbury has conceded a total of just seven runs from his second and third overs, and the young seamer again does well, yielding just three singles and thereby increasing the pressure on the batsmen. The game remains anyone's, however, while Kasprowicz and Harrison are together, and, sensing a close finish, Hollioake gives way to Clarke at the river end, in order that the captain will be able to bowl the final over himself, should the match go that far.

The penultimate over of Clarke's spell turns out to be another good one, costing just four runs and leaving the Dragons to score twenty from the last four overs, but Murtagh then slips in a full-toss to Harrison early in the next over, and the batsman takes full toll with an extra-cover drive to the boundary. This looks to have tilted the balance of the game in favour of the home side, but, fortunately for the league leaders, Murtagh keeps his cool to extract Kasprowicz's middle stump as the Queenslander attempts to heave the final ball of the 22-year-old seamer's stint away on the legside. Since only one wicket remains, Surrey should now be favourites to finish the job, though fifteen runs from three overs certainly isn't an unattainable goal for Harrison and his new partner, Dean Cosker.

This target is then reduced to ten runs from twelve balls, as four singles and a leg-bye accrue from Hollioake's next over, and the pressure passes over to Clarke, who is now to deliver the final over of a fine stint that has so far earned him figures of 8-0-19-1.

After failing to get the first ball away, Cosker takes a leg-bye from the second, putting the inexperienced Harrison on strike with nine needed from ten deliveries. With tension mounting around the ground, the 22-year-old is unable to score from the next ball, so he aims to drive the fourth delivery of the over down the ground, only to find that Clarke's yorker is right on the mark and rips out the middle stump to spark a joyous Surrey huddle and celebrations from Lions' fans around the ground. The players have secured the Sunday/National League title for only the second time since its inception in 1969, with the previous triumph having been achieved on this very ground almost seven years ago to the day, on 15th September 1996. The clinching of that trophy was the starting point for the current run of success, though on this occasion there is added satisfaction, since this triumph seals the first-ever major 'double' achieved by the Club.

As the players are presented with the trophy, and celebrate on the field - albeit in a very subdued style - the loss of the Championship can be forgotten, at least for a short while.

ADAM HOLLIOAKE'S VIEW FROM THE DRESSING ROOM

This looked to be a pretty ordinary pitch at Sophia Gardens. Correct?
AH - It wasn't great, but I guess you need to play on all types of pitches. The thing about the Championship and the NCL is that, to win them, you have to be the best side in all conditions. So, whether it's a good pitch or a bad pitch, you've got to adapt your game to suit it.

Was that a calculated assault on Dean Cosker that brought twenty-one runs from the 32nd over?
AH - Yes, I definitely targeted it. At the start of that over I had said to Ramps that I was going to really go after Cosker and try to hit twenty-four off the over, because I fancied that short straight boundary and I knew that, if it came off, it could change the course of the game.

There were bright and breezy efforts down the order from Ian Salisbury and Jon Batty. 'JB' seems to have made himself into a very handy one-day batsman - it never used to be his forte, did it?
AH - It's not just in the one-day game that he's come on - I think he's just become a more confident cricketer in general. When he first started training with me in Perth he was a 65kg guy, but he's now probably pushing 80kg, so he's a stronger guy now, which helps him to hit the ball harder. If he keeps improving at the rate he is at the moment then the sky's the limit for him.

I guess you must have been pleased with how Rikki Clarke bowled?
AH - Yes, he bowled fantastically. That's the sort of style we've been looking for from him. He now knows what is expected of him, and we need him to bowl like that week-in week-out. If he can manage that then we are a very strong side indeed.

He bowled a lot of slower balls - has he been taking lessons from you?!
AH - He's got a different type of slower ball to me, but I've been talking to him all year about using it more, and I still don't think he uses it enough. I'm trying to get him to become more unpredictable and more aggressive with his bowling, too.

You made an interesting decision to keep Tim Murtagh on after he had conceded eleven runs in an over, and he immediately got Mike Powell out. Was that an important turning point in the game?
AH - Definitely, a huge moment. Powell is another of those batsmen who likes the ball going away, and Tim was moving it back in to him, so I always fancied Tim to get him with one of those deliveries.

Just thinking about one-day cricket for the moment, 'Murts' looks like he will be a very handy bowler, because he seems equally adept at bowling at the start, in the middle, or at the end of an innings. Is that a reasonable assessment?
AH - Yes, he's a very good bowler. You will probably be surprised to hear me say this, but I think he's probably got the best temperament of anyone I've ever played cricket with. I've never seen anyone so calm under pressure, and so mentally strong to just come back and put the ball in the right place - it's a hard ask. He may not be the biggest, most in-your-face type of character but he's very tough mentally.

With the Championship gone, our celebrations looked very muted indeed. Fair comment?
AH - Definitely. I don't think there were many smiles in the changing room afterwards. It's hard to believe that, in 1996, Cardiff was where our run of trophies began, and the celebrations that ensued after that were immense. But these were subdued, to say the least, because I think, at the end of the day, we wanted three trophies so badly and we were found wanting in the end.

Any regrets later that we didn't celebrate as much as we might have done? It was still a major title, won over sixteen matches, after all.
AH - Not really. I think we appreciated winning it, and we respected the fact that we won it, but I think we also know that we probably let slip a fantastic opportunity to win three competitions, which doesn't come around very often - we just ran out of gas.

GLAMORGAN DRAGONS v SURREY LIONS at Cardiff							
Sunday 14th September				**Surrey Lions won by 8 runs**			
Surrey Lions won the toss and elected to bat				**Umpires:- Nigel Cowley & Barry Dudleston**			
SURREY LIONS							
Fall Of Wkt	Batsman	How	Out	Score	Balls	4s	6s
2-31	**S.A. Newman**	**lbw**	**b Kasprowicz**	**10**	19	2	0
1-27	**A.D. Brown**		**b Harrison**	**12**	11	3	0
6-159	**M.R. Ramprakash**	**c Wharf**	**b Dale**	**53**	93	2	0
3-49	**G.P. Thorpe**	**c Maher**	**b Kasprowicz**	**9**	19	1	0
4-61	**R. Clarke**		**b Wharf**	**4**	16	0	0
5-137	**A.J. Hollioake ***		**b Croft**	**51**	52	5	2
7-176	**J.N. Batty +**	**c Maher**	**b Dale**	**18**	21	1	0
8-189	**I.D.K. Salisbury**	**c Maher**	**b Dale**	**19**	18	2	0
	M.P. Bicknell	**Not**	**Out**	**12**	18	0	0
9-192	**F.A. Rose**	**c Wharf**	**b Dale**	**1**	2	0	0
	T.J. Murtagh	**Not**	**Out**	**0**	1	0	0
	Extras	**(1b, 1lb, 7w)**		**9**			
	TOTAL	**(45 overs)**	**(for 9 wkts)**	**198**			

Bowler	O	M	R	W	NB	Wd
Kasprowicz	**8**	**2**	**25**	**2**	-	-
Harrison	**6**	**0**	**33**	**1**	-	7
Dale	**9**	**0**	**35**	**4**	-	-
Wharf	**4**	**1**	**18**	**1**	-	-
Cosker	**9**	**0**	**49**	**0**	-	-
Croft	**9**	**0**	**36**	**1**	-	-

GLAMORGAN DRAGONS							
Fall Of Wkt	Batsman	How	Out	Score	Balls	4s	6s
1-29	**J.P. Maher**	**c Batty**	**b Bicknell**	**21**	17	2	1
3-51	**I.J. Thomas**	**c Batty**	**b Rose**	**18**	27	2	1
2-29	**A.G. Wharf**	**run**	**out**	**0**	1	0	0
4-100	**M.J. Powell**		**b Murtagh**	**40**	53	5	0
5-111	**D.L. Hemp**	**c Batty**	**b Murtagh**	**21**	44	2	0
7-130	**A. Dale**	**c Thorpe**	**b Hollioake**	**12**	25	0	0
6-114	**M.A. Wallace +**	**c Batty**	**b Clarke**	**1**	7	0	0
8-161	**R.D.B. Croft ***	**c Bicknell**	**b Hollioake**	**20**	32	1	0
9-184	**M.S. Kasprowicz**		**b Murtagh**	**20**	32	2	0
10-190	**D.S. Harrison**		**b Clarke**	**14**	21	1	0
	D.A. Cosker	**Not**	**Out**	**2**	5	0	0
	Extras	**(6lb, 11w, 4nb)**		**21**			
	TOTAL	**(43.4 overs)**		**190**			

Bowler	O	M	R	W	NB	Wd
Bicknell	**6**	**1**	**32**	**1**	-	-
Rose	**9**	**0**	**45**	**1**	1	2
Murtagh	**9**	**1**	**44**	**3**	1	2
Clarke	**8.4**	**0**	**19**	**2**	-	1
Hollioake	**8**	**0**	**29**	**2**	-	3
Salisbury	**3**	**0**	**15**	**0**	-	1

Other NCL Division One Result

While the Lions were securing the title, the Spitfires were doing their hopes of retaining first division status a power of good by annihilating their fellow strugglers, the Foxes, at Grace Road.

September 14
Leicester:- **Kent Spitfires (4pts) beat Leicestershire Foxes by 8 wickets.** Leics 98 (35.1ov; Ealham 4-19, Khan 4-26); Kent 101-2 (19.2ov).

NCL DIVISION ONE TABLE AT 14TH SEPTEMBER

Pos	Prv		P	Pts	W	T	L	A	NRR
1	1	**Surrey Lions**	**15**	**50**	12	0	2	1	7.86
2	2	**Gloucestershire Gladiators**	**15**	**42**	10	0	4	1	4.71
3	3	**Warwickshire Bears**	**15**	**32**	8	0	7	0	2.24
4	3	**Glamorgan Dragons**	**16**	**32**	8	0	8	0	-0.94
5	5	**Essex Eagles**	**15**	**30**	7	1	7	0	3.52
6	7	**Kent Spitfires**	**15**	**26**	6	1	8	0	1.08
7	6	**Leicestershire Foxes**	**15**	**24**	6	0	9	0	-8.74
8	8	**Yorkshire Phoenix**	**15**	**20**	5	0	10	0	-7.32
9	9	**Worcestershire Royals**	**15**	**16**	4	0	11	0	-0.70

21 Flat Champagne

With two trophies in the bag, it was fair to say that every other county bar the eventual winners of the County Championship - almost certainly Sussex - would swap their season for Surrey's. The campaign should, therefore, have been ending on a high, but the loss of the Championship crown seemed to have cast a huge shadow over the team's achievements, which was a great shame. Second place in the Championship was still a possibility if Essex could be beaten in the final game of the summer, though it would probably require Lancashire to slip up against Nottinghamshire, which seemed unlikely. There was, of course, nothing riding on the final NCL match as far as Surrey were concerned, though their opponents, the Leicestershire Foxes, needed a win to have any chance of retaining their first division status.

FRIZZELL COUNTY CHAMPIONSHIP DIVISION ONE - MATCH SIXTEEN

SURREY versus ESSEX
at The Oval

First Day - Wednesday 17th September
Surrey 318; Essex 112-1

The Teams And The Toss *- Surrey decide to field a very young and inexperienced side for the final match of the season, giving Championship debuts to James Benning, Ben Scott and Neil Saker, while Scott Newman - replacing the departing Ian Ward - and Phil Sampson make their first appearance of the season in the premier domestic competition. Franklyn Rose has been released after just three games for the county, Jon Batty plays as a specialist opening batsman and Ian Salisbury captains the side. Essex choose to give some of their very promising young batsmen - Alistair Cook (18), Mark Pettini (20) and Ravinder Bopara (18) - an outing, while Andy Flower skippers the visitors in the absence of Ronnie Irani. Surrey elect to bat first after winning the toss.*

The home side get away to a poor start when Scott Newman edges a scything drive at Graham Napier through to James Foster in the sixth over with the score on seventeen, but Nadeem Shahid then takes centre stage with some glorious strokeplay that sees him striking a dozen fours in racing through to a 45-ball fifty in the eighteenth over.

With Mohammad Akram and Andy Clarke having proved ineffective, Andy Flower has to turn to James Middlebrook for control, and the off-spinner does him proud, claiming wickets in successive overs shortly after the second-wicket partnership passes the hundred mark. Shahid's scintillating knock of sixty-seven ends in disappointing fashion when he reverse-sweeps at head height to backward point with the total at 120 in the twenty-third over, then Rikki Clarke shoulders arms to a delivery that spins back to hit his off stump.

Jon Batty completes a well-constructed half-century from his seventy-eighth ball shortly afterwards, but loses another partner in the penultimate over before lunch when Ali Brown skies Middlebrook to deep midwicket to become the former Yorkshire off-spinner's third victim and leave the debutant James Benning to face two balls before the break.

Lunch:- Surrey 170-4 (Batty 68, Benning 0*) from 34 overs*

After a manic morning, progress is more sedate after lunch, especially after the loss of Benning in the fortieth over with the score on 164. Having shaped up nicely in making eighteen, the 20-year-old is unfortunate to disturb the stumps with his back foot as he pushes Akram to midwicket.

While Ben Scott, the 22-year-old wicketkeeper, plays himself in, Batty does the bulk of the scoring until Napier lures him into a pull that results in a bottom-edge onto the stumps midway through the session. As the Surrey opener makes his way off the field with eighty-seven runs to his name and the score now 195-5, he is accompanied by Middlebrook, who appears to have sustained a groin injury.

Ironically, the off-spinner's replacement at the Vauxhall end, Ravinder Bopara, soon picks up the next wicket with his medium-pace seamers when Ian Salisbury's edge is brilliantly caught by Flower diving away to his right at second slip.

Tim Murtagh, the new batsman, and Scott then go on something of a run-spree, mainly at Bopara's expense, adding thirty-three in five overs before Middlebrook returns to the fray and, in partnership with Clarke and Akram, regains control in the last half-an-hour before tea.

Tea:- Surrey 294-7 (Scott 39, Murtagh 21*) from 72 overs*

Although he loses Murtagh - to a top-edged pull at Akram that results in a catch to mid-on - in the fourth over after the break, Scott goes on to complete a patient and impressive fifty from 116 balls before the Surrey innings comes to a fairly rapid end. Phil Sampson is soon trapped lbw by Middlebrook when he shuffles across his stumps and misses a push to leg, then Neil Saker is rapidly cleaned up by Napier with a ball that hits middle-and-off stumps, leaving the home side all out for 318. Having started the day so well, this represents a disappointing effort, though Scott can certainly hold his head up high as he leaves the field unbeaten on fifty-eight.

Although Sampson then strikes back for Surrey when he has Will Jefferson nicely picked up low down at first slip by Brown for a third-ball duck at the start of the Essex reply, Alistair Cook and Andy Flower quickly steady the ship before taking full toll of some indifferent bowling to bring up the visitors' fifty in the ninth over.

Cook, a tall left-hander, looks particularly impressive as he rushes through to a sensational 32-ball fifty, and, with Murtagh initially receiving the same sort of punishment that had earlier been handed out to Sampson and Clarke, Essex's total hits the hundred mark in just the fifteenth over.

Thankfully for Surrey, just eleven runs come from the last five overs of the day as Murtagh locates a better line and length, and Saker - who will be nineteen on the final day of the match - makes a fine start to his Championship career with three overs that cost just six runs.

At Hove, meanwhile, Sussex have moved within sight of the Championship crown by reducing Leicestershire from 111-1 to 179 all out - Mushtaq Ahmed taking his hundredth first-class wicket of the season in the process - and then progressing to 137-1 by the close.

Close:- Essex 112-1 (Cook 63, Flower 47*) from 20 overs*

Second Day - Thursday 18th September
Surrey 318; Essex 464

Although there's some decent bowling from Tim Murtagh and Neil Saker at the start of day two, no early breakthrough is forthcoming as Andy Flower completes a 72-ball half-century and Alistair Cook registers his highest score in first-class cricket.

We are in the twelfth over of the day, in fact, before Surrey finally strike, courtesy of Saker's maiden County Championship wicket - Cook caught behind for eighty-four after nicking a fine lifter delivered from round the wicket.

At 157-2, Essex are well placed, however, and their position improves rapidly as the new batsman, Mark Pettini, gets away to a flying start, notching five fours in his first six overs at the crease.

Ian Salisbury then enters the attack to put the brakes on for a while, before expensive spells from Rikki Clarke and Phil Sampson at the other end result in another Essex surge that sees Pettini through to an impressive fifty from 61 balls and Flower completing an excellent 144-ball century in the following over.

A tough session for Surrey at least ends on a brighter note when James Benning is brought into the attack and claims his first Championship wicket, that of Pettini, with his seventh delivery, thanks to a very good catch by Newman at third man from a top-edged cut.

Lunch:- Essex 272-3 (Flower 108) from 54.1 overs*

Despite the best efforts of Benning and Saker after lunch, Flower and Ravinder Bopara take Essex into the lead in the sixty-sixth over, and they have moved the score on to 343 before Salisbury returns to the attack and draws Bopara into a loose drive to Newman at mid-off.

With Murtagh meanwhile contributing a very good spell from the Vauxhall end, Surrey again enjoy a brief period of control, though nothing looks likely to shift Flower as he presses on remorselessly to his 150 from his 235th delivery.

Surrey desperately need further breakthroughs in the run-up to tea, but they are unable to manage any, even though Salisbury and an improved Sampson find the edge of the bat on a few occasions.

While the match situation becomes increasingly bleak for the County Champions of 1999, 2000 and 2002, champagne corks have been popping down on the south coast as Sussex have clinched their first-ever Championship title. The public address announcement informing the Oval crowd of Sussex's success is greeted with polite applause around the ground.

Tea:- Essex 407-4 (Flower 165, Foster 30*) from 93 overs*

Surrey take the new ball after the break and clean up the Essex innings with surprising haste. While Flower remains immovable, Clarke takes wickets in successive overs - James Foster lbw when hit on the back pad by a ball that nips back at him, and James Middlebrook gloving a hook through to Ben Scott - before Murtagh strikes twice in his twenty-fifth over. The scalps of Graham Napier, who shoulders arms and has his off stump knocked back, and John Stephenson, who gets a thin defensive edge to Scott three balls later, are well-deserved rewards for Murtagh, who has vied with Salisbury for the title of best Surrey bowler in the innings to date.

As Flower nears his double-century, the light starts to close in, and this possibly excuses Ali Brown for missing a reasonably easy slip catch off Rikki Clarke with the former Zimbabwe batsman nine runs short of the mark. The left-hander then loses Andy Clarke to a top-edged cut - well taken high to his left by Scott behind the wicket - off the same bowler shortly afterwards, leaving him with just Mohammad Akram for company and six runs still to find from somewhere. Luckily, however, the introduction of Sampson for Murtagh proves to be a godsend for the Essex captain, as two looseners from the new bowler are driven high over mid-on for four and then through extra cover for two, enabling him to complete a superb double-ton from 295 balls.

Sampson polishes off the Essex innings before his comeback over is complete, trapping Akram lbw for nought in light that is now poor enough to save Surrey from having to start their second innings tonight.

Close:- End of the Essex innings

Third Day - Friday 19th September

Surrey 318 and 194; Essex 464 and 49-2
Essex won by eight wickets
Essex 22pts, Surrey 6

Trailing Essex by 146 runs on first innings, Surrey's hopes of getting back into the match are destroyed within forty-five minutes by a stunning spell from Mohammad Akram.

After claiming the wickets of both Scott Newman - who is taken at short leg off bat and pad - and Nadeem Shahid - who dollies a catch to the same fielder after being beaten for pace when attempting a pull - in his second over to reduce the hosts to 0-2, he then picks up further scalps in his fifth and sixth overs to leave Surrey reeling on the ropes. Rikki Clarke becomes Akram's third victim when his off stump is knocked out by a superb yorker, then Ali Brown has his timbers rearranged by a rapid delivery that fizzes between his bat and pad as he drives. At this point, the former Pakistani international boasts the amazing figures of 5.3-5-0-4, since all of Surrey's twenty-four runs have come off Graham Napier at the other end.

Before Akram's sixth over is complete, James Benning has edged a drive to the third man boundary via the fingertips of third slip, though the young batsman soon settles down to stop the rot in company with Jon Batty, who has been helpless to do anything as his colleagues have made their exits at the other end.

Once the 29-year-old paceman has been seen off after a magnificent spell of 11-6-17-4, the rest of the Essex bowling presents few problems, and the fifth-wicket pair complete a valuable fifty partnership before taking the total into three figures during the penultimate over of the session.

Lunch:- Surrey 102-4 (Batty 38, Benning 39*) from 33 overs*

Andy Flower turns back to Akram straight after lunch and the Pakistani claims his fifth wicket in the fourth over of the session when Batty, having just upper-cut over third man for six, edges a drive through to Foster and departs for a well-played forty-seven.

Since Surrey still trail by twenty-four runs at this point, their position remains desperate... though they are soon to be put out of their misery. Within six overs the game is almost over as Akram claims another three wickets to send the home side spiralling towards a three-day defeat at 138-8. Benning falls three runs short of a debut fifty when he edges a drive to Foster in similar style to Batty before him; Ben Scott becomes the Essex keeper's third victim of the innings when he gets a thin top-edge to a hook at the final ball of Akram's fifteenth over; then Tim Murtagh has his off stump plucked out by the yorker with which the Pakistani starts his next over. Phil Sampson therefore comes out to face a hat-trick ball and is greeted by seven slips, a short leg and a leg slip, though the bowler's delivery ends up passing harmlessly down the legside.

As Akram strives for an 'all-ten', Salisbury and Sampson manage to take their side into the lead, before the eight-wicket man almost takes his tally to nine-out-of-nine in his twentieth over. Though visibly tiring, he first has Sampson edging to third man, and is then unable to hang on to a hard-hit caught-and-bowled chance, high to his right-hand side, offered by Salisbury

After one more over, the Essex hero is forced to admit defeat in his quest for 'the perfect ten' and, as Middlebrook is called up to take over from him at the Vauxhall end, the ever-sporting Oval crowd applaud his outstanding effort, and the bowler acknowledges them by raising his arms aloft.

Although the Surrey ninth-wicket pair go on to complete a fifty partnership shortly afterwards, following a run of three fours in as many overs by Sampson, the end then comes rapidly when Napier claims Salisbury lbw for twenty-nine before knocking Neil Saker's stumps awry for the second time in the match. With Surrey all out for 194, leaving Essex to score just forty-nine to win, Mohammad Akram rightly leads his team from the field having returned fine figures of 21-9-49-8.

Tea:- End of the Surrey innings

It takes Essex fewer than ten overs to knock off the required runs after tea, though Sampson does have the small consolation of picking up the wickets of Will Jefferson - brilliantly caught down the legside by Scott from a genuine leg-glance - and Alistair Cook - very well taken again by the Surrey keeper, this time from an edged drive - before Surrey succumb to the inevitable defeat. Having lost three successive Championship games for the first time since 1995, the champions of 2002 have certainly ended their 2003 season on a very low note.

Surrey 318 and 194; Essex 464 and 49-2
Essex won by eight wickets. Essex 22pts, Surrey 6

SURREY v ESSEX at The Oval — 17th to 19th September

Surrey won the toss and elected to bat — Umpires:- Alan Whitehead and Peter Willey

SURREY - First Innings

Fall Of Wkt	Batsman	How	Out	Score	Balls	4s	6s
1-17	**S.A. Newman**	**c Foster**	**b Napier**	**9**	20	2	0
6-222	**J.N. Batty +**		**b Napier**	**87**	142	14	1
2-120	**N. Shahid**	**c Pettini**	**b Middlebrook**	**67**	54	14	0
3-130	**R. Clarke**		**b Middlebrook**	**4**	9	1	0
4-164	**A.D. Brown**	**c Bopara**	**b Middlebrook**	**17**	23	0	0
5-195	**J.G.E. Benning**	**hit wicket**	**b Akram**	**18**	30	3	0
	B.J.M. Scott +	**Not**	**Out**	**58**	129	8	0
7-241	**I.D.K. Salisbury ***	**c Flower**	**b Bopara**	**14**	14	2	0
8-300	**T.J. Murtagh**	**c Napier**	**b Akram**	**21**	52	5	0
9-313	**P.J. Sampson**	**lbw**	**b Middlebrook**	**3**	14	0	0
10-318	**N.C. Saker**		**b Napier**	**1**	6	0	0
	Extras	**(7lb, 4w, 8nb)**		**19**			
	TOTAL	**(81.3 overs)**		**318**			

Bowler	O	M	R	W	NB	Wd
Mohammad Akram	**21**	**5**	**93**	**2**	1	-
Napier	**18.3**	**4**	**58**	**3**	-	-
Clarke	**7**	**2**	**32**	**0**	1	-
Middlebrook	**28**	**3**	**93**	**4**	1	-
Stephenson	**2**	**0**	**12**	**0**	-	-
Bopara	**5**	**0**	**23**	**1**	1	4

ESSEX - First Innings

Fall Of Wkt	Batsman	How	Out	Score	Balls	4s	6s
1-0	**W.I. Jefferson**	**c Brown**	**b Sampson**	**0**	3	0	0
2-157	**A.N. Cook**	**c Scott**	**b Saker**	**84**	87	11	0
	A. Flower *	**Not**	**Out**	**201**	297	20	0
3-272	**M.L. Pettini**	**c Newman**	**b Benning**	**70**	79	13	0
4-343	**R.S. Bopara**	**c Newman**	**b Salisbury**	**31**	63	4	0
5-429	**J.S. Foster +**	**lbw**	**b Clarke**	**36**	86	3	0
6-433	**J.D. Middlebrook**	**c Scott**	**b Clarke**	**3**	11	0	0
7-440	**G.R. Napier**		**b Murtagh**	**1**	3	0	0
8-442	**J.P. Stephenson**	**c Scott**	**b Murtagh**	**1**	2	0	0
9-457	**A.J. Clarke**	**c Scott**	**b Clarke**	**8**	17	2	0
10-464	**Mohammad Akram**	**lbw**	**b Sampson**	**0**	4	0	0
	Extras	**(1b, 5lb, 1w, 22nb)**		**29**			
	TOTAL	**(106.5 overs)**		**464**			

Bowler	O	M	R	W	NB	Wd
Sampson	**14.5**	**1**	**85**	**2**	1	-
Clarke	**20**	**1**	**104**	**3**	2	-
Murtagh	**27**	**4**	**89**	**2**	-	-
Saker	**16**	**1**	**71**	**1**	2	1
Salisbury	**21**	**1**	**70**	**1**	-	-
Benning	**8**	**1**	**39**	**1**	6	-

SURREY - Second Innings (Trailing by 146 runs on first innings)

Fall Of Wkt	Batsman	How	Out	Score	Balls	4s	6s
1-0	**S.A. Newman**	**c Cook**	**b Akram**	**0**	8	0	0
5-122	**J.N. Batty +**	**c Foster**	**b Akram**	**47**	102	7	1
2-0	**N. Shahid**	**c Cook**	**b Akram**	**0**	4	0	0
3-24	**R. Clarke**		**b Akram**	**18**	16	4	0
4-26	**A.D. Brown**		**b Akram**	**0**	12	0	0
6-125	**J.G.E. Benning**	**c Foster**	**b Akram**	**47**	90	8	0
7-134	**B.J.M. Scott +**	**c Foster**	**b Akram**	**5**	14	1	0
9-194	**I.D.K. Salisbury ***	**lbw**	**b Napier**	**29**	51	3	0
8-138	**T.J. Murtagh**		**b Akram**	**0**	1	0	0
	P.J. Sampson	**Not**	**Out**	**32**	49	6	0
10-194	**N.C. Saker**		**b Napier**	**0**	2	0	0
	Extras	**(7lb, 1w, 8nb)**		**16**			
	TOTAL	**(57.3 overs)**		**194**			

Bowler	O	M	R	W	NB	Wd
Mohammad Akram	**21**	**9**	**49**	**8**	3	-
Napier	**12.3**	**1**	**54**	**2**	-	-
Clarke	**7**	**1**	**19**	**0**	-	1
Stephenson	**12**	**2**	**39**	**0**	1	-
Middlebrook	**5**	**0**	**26**	**0**	-	-

ESSEX - Second Innings (Needing 49 to win)

Fall Of Wkt	Batsman	How	Out	Score	Balls	4s	6s
1-36	**W.I. Jefferson**	**c Scott**	**b Sampson**	**22**	17	5	0
2-47	**A.N. Cook**	**c Scott**	**b Sampson**	**18**	26	1	0
	M.L. Pettini	**Not**	**Out**	**4**	8	1	0
	R.S. Bopara	**Not**	**Out**	**2**	5	0	0
	Extras	**(1lb, 2nb)**		**3**			
	TOTAL	**(9.1 overs)**	**(for 2 wkts)**	**49**			

Bowler	O	M	R	W	NB	Wd
Sampson	**5**	**0**	**16**	**2**	-	-
Saker	**4.1**	**0**	**32**	**0**	1	-

Other Frizzell Championship Division One Results

Having won four more matches than any other team, Sussex were worthy winners of the 2003 County Championship title. Surrey's poor display against Essex meant that Lancashire were able to finish second, despite producing an equally dismal performance in their game with Nottinghamshire.

September 17-19

***Canterbury:-* Kent (22pts) beat Warwickshire (3) by an innings and 70 runs.** Kent 594 (Smith 213, Walker 121, Symonds 88, Key 54, Fulton 51, Trott 7-39); Warwicks 267 (Powell 61, Bell 54, Trott 53, Ealham 6-35) & 257 (Powell 110).

***Hove:-* Sussex (22pts) beat Leicestershire (1) by an innings and 55 runs.** Leics 179 (Maddy 55, Mushtaq 4-71) & 380 (Sadler 145, Masters 119, Lewry 8-106); Sussex 614-4dec (Goodwin 335*, Adams 102, Ambrose 82, Cottey 56).

September 17-20

***Trent Bridge:-* Nottinghamshire (21pts) beat Lancashire (4) by 233 runs.** Notts 376-9dec (Gallian 83, Bicknell 75, Warren 75, Pietersen 52) & 319-8dec (Franks 100*, Patel 55, Bicknell 53, Chapple 6-98); Lancs 219 (Law 51, Smith 5-61) & 243 (Sutcliffe 65, Hogg 53, Franks 4-62, MacGill 4-67).

FINAL FRIZZELL CHAMPIONSHIP DIVISION ONE TABLE 2003

Pos	Prv		P	Points	W	D	L	T	Bat	Bwl	Ded
1	1	**Sussex**	**16**	**257.00**	10	2	4	0	62	47	0.00
2	2	**Lancashire**	**16**	**223.00**	6	8	2	0	64	43	0.00
3	3	**Surrey**	**16**	**219.00**	6	7	3	0	63	44	0.00
4	4	**Kent**	**16**	**198.00**	6	5	5	0	47	47	0.00
5	6	**Warwickshire**	**16**	**171.50**	4	6	5	1	50	37	2.50
6	5	**Middlesex**	**16**	**169.00**	3	10	3	0	46	41	0.00
7	7	**Essex**	**16**	**156.00**	3	7	5	1	34	45	0.00
8	9	**Nottinghamshire**	**16**	**132.00**	2	6	8	0	36	45	1.00
9	8	**Leicestershire**	**16**	**125.50**	1	9	6	0	36	40	0.50

NATIONAL CRICKET LEAGUE DIVISION ONE - MATCH SIXTEEN

Surrey Lions versus Leicestershire Foxes at The Oval

Sunday 21st September

Setting The Scene - Surrey field a stronger side for this game than they had for the Championship match against Essex, as Hollioake and Thorpe take over from Scott and Saker. Leicestershire, on the other hand, have their strongest available eleven playing, since they need to win this game - and hope that Kent lose to Warwickshire - if they are to avoid the ignominy of being relegated in both the Championship and the NCL. When Hollioake wins the toss he decides to put the Foxes in to bat.

Leicestershire Foxes' Innings

After Sampson has Maunders caught at mid-off from the second ball of the match, it's pretty much a downhill slide all the way for Surrey for the rest of the afternoon.

Although Murtagh produces a pretty decent opening burst of seven overs, Sampson and Clarke are battered around the park during stands of 79 from 64 balls by Maddy and Hodge, and 83 from 58 balls by Maddy and Sadler, that see the score soaring to 162-2 in the twenty-first over.

Fortunately for the Lions, Benning strikes twice in that very over - the first of his spell - by having both Maddy and Nixon well caught by Batty standing up to the stumps, and the NCL champions then fight their way back into contention over the course of the next ten overs. Salisbury recovers extremely well after having twenty-one runs taken from his first two overs, while Benning adds the scalps of Sadler and DeFreitas to his collection as the Foxes slip to 200-6 after thirty-two overs.

Once these two have finished their fine spells, the visitors start to kick on again, however, with Drakes leading the way and heaping more misery on the suffering Sampson and Clarke. As a result, sixty-nine runs come from the final ten overs to take Leicestershire through to 283-9, which represents their highest total against Surrey in Sunday/National League cricket.

Surrey Lions' Innings

The Lions' openers, Newman and Brown, take twenty-two from the first four overs sent down by DeFreitas and Drakes, before the Foxes' skipper removes Newman and Shahid in the space of four balls during his third over to put the skids under the home side's reply.

To add to Surrey's woes, Thorpe is then struck down by a back spasm and has to retire hurt at the end of the ninth over, and the game is all but decided inside the next four overs when Brown edges Drakes to Nixon with the total at fifty-two and Clarke falls lbw to DeFreitas to make it 69-4.

Having played impressively in scoring twenty-five from just fifteen balls, Benning is then brilliantly caught left-handed by the diving Maddy at cover off DeFreitas, and last rites are soon being read when Hollioake edges his opposite number to slip in the seventeenth over to complete an excellent five-wicket haul for the sly old Fox.

With the game way beyond recall and the Lions' lads seemingly desperate for the season to end, the tail then folds rapidly to Dagnall, who claims three wickets in nine balls to complete the demolition of the NCL champions for 115 after just twenty-two overs of pretty miserable batting.

Surrey's spoils of the season - the Twenty-20 Cup and the NCL trophy - are re-presented on the outfield at the end of the match, but the 'celebrations' that follow are surprisingly low-key and lacking in enthusiasm for a side that has won two trophies.

SURREY LIONS v LEICESTERSHIRE FOXES at The Oval							
Sunday 21st September — Leicestershire Foxes won by 168 runs							
Surrey Lions won the toss and elected to field			**Umpires:- Alan Whitehead & Peter Willey**				
LEICESTERSHIRE FOXES							
Fall Of Wkt	Batsman	How	Out	Score	Balls	4s	6s
1-0	**J.K. Maunders**	**c Salisbury**	**b Sampson**	**0**	2	0	0
3-162	**D.L. Maddy**	**c Batty**	**b Benning**	**69**	62	12	0
2-79	**B.J. Hodge**	**c Shahid**	**b Clarke**	**43**	36	9	0
5-167	**J.L. Sadler**	**c &**	**b Benning**	**35**	27	4	0
4-166	**P.A. Nixon +**	**c Batty**	**b Benning**	**0**	2	0	0
7-230	**J.N. Snape**	**c Clarke**	**b Sampson**	**27**	54	3	0
6-186	**P.A.J. DeFreitas ***	**c Batty**	**b Benning**	**11**	16	1	0
	V.C. Drakes	**Not**	**Out**	**43**	47	3	1
8-263	**D.D. Masters**		**b Clarke**	**14**	13	2	0
9-276	**C.E. Dagnall**	**c Batty**	**b Sampson**	**9**	11	0	0
	D.S. Brignull	**Not**	**Out**	**4**	2	0	0
	Extras	**(4b, 4lb, 15w, 5nb)**		**28**			
	TOTAL	**(45 overs)**	**(for 9 wkts)**	**283**			

Bowler	O	M	R	W	NB	Wd
Sampson	**9**	**0**	**68**	**3**	-	3
Murtagh	**7**	**1**	**34**	**0**	-	-
Clarke	**7**	**0**	**64**	**2**	-	5
Salisbury	**9**	**0**	**37**	**0**	-	1
Hollioake	**2**	**0**	**16**	**0**	-	-
Benning	**9**	**1**	**43**	**4**	2	1
Shahid	**2**	**0**	**13**	**0**	-	-

SURREY LIONS							
Fall Of Wkt	Batsman	How	Out	Score	Balls	4s	6s
1-22	**S.A. Newman**	**c Nixon**	**b DeFreitas**	**8**	16	1	0
3-52	**A.D. Brown**	**c Nixon**	**b Drakes**	**27**	28	4	0
2-22	**N. Shahid**	**lbw**	**b DeFreitas**	**0**	3	0	0
	G.P. Thorpe	**retired**	**hurt**	**8**	14	1	0
4-69	**R. Clarke**	**lbw**	**b DeFreitas**	**8**	10	1	0
5-84	**J.G.E. Benning**	**c Maddy**	**b DeFreitas**	**25**	15	5	0
6-98	**A.J. Hollioake ***	**c Hodge**	**b DeFreitas**	**14**	13	3	0
	J.N. Batty +	**Not**	**Out**	**12**	17	2	0
7-107	**I.D.K. Salisbury**	**c Nixon**	**b Dagnall**	**3**	9	0	0
8-115	**T.J. Murtagh**	**c Maddy**	**b Dagnall**	**2**	6	0	0
9-115	**P.J. Sampson**		**b Dagnall**	**0**	2	0	0
	Extras	**(1lb, 5w, 2nb)**		**8**			
	TOTAL	**(22 overs)**		**115**			

Bowler	O	M	R	W	NB	Wd
DeFreitas	**9**	**1**	**40**	**5**	-	5
Drakes	**7**	**0**	**44**	**1**	1	-
Dagnall	**4**	**1**	**21**	**3**	-	-
Masters	**2**	**0**	**9**	**0**	-	-

Other NCL Division One Results

The Foxes' crushing win at The Oval was all in vain, since the Spitfires recorded an easy win over the Bears at Canterbury to maintain their place in the top flight of the NCL.

September 21

***Canterbury:-* Kent Spitfires (4pts) beat Warwickshire Bears by 104 runs.** Kent 267-7 (45ov; Smith 74); Warwicks 163 (37.2ov).

***Worcester:-* Essex Eagles (4pts) beat Worcestershire Royals by 4 wickets.** Worcs 213 (42.4ov; Kabir Ali 92); Essex 217-6 (42ov; Jefferson 74).

***Headingley:-* Gloucestershire Gladiators (4pts) beat Yorkshire Phoenix by 3 wickets.** Yorks 213-7 (45ov; Sayers 62, Ball 5-33); Gloucs 214-7 (44.1ov; Windows 91*, Thornicroft 5-42).

FINAL NCL DIVISION ONE TABLE 2003

Pos	Prv		P	Pts	W	T	L	A	NRR
1	**1**	**Surrey Lions**	**16**	**50**	12	0	3	1	2.99
2	**2**	**Gloucestershire Gladiators**	**16**	**46**	11	0	4	1	4.48
3	**5**	**Essex Eagles**	**16**	**34**	8	1	7	0	3.80
4	**3**	**Warwickshire Bears**	**16**	**32**	8	0	8	0	-0.57
5	**4**	**Glamorgan Dragons**	**16**	**32**	8	0	8	0	-0.94
6	**6**	**Kent Spitfires**	**16**	**30**	7	1	8	0	3.52
7	**7**	**Leicestershire Foxes**	**16**	**28**	7	0	9	0	-3.83
8	**8**	**Yorkshire Phoenix**	**16**	**20**	5	0	11	0	-6.96
9	**9**	**Worcestershire Royals**	**16**	**16**	4	0	12	0	-1.16

22 The Hurricane Of Change

In years to come, I suspect that players and supporters of Surrey County Cricket Club will look back on the 2003 season with pride and affection, since it saw the Club achieving its first-ever major trophy 'double' by emerging as champions in both the Twenty-20 Cup and the National Cricket League. Yet if someone who knew nothing about how Surrey had fared during the summer had attended the last two home games of the campaign they would never have guessed that the season had been so successful. Twenty-seven matches had been won and only seven lost, making it one of the best county campaigns ever recorded, yet there seemed to be a huge shadow of gloom hanging over The Oval, brought about by the late-season collapse in the County Championship. While it is quite right that the Championship is the competition that every player wants to win - and the one that matters most to the vast majority of members at every county club around the country - the reaction throughout the Club to the loss of the title was, I felt, a little extreme. Just the relatively small matter of eight years ago, everyone at The Oval would have been turning cartwheels at the thought of winning two trophies in the same season, after all! It was entirely laudable that the Club - and its supporters - set, and expected, high standards, but I couldn't help but feel that perhaps we had all become a little bit spoiled by recent successes.

As far as the players were concerned, maybe there was more to their rather downcast mood than met the eye. Clearly the loss of Ian Ward - if it were really only about budgets - wouldn't have been good for dressing room morale. Ward had been unfortunate that his contract was the one that was up for renewal at this budget-cutting moment in time - but whose turn might it be next year? It must have been a sobering and unsettling thought for anyone nearing the end of their current deal.

Without wishing to speculate too much - as I mentioned in my introduction, that is not the purpose of this book - Ward's failure to play at Cardiff, followed by a rather outspoken interview that appeared in *The Times*, suggested that the parting of the ways was not as amicable as it had been made out to be. In the article, Ward suggested that all was not well in the dressing room, which, if it were true, would certainly explain the demeanour of the players at the end of the season.

Whatever the reasons for his departure, it was a great shame to see Wardy leaving the Club, since he had been a key batsman in the Championship-winning years and gave stability to the top of a batting order packed with strokeplayers. He would certainly be remembered for any number of fine innings, but especially the epic effort of concentration that had enabled Surrey to pull off that famous against-all-odds victory at Canterbury in 2002. Although his departure would give Scott Newman a chance to impress in 2004, the Club had seemingly lost an important player, and it was no surprise that he was soon being chased by a number of counties. Given his television commitments, it was never likely that he was going to be moving too far, which is probably why a move to the new County Champions, Sussex, was completed with stunning haste and announced on 30th September. Having signed a four-year deal, Ward had stated, "The package suited my needs and my family's needs. They are a young vibrant side and they have just won the County Championship and they are going places. I felt I got a little bit stale at Surrey and I needed a new challenge. I chose Sussex for the vibrancy and for the way they are run and led." It looked to be a good move for both the player and his new county.

Apart from losing a fine batsman, Surrey had also lost a possible future captain, since Ward had appeared to be a leading candidate, if not **the** leading candidate, to succeed Adam Hollioake as skipper. This was to become increasingly relevant within a few days of Ward signing for Sussex, as Hollioake dominated the cricket news for several reasons over a period of about a week.

First, on the eve of "Adam's Journey", the 2,000-mile trek - by foot, bicycle and boat - that Adam and a few friends were undertaking in aid of The Ben Hollioake Fund, came the surprise announcement that the Surrey captain would be retiring from first-class cricket at the end of the 2004 season. In the Press Release that was issued, Adam said, "After much soul searching I have decided that 2004 will be my final year. I have many things that I want to do with my family, charity work with the Ben Hollioake Fund and my business interests in Perth. I will continue to give everything I can to the Club in the next 12 months, and in the years to come." It was revealed at the same time that Adam's final year would also be his Benefit year. The announcement of his retirement came as something of a surprise, though I wasn't the only Surrey fan who had always felt that Adam was unlikely to play on beyond the age of thirty-five. As it was, he was now going to be quitting at thirty-three. If the timing of the announcement was planned to fit in with the start of "Adam's Journey" then it was a great idea and extremely clever, since it gained maximum publicity for the guys who were going to be slogging their guts out walking, sailing, cycling and rowing all the way from Edinburgh to Tangiers. No-one would question that Adam, his father John, Matt Church, Iain Sutcliffe and Scott Welch deserved all the publicity they could get for their efforts in aid of such a great cause.

A few days into the walk, Adam was back in the news again, with another Press Release informing everyone that Jon Batty was to take over as Club captain for the 2004 season. Surrey's chief executive, Paul Sheldon said, "Following Adam Hollioake's decision to retire at the end of 2004, both he and the Club decided that it was in the best interests of the team for the captaincy to be handed over at the beginning of next year. The club is deeply fortunate to have a man of Jonathan's calibre and integrity to take on this demanding job, which he has described to me as 'one of the biggest jobs in world cricket'. We all wish him the very best of luck." Keith Medlycott had then added his own comments, stating "JB has been an integral member of the team since he joined in 1997. He has worked tirelessly on his game and has now developed into a top-class keeper and opening batsman. He is a very popular member of the squad and will no doubt draw on the experience of both Adam and the senior players in the team to ensure that we can continue to build on our recent success."

I caught up with Adam when I took part in the Watford-to-Kennington leg of "Adam's Journey" and asked him a couple of questions about his retirement and the handing over of the captaincy.

TALKING POINTS - ADAM HOLLIOAKE

Had you been considering the decision to retire for a while, or was it something you had only thought about recently?

AH - It was something I've been considering for a few years. With each passing year I knew the time was getting closer … but now I've reached the point where my family live in Australia; my wife's family live in Australia; my daughter's growing up, and my wife's trying to bring her up while I'm away every other week with no-one to help her out; and then there's the fact that I've pretty much achieved all I can achieve in county cricket, and I don't think I'll play for England again. So there were a lot of things pointing towards me retiring, and I never wanted to be someone who hung around just for the money or anything like that - I always wanted to come in, make my mark and then move on. And I've got other things I want to achieve in life as well, with The Ben Hollioake Fund being one of those things. I'm just looking forward to new challenges outside of cricket. It would have been easy for me to stay in the game and become a coach, or play until I was forty or maybe commentate or something like that. But that would be a bit too 'safe' for me.... I've never really gone for the safe option, I've always liked to take risks and go out on a limb. I really need to do those things to make life exciting for myself, otherwise I get bored and do stupid things!

What was the idea behind announcing your retirement a year in advance?
AH - I hadn't intended to announce my retirement - I wanted to leave that until the end of next year - though, obviously, I had to tell the Club in advance because they need to plan things like finding a replacement captain or a replacement all-rounder. I wanted to be as transparent as I could be with the Club, but they didn't want it to look like we were in disarray and that I'd packed up the captaincy as a result, so they wanted to announce that I was retiring and keep the public in the know, which is good. And also, of course, it gives the new captain the opportunity to take advantage of the experience I've gained over what has, in effect, been nine years as captain - so hopefully there's some useful experience there that he can draw on. 'JB' might just want me to sit in the corner and shut up, and if that's the case then I'm happy to do that as well. I just want to do whatever's best for the Club.

I then spoke to Jon Batty about stepping into Adam's shoes - a tough task if ever there was one, though he seemed to be relishing the prospect.

TALKING POINTS - JON BATTY

Have you had much experience of captaincy in your cricketing career?
JB - Captaincy is something I've always loved and, in terms of what I've done before, I've captained the second eleven, I captained Oxfordshire Under-25s, as well as some club youth teams - so I've had a bit of experience and I've always enjoyed it and had aspirations to captain Surrey. I'm very excited about leading the side.

Are you happy about taking on the role of captain, in addition to opening the batting and keeping wicket?
JB - The levels of mental and physical fitness I've achieved in recent times are going to give me a great chance of achieving it, but it's something that's going to have to be assessed with time. Just like my style of captaincy will come through and develop over a period of time, so will the way I fit in, and cope with, all three roles. I'm certainly happy with it.

What do you think you can bring to the job and what do you think your strengths will be?
JB - Well, I'm obviously a very different character to Adam - I'm probably slightly quieter, in fact probably at the opposite end of the scale from Adam! I'm very thoughtful and, tactically, I'm very aware. I want to be out there and I want to lead from the front - I want to stand up and be counted when the chips are down. But it's largely about trying to get the best out of all of our players. I think it's been said before that we have so much experience in our ranks that the side virtually captains itself, and I'm sure that when we are playing well the captaincy role won't be a problem.

Adam's always been considered something of a 'gambler', always taking the aggressive option... do you see yourself being like that?
JB - I think we've all learned a lot from Adam, in terms of "if in doubt, take the positive approach, the aggressive approach" and to take the forward step, rather than the defensive option. That has always worked well for us and I think we will continue to do that because that's the way we've developed as a side and how we've learned to play over the last seven or eight years.

And the news kept coming, as Rikki Clarke made his Test match debut for England against Bangladesh in the first Test in Dhaka, scoring fourteen, and taking a wicket and a catch, as England won by seven wickets. Coincidentally, the former Surrey off-spinner, Gareth Batty, won his first Test cap in the same match. Although it hadn't been the most sparkling debut appearance, Clarke went on to produce results in the second Test that fully justified his selection, scoring fifty-five and twenty-seven, as well as taking 2-7 and 1-4 with the ball.

Meanwhile, back at home, the ECB Groundsman Of The Year award went to new Surrey groundsman, Bill Gordon, as the pitches at The Oval were voted to be the best in both the four-day and one-day pitch categories. This was the second successive year that The Oval had come out on top, though the award had been shared with Kent in 2002. Alan Fordham, the ECB's Cricket Operations Manager said, "As well as a thrilling and memorable npower Test match against South Africa, The Oval played host to many entertaining one-day and four-day matches in 2003 thanks, in part, to superb pitches." No-one would argue with that assessment.

Further player news came when Neil Saker signed a two-year contract with the Club, following in the footsteps of Graham Thorpe who had also signed a new deal of that duration before heading out to Bangladesh with England.

Another new signing was Alec Stewart, who was appointed as the Club's Director Of New Business on 14th November. In the Press Release announcing this move, Alec stated, "I am delighted to be able to continue my long association with Surrey County Cricket Club. I hope that I can help raise the profile of the Club and support its excellent work in the local community. I am very much looking forward to this new exciting challenge." Paul Sheldon described the former Club captain's new role, saying, "We have asked Alec to help us in a number of different areas - all of which will use his great skills and reputation to attract new supporters to The Oval. He will be concentrating particularly on the immense opportunities brought about by our redevelopment project."

It would certainly be a major change for the man who had dedicated himself to Surrey and England cricket for some twenty-three years. Although he had not been able to play as often for the county side in recent years, there was never any doubt that you were always getting 100% from Alec - something that probably couldn't be said of every England player when going back to play for their county club. The immaculately turned-out 'Stewie' would certainly be missed by both England and Surrey, and there was no doubt that he would have been capable of playing on for another few years had he chosen to. His batting and keeping for Surrey in the Championship had been excellent and it was just a pity that the regular supporters of the County Club hadn't been able to give him the same kind of send-off that he had received from the crowd at the Oval Test. If the Surrey and Warwickshire fans at Edgbaston in July had been aware that they were witnessing Stewart's last county appearance then I'm sure they would have offered up a special round of applause.

Alec had, of course, done any number of interviews leading up to, and after, his final England appearance, but the focus was always, naturally enough, on his international career. I decided, therefore, that I would speak to him about his Surrey memories.

TALKING POINTS - ALEC STEWART

What would be the favourite moments of your Surrey career?

AS - I think winning the Sunday League down at Cardiff in 1996 would be the main one, because it was the first trophy of note that I'd won at Surrey. And the Benson & Hedges Cup win against Kent in 1997 would rank highly - I very much enjoyed the big partnership with Ben Hollioake in that game. Although I still felt very much a Surrey player, I didn't get to play in that many games in any of the Championship triumphs, so I think it would have to be those two that I would pick.

Which matches stand out for you?
AS - Clinching the Championship against Nottinghamshire at The Oval in 1999 would be the main one, along with that Benson & Hedges Cup final in 1997. For me, the best and most memorable games are the ones that produce meaningful wins - ones that secure a title or a trophy, for example.

What would you consider to be your best innings in the Championship?
AS - I only scored two double-centuries but they both stand out for me. The 271 not out against Yorkshire (Oval, 1997) would definitely be my best innings, but the first of my doubles, 206* against Essex (Oval, 1989), was special and important because I'd just been through a poor patch.

And in one-day cricket?
AS - I remember scoring 160 against Hampshire at The Oval in the Benson & Hedges Cup (1996), and I got another big hundred (167*) against Somerset in 1994, straight after the West Indies tour, when I whacked Caddy about a bit. Then, in more recent times, there was a ninety-odd not out against Yorkshire at Headingley (Benson & Hedges Cup, 2000) in a very tight game.

Were there any major disappointments during your years with Surrey?
AS - The main one would probably be losing to Hampshire in the 1991 Nat West Trophy final, because we've not been too successful in that competition over the years. I was also very disappointed that we didn't win a trophy while Geoff Arnold was coach - it would have been nice to win something for him to reward him for the amount of work that he put in. He was an excellent coach but we didn't have the strength of squad to win anything in those days. But now he's back at the Club I'd like to think that he might get some reflected glory. Without taking anything away from Dave Gilbert or 'Medders' or Adam, things have changed since those days - we now bring in players to strengthen the squad, but back then it was the Club's policy from the committee downwards to try and bring through Surrey born-and-bred players only. In the ideal world that's right, but if you want to win things then you have to try and get the best players available, which is what we now do.

I know you feel that there should be some fairly dramatic changes in county cricket. If it were down to you, how would you rearrange things?
AS - I'd get it down to twelve teams, that's how I'd like to see it. I think twelve teams in a four-day competition plus the two one-day competitions and the Twenty-20 would be about right. I think the Twenty-20 is excellent - I must admit that when it was first spoken about I had my reservations, but it's been good for the game - for the players and spectators. From the playing point of view, it teaches the players how to introduce new shots and how to bowl tightly at the start and at the death, which you will then see coming through in the longer form of one-day cricket… which will improve the counties and then England. The thing we most need to do if we are really going to move forward is reduce the gap between county cricket and international cricket. But while the counties run the game this is all hypothetical anyway - they aren't going to vote themselves out of business.

On a more positive note, there must be a lot of ***good*** *things about county cricket that you can see, and that you have enjoyed, over the years. What would they be?*
AS - First of all, cricket's been my hobby and I've been lucky enough to be paid for doing it… so, for twenty-three years I've been paid for doing something I'd be doing anyway. County cricket will always produce international-class players - and Surrey have done that better than most in recent times - so it gave me the chance to play for England. They always say domestic cricket is

your 'bread-and-butter' but it's very important, which is why I'm always in favour of trying to improve it. If we can improve the county game then we can improve England cricket.

I guess there are a lot of things you'll miss now you've hung your bat up?
AS - I will find out soon, I'm sure. I speak to Graham Gooch a lot and he tells me that you never replace the adrenaline rush that you get when you go out to play, whether it's for Surrey or England; when you are facing somebody bowling at 95mph; when you play in front of 80,000 people at the MCG; and you'll miss the dressing room - you'll never replace the dressing room camaraderie and humour. I've had twenty-three fantastic years and I wouldn't change anything that's happened in those twenty-three years.

If, sometime next year, the Club were to suffer a glut of injuries would you be tempted to pick up your bat and/or the gloves to help out? Or is that definitely it, as far as your playing career is concerned?
AS - Well, I suppose you should never say never, but I have said I won't play another game again, unless I can play what I call 'real' cricket, 'proper' cricket. If that situation were to arise, then I'd just have to see, but it's a hard question to answer. I'd be fit but I'm not looking to play again.

So we won't be seeing you in any charity games, or anything of that ilk?
AS - No, I'd be happy to support the charity - I'd volunteer to umpire, or go and watch, or get a signed bat or shirt for the charity - but I wouldn't want to play. The thought of putting on my whites and going into a game that isn't a 'proper' game wouldn't appeal to me at all.

Did you have offers from other counties to carry on playing?
AS - Three counties made me an offer, but just before the Oval Test I'd told Paul Sheldon and Richard Thompson that I was going to retire. Having originally said I'd like to play for another year with Surrey, I had a rethink and decided that if my England career was finished and I couldn't play at the highest level then I didn't think I'd want to just play county cricket at the age of 41, as I would be by the start of the next season. For me, personally, if you can't play at the highest level then why are you playing the game - that was my personal attitude, which was why I decided to call it a day. The chances were that I may not have been offered a contract at Surrey anyway because of the finances - if they were going to let Wardy go on that basis, then they probably weren't going to keep a 40-year-old anyway.

So I assume you weren't keen to make a final appearance for Surrey in any of the last few games of the season?
AS - The Oval Test was my farewell to cricket - by then I'd made my decision that I wouldn't carry on. I was disappointed with the side we put out against Essex at the end of the season, though. I think we should have put out our strongest possible side, because you should always look to finish as high up the table as you possibly can. And if I had been selected in that strongest possible side then I would have played. With me, if you are selected then you play - as an employee of the Club it's not about whether you would **like** to play or not.

And, finally, how are you enjoying your new life as an ex-cricketer?
AS - It's been very good. It's been quite a nice transition for me, as I'm still very much involved with sport, both with Surrey and with Merlin.

As one wicketkeeper-batsman ended his Surrey career, so, unfortunately, did another as the highly-regarded Ben Scott decided to return to his Middlesex roots in order to play more first-team cricket. His decision was entirely understandable, and not totally unexpected, and everyone wished him the best as he moved back over the river to north London.

The most sensational news of an already hectic close season then emerged on the 27th November, as Surrey announced that Keith Medlycott was leaving the Club. The Manager's statement in an official Press Release read as follows:- "It has been a privilege to have managed the side since 1998 through a period of unrivalled success. To have been part of this era gives me enormous pleasure and pride. I now feel that, following Adam's decision to stand down as captain, the time is right for me to leave to pursue other opportunities and fresh challenges. Adam and myself formed a fantastic winning partnership and it's now time for me to look forward to the future. I believe I have taken Surrey as far as I can and that under a new manager and a new captain in Jonathan Batty, the Club can continue to be successful."

This really was a bolt from the blue, since Medlycott, who had guided the team to seven trophies in six years, was leaving with a year left on his contract. Having enjoyed such amazing success, it was no surprise that 'Medders' was, at the time of his departure, the longest-serving coach/manager in county cricket, but it seemed that he had decided his time was up. With both captain and manager now gone, we had clearly reached the end of an era. The Club immediately announced that time and care would be taken in appointing the new man, and that only the very best would do for the leading county in English cricket.

After six years at the helm it would be strange not having 'Medders' around, and, rather as George Martin had often been referred to as 'the fifth Beatle', Medlycott was Surrey's 'twelfth man', in the nicest possible sense, as he took part in all the football warm-ups and enjoyed brief forays onto the field as a substitute when the official twelfth man had already been pressed into action. He certainly had more time for the fans than the average manager/coach, and his banter with the members at The Oval as he set up the video camera in the morning would be missed. Above all else, though, he would be remembered as the manager of the side that brought the coveted County Championship trophy back to The Oval in 1999, his second season in charge, after a horribly long gap of twenty-eight years.

I eventually caught up with Keith to ask him a few questions about his time as manager.

TALKING POINTS - KEITH MEDLYCOTT

I was very disappointed by the air of despondency that seemed to be around at the end of the 2003 season - amongst players, supporters, just about everyone. Of course the Championship is regarded as ***the*** *prize in Surrey circles, but we had won two trophies, nevertheless, and every side bar Sussex would have swapped our season for theirs. How did you feel about the situation?*

KM - The Championship is always number one on the list for most players, so we felt it in the dressing room as much as everyone else did. I think the level of despondency was probably over the top, but I think that was partly because we hadn't played very well for the last four or five games and it just kept eating away at us and resulted in a really disappointed environment. But I'm not despondent myself - we won another two trophies - the two trophies that we thought would be the hardest for us to win, given the loss of players that we were expecting. To win the Sunday League, having just been promoted, was an awesome achievement, and I thought the way we played one-day cricket and won tight games was fantastic. And then there was the Twenty-20 Cup, which a lot of people probably thought we were going to be too 'old' for, because we wouldn't be able to produce the breathtaking fielding and so on. To prove people wrong and play with the quality we did in that competition was a fantastic achievement. So, two trophies out of four wasn't bad, and there was too much despondency - this is a squad that is on course to win more trophies in modern times than any other county.

What would you say was your greatest achievement in your time as Surrey Manager?
KM - I think you would have to say the first Championship win in 1999. Having gone so long without winning it made it very special. But also, in a different way, I think I would say that keeping a high-quality squad together and keeping them performing has been a major achievement.

Any major disappointments?
KM - I don't think you can have too many disappointments. It might have been nice to win the C&G Trophy so that we could have completed the full set of trophies, I suppose. Probably the hardest thing has been having to let players go - either people who'd had, or who were going to have, top-class careers. With such a big, talented squad that was inevitably going to happen and it's always very disappointing to tell a player that you are going to have to let them go - no-one likes doing that sort of thing.

Do you consider the achievement of winning seven trophies in your six years in charge to be up there with the achievements of the 1950's team? They were, after all, able to concentrate their efforts on just one competition.
KM - People always like to compare eras but I don't think you can ever really do that. All I would say is that I think it would be wonderful cricket if we could see the great side of the fifties playing the modern side. Surrey were talked of as the best side in the fifties and now the current side is going to be talked of as the best side of the modern era - I think that's the most pleasing thing about the current era of success. For thirty years we didn't get our name up there, but over the last six or seven years the name of Surrey has been up there in bright colours, and I think that's important. It's a big Club and we should always be there or thereabouts, so I'm pleased that I'm leaving with things in good shape and the name right up there.

Had you been told, when you started the job, that you would end up spending six years in the role and winning seven trophies along the way, what do you think your reaction would have been?
KM - I think I'd have taken that, definitely. It's a hard, tough, competitive game, and with the Club having only just started to win trophies again, after a long spell without winning anything, I think you would have to see that as a success.

How would you most like people to remember 'The Medlycott Years'?
KM - I'd hope they would be remembered not only for the success, but also for being fun, and for the high-quality cricket that the team played. Hopefully we've provided a lot of entertainment, and I would also like to think that I've I helped to make the players a little bit more accessible to the supporters.

Would I be correct in thinking that your favourite moment from your time in charge would be the clinching of the 1999 Championship title at The Oval? If not that, then what would it be?
KM - Yes, it would have to be that, I think. It was fantastic to win it on our home ground and in those amazing circumstances. The players didn't want to come back the next day to win it, they wanted to finish it that night, and they went out and played so positively. So that would definitely be the big one. But there are lots of little moments you can look back on. I get great satisfaction from looking back at those moments where players have really risen to the occasion and won matches with an outstanding achievement and perhaps played above their normal level.

Which matches and performances particularly stand out for you as you look back?
KM - There are so many. Those that spring to mind would include Adam's amazing hundred in the C&G game at Hove not long after he rejoined us last year - it was great to see him back and playing so brilliantly; Ian Ward's terrific century with the lower-order at Canterbury in that

incredible Championship victory at Canterbury last year; Ali Brown's record-breaking 268 and the whole of that unbelievable match; a lot of the NCL games this year, where Azhar and Adam bowled so well at the death; and an example of what I meant on the previous question - Jason Ratcliffe scoring those runs at The Oval in 1999 against Somerset in near darkness when we won the game by scoring forty-nine off five overs at the end.

Do you see further interesting and successful times ahead for the Club?
KM - Yes, for sure. I think management partnerships are very important. I had a very good partnership with Adam, and I'm sure that Jon Batty and Steve Rixon will be a very good pairing, too. I have to say that a lot of what we have achieved in this successful era has been down to Adam - he's such a strong character - and I'd also like to mention Vic Dodds (the former chairman of cricket) who I think was very influential and hasn't been given the credit that he deserved.

That was a typically modest statement for 'Medders' to finish with, and I'm sure I speak for all Surrey fans in wishing him the very best for the future. Let's hope we soon see him on the county scene again, because cricket undoubtedly needs cheery and chirpy characters like him around.

Having had so much to take in - and talk about - supporters were given a break until the New Year, when it was announced that Geoff Arnold, 59, had returned to Surrey as Bowling Coach, with the former player and manager saying, "I am delighted to have been offered a two-year contract with my former Club. I am looking forward to working with the Surrey first-team bowlers as well as the Academy and younger age-group players. I hope that I can help all of them to develop their games."

On the same day, it was revealed that the Club had filled the vacancy created by Ben Scott's departure by signing the 19-year-old former England Under-19 wicketkeeper, Andrew Hodd, on a two-year contract. With his path at Sussex blocked by both Matt Prior and Tim Ambrose, this looked to be an ideal move for both Hodd and Surrey, with the highly promising youngster saying, "I am extremely excited about signing for Surrey. By playing in a side with so many talented and experienced players, I hope that I can improve my game as well as help Surrey win more silverware in the future."

So, what was next? A new sponsor for the Club and the ground. With the previous sponsors, AMP, having suffered financial difficulties and negotiated their withdrawal as, first, Club sponsors and then ground sponsors, a Press Conference was called on 26th January to reveal that Brit Insurance Holdings plc would be taking over. The deal was to be worth £500,000 a year to Surrey, making it the largest of its kind in English cricket, with the world-famous arena to be renamed 'The Brit Oval' and the sponsor's name and logo to appear on the Club's white and coloured kit from the start of the 2004 season. In the official Press Release, Paul Sheldon stated:- "This is one of the most important commercial partnerships in the history of the Club. We are looking forward to working closely with the Brit team in delivering this fantastic sponsorship opportunity. This new partnership could not have come at a better time, as next week work starts on our ambitious redevelopment of the Vauxhall end of the ground. The support we will now receive from Brit will ensure that The Brit Oval maintains its pre-eminence as one of the world's leading Test venues." In reply, Neil Eckert, the chief executive of Brit Insurance, said:- "Brit is delighted to confirm this exciting sponsorship of Surrey County Cricket Club and The Brit Oval. Together with WSM, the sports marketing consultancy, we analysed a number of sponsorship opportunities. An association with one of the leading county cricket clubs and international Test grounds proved a natural fit for the Brit brand, and the Club's proximity to the City provides us with a valuable opportunity to communicate with a key target audience."

Good news on the sponsorship front was then followed by good news on the playing front three days later when it was announced that Surrey had secured the services of their first-choice replacement for Keith Medlycott. The new Cricket Manager was to be Steve Rixon, 49, the New South Wales and former New Zealand coach, who had played in thirteen Tests for Australia between 1977 and 1985 and had enjoyed immense success with both of the teams that he had coached. Paul Sheldon stated: "We have searched the world of cricket to find the best person for this crucial position within the Club. Having spent time with him recently in Australia, I am convinced that we have found the right man to lead the team into a new era in partnership with the new Club captain, Jonathan Batty." Steve Rixon's statement read: "Having been offered roles in English cricket before, I feel this is the opportunity and challenge that really excites me the most, working for what I see as the premier county. I've been very impressed with what I've seen of Surrey so far. It's clearly a squad with high-quality players and I am looking forward to working with them. I believe we will continue to build on the winning ways of the past few years." With New South Wales seemingly the Australian equivalent of Surrey - a strong team with plenty of international players, who had enjoyed great success in recent times - it seemed that Rixon was ideally suited to the post. His two-year contract was to start in March 2004, once his contract with New South Wales had expired.

Finally, at the end of a quite incredible close season period, the redevelopment of The Oval got under way with the commencement of the demolition of the Vauxhall end of the ground at the start of February. The three major phases of the £24m project were timetabled as follows:-

2nd February 2004 to 9th August 2004: The demolition of the current Vauxhall End will be followed by construction of the ground works and some permanent seating. This will be completed in time for the International Fixtures at The Brit Oval from August to September. The permanent seats will be augmented by temporary hospitality facilities.

10th August 2004 to 4th October 2004: International Cricket at The Brit Oval to include an npower Test Match against the West Indies, a NatWest Challenge Match against India and the ICC Champions Trophy fixtures from 10th to 25th September.

4th October 2004 to 31st May 2005: The aerofoil roof structure, the 200-metre living screen, the media area, the community education facilities and the hospitality and conferencing services will be built on four floors. The new stand will be completed in time for the Ashes Test.

It seemed incredible that so much could have happened since the end of the 2003 season, but, as far as the playing side was concerned, it seemed to be a good thing that all the changes had come at once, rather than over a period of two or three years. As a result, the 2004 campaign looked like it should be very interesting, with new ideas coming from a fresh coach and captain. There certainly seemed to be no reason why Surrey's run of success shouldn't continue - given a fair run with regard to injuries - with the one-day competitions in particular looking likely to provide the Club with some more silverware. We would find out soon enough, as the new Rixon-Batty era began.

Ian Ward politely declined the opportunity to talk about his Surrey career for this book.

Appendix - Statistical Compendium

(Compiled by Richard Arnold)

COUNTY CHAMPIONSHIP AVERAGES 2003 - BATTING											
Player	**M**	**I**	**NO**	**Runs**	**HS**	**Ave.**	100	50	Balls	4's	6's	S/R
Ramprakash	**14**	**22**	**4**	**1239**	**279***	**68.83**	5	2	2310	166	13	53.64
Butcher	**6**	**8**	**0**	**527**	**144**	**65.88**	2	2	716	84	6	73.60
Stewart	**6**	**8**	**1**	**451**	**98**	**64.43**	0	5	616	75	0	73.21
Thorpe	**11**	**18**	**2**	**880**	**156**	**55.00**	1	7	1472	136	2	59.78
Batty	**10**	**19**	**4**	**794**	**168***	**52.93**	2	4	1375	131	5	57.75
Clarke	**9**	**14**	**2**	**513**	**139**	**42.75**	2	1	731	80	4	70.18
Azhar	**10**	**13**	**2**	**441**	**98**	**40.09**	0	4	538	62	8	81.97
Bicknell	**11**	**11**	**3**	**318**	**141**	**39.75**	1	0	494	44	1	64.37
Ward	**15**	**24**	**1**	**856**	**158**	**37.22**	3	1	1475	133	6	58.03
Salisbury	**14**	**18**	**4**	**455**	**101***	**32.50**	1	1	708	59	8	64.27
Saqlain	**14**	**15**	**2**	**421**	**69**	**32.38**	0	4	753	48	10	55.91
Hollioake	**13**	**18**	**0**	**567**	**122**	**31.50**	1	3	653	79	11	86.83
Tudor	**6**	**7**	**1**	**177**	**55**	**29.50**	0	1	337	33	0	52.52
Brown	**12**	**19**	**2**	**481**	**74**	**28.29**	0	5	658	64	9	73.10
Ormond	**12**	**14**	**5**	**198**	**47**	**22.00**	0	0	297	28	4	66.67
Shahid	**2**	**4**	**0**	**72**	**67**	**18.00**	0	1	72	15	0	100.00
Murtagh	**5**	**8**	**4**	**61**	**21**	**15.25**	0	0	108	13	0	56.48
Also batted:-												
Scott	**1**	**2**	**1**	**63**	**58***	**63.00**	0	1	143	9	0	44.06
Sampson	**1**	**2**	**1**	**35**	**32***	**35.00**	0	0	63	6	0	55.56
Benning	**1**	**2**	**0**	**65**	**47**	**32.50**	0	0	120	11	0	54.17
Rose	**1**	**2**	**0**	**37**	**36**	**18.50**	0	0	31	5	2	119.35
Newman	**1**	**2**	**0**	**9**	**9**	**4.50**	0	0	28	2	0	32.14
Saker	**1**	**2**	**0**	**1**	**1**	**0.50**	0	0	8	0	0	12.50
Grand Total	**176**	**252**	**39**	**8661**	**279***	**40.66**	18	42	13706	1283	89	63.19

COUNTY CHAMPIONSHIP AVERAGES 2003 - BOWLING									
Player	**Ov**	**M**	**Runs**	**Wkts**	**Ave**	Best	S/R	5Wi	10Wm
Bicknell	**326.4**	**83**	**1023**	**39**	**26.23**	5-42	50.26	3	0
Azhar	**262.2**	**48**	**994**	**34**	**29.24**	5-78	46.29	1	0
Ormond	**366.1**	**65**	**1363**	**44**	**30.98**	5-45	49.93	2	0
Saqlain	**471.0**	**100**	**1364**	**41**	**33.27**	5-46	68.93	3	0
Salisbury	**371.1**	**60**	**1224**	**33**	**37.09**	4-116	67.48	0	0
Murtagh	**115.0**	**13**	**475**	**11**	**43.18**	4-130	62.73	0	0
Clarke	**130.1**	**13**	**607**	**12**	**50.58**	4-21	65.08	0	0
Tudor	**144.0**	**27**	**532**	**10**	**53.20**	3-56	86.40	0	0
Also bowled:-									
Butcher	**12.0**	**1**	**44**	**3**	**14.67**	2-20	24.00	0	0
Brown	**9.4**	**3**	**22**	**1**	**22.00**	1-11	58.00	0	0
Sampson	**19.5**	**1**	**101**	**4**	**25.25**	2-16	29.75	0	0
Rose	**28.0**	**8**	**101**	**3**	**33.67**	3-101	56.00	0	0
Benning	**8.0**	**1**	**39**	**1**	**39.00**	1-39	48.00	0	0
Hollioake	**68.2**	**8**	**265**	**4**	**66.25**	2-32	102.50	0	0
Thorpe	**11.0**	**1**	**73**	**1**	**73.00**	1-73	66.00	0	0
Saker	**20.1**	**1**	**103**	**1**	**103.00**	1-71	121.00	0	0
Ramprakash	**8.0**	**4**	**9**	**0**	**0.00**	n/a	0.00	0	0
Stewart	**2.3**	**0**	**23**	**0**	**0.00**	n/a	0.00	0	0
Ward	**16.3**	**0**	**76**	**0**	**0.00**	n/a	0.00	0	0
Grand Total	**2390.3**	**437**	**8438**	**242**	**34.87**	5-42	59.27	9	0

NCL AVERAGES 2003 - BATTING

Player	M	I	NO	Runs	HS	Ave	100	50	Balls	4's	6's	S/R
Ramprakash	13	12	3	686	107*	76.22	2	6	877	66	9	78.22
Thorpe	13	12	4	378	79*	47.25	0	3	497	37	4	76.06
Butcher	3	3	0	116	104	38.67	1	0	134	18	0	86.57
Brown	15	15	0	491	89	32.73	0	4	420	72	14	116.90
Azhar	12	11	2	277	98	30.78	0	2	215	25	12	128.84
Ward	11	11	1	257	70*	25.70	0	1	298	35	3	86.24
Hollioake	15	15	0	377	77	25.13	0	2	379	36	17	99.47
Clarke	13	13	3	213	46*	21.30	0	0	291	20	4	73.20
Salisbury	7	4	0	62	33	15.50	0	0	59	5	3	105.08
Batty	15	11	3	113	28	14.13	0	0	129	12	2	87.60
Newman	3	3	0	33	15	11.00	0	0	49	5	0	67.35
Also Batted:-												
Saqlain	10	5	3	50	27*	25.00	0	0	99	7	0	50.51
Bicknell	11	5	3	44	14*	22.00	0	0	81	2	0	54.32
Benning	2	2	0	31	25	15.50	0	0	24	6	0	129.17
Shahid	2	2	0	19	19	9.50	0	0	23	3	0	82.61
Ormond	10	3	1	16	6	8.00	0	0	28	2	0	57.14
Murtagh	4	3	1	8	6	4.00	0	0	31	0	0	25.81
Rose	2	1	0	1	1	1.00	0	0	2	0	0	50.00
Sampson	2	1	0	0	0	0.00	0	0	2	0	0	0.00
Tudor	2	2	2	13	11*	n/a	0	0	10	2	0	130.00
Grand Total	165	134	26	3185	107*	29.49	3	18	3648	353	68	87.31

NCL AVERAGES 2003 - BOWLING

Player	Ov	M	Runs	Wkts	Ave	E/R	S/R	5Wi	3Wi
Tudor	18.0	0	102	7	14.57	5.67	15.43	0	1
Hollioake	82.5	1	443	23	19.26	5.35	21.61	1	2
Sampson	15.0	1	98	4	24.50	6.53	22.50	0	1
Azhar	89.0	4	466	18	25.89	5.24	29.67	1	0
Ormond	86.0	6	410	13	31.54	4.77	39.69	0	1
Clarke	64.0	1	396	12	33.00	6.19	32.00	0	1
Murtagh	34.0	2	200	6	33.33	5.88	34.00	0	1
Salisbury	44.0	2	210	6	35.00	4.77	44.00	0	1
Rose	17.0	1	78	2	39.00	4.59	51.00	0	0
Bicknell	91.0	9	436	11	39.64	4.79	49.64	0	0
Saqlain	81.0	0	403	10	40.30	4.98	48.60	0	1
Also bowled:-									
Benning	9.0	1	43	4	10.75	4.78	13.50	0	0
Brown	2.4	0	26	1	26.00	9.75	16.00	0	0
Ramprakash	4.0	0	23	0	n/a	5.75	0.00	0	0
Shahid	2.0	0	13	0	n/a	6.50	0.00	0	0
Grand Total	639.3	28	3347	117	28.61	5.23	32.79	2	9

TWENTY-20 CUP AVERAGES 2003 - BOWLING (BY ECONOMY RATE)

Player	Ov	M	Runs	Wkts	E/R	Ave	S/R	5Wi	3Wi
Bicknell	11.0	1	61	4	5.55	15.25	16.50	0	0
Ormond	20.0	0	111	11	5.55	10.09	10.91	1	0
Azhar	18.5	0	123	12	6.53	10.25	9.42	0	1
Salisbury	14.0	0	93	3	6.64	31.00	28.00	0	0
Hollioake	25.1	0	197	16	7.83	12.31	9.44	1	0
Saqlain	11.0	0	87	4	7.91	21.75	16.50	0	0
Murtagh	16.0	0	128	6	8.00	21.33	16.00	0	1
Sampson	15.0	0	123	4	8.20	30.75	22.50	0	0
Also bowled:-									
Clarke	4.0	0	20	0	5.00	n/a	0.00	0	0
Benning	2.0	0	12	0	6.00	n/a	0.00	0	0
Grand Total	137.0	1	955	60	6.99	15.92	13.70	2	2

TWENTY-20 CUP AVERAGES 2003 - BATTING (BY STRIKE RATE)

Player	M	I	NO	Runs	HS	S/R	Ave.	100	50	Balls	4's	6's
Azhar	5	4	1	114	57*	190.00	38.00	0	1	60	6	8
Brown	7	7	1	151	55*	146.60	25.17	0	1	103	18	6
Thorpe	5	4	0	95	50	139.71	23.75	0	1	68	11	2
Ward	6	6	0	186	50	135.77	31.00	0	1	137	24	4
Hollioake	7	6	0	74	24	129.82	12.33	0	0	57	6	2
Benning	5	5	0	73	27	125.86	14.60	0	0	58	12	0
Batty	7	6	3	64	19*	123.08	21.33	0	0	52	8	2
Salisbury	5	4	1	20	12*	117.65	6.67	0	0	17	0	1
Ramprakash	7	7	2	105	53	105.00	21.00	0	1	100	7	3
Newman	2	2	0	78	59	101.30	39.00	0	1	77	8	2
Clarke	2	1	0	15	15	65.22	15.00	0	0	23	1	0
Also batted:-												
Bicknell	3	2	2	11	10*	137.50	n/a	0	0	8	1	0
Sampson	4	2	2	7	4*	116.67	n/a	0	0	6	0	0
Ormond	5	1	0	3	3	100.00	3.00	0	0	3	0	0
Saqlain	3	2	0	5	5	100.00	2.50	0	0	5	0	0
Murtagh	4	1	0	0	0	0.00	0.00	0	0	1	0	0
Grand Total	77	61	12	1001	59	129.16	20.43	0	6	775	102	30

NCL MARGINS OF VICTORY (Overs Remaining applies only to side batting second and winning)

Match	Runs	Wkts	Overs Remaining	W/L
Essex (A)	15			W
Warwicks (H)	25			W
Worcs (A)		1	3.3	W
Kent (H)	6			W
Essex (H)		3	2.1	W
Yorkshire (H)		7	6.5	W
Warwicks (A)		6	2.5	L
Worcs (H)	79			L
Gloucs (H)	66			W
Glamorgan (H)	58			W
Leics (A)		7	16.4	W
Yorkshire (A)	2			W
Kent (A)		5	8	W
Glamorgan (A)	8			W
Leics (H)	168			L

ALEC STEWART CAREER - CHAMPIONSHIP MATCHES (BY OPPONENTS)

County	M	I	NO	Runs	HS	Ave.	100's	50's
DERBYSHIRE	13	19	5	357	60	25.50	0	2
DURHAM	3	5	1	274	151	68.50	1	1
ESSEX	20	33	6	1316	206	48.74	4	6
GLAMORGAN	13	21	0	530	99	25.24	0	4
GLOUCS	13	24	2	618	109	28.09	1	5
HAMPSHIRE	15	25	3	817	100	37.14	1	5
KENT	21	34	1	1287	170	39.00	4	5
LANCASHIRE	16	28	4	1333	126	55.54	1	13
LEICS	13	22	1	834	142	39.71	2	4
MIDDLESEX	21	37	7	1357	148	45.23	3	7
NORTHANTS	13	20	0	391	66	19.55	0	1
NOTTS	11	18	3	629	98	41.93	0	5
SOMERSET	15	22	2	610	105	30.50	1	4
SUSSEX	24	34	3	1811	199	58.42	5	9
WARWICKS	10	16	1	533	76	35.53	0	6
WORCS	15	24	3	712	82	33.90	0	7
YORKSHIRE	16	24	5	1031	271	54.26	2	4
Grand Total	252	406	47	14440	271	40.22	25	88

ALEC STEWART CAREER - LIMITED-OVERS MATCHES (BY OPPONENTS)								
Opponents	M	I	NO	Runs	HS	Ave.	100	50
Berkshire	1	0	0	0	0	n/a	0	0
British Univs	2	2	1	105	86	105.00	0	1
Bucks	1	1	0	97	97	97.00	0	1
Cheshire	1	1	0	31	31	31.00	0	0
Combined Univs	3	3	2	151	84	151.00	0	2
Derbyshire	12	11	1	462	112	46.20	1	3
Devon	1	1	1	70	70	n/a	0	1
Dorset	1	1	1	104	104	n/a	1	0
Durham	6	6	2	263	90	65.75	0	2
Essex	23	22	1	622	125	29.62	1	4
Glamorgan	15	14	2	523	119	43.58	1	2
Gloucs	21	20	1	360	89	18.95	0	1
Hampshire	18	18	0	688	160	38.22	1	5
Hertfordshire	1	1	1	66	66	n/a	0	1
Holland	1	1	0	50	50	50.00	0	1
Ireland	3	2	1	89	63	89.00	0	1
Kent	19	18	3	720	92	48.00	0	7
Lancashire	18	18	2	757	125	47.31	1	6
Leics	16	13	2	396	105	36.00	1	2
Middlesex	20	19	3	661	107	41.31	2	3
Minor Counties	1	1	1	71	71	n/a	0	1
Northants	19	18	0	350	44	19.44	0	0
Northumberland	1	1	0	55	55	55.00	0	1
Notts	14	14	2	390	77	32.50	0	4
Scotland	1	1	0	64	64	64.00	0	1
Somerset	16	15	2	686	167	52.77	4	2
Staffordshire	2	2	0	71	54	35.50	0	1
Sussex	27	25	5	796	100	39.80	1	4
Warwicks	16	16	1	306	86	20.40	0	2
Wiltshire	1	0	0	0	0	n/a	0	0
Worcs	16	15	1	247	55	17.64	0	1
Yorkshire	17	16	1	377	97	25.13	0	3
Grand Total	314	296	37	9628	167	37.17	14	63

IAN WARD CAREER - CHAMPIONSHIP MATCHES (BY OPPONENTS)								
County	M	I	NO	Runs	HS	Ave.	100's	50's
DERBYSHIRE	4	7	1	245	103	40.83	1	1
DURHAM	4	6	0	297	144	49.50	1	2
ESSEX	4	8	0	155	49	19.38	0	0
GLAMORGAN	4	6	1	260	79	52.00	0	3
GLOUCS	2	4	0	86	78	21.50	0	1
HAMPSHIRE	5	9	0	472	156	52.44	2	2
KENT	9	14	3	598	168	54.36	2	1
LANCASHIRE	9	17	1	711	158	44.44	2	2
LEICS	7	11	1	506	118	50.60	2	3
MIDDLESEX	5	7	1	269	104	44.83	1	0
NORTHANTS	3	4	0	156	79	39.00	0	2
NOTTS	4	6	1	114	55	22.80	0	1
SOMERSET	8	14	1	421	76	32.38	0	3
SUSSEX	6	11	1	383	135	38.30	1	1
WARWICKS	6	9	0	310	114	34.44	1	1
WORCS	2	3	0	153	64	51.00	0	2
YORKSHIRE	7	12	1	468	124	42.55	1	3
Grand Total	89	148	12	5604	168	41.21	14	28

IAN WARD CAREER - LIMITED-OVERS (BY OPPONENTS) includes Twenty-20 Cup								
Opponents	**M**	**I**	**NO**	**Runs**	**HS**	**Ave.**	100	50
Bucks	1	1	0	16	16	16.00	0	0
Derbyshire	9	9	0	214	53	23.78	0	1
Devon	1	0	0	0	0	n/a	0	0
Durham	6	6	1	117	41	23.40	0	0
Essex	11	11	1	188	62	18.80	0	1
Glamorgan	9	9	1	304	97	38.00	0	2
Gloucs	10	9	0	188	54	20.89	0	1
Hampshire	7	6	0	191	51	31.83	0	1
Holland	1	1	0	14	14	14.00	0	0
Kent	8	8	0	122	51	15.25	0	1
Lancashire	5	4	0	94	55	23.50	0	1
Leics	3	3	1	139	70	69.50	0	2
Middlesex	10	10	2	295	91	36.88	0	2
Northants	5	5	2	91	26	30.33	0	0
Notts	4	4	0	235	80	58.75	0	3
Scotland	2	1	0	58	58	58.00	0	1
Somerset	6	6	1	149	45	29.80	0	0
Staffordshire	1	1	0	108	108	108.00	1	0
Surrey CB	1	1	1	70	70	n/a	0	1
Sussex	12	11	1	187	46	18.70	0	0
Warwicks	8	7	0	149	50	21.29	0	1
Worcs	4	4	1	19	11	6.33	0	0
Yorkshire	7	7	0	137	81	19.57	0	1
Grand Total	**131**	**124**	**12**	**3085**	**108**	**27.54**	1	19

ALEC STEWART CAREER - CHAMPIONSHIP - PLAYING AS KEEPER v PLAYING AS BATSMAN ONLY								
	M	**I**	**NO**	**Runs**	**HS**	**Ave.**	100's	50's
Wicketkeeper	75	117	8	4443	271	40.76	7	27
Batsman Only	177	289	39	9997	206	39.99	18	61
Grand Total	**252**	**406**	**47**	**14440**	**271**	**40.22**	25	88

IAN WARD CAREER - CHAMPIONSHIP - YEAR BY YEAR								
Year	**M**	**I**	**NO**	**Runs**	**HS**	**Ave.**	100's	50's
1992	1	1	0	0	0	0.00	0	0
1997	3	4	0	102	56	25.50	0	1
1998	10	19	2	529	81	31.12	0	5
1999	17	28	3	954	103	38.16	1	8
2000	16	25	3	894	158	40.64	3	3
2001	11	18	0	561	79	31.17	0	4
2002	16	29	3	1708	168	65.69	7	6
2003	15	24	1	856	158	37.22	3	1
Grand Total	**89**	**148**	**12**	**5604**	**168**	**41.21**	14	28

NATIONAL LEAGUE RECORD IN TOP DIVISION SINCE 1998
(Includes 1998, when league was split into two at the end of the season)

Year	W	L	Total
1998	**3**	**12**	**15**
2001	**6**	**10**	**16**
2003	**12**	**3**	**15**
Total	**21**	**25**	**46**

Note:

- Last 2 games in 1998 were won after relegation had already been confirmed
- Last 4 games in 2001 were won after relegation had already been confirmed
- Last game in 2003 was lost after the title had already been secured

SUNDAY/NATIONAL LEAGUE CAREER RECORDS FOR SURREY - BATTING								
Player	M	I	NO	Runs	HS	Ave.	100	50
Ramprakash	34	33	7	1437	107	55.27	2	13
Thorpe	143	132	21	4323	126	38.95	6	29
Brown	194	189	5	5809	203	31.57	12	25
Azhar	13	11	2	277	98	30.78	0	2
Stewart	184	170	17	4652	125	30.41	7	26
Hollioake	154	141	18	3292	111	26.76	1	14
Shahid	84	79	15	1690	109	26.41	2	6
Clarke	26	26	5	536	98	25.52	0	3
Ward	89	86	9	1940	91	25.19	0	11
Butcher	94	81	14	1522	104	22.72	1	5
Bicknell	197	101	46	786	57	14.29	0	1
Newman	8	8	0	114	37	14.25	0	0
Batty	78	55	13	584	40	13.90	0	0
Benning	3	3	0	41	25	13.67	0	0
Salisbury	55	38	8	367	33	12.23	0	0
Saqlain	56	34	12	267	38	12.14	0	0
Tudor	35	25	7	186	29	10.33	0	0
Ormond	12	3	1	16	6	8.00	0	0
Murtagh	22	15	7	52	14	6.50	0	0
Sampson	8	4	0	21	16	5.25	0	0
Rose	2	1	0	1	1	1.00	0	0
Grand Total	1491	1235	207	27913	203	27.15	31	135

SUNDAY/NATIONAL LEAGUE CAREER RECORDS FOR SURREY - BOWLING									
Player	Ov	M	Runs	Wkts	Ave	E/R	S/R	5Wi	3Wi
Benning	16.0	1	101	6	16.83	6.31	16.00	0	0
Hollioake	819.1	20	4510	223	20.22	5.54	22.04	6	16
Tudor	231.2	19	1119	47	23.81	4.84	29.53	0	2
Bicknell	1414.2	103	5960	240	24.83	4.22	35.36	3	19
Azhar	90.4	4	476	19	25.05	5.27	28.63	1	0
Saqlain	414.4	21	1775	61	29.10	4.28	40.79	0	6
Murtagh	181.2	11	917	30	30.57	5.07	36.27	0	3
Brown	47.3	0	278	9	30.89	5.93	31.67	0	1
Ormond	95.0	6	435	13	33.46	4.58	43.85	0	1
Salisbury	312.1	6	1577	46	34.28	5.07	40.72	0	6
Sampson	53.0	1	290	8	36.25	5.47	39.75	0	1
Clarke	123.2	4	702	19	36.95	5.74	38.95	0	1
Thorpe	53.0	1	307	8	38.38	5.79	39.75	0	1
Ramprakash	12.5	0	78	2	39.00	6.24	38.50	0	0
Rose	17.0	1	78	2	39.00	4.59	51.00	0	0
Butcher	286.1	12	1571	37	42.46	5.50	46.41	0	3
Stewart	0.4	0	8	0	n/a	20.00	0.00	0	0
Shahid	10.0	0	74	0	n/a	7.40	0.00	0	0
Ward	9.5	0	92	0	n/a	9.68	0.00	0	0
Grand Total	4188.0	210	20348	770	26.43	4.87	32.63	10	60

Acknowledgements

Many thanks to all of the following people who have assisted me, in ways both large and small, with the production of this book. Every contribution is very much appreciated.

Thanks, first of all, to Keith Medlycott and the players, who provided all of us with some special memories and another two trophies. Special thanks to those who freely subjected themselves to my end-of-season cross-examination. I hope my books will provide you with a tangible reminder of your triumphs in years to come.

PHOTOGRAPHS
Reg Elliott
Surrey CCC
Steve Porter of The Surrey Advertiser

STATISTICS
Richard Arnold

PROOFREADING
Sue Leach

OTHER
Johnny Grave, Surrey CCC
Sam Streatfeild, Surrey CCC
Marcus Hook

All the staff at Surrey County Cricket Club who I have contact with throughout the year

Surrey C.C.C. Supporters' Club

Should you wish to become a member of the Surrey C.C.C. Supporters' Club
please write to:-
Chris Keene, 11 Limes Row, Farnborough, Kent, BR6 7BD
Membership rates for 2004:- Full Members £5, Senior Members £3, Junior Members £1
(Junior members - under 18 on 01/01/2004; Senior members - over 60 on 01/01/2004)

The Ben Hollioake Fund

Should you wish to make a donation to TheBen Hollioake Fund
please contact:-
Loraine Bicknell, Ben Hollioake Fund Co-ordinator,
CHASE Children's Hospice Service, Loseley Park, Guildford, GU3 1HS.
Tel: 01483 454213 Fax: 01483 454214
E-mail: loraine@chasecare.org.uk Web: www.benhollioake.maxmoment.co.uk

BBC London Internet Radio Coverage

Don't forget that you can hear live ball-by-ball coverage of every Surrey match on the Internet during the summer. Just go to www.surreycricket.com and follow the links to the BBC London site. Or go direct to www.bbc.co.uk/london

Sponsor-Subscribers

I would not have been able to publish ***'Two In Blue'*** without the support and financial backing of the following sponsor-subscribers. Many thanks to all of you.

Les Allen
Stuart Allen
Derek Annetts
Richard Arnold
Sarah Atkins
Keith Bain
Richard Ball
John Banfield
John Barrett
Ian Barton
Derek Beard
Derek Biscoe
Phil Booker
Peter J. Bourne
M.A. Brecknell
Colin Brown
Geoffrey Brown
Lester Brown
Justin Clark
Alan, Margaret and Adrian Clifton
Ron Cronin
Michael Culham
Michael Cunnew
Alan Curtis
Tony Dey
Paul Edwards
Reg Elliott
Keith Evemy
Paul Ferguson
Christopher G. Finch
Evelyn Fowler
Peter Franks (Shepperton)
Mark Gardiner
Dave Gardner MBE
Phil Garrard
Andrew Gasson
Brian Gee
Neil Gelder
Peter Gent
Doug Ginn
John Gough-Cooper
Ted Grant
Michael Greensmith
Chris Gudgeon
John Hall
Roger M. Hancock
Edward Handley
Julian Harding
Raymond Hart
Jacinta Hassett-Brown
Barry Hatcher
Kevin Henriques
Geoff Hetherington
Matthew Hewitt
Neil Hewitt
David Hogben
Marcus Hook
Roger Hudson
Trevor Humphreys
Elliott Hurst
Blaise Jenner
Alan B. Jones
Alan and Joyce Jones
Albert Jordan
Chris Keene
Gillian Kempster
Barrie Patrick King
Victor Klarfeld
Mr. & Mrs. Philip Krinks
Dominic Lang
Sue Leach
Tony Legall (Perth, Australia)
Charles Lehec
Stephen Lilley
Jerry Lodge
Chris Luff
Thomas Manley
Hugh Massingberd
Iain McConachie
Don McKay
Richard W. S. Miller
Steve Mills
Doug Minde
P.B. Molyneux and J.S. Wiltshire
Paul Monaghan
R.S. Mountford
David Murray
James Murray
Jim Murray
Leslie Murrell
Ken Myers
Peter Norman
Ray O'Leary
Michael N. O'Malley
Chris Payne
Wayne Pearce
John Per
A.R. Pettley
Gary Phillips
Keith Porter
Mr. William A. Powell
Alison Prater
Lorna Price
David Rankin
David E. Sawyer
Schenker
Don Scott
David Seymour
Alec Sidebotham
Cliff Simpson
Gordon Smith
Mark Smith
Richard Spiller
Rev. Arthur Stubbs
Surrey C.C.C.
Gary Sutton
John Taverner
Colin Taylor
Iain Taylor
Jim Taylor
Mike Thorn
Steve Tyler
Dr. David Waghorn
Eric W. Waldron
Brian Walton
Mary Ward
David Watts
David Webber
Peter Withey
Mr. Mark Witts
Edwin Woodcock
Steve Wooding
Andy Wotton
Billy Wright

If you would like to become a sponsor-subscriber for any future books about Surrey County Cricket Club that might be produced by Trevor Jones then please write to the author at **P.O. Box 882, Sutton, Surrey, SM2 5AW** or email him at **tj@sportingdeclarations.co.uk**

Other Books By Trevor Jones

The following books by Trevor Jones about Surrey County Cricket Club are still available and may be purchased directly from the publisher at the discounted prices detailed below.

Order from **Sporting Declarations Books, P.O. Box 882, SUTTON, SM2 5AW.**
Cheques/postal orders payable to ***Sporting Declarations Books***, please.

Pursuing The Dream - My Season With Surrey C.C.C.

The ultimately doomed Championship challenge of 1998 forms the central plank of Trevor Jones' first book, a fan's diary of a season following his team around the country. The author's personal day-by-day account of the summer includes tales of the lighter moments of his season with Surrey. Received impressive critical acclaim, including a three-ball review in Wisden Cricket Monthly.

256 pages Published April 1999
Hardback edition 0 9535307 0 1 Price - £8.99 (inc UK p&p)
Softback edition 0 9535307 1 X Price - £4.99 (inc UK p&p)

The Dream Fulfilled - Surrey's 1999 County Championship Triumph

'The Dream Fulfilled' records Surrey's first County Championship triumph for twenty-eight years. Includes twenty-four pages of full-colour photos, run charts and official Surrey CCC scorebook extracts of significant innings/events, press quotes and views from the other counties. Highly acclaimed everywhere it was reviewed, this book will be treasured by Surrey fans for years to come.

376 pages, including 24 pages of full-colour photographs Published April 2000
Hardback only 0 9535307 2 8 Price - £13.99 (inc UK p&p)

Doubling Up With Delight - Surrey's Twin Triumphs 2000

The in-depth story of Surrey's first-ever double-winning season when they added the National League Division Two title to a second successive County Championship victory. Run charts, scorebook extracts and twenty-four pages of colour photos are included in another essential volume for followers of Surrey.

312 pages, including 24 pages of full-colour photographs Published April 2001
Softback only 0 9535307 3 6 Price - £12.99 (inc UK p&p)

268 - The Blow-By-Blow Account Of Ali's Amazing Onslaught

The definitive record of Ali Brown's world record-breaking innings of 268 in the remarkable C&G Trophy match at The AMP Oval in 2002 when six other world records and countless other UK, competition, club and personal records fell.

80 pages, including 8 pages of full-colour photographs Published November 2002
Softback only 0 9535307 4 4 Price - £6.99 (inc UK p&p)

From Tragedy To Triumph - Surrey's Bittersweet Championship Success 2002

The detailed and moving story of how Surrey bounced back from the tragic loss of Ben Hollioake to secure a third Championship title in four seasons. Includes the usual exclusive interviews with the players, run charts and twenty-four pages of colour photos.

376 pages, including 24 pages of full-colour photographs Published April 2003
Softback only 0 9535307 5 2 Price - £13.99 (inc UK p&p)

Further information and a special multiple-purchase book deal can be found at

www.sportingdeclarations.co.uk

Comments can be directed to the author at **tj@sportingdeclarations.co.uk**